THIRD EDITION

GOLF COURSES
OF THE
PACIFIC NORTHWEST

The Complete Regional Golf Guide

by
Jeff Shelley

Copyright © 1997

Cover and book design by Anni Shelley
Cover illustration by Frank Gaffney

Photos by Jeff Shelley
Copy editor Mary Bischoff

Published by Fairgreens Media, Inc.
P.O. Box 15330
Seattle, WA 98115-0330
(206) 525-1294

Library of Congress Cataloging-in-Publication Data
        CIP 97-060646

Shelley, Jeff, 1950-
        Golf courses of the Pacific Northwest: The Complete Regional Golf
Guide / Jeff Shelley.—3rd Ed.
                p. cm.
        Includes index
        ISBN 0-9629329-2-2
        1. Golf courses—Northwest, Pacific—Directories. 2. Northwest,
        Pacific—guidebooks. 1. Title.

Printed in the United States of America

To Shirley's Spirit

And, once again, to Anni & Erica:

Thanks for all your love and support.

CONTENTS

Preface   7
Explanations   8
Acknowledgments   9
Regional Map   11
Climate Zones   12
In Other Words   17
    Essays & Stories on Golf in the Northwest

  1. Northwest Washington and the San Juan Islands   67
  2. Kitsap Peninsula and the Puget Sound Islands   93
  3. Seattle, Everett and Vicinity   113
  4. Tacoma and Vicinity   175
  5. Olympic Peninsula   207
  6. Olympia and Southwest Washington   225
  7. North-Central Washington   251
  8. South-Central Washington   271
  9. Spokane and Northeast Washington   291
10. Southeast Washington   315
11. Portland, Vancouver and Vicinity   343
12. Northwest Oregon   397
13. Salem, Corvallis and the Central Oregon Coast   411
14. Eugene and Southwest Oregon   449
15. North-Central Oregon   491
16. South-Central Oregon   515
17. Eastern Oregon   539
18. Idaho Panhandle and Sun Valley   553
19. Northwest Montana   581

Alphabetical Index   607
Geographical Index   615

PREFACE

This book is the culmination of over 10 years of hard work. Yeah, there are some who think writing a golf guide book is a piece of cake. It is a great job. There's just much to do to get it right.

That's why I'm so proud of this, the third edition. The first two books—so I've heard—were good, even exceptional.

But this one is special. It's taken a decade and around 150,000 miles to get here. What a ride!

After traveling to all of the golf courses, I finally feel that I can accurately document them. Because I've seen them all. This book represents an honorable—if not crazy—quest to thoroughly cover the subject, addressing each course's unique features while speaking to golfers. And with this edition, I feel comfortable that's been done.

Perhaps most importantly, the joy of seeing this book come to fruition really came from working with family—both blood and extended.

My wife Anni and daughter Erica have been true saints during the past decade (and much longer if you ask them). Anni was instrumental in creating the "look" of this work, which is the biggest book by far ever issued by our publishing company, Fairgreens Media. She kindly lent her experience in the graphic arts—and one helluva lot more—to the cause. Over the years, we've clashed many times in our cooperative artistic endeavors. What would you expect from two Irish Leos? So this book is a watershed event for us, because we worked through our differences, making the project even more rewarding.

Kudos also go to the folks who wrote the "ancillary" pieces in the "In Other Words" section. Each of the people I invited to the party are pals of mine, and I'm happy to showcase their talents. These writers represent years of experience chronicling golf in the Northwest, and their efforts are much appreciated. This is the first time I've ever used other writers. I hope you enjoy their work.

Much appreciation goes to Frank Gaffney and Mary Bischoff. Frank came up with—and then executed—the wonderful illustration used on the cover. Mary waded through tons of manuscript, helping to make my writings clearer and more grammatically correct than if they hadn't gone before her skilled eyes.

Special thanks also to Dan and Kristi MacMillan, who bail me out more often than they think. May God always be with them.

And many thanks to the readers of this book. You're the ones who keep me going.

That's it. On to other things. Hope you enjoy the third edition.

EXPLANATIONS

Ratings

The Course Ratings for a layout relate to its tee locations: F — Front, FF — Forward, R — Regular, I — Intermediate, M — Middle, B — Back, C — Championship, and T — Tournament. The yardage listed for a golf course is from the "tips"; i.e., the longest the course can play. Courses that list only Men and Women ratings are the equivalent of Back and Front.

Estimated Green Fees

The green fees in the book are categorized by Economical, Moderate and Expensive. The green-fee rating is determined when a course is at its most expensive (usually weekends and holidays), and for 18-hole rounds (regardless if the course is nine or 18 holes). The price breaks are as follows:

Economical: up to $15

Moderate: $16 to $40

Expensive: $41 and above

Walk-on Chances

This refers to how amenable a course is for "walk-on players" who show up without reservations. Though based on a facility's popularity and use (annual number of rounds), some of the busier courses are quite skilled at "working in" walk-on golfers, while others aren't.

Walkability

This new category identifies the "walker-friendliness" of a course. The bag-toting author thought those of us who actually enjoy exercise while playing golf—instead of riding around in a cart—might appreciate such a rating.

Playability

A brief overview of a course, and which golfers might gain the most enjoyment from playing it.

Waiver on Accuracy

The green fees, yardages, course ratings, and names of people in this book may no longer be correct. Prices go up, courses change, and people—pros, greens superintendents, managers and course proprietors—come and go. But golf courses are (generally) permanent; that is, once they've opened for business. You can be assured that if a golf course listed in this book is no longer around, it was at one time.

ACKNOWLEDGMENTS

Research Assistants/ Spiritual Guidance

Anni & Erica Shelley
Marliss, Molly & Mark Casteel
Doug, Casey, Maxx & Sam Shelley
Claudia & Ray Johnson
Eric & Dawn Johnson
Kristin & Nick Campbell
Kay, Steve & Stacey Wisner
Beth Macy & Brad Sandvig
Dan, Kristi, Joshua, Sarah &
    Christian MacMillan
Bob & Gloria Spiwak
John & Barb Mallon
Chris & Jeannette Smith
Dave Fischer
Woody Wilson
John Hoetmer
Loren Lippert
Dan Wenzlaff
Steve Stipe & Gail Welsh
Bill Young
Del Jordan
Keith Kaluza
Webb Nelson
Walter Loomis
Darrell, Phyllis & Stephanie Pray
Gordie Hulbert
Charlie & Becky Johnson
Rob Heidt
Mike Root
Steve Taylor & Sue Oberlink
Jim & Carol Miller
Gary Dickerson
Marianne Sao & Bud Maletta
Henry Liebman
Ron & Katie Stull
Scott Smith
Bruce Christy

Writing Buddies

John Peoples
Dan Raley
Blaine Newnham
Craig Smith
Paul Ramsdell
Bob Robinson

Associates & Business Folks

Mike Riste & Dorothy Brown
    at B.C. Golf House
Jim Apfelbaum
John Bodenhamer, John Saegner
    & everyone at PNGA Hq.
All the folks at Oregon Golf
    Association
John Zoller, Jr.
John Bracken
Gerry Cichanski & Mithun Partners
Chris Duthie
Buzz Campion & Jacobsen/Hardy
Bruce McLaughlin & Hawaiian Island
    Golf
John R. Johnson
Frank Keenan
Bob Marlatt & *Inside Golf*
Jack Moss—BMR Associates
Kelly O'Mera
Ron Coleman & Golf Resources
Larry Gilhuly & the USGA
Jerry Fehr & Washington Junior Golf
    Association
Dick Kanda
Kendra Hogue & *Portland Business
    Journal*
Randy Klein
Rob Perry
Valerie Ryan Media Services
Sound Golf
John Straun
R.W. Thorpe & Associates
Scott Fivash & *Washington CEO*
Craig Swanson
Dave Holcombe & Scanner

Golf Course Architects

Graham Cooke & Associates
Robert Cupp
Jim Engh
John Fought
Keith Foster & Associates
Jack Frei
Robert Muir Graves
John Harbottle III
Keith Hellstrom
Lynn William Horn
Tom Johnson
Rees Jones
Robert Trent Jones, Jr.
Jim Kraus
Lisa Maki
Bunny "Gene" Mason
Bill Overdorf
William Robinson
John Steidel
Peter L.H. Thompson
Carl Thuesen
Rick Verbarendse

And all the professionals, managers, greens superintendents, members and owners of Pacific Northwest golf courses and clubs who so kindly assisted me in this endeavor.

REGIONAL MAP

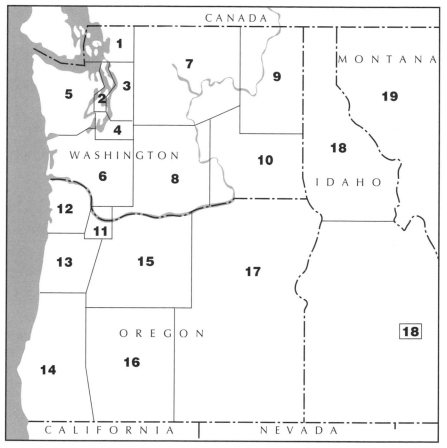

1. Northwest Washington and the San Juan Islands
2. Kitsap Peninsula and the Puget Sound Islands
3. Seattle, Everett and Vicinity
4. Tacoma and Vicinity
5. Olympic Peninsula
6. Olympia and Southwest Washington
7. North-Central Washington
8. South-Central Washington
9. Spokane and Northeast Washington
10. Southeast Washington
11. Portland, Vancouver and Vicinity
12. Northwest Oregon
13. Salem, Corvallis and the Central Oregon Coast
14. Eugene and Southwest Oregon
15. North-Central Oregon
16. South-Central Oregon
17. Eastern Oregon
18. Idaho Panhandle and Sun Valley
19. Northwest Montana

CLIMATE ZONES MAP

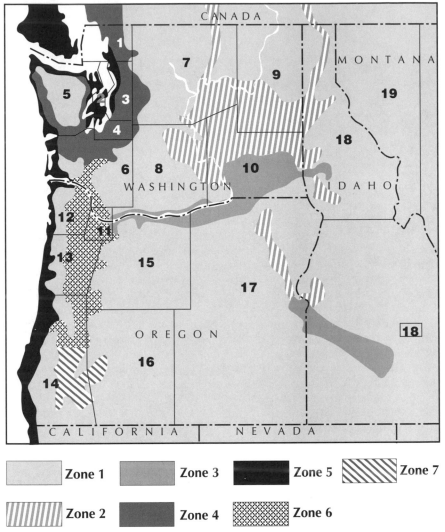

CLIMATE ZONES

Climate plays a critical role in determining when and where to golf. The Pacific Northwest is blessed with a variety of climates—from those that enable year-round play to those that limit golf seasons to a brief six months. As a rule, golf courses located from the shores of the Pacific Ocean to the western foothills of the Cascade Mountains are open 12 months a year. Courses east of the Cascades generally shut their doors before winter, then open again in spring. The factor that usually determines when a course will close is frost on the greens; footprints from people walking on frozen greens blacken and destroy the turf.

There are no hard and fast rules, however, guiding the openings and closings of the region's golf courses. Indeed, heavily-bundled diehards have been caught putting orange balls on snow-covered greens in the dead of winter. Some courses lie in climatically unique "banana belts" with more amenable weather than areas just a few miles away. In the mid-1990s, heavier-than-normal rains combined with excess snowmelt to wreak all sorts of havoc on the region's golf courses. Previously isolated to west-of-the-Cascades areas, the recent flooding stretched into eastern Washington, northwest Montana and southwest Oregon, washing over riverbanks and dikes, and dumping silt and other debris on several courses.

To find out when to golf in the various areas of the Northwest, refer to the climate zone map and the following descriptions to get a good idea of which courses are open during the year. Here's hoping that the region's weather patterns stabilize, and that Northwesterners can get back to the more reliable golf seasons described below.

Zone 1. Very Cold Winters, Magnificent Summers

Though averaging 50 degrees Fahrenheit year-round, this climate zone has some of the wildest temperature fluctuations—120 degrees and more—in the United States. The ground begins to freeze in mid-November, and thaws in March or April. In summer, temperatures over 100 degrees may occur, though balmy 70- and 80-degree days are more the norm. Yearly precipitation averages from 8 to 15 inches, with most in the form of winter snow. Rain showers during the six-month golf season are rare. Winds high enough to affect golfers generally are not a problem, though courses on exposed plateaus or in valleys may be swept by prevailing winds in spring and fall.

Zone 1 Golf Courses. Low annual precipitation. Closed from November 15 through April 15. Bring sunscreen in summer.

Zone 2. Frigid Winters, Steamy Summers

The zone 2 climate is often dictated by continental air masses and features four distinct seasons. Winter is often bone-chilling, spring quite windy, summer cloudless and hot, and fall quite pleasant during the day and frosty at night. Although similar in many ways to zone 1, zone 2 regions are not quite as mountainous. The average yearly temperature is 50 degrees Fahrenheit, and mean precipitation ranges from Spokane's 17 inches to Yakima's eight inches, most of which falls as winter snow. Prevailing winds usually kick up in spring and fall. The growing season for plants in zone 2 is 150 days. Frost usually disappears midway through March and returns in November or December.

Zone 2 Golf Courses: Generally low annual precipitation. Closed from December 1 through March 15. Bring sunscreen in summer.

Zone 3. Minor Banana Belts with Sometimes-Icy Winters

Zone 3 regions are lower in elevation than areas in zones 1 and 2. Pacific air, bypassing the Cascades through the Columbia River Gorge, washes over zone 3, preventing extremely low winter temperatures and bringing more rainfall during a typical year. Although sub-zero stretches do occur, average winter days in zone 3 hover around 15 degrees Fahrenheit. In years with mild winters, golf courses at Hood River and Milton-Freewater have remained open year-round, and facilities in the Tri-Cities and Walla Walla have enjoyed extended seasons. At the height of the golf season, temperatures in July and August can top the 100-degree mark, with courses bordering rivers and lakes quite muggy. The growing period for plants in zone 3 is about 160 days, though Walla Walla's extends almost 220 days.

Zone 3 Golf Courses: Low annual precipitation and occasional balmy spring and fall. If there's no snow on the ground and it is above freezing, give them a call, as a banana belt course might be open. Bring sunscreen in summer.

Zone 4. Mild, Multi-Influenced Climate

Geographical factors play major roles in determining the weather in zone 4. Its proximity to Puget Sound and the Pacific Ocean, and abutment on the east and west by the Cascade and Olympic mountains, respectively, allow zone 4 to be influenced by marine systems, continental air masses, convergence zones, and higher-elevation weather patterns. The weather caused by zone 4's locale results in generally mild conditions and rainfall totals upwards of 50 inches. For golfers, this means lush fairways and greens year-round, but damp footing in spring and winter. In summer and fall, courses are generally much drier. Zone 4's growing season averages 230 days, and the climate is one of the world's best for growing perennials and bulb flowers. Expect much color on zone 4 courses in spring and summer.

Zone 4 Golf Courses: Moderate to high annual precipitation. Generally open year-round; call if frost is on the pumpkin. Pack an umbrella.

Zone 5. Moderated by Puget Sound and the Pacific Ocean

Although on the same latitude as icy Duluth, Minnesota, zone 5 is protected from extremely cold winters by Puget Sound and the Pacific Ocean, affording mild winters, regular rain showers, and a 12-month golf season. There are several banana belts here, with Sequim on the Olympic Peninsula averaging less than 17 inches of rainfall annually. Conversely, Seattle receives 38 inches of annual precipitation. Winters are usually wet and mild, with temperatures around 40 degrees Fahrenheit. When cold spells do occur, they last only briefly, and temperatures rarely drop below 20 degrees. Typically, golf can be played year-round in zone 5; 60- to 70-degree summer days—ideal conditions for the sport—are frequent. The growing season extends up to 250 days and even longer in areas near salt water.

Zone 5 Golf Courses: Moderate to high annual precipitation. Open year-round, unless there's frost. Pack an umbrella.

Zone 6. The Mild Willamette Valley

The mountains bordering the Pacific Ocean in zone 1 help provide a buffer that moderates coastal winds and lessens rainfall in zone 6. Also, the Willamette River helps ease winter's chill and allows year-round golf. Annual precipitation totals upward of 40 inches, which helps keep courses quite green through all four seasons. Summer temperatures in zone 6 are slightly warmer than those in zone 5, and the growing season extends almost 260 days.

Zone 6 Golf Courses: Moderate to high annual precipitation. Open year-round, unless there's frost. Pack an umbrella.

Zone 7. Oregon's Rogue River Valley

Zone 7 offers the four distinct seasons of zones 1 and 2 without the excessively frigid winters. There are mountains in this zone, but its proximity to the Pacific Ocean as well as its more southerly latitude create a less rigorous climate than is found in other alpine climes of the Northwest. Medford averages 53 degrees Fahrenheit year-round and has just over 20 inches of precipitation a year. Because of frozen ground, zone 7 golf courses are usually closed from December to March, though some venues are open during unusually warm winter stretches. Zone 7's growing season averages about 160 days.

Zone 7 Golf Courses: Low to moderate annual precipitation. Not much snow in winter, but plenty of frost. If it's warm in February, call for a tee time. Generally, forgo the umbrella, but bring sunscreen in summer.

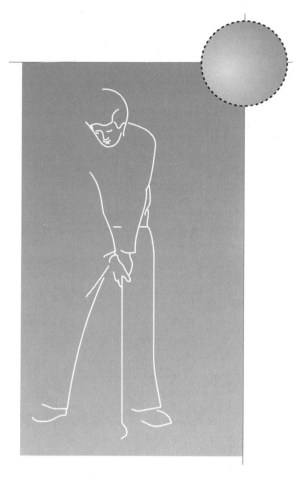

In Other Words

A selection of essays,
stories and tidbits on golf
in the Pacific Northwest.

Simplifying "The Rules of Golf"

The following appeared as "The Rules of Golf" on a local computer bulletin board in Elkton, Maryland. The author was unaccredited, though there are any number of golfers who could have written it.

1. A ball sliced or hooked into the rough shall be lifted and placed in the fairway at a point equal to the distance it carried or rolled into the rough. Such veering right or left frequently results from friction between the face of the club and the cover of the ball, and the player should not be penalized for erratic behavior of the ball resulting from such uncontrollable mechanical phenomena.

2. A ball hitting a tree shall be deemed not to have hit the tree. Hitting a tree is simply bad luck and has no place in the scientific game. The player should estimate the distance the ball would have traveled if it had not hit the tree and play the ball from there, preferably from a nice tuft of grass.

3. There shall be no such thing as a lost ball. The missing ball is on or near the course somewhere and eventually will be found and pocketed by someone else. It thus becomes a stolen ball, and the player should not compound the felony by charging himself with a penalty stroke.

4. If a putt passes over the hole without dropping, it is deemed to have dropped. The law of gravity holds that any object attempting to maintain a position in the atmosphere without something to support it must drop. The law of gravity supersedes the law of golf.

5. Same thing for a ball that stops on the brink of the hole and hangs there defying gravity. You cannot defy the law.

6. Same thing goes for a ball that rims the cup. A ball should not go sideways. This violates the laws of physics.

7. A putt that stops close enough to inspire such comments as, "You could blow it in," may be blown in. This rule does not apply if the ball is more than three inches from the hole, because no one wants to make a travesty of the game.

The Wild Side of Northwest Courses

by Craig Smith

On Northwest courses, eagles appear in trees more often than on scorecards, and a round of golf can be a walk on the wild side. Whether it's the family of foxes that lives on the West Seattle course in the middle of a metropolitan area of two million people, or the rattlesnakes that occasionally are seen on courses east of the Cascades, golf and nature in this corner of the nation go hand in paw. The fun of seeing a wild animal can even take the sting out of a three-putt. Well, maybe sometimes.

Animals account for some lively golf stories, such as Ron Caperna's 'par by a hare,' which he accomplished in 1967 at the Prineville Golf & Country Club in central Oregon. Caperna, a big hitter and then pro at Astoria Golf & Country Club, was trying to reach the 274-yard 5th hole from the tee. He was egged on by fellow golfers and spectators who wanted to see if one of the Paul Bunyans of Northwest golf could reach the green. Instead, Caperna uncoiled and topped the ball. The shot appeared headed out of bounds into sagebrush but struck a jackrabbit and stayed in-bounds. The rabbit was knocked cold.

That was the first of two miracle shots on the hole. Caperna muscled his second shot over the green, but it struck a bell used to signal golfers and stayed in. Caperna then chipped on and sank his putt for par. Caperna had started the round with four bogeys before the rabbit's-foot par launched him on a string of 11 straight pars. "I couldn't do anything right until I hit the rabbit. Then for a long time I couldn't do anything wrong," he said.

Sherm Bucher of Portland once had a seagull fly off with one the best shots of his life. Bucher, described by a friend as a competent golfer who somehow struggles on water holes, one day hit a splendid shot to within five feet of the cup on the par-3 17th hole at Eastmoreland Golf Course in Portland. But as he was walking over the bridge to the green, a seagull swooped down, grabbed the ball, took it over the pond and dropped it. Splash!

Hawks have been known to steal balls at the Walla Walla Country Club. Mark Denton of Missoula, Montana encountered different winged thieves—ravens—after he began hitting balls onto a hillside near his home in the spring of 1996. After hitting 300 to 400 balls onto the hill in a period of two to three weeks, Denton grabbed three five-gallon containers and went out to retrieve them. They were gone.

"I was looking around and I couldn't find any of them," he told a reporter. "I kept going higher up the hill and higher up the hill and I should have been stepping on them. Balls should have been all over, just like granules of sand in the ocean." Denton's hunch: "The ravens must have thought they were eggs and flew off with them."

Canada geese have become an increasing nuisance on Northwest golf courses in the 1990s. Once considered migratory fowl that were a treat to see, the geese now seem as common as robins. They are considered pests that are content to hang around all year, eating and defecating on golf courses.

One of the best goose stories involves John Monson, the former superintendent of Seattle's Broadmoor Golf Club who has been facilities manager for the Seattle Seahawks for years. He was playing Broadmoor in the mid-1970s when he hit a goose dead solid in the body while playing the club's long par-4 10th hole. One of his playing partners was Larry Gilhuly, now greens director for the USGA Western region.

"John lost about 100 yards because it hit the goose," Gilhuly recalled. "Then he hit the same kind of shot and it hit the same goose in the same spot. We were dying laughing. The chance of hitting a goose is remote enough, but hitting the same goose twice on the same hole? The goose just kept on going. We told John he had shot a double-goose."

Gilhuly, who worked at that time for Monson at Broadmoor, has another goose story. One day he was herding geese toward an exit point at Broadmoor that happened to be near a deep practice bunker. The geese would take flight when they got near the edge of the fence and often relieved themselves as they went airborne. Gilhuly thought no one was in the bunker. Surprise! Peggy Conley, a former Curtis Cup player, was in it when the geese took off over her. "Somewhat embarrassing," is how Gilhuly describes the situation.

A much more welcome bird on Northwest courses is the bald eagle. During the 1996 Ernst Championship hosted by Fred Couples at Inglewood Golf Club in Kenmore, an eagle flew over the 18th green as Phil Mickelson attempted an eagle putt. Some writers covering the event immediately started quietly rooting for the putt to drop because it was such an obvious angle to their stories. Mickelson missed the putt, but won the playoff.

At the Semiahmoo Golf & Country Club in Blaine golfers are almost guaranteed of eagles—viewing them, that is. At least three families of eagles lived on the course in the mid-1990s.

In the late 1950s and early 1960s, peacocks lived off the 9th hole at Inglewood and used to shriek, "Help! Help!" Snohomish Golf Course was home to a crow in the 1980s and early '90s that sounded like a baby. There are so many pheasants around Pendleton Country Club that the club logo features them.

Elk are a problem on many Northwest courses. One facility that decided it had had enough was Tokatee Golf Club in Blue River, Oregon, located about 45 miles from Eugene. In the mid-1980s, more than three miles of seven-foot fence were put up around the course to keep the elk out.

"There had been a herd of probably 30 elk," said superintendent Ray Telfer, who has been at the course since it opened in 1965. "They would come onto the course, mostly at night. It was like they used to play games on mounds around the greens and the mounds along fairways." The frolicking elk damaged greens and fairways. Telfer said, "As far as I'm concerned, the fence probably has paid for itself."

At Hidden Lakes Golf Resort in Sandpoint, Idaho, 50 to 60 elk live on the general property and are replaced by moose on the same day every year. "It's like the swallows of Capistrano," said Ken Parker, director of golf. "Every year on May 15, the elk leave and the moose arrive. There are 10 moose that live on the property. It's rare when the moose aren't seen on a daily basis."

Deer are a common sight at the Pumpkin Ridge complex west of Portland. During medal-play playoffs to determine berths for match play at the 1996 U.S. Amateur won by Tiger Woods, a half-dozen deer were among the spectators as golfers teed off on the 12th hole.

Jim Gibbons, executive director of the Oregon Golf Association, recalled a 1995 collegiate tournament sponsored by PING at Pumpkin Ridge during which deer roamed the property. "Some players from the South and places like New York never had seen deer," he said. "They were taken aback and they'd yell to their teammates, 'Hey, look over there.' Players from the Northwest are used to seeing deer," Gibbons said. "They would look over and say, 'Well, they are supposed to be here.'"

During the 1995 U.S. Open Qualifier at Sahalee Country Club in Redmond, Washington, two deer wandered across a green after a group of golfers had started to play the hole. The deer made hoof marks on the green and the golfers asked if they could be repaired. The ruling: Not until after the hole was finished. Fortunately, the hoof marks didn't come into play.

Fish on a fairway? It happened several years ago at the Oswego Lake Country Club south of Portland. During the Oregon Open, the skies opened and the ponds on the course overflowed. Play was halted, but when it resumed one golfer found a 10-inch rainbow trout in the middle of a fairway. He picked it up and carried it back to a pond.

One of the best courses for wildlife is the semiprivate Juniper Golf Club in Redmond, Oregon. Bob Wanker, a member since 1978, said the wildlife increases his enjoyment of the course "about 1,000 percent." Wanker, who has a naturalist's knowledge of the wildlife on his course, comments, "Most golf courses are environmentally friendly." Juniper Golf Club is on the Deschutes River and has four kinds of snakes (including an occasional rattler), coyotes, porcupines, deer, antelope, various hawks and eagles, ospreys and hundreds of quails. Emperor butterflies migrating north from Mexico fly through the course every year. "It's something to watch those butterflies come in during the spring," Wanker said.

A funny sight is watching birds such as robins and starlings peck at juniper berries, then drink water. "It's like gin," he said. "They just get hammered. They even fall out of trees."

Urban courses have their share of wildlife, too. A family of foxes has called West Seattle Golf Course home for years. They weren't the favorite sight of some male golfers in 1995, though. A woman exhibitionist living in a nearby apartment could be seen from the course. She used to put on a show for golfers until the day police knocked on her door and put an end to the proceedings.

One of the all-time Northwest golf-course animals wasn't wild at all. It was a Brittany spaniel named "Divot," who hung out at the Riverside Golf Course in Ferndale, Washington. Divot would jump into power carts, press the accelerator and take off down a fairway while the golfers were playing a shot. The dog never did learn how to operate the brake.

Craig Smith is a 20-year veteran of the sports staff at the Seattle Times, covering golf since 1995. The 52-year-old lives in Kirkland with his wife Julie and their teenage sons Stuart and Elliott. After graduating from Bothell High School and the University of Washington, Smith worked at the Seattle P-I, Associated Press, and newspapers in Charleston, West Virginia and Fairbanks, Alaska. The men's club member at Bellevue Municipal Golf Course carries an 18 handicap, and plays bogey golf at public courses throughout the Puget Sound area.

Anecdotes from a Golf Pro

by Dave Fischer

[The author asked a golf pro friend of his, Dave Fischer, to tell a few anecdotes from his collection of golf experiences. Dave is a fine storyteller who embellishes his memories with great zeal. The Greg Norman lookalike has played with and taught golf to everyone from the rich and famous in Palm Springs to cowboys who moseyed in off cattle ranches in Big Sky Country. Here are a few of Dave's more colorful tales.]

While working on the driving range at El Dorado Country Club in Indian Wells one afternoon, a member asked me to watch him hit a few shots. He said he was getting on in years and was having trouble seeing the ball.

After each shot he would ask how far the ball was going. "About 125 yards, Mr. McCarthy," I replied.

"That can't be right," he would grumble. "I hit it a lot farther than that on the course." I said, "Well, I measured the yardage this morning."

I didn't think much of it until a week later when I had the good fortune to play nine holes with Mr. McCarthy and his usual playing partners, Ernie Vandeweghe (grandfather of former NBA player Kiki Vandeweghe and Tauna Vandeweghe, a swimming gold medalist in the 1976 Olympics) and Ron Marra. Hitting second, right after me, Vandeweghe knocked his shot 215 yards right down the middle of the fairway. As he walked by me he whispered, "Get in the cart."

We sat down and as soon as McCarthy hit his tee shot we took off. Vandeweghe made a beeline for McCarthy's ball and as we approached it, he grabbed what looked like a large pair of pincers and clamped onto the ball. We traveled down the fairway another 100 yards before Vandeweghe dropped the ball. He looked at me and said, "Don't say a word to him or else!"

This went on for the entire nine holes, and then it dawned on me, "This is where the missing yards from the driving range are going." When we finished I walked up to Mr. McCarthy and said, "You were right. There must be something wrong with those range balls. You hit it much farther on the course."

While working at Rio Hondo Country Club in Downey, California, I had the distinct pleasure of golfing with Fernando Valenzuela, the great Dodger pitcher. Being fellow lefties we hit it off great. I was really surprised at how well he could hit the ball, especially when during every swing he would look to the heavens on his takeaway. He didn't speak much English, so conversation was minimal. But he would cuss on occasion.

I really felt that he liked me, because every time I made a putt to beat him on a hole, he would call me "Puto." I think that's Spanish for putter.

Every once in a while you meet living legends and observe them being human. Clint Eastwood was in the desert for the Bob Hope Chrysler Classic a few years ago and was playing a practice round at El Dorado. We fixed him up with a cart and tee time and sent him on his way. He jumped in and took off looking for the snack bar to get a cold drink before starting.

There are two turn-offs from the pro shop to El Dorado's snack bar. One will take you there and the other goes to the main dining room. If you miss the first turn, your cart ends up on the sidewalk. And with enough speed, you can almost take the steps all the way into the clubhouse dining room. Mr. Eastwood missed the first turn just as he was starting to accelerate and made a beeline up the steps.

Some tales from the pro shop:

Have you ever seen those big bags of wedges and woods that golf shops have inside the door? You know the ones: they're packed with 50 clubs in a space that should hold no more than 15. Ever seen anyone try to pick the whole bag up and carry it out of the shop thinking it's a rental set? I have.

Then there was the incident involving a demo driver. Every time the guy trying it out would hit the club, he'd walk out onto the driving range to pick up the head cover.

Or the beginning golfers who, after their lessons, decide to play nine holes. Upon putting out on the 9th hole, I've heard them ask, "Since we still have some of those striped balls left in our basket from the first time around, can we play a few more holes?"

My all-time favorite though is the group of guys who take carts and feel they have to take their clubs off the cart before teeing off on every single hole!

Lessons are a great time for an instructor to get back in touch with what it was like when they just started playing golf. What we now take for granted may not be so obvious to the next person. I've given lessons to women in high-heeled shoes because they were on their lunch breaks. Men have shown up barefoot and in swimming trunks because the weather was so nice. I even gave a lesson to a gentleman in a three-piece suit two hours before his wedding.

The movie actress, Andie McDowell, took lessons from me in Montana. We managed to get to the point where she understood you can't train a golf ball like you train a horse. Towards the end of our lessons, she rarely talked to the ball anymore. I'm also glad she stopped whipping me when I gave her bad advice. I'm just kidding about that . . . I never give bad advice!

The coastal region of Southern California has greater extremes in weather than the desert. But for the avid golfer, it's just another challenge on the way to that great course in the sky. I have seen instances after a torrential downpour where, if you are playing slowly, the kayakers behind you rudely force their way past.

There have been a great number of people I've had the honor and privilege of playing golf with. Hall-of-fame football players, baseball stars, movie stars, giants of industry, and others. These have mostly happened by accident, but some were planned.

One of my most memorable rounds was with Mrs. Patty Haggar of Haggar Slacks. During play on the 13th hole at El Dorado, after I hit a daring three iron over the pond guarding the right side of the green to set up an eagle putt, Mrs. Haggar looked at me in wonder and amazement and said, "Dave, can I ask you something?"

"Sure," I responded. I'm thinking she's about to ask how I had managed such a great shot and not be on the PGA Tour. Instead, she asked, "What kind of pants are you wearing?" I told her, and she turned to a friend in the cart and said, "See, if those were Haggar's they wouldn't be wrinkled!"

Pranks by golfing buddies are always fun. A classic caper involving two PGA professionals comes to mind. One of the pros was a very good putter and a decent player. He had a vanity plate on his car that read, "Mr. 1 Putt." You would be surprised how easy it is to convert a "1" to a "4" with black electrical tape. Mr. One Putt didn't notice until a member asked him how good of a pro could he be if he four-putts every green.

Seven years after playing his first round of golf at Forsyth Country Club in Montana, Dave Fischer received his Class A card from the PGA, a remarkable achievement. Currently the head pro at Dunham Hills Golf Club in Hartland, Michigan, the Wisconsin native apprenticed at El Dorado Country Club in Indian Wells, California, and at the Meadow Lake and King Ranch courses in western Montana. He then moved to The Children's Course in Gladstone, Oregon before heading east to Michigan. Among his biggest thrills in golf are playing a round with Fernando Valenzuela and caddying in the 1992 Bob Hope Chrysler Classic. During his relatively brief golf career, Dave has met such celebrities as Gerald Ford, Bob Hope, Clint Eastwood, Arnold Palmer, Greg Norman and actress Andie MacDowell.

A Kindred Spirit

by Jeff Shelley

Outside of a handful of golf pros, superintendents, amateurs, golf association administrators, purveyors of golf equipment and writers of golf guide books—including myself, perhaps no other person in the Northwest is as devoted to the sport in our region as Loren Lippert. At the age of 65 in October 1996, the retired Salem postal carrier had played 942 golf courses, including all the layouts opened then in Oregon and Washington, most in Idaho, and many in Montana. Other areas of Lippert's intense concentration are Hawaii (all the courses but those on Oahu), Scotland, England, Mexico and Palm Springs.

So why, Loren, are you so obsessed? "I don't hunt or fish, nor do other activities that are time-consuming," he says. "Also, every golf course is different, not like bowling or tennis where the 'stadium' is the same." Lippert adds, "Once I played every course in Oregon, I felt I had to keep going." With that confession in mind, Loren's total number of courses played will grow as he continues his quest.

Appropriately, Loren's first round of golf occurred on one of the region's throwback tracks, the Woodburn Golf Club. This nine-holer west of Woodburn is one of two courses in the Northwest that still uses sand greens. (The other is the remote Pend Oreille Golf & Country Club in Metalline Falls, Washington—which Lippert's also played.)

Lippert's odyssey began while in high school. After moving to Salem from Woodburn, he linked up for golf outings with classmates Kent Myers (who went on to a storied career in amateur golf), friend Bob Albrich, and brother Ed, who recently retired as a Botany professor at Portland State University. Other Salem High School students at the time included Bunny Mason, longtime club professional and course designer, and Paul Sundin, who went on to become the head pro at Salem Golf Club for many years.

Loren had a car in those days and would drive his pals to different courses around Salem. He'd also accompany the Salem High team to golf matches, "just to be on the golf course." While in the Army in the early 1950s, Lippert was stationed at Fort Lawton in Seattle and, on weekends, would play different Puget Sound courses. After marrying Edna (bless her heart) and joining the postal service, Loren had one week more of vacation than his wife. Edna kindly allowed him to use that extra time for golf outings.

On June 28, 1963, Loren, his brother and Albrich set an endurance record that may never to broken; the threesome played nine courses in one day! Starting with a 5:10 a.m. tee time at Illahe Hills in Salem, the trio went on to play the courses at Salem, McNary, Senior Estates, Woodburn, Evergreen, Santiam, Battle Creek and Oak Knoll. Each round was nine holes, and the group walked all 81 holes. The 115-mile golf trip ended at 9:30 p.m. Incredibly, Loren used just one ball throughout the day.

Another stamina-defying adventure occurred in Seattle in the 1960s, when Lippert played 18-hole rounds at Broadmoor, Overlake and Glendale in a single day. Several times he's played four or five courses a day. Over the years, the grandfather has accumulated six boxes of scorecards and notebooks with commentary on his golf rounds and travels. Loren has 170 golf books, only three of which are not travel-related. He showed me a copy of the second edition of *Golf Courses of the Pacific Northwest*, each course listed in the index had beside it a carefully drawn asterisk to show Loren had played it.

While going through the list, we discussed the book and the memories conjured up by the courses in it. I told him of my plan back in 1986 (when work on the original edition began) to play all the golf courses in the Northwest. I felt then (and still feel) that playing a course is necessary to properly 'capture' its essence. After a first day that included 27 holes of walking, playing, taking notes, packing a camera and clubs, and traveling over 500 miles to get to two Oregon courses (Elkhorn Valley and Tokatee—I took the wrong route), my approach was soon altered. It had to be or the book wouldn't get finished within my lifetime. I've since played whenever possible (about half the courses in the book), while touring the others in a cart, noting all the holes and taking photos of particularly arresting scenes.

I also mentioned an aborted attempt to include British Columbia courses in the book, expecting to find only 75 or so layouts. After blithely driving up to Vancouver from my Seattle home and taking notes on six layouts, I found a B.C. golf map. The map was dotted with over 200 tracks and the area was as big as the rest of the Northwest combined! Loren laughed as I recalled driving sheepishly back home, wisely determining that including B.C. would result in an unwieldy encyclopedia that publishers would balk at printing.

Loren also lent knowing sympathy when I described some of my golf trips. Traveling a total of 150,000 miles to visit the courses in the book has involved several marathon outings. One four-day trip to Montana (I've made about 10 in all to Big Sky Country) spanned 2,300 miles and 18 tracks. Another to Sun Valley via Hamilton, Montana was also that long. Sojourns to eastern Oregon have stretched upwards of 1,500 miles, with some 20 golf courses visited and photographed. A recent five-day jaunt to southwest Oregon spanned 1,500 miles and 25 courses.

Like myself, Loren doesn't restrict his golf destinations to regulation-length tracks. Indeed, he's played a total of 107 par-3s. Perhaps most remarkable are the venues he's played that no longer exist (see list below). The 11 handicapper, who's been as low as a 6, savors being dedicated to the task. And what a glorious chore it's been.

As for the future, Loren says, "As long as my wife allows me, I'll keep going. It always bugs me if there are golf courses I haven't played. I'll keep going to the new courses, particularly in Washington and Oregon." Of the golf facilities that will be opening in the years ahead, he comments, "It always blows me away that they keep adding golf courses. At one time or another, I had played all the golf courses in Vancouver, Las Vegas and San Francisco. Now, those cities all have new courses I haven't played."

Such is the dilemma, and the motivation, of this kindred spirit. Though viewed by some as being almost maniacal in our quest, Loren and I envision common horizons which move closer with each new course played.

Courses Played by Loren Lippert that No Longer Exist

Oregon. Thunder Bay (Seal Rock), Cherry Lane Park (Medford), West Hills Muni (Portland), Lloyd GC (Portland), Alderwood (Portland), Golf Land (Beaverton), Pendleton CC (original course), Ontario GC, Knox Butte (Albany).

Washington. Kelso Elks Memorial, Mountain View (Lacey), Poulsbo GC, Birch Bay Golf Resort, Meadowbrook (Seattle), Juanita GC (Kirkland), Brookside (Avondale), Holiday GC (Tacoma), Highland GC (Tacoma), Lake Chelan (original course).

Par-3 Courses. Hoyt Park Pitch & Putt (Portland), Piluso's Pitch & Putt (Portland), Wilson-Edgewater (private par-3 in Lee's Camp—near Tillamook), Clear Lake (Salem), West Hills Par-3 (Albany), Stanley Park Iron Course (Sherwood), Country Squire (Eugene), Veteran's Domiciliary Par-3 (White City), Sunset Par-3 (Spokane), Plantation Par-3 (The Dalles).

Some Lippert Recollections

"Only twice have I caddied for money. Once in the Oregon Tournament of Champions at Salem Golf Club, I carried for Lloyd Mattison from Laurelwood in Eugene. The other time was at Columbia-Edgewater in the Boy's Club Chapman. I carried two days for Gene May, pro at Longview CC, and Dick Price, a well-known amateur. This team won the tournament. Bunny Mason set me up with both jobs.

"I once left my billfold with several hundred dollars cash (which I was going to take on a vacation to Palm Springs the next day) on the first tee at Elkhorn Valley in Lyons, Oregon. Didn't miss it until four holes later. Ran all the way back to find it still there! Other players hadn't teed off from the back markers where I'd left it.

"At Hidden Valley CC in Reno, I finished late and realized I left my wedge beside a green several holes back. I took off to retrieve it. Though I found it, it was real dark by then. The gates were locked and the only way out was through the clubhouse, where a formal dance was in progress. Embarrassing as it was, I walked through the dance floor and out the front door. I picked up my clubs the next day.

"While stationed at Fort Lawton in 1951, I was hitting balls on a grassy strip across the street from some barracks, when I sliced an iron shot that broke through a window of a sergeant who was napping in the room of a barracks that wasn't mine!

"I witnessed three birds struck by golf balls. One was a duck at Salem Golf Club hit by Dr. Bates. Another was at Fort Lewis GC. This one was hit 'on the wing.' And another was hit on the fly by a member I was playing with at Canyon CC in Palm Springs.

"I once placed my watch on the first tee marker at the Eden Course at St. Andrews, and didn't miss it until after the round, by which time the starter's house was closed. The next morning I went back and someone had indeed turned it in.

"One evening in Hope, Alberta, I was told that the local course was closed. I asked why and was told that the mosquitoes were 'out.' The pro said to go ahead to play a hole or two if I wanted. Well I did, and the winds came up and kept the mosquitoes away. I played the beautiful nine-hole course and got stung only once.

"At the North Canyon CC in Palm Springs, I changed my shoes in what turned out to be the ladies locker room. After the round, I couldn't find my bag and shoes. After telling the pro, he retrieved my stuff. I did not see any ladies on the course that day, but it *was* an embarrassment.

"I've mentioned golfing with my brother Ed. He's accomplished something probably not done by many Americans. He has played every course that has held the British Open.

"On September 24, 1983, I started playing golf on Oahu and in 12 days had played 18 courses.

"The trip I took this July (1996) included 33 courses in 17 days. Three of those courses I went to twice because I only had time for nine holes in the evening. I played the other nine on another day.

"Untold thanks must be given to my great wife, Edna, for allowing me these golf trips. Now to the course."

Loren Lippert

The Glamorous Golf Writer—With Children

by Daniel MacMillan

[I asked fellow golf book author and good friend, Dan MacMillan, to write about his unique method of travel. While I generally go alone, Dan takes many research trips with his three children: Joshua age 7, Sarah 4, and 2-year-old Christian. Dan's books, *Golfing in Washington, Golfing in Oregon, Golfing in Idaho & Montana, and Golfing in British Columbia,* cover a vast geographical area. He estimates that the kids have escorted him on 15 trips over the years. Most of the time his wife Kristi goes along. One of the family's Idaho excursions involved 3,000 miles over 10 days. Another nine-day, 6,000-mile adventure took the MacMillans around the massive state of Montana (Dan notes they "saw" the Wyoming and North Dakota borders). Dan says his children "go everywhere with me. They're surgically attached to my arms." Here then is a typical travel day for this golf writer—with children.]

I don't know how often someone has remarked that I have the greatest job in the world: playing golf all day, writing about it and getting paid. But while sitting in another fast food restaurant looking at cold fries and an undercooked hamburger, I began to wonder if life on the road is all it's cracked up to be. Sure, I enjoy the early-morning drives to new golf courses, and the challenge of finding a track so obscure that only the locals know about it. I find myself drifting back to the days of bringing my clubs along and actually playing golf on a research trip. Getting to tee it up on a brand-new track with no divots, no ball marks. Maybe the course hasn't yet opened and I'm the first to play it. As I drift off to that glorious time, reality strikes me like a two-iron between the eyes.

"Dad, I don't like my fries and Sarah drank some of my pop!" interjects Joshua.

"I did not!" Sarah shouts back. "Joshua's looking at me and copying everything I say!"

"Did so!"

"Did not!"

"Are we done Dad? How many courses do we have to go to today? I'm tired of driving and want to go home. Is the hotel close?"

I glance at my watch. It's only 11:45 a.m. The day isn't half over. As I look over the restaurant booth we're sitting in, I see Kristi coming toward me with a tired look on her face, her hands filled with our newest bundle of joy, little Christian Rogers. On this day, life with Christian has not been pleasant. The boy does not like riding in the car. "What infant doesn't like to ride in the car?" I ask myself.

I wonder just how many times a kid can go to the bathroom as I unfold a Montana state map and look for the nearest route to the next golf course. Then I realize that we are, at best, four days and 26 courses away from home. If Christian was going to continue crying on this trip, Kristi and I were heading to the nearest bridge and jumping off. What was I thinking when I brought these people along?! I informed the troops it was time to go. Over moans and objections, I reminded them that the sooner we got going, the sooner we'd reach the hotel and go swimming! I've learned that bribing the kids in times like this has become one of my greatest talents.

The children are loaded and away we go—hitting the road en route to the latest and greatest course ever built. Then I hear the hum of the TV-VCR starting up and the Lion King theme blaring Elton John's voice. How many times have I heard this thing? From my driver's seat, I've learned all the movie's characters in and out. Just once I'd like Simba to eat the pig. Just once I'd like the kids to try a different tape that didn't begin with the "Wonderful World of Disney" anthem.

Much of the day is filled with quick stops at local golf courses, talking with the owner, pro or manager and picking up the scorecard, layout and any other information that may be useful in my Golfing in Idaho & Montana book. The local pro tells me how lucky I am that my family goes on these trips with me. Buddy, if you only knew. . .

Potty breaks are a constant concern. It seems that whenever I'm making good time to the next course, my wife says one of the kids must find a facility. My ever-present rejoinder, "Why didn't you go at the golf course?" Joshua says, "I didn't have to go then!" Four-year-old Sarah announces, "I forgot." Joshua sometimes chimes in with, "You didn't tell me to go."

Thankfully, my watch says it's almost five o'clock. Time to head to a hotel for some relaxation and dinner. Suddenly I realize we're almost three hours from the nearest major city. I think to myself, they're not kidding when they call this Big Sky Country because there's nothing out here but farmland and clouds. Now I must face the kids and explain we're only one Lion King movie and three Barney videos from the hotel. This tactic is crucial: Never mention how many hours there are to go, and always relate time in terms of movies and video tapes.

Just then I remember what swimming entails. Oh, how I dread the swimming, when I must go into the pool with the kids and the water is always colder on me than them. How can they have so much fun when their lips are blue? I hear Joshua say he can't wait to put on his swimming trunks and jump into the water. My hopes that they'll forget swimming are dashed. How can kids recall every detail of every promise ever made to them when they can't remember to put their toys, clothes and books away?

The drive to the hotel is shorter than expected. I'm very thankful Montana doesn't have a speed limit. Unloading the van is the final terrible job of the day. Bottles, garbage, dirty diapers and just plain kid stickiness is everywhere. How can kids be so dirty?, I ask myself. When I was their age, I was never this soiled. After checking in at the front desk, we haul what seems to be all of our worldly belongings to the room. My wife and I tote the blankets, the "woobies," the stuffed bears, the dinosaurs and Barbie clothes, and collapse in the nearest easy chair. Not two seconds later the kids are jumping on my lap—bathing suits on, life jackets in hand and ready to be strapped on, towels draped over shoulders, saying, "Are you ready yet Dad?" "Come on Dad, it's time to go!" I wish these kids would get ready for school that fast.

I head down to the pool with three kids in tow. Excitement and the smell of chlorine are in the air. I turn the corner and see the pool: much nicer than usual. The kids have been waiting all day for this. After overcoming the initial shock of the lukewarm water, I unwind from another hectic day. I look at my three kids, trying to envision the world through their eyes. A swimming pool, mom and dad—the only things that matter to them at this moment. I realize why I started writing golf books in the first place: so I could spend more time with my family.

Suddenly recharged, I realize that guy in the golf shop was right. I am very lucky! From now on, every time someone says I have the greatest job in the world, I'll agree. I get to watch my kids grow up and see every one of their games and school events. I was there for their first-ever steps, and I've heard the first words uttered by each child. What dad has had the opportunity to pursue a career he loves, while seeing his children grow up at the same time? Life on the road will never be the same. And with this motley crew, I'm glad it won't be.

Daniel MacMillan is the author of several golf guides: Golfing in Washington, Golfing in Oregon, and Golfing in Idaho & Montana. His first book was published in 1986. Born in Seattle, Dan moved to Anchorage as a toddler and was raised in Alaska until age 15. He moved back to Seattle and graduated from O'Dea High School a year after a well-known classmate, Fred Couples, in 1978. He later attended Shoreline Community College. As a youth, Dan played baseball, basketball and football. He picked up golf in 1982. Today, Dan enjoys all sports, especially coaching his three children—Joshua, Sarah and Christian—in soccer and Little League baseball. Dan and his wife, Kristi, recently celebrated their 10th wedding anniversary.

The Travails of a Greens Committee Chairman

by Blaine Newnham

There is no more ridiculous and important position at a golf club than the chairman of the Greens Committee. I've done that job for three years now. I'm the liaison between the golfing members and the course superintendent. I'm the course ombudsman, the flak catcher, the guy who knows it all and doesn't know anything. I worry about everything from goose poop to moss, from broken sprinklers to broken mowers, from drainage to dandelions, even though I personally can't do much about any of them.

The only thing I know for sure is that my game has gone down the drain. I never get to practice. If I'm not in motion for more than 20 seconds, I'm hit with suggestions, questions, complaints—mostly the latter.

Every club has a Greens (or Green) Committee. We have a half-dozen members who attend monthly meetings. We oversee an annual operating budget for course maintenance of $450,000, plus another $50,000 or more in capital expenses. We're charged with the playability of the course, a mission we take seriously, but one over time mitigated with respect for reality and lightened with a sense of humor.

The members want everything but a raise in their dues. They don't want to hear that the John Deere tractor has 200,000 miles on a frame held together with duct tape. Or that a new one costs $44,000. They complain about the greens being punched and sanded when without the process they'd eventually look like a runway at SeaTac Airport. They want a smooth putting surface but aren't willing to get rid of their steel-spiked shoes. They want their balls to roll forever down the fairways in the summer, but they don't want brown grass. They don't want goose poop on the grass, but they aren't willing to unleash our prize dog on the source of the problem.

Mostly, they want different things. The women's division at our club worries about things like ball washers, and drinking fountains and rest rooms. They are organized, efficient, unrelenting. The men are neither organized nor efficient. All they want is to keep the course in great shape all the time. No temporary greens or tees, no water in the sand traps; just have the course ready when we're awarded the U.S. Open.

Truthfully, our members aren't unreasonable. They stayed with us through one winter when we had four greens closed because of a terrible moss mess. Basically, we told our superintendent we'd back him any way we could: close the greens, bring in help from the USGA, even resod a green or two if we had to. But the problem had to be corrected by spring.

Our superintendent is great, a young guy who's still with us. He cares about the golf course beyond his responsibility and paycheck. He nearly cried the day the two of us walked across two greens after they'd been hacked with axes in an angry and wanton display of vandalism. I held his hand. That's what I do. He also cares about birds and squirrels, winning a national award for his environmental sensitivity.

Even though we get plenty of suggestions from the members, we don't tell him how low to cut the grass or how much fertilizer to use. He knows we want the greens as fast as possible, but that we want them healthy more than we want them fast. He reaches a compromise between the grass blade and putter blade.

I had one member complain about the pale color of the grass on the fairways. "Tell the superintendent we need to put lime on the fairways. It's what we put on our lawn at home." So I broached the subject with our superintendent. "Are we using lime?" I asked. "About six million pounds a month, or something," he responded.

As summer turned into fall one year, one particular fairway was flooded with water. A member said he couldn't believe we were still irrigating that hole when it was raining. I assured him we weren't. Later I found out our computerized watering system had gone bonkers—I think slugs had sacrificed their slimy bodies to short our electrical system—and, indeed, we were watering that fairway even when it rained.

Our Greens Committee meetings are never short. The simple matter of goose poop can take hours. We talked about noisemakers, fences around ponds, chemicals to make the grass unappealing, having something new and different for Thanksgiving dinner. The solution was right in front of us: Dozer, the dog. Dozer belongs to our assistant superintendent, who found him alongside the road. For some reason, perhaps because he looks and walks like a wolf, the geese don't understand just how kind and lovable he is. Dozer has done the job.

My interest is in improving the course, lengthening tees, adding sand traps. Like a lot of golfers, I'm a closet architect. It reminds me of what one wag said about writers: Every journalist has a book inside of him, and that is exactly where it should stay. Golfers shouldn't design holes. And I don't. But we've gotten together as a committee to talk about the kind of course we want, and brought in professional help to make it happen.

There is a tremendous challenge for an older course to retain its basic characteristics while keeping up with the challenges offered by modern golf course design. There is competition out there. Our members ponied up to buy a piece of land so we could remake a short, stupid par-4 into an interesting par-5.

The design fell to our committee. The project was complicated— buying the land, getting city approval, finding an architect and builder, keeping the old hole open while we built the new one—but rewarding. More so than the fight we had with adjacent property owners who had their backyard lawns in play, or the neighbor who said he would sue us because we were bouncing balls off his roof and deck. We made significant changes to the hole—new tee, new hazard—partly because the neighbor said he would share in the cost, which, of course, he never did.

As a Greens Committee we have decided to have as much fun as we can, and to make as big an impact as we can on the course. Since we don't get to play it much anymore.

Blaine Newnham is a longtime sports writer in the Northwest. Following graduation from the University of California-Berkeley in 1963, Newnham went to work for the Oakland Tribune from 1965-71, covering the Oakland Raiders. He moved to Eugene to become the sports editor for the Register-Guard from 1971-82. In 1983, Newnham moved to the Seattle Times, working as the assistant managing editor for a year. Missing sports, Newnham became an associate editor for the Times and has been doing a sports column three or four times a week ever since. The 13 handicapper has been a member of Wing Point Country Club on Bainbridge Island for several years. He counts among his golf highlights: following Ben Hogan for a round in the 1966 U.S. Open at Olympic Golf Club; spending 10 days playing golf in Ireland with old college buddies; covering the U.S. Open, British Open and Masters; and getting a hole in one at the Blue Rock Springs course in California. Newnham says he's very lucky to have a "golf-tolerant" wife, Joanna, as well as three grown children, Nicole, Lisa and D. Jay.

Fir State Golf Club

by John Peoples

One of sports' most enduring myths is that all competitors have equal access to a level playing field. Hard work, desire and talent are the things that separate individuals from one another.

But race has always played a role in American sports, a fact underscored in 1997 when Major League Baseball celebrated the 50th anniversary of Jackie Robinson's first season with the Brooklyn, and later Los Angeles, Dodgers. Whether you view that historic event as old news or recent often depends on which side of the color barrier you were born on.

While Robinson's arrival on the Dodgers' roster was a national event, a small group of African American golfers in Seattle made local history in 1947 when they got together to form the Fir State Golf Club. Many of the founding members were former military veterans who had learned the game in other parts of the country, but weren't allowed to join the men's clubs at the city's municipal courses—Jefferson Park, Jackson Park and West Seattle.

"We were allowed to play the courses, but we couldn't get in the men's clubs," said Bob Duckworth, a former Fir State president. "You had to be a member of a recognized club to get a handicap and you needed a handicap to play in local (amateur) tournaments sanctioned by the PNGA."

The club celebrated its 50th anniversary during its annual championship tournament in the summer of 1997.

Fir State, which is the second-oldest predominantly African American golf club in the western U.S., began with 15 members—13 men and two women. Portland's Leisure Hour Golf Club, organized in 1945, is the oldest club. In 1953, Fir State and Leisure Hour helped found the Western States Golf Association, which today is comprised of 31 predominantly African American clubs in Washington, Oregon, California, Arizona, Colorado and Nevada, and has more than 1,500 members. Beside running a handicap service, WSGA sponsors annual championships for men, women and junior golfers.

Fir State is based at Jefferson Park on Seattle's Beacon Hill, and has its own clubhouse less than two miles from the course. The club has play-days at courses throughout the Puget Sound region and had just over 100 members in 1996. Wilbert Ponder and Jabo Ward are founding members who are still very active, and Al Hendrix, the father of Seattle guitar legend Jimi Hendrix, also is a longtime Fir Stater. NBA legend Bill Russell and ex-NFL standout Kenny Easley are former members of the club.

Fir State members have a long history of helping youngsters of all races get started in golf. Baseball star Ken Griffey Sr. is the chairman for the club's annual celebrity golf tournament, which generates money for the club's extensive junior program. The club provides junior players with instruction, clubs, green fees, transportation to out-of-town tournaments and scholarships. It had 80 youngsters enrolled during the summer of 1996. In 1992, a then 16-year-old Tiger Woods conducted an eye-opening exhibition at Jefferson Park for the 300 youngsters in attendance.

Three Fir State juniors won titles at the 1996 WSGA youth tournament in Sacramento, including Tyson LaNore in the 15-17 age group. LaNore, who won the Seattle's Metro League championship in 1995, qualified for and competed in the Maxfli PGA Junior Championship at Disney World in Florida.

LaNore and Fir State's other juniors are following a trail blazed by Bill Wright Jr., one of Fir State's first juniors. Wright's parents were founding Fir State members. In 1955, Wright finished second to Don Bies—who went on to win tournaments on the PGA and Senior PGA tours—in the Seattle High School Championship. Wright's high school career was cut short because of his race—he was banned from further competition because he was not a member of a club sanctioned by the PNGA. Despite that roadblock, in 1959 Wright became the first African American to win the USGA Public Links Amateur championship.

PGA Tour star Fred Couples learned to play golf at Jefferson Park, and says playing against adult Fir State members as a youngster helped him develop his game. "I owe a lot to them," Couples said. "They were among the first adults who accepted me and treated me as an equal. They were good players who didn't mind letting a kid tag along. They were patient with me."

Two former Fir State juniors have embarked on careers as golf course professionals. Thaddeus Gray, who works at a course near Indianapolis, was the first black golfer from the Northwest to earn full membership in the PGA of America. Landon Jackson, who returns each summer to conduct a junior clinic the day before the Fir State Celebrity Classic, is an assistant professional at the fabled Pebble Beach Golf Links.

A Seattle native, John Peoples has been a Northwest journalist since 1985. Among the beats Peoples covered during his 10 years with the Seattle Times were the Seattle Supersonics and the NBA, unlimited hydroplane racing, college and high school football, and golf. The saddest moment of his career as a golf reporter occurred in 1989, when he won a lottery for reporters to play Augusta National the day after that year's Masters. Unfortunately, his round was washed out by torrential rains. In 1995, Peoples left the Seattle Times and went to work for Microsoft's online newspaper, MSN News, as  *a copy editor-reporter. MSN News became MSNBC on the Internet in July 1996 (www.msnbc.com). While at MSNBC, Peoples has covered the NBA, the Atlanta Olympics and Major League Baseball. The University of Washington graduate is married to Julie Selman; they have one child, Nathan. John is a member of the Jefferson Park Men's and Fir State golf clubs.*

Reflections on an "Old Man's Game"

by Dan Raley

Old man's game. To me, that was golf.

For most of my childhood and early adulthood, I would ride up the narrow tree-lined road that leads into Kenmore's Inglewood Golf Club and shrug. I was headed for dinner, a party, a family visit.

Tee time? No way. Old man's game.

I went to Inglewood for more than a few Thanksgiving dinners, forced by my mother to wear a hideous red sport coat that drew snickers from cousins I barely knew. Little did I know that golf fashion, unlike your typical fairway, has no boundary, no out-of-bounds stakes.

My grandparents' 50th wedding anniversary was held at Inglewood, as was my cousin Tim Barron's wedding reception; festive, sentimental celebrations that lasted long into the night. I hardly knew the place during normal waking hours. And for more times than I can remember, I was invited for evenings at my great uncle Joe Barron's house that bordered the ninth fairway. Inglewood meant pheasant feathers and a tour of Joe's prized bird pens—which sat behind the house, not birdies and tee shots.

Old man's game. I played varsity football, basketball and baseball at Roosevelt High School in Seattle. Casually, my grandfather, Jim Barron, would mention golf to me. No time. No interest. No chance. I had a scrimmage, a pick-up game or a doubleheader waiting. I would half glance at the golf bag he stored in the basement, the one holding the wooden clubs. Nothing clicked.

The Barron family owned Inglewood Golf Club from 1940 to 1972. Joe Barron was the proprietor and my grandfather's older brother, which meant my late mother was a Barron, which means I'm half Barron.

But for 31 years, I stubbornly wasn't a golfer. I had absolutely no clue what I was missing. I finally came to my senses, or lost them. Today, I consider golf my addiction, if not my mistress and religion. My name is Dan Raley, and I'm a golfaholic. Please, don't anyone try to save me. My case is terminal.

I have played Augusta National and Pebble Beach, and nearly 100 other golf courses in 10 different states. I don't play tournament-level golf, but I keep coming back. I can shoot 100, but it won't keep me away. Pleasure far outweighs any personal embarrassment. I almost couldn't leave the course last August after shooting 83—one of my personal bests—at Redmond's Willows Run Golf Club.

For most of a decade I have made golf an integral part of my work, covering three Masters tournaments and three U.S. Opens for Seattle's morning newspaper. I have talked to most of the great ones, drawing the ire of Fred Couples and Greg Norman for my supposed impertinent take on things, and receiving a highly complimentary letter from Chi Chi Rodriguez praising my sensitivity. Sometimes you just never know whether you're going to hook or slice when you tee it up.

I have stolen away for Arizona golf vacations; sneaked out from work to chase the little white ball; visited driving ranges at 2 a.m.; and dragged myself out of bed at 4 a.m. to make a tee time 100 miles away—all signs of a golf extremist. Isn't it wonderful?

On Sunday, my sermon is the last few holes of the televised PGA Tour event. On the rare occasion I can't watch golf live, my video recorder is working furiously, providing me with a much-needed fix later. A tape of Tiger Woods' first tour victory now sits prominently on an overcrowded bookshelf, next to my complete set of Dirty Harry movies.

Joe and Jim Barron, if they were alive today, would be totally flabbergasted. So would a third brother, the late Ralph Barron, who once served as president of Broadmoor Golf Club and lived his final years in Palm Springs for one reason. Golf.

And, yes, I have played Inglewood a half-dozen times, the most memorable a deeply sentimental round with my brother, Tom Raley, and cousins Mark and David Barron a few years ago. A rematch is in the works.

So what happened? Golf was definitely a family thing, but somehow the roots didn't take right away in me. My late father, Bill Raley, was a golfer, as was his father, Jim. I have family correspondence to prove it. My dad found time for at least nine holes every Friday afternoon at Stanford Golf Club while attending that university's prestigious law school. He dutifully reported each round to his father in weekly letters.

Tragedy also stunted my golf growth. My father, who played the game steadily with his father, was killed in a car accident in Port Angeles when I was nine. There was no chance for him to pull the golf blinders off me.

Inglewood was the first I'd ever heard of the game. The club was a mystical place, but more because of Joe Barron's unique interests. He wasn't much of golfer, playing no more than a round or two a year. Instead, he conducted business wisely and filled the place with birds, stocking pens with pheasants, geese, ducks and swans. At night, their howls and screeching could be heard echoing up one fairway and down another. A kid couldn't visit without leaving with a handful of brightly-colored pheasant feathers.

Joe Barron was an Iowa farm boy turned businessman who saw a failing Inglewood as a wise investment. A group of Seattle Golf Club members had broken off and built the club, requisitioning Canadian architect Arthur Vernon Macan to build it. Joe Barron purchased the then 21-year-old country club—once known for its opulent parties and other excesses—for $100,000. He borrowed heavily to pull off the deal, but initially was uncertain if he could make the place work.

World War II helped get Inglewood back on its feet. With fighting raging overseas, Joe Barron leased the club to the federal government, which turned it into a makeshift military camp. Coast Guardsmen were housed there from 1943 to '46, using it for "R&R." The government became responsible for the club's property taxes. Military personnel took care of course upkeep—though very little golf was played, mowing fairways and conditioning greens.

Joe Barron oversaw it all. His wife Ruth was put in charge of a military commissary set up in the pro shop. Sons Jack and Mark helped out everywhere else, working in the club office and commissary. After the war, Inglewood finally became a popular place for local golfers, later drawing PGA Tour dates in the mid-'60s. Ben Hogan, Ralph

Guldahl and Sam Snead were among the high-brow players who were tested by the hilly course.

The club flourished in the hands of the Barron family for more than two decades, until Joe Barron died in 1968. His sons sold the club to the membership four years later. The pheasants disappeared, but not the Barrons. The sons, as well as their sons, received lifetime memberships as part of the sale, though none were frequent players.

Meantime, I continued to resist the game as I moved on to Western Washington University. It mattered little that my college roommates constantly sneaked away from class to get in a round here and there. Old man's game.

Finally, in 1985, I was practically kidnapped by two foursomes of friends and taken to Tacoma's North Shore Golf Course. I had never touched a club before, never stepped onto a fairway. One guy loaned me shoes, another had clubs ready. I got a few quick pointers and was pushed onto the tee box.

I still wasn't sure what the attraction was until the sixth hole. It's a downhill par-3 of 150 yards. After shanking everything in sight on the previous holes, I somehow lofted a tee shot that settled just off the green, then proceeded to chip close and drop the putt. Par.

The rush was like heroin, or so I'm told. There was no turning back. The need for a quick fix was overwhelming. I started playing as often as three times a week. I took lessons and started practicing. I bought a set of old clubs for $50. And later bought a set of Ping irons when I broke 100, a set of metal woods when 90 was conquered. I'm still waiting to break 80.

But that's the beauty, and irony, of it all.

I don't play football, basketball or baseball anymore. Hey, I tossed the red sports coat years ago. Lucky for me, I didn't become an old man before I discovered golf.

Dan Raley has been a Seattle Post-Intelligencer reporter for 18 years, covering college football, the Mariners, murder and, his favorite assignment, golf. P-I golf duties have sent him to three Masters tournaments, three U.S. Opens, the Washington State Open, the LPGA's Safeco Classic and the now-defunct Senior PGA Tour's GTE Northwest Open. In 1991, Raley placed second in feature writing in the Golf Writers Association of America yearly awards for a story chronicling the seamy side of Augusta, Georgia. Now a 17 handicapper, Raley was picked via a lottery in 1987 to play Augusta National. Unfortunately, it was his first year of golf. But it wasn't a total disaster as he birdied a hole.

Tacoma's Deep Roots in Northwest Golf

by Paul Ramsdell

To the unknowing, something might seem strangely out of place with the following:

St. Andrew's, Shinnecock Hills, Newport Golf Club .... Tacoma. Yes, Tacoma.

Any discussion of the early history of golf in this country needs to include Tacoma. And ever since 1894 when the Tacoma Golf Club was formed, Tacomans have continued to have an impact on golf in the Northwest and beyond. And there are even theories that golf started in Tacoma long before 1894, and long before anywhere else in North America.

"I don't think people realize that some of these clubs are a hundred years old," said John Bodenhamer, executive director of the Pacific Northwest Golf Association, itself steeped in Tacoma history in that it was formed in Tacoma in 1899. "A lot of people back East probably don't realize there were people out here in the 1890s."

They do at Golf House, the museum and library in Far Hills, New Jersey, established by the United States Golf Association. Just to the right of the entryway is a framed front page of the old *Tacoma Ledger* newspaper from 1898. The whole page is about activities at the Tacoma Golf Club and how the sport at the time was booming across the country.

GOLF magazine recently came out with its selections of the "golfiest" places in each state. Washington's, of course, was Tacoma Country & Golf Club because of its history. The histories of neighboring states seemingly aren't quite as deeply rooted, with relatively new layouts being selected: Pumpkin Ridge in Oregon, and the island green at the Coeur d'Alene Resort for Idaho.

The History

Golf in Tacoma in the 1890s isn't all that exciting to Michael Riste, the president of the British Columbia Golf House Society. He's been studying hints that golf might have been played by Scotsmen working for the Hudson's Bay Trading Company in the Steilacoom area in 1846 and 1847.

In a 1920s' minutes book from British Columbia's Victoria Golf Club, there's a reference to all this. Riste has been searching for more evidence regarding John Heath, who ran the Hudson's Bay Company's Fort Nisqually. "Wherever the Scots went in the world, the first thing they did was build a golf course," Riste said. "Heath was the one who imported the golf clubs and built a six-hole golf course at the fort. If that can be proved, and I'm really confident it will be proven, that will be the first reference to golf being played in North America."

While there's proof that a golf club was formed in Charleston, South Carolina before the 1840s, and they held a "Golf Ball" social event, there's no proof golf was actually played or a golf course was built. That leaves the Royal Montreal Golf Club in 1873 as the first course in North America. The longest continuing club in operation in the U.S. is the St. Andrew's Golf Club in Hastings-on-Hudson, New York.

A scant six years later, the Tacoma Golf Club was formed by a group of men led by a Scotsman, Alexander Baillie, making it the oldest American club west of the Mississippi River. The course was located in South Tacoma near where Junett Street now lies. The original clubhouse consisted of four side-by-side buildings; two of those buildings are still in use today as private residences.

Legend has it that Baillie was responsible for obtaining the equipment to play golf, and had clubs and balls imported from Scotland. When the equipment arrived, the customs agent had no idea what they were, and was unconvinced by Baillie's description of the game. So he entered the equipment as farm tools, figuring they'd be used to dig up the ground one way or another.

In 1904, the Tacoma Golf Club moved to its current site on the eastern shore of American Lake, and merged with the Tacoma Country Club to become the Tacoma Country & Golf Club. A sense of history pervades the place. The lounge is named the Alexander Baillie Room and old trophies are prominently displayed throughout the clubhouse. "I think everybody is aware it's one of the oldest golf clubs," manager Robert S. Hollister said of the current membership. "It's a big part of the heritage of the club, the history and the tradition."

That tradition is carried on in biannual team matches with the Victoria Golf Club, "which is the oldest international team match in the world, supposedly," Hollister said. Victoria was first invited down to Tacoma in 1895, and Hollister said it was the first international team match played on this continent.

Two members of the Victoria Golf Club came to Tacoma a few years later as well—on February 4, 1899 in fact, when the Pacific Northwest Golf Association was formed. They were joined by members of Tacoma Golf Club and two members from Waverley Country Club in Portland. Members from Seattle Golf Club and Spokane Golf Club were invited, but didn't attend. Only the Royal Canadian Golf Association (1894) and the USGA (1895) are older than the PNGA on this continent. The Western and Metropolitan golf associations were also established in 1899.

In April of that year, the first PNGA Championships were held, again at Tacoma, with about 20 male and female golfers in attendance from the three clubs, plus representatives from Seattle and Spokane.

The Players

The list of interesting golfers out of the Tacoma area runs long and wide—starting with Jim Barnes and his major championships and to the Tour life of Ken Still. And while the list of accomplishments achieved outside the region by Tacoma golfers is impressive, just as impressive are the feats by Tacoma golfers in Northwest tournaments.

"Long Jim" Barnes, a native of Cornwall, England, came to Tacoma Country & Golf Club as its head pro in 1911 and stayed until 1915. After that, he moved to Philadelphia and went on to fame, becoming the first person to have his name engraved on the Rodman Wanamaker Trophy as the winner of the first two PGA Championships. In the first PGA Championship in 1916 at Siwanoy Country Club in Bronxville, New York, the finals in match play came down to Barnes and Jock Hutchison Sr., a native of St. Andrews, Scotland. The match was even coming down to the last hole and both faced five-foot putts. Hutchison missed, and Barnes made his for a 1-up victory.

There were no PGA Championships in 1917 and 1918 because of World War I, but Barnes came back in 1919 at the Engineers Country Club in Roslyn, New York. At 6-foot-4, Barnes towered over his opponent in the finals, 5-foot-3 Fred McLeod, who Barnes beat 6 and 5. Barnes reached the finals again in 1921 and 1924, but couldn't duplicate his earlier triumphs.

Barnes won the 1921 U.S. Open at Columbia Country Club in Chevy Chase, Maryland, by a wide margin, with a winning score of 289. Second went to McLeod and Walter Hagen, both nine strokes back. Barnes played in 17 Opens and finished in the top five four times. He also won the British Open in 1925. In all, Barnes won 21 tournaments in the era of Jones, Hagen and Sarazen, and is the only U.S. Open champion to have the trophy presented to him by a sitting American president, golf nut Warren Harding, in 1921.

Ken Still was another golfer who ventured out onto the national scene with success. Unlike Barnes, however, Still grew up in Tacoma and remains a resident. Still won three PGA Tour events, the Florida Citrus and Greater Milwaukee opens in 1969, and the 1970 Kaiser Open. Even so, his greatest thrill came not in winning a tournament, but in starting one.

"Number one (thrill) was hitting the initial tee shot in the 1969 Ryder Cup. I hit the first tee shot when (Lee) Trevino and I were partners," Still said of the biannual matches played that year at Royal Birkdale in Southport, England. "They had just played both national anthems, and there were between 50,000 and 60,000 people standing there. They said, 'Still, USA,' and I must tell you I was shaking like a leaf in a 100-mph storm. But I hit it right down the middle about 250 (yards). I couldn't believe it."

Still went on to win more than $1.4 million on the regular PGA Tour and Senior PGA Tour before going into semi-retirement after the 1996 season. His best years were from 1969 to 1971 when he won the three tournaments. Also in that span he finished fifth in the U.S. Open and tied for sixth in the 1971 Masters.

"Having a chance to win the Masters, that was a thrill," Still said. "I had a two on 12 on Sunday and was two shots out of the lead then." He couldn't get much going afterward, however, and his bogey on the 18th dropped him five strokes off the pace with a 72-71-72-69, 284.

Two other Senior PGA Tour stars with Tacoma connections were George Lanning and Walter Morgan. Lanning was in the Air Force and based at McChord Air Force Base when he retired after 21 years of service in 1968. He eventually became the head pro at Oakbrook Country Club and shot course-record 60s at both Oakbrook and Tumwater Valley. He played on the Senior Tour for nine years before suffering a fatal heart attack at the age of 58. He was 34th on the Senior PGA career money list at the time with more than $700,000 in earnings.

While in the Army, Morgan managed Fort Lewis Golf Course from 1977 to 1980. He broke through on the Senior PGA Tour with his first victory coming in Seattle at the GTE Northwest Classic in 1995. He finished 27th on the money list that year with $423,000, and then played spectacularly in 1996, winning two tournaments and $848,000, finishing tenth on the money list.

Tacoma-area players who didn't venture out onto professional tours full-time didn't do it out of a lack of talent. The most impressive resume belongs to Chuck Congdon, who spent 30 years—from 1935 to 1965—as the head pro at Tacoma C&GC. He was known equally for his playing and teaching abilities. As a player, Congdon, who got his start in golf as a greenskeeper at the old Green Acres course in Bothell, north of Seattle, dominated Northwest tournaments. He also captured the 1947 Portland Open and 1948 Canadian Open at Shaughnessy Heights in Vancouver, B.C., by three strokes. Congdon won seven British Columbia Opens, four Washington State Opens and the 1960 national senior title.

Jack Walters, a member of Fircrest Golf Club, won the national left-handers' tournament in 1953. His involvement in the National Association of Left-Handed Golfers helped bring its national tournament to Fircrest in 1960 and 1973; Walters won the 1960 affair.

Other historical names from the Tacoma area include Ockie Eliason, who spent 20 years as the head pro at Allenmore before retiring in 1986. He was a mentor for Still and other top-notch Northwest golfers, and was a fine player in his own right. John Rudy spent 32 years as the head pro at Fircrest. Then there was Al Feldman, who once held the titles to the British Columbia, Montana, Oregon and Washington opens all at the same time over the 1966-67 golf seasons, a feat accomplished when he was 55 years old. Chuck Hunter Jr., a 20-year-old out of Tacoma C&GC at the time, made the finals of the 1959 Western Amateur, beating Pete Dye—later known for his golf course designs—in the semifinals.

The Tournaments

The nation's best touring pros have come to Tacoma—specifically Fircrest Golf Club—three times. The Tacoma Open was held at Fircrest in 1945 and 1948, and both have unique spots in history. The 1960 Carling Open brought Arnold Palmer and the rest of the country's best golfers to Tacoma.

Byron Nelson made a stop at Fircrest in 1945 during his incredible season in which he entered 30 tournaments and won 18, including 11 in a row. Seven times Nelson was runner-up that year, and he finished in the top-10 in every tournament. His worse event, however, was the Tacoma Open, where he tied for ninth with a 1-under 283. He made up for it by winning the Seattle Open the following week with an incredible four-day total of 259.

Up until 1994, the 1948 Tacoma Open held a spot in the PGA Tour record books. Ed Oliver won that event in a five-way playoff with Congdon, Cary Middlecoff, Fred Haas and Vic Ghezzi, tying for the biggest playoff until the rain-shortened Byron Nelson Classic.

After playing in the Tacoma Open, Ben Hogan came away impressed with Fircrest. "He said it was the best three starting holes he'd ever played on any golf course," said Ken Still. "Obviously, that's probably changed by now, but I'll tell you something, 1-2-3 today are still no picnic." The first hole is an uphill, 500-yard par-5. That's followed by a hilly 450-yard par-4 and an uphill 200-yard, par-3. "Anything at even-par or better on the first three holes at Fircrest, you've played golf," Still said.

Don January certainly played some golf through some early morning fog during the opening round of the Carling Open, carding a course-record 63 that has since been matched by member Clint Names. January, however, faded with a 75 on the second day and fell out of contention.

The Courses

It took some 20 years for another golf course to be built in the area after the initial Tacoma Golf Club. Lakewood and Fort Steilacoom courses were built in 1913 and 1914, respectively, but have since disappeared. Of courses still in existence, Meadow Park was built in 1917. Fircrest, built in 1923, was designed by Arthur Vernon Macan, who developed numerous courses in the Northwest and Canada. His first was Royal Colwood in Victoria, B.C., and those two clubs compete in a home-and-home match to this day. University (1926), Linden (1927), Brookdale (1931) and Fort Lewis (1937) followed.

In recent years, some of the state's top courses have opened in the area, with Canterwood in Gig Harbor, McCormick Woods in Port Orchard, Indian Summer in Olympia, The Classic in Spanaway and Gold Mountain's Olympic Course in Gorst.

The First Family

No history of Tacoma golf would be complete without the Harbottles, Tacoma's first family of golf. It's difficult to determine with whom to start. Pat Lesser Harbottle was one of America's best female amateurs in her youth and claimed the national title in 1955. Or John Harbottle, who is one of the best senior amateurs in the country. Together, their list of accomplishments in golf is very impressive. Then there are the five Harbottle children, two of whom are in the golf business. John Harbottle III is a rising star as a golf course designer, with his Stevinson Ranch Golf Club in California being named in 1995 as one of the top-10 new "upscale" courses in the country by *Golf Digest*. Rob Harbottle is an assistant pro at Astoria Golf Club in Oregon.

Pat Lesser Harbottle dominated the amateur golf world in 1955 with a victory in the Western Amateur, followed shortly by her U.S. Amateur title. In the U.S. Amateur at Myer's Park Country Club in Charlotte, North Carolina, Harbottle was so dominating she won her quarterfinal match, 7 and 6; her semifinal match, 6 and 5; and the finals, 7 and 6.

The Lesser family moved from Hawaii to Seattle when Pat was 12, and she eventually played on the men's golf team—the No. 1 player at times—at Seattle University. A recent issue of *Golf Journal* recounted an incident after a match when a reporter asked a player from the University of Oregon for his reaction after being "beaten by a woman."

"I wasn't beaten by a women," he responded testily. "I was beaten by a 72."

Also on that Seattle University golf team was Tacoma native John Harbottle. Eventually, John and Pat married; John is a dentist in Tacoma and they have a home on the second fairway at Tacoma C&GC. Between them, the Harbottles have won 34 club championships at Tacoma, with Pat winning 19 and John 15. John has an equally amazing record as a senior amateur. He set the record for low round in the medal portion of the U.S. Senior Amateur in 1993 with a 68 at Farmington (Virginia) CC. Then he went out the next day and did it again. Needless to say, he holds the record for the lowest 36-hole medalist score with his 136 being five strokes better than the second-best 141.

He also was the medalist at the 1988 U.S. Senior Amateur and finished runner-up in the match-play portion in 1986. He dominated the Washington State Senior Men's Amateur in 1988, 1995 and 1996, winning the latter two tournaments by four and seven strokes, respectively. Harbottle also won the PNGA Senior Amateur in 1988, '90, '91 and '93.

"Obviously, it has enriched us very much," John said about having golf play such a major role in the family's life. "Just the opportunity to meet people and travel." And they have become well-known through those travels. "When you go around the country," Hollister said, "a lot of the senior golfers know John and, of course, the women know Pat Lesser Harbottle."

Family outings centered around golf when the children were young and at home. "I'm so glad I found out how to play golf before I got married and had children," Pat said. "It's been a lot of fun for me since the time I started playing. Just having golf a part of my life, and John's too, is a very big thing." According to a story from Pat, some thought having children might have improved her swing. Her swing always came quickly inside, but when she was pregnant with John III, her first child, she was forced to start her swing more outside. Ken Tyson, a local pro who designed and operated several golf courses in the Tacoma area, said he'd never seen her swing the club better before she was pregnant.

John's dentistry skills came in handy at a golf tournament once. He was playing in that 1960 Carling Open when Los Angeles touring pro Smiley Quick lost a gold cap from a front tooth during the tournament. Someone summoned Harbottle, and they both went to his office to fix the problem. Smiley was smiling again, and Quick.

Yes, folks, sometimes the truth is stranger than fiction, just as some people might think about Tacoma being a birthplace of golf.

Paul Ramsdell is the assistant sports editor and golf writer for the award-winning sports section of The News Tribune in Tacoma. After graduating from the University of Oregon in 1979, Ramsdell went on to become sports editor at the Pendleton East Oregonian and the Lewiston (Idaho) Morning Tribune, and then assistant sports editor at the Eugene Register-Guard, the Arizona Daily Star in Tucson, and Tacoma in 1987. He is a member of Fircrest Golf Club in Tacoma, and resides with his wife Margaret in Gig Harbor.

The Lost Courses of the Northwest

by Michael Riste

Since golf was introduced to the Northwest (Washington, Oregon, Idaho and Montana) in 1892, how many golf courses were built over that 100-year period? Is the number 200, 300, 500, 700, 900 or 1,000? Research indicates that approximately 700 courses were built during that time. This article recognizes some of those courses that did not survive the previous century, and traces the reasons for their downfalls.

Some Background on Golf's Early-Day Boom

Prior to 1913, golf in the Northwest was primarily a game for wealthy business people. Two events occurred that greatly influenced the spread of the sport throughout the region. When Francis Ouimet won the U.S. Open in the fall of 1913, golf became front-page news around the country. The subsequent Harry Vardon-Ted Ray exhibition tour through the Northwest further promoted the game in the region.

Equally important to golf's popularity over the next 20 years was the increased use of the automobile. A phrase coined by one local course showed the rising role of the car in golf: "One may now travel 15 miles comfortably and quickly, and what once was a place out in the country is within easy reach. The automobile permits the golf nut to belong to a distant club and still have time in the afternoon to go to it, play his game and return for dinner." Golf would never have gained such appeal during the horse-and-buggy days.

Earlington & UW Courses

The first course to be constructed as a direct result of the influence of the automobile was Earlington Country Club. Located about 12 miles from downtown Seattle off Rainier Valley Boulevard, this club began as an automobile organization and, in 1911, introduced golf. By 1914, Earlington's sporty nine-hole layout was one of the most popular courses for those who weren't members of Seattle Golf Club. After growing to 18 holes in the 1920s, the course went on to host many state events over its 50-year history. When suburban sprawl closed Earlington in the 1960s, Seattle-area golfers lost a real gem.

The University of Washington course was constructed prior to the Vardon-Ray exhibition, and those who played it were mainly dedicated golfers on the school's staff. The course was closed in 1915 because of World War I. But upon reopening in 1920, a strong and enthusiastic organization with 250 golfers developed. The tricky, well-manicured course survived until Husky Stadium was erected on the site.

Golf's Popularity Begins in Tacoma

Immediately following the Vardon-Ray matches in Tacoma, young prospering businessmen were smitten with "golf-itis." The Lakeside, Lakewood (also called Lochburn) and Fort Steilacoom courses in Tacoma were built within three months of the match. Though primitive by today's standards, these courses helped Tacoma become the fastest-growing golf area in the Northwest. But demands for residential land and fragile organizational structures conspired to halt operations at these courses, and none survived the 1920s.

Though closing their doors relatively quickly, these courses played an important role by proving that an average person was interested in the game. The members of these early Tacoma clubs unknowingly broke the myth "that golf was only for the rich." Soon, new clubs supported by working-class individuals began to emerge throughout the region.

Trading Golf Courses for Houses

Many early-day courses were located close to towns, and several layouts were lost due to expanding city limits. This was the case with the initial country clubs in Spokane, Tacoma and Eugene, along with Waverley in Portland. The Seattle Golf Club sold its Laurelhurst site for housing when the club moved to the north end.

In many instances, the original site of a club was converted into another golf club. Olympia Country and Golf Club moved to its current Butler site in 1925. The Mountain View club was formed the following year and operated a nine-hole course at Olympia's original site. Mountain View died in the 1960s. This also occurred when the Yakima Country Club moved. The Country Club of Seattle on Bainbridge Island is the oldest Washington course in its original location. Gearhart Golf Links in Oregon, Hayden Lake Country Club in Idaho, and Butte Country Club in Montana are the longest-operating courses in their respective states.

Some Original Oregon Courses

The Central Oregon Golf Club was built between 1905 and 1910 at the Deschutes Junction near Bend. Little has been uncovered about this early course, but one could surmise it was probably built by transplanted Scots who brought their "tools of the game" when settling the area. The course was closed in the 1920s. Another course which disappeared long ago was built in Pendleton, circa 1903, west of the city.

The *Oregonian* newspaper reported in 1914 that courses were located in Medford, Klamath Falls, Baker, Albany, Astoria and Salem. Another on the coast was called The Breakers. Unfortunately, little information has been uncovered about these early courses, and their existence is known only through reports of inter-club matches played against surviving clubs.

Seminal Military Venues

The military influence in the development of Northwest golf cannot be overlooked. The first course of this type was built in 1894 at Esquimalt, B.C., by the Royal Engineers. It helped spawn the construction of the Barracks course at Bremerton in 1902. By 1912, inter-club matches were played by soldiers stationed at Esquimalt, Bremerton and Fort Lawton in Seattle. (There is still strong sentiment among many Seattleites that a golf course should be at Fort Lawton.) Perhaps some "archaeological digging" will uncover old golf balls on the property.

In 1922, the second course at Fort Vancouver (Washington) was built. Jack Moffat, the region's first golf pro, constructed Vancouver's original course, Ellsworth Links. All of these early-day military courses were closed by 1940.

The Age of Expansion

In the 1920s and 1930s, golf courses were constructed for two principle reasons: to satisfy the desire of the Pay-As-You-Play (PAYP) golfer, and boost tourism. In fact, approximately 170 courses were built during this period. And the majority survive today.

Region's First Municipal Facility

In 1913, the Seattle Parks Board hired a Spalding representative, Tom Bendelow, to lay out a municipal golf course on donated land. The Parks Board Commissioners had little golf experience, so they were apprehensive when the course was ready for play in the fall of 1914. The commissioners decided to postpone the grand opening until May 1915, as they believed the course would not raise enough revenue over the winter months to cover construction costs. They were pleasantly surprised when, during the seven-and-a-half-months Jefferson Park Golf Course was open in 1915, an incredible 47,000 rounds of golf were played on the links. The board showed a profit rather than the anticipated loss.

The success of Jefferson Park spawned the development of PAYP courses throughout the Northwest in the 1920s and '30s. The majority of these operations were initiated by entrepreneurs hoping to make a buck. In most instances, the value of a course resided in the property underneath it. Thus, when a golf property's worth rose to the point where it could be sold for housing, the course died. The first course to meet this demise was the West Side Golf Club in West Seattle, which existed from 1916-1925. The layout commanded panoramic views of the Puget Sound as well as the snow-capped Olympic and Cascade mountains.

Proliferation of PAYP Courses

PAYP courses sprang up in Portland, Tacoma and Seattle in great profusion, serving as examples of free enterprise at work. These layouts included City View, Inverness, Lloyd's, Ruby's, Monagh Lea, Peninsula and West Hills in Portland; Glengarry, Green Fairways, Parkland and Steilacoom Lake in Tacoma; Greenacres, Juanita Beach, Lake Garrett, Lake Ridge, Lake Wilderness, Lakewood, Meadowbrook, Overbrook, Parkrose, Queen Anne, Redmond and Cedar River in Seattle. These courses were all examples of profitable and interesting layouts that did not survive the 1970s because they made their owners more money as housing lots than as fairways.

Some Details on these "Ghost" Courses

Let's take a look at a few of these former courses.

Did golf begin in Holland or Scotland? Perhaps this argument arose when some residents in the Peninsula area of Portland first met to form a golf club. To satisfy both opposing groups, the founders decided to build the Windmills Golf Club, which featured a touch of Holland. In fact, the course's site was diked fields near the Columbia River. The windmills adorning the course were used for decoration and irrigation purposes.

The Inverness Golf Club, Portland's second 36-hole layout (after Glendoveer), opened to great fanfare in September 1930. Dedicated by Governor Norbald, the course was divided into an 18-hole public facility and an 18-hole private club. In 1931, the nation's best public links golfers gathered at Inverness for the inaugural Western Public Links Championship.

In 1930, Ralph Lloyd, a Los Angeles capitalist, promised to transform the unsightly surroundings of Sullivan's Gulch in Portland into a golfer's paradise. Arthur Vernon Macan was given the task of turning this small canyon into a golf course. Moving thousands of yards of dirt and material, George William Otten, under Macan's direction, created a series of benches used for "rest stops" to mitigate the many uphill hikes. True to form, Macan left his mark through the tricky greens he designed.

Selling a wide range of products over a 10-year period provided L.H. Friedman with the necessary business background to run a golf club. After being bitten by the golf bug in 1930, Friedman leased 100 acres near White Center south of Seattle and entered the golf business. He hired Francis L. James to design and construct the course. In order to promote his course as having the area's best greens, Friedman copied the greens-construction methods used at the finest local layouts. His intense research succeeded, and Friedman built the best PAYP course in the greater Seattle area. Friedman's first golf professional at Lakewood was the legendary Chuck Congdon, who stayed for two years before moving on to Meadowbrook, another PAYP operation near Bothell. Congdon later enjoyed a long and successful career at Tacoma Country & Golf Club. Located on a gently rolling piece of property alongside Bothell Highway, Meadowbrook opened in 1931.

Golf's Broadening Appeal

In the 1920s and '30s, local newspapers reported that the reason for building a golf course was "to encourage the motorist to stay overnight to play the local links." This was certainly the first time that golf was considered an economic benefit to a town or area. Each local links hyped itself as the "best-maintained" and "most-interesting" course on the Pacific Coast.

It is the author's belief that every small town in the Northwest built a golf course during the 1920's and 1930s. An underlying role, which is not often espoused by golf historians, is that early-day courses also served as community centers for their towns. Golf is probably the only sport enjoyed by all groups—young and old, male and female, and local citizens would meet at the neighborhood course for a game of golf and social engagements.

The following Northwest courses were built as "town centers": Athena, Beachway (Grays Harbor), Briarcliffe (Longview), Coweeman (Kelso), Cowlitz County, Donahue, Edgewater (Everett), Grandview (Yakima), Hermiston (Oregon), Knickerbocker, Lakeway (Bellingham), Mercer Island, Moby Dick (Ocean Park), North Bend (Washington), Omak, Ontario (Oregon), Pasco, Pilot Rock, Port Dock (Gray's Harbor), Ritzville, Riverside (Yakima), Silverton (Oregon), Stillwater (Longview), Torwoodlea (Seaview), Warden and Willowbrook (Ellensburg).

Help From the Federal Government

In an effort to spur economic development following the Great Depression, President Franklin Roosevelt established various federal agencies to get people back in the workforce. Besides the Civilian Conservation Corps (CCC), which generated thousands of jobs for needy Americans, the Works Progress Administration (WPA) had the broadest regional impact. The WPA put up federal funds to support construction projects for post offices, public buildings, airports, highways, schools, and even the Mercer Island Floating Bridge.

WPA workers also built a handful of Northwest golf courses. These PAYP-type courses were located in rural areas that were particularly hard-hit by the Great Crash. Four WPA-built layouts in use today include the Fort Lewis and Pomeroy courses in Washington, Baker City Golf Club in Oregon, and Polson Country Club in Montana.

Some Late, Great Macan Masterpieces

The last collection of private and semiprivate golf courses that died due to economic factors included some extremely fine layouts. Alderwood in Portland would probably head the list. Designed in 1925 by Macan, the Northwest's most prolific golf course architect, Alderwood had a glorious run during its 40-year history. In 1925, Macan wrote this mission statement for Alderwood: "To provide a severe test of golf for the best players and, at the same time, leave the weaker players in peace to get their fives and sixes, is my ultimate goal."

Alderwood co-hosted the 1932 PNGA Championship with another Macan course, Columbia-Edgewater. In 1937, Alderwood had the distinction of being the first Northwest club to conduct the prestigious U.S. Amateur Championship. Using, as Macan envisioned, more brains than brawn, Johnny Goodman survived the tricky, well-maintained layout to win the tournament.

Few people are aware that Macan designed the Chehalis Golf Club. He once said in Northwest Golfer magazine, "One of the outstanding small community golf clubs of the Northwest, one that is attracting favorable attention and comment from neighboring clubs, visiting players and others, is the Chehalis Golf Club." Macan was proud of how Chehalis reflected his talent to design a course that everyone— high- and low-handicap players alike—enjoyed playing. "The fairways were wide, the rough wasn't bad and the greens were large and of a higher standard than most in the state. Somehow, low cards were hard to get at Chehalis." James Black, brother of Davie and John Black, a prominent golfing family in Canada and California, was the first professional at Chehalis. Sadly, the course didn't make it through the 1950s.

The Northwest's Own "17-Mile Drive"

In order to attract tourists traveling along Pacific Highway "to stay in town another night," several golf clubs were constructed along the busy north-south road. Its highway locale enabled Chehalis's members to have tourists make up for any revenue shortfalls, and allowed them to play the course for $3.00 a month. The Cowlitz County course built in 1924 and the Coweeman course in 1931 are two other examples. The Coweeman in Kelso covered 106 acres. A local newspaper reports, "From the highway (Coweeman) had the appearance of an amphitheater, the floor of which was level meadow land and all about rose-wooded hills, clothed with evergreen trees, with many clearings on the terraced sides and attractive homes nestled in the foliage."

The Northwest Golfer and Country Club magazine extolled the Clark County Country Club as one illustrating a high degree of "Spirit of

Comradeship." The club providing citizens "with a beautiful playground, a perpetual source of outdoor exercise, health and happiness." The clubhouse served the community as a center of activities. The 170-acre site in southwest Washington was just north of the Salmon Creek Bridge along Pacific Highway, about five miles north of Vancouver. The course was co-designed by John and Don Junor, who made use of three distinct elevations on the property. The front nine was on the lowest bench, while about 35 feet above it was the clubhouse and three holes. The remaining holes were on the uppermost tier, giving players scenic views of nearby mountains. Unfortunately, this course died when Interstate 5 was built through Vancouver.

Multnomah Golf Club

While Macan was building Alderwood and Columbia-Edgewater in 1924, he was asked to survey property near the present Portland Golf Club. In Macan's opinion, the 100-acre tract off Canyon Road, selected by the Multnomah Amateur Athletic Club as the site for their 18-hole course, had excellent possibilities. For some reason, Macan's plan was rejected in favor of Willie Locke's design. During its early years, the Multnomah Golf Club suffered internal strife as the same board governed both the athletic club and the golf club. In 1927, the golf club became a separate entity. During its too-short 20-year history, Multnomah hosted many state championships.

Willapa Harbor Courses

The final area of lost courses surveyed here was around Willapa Harbor in southwest Washington. In 1931, a new fast-ferry service from Astoria to the north beaches along the Washington coast made this area a travel destination for people from Portland to San Francisco. Selecting a fertile tract of land beside the harbor, William Parent built the attractive Moby Dick course. Parent catered to the golfer's gastronomic preferences by serving fresh crab, razor clams and salmon in the clubhouse dining room.

It would be difficult to find a more unusually named golf course than Torwoodlea. Torwoodlea was derived from a combination of Scottish terms: "tor" meaning hill, "wood" for forest, and "lea" for green meadows. The course near Seaview opened with great fanfare in June 1931 with an exhibition match pitting Frank Dolp and Eddie Hogan— both PNGA champions—against John Robbins and Howard Bonar. The nine-hole links was well supplied with water hazards, while trees protected it from winds off Willapa Harbor.

One Reincarnation

As stated earlier, the Northwest has lost approximately 100 courses over its century-long golf history. Around 1910, land speculators from Portland descended on the Tokeland area with grandiose ideas for a "Coney Island" resort. The idea died, but Maude Kindred created recreational amenities for her Tokeland Hotel and the surrounding property. Among Kindred's resort-related projects was a nine-hole golf course. The Great Crash and subsequent Depression led the property into decline, and the course was closed.

In 1986, Steve Nelson was building a house near the Tokeland Hotel. While cutting nearby grasslands, he kept ruining his equipment on mounds dotting the land. "At first I started going around these lumps.

Then I figured out that these were the greens from the old course." Vic Vaughn, a local resident before attending the University of Washington in the late-1920s, recalls playing the Tokeland links. Once all the greens had been located, the course routing was quite evident. Nelson has yet to open the nine-hole, 3,150-yard course.

A Final Note

Until every newspaper published over the years in every small Northwest town has been read, we will never know how many golf courses were lost over the past 100 years. I believe two things are absolutely certain: Golf was not a trivial game played by a few wealthy individuals, and the game and its facilities played a significant role in the social and economic development of the Northwest. If any reader can relate information about the lost courses of the Northwest, I would like to hear from you. I am now preparing a data base for all Northwest courses built prior to 1940, and your help would be greatly appreciated. Please forward your notes and historical evidence to Michael Riste, B.C. Golf Museum, 2545 Blanca Street, Vancouver, B.C., V6G 2B4.

Michael Riste is a native British Columbian who has been researching Northwest golf and collecting golf memorabilia since 1963. He began caddying at Capilano Golf & Country Club in 1961. Upon graduating from high school in 1965, Riste became the first Canadian awarded a Chick Evans Scholarship, later attending the University of Washington and earning a Bachelor of Science Mathematics degree. In 1987, Mike began transforming the original clubhouse at Vancouver's University Golf Club into the B.C. Golf House. He went on to be the director and past president of the B.C. Golf House Society, the director of the Golf Collectors Society, and a member of the PNGA Hall of Fame Committee.

A Glance at Oregon's Rich Golf History

by Bob Robinson

Dale Johnson, a retired former executive of the Oregon Golf Association and Pacific Northwest PGA, remembers vividly the first time he saw Tiger Woods play golf. "It was at the Eddie Hogan Cup Junior Matches when Tiger was 14," Johnson said. "He played Riverside (Golf & Country Club) like he owned it. I remember going home and telling my wife, 'Phyllis, I've just watched the best kid player I've ever seen.'"

Little did Johnson know at the time that Woods would become a part of golf history in Oregon, a history laced with ties to the greats of the game. After winning twice on the PGA Tour in late 1996, Woods talked about his learning habits while growing up. "I've always studied great players of the past—Tom Watson's putting in his prime, Lee Trevino's wedge play, Jack Nicklaus' long irons," he said. "I know there always are going to be things that I can learn about the game."

Woods had already learned that Oregon was a prime setting for him to make his own brand of history. First, he did it in the 1993 U.S. Junior Amateur at Waverley Country Club, claiming his third title in a row with a dramatic rally and a 19th-hole conquest of Ryan Armour. No one else has won that tournament more than once.

As if that "three-peat" wasn't enough, Woods did it again in Oregon, becoming the first player to win three U.S. Amateurs in succession when he edged Steve Scott in 38 holes in the 1996 final at Pumpkin Ridge Golf Club near North Plains. Against Scott, Woods put together one of the incredible rallies that had typified his play in U.S. Golf Association championships. He was 5-down after 18 holes and 2-down with three holes to play but still won, thanks mostly to a 7-under-par 65 in the afternoon round.

Already, Woods had become one of the game's biggest attractions. The Amateur at Pumpkin Ridge was the best-attended one in history. "Oregon has been awfully good to me," Woods said in an understatement.

He might have included nearby Vancouver, Washington, in his analysis. Woods played as an adult in his first amateur tournament at Royal Oaks Country Club—the Pacific Northwest Amateur when he was 18. Woods was medalist, then rattled off birdies as if they were going out of style on his way to the event's match-play title. In the scheduled 36-hole final, he shot a 9-under-par 63 in the morning round and went on to crush University of Oregon golfer Ted Snavely, who was 1 under par for 26 holes and lost, 11 and 10. At the finish, Snavely smiled and showed no dejection. Though overwhelmed, Snavely knew he had faced an opponent who was anything but ordinary.

Golf history visited Oregon long before Woods' USGA feats, going all the way back to 1913 when Henry Vardon and Ted Ray played an exhibition match at Waverley. It was after that appearance of two of the game's biggest names of the time that newspapers in the state began treating golf as a significant sport.

Over the years, Oregon has been blessed with outstanding golfers and events of national significance, such as the 1946 PGA Championship, 1947 Ryder Cup Matches and 1982 U.S. Senior Open at Portland Golf Club.

There have been many other USGA championships, including a dramatic, down-to-wire battle between Lanny Wadkins and Tom Kite for the U.S. Amateur title in 1970 at Waverley. The Amateur had a stroke-play format in those days, but it was like match play over the final nine holes as Wadkins and Kite, destined for later greatness as pros, battled it out in the final twosome. Finally, they stood on the green of the par-5 18th hole with Wadkins one shot ahead. Wadkins provided the clincher by sinking a 20-foot birdie putt. The boyish-looking Kite smiled broadly before walking over to congratulate Wadkins. Then he sank a 10-footer for a birdie that kept him one stroke back.

The women have had their moments in Oregon, too. Jackie Pung won at Waverley in 1952 and Juli Inkster did the same in 1981 in a tournament remembered for its unusually hot weather. Nancy Lopez claimed the U.S. Girls Championship at Columbia-Edgewater Country Club in 1974.

Big names have been a part of Oregon's golf history in many other ways.

Gene Sarazen: In its early days, the Oregon Open was considered a PGA Tour event. That brought Sarazen to Columbia-Edgewater in 1930 where he claimed the title in a playoff with Leo Diegel. Earlier, Tommy Armour won the 1927 Oregon Open crown at Waverley.

Ben Hogan: The legendary "Wee Ice Mon" won the 1946 PGA Championship at Portland Golf Club, then was back a year later to lead the U.S. to an 11-1 win over the British team in the Ryder Cup. A playing captain, Hogan decided to sit out the singles. He said of being a spectator, "I was never so nervous as I was today." Earlier, Hogan and Sam Snead were Portland Open winners in the 1940's at Portland GC, Hogan once shooting a record-setting, 27-under-par 261.

Jack Nicklaus: Nicklaus won three tournaments in his first year as a pro—the U.S. Open, Seattle Open and Portland Open. In the latter at Columbia-Edgewater, he survived a two-shot penalty for slow play to win by one over George Bayer. Nicklaus went on to win three Portland Open titles, the last two at Portland GC.

Billy Casper: He, too, was a three-time Portland Open titleist, the last in 1961, but is better remembered for his victory in the 1969 Alcan Championship at Portland GC, earning a $55,000 check that was the largest in golf at the time. He was the beneficiary of one of the game's most famous collapses when Lee Trevino blew a six-shot lead with three holes to play. Casper made birdies on the last four holes while Trevino was finishing bogey, triple-bogey and par on the last three holes.

Cary Middlecoff: The lanky Middlecoff couldn't approach Hogan's record total at Portland GC, but he dominated the field as he won the 1955 Western Open in an 18-under 272.

Contributing mightily to Oregon's golfing past have been the tireless efforts of the game's supporters from Portland. The Trembling Twenty, a group that made possible the Portland Opens and Alcan Championship, and Tournament Golf Foundation, Inc., managing sponsor of 25 years worth of LPGA tournaments, are the major ones.

The LPGA made its first appearance in Oregon at Eugene Country Club, then began its Portland run in 1972. Kathy Whitworth, JoAnne Carner, Donna Caponi and Lopez became popular figures in

Oregon after multiple victories in the state.

Before the Trembling Twenty and Tournament Golf Foundation, Inc., there was the late Robert Hudson personally footing the bills for the British team to come to Portland for the 1947 Ryder Cup Matches. "The matches might have died except for Bob Hudson," said Tom Watson, who prides himself on his knowledge of the game's history. Hudson also started the Hudson Cup Matches, which have become a fixture in the Pacific Northwest, annually pitting the area's top club pros and amateurs against each other.

Over the years, many Oregon golfers have made news on a national scale, going all the way back to such pioneering amateurs as Doc Willing, Rudie Wilhelm and Frank Dolp. Willing even beat the Tour pros when he won the 1928 Oregon Open.

Then, in 1952, Bruce Cudd and Dick Yost from Columbia-Edgewater were picked to play on the Walker Cup team. The only previous players from the same club to make the team in the same year were Bobby Jones and Watts Gunn of Atlanta Country Club.

Among Oregonians to win national championships have been John Fought (1977 U.S. Amateur), Mary Budke (1972 U.S. Women's Amateur), Fred Haney (1971 U.S. Public Links Amateur), Bob Allard (1972 U.S. Public Links Amateur) and Eric Johnson (1980 U.S. Junior Amateur). Budke was such a dominant player in the state that she won eight Oregon Amateur titles in a nine-year period, her only miss being a year in the middle of the run in which she didn't enter.

As of late 1996, Peter Jacobsen of Portland and Bob Gilder of Corvallis had each won six times on the PGA Tour. Jacobsen had a spectacular year in 1995 with two victories and more than $1 million in earnings. Tom Shaw, who grew up in Milwaukie, also won four times on the regular tour before moving on to success on the Senior PGA Tour.

Begun in 1986 at Portland Golf Club, Jacobsen's Fred Meyer Challenge has become nationally recognized for its best-ball format. It's also lured golf's greatest players to first Portland Golf Club and then, starting in 1992, Oregon Golf Club in West Linn. The event, won in 1995 and 1996 by the team of Greg Norman and Brad Faxon, has raised nearly $5 million for local charities.

No look at Oregon's past in golf would be complete without mention of the late Bob Duden of Portland and Kent Myers of Lake Oswego. If Duden had come along at a different time, he might have become a legend on the senior tour. As it was, he became a legendary figure in the Pacific Northwest where he consistently contended for regional titles over four decades. Duden won 23 major regional tournaments, including the Oregon Open eight times.

"Conditioning?" Duden once said. "I don't do much besides playing golf. I just go out and play, and I usually walk with my handcart. I only use an electric cart if I play 36 holes." And he kept right on doing that until his death in 1995 at age 74. His death ended an ever-climbing hole-in-one total. Duden had 22 aces over his lifetime, including one on a par-4 hole at Glendoveer Golf Course.

Duden lost a chance to add to his wealth when his croquet-style putter was outlawed by the USGA in the 1960's. The USGA didn't actually ban the putter, but it made the style obsolete by making it a rules violation for a player to straddle the line of a putt. "That decision cost me plenty," Duden said a few years later.

Myers' major claim to fame was an uncanny ability at match-play, which led to four Oregon Amateur titles spread over three decades and some exciting victories in Hudson Cup matches against the pros. One of his trademarks was a special putting style that he used occasionally in the heat of battle—holding the putter behind him and extending the shaft between his legs. He putted well that way and the psychological effect on opponents was stunning. "Golf was so difficult when I started that I decided I was going to whip it," Myers said in a 1988 interview. "I'm still trying."

Bob Robinson has been a sports writer at The Oregonian for 36 years and the golf writer there for 30 of those years. He's covered the Masters, the U.S. Open and PGA Championship several times each, in addition to many Northwest golf events. Robinson was the beat writer for the Portland Trail Blazers when they won the NBA championship in 1977, and had two books published after that season—World Champions (Graphic Arts of Portland) and Bill Walton—Star of the Blazers (Scholastic Press of New York). Bob was selected Oregon Sports Writer of the Year in 1977 by the National Sportscasters and Sports Writers Association. Bob is a University of Oregon graduate who began his career as an assistant news editor, city editor and sports editor at the Capital Journal in Salem before moving on to The Oregonian.

The Charms of North-Central Washington

by Bob Spiwak

North-central Washington oozes down the east slopes of the Cascade Mountains and comes to rest, nominally, where the Columbia River dives south from Canada. From north to south, it begins at the Canadian border and comes to rest shy of Hanford's atomic works. This is fortunate, because a slice into Hanford can transform a Titleist into a glow-in-the-dark spheroid—what with radioactivity and all that.

It is a land of diversity. Jagged, sky-scratching mountains give way to desert country with the nation's fruit basket in between. Okanogan, one of the largest counties in the U.S., stretches across the area. It is larger than Connecticut and Rhode Island yet has but one 18-hole golf course. There are four public nines. There's also two private nine-holers outside the town of Winthrop, population 345.

The region receives 10 to 14 inches of precipitation a year, most of which is snow. The farther west you go into the Cascade foothills, the deeper the snow becomes, with colder temperatures and winters that seem interminable. Now this is fine for skiers, but it does leave things wanting for golfers. I happen to be a golfer, happen to own the more private of the two courses mentioned above (which was converted in 1997 to a private lesson facility and arboretum), and happen to go just a bit bonkers after Christmas when my friends in more southerly climes call to brag about their career four-wood shots hit earlier that day. Living in this climate can be frustrating for a golfer.

The local high school golf team is a case in point. While virtually every other team is practicing on grass—brown or green—by the middle of March, these poor kids are hitting wiffle balls in the school gym. There's still a foot or more of snow on the ground at this time. Thus unprepared, they must venture forth to compete against schools whose students have never seen a wiffle ball, let alone smote one with a golf club for hours on end.

The first courses to open are more than a hundred miles to the south, along the temperature-modifying Columbia River. Early in February, when the PGA Tour is basking in Palm Springs, local golfers will meet on the street and wonder aloud if Rock Island, Crescent Bar or Desert Aire might be open. If one is, plans are made to gather a foursome and set up a game.

There are certain parameters involved in these excursion plans. While all are aware that the journey to and from the course will take an hour longer than walking the 18 holes, the trip itself is contingent upon the weather. Bear in mind that at this time of year we are wading through at least three feet of snow at home. First, in the name of safety, there cannot be more than four inches of snow on the highway. Secondly, the temperature must be at least 22 degrees, for we can count on it being 10 degrees warmer at our destination. Third, visibility on the highway must be at least the length of three telephone poles through the falling snow. If these conditions are met, we go.

With down vests and jackets we resemble a quartet of Michelin men. Our mittens contain handwarmers, and wool caps are pulled over our ears. We hit our frozen rocks down the fairway and revel in it, uttering inane comments like, "Boy, it sure feels good to be out again." Never mind that fingers are numbed by contact with shafts, or a thin hit will resonate through the body and loosen fillings—we are golfing again.

I have a bit of an advantage; being a fairly inept golfer, I need it. Although my pitch-and-putt course is buried under feet of snow, I keep a small patch plowed throughout the winter. If it isn't too cold, I take a bucket of heated balls and a small mat out to the plowed area every week and hit a few into the white beyond. In spring, as the snow melts, they pop up like 90-compression Easter eggs to be gathered.

But golf in north-central Washington is not only about winter. Because the season is so severe, it may be that we appreciate the coming of spring more than, say, a golfer in Honolulu, which has no spring. (I mention Hawaii because there are some shameless Northwest golfers who will flee the winter and head there, Florida or the Southwest, and never know the joy of a well-hit iron running 300 yards down a frozen fairway.)

This being mountain and desert country, the ground drains quickly. Our fellow hackers on the soggy side of the Cascades must endure, until June or so, having their balls plug, lost forever in mucky, muddy fairways. Rooster tails follow putts across the greens. Golfers there wear spiked rubber boots and are encased in Gore-Tex from head to ankle, like so many high-tech mummies.

In spring, the mountains block the incoming moist Pacific air and the rain peters out as it crosses the Cascade crest. While it is pouring in Seattle, it is hot and sunny in this country. And it gets hot in a hurry. In my three decades here the temperature has ranged from 32 below zero to 110 degrees above. These are extremes, and summer days are usually in the 80's. And, as winter retreats northward, other courses begin to open. The drive to the nine-holers at Rock Island and Crescent Bar are a thing of the past for this season. Desert Canyon—ranked among the top-five courses in the state—opens and, soon after, Lake Chelan. Both involve drives of little more than an hour. By mid-April, the local public Bear Creek nine, a mere 10 minutes away, begins greeting players. Bear Creek is usually the last course in the state to open. There may be a desultory snow flurry or two after it opens, but these chilly intrusions only serve as final exclamation points to winter's end.

Suddenly, the region is green. A tide of pink and white and red blossoms washes over the branches of apple, pear, cherry, apricot and peach trees which follow the Columbia north through the thousands of orchards along the way. The bald eagles depart; the geese, swans and white pelicans arrive. Putts are accompanied by birdsong.

The marmots emerge from a seven-month hibernation. I don't know of a course in north-central Washington that doesn't have these fat rodents scurrying about, cute little guys that laze on rocks and nibble the grass. Cute they are, until it dawns on you that your missing ball is probably down in one of their burrows. It is not good policy to reach in to find it either, or you might find a *Crotalus pacificus* zealously protecting its new-found Pinnacle.

The Pacific Northwest rattlesnake is quite a benign fellow, rarely looking for a fight. They are quite shy and on the small side, their bite hardly ever fatal to humans. But they will protect themselves and, therefore, reaching into unseen places—especially among rocks—is a bad idea in this country. Many courses in the region have bull snakes cruising about. Golfers seem unable to resist poking them with a club. Their response is to flatten their heads and hiss menacingly. Some are killed by golfers, either being mistaken for rattlers or just out of sheer mean spirit. There would be a lot more mouse damage on the courses were it not for them and their rattling cousins.

Deer are frequently spotted on the courses. Their dainty little hooves make divots in the greens, and their cute little noses twitch above teeth that consume flowers and shrubs on the course. For all the nuisance they can be, there is something about deer that makes the grouchiest golfer forget a four-putt on the hole before. Coyotes will sometimes use a fairway as the shortest route between points A and B. And, speaking of B, bears are occasionally spotted.

Ponds and lakes attract waterfowl, and in early spring duck and goose parents are followed around the waterways by a clutch of youngsters, bobbing like corks in their parents' wake. Herons plod in slow motion through the wetlands, watched with mild interest by a family of long-eared owls in the aspens on the pond bank.

The advent of summer lessens the wildlife sightings. The courses become more crowded as vacationers arrive. The diversity of the area's golfing venues is contained within the text of this book, course by course. There is something for every golfer. Desert courses reminiscent of Arizona and Palm Springs. Treeless links-type layouts are here, as are lush verdant fairways lined with spreading maples and evergreens, like courses east of the Mississippi.

The common attribute shared by almost every north-central Washington course is the view, or better yet, the views. There is not one from which mountains cannot be seen. Those abutting the North Cascades—from Winthrop south—offer some of the most spectacular mountain scenery in the world. At Desert Canyon, the peaks are counterpointed by the flowing Columbia River 600 feet below. At mile-wide Banks Lake, the Grand Coulee's basalt columns flank the blue waters of the 60-mile-long reservoir. Lake Chelan offers a continuing vista of snowy mountains, the fjord of the lake, waves of orchards and brown foothills. Bear Creek in the Methow Valley is surrounded by majestic peaks and lies at the terminus of a magnificent valley carved by glaciers during the last ice age.

Being on the downslope of the mountains, the region can frequently be windy. When the wind is up, it's time to put on the golfer's thinking cap. A "two-club" wind is not at all uncommon, and there are times when a three wood is a wiser choice than a five iron.

The sun is hot, and the air is clear and very dry. You may not be aware of perspiration, especially if the wind is up. This is the ideal scenario for a big-league sunburn, and sunscreen should be applied liberally, even if you're riding in a golf cart.

The major annoyances of the region's courses are yellow jackets and bald-faced hornets. The yellow jacket is a familiar creature that has the propensity to sneak, sometimes in numbers, into beverage cans. They seem to do this when one is on the tee, and can offer varying levels of surprise when a drink is quaffed after a shot. The hornets, black with a white face, are aggressive in the extreme. Proceed carefully into brushy areas to avoid meeting them.

All this is but a sampler of golf in north-central Washington. While we may have one of the shortest golf seasons in the nation, us locals have learned to adapt to off-season golf. When the weather warms, there's no finer place on the planet in which to spoil a good walk.

Bob Spiwak took up golf in 1953 as a respite from the rigors of selling bibles door-to-door in North Dakota. He's been a fanatical golfer ever since. Spiwak has written articles for almost every golf magazine in the Western world, although few have been published (just kidding). He has rubbed elbows with many famous golfers because they would not shake his hand. His most treasured golf antiquity is a nod he got from Gerald Ford at the 1990 Golf Summit. Spiwak lives in Mazama, Washington, with his wife, four cats, a dog, a small rabbit and a big handicap next to the clubhouse at Whispering Rattlesnakes Golf & Flubbers Club.

The Northwest's *Very* Private Courses

by Jeff Shelley

The Northwest—at least as defined by this book—encompasses about a million square miles. The region is inhabited by thousands of property owners, many of whom possess unused expanses of land. Politically-correct people often refer to these tracts as "open space," a term sometimes applied to golf courses which, after all, are just grass and trees with some sand and water hazards thrown in to irritate their users.

We golfers like to view these stretches of mowed-low greenery as something other than just any old open space. And the region has a few people who, through either wealth or hard labor, have turned parts of their property into their very own golfing grounds. These "very private courses" range from modest par-3 layouts squeezed onto outsized back yards to manicured 18-holers on personal estates. Some courses are maintained by professional greenskeepers while others are hand-cut by the owner. Regardless of the scope of these layouts, the story behind each reveals something about the folks who started them.

Among the more high-profile of these ultraprivate courses—despite its remote location—is **Crystal Lakes** in Fortine, Montana. The 6,500-yard track had been part of a resort near the Canadian border before Jim Smith bought it in 1989. One of the reasons that Smith, an aviation buff, acquired the 1,200-acre resort was because it had a 5,000-foot-long runway, a feature also noticed by the jet-setting Arnold Palmer, who, on occasion, would alight at Crystal Lakes for a round of golf. Some men's club members complained to Smith that noise from his airplane interrupted their golf rounds. Smith replied, "Fine, I'll take care of the problem." And boy did he ever, closing the 200-acre golf course to all but himself, family members and friends. Smith continues to maintain the layout as well as the resort, playing golf after flying in from his Colorado home.

The layout features two different nines. The original holes (played as the back side) are long but traditional, with some sand traps and water hazards (ponds, streams and a large lake) on six holes. Conversely, the Bill Robinson-designed front nine is modern and impressive, with 40 bunkers, lakes on six holes, and some 10,000-square-foot greens. Here also resides one of the region's best par-5s. The 516-yard 4th begins in the middle of a lake at an island tee reached by a 60-foot-long bridge. One's drive must carry at least 175 yards over water to find the fairway. The hole is a double-dogleg that goes right, then left, and is amply bunkered along the way. The 4th ends at a raised green ringed by seven traps. It's too bad Crystal Lakes was taken off the region's rota of public golf courses, if for no other reason than this hole.

Another terrific 18-holer is **Caledon** near Arlington, Washington. The 6,300-yard, par-72 track is part of a private getaway owned by two brothers, who bought it in 1995. The 380-acre Caledon estate was built by Donald Saunders who, after selling his ownership share in Bayliner Marine in late 1986 to the Brunswick Corporation, began building a recreational paradise for himself.

Among the features Saunders put into Caledon are the world's largest quarter-scale railroad system, which has two miles of track; a nine-bay roundhouse for the rail cars; a Le Mans-style go-cart track; a helicopter landing pad; caretaker's house; several outbuildings; a swimming and fishing lake; and a golf course of his own design. The 14,000-square-foot lodge is essentially a party house filled with antiques and entertainment rooms. According to a brochure produced when Saunders put the property on the market in 1994, the furnishings include 17th Century Flemish panel tapestries; an early 18th Century Italian monastery dining table of plank oak; three hand-colored botanical engravings by Basil Bresler published in 1613; a mid-19th Century Japanese altar; and other antiquities.

The lodge has a 200-seat banquet room, a disco dance area, a huge game room, a tavern removed intact from Everett's waterfront, an early-day soda fountain from Colfax, Washington, a conservatory/art studio/workout room with a stone fireplace, and five bedrooms—each decorated in a different motif. The lodge and surrounding grounds, which were advertised in the *Wall Street Journal*, also came with an undeveloped 950-acre parcel zoned for housing.

The fairways wind over hills and dales above the south fork of the Stillaguamish River. Saunders designed the course from a helicopter, instructing the construction crew where to place fairways, cut trees and move dirt while hovering overhead. Since its 1992 opening, the layout has been tended by a full-time crew. Caledon's holes—plied only by the brothers and their guests—are lined by cedars, firs and maples. There are no bunkers, but water hazards and corridor-like fairways would probably earn the unrated course a slope of 125 to 130. A pond fronting the raised 18th green is stocked with rainbow trout, and higher parts of the course offer incredible views of mounts Baker and Pilchuck.

Another high-end, very private Northwest course is a Jack Nicklaus-designed nine built by a Seattle industrialist. Under construction in 1995-1997, the course occupies part of a $26-million estate on **James Island** in the San Juans. While in the Seattle area to check up on the Snoqualmie Ridge TPC track near Issaquah, Nicklaus flew up to James Island to oversee progress on this layout.

Though not within the Northwest as defined by this book, another personal course is worth mentioning. **Dennis Washington**, a Montana magnate who owns railroad right-of-way land throughout the West, hired Robert Trent Jones, Jr. to build a $2-million, nine-hole track on Stewart Island in southwest British Columbia. The 15-acre layout has crisscrossing fairways and spectacular water views, according to an article in the *Wall Street Journal* that discussed ultra-private courses.

One of the more high-profile celebrities to acquire a golf course of his very own is Seattle-born rock star Steve Miller. For $4.35 million, Miller purchased the **Whittier Estate** on Carter Beach Road near Friday Harbor in May of 1996. The 26-acre reserve on San Juan Island boasts a 6,000-square-foot mansion and a 1,000-yard par-3 nine. The layout sits on manicured waterfront property with moorage for Miller's 62-foot yacht, *Abra Cadabra*.

Ultra-private courses are not the exclusive domain of the rich and powerful. Indeed, many reflect the fancies of their golfer-owners. Perhaps the region's most written-about personal course is **Whispering**

Rattlesnakes Golf & Flubbers Club in Mazama, Washington. This whimsically-named layout was designed and built by Bob Spiwak, the well-known golf writer and humorist who contributed a piece to this book. Sadly (to those of us who were lucky enought to have played it), Spiwak closed the difficult, five-acre par-3 nine after the 1996 season, saying he was tired of maintaining it. Also, after 10 years of hosting two tournaments annually, Bob found that the hassle of staging these events exceeded the rewards, even though the Mazama Invitational was an important fundraiser for a local Montessori School.

In 1997, Spiwak—much to his wife Gloria's delight—renamed the course Whispering Rattlesnakes Arboretum and Golf Academy. Instead of seeing nicely mowed bentgrass greens with flagsticks popping out of them, motorists along Highway 20 west of Winthrop will now observe exotic plants and gardens. Spiwak retained two greens for personal use and golf lessons. Whispering Rattlesnakes, written up in such publications as *Back Nine* and *Golf Course News*, featured ponds, greenside bunkers and streams. The head pro was Wiffi Smith, an LPGA star in the 1950s who as an amateur won the U.S., British, French and Mexican Amateurs. Also the head pro at Cloverdale Golf Club in Arlington, Wiffi is the golf instructor for several LPGA Tour players.

On about the same scale as Whispering Rattlesnakes is Chuck Burleson's six-acre par-3 near Battle Ground, Washington. Called **Duffer's Golf**, Burleson's nine-holer came about after he logged off a hillside on his property. Friends saw the clearing and suggested he turn it into a golf course. Burleson, who's played only a few courses other than his own, built the layout for slow-going hackers like himself. The short track features tiny greens; a pond enters play on several holes. Several tee shots must be judiciously placed to avoid overhanging tree branches.

A newer private nine-hole track called **Tanwax** lies off Highway 7 near Yelm. The owner, Ray Hendrickson, built what he thought might become a public course. Unfortunately, Hendrickson didn't have a conditional-use permit from Pierce County to operate it as such, so it's now used only by the owner and his friends.

Another recently-built layout is **Rocky Hills Golf Course.** The six-hole, 978-yard track lies off Simon Road, southeast of Snohomish. Dean Pratt, a retired custom homebuilder, converted a part of his 20-acre plot into a golf course. Pratt had raised beef cattle on the property, but says he "got sick of cows" before starting the short course with four par-3s and a pair of 180- and 300-yard par-4s. The 180-yarder is a sharp dogleg with a sloping-away green. Pratt built eight greens and 11 tees to give the holes different looks. He allows golfers to come by and play all day for a $5 contribution, which Pratt uses to buy gas for his mower. He also charges players $1 a swear word. If you're interested in playing Rocky Hills, call (360) 568-6279 and Dean might let you on.

Robert Munn's **Horse Heaven Country Club** is a nine-hole, par-34 track that begins in his back yard, then winds around his house and through his daughter's yard next door. The course in Paterson, a small central Washington town in Benton County, has two par-5s, three par-4s and four par-3s. The layout occupies once unwatered pasture; the lush tract now sports bluegrass fairways, bentgrass greens and over 40 different types of trees along fairways. A 250-yard-long creek winds across several holes, and bulges into a pool filled with bass and Japanese koi. The 18-acre course is on part of Munn's Sun Heaven Farms and Sun Set Produce, a 3,500-acre concern that grows onions, potatoes, corn and sugar beets. The course was designed by Munn's son, Randy; family members and hired workers built it. Horse Heaven Country Club is a popular spot for Munn family parties, reunions and church events. Munn allows only residents of the Horse Heaven area to play his exquisitely-conditioned layout.

Another fine personal course is a par-3 nine in **Port Orchard**. Designed and built by Joe Ladley, a retired veterinarian, the course is part of a 27-acre estate that includes a 4,500-square-foot home, a 2,500-square-foot guest house, seven-car garage, horse stables, tennis court and trout-stocked lake. In early 1997, the property was on the market for $1.65 million. The estate offers striking views of the Olympic Mountains, Seattle's skyline, Puget Sound and Vashon Island. When building the course off Southeast View Park Road, Ladley removed over 100 alders and repositioned more than 100 tons of rocks. He did virtually all the work himself; the fairways and greens are now maintained by paid staff. The course involves several water and sand hazards, and is said to be immaculate.

While each of the above owners had their own motivations for building personal courses, perhaps the most unusual is that of Bert Hotchkiss, of Sweet Home, Oregon. Hotchkiss built **Fernwood Golf Course** in 1988 so he could visit the remote nooks and crannies of his 44 acres, places that would otherwise go unappreciated. Hotchkiss deliberately built tees—27 in all—that require him and guests to travel through woodlands to get to them. Featuring nine beautifully-tended bentgrass greens built to USGA specs, the course, with three tees per hole, involves the Green, Blue and Gold nines. While padding around the rural layout, Hotchkiss and guests see turkeys, deer and rabbits. In April and May, Hotchkiss closes the course and grows hay on the fairways. Once the hay is mowed and sold off, golf returns.

An author who's penned two best-selling personal-philosphy books, Hotchkiss spends a month each year traveling the country in a motorhome selling his current title *(Your Owner's Manual)* and lecturing on the powers of self-awareness and personal responsibility. Nearby residents are allowed to play Fernwood for free, provided they call ahead. Of this policy, Hotchkiss says, "I probably wouldn't have met as many local people if the golf course had not been built."

Fernwood invitees will be assured of solitary rounds as Bert allows only one group on the course at a time. The unique layout, which has ornamental trees planted around it (including one on the corner of a green), boasts elevated tees, lovely views of a lush valley, and a trout-stocked pond with a fountain. One severely tilting green called "Squirrelly" harbors humps, a wild slope and a very tall tier. Bert recommends players negotiate this putting surface by saying something nice to a deceased aunt buried nearby. (The praise works; I sunk a tough, side-snaking eight-footer after following Bert's advice.)

There are probably other personal golf courses in Northwest places, maybe even one down the road from your house. It's certainly a strong likelihood that these ranks of "privateers" will grow as the golf bug does its inexorable march through the populace. More Northwest landowners will probably build their very own fields of dreams, and the region's golf scene will be richer for it.

Author's Note: If any reader knows of any more such "very private courses," please forward the information to the author at: Fairgreens Media Inc., PO Box 15330, Seattle, WA 98115-0330. Thanks for your help.

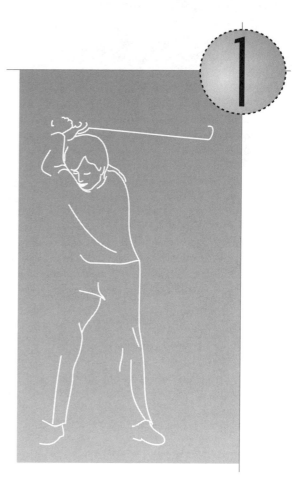

NORTHWEST WASHINGTON & THE SAN JUAN ISLANDS

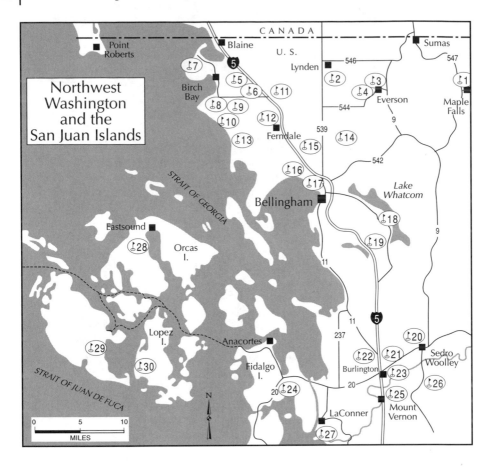

1. **Peaceful Valley Country Club** — public 9
2. **Homestead Golf & Country Club** — semiprivate 18 & driving range
3. **Raspberry Ridge Golf Community** — public 9
4. **Evergreen Golf Course** — public 9
5. **Loomis Trail Golf Club** — private 18
6. **Grandview Golf Course** — public 18
7. **Semiahmoo Golf & Country Club** — semiprivate 18 & driving range
8. **Sea Links** — public 18 (par-3)
9. **Birch Bay Village Golf Course** — private 9
10. **Rodarco Golf Range** — driving range
11. **Dakota Creek Golf & Country** — public 9
12. **Riverside Golf Course** — public 9
13. **Sandy Point Golf Course** — private 9 (par-3)
14. **Shuksan Golf Club** — public 18 & driving range
15. **North Bellingham Golf Course** — public 18 & driving range
16. **New World Pro Golf Center** — public 9 (par-3) & driving range
17. **Bellingham Golf & Country Club** — private 18
18. **Sudden Valley Golf & Country Club** — semiprivate 18 & driving range
19. **Lake Padden Municipal Golf Course** — public 18 & driving range
20. **Gateway Golf Course** — public 9
21. **Avalon Golf Club** — public 27 & driving range
22. **Skagit Golf & Country Club** — private 18
23. **Cooper's Golf Range** — driving range
24. **Similk Beach Golf Course** — public 18 & driving range
25. **Eaglemont Golf Course** — semiprivate 18 & driving range
26. **Overlook Golf Course** — public 9
27. **Shelter Bay Golf Course** — private 9
28. **Orcas Island Golf Club** — semiprivate 9
29. **San Juan Golf & Country Club** — semiprivate 9 & driving range
30. **Lopez Island Golf Club** — semiprivate 9

Demarcated by the Canadian border and the Snohomish County line, this area of the Northwest is blessed with scenic coastlines, attractive islands and unimpeded mountain vistas. All these features help make it a recreational and trade destination for both Americans and Canadians. Northwest Washington enjoys a moderate climate (zone 4 for Bellingham-Blaine, zone 5 for the San Juans). Golf is usually a year-round sport, but be prepared for rain especially in spring and fall. The alpine reaches along the North Cascades are in zone 1. Several golf courses opened during the early 1990s, with Whatcom County leading the way. The influx of golf holes has been a dual-edged sword, however. Golfers are thrilled by the new tracks and their relatively low playing fees. But, due to an unfavorable exchange rate with the Canadian dollar, some operators have had to offer incentives and price discounts to attract players—either American or those from north of the border. Land has become so expensive in the San Juans, it's unlikely (other than that occasional private layout built by a tycoon on estate property) that new courses will be built here in the near future.

Public Courses

Avalon Golf Club

27

1717 Kelleher Road, Burlington, WA 97233. (360) 757-1900 or 1-800-624-0202. Brian Kruhlak, pro. 27 holes. Course ratings: South/West (6,576 yards, par 72) men—C71.8/129, B70.0/124, M68.7/118; women—FF74.8/127, F72.2/122; North/ South (6,771 yards, par 72): men—C73.1/132, B71.3/127, M69.6/124; women— FF75.6/133, F73.2/127; North/West (6,597 yards, par 72) men— C72.3/125, B70.3/ 121, M68.7/117; women—FF74.6/129, F71.67/122. Year Opened: 1991 (West & South nines), 1992 (North Nine). Architect: Robert Muir Graves. Moderate, credit cards. Reservations: Call five days ahead. Walk-on chances: Fair. Walkability: Excellent. Playability: Enjoyable for all play levels—just be sure to pick the right tees.

This namesake of King Arthur's paradise is a great place for golf. The first-rate facility, owned by Ron and Susan Hass, lies east of Interstate 5 off the Cook Road exit north of Burlington, and sprawls over Butler Hill. From the South Nine, golfers enjoy wonderful vistas of the Skagit Valley and Cascade Mountains. Besides 27 holes and a grass-teed driving range, Avalon Golf Club has an attractive clubhouse with a restaurant. Golfers are sent off 10 minutes apart, and the three nines are used all the time to help spread out play.

The 233-acre site was transformed into an entertaining golf course by architect Robert Muir Graves. Thirty-year-old trees and some ancient firs define fairways. Avalon's wooded character extends to the tree stumps squatting in target zones; a snag at the South Nine's 5th hole contains a never-removed sawblade, the logger's equivalent to Excalibur, if you will. The West and South nines opened in July 1991; the North side in spring 1992. Avalon will remain devoted to golf; no homes or resort facilities are planned. Each hole has multiple tees, and the bentgrass greens can be slick when mowed low. Fairways offer good lies on island-like routes lined by mounds and trees; the layout has very few OB markers. Errant golfers don't need white stakes to penalize them when off the beaten path, as thick underbrush lines most Avalon holes.

This is a shotmaker's course, and players are advised to be prudent when wielding a driver. Wind plays a subtle but important role at the hilltop track; Puget Sound westerlies will skew shots hit above tree tops. A challenging South hole is the 4th, a 519-yard par-5 with a narrow and rolling dogleg-right fairway. The tee-shot "garden spot" located 240 yards out is squeezed by two huge stumps. A pair of bunkers—75 yards from the trapped-left 4th green—gathers second shots from players unaware that the traps exist. The West Nine begins with an interesting hole, a 363-yard par-4. This 90-degree dogleg-right sneaks around two hidden ponds. A stand of trees before the water hazards stymies attempts to drive the green, while a tiny landing area makes cautious golfers use a mid-iron from the tee. The raised and trapped-rear 1st green is wide but shallow, and it slopes steeply toward the fairway and a sand trap.

The longest of the nines at 3,396 yards, the North side has nearly two dozen sand traps and three ponds. The largest water hazard imperils portions of the 6th, 7th and 8th holes. The top-rated 6th, a 594-yard par-5, features a fairway that runs straight for 450 yards, while skirting a bunker and "jailed" OB along the right and tree stumps left. The hole eventually curls around a large pond to a mound-ringed, untrapped green. Another dandy is the 7th, a 408-yard par-4. Once past a pond right of the tee, the fairway, perhaps Avalon's narrowest, burrows through trees. An unseen creek crosses the hole 100 yards from a large left-sloping green with a steep right flank and a trap on its left side.

Dakota Creek Golf & Country   9

3258 Haynie Road, Custer, WA 98240. (360) 366-3131. 9 holes. 2,379 yards. Par 35. Grass tees. Course ratings: men 64.3/112, women 65.9/112. Year Opened: 1988. Architect: Pam Magee. Economical, credit cards. No reservations. Walkability: Good. Playability: Though there's plenty of trouble to get into, this course isn't as long as others in the area and might be more appropriate for beginning-intermediate golfers.

There is no "Club" in the name of this 1988-opened facility, as owners Pam and Frank Magee wanted to connote a place of relaxation without the exclusivity of a club. Located in a rural part of Whatcom County, the Dakota Creek area is home to raccoons, deer, red foxes, blue herons, hawks and eagles. On-course ponds are stocked with salmon and trout. On clear days, Cascade panoramas are enjoyed from several promontory-perched tees. The Magees' property had been a blackberry- and alder-snarled wilderness before it became a nine-hole golf course. The couple has gradually been working on a second nine; as of 1997, a few holes had been built with the remaining work to be phased in over the next couple of years.

Dakota Creek's current layout penalizes those straying into the feral, fairway-side rough. Also of concern are several creeks, steep terrain, strategically-placed ponds, a few sand traps and well-canted greens. The layout's bunkers serve less as hazards and more as catch basins for balls headed into jail. Dakota Creek's toughest hole is the 7th, a 312-yard par-4 that doglegs left through alders past a pond along the right. Very tight at the turn, the fairway rises to a tiny, tree-ringed green with a narrow entry and steep front slope, and another pond off to the right.

Eaglemont Golf Course - semiprivate

18 *4127 Eaglemont Drive, Mount Vernon, WA 98273. (360) 424-0800 or 1-800-368-8876. Mike O'Laughlin, pro. 18 holes. 7,006 yards. Par 72. Grass tees. Course ratings: men—T73.9/136, C72.2/130, M71.0/125, FF69.9/122; women— FF75.6/137, F71.4/122. Year Opened: 1993 (original nine), 1994 (second nine). Architect: John Steidel. Moderate (expensive on weekends), credit cards. Call for reservations. Walk-on chances: Good. Walkability: Carts included with green fees for good reason. Playability: Holes range from intermediate to very penalizing.*

Eaglemont, a sprawling layout southeast of Mount Vernon, continues to generate reactions at the opposite ends of the spectrum from the golfers who play it. There are those who find Eaglemont's hilly, cart-necessary layout intriguing, with hole after challenging hole continually piquing their interest. Then there are those who end

Eaglemont's 2nd hole is a 380-yard par-4.

up denigrating the track as a contrived mish-mash of pretentious holes ill-fit for a site that honors a proposed residential development over golfing integrity. How else to explain the "forced" carries, lengthy between-hole distances, and bagful of blind (and unfair) shots?

Which side you're on depends upon one's success at Eaglemont, the amount of balls lost during a round, and the ability to adapt to side-, up- and down-hill lies. It may also have to do with how much cash you've got in the bank and your feelings about cart-mandatory policies. I dislike the latter, but am fully cognizant of why Eaglemont's proprietors—Sea-Van Investments—vetoed walking: workers would probably have to extricate stragglers at the end of each day if they weren't riding vehicles to carry them through.

The 680-acre Eaglemont project is still a work in progress, with the professional staff and food service operating out of a temporary clubhouse. Site preparation has been done for a new 22,000-square-foot clubhouse near the current 4th hole; until a new clubhouse opens—perhaps by 1998—the first hole will remain a 181-yard par-3, an unusual opener for a 7,000-yard course. Sales of residential lots have lagged since Eaglemont's late-1993 opening, so many of the 650 homesites remain undeveloped. A few homes have been built along the 10th and 11th holes. A third nine is also planned, but it won't be built until more homesites are sold.

One of the benefits of a hilltop track like this are the views. Here, golfers can glimpse the Olympics and Cascades from many holes. On a recent visit in 1995, I found Eaglemont's fairway turf a bit yellow and with some bald spots. The tees and greens, however, were immaculate and richly verdant. Eaglemont has many of the features found in upscale golfing reserves, with paved cart paths, color-coded flags showing pin placements, well-conceived signage, and a spacious driving range. Its friendly head pro, Mike O'Laughlin, runs the pro shop with considerable gusto and has a great regard for the course. The course has hosted several tournaments over the years; in 1997, it held the Washington State Best Ball Tournament.

John Steidel's design for Eaglemont features target-type, multi-part fairways routed through wetlands and barancas. Longer hitters will find Eaglemont to their liking, but accuracy for all is a must. A good example of Eaglemont's confounding nature is the 3rd hole, a 480-yard par-5. From the tee, one views a steep and rocky hill. Players must shoot over this scree to reach a hidden fairway that sits about 100 feet above the tee. Once on top, the fairway slopes left toward trees, with another rocky hill along the right. The last 150 yards of the gradually ascending hole are narrowed by trees left and the aforementioned hill right. About 80 yards from the green sits a tall (and unnecessary) tree in the middle of the fairway, one that may penalize players who've hit two good shots up to that point. The 3rd hole ends at a small, left-sloping green trapped front and rear.

No matter how you view Eaglemont, it'll probably vary from that of your playing partner. This much is certain: No one has left the course with a ho-hum reaction.

Evergreen Golf Course

9

413 East Main Street, Everson, WA 98247. (360) 966-5417. 9 holes. 2,145 yards. Par 31. Grass tees. No course ratings. Year Opened: 1959. Architects: Clint & Jerry McBeth. Economical. No reservations. Walkability: Excellent. Playability: Ideal for beginners.

An executive-length nine at Everson's east end, Evergreen is overseen by long-time owner and the course superintendent Jerry McBeth. Evergreen is closed from November through mid-March. If the clubhouse is unoccupied during the season, a pay box by the door accepts green fees. Evergreen, built in 1959 by Jerry and his late father, Clint McBeth, occupies about 30 acres of flat land dotted with trees. Its small greens are untrapped affairs, and the fairways are short but, with adjoining OB, narrow. Evergreen's primary hazard is a creek that enters play at the 1st, 3rd, 6th and 7th holes. The easy-to-walk layout contains five par-3s and four par-4s. Evergreen's toughest hole, the 7th, is a 405-yarder with a creek-fronted tee and a tree-lined fairway.

Gateway Golf Course

9

839 Fruitdale Road, Sedro-Woolley, WA 98284. (360) 856-0315. Wellington Lee, pro. 9 holes. 3,050 yards. Par 36. Grass tees (mats in winter). Course ratings: men— B67.9/115, M66.7/113; women—M72.2/118, F67.6/108. Year Opened: 1972. Architect: Al Fredlund. Economical (moderate on weekends), sr. rates. No reservations. Walkability: A couple of hills, but not too bad. Playability: Lovely views from higher points of nine-hole course.

Gateway, named for its proximity to the "entrance" to Washington's major mountain range, is on Sedro-Woolley's northeast end off Highway 20 (North Cascades Highway). The course is owned by Sotero and Anita Lee; their son Wellington, also the head pro at Kayak Point, comes in for lessons on occasion. Anita runs the place pretty much on her own as Sotero, who doesn't golf, serves as a counselor general in Beijing, China, and is gone much of the time. The Lees had discussed building a second nine on neighboring land, but in early 1997, were thinking of selling Gateway as Anita has tired of driving to the course from her Edmonds home.

Gateway was designed and built by Al Fredlund, who opened it in 1972. Gateway is a center of local golf activities, with members competing in all sorts of tournaments. Gateway's Industrial League, comprised of teams sponsored by local businesses and initiated in 1977, is capped by a championship and banquet. One of the nation's top girl amateurs, Kelli Kamimura, learned golf at Gateway. She and her younger sister, Jennifer, also a top player, began working with the course's then-head pro, Rudy Franulovich, when they were very young. Though Franulovich died in early 1996, Kelli and Jennifer continue using Gateway as their "home" course.

The nine holes occupy a former cow pasture and swamp. Its terrain encompasses a low-lying meadow and a tree-dotted hill. Players can use most clubs in the bag on the "18-on-9" track, which has two tees per hole and measures 6,100 yards over two trips. A ditch winds through the flat portion of the course, and a pond abuts the 5th green. Most of the these knoll-perched greens have steep sides. The top-rated hole is the 4th, a 401-yard par-4 that stretches over undulating terrain to a rolling green fronted by the ditch.

Grandview Golf Course

18

7738 Portal Way, Custer, WA 98240. (360) 366-3947. 18 holes. 6,404 yards. Par 72. Grass tees. Course ratings: men—B70.3/116, M69.4/114; women F71.2/ 120. Opened: 1950s (original nine), 1974 (second nine). Architects: Fred Muenscher (original nine); Lonnie Montgomery (second nine); Golf Concepts (remodel). Moderate, jr./sr. rates, credit cards. Reservations: Call a week ahead. Walk-on chances: Fair. Walkability: Flat track is easy on the ambulatory. Playability: Good spot for beginning-intermediate golfers to test their wings.

Located four miles north of Ferndale, Grandview Golf Course sits on the west edge of Interstate 5 near the Custer exit. Fred Muenscher started Grandview with a few holes atop a cow pasture in the 1950s, later extending the course to nine holes. In 1972, Lonnie Montgomery bought the facility and, in 1974, added a back nine. In 1991, a Vancouver, B.C. partnership purchased Grandview and proceeded to build new holes and greens, improve drainage, install a computerized irrigation system, and add 300 yards to the former run-of-the-mill course. Bellingham-based Golf Concepts did the design and construction work.

All-new holes or rebuilt greens now occupy the 1st, 9th, 10th, 16th, 17th and 18th. The new greens are quite different from Grandview's originals, having more size and contour as well as mounds and traps around them. All of the old greens slope toward the front—ramp-like onto fairways—with steep rear edges. A creek on the course has been diverted into ponds, which toughened up the course and aided drainage. Twelve greenside bunkers were also added.

Wildlife visitors include geese, frogs, ducks, rabbits and moles; a few bald eagles occasionally circle fairways. Nice views of the Cascades are available from several junctures. Grandview crosses a flat meadow but, with the addition of man-made hazards, now has much more character. Among its sterner challenges is the 7th, a 532-yard par-5 where golfers can catch the best mountain vistas. The tee shot at this dogleg-right must be well-placed, as trees and OB are off to the left and a pond lurks inside the turn. Once around the bend, a creek lines the hole on the left. A tall fir looms in mid-fairway, 75 yards from a two-tiered green guarded right-rear by a pond. Grandview's 16th, a 479-yarder, is one of the Northwest's longest par-4s. Rated the course's second-toughest hole, the 16th has a pond right of the tee and a ditch crossing the fairway 150 yards out. The dogleg-left hole winds toward an evergreen sitting 50 yards from a mound-ringed, right-front-sloping green.

Homestead Golf & Country Club - semiprivate

18

673 Mayberry Drive, Lynden, WA 98264. 1-800-354-1196. Joe Sievers, pro. 18 holes. 6,927 yards. Par 72. Grass tees. Course ratings: Men—C73.2/129, B71.0/ 125, M69.0/119; women—M74.2/128, F72.0/124. Year Opened: 1993 (original nine), 1995 (second nine). Architect: Bill Overdorf. Moderate, jr./sr. rates, credit cards. Reservations: Call a week ahead. Walk-on chances: Fair. Walkability: Excellent. Playability: Fine for all players, but everyone should know where they're going 'cause there's plenty of trouble to be found here.

A newer facility northeast of Lynden, this course is the centerpiece of a 350-acre planned unit development. Besides an outstanding golf course, Homestead features a large clubhouse. Soon-to-open facilities include a 40-unit hotel, athletic club, RV park and swimming pool. Roughly half of the 600 proposed single- and multi-family housing units have been built and sold; none of the houses are between fairways. Homestead's residences have been attractive as the city of Lynden has experienced a 30 percent increase in population since 1990. Many younger (and primarily Canadian) families are moving here. The backer of the project is Homestead Northwest, a local corporation headed by Jim Wynstra and Bob Libolt. The semiprivate club offers unlimited-golf memberships to lot buyers and non-residents, with public play allowed. Groups are spaced a relaxing 10 minutes apart.

Homestead occupies a former strawberry field and dairy farm. The agricultural heritage of the site continues with a nearby dairy operation. Uninterrupted views of the Cascades are available on clear days. The course architect is Lynden resident, Bill Overdorf, who's designed such stellar Western Washington layouts as the Classic Country Club in Spanaway, Raspberry Ridge in Everson, and Meriwood in Lacey. Homestead's two nines are separated by Depot Road; the original (front) nine is east of Depot, while the newer back nine lies on the west. Both sides are amazingly mature considering their relative youth. Fairway turf is thick and rich, wonderful flower gardens dot the grounds, and the greens can be mowed low if superintendent Chris Lovgren so desires.

Homestead can play tough. Its primary sources of difficulty are the many ponds which tighten the grip; dozens of grass and sand bunkers; and some wildly undulating greens. Overdorf's wily design finds ponds lurking in hidden swales within driving zones and sneaking in front of greens. Some ponds enter play on more than one hole. Most putting surfaces are huge and, since the flags are not color-coded to show pin placements, players must be confident in their choices of clubs. Homestead is not for the faint of heart, nor is it for the golfer who owns only a few balls.

Among the more memorable holes—and there are many—is the top-rated 3rd, a 527-yard par-5 with a pond-fronted tee. Two huge bunkers sit along the left driving distance out, and grass bunkers occupy mounds along the right with OB a concern there also. Another pond on the left starts at the 150-yard mark, then winds up to guard the left-front of a rolling green trapped right and rear. The 421-yard, par-4 10th has a liberal landing area for tee shots, but sand traps line both sides of the fairway and its slick front-sloping green is also well-bunkered. Homestead's signature hole is the 18th, a dandy 525-yard par-5 with four ponds and sundry traps along its perilous route. In 1996, the hole was featured in a pictorial essay of the nation's most-interesting "island" holes in *Golf Digest*. The dogleg-left winds around a pond, with another outside the turn, before the fairway broadens 150 yards from a water-engirded island green with a hump in the middle and a frontward tilt. This aqueous hole concludes the tough and entertaining Homestead track, one of the best to enter the Northwest golf scene in recent years.

Lake Padden Municipal Golf Course

18 *4882 Samish Way, Bellingham, WA 98225. (360) 676-6989. Kene Bensel, pro. 18 holes. 6,575 yards. Par 72. Grass tees. Course ratings: men—B72.0/124, M69.9/ 120; women—M75.4/129, F71.9/122. Year Opened: 1971. Architects: Glen Proctor & Roy Goss; John Steidel (remodel). Economical—Whatcom County residents (moderate for non-residents), jr./sr. rates, credit cards. Reservations: Call a week ahead. Walk-on chances: Ok for singles. Walkability: Good. Playability: Excellent test for all concerned.*

This city-run facility lies about four miles southeast of town in the Lake Padden Recreational Area, a woodsy fun zone for the horsy, tennis, camping and swimming sets. After undergoing a course-wide renovation between 1991 and 1995, Lake Padden steps up to Bellingham's loaded golf table with a plateful of challenges. Besides giving Lake Padden Golf Course a new life, the $1.7-million upgrade has lent the former unadorned track a contemporary character. Overseen by Kennewick architect John Steidel, the remodel work resulted in a reversal of the nines, a computerized irrigation system, and dozens of new tees to satisfy players of various abilities. A yearly topdressing program has greatly improved the course's play in winter. The clubhouse and pro shop were given a new coat of paint; informative signs define hole configurations; and a computerized reservation system has created a much fairer way to get a tee time at a course ranked among Bellingham's busiest. The work at Lake Padden leads me to consider it on a par with Spokane's venerable Indian Canyon. The players in the annual Bellingham Amateur will probably concur; average scores have skyrocketed since the improvements were made.

Though bunkers, mounds and reconditioned turf now grace the course, Lake Padden still gains its character from the towering trees along its 170 acres of fairways. Golfers often spot rabbits, deer and various birds along these arboreal routes. "Padden's" challenge begins immediately with the 1st, a 421-yard par-4 rated the toughest. This long and tree-lined hole bends slightly to the left on a path lined by traps. The latter part of the fairway gradually tapers before reaching a greatly undulating green bunkered on the right. The 6th, a 381-yard par-4, runs downhill and to the right, skirting a sinuous bunker outside the turn. For accuracy, use a long iron or five-wood from the tee as dense jail borders the hole. Once around the corner, wetlands loom along the left before the 6th ends at a right-rear-sloping green bunkered right-front.

The 12th through 16th are Lake Padden's extended version of Amen Corner. The 12th, a 380-yard par-4, is an uphill dogleg-left that ends at a front-sloping, trapped-left and -rear green fronted by a pesky fir. The 13th, a 171-yard par-3, runs uphill past a pair of bushy cedars left-front of a rolling, skinny-but-deep green. The 14th, a 530-yard par-5, is long, winding and on the narrow side. Its last 150 yards slope left and rise to a bowl-shaped green ringed by trees. The 218-yard, par-3 15th (the course's fourth most-difficult hole) features a small, hogbacked green trapped laterally. And the 521-yard 16th is a slightly uphill par-5 that requires several accurate shots to reach a diminutive, left-tilting green trapped twice in front.

Lopez Island Golf Club

Airport Road, Lopez, WA 98261. (360) 468-2679. 9 holes. 2,701 yards. Par 35. Grass tees. Course ratings: men—B65.2/110, F62.8/105; women—B69.9/122, F67.0/114. Year Opened: 1958. Architects: the McCanagy family. Moderate, jr. rates. No reservations. Walkability: Easy. Playability: Good.

9

This rural course sits on the southwestern edge of Lopez Island, one of the most scenic of the San Juan Islands and heaven to bicyclists who can traverse its gently sloping roads en route to dozens of lovely coves. Lopez Island Golf Club, owned by about 230 members and overseen by a board of trustees, has benefited from several improvements and some hole reroutings in recent years. Built in 1958, the 40-acre course was designed and constructed by the McCanagy family, which founded it. Club members bought the course in the early 1980s. Although situated next to a small airport, Lopez Island's course is one of the most sedate in the Northwest. Deer and rabbits abound; eagles and hawks fly overhead.

Like other older tracks near coastlines, Lopez Island Golf Club has some weeds and patchiness. But who cares? This course is the only one on the island and it's fun to play, with several holes containing wildly undulating greens. Noteworthy among the stiffer tests is the 3rd, a 341-yard par-4. A sometimes-dry pond looms 225 yards off the tee, and its small green sits within a pocket of trees. The 9th, a par 4 of 292 yards, is a sharp dogleg-right. A pond outside the turn is a problem, but the large, left-sloping green can be reached with a long and high drive.

North Bellingham Golf Course

18 *205 West Smith Road, Bellingham, WA 98226. (360) 398-8300 or 1-800-469-9517. Howard Russell, pro. 18 holes. 6,816 yards. Par 72. Grass tees. Course ratings: men—C72.1/124, M68.9/119; women—M74.4/124, F68.7/112. Year Opened: 1995. Architect: Ted Locke. Moderate, jr./sr. rates, credit cards. Reservations: Call a week ahead. Walk-on chances: Fair. Walkability: Nice, tight layout pleasing for the ambulatory. Playability: Great for intermediate to skilled sticks, and not a bad place for beginners to assay their emerging skills.*

This new links-like layout north of Bellingham and off Guide Meridian occupies the former Wilder Ranch, a farm operation that produced hay and silage. The course's owner and developer, Caitac U.S.A. Corp., has 600 acres in all. Caitac, which is actually the Teraoka family, has plans for 1,350 single- and multi-family residences (to be placed outside the golf course). But the house-building probably won't occur until after the turn of the century. Also on the drawing board is a third nine, which may come on-line sooner. The course was designed by Vancouverite Ted Locke, and was built by Teufel/Leahy Golf, which has offices in Portland and Everett. Rich Jahnke, formerly of Loomis Trail, is the superintendent, the head pro is Howard Russell, and Terry Teraoka manages the facility.

In its first year of operation, the staff learned that 70 percent of its players were from across the border. Its international playlist stems from the fact that Vancouver-area courses cost upwards of 50 bucks (Canadian) a round. North Bellingham's about 10 smackers less, even with the exchange rate. Yet the prime reason for the migration is that this is an enjoyable course with fast and true greens, 12 ponds that complicate play on half the holes, dozens of white-sand bunkers, and well-conditioned turf that drains well in spring and fall. There are no big elevation changes at North Bellingham, so this is also an easy-to-walk track. To further enhance the package, the proprietors offer reasonably-priced unlimited golf packages. The facility is augmented by a 6,000-square-foot clubhouse with a pro shop, food service, bar and banquet areas.

Golfers here might spot Mount Baker and other Cascade spires along with deer, coyotes and various birdlife, including hawks. The coyotes were a pain during construction when they chewed up some greens, but have since lessened their visits. Wind often plays a crucial role at North Bellingham, which has a nice mix of holes that run both east-west and north-south. Locke fashioned large tees—four per hole—to make it a true player-adaptable layout. North Bellingham's signature hole may well be the 16th, a 216-yard par-3 that requires a tee shot over wetlands to reach a large green. The 17th is also a dandy. The 513-yard par-5 winds leftward along a narrowish, bunker-laden route before ending at a mid-sized, well-trapped green with subtle undulations.

Orcas Island Golf Club - semiprivate

9 *Route 1, Box 85, Eastsound, WA 98245. (360) 376-4400. 9 holes. 3,060 yards. Par 36. Grass tees. Course ratings: men B67.6/114; women—B72.8/125, F71.2/118. Year Opened: 1949. Architect: Bob Blake, Sr. Moderate, credit cards. Call for reservations. Walk-on chances: Good. Walkability: No major problems. Playability: Relaxing, good time at rural layout.*

Playing this course at the north end of Orcas Island during the off-season is a snap, but call in advance during the summer months as the island comes alive with tourists and vacation-home owners. The layout was designed and built by Bob Blake, Sr., and is now run by Blake's son, Bob, Jr. Bald eagles, hawks, herons and other endemic birdlife circle Orcas's fairways, and deer roam freely.

The mid-length dual-tee course, which extends 5,804 yards over 18 holes, crosses a bowl-shaped site whose periphery is lined by evergreen trees and a few homes. Several holes cross a hilltop, resulting in sloping fairways and greens with precipitous sides. Good tests include the 1st, a 466-yard par-5. From the raised tee, golfers view a rolling dogleg-right fairway that descends to a small, front-sloping green bordered left by a pond. The top-rated 2nd, a 394-yard par-4, contains a ditch-like, left-turning fairway that heads to a squarish green guarded left by a pond. The longest hole on the course is the 9th, a 542-yard par-5 that curls left around trees, harbors a depression in mid-fairway, and has a road crossing it 75 yards from a knoll-perched green.

Overlook Golf Course

1785 State Highway 9, Mount Vernon, WA 98273. (360) 422-6444. 9 holes. 2,540 yards. Par 35. Grass tees. Course ratings: men—B61.2/101, M60.4/97; women—M63.3/102, F60.6/96. Year Opened: 1985. Architect: Neil Hansen. Moderate, sr. rates. Reservations: Call two weeks ahead. Walk-on chances: Good. Walkability: Good. Playability: Ideal for infrequent golfers on vacation or habitués needing a quick nine-hole fix.

Located southeast of Mount Vernon, Overlook Golf Course crosses a hill on the opposite side of Highway 9 from Big Lake, a popular resort. Narrow, sloping fairways and small, rolling greens make this a fine executive-length layout. Trees dot the course, but Overlook's hilly contours are the predominant obstacles to par. The owner, designer and builder of the course is Neil Hansen, a retired Air Force major. Hansen is in the process of gradually shaping new holes for a back nine.

Overlook lies in scenic, pastoral surroundings, with Mount Baker's snow-capped spire on display during clear weather. The 1985-opened course occupies portions of the Hansen family's former 135-acre dairy farm. Good holes include the 1st, a 478-yard par-5 that bends slightly left over a rolling, left-sloping route. Overlook's 7th, a 359-yard par-4 rated its toughest hole, is abutted on the left by a creek that also enters play on three other holes.

Peaceful Valley Country Club

8225 Kendall Road, Maple Falls, WA 98266. (360) 599-2416. 9 holes. 2,467 yards. Par 33. Grass tees. Course ratings: men 61.0/94, women 65.1/103. Year Opened: 1979. Architects: Founders. Economical, jr./sr. rates, credit cards. Reservations: Call a week ahead. Walk-on chances: Good. Walkability: Good. Playability: Suitable for beginning to intermediate golfers.

Peaceful Valley's development lies just south of Sumas and the Canadian border, occupying both sides of Highway 547. The course is on the west side of the road and is overseen by a homeowner-comprised board of directors. Over half of Peaceful Valley's lot owners are Canadians. Besides an executive-length golf course, Peaceful Valley's recreational facilities include an Olympic-size swimming pool, sauna, Jacuzzi and hiking paths around a forested enclave at 1,000 feet above sea level. Lot owners enjoy unlimited access to the golf course.

The layout was built in 1979 on an 80-acre meadow; its original butch-cut greens have since been modernized. (There have been recent efforts to sell the course and remaining residential acreage. Also discussed were plans to add another nine holes. As of this writing, neither activity has occurred.) A good course for beginning to intermediate hackers, Peaceful Valley sits on a porous gravel base that drains well in winter. Players enjoy views of the Sisters, a triad of snowcapped crags to the east, while birds, rabbits and deer frequent the course. Five holes have sand traps. There are no water hazards on the dual-tee nine, which plays to 4,628 yards over two circuits. Perhaps its stiffest test is the 9th hole, a 426-yard par-4 with a generally straight fairway leading to a well-canted green.

Raspberry Ridge Golf Community

9 *6827 Hannegan Road, Everson, WA 98247. (360) 354-3029. Bill Robins Jr., pro. 2,825 yards. 9 holes. Par 34. Grass tees. Course ratings: men—B65.1/106, M63.9/104; women—M68.5/112, F67.3/110. Year Opened: 1984. Architect: Bill Overdorf. Economical, jr./sr. rates, credit cards. Reservations: Call a week ahead. Walk-on chances: Good. Walkability: Quite good. Playability: Enjoyable for players of all skills.*

The 1984-built course is owned by Bill Robins, Sr. His son, Bill Robins, Jr., maintains the course and runs the pro shop. Located southwest of Everson, Raspberry Ridge is bordered by homes and condominiums. The Bill Overdorf-designed track is imperiled by seven ponds and nearly 30 sand traps—considerable hazards for a short nine. The course and adjoining neighborhood occupy over 80 acres of a one-time raspberry farm, and are split by Hannegan Road. The first four holes lie to the east, with the remaining five on the west accessible via a tunnel under Hannegan. Raspberry Ridge is appointed with a comfy clubhouse and popular restaurant.

The dual-tee course, which over two circuits extends 5,410 yards, boasts paved cart paths and excellent year-round conditioning. Tough holes include the 2nd, a fairly straight 370-yard par-4 that passes three traps along the right en route to a well-bunkered green guarded left-front by a pond. The 4th, a 310-yard par-4, is a dogleg-right with a pond in mid-fairway. Bunkers on both sides of the fairway further squeeze the hole. The clover-shaped 4th green is ringed by three traps. The top-rated 7th, a 390-yard par-4, has a pair of water hazards pinching its fairway; a bunker past the ponds penetrates the hole's right edge. The elongated 7th green— a double green set-up shared by the 5th hole—is guarded laterally by sand.

Riverside Golf Course

9 *5799 Riverside Drive, Ferndale, WA 98248. (360) 384-4116. 9 holes. 3,000 yards. Par 36. Grass tees. Course ratings: men 66.9/103; women 70.4/112. Year Opened: 1929. Architect: Don Fryer. Economical, jr./sr. rates, credit cards. No reservations. Walkability: Good. Playability: Good course for beginner and intermediate hackers; a bit damp in the winter.*

Riverside, located off Interstate 5's Ferndale exit, enjoys a colorful history. After being built in 1929 by Don Fryer, it became the site of a popular roadhouse where couples from the Canadian border to Bellingham would go to be married and to party and dance. The course was rearranged in the 1960s when the Scottish Lodge was built on its southern end. The old-style clubhouse at Riverside Golf Course, which is owned by Jeanne Olson Estie, still serves good food and cheer.

The flat track occasionally floods when the adjoining Nooksack River rises over its banks. Two men's tees and a ladies' tee give Riverside an "18-on-9" format. Top holes include the 2nd, a 313-yard par-4 that winds rightward around a pond. The 8th, a 496-yard par-5, runs fairly straight to a mid-sized green guarded along the right by a pond.

San Juan Golf & Country Club - semiprivate   9

2261 Golf Course Road, Friday Harbor, WA 98250. (360) 378-2254. Steve Nightingale, pro. 9 holes. 3,194 yards. Par 35. Grass tees. Course ratings: men— B71.0/115, M68.6/110; women—M74.3/118, F70.3/109. Year Opened: 1963. Architects: John & Myrtle Jackson. Moderate, credit cards. Reservations: Call a day ahead in summer. Walk-on chances: Fair. Walkability: Good. Playability: Lovely views and nice course combined in enjoyable golf experience.

San Juan Island's only golf course lies on the island's southeast side, four miles from Friday Harbor. Set amid homesites along a bluff, San Juan Golf & Country Club offers choice views of Griffin Bay and, on particularly cloudless days, Lopez Island. The 65-acre layout was designed and built in 1963 by John and Myrtle Jackson on their former farm. Club members bought it from the Jacksons in 1973. Older members recall the original greens as rough-hewn, close-cropped patches but, thanks to dedicated efforts by the greens crew, San Juan's course has developed into a fine golfing venue.

Lovely gardens grace this easy-to-walk layout, which is equipped with four sets of tees. Over two circuits from the tips, it stretches 6,634 yards. As the fairway-side trees mature, San Juan's difficulty will increase. Noteworthy holes include the 1st, a 490-yard par-5 with a fairway pinched by trees at the 200-yard mark. Long hitters beware: in this seemingly benign juncture nests a good-sized pond. The hole then bends uphill to the right toward a raised and ridged green. San Juan's 9th, a 437-yard par-4, is a narrow, left-turning affair that winds around a fat pond to a raised, steep-sided green guarded by a bunker right and pond left.

Semiahmoo Golf & Country Club - semiprivate   18

8720 Semiahmoo Parkway, Blaine, WA 98230. (360) 371-7005 or 1-800-770-7992. Brian Southwick, pro. 18 holes. 7,005 yards. Par 72. Grass tees. Course ratings: men—C73.6/130, B70.9/125, M69.3/120; women—M74.7/128, F70.7/121. Year Opened: 1987. Architects: Arnold Palmer & Ed Seay. Expensive, credit cards. Call for reservations. Walk-on chances: Ok for singles. Walkability: Fairly good for the fit, with some lengthy between-hole hikes. Playability: Its resort orientation and multiple sets of tees make the course suitable for all players.

The Palmer and Seay-designed course here is an integral part of the Resort at Semiahmoo, a full-service facility within coastal woodlands beside Drayton Harbor and the Georgia Strait. On-site amenities include the 200-room Inn at Semiahmoo, convention spaces, restaurants, lounges, a large clubhouse, 300-slip marina, indoor and outdoor tennis, racquetball and squash courts, saunas, steam rooms, weight-training facilities, an indoor running track and outdoor swimming pool. More and more new homes have been popping up at Semiahmoo since its golf course opened in 1987.

Semiahmoo's layout has received many accolades over the past decade. Recognition came in 1995 when *Links* magazine gave it a "Best of Golf Award," which goes to the 75 best resorts in the U.S., Canada, Mexico and Caribbean. It's also been touted by *Golf Digest* and *Western Links* magazines. Besides an experienced pro shop staff, Semiahmoo has a golf instruction facility headed by Jeff Coston. Both in 1995 and '96, Coston received the highest honor accorded by the Northwest Section of the PGA when he was named its Maxfli Player of the Year. Coston garnered the points-based award after winning the Oregon Open, earning runner-up finishes in the Washington and Northwest opens, and placing high in Spokane's Rosauer Open. He also won the 1996 Club Car Western Washington Section Championship at Indian Summer.

Certainly Semiahmoo has all the earmarks of a first-class golf resort. It also has the high prices to match. In August 1994, my wife and I spent two nights in one of Semiahmoo's regular rooms. We played one round of golf with a cart, and had a dinner and lunch along with a few drinks during our stay. We also rented bicycles for a tour along Drayton Harbor and through nearby forests. We were quite shocked to learn upon checkout that our room, board and sundry activities totaled nearly $800. Overall, our stay was fine, though the food was rather pedestrian and the service below par. Another quibble is the haughty treatment given by the golf course staff to its guests; when paying Semiahmoo's high fees, players should expect a little friendliness. The course was in decent shape, though its greens were in the throes of being taken over by *poa annua*. (For years, Semiahmoo's greens staff hand-culled poa from the all-bentgrass greens and fairways. In 1994, they bowed to the inevitable; the full poa takeover is now complete and the greens are just fine.)

Semiahmoo's layout is quite nice, with plenty of water and sand to impress shotmakers. Variable tees allow golfers of all abilities to circuit the course, which can be played anywhere from 5,300 to 7,000 yards. Groups are spaced 10 minutes apart, and wildlife such as deer, shorebirds, and bald eagles are on display. Good tests include the top-rated 4th, a 417-yard par-4 with a moguled, right-bending fairway and a green guarded left and rear by vast traps. The well-trapped fairway at the 574-yard, par-5 13th is a virtual half-circle that curls leftward around a forest to a small green in trees. A 211-yard par-3, the 15th leads to a hogbacked green squeezed by three sand hazards.

Shuksan Golf Club

18 *1500 East Axton Road, Bellingham, WA 98226. (360) 398-8888. Rick Verbarendse, director of golf; Joe Holdridge, pro. 18 holes. 6,537 yards. Par 72. Grass tees. Course ratings: men—B70.4/121, M67.6/115; women—M72.7/123, F67.7/112. Year Opened: 1994. Architects: Rick Verbarendse & Rick Dvorak. Moderate, credit cards. Reservations: Call a week ahead. Walk-on chances: Fair. Walkability: Overall good, but some steep ascents led owners to include a cart in green fees. Playability: Pretty daunting for beginners, with intermediate-good "sticks" having their hands full.*

Located northeast of Bellingham, Shuksan is one of the finest additions to Northwest golf in the past decade. Co-designed by its director of golf Rick Verbarendse, and owner Rick Dvorak, Shuksan features 18 holes creatively arrayed around a bowl-shaped site. The former farm parcel, which grew corn and hay and served as grazing land, is split by Ten Mile Creek, a slender rivulet that enters play with alarming regularity. (In order to get permits to build a golf course along this riparian zone, Verbarendse and Dvorak worked closely with the state Fish and Wildlife Department, which continues to monitor the salmon in the creek.)

From higher holes overlooking the valley, golfers enjoy vistas of the Cascades to the east. Named after one of that range's peaks, Shuksan features a wonderful clubhouse made of wood and rock. Other nice touches—including 10-minute-apart tee times, concrete cart paths, and a grass-teed driving range—led *Golf Digest* to award Shuksan Golf Club four stars in its *1996-'97 Places to Play* guide.

Shuksan's site is a mixed geological bag; during construction, peat, sand, sandstone, clay and coal beds were unearthed. Prevailing winds are slight westerlies, though more full-throated winds occasionally howl out of British Columbia's Fraser Valley to toughen the course even more. The front nine is not as liberally bunkered as the back, but that discrepancy is more than adequately compensated by the water hazards stemming from Ten Mile. The top-rated hole, the par-5 4th, is a 541-yarder with a narrow and slightly uphill fairway that winds between trees left and mounds right. Wetlands bordering the hole further squeeze the fairway, which leans to the right over its last leg. The 4th gradually ascends leftward to a hill-cut, wide-but-shallow green guarded left-front by trees and at the rear by a pot bunker.

Several towering elevated tees characterize Shuksan's back side, with the par-4s at the 10th and 12th offering spectacular eastward panoramas. Probably the toughest hole on the course is the 13th, a 535 yard par-5 that's devilishly tight and visually deceiving throughout. A pack of firs along the right 150 yards out, and a pond left of the left-sloping landing zone, cause some serious white-knuckling (and hooking, slicing, sclaffing, etc.) on the tee. The narrow 13th then winds rightward along a path defined by an unseen creek in a depression along the left. Stay to the right here! That creek eventually crosses the fairway to feed into a pond close by the right flank of a thin and shallow green lined left by mounds. No bunkers are found on the 13th, but none are needed at a course which employs tipped topography and a

Among Shuksan's more brutal holes is the 392-yard, par-4 10th.

trickling creek to full advantage.

Similk Beach Golf Course

18 *1250 Christiansen Road, Anacortes, WA 98221. (360) 293-3444. Dick Freier, pro. 18 holes. 6,205 yards. Par 72. Grass tees. Course ratings: men—M67.1/107, F65.9/105; women F71.1/111. Year Opened: 1927 (original nine); 1955 (second nine). Architect: R.D. Turner; Bill Overdorf (remodel). Moderate. Call for reservations. Walk-on chances: Good. Walkability: Very good. Playability: Links-like layout suitable for all types of players.*

Located east of Anacortes, Similk Beach has been gradually upgraded over the years. Opened as a nine-holer in 1927, Similk Beach was expanded to 18 and revamped in 1955. It now employs only three original holes. In 1947, longtime Anacortes resident and oyster company owner, Earl Morgan, acquired Similk Beach from his father-in-law, R. D. Turner, who conceived and built the course. The layout occupies a narrow spit enclosed on the north by Fidalgo Bay and on the south by Similk Bay; Highway 20 passes right before its entry.

The course contains a decent array of golf holes thanks to some recently-added ponds. New tees are gradually being built to lengthen the course. The layout is characterized by ravine-like holes, whose high sides sink toward fairway midsections and cause awkward lies. A dry ditch bisecting the course also enters play. Tight fairways and slick, raised and mound-ringed greens typify the links of Similk Beach. Among its more intriguing challenges is the 3rd, a straight-running 528-yard par-5 that ends at a small, rolling green. Perhaps the toughest hole is the 7th, a 516-yard par-5 that winds leftward around a pond to a slick and rolling putting surface.

Sudden Valley Golf & Country Club - semiprivate

18 *2145 Lake Whatcom Boulevard, Bellingham, WA 98226. (360) 734-6435. Greg Paul, pro. 18 holes. 6,553 yards. Par 72. Grass tees. Course ratings: men—B71.8/126, M70.0/123; women—M75.7/130; F72.8/124. Year Opened: 1971. Architect: Ted Robinson. Moderate, jr. rates, credit cards. Reservations: Call a week ahead unless a resort guest. Walk-on chances: Ok for singles. Walkability: A few uphill hikes but, after those, it's downhill all the way. Playability: Mid- and low-handicappers will definitely be challenged.*

Sudden Valley features two distinctly different nines. The front side occupies a meadow beside Lake Whatcom, while holes 10 through 18 span a forested hill overlooking the lovely lake. Both nines offer great eastward vistas of the shimmering water body as well as the Cascades. The semiprivate course was designed by notable architect Ted Robinson, and opened in 1971. The layout is part of a resort that caters to overnight guests and homeowner-members who dwell around the course. Besides an exceptional golf course, on-site recreational venues include an ice rink and putt-putt course, tennis courts, swimming beaches, spa, pool and marina.

Due to its difficulty and facilities, Sudden Valley has hosted such tournaments as the Washington State Open and Washington State Amateur. Among the best holes on the relatively flat front nine is the 5th, a 421-yard par-4 that doglegs left. A creek crosses the fairway at a juncture where the hole veers to a tri-trapped green backed by Lake Whatcom. A hole representative of the woodsy back side is the 15th, a par-4 of 420 yards with elevated tees that stagger-step down a steep escarpment. The hole turns sharply left on a route that runs between trees inside the dogleg and traps outside the turn. The 15th green is a well-bunkered, teardrop-shaped affair.

The 17th, a par-5 of 488 yards, is a perilous journey that begins with a very tight, tree branch-squeezed chute in front of an 80-foot-high tee. The hole is crossed by a creek at the 250-yard mark, while a bunker along the left further squeezes the landing area. Once past the creek, a long pond borders the left edge of the hole. The smallish, gently sloping 17th green is trapped front-right and left. The putting surfaces at Sudden Valley are not wildly undulating, but they're hard to read even though the course is positioned alongside Lake Whatcom.

Private Courses

Bellingham Golf & Country Club

3729 Meridian, Bellingham, WA 98225. (360) 733-5381. Dean Russell, pro. **18**
18 holes. 6,473 yards. Par 72. Grass tees. Course ratings: men—B71.0/123, M69.8/
120; women—M75.3/129, F72.7/124. Year Opened: 1912 (original nine); 1925
(second nine). Architect: John Ball; Bill Robinson & Golf Concepts (remodels).
Members, guests & reciprocates.

With its first nine holes and clubhouse opened in 1913 and the second nine in 1925, Bellingham Golf & Country Club is the oldest course in Whatcom County. The course has undergone several revisions in recent years, including a computerized sprinkler system. Future changes include new bunkers and perhaps the rebuilding of a few greens. Unique aspects of the layout include only one dogleg-left fairway; a par-3 as the 18th hole; and a par-37 front nine and a par-35 back. Holes one through nine circuit around the interior back nine, and Whatcom Creek crosses six holes.

The 142-acre course spans gently rolling ground on Bellingham's north end. The parkland-type course, with towering firs and other trees lining fairways, is close to Interstate 5 and Bellis Fair Mall. Because of its enduring role in Northwest golf, the club has hosted some significant events, including the Washington State Amateur, Washington State Open, Washington State Women's Amateur, various PNGA tourneys, and the Hudson Cup matches in 1992. Among Bellingham's more acclaimed players is Frank Sadler, a former boxer and the club's head pro from 1936-1971. A fine player in his day, Sadler helped initiate the National Seniors Tournament, which was held here in the mid-1940s. Other outstanding golfers were Connie Guthrie, a medalist in many state and regional events. Celebrity visitors have included golf pros Walter Hagen, Jock Hutchinson, Jim Barnes, Stan Leonard, Porky Oliver and Chuck Congdon as well as LPGA greats Patty Berg and Carol Mann. The comedian Bob Hope played the course in 1978.

Bellingham's efficiently arrayed course is quite walkable, and drains reasonably well during the rainy seasons. Featuring an interesting mix of new (large and saddle-shaped) and old-style (small and raised) greens, the course involves plenty of bunkering and water hazards. Good holes include the 2nd, a 370-yard par-4 that runs uphill to the right. A bunker squeezes the fairway at the 150-yard mark; here, the hole curls rightward on a path that skirts two bunkers left. The humped-in-the-middle, steeply left-front-sloping 2nd green is trapped at both front entries. The pretty 3rd, a

335-yard par-4, starts at an elevated tee then winds narrowly around to the right, passing trees right and a pond left. A good drive will earn a peek at the green, which is flanked left-front by a pond and is trapped right-front and right-rear.

The 4th, a 347-yard par-4, ascends over rolling ground once past a pond off the tee. The pond tapers into a creek, which then bulges back into a pond that guards the fairway's left-hand side. A bunker sits 100 yards at the right-front of a steeply two-tiered, hill-cut green protected by a waterfall and creek left and a trap right-front. The 7th, a 523-yard par-5, is a lengthy right-bender that curls around trees and jail. Bunkers lurk outside the turn about 250 yards out. The fairway descends to a creek-fronted, hill-cut green trapped twice left, and once each rear and right. The top-rated 9th, a 433-yard par-4, is straight, wide and slightly uphill. At the 150-yard mark, the fairway bends slightly right to a small and round, domed green.

The 10th, a 403-yard par-4, has Whatcom Creek off the tee and an uptilted, tree-lined fairway. A bunker sits along the right about 180 yards from a round and wavy green that leans toward a deep bunker at the right-front. The flat 12th, a 402-yard par-4, bisects trees right and the driving range left. Rated Bellingham's second-toughest hole, the 12th concludes at a small, undulating green trapped laterally. The attractive 14th, a 348-yard par-4, is narrowish and rolling en route to the 150-yard mark. Here, the hole turns 45 degrees to the right. Whatcom Creek crosses the fairway 75 yards from a mid-sized, two-tiered green trapped right and left-front.

The interesting 16th, a 392-yard par-4, starts at a raised, creek-fronted tee. The fairway goes straight for 250 yards or so, then zig-zags very tightly (about 20 yards from branch to branch) to a mid-sized green guarded closely on the right by trees. One must be able to work the ball on the second shot at Bellingham's 16th. The tricky 17th, a 324-yard par-4, bends a bit left and somewhat downhill off the tee. Whatcom Creek crosses the hole 60 yards from a small, front-sloping green in a depression. A berm backs this putting surface, which is trapped in front. The par-3 18th is a 199-yarder that descends slightly to a rolling, skinny-but-deep green in a swale. Bunkers—unseen from the tee—occupy the green's right-front, right and left edges. The trap on the left is very deep.

Birch Bay Village Golf Course

9 *8169 Cowichan Road, Blaine, WA 98230. (360) 371-2026. Galen Reimer, pro. 9 holes. 2,120 yards. Par 33. Grass tees. No course ratings. Opened: mid-1980s. Architect: Bill Overdorf. Homeowners & guests.*

Birch Bay Village Golf Course is part of a housing development inhabited mainly by retirees. The village lies next to scenic Birch Bay. The nine-hole course, a challenging executive-length track on 38 acres, houses three ponds that enter play on virtually every hole. The Bill Overdorf-designed layout was recently upgraded with a new irrigation system, sand traps, and bridges over the waterways. The course contains three par-3s—ranging from 175 to 180 yards, and six par-4s from 245 to 300 yards. The generally flat, well-tended venue is frequented by shorebirds and deer.

Loomis Trail Golf Club

4342 Loomis Trail Road, Blaine, WA 98230. (360) 332-1608. Jerry Palumbo, pro. 18 holes. 7,137 yards. Par 72. Grass tees. Course ratings: men—C74.9/139, T72.3/133, M69.4/125; women F72.4/129. Year Opened: 1993. Architect: Graham Cooke & Associates. Members & guests.

18

Opened in April 1993, this private club lies about a mile northwest of Interstate 5's exit 270. Over its few years of operation, the course changed hands and underwent major revisions from its original configuration. Loomis Trail is currently owned by Arctic King, a division of Kaiyo International Investment Corporation, a Japanese company with diversified business interests. Graham Cooke & Associates designed Loomis Trail's course, and American Golf Construction of Plano, Texas, built it. Soon after it opened for play, the exclusive club (it's very difficult to get on) was appointed with a 44,000-square-foot clubhouse with 18 overnight units, exercise facilities, and dining areas. In 1995, the owner was contemplating the development of 188 single-family homesites on land alongside the course.

The 200-acre layout winds across terrain with a mere 20 feet in elevation change. The course, previously the home of an equestrian facility, Doran Stables (thus its "trail" designation), has many man-made hazards and target-type, multisectioned fairways. Eighty sand traps and 10 grass bunkers guard fairways and greens. Strategically-placed trees—most of which are second-growth firs and pines—inhibit play, and 40 acres of ponds and channels are a constant concern. A signature trait of Loomis Trail is its bentgrass tees, greens and fairways, one of the few Northwest layouts fully appointed with such turf. *Poa annua* grows along the edges of holes, but not in the fairways. Several miles of 8- to 12-foot-wide concrete cart paths wind throughout the course.

Loomis Trail's greens are among the best in the Northwest. Having uniform speed and some undulations that are not wild enough to make them unfair, these huge targets putt very true. One negative aspect of the course (at least for first-time players) are the water hazards. Though these canals and ponds vary in width from eight to 20 feet, the inward-sloping contour of the border areas actually doubles the size of the hazard. If a ball lands anywhere near water, it's probably in the drink. (One way to mitigate this would be to let the grass grow along the edges of the hazards, thus impeding roll.) The bunkers are filled with soft, fluffy sand that generates fried-egg lies. But the worst aspect of the traps is their cuts, some of which tower a foot above the surface of the sand. If hitting from the edges of Loomis Trail's bunkers, it's like trying to scale a wall. Another detriment to the course is the concrete cart paths along the holes. Besides shrinking already tight target zones, these roadways tend to deflect well-hit shots into unrecoverable jail. These quibbles aside, Loomis Trail ranks among the region's best-maintained and toughest tracks. Fairway lies are remarkable, and the firm greens are magnificent. (A friend commented during our round, "These greens are hard and the fairways are mattresses").

Views of Mount Baker are available from many junctures of the course, and it's visited by eagles and blue herons. Outstanding holes at Loomis Trail, which was named by *Golf Digest* as its "Best New Private Course" in 1993, include the top-rated 2nd, a 562-yard par-5. This narrow, tree-lined dogleg-right is guarded along the right by a canal that fattens into a pond 280 yards out. A bunker squats along the left 90 yards from a wide-but-shallow, 10,000-square-foot green bunkered left and guarded right by a pond. From the back (black tees), Loomis Trail's par-3s are truly gargantuan.

The longest of them is the 12th, a 257-yarder that requires titanic strength with a driver to reach the green, particularly when winds off Birch Bay (from the left) are aloft. Lined all along the right by a pond and left by wetlands, the hole ends at a tilted, rolling green with a pair of pot bunkers left-front and a trap left-rear. Perhaps the nastiest hole on the course is the 17th, a 472-yard par-4. Not only does the long 17th head slightly uphill, but its landing area is squeezed by two bunkers along the right and trees left. A channel crosses the fairway at the 170-yard mark. The 17th green—which is linked to the 10th green—contains two spurs and is laterally trapped.

Sandy Point Golf Course

9

Box 1418, Ferndale, WA 98248. (360) 384-3921. 9 holes. 1,000 yards. Par 27. Grass tees. No course ratings. Year Opened: 1965. Architects: Club founders. Homeowners & guests.

Sandy Point Golf Course is the centerpiece for homeowners dwelling in a proprietary community west of Ferndale. Begun in 1965, the Sandy Point development contains over 800 homes for year-round and vacationing residents. The neighborhood overlooks Puget Sound, where homeowners have access to a marina. Sandy Point's layout spans terrain that ranges from flat to gently rolling. The course is equipped with grass tees, and its greens are postage-stamp in size. With its locale beside the sound, the venue is visited by birds and deer.

Shelter Bay Golf Course

9

Box A, La Conner, WA 98257. (360) 466-3805. 9 holes. 1,000 yards. Par 27. Grass tees. No course ratings. Opened: 1970s. Architect: Osberg Construction. Homeowners & guests.

This nine-hole par-3 is enjoyed by homeowners living in the like-named subdivision around it. Begun in the early 1970s by Osberg Construction Company of Seattle, Shelter Bay's development now has 1,100 residents and 600 homes. Occupying 450 acres and platted for 935 homesites, the retiree-dominated neighborhood is linked to the charming and historic town of La Conner—across the Swinomish Channel—via Rainbow Bridge.

Besides the par-3 golf course, the Shelter Bay community has two swimming pools and three tennis courts. Two marinas beside the channel are also used by residents. When this course was built, it contained greenside sand traps, but they've since been sodded over to simplify play.

Skagit Golf & Country Club

18

1493 Country Club Drive, Burlington, WA 98233. (360) 757-4081. Dave Bobillot, pro. 18 holes. 6,151 yards. Par 71. Grass tees. Course ratings: men—B68.7/118, M68.0/117, FF66.6/114; women—M74.0/123, FF72.4/119, F70.6/115. Years Opened: 1918 (original nine); 1971 (second nine). Architects: Charlie Weist (original nine); Skyko Development Company (second nine). Members, guests & reciprocates.

A private layout traversing a hillside west of Interstate 5 and Burlington, Skagit is readily accessible off Highway 20 at Avon-Allen Road. Skagit's roots date back to just before the Roaring Twenties. Founded in 1918, the club was notorious for its slot machines, illicit liquor and high-fashion parties. Sheep, deer and cattle shared the nine-hole course with the founding golfer-members. The original clubhouse burned down in the early 1950s, and Skagit was later purchased by Andy and Polly Anderson in 1957. A temporary clubhouse was built where the cart shed now sits; Andy Anderson later built the current clubhouse. The course was open for public play at various times during this period.

In the 1960s, the club was sold to Skyco Development Company, which purchased the land for the second nine (played as the front) and developed houses on the periphery. Members bought the course from Skyco in October 1968, and it has been a proprietary concern ever since. Skagit's fairways wind past the nicely-tended backyards of the surrounding homes. With its perch atop a promontory, golfers enjoy vistas of Cascade foothills, Skagit Flats and southern and western scenes. Deer, rabbits and eagles visit the grounds. Because of its position amid a neighborhood, the course involves some lengthy between-hole hikes. Overall though, the generally flat layout is easy to walk. Skagit is a bit wet during the rainy season; when I visited the course in October 1996, many players were wearing spiked boots.

The course has undergone several recent improvements. Upcoming work, by greens superintendent Greg Miller, includes building a back tee at the 13th hole (making it a 178-yard par-3), and adding another 3,000-square-feet to the green. Unique aspects of Skagit's course include two consecutive par-3s at the 13th and 14th holes, and many greens bunkered rear. Notable tests include the top-rated 3rd, a 373-yard par-4 with a pond-fronted tee and a narrow, tree-lined fairway that gradually rises to a small, front-sloping green. The 4th, a 341-yard par-4, is lined on the right by houses and OB. The rolling 4th green tilts left-front, has traps right-rear, left-rear and left, and is closely guarded left-front by a pond.

The 9th, a 534-yard par-5, runs straight and a bit downhill into the prevailing wind (out of the west). After passing a bunker along the left at the 250-yard mark, the hole curls slightly right to a large, front-sloping green trapped twice left and once each right and right-rear. The 10th, a 383-yard par-4, follows a straight and climbing path that skirts OB and houses on the right en route to a small, front-right-sloping green lined left by a pond. The 12th, a 388-yard par-4, has a narrowish, right-sloping fairway that bisects trees left and backyards/OB right. The hole ends at a rolling, right-leaning green pinched by trees left and a steep bank right.

The pesky 14th, a 139-yard par-3, rises up to a ridge-perched, skinny-but-deep, two-tiered green with a big and deep bunker before it. The 15th, a 403-yard par-4, rises slightly and runs straight. Playing very long in the winter—with no fairway roll to abet the cause, the 15th stretches out to a small, right-rear-sloping green trapped left-rear. The 16th, a 395-yard par-4, traverses a rolling, right-sloping path that passes a pond along the left that resides on the 17th hole. The final 100 yards tilt steeply rightward to trees before curling left to a tiny, right-front-sloping green. The 17th, a 349-yard par-4, starts at a raised tee, then descends along a path between a pond left and OB right. The fairway winds leftward to a wide-but-shallow, figure-8-shaped green trapped front and right. Nice southerly views are on tap at the 18th, a 475-yard par-5 with a pond-fronted tee. The hole rises to the 200-yard mark, then drops steeply down to a left-sloping, V-shaped green trapped once right-front and twice left-front. The lips on these traps are quite high.

Par-3 Courses

New World Pro Golf Center

9 | *5022 Guide Meridian, Bellingham, WA 98226. (360) 398-1362. 9 holes. 947 yards. Par 27. Grass tees. No course ratings. Economical. No reservations. Driving Range.*

This par-3 venue lies north of Bellingham off Guide Meridian. The course—with holes ranging from from 73 to 122 yards—is played mainly by families, seniors and beginners. Open from May through November, New World Pro Golf Center has a driving range with 15 covered stalls and six grass tees. The short, flat track has a few trees entering play. Through the course runs a dry-in-summer drainage ditch that floods in winter, making the course unplayable during that time.

Sea Links

18 | *7878 Birch Bay Drive, Blaine, WA 98230. (360) 371-7933. Craig Wood, pro. 18 holes. 2,701 yards. Par 54. Grass tees. Course ratings (for local use only): men 50.7/67, women 50.7/67. Economical, sr. rates, credit cards. Reservations: Call up to a week ahead. Walk-on chances: Good.*

The 18-hole par-3 course at Sea Links is one of the most entertaining tracks of any length in the Northwest. Golfers of all abilities are challenged by the course, which gains difficulty from the westerly winds off Birch Bay, tiny bentgrass greens, assorted water-laden channels, and ample bunkering. The course adjoins the Sea Links Restaurant and lies off Birch Bay Drive, a thoroughfare that leads to cottages, condos and other tourist-oriented enterprises. Sea Links is owned by its head pro, Craig Wood. Recent improvements include some new tees.

Sea Links opened with nine regulation-length holes in 1933, then a second nine of equivalent yardage was built the following year. A local man, Bob Vogt, built and operated the original Sea Links course after his father, Grover, gave him the land. Green fees for that course—at that time Whatcom County's most-popular—were 25 cents. In 1984, its then-owner shortened the layout to allow for homesites. The natural bounty that is part and parcel of Birch Bay—deer, Canada geese, rabbits, sandpipers and shorebirds—continues to please players at Sea Links.

DRIVING RANGES

Cooper's Golf Range

1899 South Burlington Boulevard, Burlington, WA 98223.
(360) 757-1854. Ken Harrsch & Mark Flitton, pros.

Rodarco Golf Range

8020 Kickerville Road, Blaine, WA 98230.
(360) 332-2665. Roger Cook, pro.

UPCOMING COURSES

Blaine—West Semiahmoo (1999). Originally proposed in the late-1980s, this course, designed by Tom Weiskopf and Jerry Morrish, still lacks a suitable water source. The public 7,000-yard layout would be located beside the Resort at Semiahmoo.

Conway—Starbird Golf Club (1999). The backers of this Tom Johnson-designed golf course and 96 homes have undergone much scrutiny from the state and Whatcom County officials. A local group has also appealed previous approvals of the 311-acre project off Starbird Road, but recent negotiations may pave the way for development.

Custer—Rolling Hills (1999). Development of a private 18-hole course, 53 single- and multi-family homes, an equestrian center and sports complex has been held up by an inability to secure water rights from the state.

Mount Vernon—Chuckanut Crest Golf Course (1999). A Bill Overdorf-designed 18-hole layout is planned for this 320-acre project north of Bow Hill Road. The project has all the permits as well as water rights, but financing has been an issue. The site, across the street from a casino run by the Upper Skagit Indian Tribe and Harrah's, also involves housing.

Point Roberts — Point Roberts Golf Club (1999). This golf and residential project has been on and off the drawing board for several years. At last check, the site off Marine Drive had been sold. The backers originally wanted to build a 6,900-yard golf course designed by Ted Robinson, though it's uncertain whether plans for the course are still afoot.

KITSAP PENINSULA &
PUGET SOUND ISLANDS

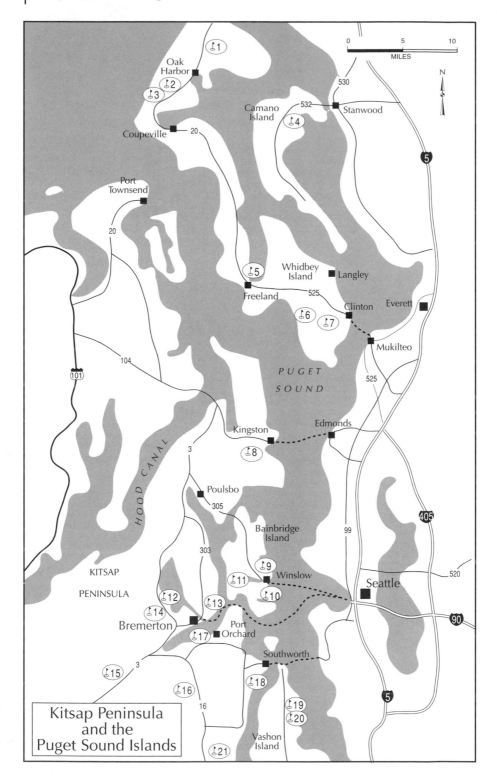

Kitsap Peninsula
and the
Puget Sound Islands

1. **Lam's Links** — public 9
2. **Gallery Golf Course** — semiprivate 18 & driving range
3. **Whidbey Golf & Country Club** — private 18
4. **Camaloch Golf Club** — semiprivate 18 & driving range
5. **Holmes Harbor Golf Course** — public 18 & 9-hole putting course
6. **Useless Bay Golf & Country Club** — private 18
7. **Island Greens** — public 9 (par-3)
8. **Woodall's World Driving Range**
9. **Wing Point Golf & Country Club** — private 18
10. **The Country Club of Seattle** — private 9
11. **Meadowmeer Golf & Country Club** — semiprivate 9
12. **Northwest Golf Range** — driving range
13. **Rolling Hills Golf Club** — public 18 & driving range
14. **Kitsap Golf & Country Club** — private 18
15. **Gold Mountain Golf Course** — public 36 & driving range
16. **McCormick Woods Golf Club** — public 18 & driving range
17. **Village Greens** — public 18 & driving range
18. **Clover Valley Golf & Country Club** — public 18
19. **Vashon Island Golf & Country Club** — private 9
20. **Vashon Island Driving Range**
21. **Horseshoe Lake Golf Course** — public 18 & driving range

The Kitsap Peninsula and the Puget Sound islands of Whidbey, Camano, Bainbridge and Vashon are popular getaway spots. Permanent residents, summer homeowners and weekend tourists commingle in a classically beautiful Puget Sound setting. Many Bainbridge and Vashon islanders commute to Seattle via Washington's state ferry system, the nation's largest. Naturally lush with ample year-round rainfall, the golf courses in temperate zone 5 generally don't lack for irrigation. There are a few banana belts, however, so while it may be pouring in Port Orchard the sun could be lighting up Bainbridge Island. Several projects have been under consideration during the 1990s, but because of eco-minded locals, limited financial options, and the penurious parceling of water permits from the state's Department of Ecology, these proposed golf courses have been slow in reaching fruition.

Public Courses

Camaloch Golf Club - semiprivate

18 *226 NE Camaloch Drive, Camano Island, WA 98292. (360) 387-3084 or 1-800-628-0469. Gary Schopf, pro. 18 holes. 6,119 yards. Par 71. Grass tees. Course ratings: men—B70.0/125, M68.7/122; women F70.9/122. Year Opened: 1973 (original nine); 1990 (second nine). Architects: Ralph Heddelstadt (original nine), Bill Overdorf (second nine). Moderate, jr./sr. rates. Call for reservations. Walk-on chances: Fair. Walkability: Good. Playability: Suitable for all play levels; just be sure there are enough balls in the bag when playing Camaloch's water holes.*

Camano Island is separated from the mainland by the Stillaguamish River, and this course lies just over 12 miles west of Interstate 5 on the west side of the slow-moving "Stilly." Camaloch Golf Club is owned by members living in the like-named neighborhood that envelops the course's eastern edge. Elmer Hovik developed Camaloch and opened the original Ralph Heddelstadt-designed nine holes in 1973. When a Bill Overdorf-designed nine opened in 1990, the 86-acre layout underwent a major personality change, one that has attracted more players. The new nine has considerably more water and sand hazards than the original holes, and contains larger greens and tighter fairways. The original holes are noted for their domed, elevated putting surfaces.

Camaloch features some lengthy par-4s on the front nine, while restrictive, white-knuckle holes characterize the back. The top-rated hole is the 6th, a straight-running and left-sloping, 413-yard par-4 through trees. The narrow fairway ends at a raised, right-sloping green trapped twice at its right-front edge and once left. Camaloch's mirror-image 15th and 16th—a par-5 and par-4 occupying a rectangular, forested-in parcel on the course's southwest end—are separated by a large pond toward which both fairways tilt. The 449-yard 15th is guarded along its right by the lake, as is the reversing 16th. Densely-treed OB guards the left edges of both holes. The 15th ends at a hogbacked, swale-fronted green lined by three traps. At the 419-yard 16th, an arm of the pond crosses the fairway 140 yards from a tri-trapped green.

Clover Valley Golf & Country Club

18

5180 Country Club Lane SE, Port Orchard, WA 98366. (360) 871-2236. Pat Nixon, pro. 18 holes. 5,317 yards. Par 69. Grass tees. Course ratings: men 64.9/102, women 66.8/106. Opened: 1960s (original nine); 1970s (second nine). Architects: Members. Economical (moderate on weekends), jr./sr. rates, credit cards. Call for reservations. Walk-on chances: Good. Walkability: Good. Playability: Improving; suitable choice for beginning-intermediate sticks.

The 1960s-built Clover Valley was purchased in 1991 by Andrew Yang. Located near an established neighborhood, the layout crosses a bowl-shaped parcel intersected by Salmonberry Creek. Before Yang acquired it, the layout had been rerouted several times over the years, resulting in a confusing layout with rows of poplar trees crossing holes. The 95-acre site was developed into a private golf course by founding members. After encountering financial travails following the addition of a second nine, the members opened Clover Valley to the public. The facility also includes a clubhouse, snack bar, pro shop and banquet area, and is not far from the Southworth ferry terminal.

Salmonberry's position on the course results in flooding after heavy rains. Because of the wet and unplayable conditions, head pro Pat Nixon and Yang developed a scheme that reduces the layout to the nine driest holes during these extended periods. The abbreviated track involves the 1st, 8th, 9th, 10th through 14th, and 18th holes. In 1997, the original 1st tee was restored—shrinking the length of the driving range to 125 yards, thus bumping Clover Valley's par from 68 back up to its original 69. On average, Clover Valley hosts 20,000 rounds a year.

Gallery Golf Course - semiprivate

18

Golf Course Road, NAS Whidbey Island, Oak Harbor, WA 98278. (360) 257-2178. 18 holes. 6,350 yards. Par 72. Grass tees. Course ratings: men—B70.1/121, M69.0/120; women—M74.8/126, F71.1/118. Year Opened: 1947. Architects: Various contributors. Moderate, credit cards. Call for reservations. Walk-on chances: Fair. Walkability: Not bad overall, outside of a few uphill hikes. Playability: Beautiful panoramas and some neat holes result in an entertaining track.

Gallery Golf Course is a fun 18-hole layout located on the Whidbey Naval Air Station near Oak Harbor. The course, long a military personnel-only venue, was opened for limited public play in 1992. As with most semiprivate facilities, public access is governed by its "members" which, in Gallery's case, are military personnel, Department of Defense workers and their guests. Because of the priority given to its primary users, public players interested in playing the course should call ahead for tee times.

The effort needed to play Gallery is worth it. Though the track is not overly daunting, golfers here enjoy some of the most spectacular views in Northwest golf as just to the west lie Puget Sound and the Strait of Juan de Fuca. Other than a few forested holes on the back nine, just about every place on this course offers unimpeded western vistas. (When I visited it during the summer of 1995, a pro shop employee dubbed Gallery the "poor man's Pebble Beach." From a panoramic standpoint, I couldn't disagree.)

Designed by Navy Seabees and other military personnel stationed at the base, Gallery opened with nine holes in 1947. Nine more holes—each designed by the manager at the time or by local servicemen/golfers—gradually opened over subsequent years. Several improvements have been implemented of late, including the planting of young trees which, when mature, will further tighten the fairways. Though located on a military installation, Gallery is very quiet, with lots of wildlife on display because of its water-side locale.

One of Gallery's more interesting holes is the 4th, a 475-yard par-5 that doglegs rightward around a barbed-wire compound bearing "Radiation" signs. Don't know what's in there, but don't recommend golfers scale the fence to retrieve mishit balls. Two bunkers lurk farther down along the right edge of the fairway, which ends at a small, right-sloping green. One of Gallery's sternest tests is the 15th, a 246-yard par-3 rated the second-toughest hole. A magnificent elevated tee begins the 15th, and the chute-like hole is lined by tall trees on both sides. The 15th green is large and untrapped, but when winds come off Puget Sound from the west (left), finding the putting surface is chancy at best.

Gold Mountain Golf Course

36 *7263 West Belfair Valley Road, Gorst, WA 98337. (360) 674-2363 or 1-800-249-2363. Scott Alexander, pro. 36 holes. Course ratings: Cascade Course (6,717 yards, par 71) men—B71.9/120, M68.6/116; women—M73.8/122, F70.0/116; Olympic Course (7,003 yards, par 72) men—C73.1/128, B70.6/122, M68.0/116; women F69.2/115. Grass tees. Years Opened: 1972 (Cascade); 1996 (Olympic). Architects: Ken Tyson (Cascade); John Harbottle III (Olympic). Moderate, jr./sr. rates, credit cards. Reservations: Call a week ahead. Walk-on chances: OK for singles. Walkability: Fair, with some hills encountered on both courses. Playability: Washington's first 36-hole facility contains two outstanding and affordable tracks.*

Owned by the city of Bremerton, this 36-hole venue off West Belfair Valley Road, northwest of Gorst, has the highest bang-for-the-buck quotient in Northwest golf. Even though having green fees a few bucks cheaper than its magnificent new sister course, Gold Mountain's original Cascade layout can hold a candle to any course. Augmented by a full-service clubhouse and grass-teed driving range, Cascade had hosted over 71,000 rounds annually before Olympic opened in fall 1996. One of the strongest motives for building Olympic was to ease the demand on Cascade, which became so great that the city turned away 34,000 players a year; there was just no room for them. Gold Mountain's success can be traced to head pro Scott Alexander, a friendly and effective front man. In 1997, Scott was named by the Western Washington chapter of the PGA its public course merchandiser of the year and the golf professional of the year. Scott's brother John Alexander was the greens superintendent during the crucial grown-in period of the Olympic course. John, a fine golfer who played in the 1991 U.S. Publinx Championship, left at the end of 1996 to become the superintendent at Waverley Country Club in Portland.

The Cascade 18 opened in 1972. Designer Ken Tyson leased the course until 1983, at which time the city took over the operations and began upgrading it. The dry-in-winter venue occupies well-treed terrain that ranges from flat to moderately rolling. Though its hills are not mountain goat-type affairs, Cascade can be an arduous walk, particularly if one is having a bad round. Golfers at this 100-plus-acre layout will encountered 30-plus bunkers, two ponds and some large greens. These saucer-like swards are well-mounded peripherally and can be fitted with tough pin placements.

Recent changes to Cascade include a new pond at the 367-yard 4th hole and another tee at the par-3 17th. Good tests include the top-rated 5th, a 423-yard par-4 with a tree-lined, up-and-down fairway leading to a green that tilts rightward to a sand trap. The 9th, a 507-yard par-5, runs straight for 425 yards on a gradually tree-squeezed route. The fairway then curls sharply left to a large, front-sloping green ringed by three traps. The 10th, a 418-yard par-4, initially heads uphill, then flattens and doglegs right, skirting dense jail on the right. The 10th concludes at a bi-trapped green that leans steeply toward a swale in front. Cascade's 18th, a 550-yard par-5, is an excellent closer. Its canyonlike fairway—with steep and tree-lined edges—crosses rolling terrain before turning left and rising to a knoll-perched green trapped right rear.

Olympic occupies 180 acres west and south of the Cascade. To my thinking, this is one of the finest Northwest courses to open in recent years. After playing the course and looking through my notes, I ran across this telling summation: "One helluva muni!" Harbottle fashioned a wonderful variety of holes for the 7,000-yard track, the risks and rewards of which are clearly displayed from the tees on all but a handful of holes. The layout, built by Bob Soushek of Fore Inc., winds through forested watershed property. There's no chance that fairway-side houses will impair the golf experience.

The $5-million layout is irrigated by treated wastewater; about the only place I noticed a smell was on the left side of the 15th fairway, an area protected from the winds by trees. Elsewhere, the prevailing westerlies sweep across the course to play an integral role. Also complicating Olympic are sundry water hazards and bunkers of all shapes and sizes. Many angles, slopes and humps define the greens, which average 6,500-square-feet in size. You'll need a fertile imagination to figure out the breaks on these putting surfaces. Paved cart paths, excellent signage (including yardage distances on sprinkler heads), and superior conditioning are also hallmarks of the Olympic course, which in January 1997 was named in Golf Magazine's list of the "Top Ten Layouts You Can Play"—for courses opened in 1996.

Among the more interesting holes, and there are literally a dozen and a half of them at Olympic, is the beautiful 2nd, a 521-yard par-5 that begins at an elevated tee and heads off into a facing wind. Swales front the tee and line the left edge of the fairway, which is squeezed by trees along the right. The hole gradually rises over rolling ground, passing a huge bunker in the right half of the fairway at the 130-yard mark. The untrapped putting surface at the 2nd is raised and steep-sided. The 3rd, a 251-yard par-3, starts at a towering tee then drops down to a vast, right-front-sloping, hogbacked green guarded left-front by a pair of huge bunkers. The bigger of these two traps is the deepest on the course. The 5th, a 515-yard par-5, is an uphill dogleg-right with a big dip off the tee. The hole winds around trees and passes two bunkers on the left at the 150-yard mark. The fairway is tapered by trees as it descends to a long, rolling and rear-sloping green guarded by pot bunkers left-front, right (two), and steep rear and right sides. From beyond 150 yards, the 5th green is hidden.

The top-rated 8th, a 467-yard par-4 with another tall tee, has a good-sized landing area delineated by a creek and pond on the right. The last 170 yards are narrow and uphill, while the final 110 yards are lined along the right by a pond. The 8th ends at a smallish and undulating green ringed by three pot bunkers; the pond runs up to the green's right-front edge. Though short, the right-turning, 305-yard 9th is tough on the imprudent. A pond sits at the turn and four pot bunkers lurk on the other side of the water. From the elevated back tees, a 225-yard carry is needed to reach the bunkers. The safest route is left of the pond with a long iron or 5-wood. Trees line the right-front edge of the kidney-shaped, trapped-left 9th green, thus stinting corner-cutting drives. A series of grass traps lie between the trees and green.

It's a fairly steep hike from the 9th green to the 10th tee, but the effort—after a breath-catching pause—is worth it. The 10th, a 466-yard par-4, has water right of its raised tee and then bends uphill to the right. At the 175-yard mark, the left-sloping hole winds left and descends to a skinny-but-deep, two-tiered green protected by a pot bunker left. The 16th, another gargantuan (464-yard) par-4, runs over wide and flat ground for 210 yards, then drops over rolling ground. A chunky bunker sits 30 yards from the right-front edge of the huge (120-foot deep), humped-in-the-middle 16th green, which is further imperiled by two traps right-front.

Upcoming tournaments (possibly including state, regional and national—the U.S. Publinx is a distinct possibility) may be decided at the 18th, an Olympian 621-yard par-5. The hole starts out wide and left-sloping, running slightly uphill off the tee. A depression along the left in the landing area is termed a "dungeon" by Harbottle. The last 150 yards go steeply down to a mid-sized green with three pot bunkers and a lake along the right. Another pot bunker lurks left. Aim left-front of the green and the ball might roll to the desired spot. Behind the 18th green is a grassy, amphitheater-like area that can hold several thousand spectactors. Here's hoping that a big-time tournament comes soon to this great new course, which must rank among the nation's finest municipally-owned facilities.

Holmes Harbor Golf Course

18 *5023 Harbor Hills Drive, Freeland, WA 98249. (360) 331-2363. Bill Carbonell, pro. 18 holes. 4,371 yards. Par 64. Grass tees. Course ratings: men—B62.0/109, M61.0/107; women—B64.8/114, M62.9/110, F60.3/104. Year Opened: 1993. Architect: William Robinson. Moderate, jr./sr. rates, credit cards. Reservations: Call five days ahead. Walk-on chances: Good. Walkability: Too many long hikes for such a short course; be aware that the 9th green is a long way from the clubhouse. Playability: Course ranks quite high in the fun equation, but enjoyment negated somewhat by high playing costs.*

Executive-length Holmes Harbor lies in a banana belt of sorts at Whidbey Island's south end. At 50 miles from tip to tip, Whidbey is the nation's longest island. Holmes Harbor Golf Course is a resurrection of a regulation-length layout that had occupied the site from 1939 through the mid-1980s. Financial troubles doomed the first course, which originally sported sand greens. The savior of golf in this area by Freeland is Sikma Enterprises, headed by former NBA player Jack Sikma. After acquiring the site in the late-1980s, Sikma hired Florence, Oregon, architect Bill Robinson to design a short track, which was built by Sikma's director of maintenance Bill Campell and Sikma's business partner, Terry Otey. Campbell and Otey helped build Harbour Pointe in Mukilteo, another Sikma-operated venue.

The result is a fun-filled golf experience on an island that is one of Puget Sound's loveliest. Great eastward views of Holmes Harbor are available from the course and the deck of the clubhouse. Behind and alongside the clubhouse is a nine-hole natural-turf putting course designed by Campbell. Wildlife visitors include bald eagles, rabbits, deer, raccoons, quails and muskrats, the latter of which frequent a pond at the 4th hole. The golfing experience at Holmes Harbor is fine, with two caveats. It's priced too high, with weekend rates at over $30 for 18 holes and a shared cart: too much for a short course. Another problem is the position of the 9th hole, which is far removed from its customary position beside the clubhouse. If only playing nine holes at Holmes Harbor, the hike from the 9th green to the parking lot is either on the paved entry road or along the 9th and 18th holes, a potentially dangerous proposition.

Those observations aside, Holmes Harbor is an entertaining track, with thought-provoking holes, hazards galore and some devilishly slick and sloping greens; in sum, an excellent short-game test. The course's top-rated hole is the 373-yard, par-4 11th, whose downhill fairway is lined on the right by a drop-off. At the 130-yard mark, the hole descends to a pond-guarded and steeply front-tilting green with a pot bunker at the rear. The longest hole—and Holmes Harbor's only par-5— is the 487-yard 18th. This dogleg-left follows a slight downhill path that has three ponds along the left to deter any ideas of corner-cutting shots to the green. A long, sinuous bunker sits behind the greatly undulating 18th green, which is guarded front-left by the last of the three ponds. A neat closing hole.

Horseshoe Lake Golf Course

18

15932 Sidney Road SW, Port Orchard, WA 98366. (253) 857-3326 or 1-800-843-1564. Chris Morris, pro. 18 holes. 6,005 yards. Par 71. Grass tees. Course ratings: men—B68.0/115, M66.0/108; women—M70.8/117, F68.0/112. Year Opened: 1992. Architect: Jim Richardson. Moderate, jr./sr. rates. Reservations: Call a week ahead. Walk-on chances: Fair. Walkability: Front nine fine, but cart provided for steep back side. Playability: Good for all play levels.

Horseshoe Lake is a full-service facility off Highway 16's Purdy exit. Besides an enjoyable 18-hole course, the venue has a clubhouse with a popular restaurant and bar and a grass-teed driving range. The 125-acre venue lies across the entrance from a Kitsap County-operated park and recreational area, also called Horseshoe Lake. The proprietor of the golf development is Gig Harbor realtor, Robert Roland. The course was designed by Jim Richardson, and was built by Bob Soushek of Fore, Inc. The course opened as a 5,800-yarder; three back tees (at the 3rd, 15th and 16th) holes have stretched it beyond 6,000 yards.

Horseshoe Lake's fairways wind through second-growth forest, and are crossed by such wildlife as deer, ducks, beavers and frogs. Salmon-bearing Minter Creek intersects the property, dividing the 14th through 16th holes from the rest of the course. These holes run up and down a steep hill, and for that reason, green fees include a power cart for the back nine. Though still on the short side, Horseshoe Lake penalizes errant shooters. Target zones are tight, ball-hiding woodlands and scrub growth line fairways, and awkward lies are commonplace. When the course first opened there were quite a few rocks in fairways. In the last couple of years, however, the rocks have settled (as they're wont to do as a golf course ages) and Horsehoe Lake's turf is now quite nice.

This layout, Richardson's first design, is well conceived, though some of the par-4s and par-5s are similar. The course is separated into the front Uplands Nine and Minter Canyon Nine. The pastoral venue is quiet and features unhurried play. Among its top holes is the 6th, a narrow and rolling 505-yard par-5. A pond sits driving distance out along the left, and the fairway slopes toward it. Once past this juncture, the 6th curls sharply and tightly rightward to a rectangular, tree-tucked green. The top-rated 7th, a 400-yard par-4, is a severe and narrow dogleg-left. The latter leg of the fairway tapers before arriving at a tree-ringed, plateaued green with steep sides. One of the best holes on the Minter Canyon side is the 12th, a 495-yard par-5 along a ridgetop. The 12th's steep-sided, dome-shaped green sits on a bluff that offers nice views of a forested valley.

Lam's Golf Links

9

585 West Ducken Road, Whidbey Island, WA 98277. (360) 675-3412. 9 holes. 1,347 yards. Par 28. Year Opened: 1976. Architect: Bill Lam. Grass tees. No course ratings. Economical, sr. rates. No reservations. Walkability: No problems at all. Playability: Good spot for beginners or linksters after a quick fix.

This short track lies off Highway 20, a mile south of spectacular Deception Pass at Whidbey Island's north end. Begun in 1976 by Whidbey native Bill Lam, the course occupies 15 acres of fields and a former chicken farm. Appropriately, Lam's Links operates out of a clubhouse that was once a chicken coop. When this aging structure is untended by Lam or his staff, green fees are paid on the honor system.

Lam, who helped build the island's two country clubs—Whidbey and Useless Bay—while working with Kreig Construction, used his course-building knowledge for these "links." When viewed from the side, the otherwise flat site is punctuated by nine mushroom-like greens and nine raised tees. Some of the small, steeply sloping putting surfaces have multiple tiers, and the fairways are pinched by evergreen, fruit and deciduous trees. Two tees at each hole allow players to manufacture 18-hole rounds. Three man-made ponds enter play on five holes, with two water hazards imperiling the 7th. The eight par-3s range from 101 to 195 yards (front-nine yardages), with the course's only par-4, the 2nd, stretching 260 yards (280 yards as the 11th).

McCormick Woods Golf Club

18

5155 SW McCormick Woods Drive, Port Orchard, WA 98366. (360) 895-0130 or 1-800-323-0130. Ernie Taylor, pro. 18 holes. 7,012 yards. Par 72. Grass tees. Course ratings: men—C74.1/135, B72.3/129, M70.0/124, FF68.1/120; women—FF73.6/ 127, F71.1/122. Year Opened: 1986 (original nine); 1988 (second nine). Architects: Jack Frei. Moderate, (expensive on weekends), sr. rates, credit cards. Reservations: Call five days ahead. Walk-on chances: Fair. Walkability: A few lengthy jaunts but not bad considering the course's epic scope. Playability: Definitely a test for anyone who steps onto it.

Located southwest of Port Orchard, this 18-hole venue is an integral part of a self-contained development totaling 1,300 acres, 500 of which are devoted to natural woods, wetlands, parks and open space. The product of owner and developer Gene Hooker, and his wife, Therese ("McCormick" is Therese's maiden name), McCormick Woods opened its front nine on May 1, 1986; the back nine opened in spring 1988. The course operated out of a temporary clubhouse until 1995, when a spacious 24,000-square-foot structure was completed. Besides a pro shop, banquet rooms, lockers and lounge, the clubhouse features Mary Mac's Restaurant & Bar, an upscale eatery. As the course has evolved over its initial decade, more and more houses are popping up alongside fairways. The development is slated to ultimately contain 1,189 homes.

The front nine contains five tees per hole; holes on the back side have up to seven tees, all of which are rotated to minimize sod damage. McCormick Woods is graced by dozens of white-sand bunkers; salal, a flat-leafed groundcover that maliciously veils golf balls, thrives along fairway peripheries. The course harbors over 100 bird species, including bald eagles, hooded mergansers, American kestrels, cormorants, grebes, herons, hawks, owls, woodpeckers and turkey vultures. Bird feeders are located throughout the grounds, and deer, cougar, coyotes and beavers frequent the wooded back nine. McCormick Woods ranks among the top Northwest courses in customer service. From the time players arrive at the pro shop to the greeting they receive by the starter at the first tee, the guests at this course are made to feel special.

McCormick Woods is routinely placed among the state's "Top-5" rankings by national golf publications such as *Golf Digest* and *GOLFWEEK*. It received an exalted four-star rating in *Golf Digest's* "Places to Play" 1996-'97 edition. And the laudatory reviews are deserved. Noteworthy holes include the 427-yard 3rd, a rolling par-4 rated the course's most difficult. The dogleg-right fairway ends at a green guarded along the left by a pond and on the right by a trap.

The 9th, a tough-driving 575-yard par-5, doglegs 90-degrees to the left. The initial stretch of the fairway crosses a ridge and, at the turn, the hole descends steeply toward a seasonally-filled creek. "Jail" inside the dogleg severely penalizes inadequate corner-cutters. After the turn, the hole rises to a laterally-trapped putting surface linked to the 18th green. Back nine tests include the 15th, a 432-yard par-4 that is a precise, 90-degree dogleg-right. This difficult driving hole requires a 250-yard tee shot that must avoid trees and a bunker inside the turn. The small, two-tiered 15th green is backed by a hidden pot bunker and trapped twice on the right.

Meadowmeer Golf & Country Club - semiprivate

9

8530 Renny Lane NE, Bainbridge Island, WA 98110. (206) 842-2218. Tom Mueller, pro. 9 holes. 2,968 yards. Par 36. Grass tees. Course ratings: men—B/M66.7/119, M/F64.9/115; women—B/M71.8/123, M/F69.6/119. Year Opened: 1972. Architect: Sam Clarke. Moderate, jr./sr. rates, credit cards. Reservations: Call a week ahead. Walk-on chances: Fair. Walkability: No problems. Playability: Pleasant nine holes amidst a neighborhood.

The course at Meadowmeer Golf & Country Club winds through a 120-home subdivision; both the course and the like-named neighborhood were developed by Sam Clarke. Meadowmeer opened in 1972 as a six-holer; three holes were added later. Since it is owned by over 400 members, call for tee times during the summer as member-only events may be underway. The course occupies 60 acres of gently rolling land that was once a strawberry farm; good drainage makes it one of western Washington's driest venues. The well-appointed course has paved cart paths and manicured fairways, greens and traps.

Sam Clarke is to be commended for his layout, which weaves discreetly between homes. A unique trait of the course are the vision-blocking hills fronting the tees on some par-4s. Good tests include the 1st, a 355-yard par-4 bordered left by homes. Its straight and rolling fairway ends at a trapped-left, mid sized green with a steep back edge. The top-rated 5th, a 386-yard par-4, is a narrow dogleg-left that curls around a large trap to a raised green with cascading sides. The 8th, a 210-yard par-3, features a hill-perched tee, potentially shot-rejecting trees near mid-fairway, and an amply bunkered green with a high front flank.

Rolling Hills Golf Club

18 *2485 McWilliams Road, Bremerton, WA 98310. (360) 479-1212. Tedd Hudanich, director of golf; Roger O'Hara, pro. 18 holes. 5,910 yards. Par 70. Grass tees. Course ratings: men—B67.9/115, F65.9/110; women—B73.5/122, F71.0/117. Year Opened: 1972. Architect: Don Hogan. Moderate, credit cards. Reservations: Call a week ahead. Walk-on chances: Fair. Walkability: Good. Playability: Course upgrades improving year-round play.*

Rolling Hills Golf Club lies northeast of Bremerton off Highway 303. Owned by Don Rasmussen, this community-oriented public facility hosts around 55,000 rounds a year, with local golfers responsible for most of the play. Navy personnel and civilian shipyard workers from Bremerton's waterfront compete in leagues and tournaments, and the men's and women's clubs are large and active.

The Don Hogan-designed course has been upgraded with flower gardens and landscaping enhancements. An ongoing drainage-improvement project has resulted in better winter playing conditions. A new bunker was added alongside the 3rd fairway, and upcoming plans include mounding along holes. The layout, called Bremerton East Golf Course when it opened in the early '70s, is moderate in length and overall difficulty, but many good "sticks" have difficulty "eating it up" as its small greens are slick and elusive. The depressions around the course, originally destined for bunkers, are being gradually filled with sand. Two ponds and a ditch also compete for errant shots on the 100-acre track.

The name of the course aptly describes its topography, which is defined by a hillside offering views of the Olympic Mountains and the city of Bremerton. A sampling of its toughest holes should include the 8th, a 375-yard par-4 that descends past OB along the right to a quick and rolling green. Another good test is the dogleg-left 10th, a 560-yard par-5 that skirts the driving range. A water hazard crosses the hole at the turn, and the mid-sized green is trapped in front.

Village Greens Golf Course

18 *2298 Fircrest Drive SE, Port Orchard, WA 98366. (360) 871-1222. Doug Hathaway, pro. 18 holes. 3,255 yards. Par 58. Grass tees. Course ratings: men 57.1/81, women 57.2/80. Year Opened: 1957. Architects: Original founders. Economical, jr./sr. rates. Call for reservations. Walk-on chances: Good. Walkability: Excellent. Playability: Good short-game test.*

Village Greens is a tidy 18-hole layout with 14 par-3s and a quartet of 200-plus-yard par-4s. Owned by the Kitsap County Parks Department, Village Greens is a well-conceived golf park encompassing 48 acres. It was built in 1957 and deeded to the parks department in the 1960s.

The short course is dotted with assorted greenside bunkers and flower gardens. Though manually irrigated, Village Greens lives up to its name, thanks in part to steady year-round rainfall. The greens are quite small and elusive; their diminutive size and convex structure make them difficult targets to hit—and stay on—with any consistency. Most of the fairways are mere tree-lined hallways and some, if measured across from branch to branch, are less than 10 yards wide.

Private Courses

The Country Club of Seattle

At Restoration Point, Bainbridge Island, WA 98110. No phone. 9 holes. 900 yards. 9
Par 27. No course ratings. Year Opened: 1896. Architect: Josiah Collins. Members
& guests.

This publicity-shy, ultra-private golf club is one of the most unique in the United States. When established in 1891 as "The Country Club," the charter stipulated a maximum of 16 members, a total sustained for over 100 years. The club's current members are second-, third- and fourth-generation descendants of the founders. As outlined in a book written by T. M. Pelley, entitled "The Story of Restoration Point and The Country Club," the original course spanned five-and-a-half acres. By 1956, the club had expanded its holdings to over 250 acres; most of the land is now occupied by homes. The club's early-day activities included swimming, tennis and baseball, and the members owned vacation cottages. The clubhouse, probably the first in the Northwest when erected on Bainbridge Island's eastern shore in the mid-1890s, contained sleeping rooms.

A golf course at The Country Club of Seattle was begun in early 1896 when a few members, led by Josiah Collins, planted tin cans in the ground for two holes. By October 1896, the "layout" was expanded to six holes. In 1915, three more were added and the other holes were reconditioned. The first fairways were rough-hewn pastures, with one hole requiring golfers to launch their gutta-percha balls over a bog off the tee. The club held its first tournament in 1896, with Henry Meserve the winner after shooting a 25 on the six-hole layout. The present-day course has changed little over its century of existence. Still equipped with sand greens, the short layout is preserved as if in a time capsule. The course is visible from the Seattle-Bremerton ferry run; look north while the boat winds around the tip of Bainbridge Island and observe the club's "brown greens."

Kitsap Golf & Country Club

3885 NW Golf Club Hill Road, Bremerton, WA 98312. (360) 373-5101. Mark 18
Sivara, pro. 18 holes. 6,312 yards. Par 71. Grass tees. Course ratings: men—B70.1/
120, M69.6/118; women—M75.1/129, F72.0/122. Years Opened: 1929 (original
nine); 1962 (second nine). Architects: Members. Members, guests & reciprocates.

With its first nine holes opening in 1929, this club is the oldest course on the Kitsap Peninsula. Besides a nice clubhouse, driving range and swimming pool, Kitsap's members have access to an interesting golf course located northwest of Bremerton off Chico Way. The layout, which features two different but very tight nines, enjoys paved cart paths, nice flower gardens, good signage and a lot of character. The original front side and the clubhouse occupies a hilltop, while the 1962-opened back nine winds down, around and along the base of the promontory. Chico Creek plays a major role in holes 10-18. The course record, a 62, was set in 1996 by Ryan Kelly, a player on Oregon State University's golf team.

Kitsap's golf operations have been overseen by Mark Sivara since 1989. The Tacoma native helps oversee such annual events as the Kitsap Amateur, a two-day event in June with a field of 224 players. The Haselwood Partnership Championship is a popular member-guest tourney, and the two-day Women's Invitational in June has a full field of 144. Non-member events at Kitsap have included such major tournaments as the Washington State Amateur.

Kitsap starts off with a par-3, one of the few courses in the Northwest so configured. The 181-yarder has its elevated tee and hill-cut green separated by a canyon. The elusive putting surface is trapped left-front. The 2nd, a 400-yard par-4, skirts trees and jail along the left. At the 140-yard mark, trees lurk along the right and the fairway winds narrowly down to a round, front-sloping green lined by trees left and a trap right. The top-rated 4th, a 422-yard par-4, heads slightly uphill off the tee and then flattens out. The tree-pinched route eventually drops down to a hill-perched, front-left-sloping green with a swale left-front. The 7th, a 424-yard par-4, has a pond along the right and OB left of its right-sloping fairway. The hole goes directly to a knobbed, steep-right-sided green protected by a pond left. Two bunkers sit outside the turn of the 9th, a 333-yard par-4. The left-sloping hole bends rightward 90 degrees around dense forestry to a radical, two-tiered green. A trap along the left is actually a catch basin for misdirected shots to this smallish, sidehill-cut target.

One of the Northwest's wildest holes is the 10th, a 431-yard par-4 that begins Kitsap's entertaining back nine. Once off its elevated tee, the 10th skirts jail left and the driving range right along a slight descent. At the 200-yard mark, the hole veers left and drops down about 180 feet to a large, rolling green with a tree-squeezed throat. The 11th, a 549-yard par-5, is a lengthy right-bender that winds between a jailed hill left and two huge firs right. The rolling fairway gradually bears to the right. At the 150-yard mark, the hole descends to a V-shaped, front-left-sloping green trapped right-front.

The par-4s at the 12th, 13th and 14th holes are quite interesting. With their corrugated contour, abbreviated length, tiny and wavy greens, and deep bunkers, these holes are like those found on Waverley's links. The 296-yard 12th heads off a Chico Creek-fronted tee on a sharp dogleg-right path around trees. The greatly moguled fairway bends around to a concave, trapped-front green set closely against an OB-fenced corner of the club's property. At the 13th, a 274-yard par-4, Chico Creek crosses the hole diagonally, and OB lurks off to the left. The fairway rises to a tight tree-pinched landing area for drives, then continues to a miniscule, ridge-perched green ringed by a swale left and a trap left-front. The 14th, a 382-yard par-4, has three huge firs right in front of the tee, while another line of evergreens squeezes the hole along the left. Once past the firs, the fairway goes straight to a raised, front-tilting green trapped left-front.

The 15th, a 408-yard par-4, heads toward two goalpost-like Douglas firs at the 175-yard mark. Once beyond this tight juncture, the hole drops slightly to a skinny, front-tilting green trapped twice right and once left. Though ranked Kitsap's 18th-toughest hole, the par-3 17th is dicey. The 166-yarder rises past a towering, treed hill along the right to a hill-cut, deep-but-skinny green trapped twice left. The putting surface has a hump in its front third, which veils its actual depth. The 18th, a 360-yard par-4, makes Everett Country Club's notorious "Hogan's Alley" (the par-4 16th) look like an airport runway. Indeed, the cart path skirting this route eats up about a third of the fairway, a sunken, chute-like affair between two treed bluffs. Over the final 100 yards of this right-bending hole, the path angles up to a small, hill-cut and very slick, right-sloping green. Slicing and hooking is not permissable on Kitsap's home hole.

Useless Bay Golf & Country Club

5725 South Country Club Drive, Langley, WA 98260. (360) 321-5958. Bill Davis, pro. 18 holes. 6,389 yards. Par 72. Grass tees. Course ratings: men—B70.1/119, M69.0/116; women—M74.4/128, FF71.2/121, F70.9/121. Year Opened: 1967 (original nine); 1974 (second nine). Architect: Howard Sievers; Bill Teufel (remodel). Members, guests & reciprocates.

18

Useless Bay Golf & Country Club is a lovely course that traverses scenic property west of Langley. The club's namesake waterbody was dubbed by Captain George Vancouver in 1792. It seems that when the keel of Vancouver's boat hit bottom before his anchor could, Vancouver named the bay in disgust. The current back nine was once part of the bay; smaller ships often docked beside the area now housing the 13th green. The private facility was built and designed by Howard Sievers, who owned a sand and gravel company. Sievers originally wanted to weave fairways through a subdivision on his 540 acres, but because the soil didn't percolate, his plans were tabled. Vestiges of the unrealized development remain on the property. Fire hydrants sit unused along dirt roads which lead nowhere. The smattering of homes that have been built around the course all use septic systems.

Despite its founder's unfulfilled dreams, Useless Bay has evolved into a fine golfing facility, with its membership enjoying a wonderful course and a beautiful clubhouse. Though some members live in Puget Sound's metropolitan areas, many make frequent trips to Whidbey for golf and relaxation. (Islanders say that when they go to the mainland, they're "returning to the United States.") This part of Whidbey is home to eagles (which nest in trees on a nearby bluff), many shore birds, and rabbits. Useless Bay is registered as an Audubon Society course.

Useless Bay's golfing grounds have been enhanced over the years. A sanding program has greatly enhanced drainage at this traditionally wet course. The layout spans a bowl-shaped site, which creates a wide variety of holes and shot selections. Play is frequently interrupted by water hazards in the form of fat ponds and slender canals in and around landing zones. The top-rated hole is the 6th, a 453-yard par-4 that begins at an elevated tee. The fairway runs long and straight, with OB on the right. A pond lurks along the hole's left side, 150 yards from a large right-front-sloping green.

Two par-4s on the back nine stand out for their difficulty. The 15th, a 407-yarder that ranks among the region's nastiest par-4s, requires a tee shot that must carry—depending upon the tee used—200 to 250 yards over water into a prevailing wind. A pond sits driving distance out along the left. This water hazard later crosses in front of the green, resulting in a knee-trembling long iron for those trying to make this hole a two-shotter. The wide-but-shallow 15th green is trapped left-front. Useless Bay's 413-yard 18th is an uphill, slight dogleg-right that winds between water left and white-staked wetlands and homes right. The fairway is narrowed over its last 130 yards by wetlands along the right before it ascends to a hill-cut, and steeply front-sloping, ultra-slick green.

Vashon Island Golf & Country Club

9

24615 75th Avenue SW, Vashon, WA 98070. (206) 463-2006. Steve Englund, pro. 9 holes. 3,006 yards. Par 35. Grass tees. Course ratings: men—B67.6/114, F64.7/ 108, women—B72.9/118, F69.3/111. Year Opened: 1929. Architect: Founding owner. Members, guests & reciprocates.

Vashon Island Golf & Country Club spans a well-treed slope in the center of Maury Island, a slender crescent-shaped isle connected to Vashon's east edge by a thread of land. Currently a dual-tee nine that extends 5,870 yards over two circuits, Vashon's only golfing venue may one day be augmented by a back nine. The members have continued discussions with King County over acquiring 40 neighboring, county-owned acres for the expansion. So far, the county has balked at selling the parcel because it's used for equipment storage.

In mid-1997, the club completed work on a public driving range. The practice facility lies across 75th Avenue S.W. from the course, and has a separate operations building. A drainage project begun in 1992 continues, improving play on the layout during the wet months. Vashon Island Golf & Country Club has 300 golfing members, and there's room for 50 more. In addition, the club has 100 social members, making it one of the island's prime social gathering spots.

Vashon's course was begun in 1929 as a public facility. In 1965, its then-owner, Howard Williams, encountered some financial difficulties and sold the course to the founding members. Ever since that time, Vashon has been a private venue. Players here enjoy nice views of Puget Sound and may catch glimpses of Seattle's skyline and Mount Baker, particularly from the 1st hole. Deer often cross Vashon's fairways. Vashon's rolling, well-treed layout contains eight sand bunkers and a pond. Two grassy gullies impede play on seven holes, appearing in landing zones, off tees and before greens.

Whidbey Golf & Country Club

18

1411 West Fairway Lane, Oak Harbor, WA 98277. (360) 675-4546. Chuck West, pro. 18 holes. 6,427 yards. Par 72. Grass tees. Course ratings: men—B71.0/120, M69.6/117; women—B74.6/128, F70.6/120. Year Opened: 1962 (original nine); 1979 (second nine). Architects: Hank Garletts & Ken Putnam (original nine); Norm Mattson (second nine); Bill Overdorf (remodel). Members, guests & reciprocates.

Whidbey Golf & Country Club lies at the south end of Oak Harbor on the former Loerland Dairy Farm. Indeed, the original clubhouse was Loerland's dairy barn and the lounge was a milking parlor for cows. Unfortunately, in late 1996, these structures burned to the ground, incurring $1 million in damage. At press time, the members weren't sure when a new clubhouse would be constructed. Whidbey's golf operations will be conducted out of a temporary structure until a new clubhouse is built.

The club evolved in the early '60s through the efforts of a handful of local golfers, who felt another course on the island was needed. Much of the work on the initial nine was donated; one of the founders, Hank Garletts, designed the first set of holes with help from golf architect, Ken Putnam. After that portion of the course had been in operation for about 15 years, surplus club land was sold as housing lots to help finance the second nine. Whidbey member Norm Mattson designed the second set of holes, which was built by Kreig Construction.

Though homes line portions of the course, the layout is decidedly pastoral and golf is unimpeded by civilization. In the late-1980s, architect Bill Overdorf oversaw a master plan that involved new greens and tees. Though Whidbey doesn't have a plethora of bunkers, seven ponds demand accuracy from players. An interesting hole is the 5th, a 349-yard par-4 that curls left around a long lake. Out-of-bounds lurks outside the turn before the fairway ends at a wild-looking, left-sloping green guarded left by the pond and right by a bunker. Rated the course's second-toughest hole, the 430-yard, par-4 14th harbors a pond that borders the fairway's left edge all the way up to the 125-yard mark. Entry to the oval-shaped, untrapped 14th green is squeezed at its left-front entry by pudgy willows. Views of the green from the pond-fronted "tips" of the 17th, a 200-yard par-3, are blocked somewhat by trees. This putting surface is large and bunkered left.

Wing Point Golf & Country Club

18

811 Cherry Avenue, Bainbridge Island, WA 98110. (206) 842-7933. Jim Swagerty Jr., pro. 18 holes. 6,000 yards. Par 71. Grass tees. Course ratings: men—B68.1/124, M66.9/122, FF65.5/119; women—B74.0/128, M72.6/126, FF70.8/122, F68.9/118. Years Opened: 1903 (original six); 1991 (second nine). Architects: Founding members (original nine); Jack Frei (second nine); Bill Teufel (remodel of original nine). Members, guests & reciprocates.

Located on the southern part of Bainbridge Island, Wing Point Golf and Country Club offers glimpses of Puget Sound from its higher elevations. When the course opened in 1903 with six holes, it sported sand greens. In 1963, the original holes were rebuilt and the greens converted to grass. Seattle golf architect Bill Teufel designed this step in Wing Point's evolution. In May 1991, Wing Point received a new—and long-awaited—second nine (now played as the front). Architect Jack Frei—whose work includes McCormick Woods and Desert Canyon—designed these holes.

The course now offers interesting representations of old and new golf architecture. The traditional back side is classical Northwest, with tree-lined fairways and generally small, steep-sided greens. Teufel added bunkering to modernize these holes. In general, holes 10 through 18 are longer than their counterparts. Frei's addendum was creatively woven within a fairly small plot defined by forestry, homesites and wetlands. These holes feature well-trapped and rolling greens, and some sneaky water hazards.

In early 1997, the members were moving forward with a plan to add yardage to Frei's front nine. The proposal includes rebuilding the 4th hole, converting it into a 480 yard par-5 from a short par-4. Lengthening of the 4th stretched Wing Point's layout to over 6,000 yards from the tips and bumped its par to 71. Despite these modifications, the course will remain a shotmaker's track, not a long-ball hitter's venue.

Commencement of the course upgrades was stalled in late 1996 when vandals ravaged seven greens and broke and overturned benches, ball washers, irrigation boxes and bird feeders. The floor of the swimming pool was also damaged. Only nine holes were in play for six months. According to greens superintendent, Bill Schilling, who made the repairs with help from his staff, the malicious nature of the vandalism was the worst he'd ever seen. This sad tale ends on a happy note: the vandals were caught and prosecuted, and Wing Point should emerge from the experience better than ever.

Par-3 Courses

Island Greens

3890 East French Road, Clinton, WA 98236. (360) 579-6042. 9 holes. 1,355 yards. Par 27. Grass tees. No ratings. Economical. No reservations.

Island Greens lies near the Clinton ferry terminal at Whidbey Island's south end, off Highway 20 and Cultus Bay Road. The genesis of the course is unusual. One day, Karen Anderson told her "hardcore-golfer" husband, Dave, to "clean up" the 20 acres beside their home. The next thing she knew, Dave had fashioned three fairways by removing immature alders and scrub growth within a stand of evergreens.

After six more holes were added, Island Greens opened on Father's Day 1989. The site was once used for the family's horses, cattle, sheep and pigs. While admirably creating a golf layout on a bowl-shaped parcel, the Andersons are seeking to ensure that the course doesn't harm the environment. Much to the satisfaction of Island County officials, a wetlands in the plot's midsection was untouched, and a holding pond—also an on-course water hazard—is an irrigation source. Only the putting greens—which are modern in scope and subtly contoured—are fertilized. The Andersons considered using sheep to "mow" fairways, but thought that the animals might get hurt by flying golf balls.

Local wildlife visitors include birds and deer. Besides the pond, the forested par-3 is dotted with pot-type sand and grass bunkers. Each hole offers three sets of tees, and the Andersons encourage the use of Cayman balls, which travel only half the distance of regular balls but enable the use of longer clubs. Island Greens's toughest test is the 8th, a 220-yarder that bypasses the pond, the Anderson's house and a tree grove along the left en route to a small, front-sloping green.

Driving Ranges

Northwest Golf Range

368 NE Bucklin Hill Road, Bremerton, WA 98310.
(360) 692-6828. John Chafin, pro.

Vashon Island Driving Range

24615 75th Avenue SW, Vashon, WA 98070.
(206) 463-2006. Steve Englund, pro.

Woodall's World Driving Range

8400 NE West Kingston Road, Kingston, WA 98346.
(360) 297-4653. Ted Wurtz, pro.

Upcoming Courses

Camano Island — Campbell Project (1998/1999). In mid-1996, a local resident was moving forward with plans for a nine-hole par-3 course, 113-slip RV park and a small pro shop on a 30-acre parcel off Chapman Road.

Indianola — White Horse (1999). In late 1996, Kitsap County Commissioners approved this controversial 450-acre golf-residential project. A King County judge later upheld the ruling, thus allowing the developer to proceed with plans for a championship-length 18, 224 homes, driving range, clubhouse, tennis courts, equestrian area and swimming pool.

Port Orchard — Tallamach (1999/2000). In late-1996, following the results of a feasibility study, Kitsap County officials turned down an opportunity to purchase this site and proceed with the development of an 18-hole golf course. The fully-permitted 170-acre site is owned by local residents, including Gold Mountain's head pro Scott Alexander, who may still proceed with the $7-million project.

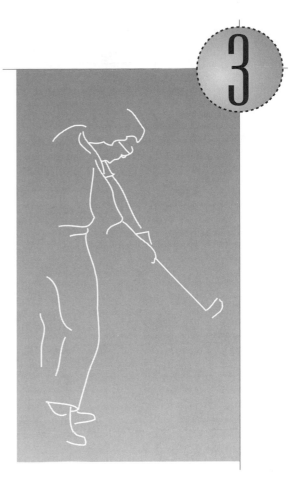

SEATTLE, EVERETT & VICINITY

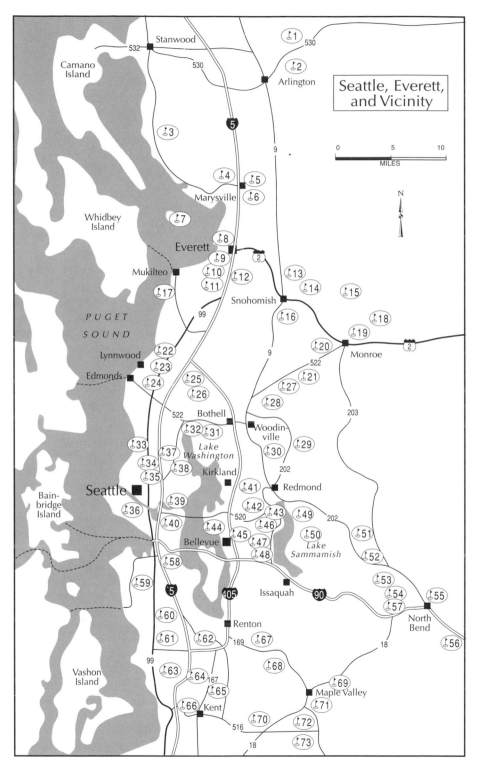

Seattle, Everett, and Vicinity

1. **Cloverdale Golf Club** — public 9
2. **Gleneagle Golf Course** — public 18 & driving range
3. **Kayak Point Golf Course** — public 18, 18-hole putting course & driving range
4. **Battle Creek Golf Course** — public 18, 9 (par-3) & driving range
5. **Cedarcrest Municipal Golf Course** — public 18
6. **Marysville Golf Center** — driving range
7. **Hat Island Golf Club** — private 9
8. **Legion Memorial Golf Course** — public 18
9. **Everett Golf & Country Club** — private 18
10. **Walter E. Hall Memorial Golf Course** — public 18
11. **Longshots Driving Range**
12. **Super Range** — driving range
13. **Lobo Country Club** — public 9 (par-3)
14. **Snohomish Public Golf Course** — public 18 & driving range
15. **Flowing Lake Golf Course** — public 18
16. **Kenwanda Golf Course** — public 18
17. **Harbour Pointe Golf Club** — public 18 & driving range
18. **Blue Boy West Golf Course** — public 9
19. **Monroe Golf Course** — public 9
20. **Iron Eagle Sport Center** — driving range
21. **Echo Falls Country Club** — semiprivate 18 & driving range
22. **Lynnwood Municipal Golf Course** — public 18 & driving range
23. **Ballinger Park Municipal Golf Course** — public 9
24. **Nile Golf & Country Club** — semiprivate 18
25. **Kaddyshack Golf Center** — driving range
26. **Mill Creek Country Club** — private 18
27. **Wellington Hills Golf Course** — public 9
28. **Gold Creek Tennis & Sports Club** — driving range
29. **Bear Creek Country Club** — private 18
30. **Red Wood Golf Center** — driving range
31. **Inglewood Golf Club** — private 18
32. **Wayne Public Golf Course** — public 18
33. **Seattle Golf Club** — private 18
34. **Puetz Evergreen Golf Range** — driving range
35. **Green Lake Golf Course** — public 9 (par-3)
36. **Golden Bear Family Golf Center at Interbay** — public 9, 18-hole putting course & driving range
37. **Jackson Park Municipal Golf Course** — public 18 & 9 (par-3)
38. **Sand Point Country Club** — private 18
39. **University of Washington Driving Range**
40. **Broadmoor Golf Club** — private 18
41. **Willows Run Golf Club** — public 18 & driving range
42. **Bellevue Municipal Golf Course** — public 18 & driving range
43. **Brae Burn Golf & Country Club** — private 9
44. **Overlake Golf & Country Club** — private 18
45. **Glendale Country Club** — private 18
46. **Tam O'Shanter Golf & Country Club** — private 9
47. **Crossroads Park Golf Course** — public 9 (par-3)
48. **The Golf Club at Newcastle** — public 36 & driving range

49. **Sahalee Country Club** — private 27
50. **Plateau Golf & Country Club** — private 18
51. **Carnation Golf Course** — public 18 & driving range
52. **Tall Chief Golf Club** — public 18
53. **Snoqualmie Falls Golf Course** — public 18 & driving range
54. **Twin Rivers Golf Course** — public 9 & driving range
55. **Mount Si Golf Course** — public 18 & driving range
56. **Cascade Golf Course** — public 9
57. **Snoqualmie Ridge TPC Golf Course** — private 18
58. **Jefferson Park Municipal Golf Course** — public 18, short 9 & driving range
59. **West Seattle Municipal Golf Course** — public 18
60. **Glen Acres Golf & Country Club** — private 9
61. **Rainier Golf & Country Club** — private 18
62. **Foster Golf Links** — public 18
63. **Tyee Valley Golf Club** — public 18 & driving range
64. **Southcenter Golf** — driving range
65. **EagleQuest at Golf Park** — driving range
66. **Riverbend Golf Complex** — public 18, 9 (par-3) & driving range
67. **Maplewood Golf Course** — public 18 & driving range
68. **Fairwood Golf & Country Club** — private 18
69. **The Course at Taylor Creek** — public 9 & driving range
70. **Meridian Valley Country Club** — private 18
71. **Elk Run Golf Course** — public 18 & driving range
72. **Lake Wilderness Golf Club** — public 18
73. **Druids Glen Golf Club** — public 18 & driving range

This is the Northwest's most densely populated area, with over 3.5 million people. And Seattle, Everett and environs continue to grow. The area's popularity owes to its proximity to water (Puget Sound and Lake Washington), breathtaking vistas of the Olympic and Cascade mountains, and mild climate. An excellent and diversified economy—greater Seattle is the nation's leader in the aerospace and computer software industries—also helps. Its location within mild climate zones 4 and 5 enables golf to generally be a year-round activity. Seattle averages 36 inches of annual rainfall, but its drizzly, gray skies lead many denizens to head south for the winter.

The area still lacks the number of golf holes needed to slake the appetites of its hackers. But several interesting new facilities—public and private—will help, as will new back sides at existing nine-hole tracks and major remodels to several of the older municipal courses. A possibly encouraging development—the city of Seattle turning its three muni facilities over to the non-profit Municipal Golf of Seattle—was a dud initially as green fees were raised and the course renovations took too long to get implemented. Hopefully, that will change in the years ahead and the much-needed infrastructural upgrades (new tees and greens, drainage improvements, irrigation systems, etc.) will get done.

Public Courses

Ballinger Park Municipal Golf Course

23000 Lakeview Drive, Mountlake Terrace, WA 98043. (425) 775-6467. 9 holes. 2,656 yards. Par 34. Grass tees & mats. Course ratings: men 64.2/100, women 66.9/105. Year Opened: 1959. Architect: Mountlake Terrace Parks Department; Bill Overdorf (remodel). Moderate, jr./sr. rates, credit cards. Reservations: Call a week ahead. Walk-on chances: Fair. Walkability: Once remodel is completed, former ankle-spraining course should be a thing of the past. Playability: If taken to fruition, all-new layout will shock former players.

This muni facility is situated beside Lake Ballinger, an attractive pond rimmed by homes, a fishing park, and the Nile Golf & Country Club. The 1959-built, nine-hole course used some of the greens from the old Meadowbrook Golf Course in northeast Seattle as turf for its tees. The facility, which includes an expansive clubhouse with banquet space, food service and offices for the city of Mountlake Terrace, is operated by Ballinger Recreation, Inc. (BRI), headed by Jan Japar and Mimi Racicot. BRI also operates Wellington Hills in Woodinville.

In early 1997, BRI and the city escaped a contentious period which involved a breach-of-contract lawsuit filed by BRI. The suit was settled out of court when the Mountlake Terrace City Council approved a plan that turns the course over to BRI on a 28-year lease. The agreement calls for BRI to spend $1 million in much-needed renovations to Ballinger Park's layout. The city paid BRI $300,000 to settle the suit, and agreed to pay another $250,000 toward the course improvements when BRI has its permits and financing in order. Should the permitting or financing not be worked out, the city will pay BRI an additional $225,000 to buy out the company, and Ballinger Park would revert to the city.

While the agreement took effect January 1, 1997, the city said it would return the course to decent shape after it was badly flooded in December '96. The water from Lake Ballinger washed over its banks and crossed the entire course all the way up to the clubhouse. The 34-acre track has historically suffered from poor drainage and seasonal flooding, but the most-recent inundation was the worst anyone can remember. The course's generally poor playing conditions, which went unaddressed during the rift between the city and BRI, caused it to go from 61,000 rounds in 1987 to 41,000 in 1996.

Overdorf's plan calls for restoring wetlands and the lake's shoreline. Retention ponds will be added to help the course better recover from flooding. The general layout will be completely reversed; instead of heading east to west, the holes will go north and south. About 100 yards will be added to the revised track, which will feature all-new bunkers, tees and greens. The project will require that the course be shut down for a 15-month period. If all goes well, an all-new Ballinger Park course will reopen in 1999.

Battle Creek Golf Course

27

6006 Meridian Avenue North, Marysville, WA 98270. (360) 659-7931 or 1-800-655-7931. Jim Pulliam, pro. 18 holes. 6,575 yards. Par 73. Par-3 Nine: 1,113 yards, par 27. Grass tees. Course ratings: men—B71.4/125, M69.5/121; women F70.9/124. Year Opened: 1990. Architects: Dave Richards, Bruce Richards & Fred Jacobson. Moderate, jr./sr. rates, credit cards. Reservations: Call a week ahead. Walk-on chances: Fair. Walkability: Fair, with some uphill treks and distances between greens and tees. Playability: Suitable for players of all abilities.

Named after the headwaters of nearby Battle Creek, this 175-acre golf facility offers a regulation-length 18, a par-3 nine and a driving range. Battle Creek is owned by the Richards brothers, Dave and Bruce, golf professional Fred Jacobson, and former University of Washington quarterback Bill Douglas. Designed by the Richardses and Jacobson and opened in April 1990, Battle Creek hosts approximately 45,000 rounds a year. The par-3 nine lies in the middle of the 18-hole layout, and features tight, tree-lined fairways and diminutive fir-ringed greens.

The regulation track winds around wetlands and spans several hills. Its generally mid-sized greens are uncontrived and fair, but the putting turf is bumpy and patchy. When I played Battle Creek at its grand opening, the greens were too immature; the owners should have delayed opening the course to better establish the putting surfaces. On my most recent visit, in late-1996, the greens were still in poor shape. They hadn't been mowed for awhile and, because of water retention, were badly spiked and dented by footprints. Putts drifted off-line and were very slow. The primary problem with Battle Creek's greens is that trees are too close to them. Sunlight has a tough time reaching the turf and, as a result, the greens don't dry out nor enjoy proper growth. That's an unhappy combination for turf so frequently trampled upon.

The problem with the greens is unfortunate since, overall, Battle Creek is a nice layout. There is considerable length (which increases significantly during wet weather as there's no fairway roll) as well as some tough par-4s. The forested course is quiet and pastoral; no homes are along the fairways. In recent years, the owners have cleared out peripheral woods to allow players decent lies on pine needles and seemingly good recoveries. Unfortunately, there's little daylight between you and the fairway as the trees are so tightly packed: kind of like being in a carpeted jail cell.

Among Battle Creek's better tests is the 4th, a 427-yard par-4 with a slightly downhill, right-bending fairway. The tree-lined hole plays quite long en route to a large green trapped left-front. You can't see the fairway from the back tee blocks on the 8th, a 398-yard par-4. Once out in the landing zone, the rolling 8th winds downhill past OB (a road) left and trees right. A big wetlands runs up to front its wide, trapped-left-rear green. The 10th, a 544-yard par-5, goes straight over left-tilting ground. The fairway stretches out for 350 yards or so, then winds left to another tree-ringed green.

Battle Creek's signature hole is the 12th, a 185-yard par-3 whose tee and green are separated by a deep chasm filled with dense vegetation. A huge, ball-rejecting boulder squats before the sizable green, which is surrounded by conifers. The 13th, a 480-yard par-5, begins at an elevated tee that offers lovely views of Puget Sound and Whidbey Island's southern tip. A wide wetlands lurks 275 yards out, then the fairway broadens and rises to a big green fronted by a swale. The 14th, a 400-yard par-4, has ponds along both sides of the fairway about 140 yards out. The hole then slopes rightward en route to a hill-cut, right-sloping green trapped left-rear. The putting surface also has a steep right side. The home hole, a 421-yard par-4, features a left-curling fairway that slopes left toward trees. At the 125-yard mark, the route is crossed by a fairway-wide wetlands. This detritus—home to probably thousands of mishit balls—runs up to the front edge of a wide-but-shallow, front-sloping green.

Bellevue Municipal Golf Course

18

5500 140th Avenue NE, Bellevue, WA 98005. (425) 451-7250. Martin Raab, Casey Anderson & Steve Hubbard, pros. 18 holes. 5,535 yards. Par 71. Grass tees & mats. Course ratings: men—M66.5/110, F64.4/107; women—B71.1/117, F68.6/111. Year Opened: 1968. Architect: Dave Kent; John Steidel (remodel). Moderate, jr./sr. rates. Reservations: Residents call on Monday between 7 to 9 a.m. for following week; nonresidents call after 9 a.m. for following week. Walk-on chances: Ok for singles. Walkability: Good, but muddy in winter. Playability: Suitable for all skills, but remember to take evasive action if hearing any "Fore!" warnings.

Owned by the city's parks department, this course lies northeast of downtown Bellevue. It averages over 85,000 rounds a year, making it one of the region's busiest facilities. The layout was designed by the late Dave Kent, a golf architect from California. Since opening in 1968 in a then-rural part of Bellevue, the facility has evolved into an urbanized playground bursting at the seams. Most days of the year the tee-time slate is full. If arriving at "Bell Muni" without a reservation, be prepared to wait awhile before being paired with other golfers. Headed by Martin Raab, Bellevue's teaching pros may give more lessons than any staff in the Northwest.

A recent upgrade, if that's what you want to call it, is the addition of a Puget Sound Power & Light substation along the right side of the 18th hole. Built in 1997, the structure was originally thought to infringe on the course, but the 315-yard 18th generally remains the same. That side of the fairway was elevated, with bunkers added near a wall between the substation and the field of play. The city of Bellevue received $875,000 from Puget Power for the project as well as other course improvements. The money was used to redesign the 2nd hole, a traditionally wet route behind Bellevue's mat-teed driving range. Designed by the parks department, the fairway was raised, a new back tee added 10 yards to the still-short par-4, and three traps line the right side. Also, a new 4th tee was built with artificial turf material into which a tee can be placed. This new tee is a significant improvement over the black rubber mat previously in use there.

Bellevue's considerable traffic requires it to liberally use mat tees in winter. During a recent round here in December 1995, 12 temporary greens were in use and mats were used on every hole. Another quibble is a city requirement that allows fivesomes. Though the course was boggy and the fees remained at $18 a pop, the pro shop sent out fivesomes every six minutes or so. The round took well over five hours to complete.

In summer, Bellevue's track is fairly decent, presenting a moderate challenge to all concerned. The fairways dry out and the already-short course plays even shorter. Among its better tests is the 7th, a par-5 of 480 yards. The hole begins with a tree-pinched fairway that opens onto a wide area before curling rightward to a bi-trapped, tree-ringed green. The 460-yard, par-5 14th doglegs 90-degrees to the right and ends at a well-bunkered, undulating green. The city used some of Puget Power's money to buy property along the 14th's right side. The acquisition allows golfers to actually retrieve—and perhaps play—errant shots instead of vainly looking at their balls through a chain-link fence.

Blue Boy West Golf Course

9

27927 Florence Acres Road, Monroe, WA 98272. (360) 793-2378. 9 holes. 2,199 yards. Par 31. Grass tees. Course ratings: men—B61.2/98, B/M60.8/96, F60.4/94; women—B64.2/109, B/M62.7/106, F61.2/103. Year Opened: 1992. Architects: Doug Smith & Chuck Nolan; Dick Moultrie (remodel). Moderate, jr./sr. rates. Reservations: Call two weeks ahead. Walk-on chances: Good. Walkability: Good. Playability: Enjoyable place for the whole family.

The executive-length Blue Boy West occupies a 30-acre pasture once grazed by dairy cattle and, later, by thoroughbred horses. Named after a prize hog in the old flick, "State Fair," Blue Boy Ranch was a dairy operation before Monroe veterinarian, Dr. William Smith, purchased it in the early 1970s and began raising beef cattle and horses. Many structures from the old dairy farm are still in use: the milkhouse has been renovated into the starter's shed and a barn is the clubhouse. The course originated with a few golf holes used by friends and family. When Dr. Smith moved the livestock to eastern Washington, he gave his sons, Doug and Ernie, the go-ahead to build a public golf course on the property. The sons received help from local greens superintendent, Chuck Nolan; the course was later re-routed by Bill Moultrie.

Blue Boy West has a few sand traps, some wildly undulating bentgrass greens, gully-fronted tees, and nice Cascade Mountain vistas. Westerly winds sweep over the dual-tee course, which plays 4,398 yards over two circuits, to skew shots off line and into trouble. Blue Boy West's layout includes five par-3s and four par-4s. The longest holes are the 2nd and the 4th, at 350 and 370 yards, respectively. Some tees are located in the backyards of the Smith family's residences. Blue Boy West maintains an enjoyable, low-key ambiance appropriate for its countryside locale and players of all abilities.

Carnation Golf Course

1810 West Snoqualmie River Road NE, Carnation, WA 98014. (425) 333-4151 or 583-0314 (from Seattle). Dan Tachell, director of golf; Chad Tachell, pro. 18 holes. 5,996 yards. Par 71. Grass tees. Course ratings: men—B67.6/113, M65.1/104, F60.9/ 91; women—B72.6/118, M69.9/113, F65.0/103. Year Opened: 1967. Architect: Bob Tachell. Moderate, jr./sr. rates, credit cards. Call for reservations. Walk-on chances: Fair. Walkability: Good. Playability: Suitable for players of all skills.

18

The 18-hole layout here lies about two miles from Carnation, off the Redmond-Fall City Highway. Carnation has always been owned and operated by the Tachell family. The late Bob Tachell designed and built the course with help from his wife Eva; son Dan now runs it as the director of golf. Dan's son Chad is the pro, and daughter Stephanie runs the pro shop. Another son, Jeff, is the head pro at nearby Twin Rivers Golf Course. The Tachells received their background from Bob who, in the 1950s, built and operated the now-defunct Meadowbrook Golf Course in north Seattle.

Situated on a Snoqualmie River floodplain, Carnation is usually inundated in winter, causing a golf season that runs from May to October. During its "prime" time, the course hosts about 40,000 rounds. The torrents of November 1995 and February 1996 may have caused the heaviest damage in Carnation's history. Even the clubhouse was awash by the rising river, and the 17th tee was wiped out (it's since been rebuilt). The Tachells prepare the course for the expected floods, removing benches, signs and ball washers. In 1990, a raging Snoqualmie carried away a bridge at the 2nd hole to the city of Everett, 15 miles away.

But, like its owners, the layout is surprisingly resilient, with the turf in good playing shape after the Snoqualmie River returns to its banks. The course has received several improvements in recent years. A major addition is a driving range, which necessitated the rebuilding of the former 13th, 16th and 17th holes. The course's riverside locale allows regular visits from ospreys and hawks, with deer also on display. Lowing cattle from nearby farms contribute to the countrified ambiance of a course which was formerly a sheep pasture.

Carnation has a fairly open front nine and a more forested back. Noteworthy holes include the 237-yard par-3 4th, which requires a long and well-placed tee shot to find a small, trapped-right green. The 8th is a 456-yard par-5 bordered along the left by the Snoqualmie. The fairway, which bends slightly left, crosses rolling ground en route to a mid-sized, tree-squeezed green. Perhaps Carnation's best hole is the par-5 18th, a 511-yarder. The wide and flat fairway curls left to a diminutive, fir-ringed green behind the clubhouse.

Cascade Golf Course

14303 436th Avenue SE, North Bend, WA 98045. (425) 888-0227. 9 holes. 2,514 yards. Par 36. Grass tees. Course ratings: men 62.8/93, women 66.4/107. Year Opened: 1954. Architects: Emmett Jackson; Fred Lawrence & Leroy Jorgenson (remodel). Moderate, jr./sr. rates. Call for reservations. Walk-on chances: Good. Walkability: Excellent. Playability: Great starter course for beginners.

9

Family-operated Cascade is set in pastoral environs just off Interstate 90 east of North Bend. The owners since 1987 are Fred and Carol Lawrence and Joyce and Leroy Jorgenson, who've added a pro shop to the clubhouse and upgraded the 36-acre layout with all-grass tees. The layout was designed and built by Emmett Jackson, who managed the nearby Mount Si course in the 1940s and '50s. Besides relatively quick rounds of golf, people come here for a "Tony Burger," named after former manager, Tony Pillo, who gained popularity with a sandwich filled with ground beef and Parmesan and American cheeses. Sadly, Pillo passed away in October 1996.

Cascade's track is flat and easy to walk, an ideal set-up for beginners, who can smack the small spheroid with relative impunity. If teeing off during non-peak hours, the shortish track can be played in just over an hour. Deer occasionally visit the site which, despite its locale beside I-90, is quiet. The course has fairly disparate front- and back-nine tees, and plays to 5,028 yards over two circuits. Good tests include the 1st, a straight-running 420-yard par-4 that ends at a rolling, mid-sized green. Perhaps the toughest hole is the 355-yard, par-4 5th, which winds leftward over rolling ground and past homes along the right to a trapped-left green. The 277-yard 7th is a tricky little hole. The dogleg-right par-4 winds narrowly between trees; a hidden pond lurks at the right-front of a small green trapped left-front.

Cedarcrest Municipal Golf Course

18

6810 84th Place NE, Marysville, WA 98270. (360) 659-3566. Don Shaw, pro. 18 holes. 6,000 yards. Par 70. Grass tees. Ratings of remodeled course not available. Year Opened: 1927. Architect: Tom Quast; John Steidel (remodel). Economical (rates to change after reopening). Reservations: Call a week ahead. Walk-on chances: Ok for singles. Walkability: Though yards were added, course is friendly for bag-packers. Playability: Should be much improved after major remodel completed.

The original 1927-opened Cedarcrest was a traditional municipally-owned course with a perfunctory set of holes. In June 1996, the city of Marysville closed the facility to begin a $3-million, 16-month makeover. The project, designed by architect John Steidel and built by Evans-Hall, involved drainage improvements, a new irrigation system, a remodel of several holes, 16 new greens, and a stretching of the par-70 course to 6,000 yards. The original layout was designed and built by Tom Quast, the father of one of the Northwest's most-accomplished all-time golfers, Anne Sander.

Improvements were needed as the facility, which hosts 70,000 rounds annually, experienced serious congestion. The course occupied about two-thirds of a 116-acre plot, and several junctures were often clogged with players. Foursomes quickly backed up, causing some long waits at tees. During one mid-week round here in 1994 it took me over two hours to play five holes. The cashier omitted to tell patrons that a tournament of once-a-year players had just started. At the 2nd hole, I ran into other disgruntled patrons, and the wait began. After five holes it appeared as if it was going to be a seven-hour round, so I went to the pro shop for a refund or rain check. Don Shaw, Cedarcrest's head pro, pointed to a strict "no rain checks" sign above the cash register. I, and several others, left the course in disgust, receiving very little "bang" for our buck.

It'll be interesting to see the next step in Cedarcrest's evolution (the work was underway as this book went to press). Steidel does excellent work on remodels (Whitefish Lake in Montana, Maplewood, etc.), and Evans-Hall (Seattle Golf Club's remodel, Creek at Qualchan, etc.) is a skilled builder of golf courses. The site, a gentle west-facing slope east of Marysville, has possibilities. The structural and physical aspects of Cedarcrest are probably handled. But the all-important customer service area also needs to be addressed. Maybe with the new course, Cedarcrest will get its operational act together and make the golfing experience—and not the generation of rounds—the priority.

Cloverdale Golf Club   9

26718 115th NE, Arlington, WA 98223. (360) 435-2539. Wiffi Smith, pro. 9 holes. 2,930 yards. Par 35. Grass Tees. No course ratings. Year Opened: 1994. Architects: Rick Witscher & Wiffi Smith. Moderate. Call for reservations. Walk-on chances: Good. Walkability: Good. Playability: Enjoyable for all age groups and abilities.

Located in rural Snohomish County, this course is on the site of Cloverdale Farms, a dairy farm homesteaded by the Croeze (pronounced "Croozy") family in 1914. In the 1970s, the Witscher family bought the 120-acre parcel. In the early 1990s, a member of that family, Rick Witscher, decided to convert the agricultural concern into a golf course when the dwindling price of milk made raising dairy cattle unprofitable. Witscher had a background in golf: his family owned land by Cedarcrest Golf Course in Marysville, where his father worked and Rick caddied.

Appropriately, Cloverdale Golf Club is a family operation. Rick is helped on and off the course by his wife Cynthia, brother Jan, sons Joe and Lee, and daughter Inga. The nine holes opened in 1994. A leg of the proposed Centennial Trail (which will open in the year 2000) runs by the course. In early 1997, the Witschers were entertaining an offer from the Snohomish County Parks Department, which would like to convert the 120-acre site into a recreational reserve. Near the course are fly-fishing lakes and the hiking and biking, "Rails-to-Trails" path. The Witschers are pleased with this development as it will lessen their financial burden.

The Cloverdale site is ideal for growing golf turf, and the Witschers have a bentgrass sod farm. Future plans include converting a dairy barn into a clubhouse; the golf operations are currently run out of a shed next to the family home. Nearby are lovely rose gardens. Food service includes hot dogs and candy bars. When I visited the course in spring 1995, neighborhood kids stopped by to purchase soda pop and sweets. One of the neat things about Cloverdale, which hosted about 25,000 rounds in 1996, is that private groups can rent the entire facility for tournaments. The head pro is Wiffi Smith, an LPGA star in the 1950s who's been rated among the nation's top-10 golf teachers by *Women's Golf Magazine*. Smith is an instructor for several LPGA Tour players and a staffmember of the Craft-Zavichas Golf School. As an amateur, Smith won the U.S., British, French and Mexican Amateurs.

As a golf historian, Rick Witscher wants his course to retain a traditional feel. You won't find yardage signs here as he feels players should be able to gauge distances to targets on their own. Cloverdale evinces other charms of a golf course from yesteryear. Its rudimentary layout has rugged gravel cart paths, old-style ball-washers, rustic benches, unmanicured bunkers, and raised, domed greens. The course encompasses a hill, with a few elevated tees offering vistas of the course and environs. The Witschers maintain a "natural" golf course, minimizing the use of herbicides and pesticides to mitigate environmental effects and runoff into the nearby "Stilly." Cloverdale was featured in a 1997 *Smithsonian* magazine article that discussed environmentally-friendly golf courses.

As might be expected, Cloverdale's greens are in excellent shape. The domed surfaces contain plenty of undulations—subtle and otherwise—to make putting a challenge. Among Cloverdale's more interesting holes is the 5th, a 540-yard par-5 with a straight fairway and a modest-sized green with a steep tier along its back quarter. The 390-yard, par-4 9th ascends slightly as it winds past wetlands and rugged rough along the left. A lagoon lurks 60 yards before a three-tiered green bunkered left-front. The back-left corner of the 9th green sits on a ledge. Tough putt from there.

Druids Glen Golf Club

18 *20410 SE 304th Street, Kent, WA 98042. Call (253) 638-1200. Travis Cox, director of golf; Eric Berry, pro. 18 holes. 7,146 yards. Par 72. Grass tees. Course ratings: men—T74.8/137, B71.8/131, M68.9/123, FF66.0/117; women—T80.7/145, B77.6/137, M74.4/130, FF70.6/121. Year Opened: 1997. Architect: Keith Foster. Expensive, jr./sr. credit cards. Call for reservations. Walk-on chances: Fair. Walkability: Quite good for such a huge layout. Playablity: Outstanding, all-bentgrass course features one of the best nine-hole sides in the Northwest.*

Previously called Remington Golf & Country Club and, later, Washington Golf Club, this facility looked like it might never come to fruition because of various legal and fiduciary entanglements. But in late March 1997, Brian Patton, owner of Willows Run in Redmond, stepped forward and purchased the place. The acquisition included a wonderful, all-bentgrass 18-hole course and a total of 350 acres. Housing was originally planned, but Patton has tabled that idea. The course was expected to open in July or August 1997 (after this book went to press), along with a driving range and a full-service, 20,000-square-foot clubhouse.

The venue began in the early 1990s as a cooperative venture between Bob and Lisa Soushek, Hiroshi Tanaka, and Quadrant, the residential-development arm of Weyerhaeuser. The course was partially built by 1993, but construction was halted because of a water moratorium (that was still in effect in early 1997) imposed by the Covington Water District. In the meantime, Tanaka's well-publicized financial woes led to a bankruptcy filing, thus reverting possession of the partially-completed course to the property's owners, Quadrant and Lakeside Industries. While Quadrant and Lakeside were trying to figure out what to do with the place, the Sousheks, owners of Fore, Inc., a respected golf course construction company, continued working on the layout.

In 1995, Scott Sasaki came along and bought the troubled project. The Bellevue resident had architect Keith Foster fine-tune the design, and Links Construction was brought in to finish the course. Sasaki converted the venue from a public facility into a private one, even selling a few memberships. In late 1996 and early 1997, however, the ownership situation became more muddled than ever as Sasaki decided to sell the place. The course's convoluted story will hopefully end with Patton, who's acquisition (under his company's name, Druids Glen L.L.C.) should herald a more predictable and upbeat future.

Patton obtained one helluva golf course, and I'm very pleased that golfers can now step foot on it. Featuring considerable length, tremendous variety, and bentgrass tees, greens and fairways, Druids Glen (a name taken from a Scottish links) is a terrific addition to the Puget Sound golf scene. Part of the reason for this assertion is that, because of all the delays and ownership changes, the turf grew free of foot traffic. Also,

Sasaki had replaced the original irrigation system with a state-of-the-art Toro unit (fed by 14 storage ponds because of the water moratorium), and over 300,000 yards of sand were placed under fairways to enhance drainage. When I played the course in October 1996 following several heavy storms, only a few puddles were found, a rare occurrence for such a new track.

The 228-acre layout winds through second-growth timber just south of the Remington subdivision, about a mile from Elk Run Golf Course. Foster designed the course to host major tournaments, reserving amphitheater-like spaces behind greens and routing fairways to facilitate the movement of spectators over fully-paved cart paths. Despite its considerable length and acreage, Druid's Glen is quite walkable, with only a few longer-than-normal hikes between holes. Great views of Mount Rainier are available from many junctures and, during my visit, elk tracks were found on some greens.

The tee boxes are cut in squares, a la those at Pumpkin Ridge. The course's signature characteristics are some spectacular par-3s; devilishly slick greens; and a back nine that's as magnificent as any set of holes in the region. Prevailing westerlies are also a factor. The 213-yard 3rd is representative of the great par-3s. A pond runs from the tee to a huge, front-banked green trapped twice at the right-front. Another front-nine dandy is the top-rated 4th, a 442-yard par-4. A pond left of the tee runs up the left side of the fairway, which is tree-lined on the right. After rising for most of its length, the hole descends over its final 125 yards to a front-sloping, high-backed green trapped right.

The stellar back nine starts with a 453-yard par-4 that, according to pre-Patton employees, cost nearly a million dollars to build because of several reconfigurations by the different owners. Drives at the 10th must carry the corner of a 14-acre pond, which curls up the right side of the landing area. Water is also out along the left, but shouldn't enter play unless one encounters "Mr. Snappy" off the tee. The water along the right bulges into the fairway at the 130-yard mark, and the 10th ends at a crowned, left-sloping green trapped right. The 11th is a nice but rugged 420-yard par-4 that heads into the prevailing wind over a moguled, bunker-lined route. The lovely 12th, a 182-yard par-3, sports a concrete block-walled, 125-foot-high tee and a V-shaped, trapped-right green fronted by a shimmering pond.

The 389-yard, par-4 13th is a beautiful hole with another pond-fronted tee, a narrow fairway, and a hill-cut green trapped twice in front. The 522-yard, par-5 14th has a fat wetlands in mid-fairway, allowing players the option of following a longer and safer route to the right, or a shorter but tighter path left en route to a tri-trapped, terraced green. The 474-yard length of the par-4 15th is exacerbated somewhat by a descending path, but this is still a very difficult hole. The 206-yard 16th is a gorgeous par-3 with a tee-to-green lake and a massive, two-tiered green surrounded by white-sand bunkers. The 17th is another nasty and long (468-yard) par-4, and the uptilting par-5 at the 18th is a worthy tournament-decider at 587 yards.

Echo Falls Country Club - semiprivate

18 *20414 121st Avenue SE, Snohomish, WA 98290. (360) 668-3030, 362-3000 (from Seattle) or 1-800-377-2420. Dave Shelton, pro. 18 holes. 6,104 yards. Par 70. Grass tees. Course ratings: men—B68.9/126, M67.1/123; women—B73.9/134, M71.8/130, FF68.5/120, F64.6/115. Year Opened: 1992. Architect: Jack Frei; Tom Johnson (remodel). Moderate, credit cards. Reservations: Call five days ahead. Walk-on chances: Fair. Walkability: Unfortunately, poor, with considerable distances between some holes and a few steep climbs. Playability: Suitable for all skills, with good "sticks" having their way on the par-5s.*

Located four miles northeast of Woodinville, this Snohomish County course is the centerpiece of an upper-end neighborhood off State Route 522. The course is owned by Scott Oki, backer of the new Golf Club at Newcastle near Bellevue. After he bought Echo Falls, Oki hired Mount Vernon architect Tom Johnson to redesign some holes and lengthen the course. Johnson's work has bumped the course's yardage to just over 6,000 yards. The original designer was Jack Frei, who also built it and co-developed the property.

The course and adjoining 79 homes occupy a tidy 203-acre plot. Many evergreens and deciduous trees were left intact to preserve fairway and residential buffers. BPA power lines border seven holes and periodically cross before tees. The facility is graced with a large, chalet-like clubhouse with banquet facilities, a pro shop and restaurant. Echo Falls' driving range sits across the street from the entrance to the course. The venue has hosted the Richard Karns Celebrity Golf Classic, a fund-raiser for the Fred Hutchinson Cancer Research Center.

Echo Falls' bowl-shaped site resulted in an odd sequencing of holes. Some of the uphill walks over asphalt cart paths are quite arduous. The par-70 layout contains six par-3s, and the greens are fairly straightforward. Ponds, trees, stumps, steep banks, feral rough, and sand and grass bunkers squeeze landing zones on the longer holes. The par-5s, which all wind downhill, are quite birdie-able by proficient players. And some of the shorter par-4s are driveable. Good tests include the 17th, a dandy par-4 that can play as long as 462 yards. The ribbonish, right-bending route follows the curvature of the lake behind the clubhouse before ending at a shallow and wide green guarded right-front by water. The home hole contains a pretty island-like, two-tiered green that sits 45 degrees from the tee. If one overclubs this 148-yard par-3, a back-left trap might prevent an unwanted ball-washing.

Elk Run Golf Course

18 *22500 SE 275th Place, Maple Valley, WA 98038. (425) 432-8800 or 1-800-244-8631. Steve Dubsky, pro. 18 holes. 5,724 yards. Par 71. Grass tees. Course ratings: men—B67.8/117, F65.5/112; women—B73.4/121, F70.6/114. Years Opened: 1989 (original nine); 1995 (second nine). Architects: Jack Frei (original nine); Pete Petersen & Roy Humphreys (second nine). Moderate, credit cards. Reservations: Call a week ahead. Walk-on chances: Fair. Walkability: Fair. Playability: Much improved from original incarnation.*

A former executive nine, Elk Run has blossomed into a full-scale golfing concern. Owned by Daryl Connell and Roy Humphreys, Elk Run has seen a new back nine opened and its original layout lengthened and thoroughly revamped. The work was done by Bob Soushek of Fore, Inc. A 12,000-square-foot clubhouse opened in 1996 with a sports bar, 160-seat banquet area and pro shop. Nice touches on the course include covered kiosk-like tee signs, paved cart paths and expansive multiple tees. The golf course occupies about 120 acres; it's engirded on several sides by homes. Veteran Northwest pro, Steve Dubsky, previously at Lake Spanaway in Tacoma, runs Elk Run's pro shop and lesson program.

The Jack Frei-designed original nine retained only three of its holes. Architect Pete Petersen and co-owner Humphreys fashioned the newer front side (called the East Nine), and remodeled the back. The East Nine circles a 60-acre gravel pit owned by King County; Elk Run's operators have a 35-year lease of the property. These holes are nicely layed out and easy to walk. For the most part, the West (back) Nine is efficiently arrayed, though there's a lengthy hike between the 16th and 17th holes. From higher-elevation holes, golfers have views of Mount Rainier.

Among the better holes on the East Nine is the 1st, a 486-yard par-5 with a pond-fronted tee. From here, the fairway heads straight for 280 yards before abruptly turning left. The hole goes downhill and then rises up to a ridge-perched, right-front-sloping green trapped twice in front. The top-rated 7th, a 496-yard par-5, runs downhill off the tee toward a wide, tree-lined landing area. At the 150-yard mark, the hole ascends very steeply to a large, left-leaning green trapped laterally. The 9th, a 364-yard par-4, descends gradually to the 175-yard mark. At this juncture, the fairway drops precipitously down to a V-shaped green with a ponds left and rear, and four bunkers around it. This is a pretty but treacherous hole.

The 11th, a 456-yard par-5, has a pond off the tee with another water hazard farther out along the left; OB and homes line the hole along the right. The left-sloping fairway curls narrowly rightward to a deep green with a trap left-front and a pond in back. The narrowish 14th, a 485-yard par-5, traverses up-angled ground along a right-bending route. A bunker along the left sits driving distance out. At the 150-yard post, the fairway winds up to the right to a deep green trapped thrice in front and once right. The 332-yard 16th is a nice two-shotter with a pond off the tee. The hole heads rightward between a tree and bunker right and a trap left. Three trees tower over the right edge of a deep and snaky green trapped front-left and right.

Flowing Lake Golf Course

18

5001 Weber Road, Snohomish, WA 98290. (360) 568-2753. 18 holes. 4,265 yards. Par 66. Grass tees. No course ratings. Year Opened: 1995. Architect: Gary Laz. Moderate. Call for reservations. Walk-on chances: Good. Walkability: Short course easy to walk except for "Heart Attack Hill." Playability: Though abbreviated, trouble can be readily found.

Family-run Flowing Lake lies next to Wonderland Park in the Three Lakes section of Snohomish County; the area is named after the Flowing, Storm and Panther lakes. Besides an entertaining par-66 course, the 77-acre venue contains a small clubhouse/pro shop and a deli serving sandwiches and espresso. "Jake's" deli was named after "Crazy Jake," a previous owner of the property. Jake was a hermit who logged the area and used mules to haul timber to nearby Flowing Lake, which once was the site of a lumber mill. Immediately prior to being converted into a golf course, the land was a Christmas tree farm. The Laz family has owned the property since 1947.

Members of the Laz family transformed the bowl-shaped site into a golfing concern. The clan includes patriarch Bob Laz, his sons Gary and Stan (who built the course and are now the co-superintendents), ex-daughter-in-law Debbie Laz, Gary's daughter Kara Laz, Bob's grandson Steve Christian, and Bob's grand-daughter-in-law Stephanie Christian. Despite this being their first foray into designing, building, maintaining and operating a golf course, the Lazes have done well. Most players have lauded the condition of the course, with women particularly smitten with the layout. Besides a tight and challenging track, golfers enjoy views of the North Cascades and glimpses of deer, ducks, geese, eagles and hawks.

The course involves a few bunkers—with more planned—and nine ponds on 12 holes. Flowing Lake is known for its small and fast, steep-sided bentgrass greens. An average round should take just over three hours to play. The top-rated hole is the 2nd, a straight-running 360-yard par-4 with a hidden pond driving distance out. The diminutive and slick 2nd green is dome-shaped. The 3rd, a 253-yard par-4, heads straight uphill to a tiny, right-sloping green. Though a par-3 of but 134 yards, the 12th is rated Flowing Lake's second-toughest hole. The 12th ascends steeply up "Heart Attack Hill" to a knoll-perched, tree-backed green guarded left-rear by a pond. Another tough test is the 13th, a 259-yard par-4 with an unseen pond in the tee-shot landing area. A tall fir towers over the left-front edge of the 13th's tidy putting surface.

Foster Golf Links

18

13500 Interurban Avenue South, Tukwila, WA 98168. (206) 242-4221. Marty O'Brien, pro. 18 holes. 4,930 yards. Par 68. Grass tees & mats. Course ratings: men—M62.3/94, Mats 60.9/91; women—M66.6/101, F65.1/98, Mats 64.9/98. Year Opened: 1924. Architect: George Eddy. Moderate, jr./sr. rates, credit cards. Reservations: Call a week ahead. Walk-on chances: Ok for singles. Walkability: Very good. Playability: Great starter's course.

Foster is a popular course near the Tukwila exit off Interstate 5. The amount of play (about 80,000 rounds annually) matches the activity on the course's periphery, which is a mixed residential-industrial zone involving trains, trucks, car traffic along Interurban Avenue and I-5, and airplanes landing at and departing Sea-Tac Airport. When built in 1925 by George Eddy, the course was in a rural part of King County. Eddy and his son Bob ran the layout until 1951, when Joe Aliment bought it. The Aliment family eventually sold Foster Golf Links to the city of Tukwila in 1977.

Foster was upgraded in the late-1980s with a $1.5-million makeover, which included a $440,000 footbridge over the Duwamish Slough. The project came about as Metro, King County's water and transportation department, layed sewage pipes through the back nine. Metro funded Foster's reconstruction. The city of Tukwila has plans to renovate the front nine.

Easy-to-walk Foster is ideal for seniors and beginning golfers. Green River borders the course and the Duwamish enters play on two holes. Foster's fairways are peppered with depressions and slight mounds, but the course is not at all hilly. Good holes include the 12th, a 336-yard par-4 bordered along the right by the slough. It concludes at a large front-tilting green trapped on the right. Trees front the green at the 15th, a meager 248-yard par-4. Though driveable with a faded tee shot, the rear-sloping 15th green is lined in front by two traps.

Gleneagle Golf Course

7619 Country Club Drive, Arlington, WA 98223. (360) 435-6713. Bob Garza, pro. 18 holes. 5,977 yards Par 70. Grass tees. Course ratings: men—B69.8/129, M67.0/ 123; women—B75.2/136, M71.8/129, 68.1/122. Years Opened: 1993 (original nine); 1995 (second nine). Architect: Bill Teufel. Moderate. Reservations: Call a week ahead. Walk-on chances: Fair. Walkability: Below-par, with several long hikes between holes. Playability: Consider keeping the driver in the trunk as tight fairways severely penalize the wayward.

Gleneagle's course winds through a housing community along a forested hill east of Arlington. The layout has been completely revamped from its days when it was called the Woodlands, a short nine burdened by a financially-checkered history. Gleneagle's course and surrounding residences have been on the up and up since Woodland Ridge Joint Venture acquired the 455-acre site in 1989. New homes are steadily being built, and an upscale clubhouse opened in 1994, the year American Golf (AGC) also took over its operations. (For an annual fee of $229, AGC offers participants discounts on green fees, power carts, equipment and apparel at this course as well as Capitol City Golf Club in Olympia and Lake Wilderness in Maple Valley.) Just a few of the original holes were retained (and improved), with the current layout, designed by Seattle's Bill Teufel, leading one to believe Gleneagle has finally extricated itself from the woods.

After playing the course in June 1995, I found it tight and tough to walk, with lengthy distances between holes. Golfers will be challenged by Gleneagle's winding, tree-lined fairways and dense peripheral rough. These latter features will probably be ameliorated as trees and scrub are removed for new residences. The long distances between greens and tees stem from the platting of lots, which will total over 1,000 at full build-out.

The layout is a needed addition to the Puget Sound public golf scene. Its rates are mid-priced, and the facility isn't too far to drive for Seattleites. The site contains up-and-down terrain, and power lines run through the property. Some of the tougher tests include the 2nd, a 489-yard par-5. This narrow, fir-paneled hole has a pond along the left driving distance out. A creek crosses the fairway 180 yards from a trapped-right green, which is guarded right-front by trees—redundant impediments to my thinking. A precise drive is needed at the barranca-fronted tee of the 6th, a 389-yard par-4. The dogleg-right has bunkers pinching the fairway at the turn, where it descends to a deep green trapped left, right-front and right-rear.

A gritty back-nine hole is the 10th, a 363-yard par-4 with trees squeezing the tee ball garden spot. The last leg of the fairway rises to a bi-bunkered green. The 471-yard par-5 14th features an elevated tee and a steeply left-sloping fairway. A pond lurks left of the tee. The fairway gradually tapers before reaching a small, trapped-right green guarded left-front by another water hazard. The 18th is a 367-yard par-4 that winds sharply left between conifers. Two traps squat outside the turn, and the hole concludes at a ridge-perched green that leans steeply toward two traps in front.

Golden Bear Family Golf Center at Interbay

9

2501 15th Avenue West, Seattle, WA 98119. Call (206)Information for phone number. 9 holes. 1,420 yards. Par 28. Grass & mat tees. No course ratings. Year Opened: 1998. Architect: Jack Nicklaus Design. Economical, jr./sr. rates. Call for reservations. Walk-on chances: Fair. Walkability: Good. Playability: Suitable for all skills.

Work finally began on this remake of the old par-3 Interbay Golf Course in early 1997. That rundown facility was shut down in 1992; five years, that's how long it took Seattle officials to figure out what to do with the place. Perhaps the wait was worth it as Family Golf Centers, a successful operator with courses and driving ranges around the nation, will see the $5.3-million project come to fruition. Family Golf inked a 25-year lease, with a five-year option, with the city to develop the course and adjoining amenities. Interbay's near-downtown site off 15th Avenue West was quite attractive to a number of national golf-development firms. Family Golf, in conjunction with Golden Bear International, was selected because of its track record, financial strength and name recognition.

Besides receiving an upscale name, the 42-acre Interbay facility features a double-decker, 80-tee driving range with heated and lighted stalls; a par-28 executive track; a 7,000-square-foot clubhouse with a pro shop, restaurant and two Jack Nicklaus/Jim Flick Instruction studios; a 210-car parking lot; and an 18-hole "Garden Golf Course" equipped with synthetic turf, landscaped peripheries, recycling ponds and waterfalls. The driving range was scheduled to open in July 1997, and the course in March 1998 (after this book went to press).

The Golf Club at Newcastle

36

15401 SE Newcastle-Coal Creek Parkway, Newcastle, WA 98059. (425) 455-0606. 36 holes. Coal Creek 18: 7,003 yards, par 72; China Creek 18: 6,946 yards, par 72. Course ratings not available. Years Opened: 1997 (Coal Creek); 1998 (China Creek). Architect: Robert Cupp. Expensive, credit cards. Reservations: Call a week ahead. Walk-on chances: Fair. Walkability: Fair, with some steep between-hole hikes. Playability: With tremendous views, a close-in location and a designer like Cupp, these two 18s will rival the best in the Northwest.

Though neither of these 18-hole courses were open when this book went to press, there is no reason to believe that the first 18 (Coal Creek) won't be on schedule for its opening in 1997. Work on the second course, China Creek, is scheduled to commence once Coal Creek is ready for play, and it should be finished in 1998. Though I've been burned when including planned courses in previous issues of this book (Interbay, Monument Hill in Ephrata, and Taylor Creek never opened during the life of the second edition), The Golf Club at Newcastle looks like a sure thing. So I'll dare include it here.

Helping to assure this new venue's inclusion is the well-heeled backer of the project, Scott Oki of Oki Developments, Inc. Oki, a former Microsoft executive and current owner of Echo Falls Country Club in Woodinville, endured the permit process to get approval for the project. Coal Creek's site preparation began in late-summer 1996, with seeding to start in spring '97. Originally slated to contain a private and a public 18, Oki altered those plans in May 1996, deciding on an upscale public venue with green fees around $70. Just before the book went to press, a membership plan was being implemented. The two-tiered program involves a $5,000 annual fee for unlimited golf and priority tee times. The second plan entails a $5,000 one-time fee ($10,000 for a family), with $125 monthly "dues" for a couple of rounds a month and priority tee times.

The 350-acre site, a former coal mine and landfill that was built up from material dredged during the construction of Interstate 90 and Highway 520, is truly special, offering spectacular views of the Cascades, the skyscrapers in Seattle and Bellevue, and Lake Washington. Nearly two million yards of dirt were moved and sculpted for the two courses, which were built by Golf Works of Austin, Texas. Robert Cupp, the designer of such noteworthy Northwest courses as Pumpkin Ridge, Crosswater at Sunriver, and the new Reserve Vineyards near Portland, says that the site has coal seams running through it. The coal seams were filled with rebar and concrete from the construction material, but no sinkholes were found prior to construction. Additionally, no methane was sensed on the 70-acre landfill.

Cupp, who was assisted on the strategic aspects of the design by Seattle's PGA Tour star, Fred Couples, says that the courses involve some elevation changes. He doesn't classify the layouts as links-like, though they will be essentially treeless. Trees are located near wetlands areas along the base of the hilly site, and 15-foot-high ornamentals will be planted. The course will feature ryegrass tees, bentgrass-fescue fairways, bent greens, and fescue roughs. It's possible that a soft-spike policy will be implemented—a la Pumpkin Ridge—during the Puget Sound's primary golf season to preserve the bentgrass greens.

Once the first course is up and running, work on a 37,000-square-foot clubhouse, designed by Bill Foley of Atlanta, will commence. The massive structure will contain a 400-seat banquet space, brew pub, restaurant, conference center and teaching area. A huge grass-teed driving range will be open when Coal Creek debuts. With Newcastle's panoramas, Cupp considers the site more dramatic than Pumpkin Ridge. He also says that Oki is committed to building something "really nice," and that it will be "first-class," good news for local linksters and visitors to the area. Despite some slopes to the courses, Cupp says Newcastle will be walkable, with no more than 20 feet between greens and tees. I've visited the site, and it's enchanting to envision the golf courses here. Oki certainly has the right guy in Bob Cupp to make his dreams come true. Sorry I can't provide more specifics about the courses. You'll just have to check this place out yourself.

Harbour Pointe Golf Club

11817 Harbour Pointe Boulevard, Everett, WA 98204. (425) 355-6060 or 1-800-233-3128. Mark Rhodes, pro. 18 holes. 6,812 yards. Par 72. Grass tees. Course ratings: men—C72.8/135, B71.6/130, M69.7/122; women—FF70.9/125, F68.8/117. Years Opened: 1989 (original nine), 1990 (second nine). Architect: Arthur Hills. Expensive, credit cards. Reservations: Call five days ahead. Walk-on chances: Ok for singles. Walkability: So-so, with hilly terrain and several long, uncomfortable stretches between holes. Playability: Tough for all concerned.

The golf course here is part of the 2,000-acre Harbour Pointe community, a sprawling development with hundreds of homes as well as business and technology parks, a boat marina, restaurants, retail shops, schools and churches. The project's ongoing development has definitely had an impact on this course. The original nine, once blissfully segregated from streets, sidewalks and rooftops, thanks to a forested buffer, has gradually seen its fairway peripheries converted into siding and rooftops. Besides altering the aesthetics of the layout, which sits on a view-encompassing promontory above Puget Sound, the residential work changed drainage patterns. When I visited Harbour Pointe in spring 1995, the removal of trees for houses had caused small mudslides over cart paths and scarred some back-nine fairways. A later visit in fall 1996—during much drier weather—found the problem not nearly as acute. On the plus side, cutting the trees has allowed more sunlight to reach the greens and opened up westward views of the Sound.

Arthur Hills-designed Harbour Pointe reaped several awards, including *Golf Digest's* "Best New Public Golf Course," upon its completion in 1991. The course received three stars in the magazine's 1996-'97 "Places to Play" supplement. The facility is owned by Golf Northwest, headed by Jack Sikma, Terry Otey and head pro Mark Rhodes. The 180-acre layout features two distinctly different nines. The mostly-flat front winds around 28 acres of wetlands, with lakes entering play on every hole. The back side, despite the gradual eradication of trees and insertion of houses, still has a woodsy feel.

Harbour Pointe features several sets of tees and slick bentgrass greens. Among its noteworthy holes is the "S-shaped" 4th, a 517-yard par-5 that initially winds to the left around a pond. Once past this juncture, the hole goes straight for 200 yards or so before bearing rightward to a large, trapped-right green. Another good par-5, and perhaps the course's toughest, is the 6th, a 514-yarder. Water crosses the right-turning fairway midway to an undulating, trapped-right green. Indicative of Harbour Pointe's residential intrusion is the 445-yard 9th hole, a dogleg-left par-4 that winds sharply around a net-protected apartment building. Maybe the nastiest hole on the back is the 17th, a sidehill, uphill 423-yard par-4 whose left-bending route is lined by trees right and houses left. Its slick, knoll-perched green is bunkered on the left.

Jackson Park Municipal Public Golf Course

27 *1000 NE 135th, Seattle, WA 98125. (206) 363-4747; 301-0472 (tee times). Mark Granberg, pros. 18 holes. 6,227 yards. Par 71. Par-3 Nine: 995 yards, par 27. Grass tees & mats. Course ratings: men—B68.6/113, M67.4/111, FF66.3/107; women—M73.2/120, F71.8/118. Year Opened: 1930. Architects: William H. Tucker & Francis L. James. Moderate, jr./sr. rates, credit cards. Reservations: Call a week ahead. Walk-on chances: Ok for singles. Walkability: Fine. Playability: Good for all talents; beginners can go to short course while others play this one.*

For years, this popular facility was run by concessionaires who leased the course from the city of Seattle. But in 1995, its operations were turned over to Municipal Golf of Seattle, a non-profit corporation. The primary purpose of MGS, which also runs the muni tracks at Jefferson Park and West Seattle, is to reinvest the profits generated by the courses into capital improvements. This means long-awaited and much-needed projects such as new irrigation systems, clubhouse upgrades, a driving range, cart paths, new tees and greens, refurbished bunkers, hole reroutings and landscaping enhancements. Unfortunately, these renovations have been slow in coming, preventing Jackson Park—as well as the other courses—from making a quantum step forward in playability.

Certainly, of all the city's courses, Jackson Park could use the thickest coat of fresh paint. The layout, designed by William H. Tucker and Francis L. James, is fine.

Indeed, Tucker and James arrayed an interesting coterie of golf holes over the 160-acre site, whose varied topography offers a full range of golf shots. Thornton Creek runs through the property, entering play on a few holes. It's just that the turf, trampled by upwards of 124,000 rounds a year (including play on the adjacent par-3 nine), needs a serious renovation. Some important work has already been done, including several new tees of contemporary dimension and scope. Western redwood cedars were planted along the 3rd hole to protect cars along 5th Avenue NE, which parallels the west edge of the course. But major capital improvements have been too slow in coming.

It'll be interesting to see how Jackson Park phases in the work—whenever it begins, since the course is so popular. Currently, its better holes include the 594-yard, par-5 12th, which starts at an elevated tee. The fairway crosses 175 yards of flat ground, then drops down a tree-lined chute past OB along the right and dense forestry left. Second shots at the 12th often come from a downhill lie, but longer-hitting players might reach a front-sloping, two-tiered green with a well-hit fairway wood. Another tester is the 17th, a 381-yard par-4 with a severely left-sloping fairway that rises between trees. Approaches to the hill-cut 17th green must be precise as the target has a very steep left-side bank and jail along the right.

Jefferson Park Municipal Golf Course   27

4101 Beacon Avenue South, Seattle, WA 98108. (206) 762-4513; 301-0472 (tee times). Pete Guzzo, pro. 18 holes. 6,122 yards. Par 70. Short Nine: 1,225 yards, par 28. Grass tees & mats. Course ratings: men—B68.3/112, M67.0/110, FF64.9/ 104; women F70.2/116. Year Opened: 1915. Architect: Thomas Bendelow. Moderate, jr./sr. rates, credit cards. Reservations: Call a week ahead. Walk-on chances: Ok for singles. Walkability: Very good. Playability: Good for all players; beginners may use short nine.

Jefferson Park is the Northwest's oldest municipal golf course. Named after Thomas Jefferson, the 128-acre facility was designed by "Old" Thomas Bendelow, a Scottish architect who crafted over 300 golf courses in 41 states and four Canadian provinces during the early part of the 20th Century. Perhaps his most famous design is the Number 1 Course at Medina Country Club in Illinois. Jefferson Park may well be Bendelow's most popular course; the facility averages over 110,000 rounds a year on its regulation 18 and short nine.

As with Jackson Park and West Seattle, Jefferson Park is operated by Municipal Golf of Seattle, a non-profit entity. And like its sister courses, Jefferson Park will hopefully benefit from capital improvements in the years ahead. Primary needs here are a new irrigation system and a general overhaul of the layout. Lying southeast of downtown Seattle, the course is within a well-established Beacon Hill neighborhood. For years, it has served as a sporting and social center for local golfers. Since 1947, Jefferson Park has been the home base of Fir State Golf Club, a predominantly African American club that has contributed greatly to Seattle's junior golfers, among them Landon Jackson, now a pro at Pebble Beach Golf Club, and Andia Winslow, a teenager with a bright future. Tiger Woods gave an exhibition to benefit Fir State in 1992. (See John Peoples' article on Fir State in this book.) In 1994, a phenom who learned the vagaries of golf at Jefferson Park, Fred Couples, staged a clinic while in town to host his own annual tournament.

Jefferson Park's traditional layout occupies 128 acres of varied topography. The front nine is fairly flat, with the back side encompassing more slopes. On many holes, huge evergreens and magnolias loom in target zones. Pot-type bunkers—with upwardly-angled edges—guard the entries and sides of many greens. One of the course's top holes is the tree-lined 7th, a 440-yard par-4 that slopes slightly right toward homes and OB. Three firs sit at the inside corner of this dogleg-left, which concludes at a rolling green. The east-facing view of Lake Washington from the 7th hole is excellent. The "garden spot" for tee shots at the 415-yard, par-4 14th is the flat portion of the fairway. From here, the hole winds leftward and downhill to a trapped-right green.

Kayak Point Golf Course

18 *15711 Marine Drive, Stanwood, WA 98292. (360) 652-9676 or 1-800-562-3094. Elwin Fanning, director of golf; Wellington Lee, pro. 18 holes. 6,648 yards. Par 72. Grass tees. Course ratings: men—B72.7/133, M71.4/128; women F72.8/129. Year Opened: 1977. Architect: Ron Fream. Moderate, jr./sr. rates, credit cards. Reservations: Call a week ahead. Walk-on chances: Ok for singles. Walkability: Okay, but you may want to cart it and save strength for making good golf shots. Playability: A stiff test for all concerned.*

Owned by Snohomish County's Parks and Recreation Department and leased to its director of golf, Elwin Fanning, this 227-acre reserve is one of the Northwest's premier public courses. In its 1996-'97 "Places to Play" supplement, *Golf Digest* gave Kayak Point exalted four-star status. The Ron Fream-designed layout was originally intended to be part of a housing development built by the Atlantic Richfield Corporation. But the subdivision, which was to adjoin a proposed oil facility on Puget Sound, never got off the ground. Thankfully, the course was completed, and it's remained a stalwart in the local golf scene ever since. Over the years, a few homes have been built on Kayak Point's peripheries, but not nearly to the extent ARCO had wanted.

Kayak Point is very popular with the area's good "sticks." On average, the facility hosts 60,000 rounds a year. Thanks to the course's success during his years at the helm, Fanning pretty much has carte blanche to make improvements. Recent upgrades include a 13,000-square-foot clubhouse with a restaurant and lounge. An 18-hole putting course was scheduled to be built in spring 1997 (after this book went to press), a time when J.D. Cline and Jim McLean were also slated to open a golf school. Future plans include a short practice nine routed around the driving range. From some of the higher points on the course, westward views of Puget Sound are available. Other endemic traits include regular visits from beavers, eagles, hawks, deer and squirrels.

With its heavily wooded and hilly terrain, Kayak Point provides an acid test for all golfers. Weather plays a part, as winds off the Sound can skew shots hit above the timber line. Among its best holes is the 2nd, a 549-yard par-5 that winds to the right off a pond-fronted tee. The tree-squeezed fairway eventually reaches a wavy, bi-trapped green. The home hole is an uphill, 418-yard par-4 that requires a 250-yard drive from the back tees to cross a well-jailed ravine. Shot-blocking firs line the right side of the fairway on the other side of this crevice, while a forested hill lurks left. At this juncture, the fairway curls uphill leftward to a sinuous green guarded by two bunkers rear and a trap left-front.

Kenwanda Golf Course

14030 Kenwanda Drive, Snohomish, WA 98290. (360) 668-1166. Curtis Creighton, pro. 18 holes. 5,336 yards. Par 69. Grass tees. Course ratings: men 65.3/119, women 70.4/126. Year Opened: 1963 (original nine), 1967 (second nine). Architect: Ken Harris. Moderate, credit cards. Reservations: Call a week ahead. Walk-on chances: Fair. Walkability: Good. Playability: Enjoyable track offers wonderful valley vistas.

Kenwanda Golf Course lies off Highway 9 about four miles south of Snohomish. From its perch atop Springetti Hill, the layout offers great views of the lush Snohomish Valley below, Mount Baker to the north, Mount Rainier south, and Snohomish River east. The name "Kenwanda" is derived from the first names of owner Ken Harris and his late wife, Wanda. The facility occupies an old farm; a few fruit trees and the original ranch house remain on the site.

Virgin firs and second-growth trees define fairways and enter play with regularity. Wildlife—which dwells along the Snohomish River and migrates up the hill—includes coyotes and deer. Other than improved conditioning, the course has remained virtually unchanged over its three decades.

Among Kenwanda's better holes is the 6th, a 141-yard par-3 that runs uphill to an elevated and narrow green that, from below, looks like the prow of a battleship—about six yards wide with steep sides: a penalizing configuration. The 15th, a 342-yard par-4, has a left-sloping fairway and a narrow green with a sloping rear end. The 16th, a 157-yard par-3, has a green in a hollow near the northern crest of Springetti. A "target"—a metal sign with concentric black circles on a white background—is mounted in trees behind the green to indicate the recommended direction of tee shots. Similar targets appear throughout the course to help golfers locate hill-obscured greens.

Lake Wilderness Golf Club

25400 Witte Road SE, Maple Valley, WA 98038. (425) 432-9405. Russell Lee, pro. 18 holes. 5,218 yards. Par 70. Grass tees. Course ratings: men—B66.1/118, M64.7/116, F63.2/113; women—M68.7/121, F66.6/117. Years Opened: 1931 (original nine), 1973 (second nine). Architects: Founding members (original nine); Ray Coleman & Jack Reimer (second nine); Pete Petersen (remodel). Moderate, jr./sr. rates, credit cards. Reservations: Call a week ahead. Walk-on chances: Fair. Walkability: Fair, with some long walks over asphalt roads. Playability: Good for beginning and intermediate golfers, though all players must beware of fairway-side homes.

Lake Wilderness has evolved—for better or worse—quite a bit over the years. The member-designed track played as a 2,700-yard, par-33 layout in its early years. In 1947, Ray Coleman bought the course and proceeded to lengthen the holes, add a new nine, and build a clubhouse during his tenure. When the renovated 18-hole course opened with a new clubhouse in 1973, Coleman retitled it Wilderness Ridge, a name suggested by his son, Ron. Ray Coleman built 11 courses in western Washington, including such fine venues as Dungeness, Twin Lakes, Fairwood and Tam O'Shanter.

In 1977, Coleman sold Wilderness Ridge to a Bellevue firm, Kinkman & McClure, who ran it until 1989, when it was sold to J.J. Welcome Construction Company of Redmond. After reverting to the course's original name, Welcome reduced Lake Wilderness to nine holes to plat 280 lots on and around the course. In 1990, the course changed hands again. A Japanese firm, Itoman Corporation, bought it and turned operations over to one its subsidiaries, SVGC (Silicon Valley Golf Course Corporation) of California. SVGC restored Lake Wilderness to an 18-hole course built on 106 acres, using a design by R.D. "Pete" Petersen. In 1994, the golf-operations giant, American Golf Corporation (AGC), acquired Lake Wilderness as part of a deal involving another Itoman course in California.

Because the homes are so close, the course has gone from a discreet track to one fully engaged with civilization. The houses have a decided effect on play, with the layout's corridor-like holes winding between backyards, cul-de-sacs, patios and garages. As a result of the close proximity of residences to flying golf balls, there are more protective nets on this course than any other in the region. On the plus side, a full-service restaurant recently opened in the clubhouse. And, for an annual fee of $229, AGC offers participants discounts on green fees, power carts, equipment and apparel at this course as well as Capitol City Golf Club in Olympia and Gleneagle in Arlington.

A hole representative of the closeness of houses is the 14th, a 307-yard par-4 that is literally a dogleg-left around a three-bedroom, ranch-style dwelling guarded by a net (the house, not the hole). Another example is found at the 18th, which has a large net along its entire length to keep golf balls from smacking cars traveling along Witte Road. To help identify the field of play, Lake Wilderness has OB markers everywhere, even within its interior. As far as golf hazards, the layout has an abundance of sand traps and strategically-placed firs. Golfers will also encounter a few water hazards, with wetlands around the 16th, 17th and 18th holes making these holes the prettiest and most engaging on the course.

Legion Memorial Golf Course

18

144 West Marine View Drive, Everett, WA 98201. (425) 259-4653. Bob Whisman, pro. 18 holes. 6,434 yards. Par 72. Grass tees & mats. Course ratings (original course): men—B69.4/113, M68.6/111; women F71.5/113. Year Opened: 1934 (original nine); 1942 (second nine). Architect: H. Chandler Egan; John Steidel & Steve Burns Golf Design (remodels). Moderate, credit cards. Reservations: Call Mondays for next seven days. Walk-on chances: Ok for singles. Walkability: Very good. Playability: Significant upgrades herald a bright future for popular muni.

Legion Memorial sits atop a hill alongside the Snohomish River at Everett's north end. The venue is named after the American Legion, which owned the course until 1940, at which time the association deeded the facility to the city. The course is operated by concessionaire and head pro, Bob Whisman. Whisman's son, Greg, is one of the Nike Tour's top players. The course hosts about 70,000 rounds annually, and was designed by H. Chandler Egan, a Northwest golf pioneer. Egan, who witnessed the opening of the original nine, died before the second side opened in 1942. In 1969 when the clubhouse was moved to its present site, the course was re-layed out. John Steidel designed a couple of new holes in the late-1980s.

In 1996, the city of Everett got serious about improving this 125-acre layout. The $3.1-million project, overseen by Steve Burns of Burns Golf Design in Florida, involves new fairways, three new lakes and several bunkers, an upgraded irrigation system, massive fairway sanding and drainage work, an enlarged parking lot, and other changes. Legion Memorial closed on May 1, 1997 (after this book went to press), with the year-long work beginning immediately. The remodel was spurred by concerns for safety along peripheral areas and to upgrade drainage and year-round playing conditions.

With all these changes afoot, there's no need to go into detail about the toughest and most interesting holes at Legion Memorial which, with all the work, will be lengthened about 400 yards from the back tees. But there'll be plenty to discuss in the next edition of this book.

Lynnwood Municipal Golf Course

18

20200 68th Avenue West, Lynnwood, WA 98036. (425) 672-4653. Dan Smith, pro. 18 holes. 4,741 yards. Par 65. Grass tees. Course ratings: men—B62.4/101, F60.6/ 97; women—B66.3/101, F62.7/96. Year Opened: 1990. Architect: John Steidel. Moderate, jr./sr. rates. Reservations: Call a week ahead for weekdays and five days ahead for weekends. Walk-on chances: Ok for singles. Walkability: Excellent. Playability: Ideal for beginners and mid-handicappers, and surprisingly fun for good "sticks."

Owned by the Lynnwood Parks Department, Lynnwood Muni is an abbreviated but fun layout situated behind Edmonds Community College. The 70-acre venue lies in a wooded area once used by local hikers and joggers. The pro shop—with a snack bar above it—is on the ground floor of the college's student union building. John Steidel designed the executive-length layout. Though imperiled with over 30 bunkers and five ponds, the course is suitable for all handicappers. Its brevity and nine-minutes-apart starting times enable 18-hole rounds to be completed in just over three hours. The course contains seven par-3s and 11 par-4s, with the par-3s—ranging in length from 115 to 215 yards—featuring small, well-bunkered greens. The par-4s, extending 280 to 379 yards, wind between trees and assorted hazards.

An interesting hole is the 3rd, a 280-yard par-4. A pond sits about 200 yards out, so a lay-up tee shot is suggested. The narrow route leads to a front-sloping, tree-ringed green guarded by three bunkers. The 5th, 6th and 7th—each 350- to 370-yard par-4s—is Lynnwood's toughest stretch. The 5th, perhaps the most difficult driving hole on the course, has an ascending, timber-paneled fairway that ends at a two-tiered, trapped-left-front green. The 370-yard 6th is a mirror-image of the 5th, though it heads slightly downhill. A pond right of the fairway is reachable by errant drives, and its good-sized, trapped-left-front putting surface bears some ticklish undulations. The 350-yard 7th harbors a pond-fronted tee and an uphill fairway that heads toward a wide-but-shallow, bi-bunkered green.

A good back-nine hole is the 10th, a 295-yard par-4 whose fairway is squeezed by ponds along both sides. The tiny 10th green is ringed by three traps. The 13th, a 378-yard par-4, bears a hidden pond driving distance out. A tree in the fairway's right half causes golfers to aim left, toward the pond. The raised 13th green is trapped on the right. Another good test for the driver is the 14th, a 379-yard par-4 lined by trees, OB and a hiking path along the left, and dense trees right. The fairway rises to a narrowly-entered and large, trapped-left green with a steep back side.

Maplewood Golf Course

18 *4000 Maple Valley Highway, Renton, WA 98055. (425) 277-4444. Gordy Graybeal, pro. 18 holes. 5,675 yards. Par 72. Grass tees (mats in winter). Course ratings: men—B67.4/112, M66.1/110; women—B72.2/122, M70.7/118, F68.7/114. Year Opened: 1927. Architect: Al Smith; John Steidel (remodel). Moderate, sr. rates. Reservations: Call a week ahead. Walk-on chances: Ok for singles. Walkability: Good. Playability: Course gaining credibility and challenge with renovations.*

Maplewood stretches across treed meadows and a foothill beside the Cedar River. Earlier this century, there were 27 holes here—Maplewood's 18 and the nine at the now-defunct Cedar River Golf Course. After World War II, the government constructed houses for returning military personnel and their families on Cedar River's course. Maplewood was originally owned by Byrd Farrell. Bob Aliment bought the course from Farrell; then the city of Renton acquired it. The popular municipal course receives over 80,000 rounds a year.

Maplewood has benefited from a $5-million makeover. A two-tiered, 30-tee driving range and 15,000-square-foot clubhouse—with the RiverRock Grill & Ale House restaurant, pro shop and 450-seat banquet room—opened in 1995. The location of the new clubhouse means that golfers no longer drive through the middle of the course to get to the pro shop, as they did with the old set-up. Also, Kennewick architect John Steidel designed several new holes. Three of these opened in 1995, and two more were thrown into the mix the following year. Further modifications are planned, including the replacement of ancient maples damaged by storms and the construction work. The upshot of all this work is that Maplewood has gone from an 5,400-yard hard-hat zone to a longer track with better-spaced holes and safer playing conditions.

Among the more interesting holes here (note that the nines may be reversed in 1997) is the 3rd, a 378-yard par-4 with an elevated tee and a fairway that curls leftward around the Cedar. The hole was considerably wider before February 1996, when the flooding river washed out 150 feet of riverbank and shrunk the fairway. Over its last 75 yards, the 3rd winds to a small left-sloping green trapped at the rear. The 5th, a 493-yard par-5, doglegs left around two big bunkers. Two traps appear along the right 75 yards from a small green trapped twice on the left. The 7th, a 561-yard par-5, runs straight into the valley's prevailing winds. A bunker and OB lurk on the fairway's left, and a pond appears at the 150-yard mark along the right. The water hazard runs up to the right-front edge of a trapped left, mid-sized green.

Good tests on the reconditioned back nine include the 10th, a straight-running 396-yard par-4 lined on the left by trees and Maple Valley Highway. The small 10th green is trapped left. The 15th, a 466-yard par-5, features a raised tee and a narrow fairway bordered on the left by trees. Over its last 150 yards, the hole narrows and curls leftward to a tree-ringed green guarded in front by a fir and bunker. The new 17th, a 200-yard par-3, runs uphill to a big front-sloping green with two tiers and a bunker left. A creek and power lines cross the hole.

Monroe Golf Course

22110 Old Owens Road, Monroe, WA 98272. (360) 794-8498. 9 holes. 2,451 yards. Par 33. Grass & mat tees. Course ratings: men 61.8/92, women 66.4/100. Year Opened: 1928. Architect: Leonard Shrag. Moderate, jr. rates. Call for reservations. Walk-on chances: Fair. Walkability: Good. Playability: Possible remodel may significantly change original course.

This layout north of Monroe is the second-oldest in Snohomish County (private Everett Golf & Country Club is the granddaddy). In 1995, the 57-acre venue was acquired by Mona Lisa Partnership of Mill Creek for $3.2 million. Company principals Ragnar Pettersson and Terry Martin plan significant changes, including the addition of 104 housing units. The homes will be built near the current 9th tee and in forests east of the first hole. Some holes will be shortened but, according to manager Tom Johnson, the course will retain its original mix of par-3s and par-4s. Holes 4-9 will be upgraded with new bunkers and a large pond. Length will remain around 2,000 yards, with par at 32 or 33. In early 1997, Pettersson and Martin still hadn't received permits for the project.

All this upheaval will greatly change Monroe, a classic old-style course with tree-tunneling fairways and small, slippery greens. It's uncertain what Mona Lisa Partnership has in mind for the old clubhouse, a former farm house with a massive stone fireplace. The previous owners—Jim and Penny Hager and Leonard and Sylvia Axtman—served up hearty breakfasts, pies and a low-key ambiance. When the previous owners sold the course, a group of local golfers who called themselves the Friends of the Golf Course made an aborted attempt to buy it. If the major renovation doesn't occur, players will still flock to Monroe's abbreviated track, a good beginner's venue that plays to 4,902 yards over two circuits.

Mount Si Golf Course

9010 Boalch Avenue SE, Snoqualmie, WA 98065. (425) 888-1541 or 391-4926 (from Seattle). Gary Barter & John Sanford, pros. 18 holes. 6,359 yards. Par 72. Grass tees. Course ratings: men—B68.5/116, M67.4/113; women—M72.6/116, F68.8/108. Years Opened: 1927 (original nine); 1930s (second nine). Architects: Pratt Family (original nine); Emmett Jackson (second nine); Harry Umbinetti & Gary Barter (remodels). Moderate, jr./sr. rates. Call for reservations. Walk-on chances: Fair. Walkability: Good. Playability: Upgraded holes enhance longtime course.

Situated in the picturesque Snoqualmie Valley, Mount Si has undergone several transformations over the years. The latest project, completed in 1994 and overseen by co-head pros and co-owners Gary Barter and John Sanford, helped ease conjestion by realigning several holes. The work included adding new tees and greens, converting a par-3 into a par-4, and toughening up the 507-yard 7th by sharpening its dogleg. The changes lengthened the course and bumped its par from 70 up to 72.

The layout is shadowed by its namesake crag to the east. Easily accessible off Interstate 90 and generally open year-round, Mount Si Golf Course receives about 60,000 rounds a year; play can be slow during the summer. The layout is popular because of its views, clean air, moderate challenge, friendly staff, and full-service restaurant/bar. Mount Si was the home course for one of the nation's most active golfers, Dave Mikkelson. Mikkelson, who died in 1988, twice received the USGA's award for posting the most official scores in the nation, topping out with 501 rounds in 1983. Almost all of his rounds were played here. The course commemorates Mikkelson's dedication with a fountain by the pro shop.

Mount Si was built by the Pratt family—one of the Snoqualmie Valley's most prominent early-day landowners—on what was then the world's largest hop farm. When Prohibition came along, the farm ceased operations and the Pratts built nine holes. Another nine was built in the early 1930s and, in 1958, Seattle-area pro Harry Umbinetti designed four new holes. Mount Si underwent another renovation in 1985, when nearly 600 yards, trees, traps and cart paths were added. Barter and Sanford acquired the course in 1989. The recent changes have improved drainage at the historically wet course. The drainage work wasn't helped by a flood in winter '96. The nearby Snoqualmie River spilled over its banks, damaging the parking lot and filling the basement of the restaurant with water. All facilities have since been repaired.

Barter and Sanford own 210 acres; the golf course occupies 110 acres while the remainder of the property is wetlands. Mount Si is frequented by deer, ducks, geese and an occasional coyote. The course is easy to walk, though fairways are marked with mounds and depressions that create awkward lies. The turf is spotty in places, owing primarily to the clayey, river-side soil underneath it. Interesting holes include the top-rated 2nd, a 521-yard par-5 that winds leftward between poplars to a mid-sized, raised green with a tier through it and grass bunkers left. The pretty 6th, a 357-yard par-4, curls rightward around woods and a lateral hazard. Over its last 125 yards, the hole is squeezed by trees and gardens en route to a small, tree-ringed green.

The 7th, a 507-yard par-5, is a 70-degree dogleg right with a dip about 100 yards from a hill-perched green. The putting surface is lined by troughs at its front and right flanks. The 12th, a 581-yard par-5, runs uphill along a left-turning route. About 450 yards out, the hole curls sharply left to a berm-fronted green guarded by grass bunkers front and right. Though rated the 18th-toughest hole, the 184-yard 17th is a tough par-3. Starting at a ditch-fronted tee, the hole ascends to a smallish green on a ledge. A grass bunker behind the putting surface gathers in long shots.

Nile Shrine Golf Course - semiprivate

18

500 NE 205th, Edmonds, WA 98020. (425) 776-5154. Randy Puetz, pro. 18 holes. 5,000 yards. Par 68. Grass tees. Course ratings: men B64.5/105, women—B68.1/112, F66.0/106. Years Opened: 1968 (original nine); 1996 (second nine). Architects: Founding members (original nine); Hank Hopkins (second nine). Moderate, credit cards. Reservations: Call a week ahead. Walk-on chances: Fair. Walkability: Good, with some hills. Playability: Much improved with new holes.

Once a private nine-holer, Nile was upgraded to 18 holes in July 1996. The work rewarded the patience of the course's owner, Seattle's Nile Temple, which endured three years of environmental reviews. The project was scrutinized by municipal, county, state and federal agencies as the 180-acre site borders Lake Ballinger and falls under the purview of those protecting such riparian zones. Aside from the permit hassles, the club went through a tough time when their popular head pro, Cobe Holmstad, passed away in early 1995. Randy Puetz took over the head pro job in December 1995, and began working out of a new pro shop in fall 1996.

Though still oriented toward Masons, Shriners and their guests, the Nile opened up for public play to help defray construction costs. Since outside play began, rounds have tripled. Members have access to a full-service clubhouse, swimming beach and fishing (trout and perch) pier on the lake. Public golfers must abide a dress code, and can order food from the restaurant. Also on the grounds is a picnic area popular with groups in the summer. When I played in a Seattle University Alumni tournament here in 1995, a large party was jamming in this fun zone; disco music boomed across fairways while kids skittered across the dance floor. The Nile also has an RV area.

Another visit in August 1996 found the revised Nile layout fun and entertaining, with several short par-3s (including the 95-yard 7th) and some par-4s in the 240-yard range. Fairway turf is fully knitted, and the new greens, though without many contours—which is too bad since adding some tricks to the putting surfaces would have made the 5,000-yard track more interesting—are large and adequately bunkered. Icons of the Nile's orientation are witnessed on the tees, which have red (women's) and yellow (men's) concrete blocks shaped like Shriner fez hats. Noteworthy holes include the 3rd, a 360-yard par-4 that winds leftward around trees and the picnic area. Lake Ballinger and a creek line the right side of the hole, which ends at a flat green. The dogleg-left 5th, a 344-yard par-4, has scrub growth off the tee. The fairway leans right toward jail before the final 150 yards ascend to a left-sloping green guarded by a hidden bunker left-front, a trap rear and pot bunker right. The top-rated 8th, a 388-yard par-4, runs downhill along a left-turning, tree-lined path. The 8th green is trapped twice on the back and fronted by a creek.

The 10th, a 376-yard par-4, has a big dip in mid-fairway; the hole slopes toward OB on the right. At the 100-yard mark, the hole rises up to a domed, hill-perched green trapped on the rear. The rolling 12th, a 326-yard par-4, turns slightly left along an uphill route skirting OB and Lakeview Drive on the left. Its big green is ringed closely by trees. The 14th, a 578-yard par-5, is easily Nile's toughest hole. Starting at a towering elevated tee overlooking Interstate 5 on the left, the hole requires a long-iron drive to avoid the wetlands and a creek which occupy much of the fairway's right side. Once past this juncture, the 14th ascends to a hill-cut green guarded left-front by trees and a bunker. The nice-looking 16th, a 320-yard par-4, heads leftward off a raised tee. A cluster of tall evergreens sits at the right-front of a mid-sized, front-sloping green trapped twice in front. An accurate drive to the left half of the fairway is needed to have a decent shot at this well-guarded target.

Riverbend Golf Complex   27

2019 West Meeker, Kent, WA 98032. Regulation 18 — (253) 854-3673; Par-3 Nine 859-4000. Brett Wilkinson, pro. 18 holes, 6,603 yards. Par 72. Par-3 Nine: 1,260 yards, par 27. Grass tees. Course ratings: men—B70.1/119, M68.1/114; women— M74.4/124, F70.1/114. Year Opened: 1989. Architect: John Steidel. Moderate, jr./sr. rates, credit cards. Reservations: Call a week ahead. Walk-on chances: Ok for singles. Walkability: Very good. Playability: Full-service facility has something for everyone.

Located on Kent's west side, Riverbend lies about a mile east of Interstate 5. The 18-hole John Steidel-designed layout is on the north side of West Meeker, while across the street are Riverbend's par-3 nine and driving range, which opened in the early 1960s as Kent Municipal Golf Course. Riverbend is owned by Kent's Parks and Recreation Department.

After enduring controversy over the operations of the course during its early years, the facility emerged from the woods when SSMD began managing it. SMDD is made up of Jim Stone, NBA coach Lenny Wilkins, Dr. Joe Drake, Del Durden, Purcell Johnson and head pro Brett Wilkinson. Riverbend's operators have instituted several changes, including a starter, a bag-tag system, and automatic tee-time reservations. SSMD operates the short nine and driving range; the range was recently retrofitted with artificial turf and the short nine got a new irrigation system. In March 1997, Kent officials decided to entertain request-for-proposals from other golf operators. SSMD's contract was to run out in December 1997 (after this book went to press).

Riverbend's regulation track annually hosts 80,000 rounds. Its popularity is justifiable, as the course encourages players to use all clubs in the bag, and there are plenty of water and sand hazards to keep things interesting. The mostly flat 130-acre site, a former cornfield, is easy to walk. A 180-foot-long bridge over the Green River links the 11th through 15th holes with the rest of the course, and a paved path along the river is used by hikers, bikers and joggers. Once the fairway-side trees mature, Riverbend's demeanor will toughen significantly. A good test is the 6th, a 554-yard par-5 bordered left by the river. The fairway is also pinched on the left by a wooded bank and along the right by a tangle of trees. The fairway runs straight for 400 yards or so, then turns abruptly left. The last leg of the 6th is tapered by trees, and its steeply front-sloping, hill-cut green is trapped laterally. The 12th, a 356-yard par-4, requires a precise drive to the fairway's right half, as a pond lines its left edge. The dome-like 12th green has water along its left-front flank and traps right and rear.

18 Snohomish Public Golf Course

7806 147th Avenue SE, Snohomish, WA 98290. (360) 568-9932, or 1-800-560-2676. Fred Jacobson, director of golf; John Brandvold, pro. 18 holes. 6,813 yards. Par 72. Grass tees. Course ratings: men—B71.7/122, M69.8/117, F67.9/114; women F73.3/125. Year Opened: 1965. Architect: Gordon Richards. Moderate, jr./sr. rates, credit cards. Reservations: Call a week ahead. Walk-on chances: Ok for singles. Walkability: Fair as tight layout involves several hills. Playability: Good test for all.

Situated about eight miles southeast of Everett, this course is one of the better public venues in the Puget Sound area. The lengthy layout sprawls over a hill near neighborhoods and horse pastures outside the historic town of Snohomish. Its tree-lined holes require length and accuracy, and its large, well-manicured greens mandate controlled play and a solid putting touch. The course crosses an elevated ridge and is occasionally swept by westerly winds. In recent years, drainage at Snohomish has been improved through a topdressing and aerating program, with new drain tile also installed.

The late Gordon Richards designed and built Snohomish, opening it in 1965 on the old Walter Bosse farm. The Richards family owns the course, having converted the original farmhouse into a pro shop and a restaurant that serves good food. The layout follows the westward slope of a prominent hill. Though a couple of gullies and swales crop up on the layout, the terrain is gently rolling. Most of Snohomish's trees are full-grown, squeezing fairways and target zones. The popular facility hosts upwards of 70,000 rounds a year.

Notable holes include the 1st, an uphill, 551-yard par-5 that requires a few long and accurate shots to reach its deceptively deep, trapped-right green. A downhill par-5 of 510 yards, the 10th doglegs left off a towering tee. The tree-lined fairway is elusive as it slopes to the right, away from the turn. The 10th green is raised and trapped on the right. The 16th, a 447-yard par-4, begins at an elevated tee fronted by a pond 125 yards out along the right. The left-tilting hole curls rightward along a narrow route to a flat, tree-tucked green bunkered left.

Snoqualmie Falls Golf Course

35109 SE Fish Hatchery Road, Fall City, WA 98024. (425) 222-5244 or 392-1276 (from Seattle). John Groshell, pro. 18 holes. 5,486 yards. Par 71. Grass tees. Course ratings: men—M65.3/105, F63.9/102; women—M70.4/117, F68.9/114. Year Opened: 1963. Architect: Emmett Jackson. Moderate, jr./sr. rates, credit cards. Reservations: Call six days ahead. Walk-on chances: Ok for singles. Walkability: Very good. Playability: Ideal for beginning and intermediate golfers.

This well-conditioned course lies west of one of the area's prime tourist meccas, Snoqualmie Falls. A flat 18-holer arrayed over a one-time cow pasture, Snoqualmie Falls was built by its co-founders, Emmett Jackson and Walt Nelson. Jackson (who also built Cascade in North Bend) and Nelson owned the course for a few years before selling it to Bill Porter, Art Russell and Terry Shannon. Current owner and head pro, John Groshell, bought out Shannon in 1972. After further exchanges of ownership shares and the death of Porter in 1994, Groshell became the sole proprietor of this popular course, which hosts upwards 70,000 rounds a year.

Groshell has implemented several improvements of late, including a new irrigation system and renovations to the restaurant. In February 1996, flooding by the nearby Snoqualmie River caused $120,000 damage to the course. Fairways were covered with silt and sand, but the layout rebounded nicely by spring. Because it has flexible private ownership, Snoqualmie Falls is the site for many private tournaments. The relatively short layout is amenable to golfers with a wide range of abilities, such as is often found in these tourneys. Because of these such events, call ahead for tee times, particularly in summer.

Linksters here enjoy choice vistas of the Cascades and Mount Si. The course, surrounded by farms and a few homes, is flat and easy-to-walk; its wide fairways often forgive errancy. The river winds around the 1st, 2nd and 5th holes, but shouldn't enter play. The venue has some short par-4s and par-5s, so there are good scoring chances. A challenging hole is the 5th, a wide 479-yard par-5 lined along the right by trees and the river. The hole crosses corrugated terrain en route to a mid-sized green guarded by three traps. The 8th is a nice 179-yard par-3. The tee shot here is usually hit into prevailing winds out of the west, and its green is closely guarded along the left by trees and a bunker. With a pond driving distance out and OB left, the 272-yard 12th is a neat par-4. Lay up with an iron off the tee, and you'll have a good chance at a birdie putt on the front-sloping green.

Tall Chief Golf Club

18 *1313 West Snoqualmie River Road SE, Fall City, WA 98024. (425) 222-5911 or 706-1881 (from Seattle). Rick Larson, pro. 18 holes. 5,412 yards. Par 70. Grass tees & mats. Course ratings: men—B64.4/102, M63.4/101; women—B68.9/110, M67.7/108, F65.8/105. Years Opened: 1964 (original nine); 1970s (second nine). Architect: Frank Avent. Moderate, sr. rates, credit cards. Reservations: Call six days ahead. Walk-on chances: Fair. Walkability: Good, with hillside holes 13-18 the most arduous. Playability: Fun rural venue not too taxing.*

Pastoral Tall Chief Golf Club is a good spot for linksters seeking a day away from the hustle and bustle of city life. Once the property of American Adventure, Tall Chief has been owned since 1989 by Mike Foster. The layout began as a nine-hole course on a former pasture; a back side was later built on a ridge to the west. The original back nine—since replaced by an American Adventure campground and the current set of holes—was reached by a tram that ran up a steep hill. The course hosts about 40,000 rounds a year, and generally enables sub-four-hour rounds.

Tall Chief offers Cascade vistas and glimpses of foxes and deer. It's also ringed by various agricultural operations; while playing the back nine, one might catch the odors emanating from a nearby dairy farm. Though not directly alongside the Snoqualmie River, Tall Chief generally floods in winter and spring. It was particularly hard hit by the floods of winter 1996. Besides having fairways six feet under water and suffering $50,000 in damage, Tall Chief lost a 200-foot chunk of asphalt from its entry road.

The front nine and first three holes of the back side cross generally flat terrain and are wide open, an ideal configuration for beginners. Tall Chief has a dozen or so sand traps, and water hazards enter play on the 1st, 7th, 9th and 10th holes. The toughest part of the course is holes 13-18, which feature tree-tightened fairways alongside a hill. Finding a flat lie on this part of the course is as rare as getting a chance to pet one of the fox pups or fawns, which emerge in spring and romp along the edges of fairways in this secluded section of the course.

Top holes include the 9th, a 450-yard par-5. The initial part of the fairway is wide, but the 9th is squeezed by a pond about 150 yards from a hill-cut, front-sloping green trapped at the rear. A good back-nine test is the 14th, a left-tilting, 443-yard par-4 that winds rightward around a forest to a tree-veiled, raised green. The 18th, a 367-yard par-4, initially crosses level ground on a route that heads toward a tall fir in the left half of the fairway. At this point, the hole curls rightward and drops down to a hidden, mid-sized green with a steep rear edge and a trap along the right.

The Course at Taylor Creek

9 *21401 244th Avenue SE, Maple Valley, WA 98038. (425) 413-1900. Dan Harrington, pro. 9 holes. 2,650 yards. Par 35. Grass tees. Course ratings: men—B66.6/122, M63.6/109; women—M66.6/120, F62.8/105. Year Opened: 1995. Architect: Brad Habenicht. Moderate, jr./sr. rates. Call for reservations. Walk-on chances: Good. Walkability: Pretty good. Playability: Plenty of dangers lurking along mid-length layout.*

A 1995-opened venue involving 63 acres northeast of Maple Valley, this course is across the road from Tahoma Junior High. The clubhouse and restaurant, pro shop and driving range were completed in 1996; an 18-hole putting course was scheduled to open in 1998. Designed by co-owner, Brad Habenicht, The Course at Taylor Creek winds around a King County-designated historical landmark, the Olson Mansion. The four-story, 8,000-square-foot former residence—site of the pro shop and clubhouse—was built in 1902 by Olof Olson, an engineer who constructed bridges and tunnels around the Northwest. In 1908, Olson built a cavernous barn on his homestead. This 45-foot-tall structure has an upper loft with a 22-foot-high ceiling shaped like one of his tunnels.

Habenicht and his 15-member development group, Taylor Creek Partners, nursed the project through five years of King County review. The site is dotted with wetlands; as these environmentally-sensitive areas were identified and re-identified by county officials, Habenicht was forced to go through several design revisions. Once the group got building permits in mid-1993, Larson-Travis Construction of Seattle began work. Habenicht, his cousin Don Habenicht and superintendent John Webber completed the course. Taylor Creek offers several greens-fee discount programs, including "players cards" that cut the cost of rounds in half.

The triple-teed layout involves several blind shots, the result of vision-blocking hills in fairways and before greens. The track spans a gently sloping hill, so players must be able to handle a mixture of down-, up- and side-hill stances. My suggestion for an 18-hole round is to play the white (middle) tees on the front. First-timers may want to initially "bunt" the ball around to stay out of serious trouble and become familiarized with the layout. During the second circuit, better players can pull out the "big dog" and let it fly. Just don't expect to get your way from either set of tees, as there's plenty of trouble to be found. One of the course's lesser characteristics is the interior OB markers on holes 3 and 4. The white stakes are intended to keep the wayward off adjoining fairways and away from cars in the parking lot, but I have a personal hang-up with interior OB.

Among the more interesting tests is the 1st, a 305-yard par-4 that winds downhill to the right. The Olson barn lurks closely to the right of the hitting zone (a few of the barn's windows have been broke). A mid-iron drive should find the middle of the fairway, thus enabling a 100-yard approach to a bi-trapped green that tilts left-rear toward wetlands. The 265-yard, par-4 3rd is a 90-degree dogleg-right that looks like a tunnel from the tee. Four bunkers guard the small, left-sloping green—which resembles the bottom of a tea cup with all the mounds around it. The 5th, a 329-yard par-4, is a tight dogleg-left. At the turn, the fairway slithers between a rock wall right and mounds left en route to a trapped-in-front, mound-lined green in a hollow. The prettiest hole on the course is the 9th, a 335-yard par-4 that ascends past waterfall-adorned ponds along the right and trees left. Over its last 150 yards, the 9th rises steeply. A creek crosses the fairway at the base of the hill-perched green, a wide-but-shallow affair trapped right-front.

Twin Rivers Golf Course

9

4446 Preston-Fall City Road SE, Fall City, WA 98024. (425) 222-7575. Jeff Tachell, pro. 9 holes. 3,557 yards. Par 36. Grass tees. Course ratings: men—B71.8/116, M68.5/109, F68.4/106; women—F68.0/103. Year Opened: 1994. Architects: Richard & Tom Rutledge. Moderate, jr./sr. rates. Call for reservations. Walk-on chances: Good. Walkability: Flat and easy-to-walk. Playability: Great place to grip it and rip it.

This nine-hole facility is named after the nearby Raging and Snoqualmie rivers. The layout was built and designed by its brother-owners, Richard and Tom Rutledge. The Rutledges originally wanted to build a full-blown 18-hole course on their 160-acre parcel, but King County's restrictive wetlands policies pared their plan to an 81-acre nine. On-site facilities include a small clubhouse with a pro shop and cafe, and a driving range; a campground borders the 5th hole. Upcoming plans include adding fairway mounding and grass bunkers around the greens.

As might be expected, this flat layout on expansive acreage has considerable yardage. If circuiting Twin Rivers twice for an 18-hole round from the back tees, it stretches 7,190 yards, making it the Northwest's longest nine-hole course. But the fairways are wide (75 to 100 yards across), and unless players are very wild, trouble is hard to come by. Indeed, it's one of the best courses around for loosing the "big dog" and seeing how far you can hit it. Besides length, the course gains distinction from its flat and round, mushroom-like greens.

Some of the tougher holes include the 2nd, a 414-yard par-4. The wide fairway skirts trees right and OB left en route to a rolling, left-tilting green. The 5th, a 560-yard par-5, is long, broad and flat. The last 130 yards of the hole curl left to a tree-fronted and oval, right-sloping green. The best hole at Twin Rivers is the 9th, a 499-yard par-5 that doglegs left around a pond. Take your vitamins before teeing off and you may chew off the corner. A safer place is to aim for a large landing area defined by a pond left and ditch right. Once past this juncture, the fairway gradually tapers before reaching a two-tiered green guarded by OB left and rear.

Tyee Valley Golf Club

18

2401 South 192nd Street, Seattle, WA 98188. (206) 878-3540. Mark Olson, pro. 18 holes. 5,318 yards. Par 70. Grass tees. Course ratings: men—B64.3/106, M63.1/104; women—B69.2/114, M67.7/110, F66.3/107. Year Opened: 1965. Architects: George Geyer, George Puetz & Roy Moore. Moderate, jr./sr. rates, credit cards. Reservations: Call a week ahead. Walk-on chances: Ok for singles. Walkability: Good. Playability: Suitable for all skills.

Situated at Sea-Tac Airport's south end, this course has a decided aeronautical ambience. Jumbo jets regularly pass above Tyee Valley, and some of its players are air farers who fill layovers with rounds of golf. A row of landing lights penetrates the course's north-south midsection, and the right side of the 5th fairway is lined by a string of orange flight towers that lead airplanes into Sea-Tac. Regulars, who have learned to communicate with a unique sign language, call the place "Thunder Valley." The layout occupies about 112 of the site's 137 acres; the remainder is wetlands. When the course was built in 1965, the only spot to build the clubhouse was its current location. Under Federal Aviation Adminstration rules, a building occupied by people must be 1,000 feet away from the nearest runway. Tyee Valley's clubhouse is just 10 feet outside the FAA's limits.

The course is owned by the Port of Seattle and leased to Golf Management, headed by Roy Moore. In 1996, the port and Golf Management began what will be a lengthy process to figure out how to reconfigure the course to prepare for a third runway at Sea-Tac. A preliminary proposal involved redesigning the 8th and 10th holes, and possibly the 15th and 16th. The port hired Ed Chaffee of Tacoma to find a way to work these holes into a plan to extend the main runway 500 feet, which would penetrate the existing course. One way to make room for a new runway would be to eliminate the nine holes east of the landing lights. The port owns 250 acres to the south—on the other side of South 200th Street—and it may opt to reposition at least nine new holes there. If plans for a third runway go through, and that's a big if, it's possible that an all-new 18- or 27-hole Tyee Valley may occupy that site. This major revision wouldn't occur until well after the year 2000.

Tyee Valley hosts an average of 70,000 rounds a year. The layout has been the site of several national cross-country events, including the 1980 NCAA Women's Championship and the 1989 and '90 American trials for the World Cross-Country championships. Top tests at this south Seattle "track" include the top-rated 7th, a par-4 of 390 yards that winds downhill to the left around a ball-snagging tree to a tiny green. The 8th, as currently configured, is a 426-yard par-4 that bends slightly rightward over rolling ground. Its undulating green is bunkered right, and a small pond guards its left-front flank. The current 10th, a par-4 of 366 yards, is imperiled by a creek and OB left, and has an elevated green with steep sides. The 12th, a 415-yard par-4, crosses wavy ground en route to a green bunkered on the right and front.

Walter E. Hall Memorial Golf Course

18

1226 West Casino Road, Everett, WA 98204. (425) 353-4653. Bob Whisman & Bruce Weir, pros. 18 holes. 6,444 yards. Par 72. Grass tees. Course ratings: men— B69.6/117, M68.6/115, F66.2/105; women—M74.5/119, F71.6/115. Year Opened: 1972. Architect: Al Smith. Moderate, credit cards. Reservations: Call a week ahead. Walk-on chances: Ok for singles. Walkability: Good. Playability: Should be considerably better—and tougher—once a major remodel is completed in the year 2000.

Hosting over 75,000 rounds a year, Walter E. Hall Memorial is one the region's busiest courses. The facility was named after Everett's first parks director. Walter Hall's son John, the city's second parks director, acquired this piece of south Everett real estate and named the course after his late father. The architect of the course was Al Smith, who also designed Glendale Country Club in Bellevue. Head pro Bob Whisman oversees this and Everett's other muni track, Legion Memorial. Walter Hall has hosted two PNGA Championships over the years, but today, because of the amount of play it receives, limits tournament play to club events.

In 1996, the city of Everett considered a complete revamping of Walter Hall in tandem with that of Legion Memorial. The plan called for doing nine holes at a time, rotating the work from "Hall" to "Legion." But in early 1997, the city changed its plans, opting instead to devote its full energies to Legion's makeover. The city still plans to renovate Walter Hall. A preliminary design called for it to receive such upgrades as new fairways and bunkers, mounding, an irrigation system retrofit, massive sanding and drainage improvements, an expansion of the cart-storage area, and a new driving range. The $3.1-million project may be initiated in 1998 or 1999, with an all-new Hall opening in the year 2000.

Until those changes are made, golfers will be faced with such challenging holes as the top-rated 4th, a 468-yard par-4 that runs straight over rolling ground. The concluding 75 yards of the hole are squeezed by trees en route to a wide-but-shallow green perched on a knoll. The 15th, a 499-yard par-5, has trees right and a pond left of its tee. The fairway traverses the side of a hill, and is crossed by a ditch before it ends at a large, untrapped green.

Wayne Public Golf Course

18 *16721 96th NE, Bothell, WA 98011. (425) 486-4714. Dave Richards, pro. 18 holes. 4,326 yards. Par 65. Grass tees & mats. Course ratings: men B60.6/97, women— B64.5/102, F64.2/101. Years Opened: 1929 (original nine); 1964 (second nine). Architects: Founding members (original nine); Gordon Richards (second nine). Moderate, jr./sr. rates. Reservations: Call a week ahead. Walk-on chances: Fair. Walkability: No problems. Playability: Good beginner's course.*

Owned and operated by three generations of the Richards family (who also help run the courses at Snohomish and Battle Creek), Wayne began with nine holes— played as the front—in 1929. Its 1,650-yard back side opened in 1964. In April 1996, the city of Bothell purchased the development rights to Wayne's front nine for $889,000. Although the city doesn't own the property, its acquisition of the development rights assures that nothing will be built on this section of the layout, and that the property will remain open as a golf course for passive and active recreation.

The 4,300-yard venue involves eight par-3s, nine par-4s, and a 447-yard par-5. Though Wayne crosses poorly-draining soil, its raised greens are well-maintained. The course is popular because of its handy location and easy challenge. It adjoins the Lake Washington-Sammamish Slough; homes and condominiums skirt the waterway. Geese and other waterfowl frequent holes along the slough. Interesting front-nine tests include the 5th, a 336-yard, par-4 hole with a slough-fronted tee. The fairway is wide and the green roosts atop a 30-foot-high promontory. The par-4 6th is a sharp dogleg-right of 307 yards. Players should use an iron from the tee as a slightly hooked wood shot will find "jail" or put them back on the 5th hole. A second-shot wedge may find the small 6th green, which is concealed in a gully. The 238-yard 9th is a tough par-3 crossed by the slough halfway to an untrapped green.

Wayne's back nine, situated on about 20 acres, is 1,000 yards shorter than the 2,674-yard front. A major detriment to this section of the course is the club-scarring tee mats at the start of nearly every hole. The 172-yard 12th is one of the region's weirdest holes. This *par-4* is a 90-degree, dogleg-right. From the tee, one must plop a half-cranked 9-iron or a wedge 90 yards straight out. (You can't cut off the "dogleg" as there are trees and a fence right of the tee.) Second shots must be lofted up to a small, trap-fronted green that sits about 20 feet above the "fairway."

Wellington Hills Golf Course

7026 Wellington Heights Drive, Woodinville, WA 98072. (425) 483-1981. 9 holes. 2,735 yards. Par 34. Mats. Course ratings: men 64.8/106, women 69.1/115. Year Opened: 1931. Architects: the Crumm family. Economical, sr. rates, credit cards. Reservations: Call a weeek ahead. Walk-on chances: Fair. Walkability: Good, just beware of ankle-spraining hollows in turf. Playability: Suitable for beginners and those seeking a quick golf fix.

9

In 1994, University of Washington officials considered opening a branch campus on this course, which it owns. But after much cogitation, the UW found another site and thus spared the nine-hole, hillside-arrayed layout from the wrecking ball. The layout is operated by Ballinger Recreation, Inc., whose principals are Jan Japar and Mimi Racicot, the same duo that runs Ballinger Park in Mountlake Terrace. Japar says that the UW may expand onto the course, but not in the foreseeable future.

The dual-tee track, which plays 5,228 yards over two circuits, is split by Wellington Heights Drive. The arterial has caused safety concerns, particularly for the motorists traveling through. The problem is particularly acute at the 1st tee. A shed and some trees block the leftward views of players, who must shoot blindly over the road—150 yards from the tee—to reach the green at this 255-yard, par-4. Another dangerous juncture is at the 6th hole, which involves a tee shot over the road to reach the fairway on the other side.

Wellington Hills is an old-style layout with relatively short holes and small, domed greens. The course was built the "old way"—on fallen timbers that now result in hundreds of ankle-spraining hollows. During one nine-hole round here, I wrenched my ankle twice. Decent holes include the 2nd, a 415-yard par-4 with a right-bending fairway leading to a heart-shaped, knoll-perched green. The dogleg-right 8th, a 400-yard par-4, has an elevated, swale-fronted tee and a shot-snagging fir in mid-fairway. The 9th, a 325-yard par-4, sports a duck pond off the tee. Its tree-lined fairway leads to a front-sloping green that leans toward a pot bunker.

West Seattle Municipal Golf Course

4470 35th Avenue SW, Seattle, WA 98126. (206) 935-5187. Matt Amundsen, pro. 18 holes. 6,635 yards. Par 72. Grass tees. Course ratings: men—B70.8/118, M69.2/116, FF68.6/114; women F72.1/120. Year Opened: 1940. Architect: H. Chandler Egan. Moderate, jr./sr. rates, credit cards. Reservations: Call a week ahead. Walk-on chances: Ok for singles. Walkability: Good, with some hilly hikes. Playability: Improving all the time.

18

From its lofty perch at 550 feet above sea level, this course offers grand views of the Duwamish Waterway and Elliott Bay. Designed by PNGA Hall-of-Famer H. Chandler Egan, the layout occupies what was once the Puget Mill Site. West Seattle is one of a handful of Northwest golf courses built by WPA labor. The layout is crossed by Longfellow Creek, and is bordered by neighborhoods on three sides. West Seattle Stadium looms over the parking lot's south edge. Like Seattle's other muni courses at Jackson Park and Jefferson Park, West Seattle is operated by Municipal Golf of Seattle, a non-profit corporation whose primary purpose is to make improvements to the city's golf facilities.

This is actually West Seattle's second course. The original West Seattle links had sand greens, and occupied a half-mile strip known as Haller Track (now Sunset

Avenue Southwest). Located atop a bluff overlooking Alki Beach, the layout began with six holes in 1914 and was later expanded to nine. The course apparently was quite tricky as a cliff bordered its left side. Golfers lost their teeing grounds in the 1920s when the property's owner converted the course into view lots. A house was built in 1925 right in the middle of the layout, and soon homes sprouted up along the bluff.

West Seattle's 130-acre site sprawls across a hillside. Recent improvements include new tees and landscaping; future upgrades may include a driving range and par-3 nine on a city-owned 12-acre plot south of the course. Certain to come soon are a new irrigation system and clubhouse improvements. West Seattle's course sits on clay-type soil, and though the turf turns boggy after heavy rains, it hardens in the summer. Old-growth madronas, maples and evergreens extend throughout the front nine—slightly less so on the back—to serve as hazards and fairway dividers. The layout also involves gullies, creeks, drainage ditches and thick-grass fairway peripheries.

Top holes include the 4th, a 503-yard par-5 that starts with a blind drive over a fairway hillock. Stay to the right side of the fairway for a clear second shot to a mid-sized and rolling green. With its rebuilt elevated tees, the par-5 12th has become a dandy 515-yarder with Longfellow Creek at the base of its tee. The rolling route initially heads downhill, then rises up to a hill-perched green flanked left by a steep bank. West Seattle's 17th and 18th holes are par-4s in the 360-yard range, with the 17th going downhill and the 18th reversing straight back up toward the clubhouse. The tougher of the two is the 18th, which has a left-leaning, right-curling fairway guarded right by OB. It ends at a tree-ringed green trapped left and rear.

Willows Run Golf Club

18

10442 Willows Road NE, Redmond, WA 98052. (425) 883-1200 or 1-800-833-4787 (within western Washington). Travis Cox, pro. 18 holes. 6,812 yards. Par 72. Grass tees. Course ratings: men—B72.3/120, M69.1/118; women F71.6/117. Year Opened: 1994. Architect: Lisa Maki. Moderate. Reservations: Call a week ahead; two weeks ahead in summer. Walk-on chances: Ok for singles. Walkability: Good. Playability: Nice mix of holes create a challenge for all concerned; look for a 45-hole Willows Run in 1998 or 1999.

This full-service facility lies west of Redmond off Willows Road, a north-south arterial lined by Redmond's various high-tech industries. Willows Run is owned by Brian and Joyce Patton; Joyce is the sister of Microsoft co-founder, Paul Allen. The course opened in July 1994, and a 10,000-square-foot structure—with food service and banquet space—began drawing customers the next year. The layout hosts over 70,00 rounds a year. It's played by locals, guests to the area and large men's and women's clubs, which number 1,000 and 200 members, respectively.

Also on hand is a driving range; head pro Travis Cox is aided by three teaching pros who give lessons at the lighted practice facility. The course hosts a Dave Pelz Short Game School each July. In 1996, Willows Run hosted the Richard Karns Celebrity Golf Tournament. This event, named after the Seattle-born actor who plays "Al" on ABC's popular "Home Improvement" show, is a three-day fundraiser for the Fred Hutchinson Cancer Research Center and Overlake Hospital. Another Willows Run event is a $1,000,000 hole-in-one contest sponsored by a local radio station. A new tournament on the busy Willows Run rota is the annual Eastside Amateur, a tournament started in 1997 for scratch golfers.

In early 1997, Willows Run was in the throes of expanding. The Pattons had filed permits with the city of Redmond for another 18-hole regulation-length course and an executive nine. The regulation track would be built on property north of the existing course and the short nine to the south; the two courses involve a total of 150 acres. Also planned is an 18-hole putting course. The Pattons hoped to receive permits for the expansion by June 1997 (after this book went to press), with construction to begin immediately. If all goes well, an expanded Willows Run may debut in summer 1998. Designed by Ted Locke of Vancouver, B.C., the new 18 will have a links flavor similar to the original course, only tougher. Some mixing and matching of holes on the two courses may be needed so both layouts can operate out of the existing clubhouse. Besides allowing golfers a quick golf fix, the par-30 executive side will be used for junior and beginner golf programs.

The Lisa Maki-designed original track was built by Bilberry-Maas Construction of Florida. The flat site was varied by building mounds along fairways, with several depressions also dotting the property. When the water table is high in spring and fall, these sunken areas become troublesome ponds and wetlands. In summer, when the water dissipates and native fescue grasses replace the hazard, getting out of these areas is still not easy. Perhaps the signature feature of Willows Run is its large bentgrass greens. In 1996, superintendent Ben Nelson began verti-cutting these massive putting surfaces, a move that will enable mowing the turf lower and quickening their pace even more. Prevailing westerlies can wreak havoc on this links-like layout, and southerly views of Mount Rainier are available on nice days.

Notable holes include the 2nd, a 541-yard par-5 with a pond along the left and wetlands right of its slight dogleg-left route. The hole is narrowed at the 150-yard mark by mounds and water right, and a pond left. The pond runs up to guard the left flank of a rolling, trapped-left green. The 7th, a 446-yard par-4, has water along both sides of its initial leg; three bunkers also lurk in mounds along the left. At the 100-yard mark, the hole curls rightward to an slick, undulating green. The 9th, a 529-yard par-5, has a wide fairway lined by wetlands and a pond on the right, with OB left. The 9th green—a long and sinuous affair linked to the 18th—is fronted by a large pond. A trap lurks right-rear of this humped-in-the-middle target.

The 11th, a 529-yard par-5, is lined left by OB; a pond/wetland squeezes the right edge of the snaky path. The pond runs up to the right-front edge of a large, teardrop-shaped green trapped right-front. The top-rated 15th is a 441-yard par-4 with a narrow right-tilting fairway. The driving area is defined by mounds left and a huge swale/wetlands right. The left-sloping, mound-ringed 15th green contains sundry humps and hollows. The 18th, a 514-yard par-5, bears wetlands on both sides. The hole ends at a small (for Willows Run) left-leaning green with a dip in its midsection. The target is pond-fronted (a la its partner on the 9th), and is bunkered left-rear and left-front. Going for the 18th green in two is one of the trickiest tasks on this enjoyable course.

Private Courses

18 Bear Creek Country Club

13737 202nd Avenue NE, Woodinville, WA 98072. (425) 881-1350. Roger Rockefeller, pro. 18 holes. 6,930 yards. Par 72. Grass tees. Course ratings: men— C74.9/136, B72.1/130, M69.8/125; women—M75.0/131, F71.9/124. Years Opened: 1983 (original nine); 1984 (second nine). Architect: Jack Frei. Members, guests & reciprocates.

Bear Creek is an integral part of an upscale Woodinville neighborhood. Opened in 1983 as a public venue, the layout went private in April 1990 after Fuji Vending/ Delicor purchased it. Fuji invested several million dollars in upgrading the golf course and associated facilities before selling the non-equity club to American Golf Corporation in 1993. AGC—the world's largest golf course operator—offers Bear Creek's 450 members playing privileges at its couple hundred other courses as well as the stability of a skilled, golf-oriented proprietor.

Bear Creek's 18-hole track was designed around the adjoining community's brick-laid cul-de-sacs and roads. Each hole is challenging, with many endemic features—hills, valleys and virgin timber—mixed in with many sand and water hazards. The Jack Frei-designed course boasts over 100 sand traps and various ponds, creeks and lakes. The back side is situated more in woodlands than the front. A power buggy is recommended at Bear Creek as green-to-tee walks over the cart paths and asphalt roads are not only lengthy, but uncomfortable as well. As noted by its high rankings, the course is tough from each set of tees. In 1993, the nines were reversed as the members wanted to start their rounds on a straight par-4, not the nasty uphill right-bender now played as the 10th.

AGC is known for its turfgrass managers, and Bear Creek's conditioning has improved during the company's oversight. Nonetheless, the course is wet during the winter and, in summer, its fairways dry out and harden. Particularly good holes include the par-5 2nd, which has plenty of hazards along its 600-yard route. The hole winds slightly leftward between trees to a laterally-trapped green shared with the 6th, a 454-yard par-4. The 389-yard, par-4 8th—along with the 247-yard, par-3 9th—is Bear Creek's signature hole. A 200-yard drive should safely alight on a flat area fronting a 130-yard-wide lake at the 8th. The second shot must carry the lake to reach a wavy green fronted by timber-shored traps. The winding 18th, a 581-yard par-5, is lined with trees and concludes at a mid-sized green guarded left by a pond and right by a vast bunker. Behind the 18th green is an array of bunkers shaped like a bear paw.

9 Brae Burn Golf & Country Club

2409 182nd Avenue NE, Bellevue, WA 98052. No phone. 9 holes. 1,283 yards. Par 28. Grass tees. No course ratings. Opened: late-1960s. Architects: Course founders. Members & guests.

Located in Bellevue's north end off 24th Street Northeast, Brae Burn Golf & Country Club is an executive-length layout used exclusively by homeowners living in the adjoining housing development. The short nine is well-treed and has eight par-3s ranging from 87 to 219 yards. Its only par-4 stretches 255 yards. Five sand traps guard its small greens, and a creek winds through the 5th and 6th holes. The well-conditioned layout is equipped with a small clubhouse.

Broadmoor Golf Club   18

2340 Broadmoor Drive, Seattle, WA 98112. (206) 325-8444. Bill Tindall, pro. 18 holes. 6,270 yards. Par 70. Grass tees. Course ratings: men—B70.5/124, M70.0/123 FF67.7/118; women—M76.3/133, FF74.7/130, F73.7/128. Year Opened: 1927. Architect: Arthur Vernon Macan; John Steidel (remodel). Members, guests & limited reciprocates.

Built in 1927, Broadmoor Golf Club is the centerpiece of a gated Madison Park neighborhood. The 18-hole course was built by the Puget Mill Company, which initiated the Broadmoor community in the 1920s. PNGA Hall-of-Famer Arthur Vernon Macan designed the horseshoe-shaped layout, which winds between homes and well-tended backyards. One arm of the horseshoe contains the front nine—with the first four holes extending to a point, and holes 5 through 9 return to the closed end and the clubhouse. The back nine is similarly arranged, with the paralleling 10th and 18th filling the closed end of the horseshoe. The course was sculpted by horse-pulled scrapers and greens were sown with creeping bentgrass. The fairways follow a sloping hillside above Madison Park, near the entrance to the University of Washington Arboretum.

Over its seven decades, Broadmoor has hosted many prestigious events. In 1945, Ben Hogan, Byron Nelson, Jug McSpaden and Sam Snead were some of the players in the first of many Seattle Opens at Broadmoor. Other contestants who played at this then-regular PGA Tour stop included Jack Nicklaus, Ken Venturi, Arnold Palmer, Billy Casper, Gary Player and Miller Barber. The 1952 Women's Weathervane Tournament found Betsy Rawls besting the legendary Babe Zaharias. Other tournaments include the 1954 Western Amateur, USGA Girls' Juniors in 1961, the Women's National Amateur Championships in 1974, and the 1996 Senior Women's Amateur. Broadmoor's head pro, Bill Tindall, has been a fine teacher and player for many years. After finishing 12th in the 1995 U.S. Senior Open, Tindall tried to qualify for the PGA Senior Tour in 1996. Unfortunately, the effort by the former University of Washington men's golf coach fell just short.

Over the years, Broadmoor's original layout has been lengthened and modernized, with the front and back nines reversed and bunkers added. Kennewick architect, John Steidel, remodeled some holes in 1984. In 1994, an all-new clubhouse was erected, and in 1997 there was a plan for a new back tee at the 1st to add some length to the par-5. Broadmoor's proximity to the arboretum has been a godsend over the years. Besides towering, native firs, the fairways are lined by azaleas, rhododendrons, pink-blossomed Kwanzan cherries, red and orange *Nyssa sylvaticas* trees and willows.

Broadmoor's course is immaculately conditioned, and its *poa annua* greens are among the slickest in the region. Though at first glance these putting surfaces don't seem to bear many undulations, there's a confounding trickiness to them that baffle the uninitiated. Lake Washington's position near Broadmoor has a decided effect on how the ball rolls on these low-cut swards. Canada geese and ducks occasionally haunt the 18th fairway, which adjoins a slough off the lake.

One of Broadmoor's toughest holes is the 7th, a 225-yard par-3 that can play like a 250-yarder when winds come out of the west (left). Though the drive is aided by a raised tee, reaching the distant 7th green in regulation is a superior challenge, particularly from the tips. Those short of the hillcut green may find one of the three deep, upwardly-angled bunkers before the midsized, front-tilting green. Another Broadmoor dandy is the 10th, a 424-yard par-4 with an elevated tee that provides nice eastward views of the lake and Cascades. The left-sloping hole tilts toward trees and sundry trouble, with homes and OB along the right. After reaching its nadir, the fairway gradually ascends along a tree-tapered path to a right-front-sloping green trapped laterally.

18 Everett Golf & Country Club

1500 52nd Street, Everett, WA 98206. (425) 259-1214. Bob Borup, pro. 18 holes. 6,266 yards. Par 72. Grass tees. Course ratings: men—B70.0/126, M69.2/124; women F73.1/126. Years Opened: 1910 (original nine); 1931 (second nine). Architects: Dr. Ottar Thomle & Francis L. James; Arthur Vernon Macan, Ted Robinson, Michael Asmundson & William Robinson (remodels). Members, guests & reciprocates.

Everett Golf & Country Club has evolved over the years to become one of the Puget Sound region's premier private venues. Founded in 1910, Everett's original layout was a rudimentary nine-holer built by members on leased property. In the early 1920s, the club bought the ground the golf course occupied while acquiring 34 additional acres. A member, Dr. Ottar Thomle, drew up a plan for nine more holes, then convinced the club to hire the notable architect, Francis L. James, to design the course. Using Thomle's routing, James designed six new holes on the 34-acre parcel, with the original nine modified to allow the placement of three additional holes. Construction was partially finished when the Great Depression hit in 1929. In 1931 the project was completed and Everett's new 18-hole layout opened for play. Much of the work was performed by members, who formed work parties to prepare the course.

Over the years, Everett's course has been fine-tuned. The original clubhouse was replaced in 1961, and the club received a driving range, based on recommendations from architect Arthur Vernon Macan, in 1962. In the late-1960s, architect Ted Robinson was hired to upgrade the course. Some of Robinson's changes were implemented, but others weren't as the economy in the Puget Sound area took a downturn at that time. Another master plan initiated in 1993 was overseen by Oregon architect, William Robinson. The project, to be concluded in 1998, adds mounding for hole definition and replaces bunker sand.

Notable tournaments hosted by Everett over the years include the Greater Seattle Open in 1966. The Everett Open in 1984 and '85 was a stop on the now-defunct Tournament Player Series. Everett hosts a major PNGA event every two or three years. One of the great players who learned the game at Everett Golf & Country Club is Anne (Quast) Sander, who has played more championship rounds than any golfer—male or female—in U.S. golf history. The club also produced Jack Westland—winner of two Washington State Amateur Championships an incredible 23 years apart—in 1924 and 1947, and who was runner-up in the 1925 NCAA Men's Championship. Westland finished second to Francis Ouimet in the 1931 U.S. Amateur, won the 1933 Western Amateur, and was a two-time member of the Walker Cup team and its honorary captain in 1961. Westland also garnered several PNGA championships, and in 1963 won the U.S. Seniors. Other golfers out of Everett's illustrious stable have included former PNGA Men's titleholder George Holland, Jeff Knudson, and Dr. Kirk Smith, a fine tournament player and holder of Everett's course record, a 62.

Everett's course winds through towering native firs as well as deciduous and ornamental trees. Though not particularly long, the well-conditioned layout gains difficulty through its tight target zones, ample hazards, and generally small, rolling greens. When mowed low, these putting surfaces are among the region's quickest. Everett is the site of one of the region's legendary holes. The 265-yard, par-4 16th is known as "Hogan's Alley" for its mere 20-yard width. The slight dogleg-left tunnels between evergreens to a small, slick green. The naming of the 16th is also interesting. The hole was originally dubbed "Maulsby's Alley," honoring club member Zene Maulsby, who twice won the club championship. In 1939, Alex Rose, the golf writer for the *Seattle P.I.*, made the reference to "Hogan's Alley" in a column, more than a year before Ben Hogan won a tournament of any significance. So who was Rose referring to? Perhaps it was a mispelling of "Haugen's Alley," after Oscar Haugen, the man who completed construction of the hole from James and Thomle's plans.

Fairwood Golf & Country Club

18

17070 140th Avenue SE, Renton, WA 98058. (425) 226-7890. Ron Hanson, pro. 18 holes. 6,314 yards. Par 71. Grass tees. Course ratings: men—B70.8/126, M69.2/ 122; women F71.8/125. Years Opened: 1968 (original nine); 1970 (second nine). Architects: Bill Teufel (original nine), Jack Reimer (second nine). Members, guests & reciprocates.

Fairwood Golf & Country Club lies within a tri-sectioned, 750-acre residential and recreational community southeast of 140th Street Southeast. The golf course is an integral part of Fairwood Greens; other neighborhoods include Fairwood Crest and Fairwood West. Quadrant developed the neighborhood, and the course was built by Ray Coleman. Fairwood's founding members helped condition the layout after it opened, policing fairways for rocks and other impediments during regular patrols. The ladies club raised funds through auctions and raffles to finance clubhouse renovations and buy locker room furnishings.

Fairwood's nicely maintained track winds between homes and yards. The houses are farther removed from the field of play than another Quadrant development, Twin Lakes Golf & Country Club in Federal Way. Like Twin Lakes, players at Fairwood must cross a few residential roads during their rounds. Fairwood features good signage, pretty flower gardens, paved cart paths and a sizable clubhouse. The course has hosted such events as the Seattle Women's Golf Association City Championships, Southwest Washington Golf Association championships, Washington State Juniors and various PNGA tourneys.

Fairwood's greens have considerable character, with the course gaining additional difficulty from ample water and sand hazards. Among its better holes is the 4th, a 389-yard par-4. The narrow right-bender has power cables paralleling it above on the right as it winds through trees to a ridge-perched green that tilts rightward to a bunker. The 6th, a 370-yard par-4, veers to the right along a path that skirts OB and homes on the right. The hole curls around to a rolling, front-left-sloping green trapped left-front. The 9th, a 544-yard par-5, heads downhill along a dual-ledged fairway; the right side tilts toward jail and the left side—lined by houses and OB—is fairly flat. At the 225-yard mark, the left-leaning fairway ascends to a mid-sized, undulating green guarded by big traps front-left, front-right and left.

The 10th, a 564-yard par-4, is a slight downhiller between trees. Once past the driving range on the right, the hole bends uphill to the left. At the 200-yard mark, trees pinch the fairway, which then bears leftward along an ascending path to a deep-but-skinny green trapped left-front. Trees squeeze the green's left-front entry. The 12th, a 175-yard par-3, is a pretty hole with an elevated tee fronted by a pond. The ridge-perched green leans steeply frontwards, and is trapped left-front and left. The fairway at the 14th, a handsome 385-yard par-4, ventures off a raised tee toward a bunker-pinched landing area. The hole heads toward a big swale at the 100-yard mark, then rises to a slick, front-left-sloping green trapped left. A fat maple tree sits at the green's right-front entry. Fairwood's 15th, a 352-yard par-4, contains a tight right-turning fairway lined by deep jail along the right. Houses, OB and two bunkers lurk at the turn, which is 75 yards away from a hill-cut, smallish green trapped left.

Glen Acres Golf & Country Club

9

1000 South 112th, Seattle, WA 98168. (206) 244-3786. Bart Turchin, pro. 9 holes. 3,060 yards. Par 36. Grass tees. Course ratings: men 69.5/122, women 73.2/127. Year Opened: 1924. Architect: Arthur Vernon Macan. Members, guests & limited reciprocates.

Well-established Glen Acres in Seattle's south end is ringed by condominiums and townhouses. Wonderful views of Seattle's skyline and Elliott Bay are available from higher points. Glen Acres lies about two blocks west farther up the hill from Rainier Golf & Country Club. The course is owned by the Glen Acres Home Association and has 300 members. In October 1996, the association, seeking a more efficient operation, turned over management of the course to Golf Resources, the firm run by longtime Northwest pros, Ron Coleman and Ron Hagen. Head pro Bart Turchin is a fine player; in 1996, he and apprentice David Roberts won the Cobra Washington State Pro-Assistants Championship.

By the looks of its classic chalet-like clubhouse, swimming pool and course, Glen Acres must have been a premier Seattle-area club during its heydays. Originally called Glendale Country Club, it was founded by prominent members of Seattle's Jewish community. Out of a desire to play an 18-hole course—which never could happen at Glen Acres' house-ringed site, 250 members left in the mid-1950s and took the club's original name with them. The 18-hole venue at Bellevue's Glendale Country Club resulted from that exodus, and this nine-holer was renamed Glen Acres.

The dual-tee layout stretches 3,060 yards on the par-36 front side, and 3,028 on the par-35 back. As indicated by the above ratings, Glen Acres plays tough. Its challenge stems from some radical, steeply-tipped greens and wavy fairways. Towering trees line most holes, and a flat lie is nigh impossible to find. Over its long life, the course record remains a 64, set by member and former golf pro, Bill O'Brien. In fall, the course is ablaze in oranges and reds, with maples and other ornamentals colorfully framing holes.

Particularly good tests include the 3rd, a 375-yard par-4 that runs straight uphill. At the 150-yard mark, the fairway tilts even more severely up to a rolling, humped-in-the-middle green trapped twice in front. The left side of 3rd green is quite steep. The top-rated 4th, a 541-yard par-5 that extends 557 yards when played as the

13th, is a lengthy downhiller lined by trees. The hole gradually makes its way to the base of a hill at the 75-yard mark, then rises up to a wild-looking, front-canted green trapped twice in front.

The 7th, a 457-yard par-5 (a 390-yard par-4 as the 16th), has OB and houses left of its narrow, tree-lined route. Over its concluding 125 yards, the hole ascends sharply to a large and flattish (for Glen Acres) green trapped right-front. The 9th, a 320-yard (365 as the 18th) par-4, contains a well-treed chute for tee shots. The right-sloping fairway leans toward a fountain-adorned pond. Over its final 75 yards, the fairway goes up to a steeply front-sloping green guarded by huge traps at the right-front and left-front. The 9th/18th holes typify Glen Acres' interest-piquing, old-style holes.

Glendale Country Club

13440 Main Street, Bellevue, WA 98005. (425) 746-7377. Stan Hyatt, pro. 18 holes. 6,502 yards. Par 72. Grass tees. Course ratings: men—B71.2/135, M70.2/ 132, F67.4/126; women—M76.3/138, FF73.1/131, F72.8/131. Year Opened: 1957. Architect: Al Smith. Members, guests & limited reciprocates.

This private club was formed when members of the original Glendale Country Club in south Seattle wanted to play an 18-hole golf course. Starting with 250 charter members, Glendale soon enjoyed a full membership. The original Glendale club was renamed Glen Acres. The Al Smith-designed layout stretches over rolling hills of former farmland next to the Bellevue Farm Park, west of downtown. Aside from an occasional coyote, Glendale's wildlife is limited to various birds and spawning salmon in Kelsey Creek. These fish—tipping the scales at 35-40 pounds— arrive about a day after they begin their upland journey from Lake Washington.

As noted by its ratings, Glendale is a difficult track, with Kelsey Creek winding through the layout and entering play on several holes. Over 50 bunkers and a pond also dot the layout, which has some fine golf holes. The sizes of the greens vary and, when mowed low, are very slick. Another contributor to Glendale's challenge is its tipped topography, which leads to off-kilter lies and requires swing adjustments. Glendale has hosted significant tournaments over the years, including Hudson Cup matches, the Men's Pacific Northwest Amateur, Northwest PGA and Washington State Open. Over 1996-97, the clubhouse underwent a $1.5-million remodel.

Among the top tests at the well-conditioned course is the 1st, a nasty 386-yard par-4 with a fairway that slopes severely left toward trees; OB lines the hole on the right. About 100 yards from the green's left entry is a pack of shot-blocking firs. The small and fast, plateaued 1st green is guarded by three traps and has a steep back end. The 3rd, a 422-yard par-4, sports a downhill and left-curling fairway lined by OB on the right. Trees squeeze the left side of the hole all the way to a raised green trapped twice in front.

A valley separates the tee and green at the pretty but treacherous 11th, a 179-yard par-3 with a severely left-front sloping green ringed by three traps. The 501-yard, par-5 12th doglegs right around trees. Kelsey Creek is along the right as the hole horseshoes around to a knoll-perched green protected left-front by an evergreen and right by a bunker. The 14th, a 336-yard par-4, is a very tight driving hole that leans left toward trees. The fairway curls right toward a smallish, kidney-shaped green engirded by three bunkers. The 16th, a 370-yard par-4, has the stream off the tee. The creek then winds along the fairway's left edge before the hole ends at a green trapped twice in front. The putting surface is further guarded on the left by the sneaky creek.

Hat Island Golf Club

9 *1016A 14th Street, Everett, WA 98201. (425) 339-8485. 9 holes. 2,335 yards. Par 35. Grass tees. No course ratings. Year Opened: 1962. Architect: Jack Reimer. Property owners & guests.*

The tidy track here lies on mile-long Hat Island, identified on sailing charts as Gedney Island. Shaped like an inflated beret, Hat Island contains 150 homes and nine miles of roads. Indians once used it as a stopover while on fishing expeditions and, during Prohibition, Hat Island harbored bootleggers. It has been privately owned since the early 1960s. Located in a banana belt, Hat Island misses most of the weather systems coming from the north and south. The island once had a thriving rabbit population, but wild cats have since eradicated most of them.

The Jack Reimer-designed course—which can only be played by Hat Island homeowners—was built by Ray Coleman. A retired Air Force master sergeant, Wayne Parkhurst, maintained and managed the course for years; Ray Carnevali now runs the place. Since it lies close to saltwater, golf balls don't travel far at the layout, which has two par-3s, six par-4s and a 470-yard par-5. The course crosses mostly flat topography and its greens are ringed by trees. The club's big events include Yacht Club men's days on the Fourth of July and Labor Day.

Inglewood Golf Club

18 *6505 Inglewood Road NE, Kenmore, WA 98028. (425) 488-7000. Rick Adell, pro. 18 holes. 6,722 yards. Par 73. Grass tees. Course ratings: men—C72.9/131, B71.6/ 128, M69.3/122; women—M75.4/128, F70.2/121. Year Opened: 1921. Architects: Bob Johnstone & Arthur Vernon Macan. Members, guests & limited reciprocates.*

Inglewood Golf Club spans a well-treed hill at the northeast end of Lake Washington. (For years called Inglewood Country Club, the club's name was changed in 1996 to better reflect its orientation and facilities.) Partially visible from a few fairways, the lake is a landing strip for seaplanes that occasionally drone overhead. Inglewood was co-designed by Bob Johnstone and Arthur Vernon Macan and opened in 1921. The club enjoyed a full membership until the Great Crash in 1929, after which it plummeted to 48 members. When the original corporation disbanded in 1942, Joe Barron bought the club for $100,000. The Barron family ran it for several decades before selling Inglewood back to the members in 1970 for $2.2 million. (For more on Inglewood's history, see Dan Raley's piece in this book.)

Inglewood has encountered its share of colorful anecdotes over the years. In the 1950s, a member bled to death on the 9th hole when his club broke and imbedded in his leg. His cries for help went unanswered as some peacocks on adjoining property routinely screeched in a sound similar to someone in pain. To make matters worse, a doctor played past the dying man, thinking he was just taking a nap. While the course was closed during World War II, sheep were allowed to graze on the greens to keep them short, and the clubhouse was used for R&R by Coast Guardsmen. In 1954, a light plane made an emergency landing on the 18th fairway and had to be dismantled for removal.

The 13th hole at Inglewood is a 367-yard par-4

In 1974, police raided a house of ill repute beside the 10th fairway. Before the place was closed by police, "Johns" often parked their golf carts in front of the house. In 1952, a deputy sheriff was shot and killed and two other deputies were wounded when the club's dishwasher mistook them for safecrackers returning to the scene of a crime. An hour earlier, the dishwasher and two watchmen had been tied up by four men who made off with $6,800 from the club's safe and 25 then-legal slot machines. During a tournament in the 1950s, the players and gallery reached the top of the hill on the 4th hole and came upon a man and woman passionately entwined on the green. Since then, the 4th hole has been called "Lover's Lane."

Inglewood's 1926-built clubhouse underwent a major renovation in 1994, though it retained its unique Spanish-style motif. The club is quite active as a tournament host. In 1996, Inglewood held the Ernst Championship hosted by (Seattle native) Fred Couples. Comprised of 27 of the PGA Tour's best players, the unique two-dayer (renamed the Fred Couples Invitational in 1997) is held on the Monday and Tuesday prior to the International in Denver. Other noteworthy events have included the 1963 and '65 Seattle Opens, Ladies Valhalla Open in 1967, 1969 Northwest Open (a former PGA Tour stop), and the GTE Northwest Classic, a Senior PGA Tour event whose last year was 1995. Since 1977, Inglewood has been overseen by head pro Rick Adell. In late 1995, the club hired Tom Christie (formerly of Sand Point and Riverside in Portland) as superintendent. In 1996, the membership elected its first woman president, Deborah Chase.

Christie's primary mission was to continue improvements at a course that endured some difficult times. Acquiescing to the complaints (which many insiders considered sour grapes) by the PGA seniors about Inglewood's notoriously slick greens, the members decided to accept a free offer by Bruce Devlin and Butch Baird to redo four greens. The intent was to "soften" the putting surfaces by removing tiers and reducing slopes. Begun in 1990, the project, according to one member, turned into a "disaster" as repeated attempts to grow turf on the rebuilt greens failed. In my opinion, Inglewood's greens should have been left alone. Sure, some of the putting surfaces were quite tilted and, when mowed low, exceedingly fast. But the small greens were appropriate for a course built in the 1920s. Tacoma-based architect John Harbottle redesigned the aforementioned 1st, 2nd, 13th and 14th greens and, by 1996, the greens crew had completely reestablished the turf.

Inglewood's challenge will always reside in its topography. Side- and uphill lies and awkward stances make hitting any club a real challenge. The cant of the terrain is certainly observed at the 5th, a 412-yard par-4 that bends rightward around trees and tilts steeply to the right. At the 150-yard mark, the hole descends toward a narrow redan green with deep hollows alongside it. Probably the toughest par-3 on the course is the 16th, a 216-yarder that rises slightly to a front-leaning green trapped right-front and left. Seattleite Don Bies had a one-stroke lead on the final round of a GTE Northwest Classic, only to bogey Inglewood's 16th and let the tournament slip away. The local fans were dismayed at this development, but Inglewood's track has inflicted pain on many players.

Meridian Valley Country Club

18 *24830 136th Avenue SE, Kent, WA 98042. (253) 631-3133. Dave Gibson, pro. 18 holes. 6,652 yards. Par 72. Grass tees. Course ratings: men—B72.4/134, M70.3/ 130, FF69.7/129; women—FF75.1/132, F73.1/129. Year Opened: 1967. Architect: Ted Robinson. Members, guests & limited reciprocates.*

Meridian Valley Country Club lies east of Kent on a scenic, bowl-shaped site. Though amply suburbanized by peripheral houses—none are within its interior, this private Ted Robinson-designed course retains a laid-back, pastoral ambience. Meridian Valley might not rank among the top-five works in Robinson's portfolio—which includes magnificent Sahalee in Redmond, but fits comfortably within his sec-ond-echelon file. The course's efficient routing and ample hazards, decent length, and varied topography give it much character. Ongoing upgrades have continued to improve playing conditions and toughened up the track substantially.

Meridian Valley contains the best traits of 1960's-era course designs. Crossing a mix of hilly and flat terrain, the layout involves over 50 sand bunkers and nine water hazards. In other words, it enjoys the epic, penal scope characteristic of the sprawling "golf communities" built in the '60s. The greens—averaging 6,000-square-feet in size—are large and contemporary in contour, and were built to USGA specifications. And the wide set-backs between fairways and peripheral residences indicate that land was plentiful and affordable, with golf a priority of the developers (a group of Kent businessmen).

The par-72 course is certainly among the most popular stops on the LPGA Tour, which comes here each September for the Safeco Classic. The well-attended four-dayer has been won by such luminaries as Judy Dickinson, Jan Stephenson, Pat Bradley, Beth Daniel, Julie Inkster, Patty Sheehan and Kirkland native, JoAnne Carner. While skipping other late-season tournaments, many of the tour's biggest stars plan on coming to Meridian Valley, one of their favorite courses. Another high-profile event is the USTravel Golf Invitation, a two-day tournament featuring nine-hole guest appearances by such folks as Jack Nicklaus, Arnold Palmer and Dave Stockton. Top club events include the Meridian Valley member-guest in June, and the Green River Community College Foundation Pro-Am. Meridian Valley has also hosted numerous state and regional tournaments.

The women professionals (who play the course at approximately 6,200 yards) and Meridian Valley's members are tested by the layout's constant challenge. Many holes are narrow and tree-lined, with fairways following various slopes. The aforementioned sand and water hazards impede low scoring, and the greens are among the best in Puget Sound golf. Meridian Valley's signature hole is the 18th, one of the region's prettiest holes. A downhill 524-yard par-5, the home hole begins at a panoramic tee where players can glimpse Mount Rainier and a manicured course. The island-like 18th green is bordered by water on three sides.

Mill Creek Country Club

15500 Country Club Drive, Mill Creek, WA 98012. (425) 743-5664. Tom Sursely, director of golf. 18 holes. 6,349 yards. Par 72. Grass tees. Course ratings: men—B70.8/128, M69.8/124, FF67.4/118; women—M74.9/138, FF73.0/126, F71.7/123. Year Opened: 1976. Architect: Ted Robinson. Members, guests & reciprocates.

18

Mill Creek Country Club is an integral part of a burgeoning community between Seattle and Everett. Originated by a Japanese group, United Development Corp. (UDC), and initially named Olympus, the area was intended to be a quiet retirement enclave. Today, Mill Creek is an incorporated city with a population of nearly 9,000, with residents ranging from retirees to young families with children. Strict covenants overseen by the Mill Creek Community Association retain UDC's original philosophy for the town, which has been annexed several times over. Considered filled up when it reaches 10,000 residents, Mill Creek has its own fire station, police department, library, shopping outlets, churches and post office. This golf club offers only non-proprietary memberships.

One of UDC's strictest and most unusual covenants for Mill Creek regulates the removal of vegetation. The avenues and residential yards in the development look as if they were dropped from the sky into a dense forest. UDC's rule also applies to this Ted Robinson-designed golf course, a penal-type affair with towering evergreens located in target zones, before greens and inside doglegs. Golfers definitely need to be able to "work the ball" both left and right to circumvent these impenetrable barriers. Mill Creek's greens, though elusive, are fairly straightforward. Mill Creek has proven to be a good spot for testing upper-echelon players, hosting such events as U.S. Open Qualifying, U.S. Amateur Qualifying, PNGA Girls' Juniors, PNGA Senior Men's, Washington State Senior Women's, U.S. Girls' Junior Championships and the Women's Western Golf Association Junior Championship.

A stern Mill Creek test is the narrow 3rd, a 488-yard par-5 with a tree-squeezed fairway with a bunker along the left. A creek crosses at the base of the hill-perched 3rd green, which is trapped laterally. The top-rated 7th is a 416-yard par-4 that doglegs 80 degrees to the right around a bunker and houses. The hole eventually ascends to a ridge-roosting green trapped right. A perhaps unfair element of the 7th are the trees that guard the left-front of the green 65 yards out, blocking half the entry to the target. The 15th, a 337-yard par-4, follows a ravine-like, dogleg-right path. A pond lurks along the right driving distance out, while another water hazard fronts a wide-but-shallow green bunkered rear.

The 16th, a 203-yard par-3, has an elevated tee and a big dip in its midsection before running up to a good-sized green fronted left by a fir tree and right by a bunker. Called "Logging Run" (all of Mill Creek's holes have names), the 17th is a 479-yard par-5 with an elevated tee that falls off toward a right-sloping fairway lined on the right by a bunker. The tree-pinched throat entering the 17th green is further imperiled by two bunkers. Mill Creek's home hole—"You Gotta Be Kidding"—is a 365-yard par-4. The 18th starts at a raised tee fronted by a deep, jailed depression. The right-turning route rises steeply up to a knoll-perched, two-tiered green trapped left.

18 Overlake Golf & Country Club

8000 NE 16th Street, Bellevue, WA 98004. (425) 454-5031. Ron Hoetmer, pro. 18 holes. 6,712 yards. Par 71. Grass tees. Course ratings: men—T71.9/129, B71.2/127, M69.6/123, FF67.8/117; women—FF73.2/127, F70.4/123. Year Opened: 1953. Architect: Arthur Vernon Macan; Robert Muir Graves (remodel). Members, guests & reciprocates.

The original "Overlake Golf Club" opened in 1927. The architect for that 18-hole course—which had nothing to do with the current Overlake Golf & Country Club except for the location—was Francis L. James. James and his sometime partner, William Henry Tucker, designed such seminal Puget Sound layouts as Olympia Country & Golf Club, Sand Point Country Club and Jackson Park Golf Course. Overlake was in full swing as a social and sporting scene for Eastsiders and Seattleites—many of whom arrived by small boat or ferry—until 1935, when the Great Depression forced the club's closure.

The course was converted into pastureland for horses and Hereford cattle by two subsequent owners who bought the site after the club's demise. Norton Clapp of the Weyerhaeuser family then acquired the property. Clapp knew about the previous course, and met with some local men who wanted to create another golf club. In 1952, Clapp agreed that another private golf club was needed and, for a nominal fee, leased the 132-acre site to the newly-formed Overlake Golf & Country Club. The club's founders hired Arthur Vernon Macan of Victoria, B.C. to design a new layout.

Macan routed the new holes north and south, a move which eliminated many of the arduous uphill walks found in the first course, which ran east to west. Overlake's greens are well-known for their domed shape and slickness, but they weren't designed that way. As remembered by the club's first president in 1953—Stan Stretton, the configuration of the putting surfaces developed because they were seeded before the topsoil had settled. Another anecdote recalls the "work days" that had early-day members wielding shovels, rakes and saws to fill holes, pick up rocks and trim trees. Overlake's new course opened on June 27, 1953, a time when Bellevue had about 1,000 inhabitants. But the city—along with Mercer Island and neighboring communities—was expanding thanks to the completion of the Lacey V. Murrow Floating Bridge, which spans Lake Washington and links the Eastside to Seattle. The club's original staff included a couple of legendary Northwest golf professionals. Head pro Gordon Richards, who passed away in late-1995 at the age of 87, and assistant Les Moe generated much interest in the new club, and Overlake soon flourished.

Overlake's course has been fine-tuned and improved (primarily through a remodel by Robert Muir Graves) in recent years. Its original clubhouse, a small cottage augmented by an old barn for larger club functions, was replaced on July 30, 1960 by a new 11,000-square foot clubhouse. That structure burned down in 1971. A replacement clubhouse was built and later extensively remodeled in 1993. Tournaments hosted by the club include the Washington State Open, Northwest Open,

PNGA Mid-Amateur, Seattle City Ladies, Women's State Amateur and the 1994 and '95 Ernst Championship Hosted by Fred Couples. Seattle native Jeff Gove, who gained a berth in the 1995 Couples' tournament by winning the Washington State Open, shot a remarkable 61 on the second day, earning a surprising runnerup finish behind winner John Cook and setting a new course record. Incredibly, there was not a single 5 on Gove's card at the end of his magical day at Overlake.

Though generally flat, Overlake's course gains difficulty from its well-guarded and deceptively undulating greens. Tougher tests include the 5th, a 219-yarder that ranks among the region's best par-3s. The hole ascends to a cut-in-a-hillside green bunkered right-front. The right-tilting green has a steep bank on its right flank, with OB and trees close to the left. The top-rated hole is the 7th, a 424-yard par-4 with a straight-running fairway that slopes left toward trees. The last 150 yards taper and curl slightly right to a steep, right-front-sloping green trapped left and right. The pretty 14th is a treacherous 404-yard par-4. Willows left and short pines and firs right squeeze the fairway over its initial run. At the 125-yard mark, the hole curls narrowly left between ponds; the pond on the right is veiled by pines. The skinny and deep 14th green is imperiled by three bunkers—left, right-front and rear, while a pond sits on the left.

Plateau Golf & Country Club

Off SE 8th Street, Redmond, WA 98053. (425) 836-4653. Ray Bloom, pro. 18 holes. 7,122 yards. Par 72. Grass tees. Course ratings not available. Year Opened: 1997. Architects: Masatugo Saito & Perry Dye. Members, guests & reciprocates.

18

This new private club lies on the Sammamish Plateau, about a mile east of 228th Street off Southeast 8th Street between Redmond and Issaquah. The course is part of a 577-acre project that also involves 230 single-family homes. Quadrant Corp. is developing the housing; 55 lots are on holes 3-7, while the rest of the course will be kept in its natural state. The golf portion of the project is backed by Taiyo Golf Development, a Japanese company that owns 25 golf courses world-wide. One of Plateau's perks is that its members have playing privileges at Taiyo's other courses.

Plateau is a true country club, one with a swimming pool, outdoor tennis courts, health club, child-care facilities, a 37,500-square-foot clubhouse and a championship golf course. The 220-acre layout is designed by Masatugu Saito, Taiyo's in-house golf architect, with Perry Dye as a design consultant. Dye was involved in a course Taiyo developed in Singapore and was brought into the project in 1996. Plateau's track was built by Bob Soushek of Fore, Inc., and the superintendent is Joseph Roloff, previously with Meriwood in Lacey. Plateau was scheduled to debut with the original (back) nine in July 1997, with the second (front) nine later that fall (after this book went to press). Plateau's backers will open the course with a temporary clubhouse, with work on the final structure to be finished by mid-1998.

Prospective members have found Plateau's various recreational venues quite attractive. As of early 1997, over 150 of the golf memberships (of 600 total for golf, tennis and social) had been reserved. Many prospective members like the location of the aptly-named club, which is near thousands of newer homes in a growing section of east King County. Also of interest is the club's family orientation. Plateau will have child-care facilities as well as a game room for kids. The clubhouse will also contain a health club, banquet facilities, business meeting rooms and full concierge services.

The golf course winds around wetland areas called Beaver Dam and Saddle Swamp. (When originally announced, the club's "working" name was Beaver Dam.) All told, several hundred acres were left untouched as open space, so playing this course will be an outdoorsy experience. The site involves up and down terrain, with dense fir, alder and maple along the fairways. Views of the Cascades are on display, and deer regularly visit the grounds. The layout has five tees per hole, and is walkable, with close green-to-tee distances. The track involves seven lakes and over 80,000 square feet of bunkers. Since the track was under construction while the book went to press, I won't analyze individual holes. But after visiting the site, and watching Taiyo patiently wade through eight years of permit processing with King County, it isn't far-fetched to regard Plateau's arrival as a welcome one on the Puget Sound golf scene.

Rainier Golf & Country Club

18 *1856 South 112th, Seattle, WA 98168. (206) 242-2800. Keith Williams, pro. 18 holes. 6,352 yards. Par 72. Grass tees. Course ratings: men—B71.1/132, M70.3/ 130; women—M75.7/135, F73.3/130. Years Opened: 1921 (original nine); 1924 (second nine). Architects: Bob Johnstone & Arthur Vernon Macan. Members, guests & limited reciprocates.*

Rainier was founded in 1919 by Charles A. Reynolds, a realtor who donated the 120-acre site for the course. The first nine (now played as the back) opened in 1921; the second, now-front nine was completed in 1924. Initial memberships were $300, with dues of $5.50 a month. Women played for free. Reynolds was abetted in the founding of Rainier by golfers from Jefferson Park, which they felt was becoming too crowded. Once it got going, Rainier quickly developed into one of the region's most popular clubs.

During the Depression, however, the club almost went under. Members were asked to pony up $1,200 apiece to save it from bankruptcy. But the money wasn't raised and the club looked like it would have to be closed. Fortunately, a wealthy member, a Mr. Fisher, rescued Rainier by purchasing the entire club. Once the Depression years passed, Fisher gave the club back to the members and it's stayed quite solvent ever since.

Rainier's layout crosses a hill northeast of Burien, about two blocks below the private nine at Glen Acres. It's under the path of airplane flights landing and taking off from Sea-Tac Airport, so the golfing experience can be somewhat noisy. A classic Northwest course—with tree-lined fairways, small greens and rolling topography, Rainier features prime views of its namesake mountain to the southeast. Though the layout is ringed by homes, no residences are within the course proper. Front-nine holes are fairly flat, except for the last three, while the back nine can be characterized as gently rolling. There's lots of variety to be found on this layout which, to me anyway, is one of the more enjoyable in the greater Seattle area. Dotted with over 80 sand traps and one pond, the track can play difficult, particularly for women, whose tees are not that far ahead of the men's.

The course record of 63 was set in the 1940s before many of the bunkers were in place and the firs, spruces and elms had matured as they are now. Awkward fairway lies are common, and Rainier's greens are among the quickest in the Puget Sound. The course's traditionally poor drainage has received considerable attention of late, such that Rainier now plays great year-round. Other upgrades have included a pond before the green at the 16th, a 525-yard par-5, and an expanded driving range. Perhaps the toughest hole here is the 11th, a nasty 432-yard par-4 that plays much longer than its yardage. Winding over a flattish and wavy, left-leaning route interrupted by a ridge, the hole ends at a very skinny and slick, trapped-left green.

In recent years the members have refurbished the club's two swimming pools, remodeled the clubhouse (adding a deck off the lounge), and improved food service. The club has hosted some significant tournaments over the years. In the early-1960s, the LPGA Tour stopped by for the Ladies Western Open. The contestants in this seminal event included Patty Berg and Kirkland-born JoAnne (Gunderson) Carner. Rainier has also been the site of various PNGA events, including the 1989 Washington Junior Golf Championship (when a 7-year-old girl shot a hole-in-one).

Sahalee Country Club

21200 NE 28th, Redmond, WA 98053. (425) 453-0484. Jim Pike, pro. 27 holes. 6,913 yards (North/South Course). Par 72. Grass tees. Course ratings (North/South Course): men—T74.0/135, B73.2/133, M71.6/130, F68.8/124; women—M77.0/ 136, F73.6/129. Year Opened: 1969. Architect: Ted Robinson; Rees Jones (remodel). Members, guests & limited reciprocates.

Sahalee Country Club is one of the Northwest's premier tracks. Often rated by *Golf Digest* as the top golf course in Washington state, Sahalee has been a fixture in the magazine's listing of top-100 American courses since 1979. The beautiful but tough layout is a wonderful place for hardcore golfers; its constant challenge and endless variety require thorough concentration for players to have any hope of success. It'll certainly be interesting to see how the "big boys" score when the PGA Championship comes to Sahalee in 1998. In preparation for that major event, which will be attended by 25,000 spectators, the club and the PGA invested millions in a new irrigation system, significant drainage improvements, new bunker sand, and many landscaping enhancements. Well-known architect Rees Jones redid four tees on the North and South nines, which will be used for the tournament. The East nine will be closed during the event for parking and hospitality tents.

Sahalee Country Club is devoted to golf. Members have at their disposal a spacious clubhouse, an expansive grass-teed driving range, and 27 holes of manicured golfing grounds. Swimming pools and tennis courts are not part of the equation. Just golf. The fairways wind discreetly between well-tended backyards of a like-named housing development. The residential community spans 200 acres and includes 500 homes and 50 condominiums. The gated neighborhood is festooned with towering pines and cedar trees, rhododendrons, shrubs and ornamental species. Not all residents belong to Sahalee; some are here for the secure suburban environment.

The Ted Robinson-designed layout is very efficient; though hilly in parts, it's easy to walk, with short jaunts between greens and tees. Superintendent Tom Wolff does an exceptional job conditioning Sahalee: short-cropped fairways offer easy-to-pick lies, while the greens, though slick, are receptive to approaches. When I played the course in fall 1995, just before the commencement of winter rules, the grass along some fairways was allowed to grow upwards of six inches in height. The conditions weren't so much a simulation of a PGA Championship as of a U.S. Open. Any ball hit off the mowed-low paths were hopelessly buried in deep grass, and merely returning to the fairway was often the only option. This isn't the usual status of Sahalee, but it sure was interesting to see just how tough the course could be set up. Jack Nicklaus still holds the course record, a 67 from the tournament tees, set during a Seattle Symphony benefit with Arnie Palmer, Don Bies and Sahalee's former pro, Rick Acton.

Members are allowed to play any of the three nines. The most difficult configuration is the North/South, as attested above by the high ratings. Sahalee's difficulty stems from its tight, tree-lined fairways; precise target zones; length; tilted topography; and seven ponds and over 75 sand traps. Perhaps its signature hole is the North Nine's 1st, a 401-yard par-4. The tree-squeezed dogleg-left winds downhill to a pond-ringed green trapped rear-left.

The belief by Sahalee's 500 members in the playing abilities of its long-time head pro, Rick Acton, came to fruition in late 1995 when Acton qualified for the PGA Senior Tour. Acton placed third in his first event, the Royal Caribbean Classic, and finished the year 31st on the money list, automatically qualifying him for another year on the tour. A former regular on the PGA Tour as well as a member of the U.S. Ryder Cup team, Acton had been at Sahalee since 1983. During that time, he has won—at least once—just about every major Northwest tournament. He joins other Northwest-bred golfers such as Bies, Tom Shaw, Kermit Zarley and Ken Still on the senior circuit. Acton was replaced as the head pro by Jim Pike. Acton's new Sahalee title is senior teaching professional; the time he has to teach will be determined by his Tour schedule.

18 Sand Point Country Club

8333 55th NE, Seattle, WA 98115. (206) 523-4994. Ron Stull, pro. 18 Holes. 6,004 yards. Par 71. Grass tees. Course ratings: men—B69.7/123, M68.3/120, FF67.4/119, F66.2/117; women—B75.4/134, M73.6/130, FF72.4/127, F71.1/124. Year Opened: 1927. Architect: Francis L. James; Robert Muir Graves & John Harbottle III (remodels). Members, guests & limited reciprocates.

Sand Point lies in northeast Seattle. Designed by prominent early-day architect, Francis L. James, Sand Point's layout sits within an enclosed neighborhood with 203 houses. Built in the 1920s by developer, Sam Hayes, the community and course occupy a prominent hill that offers wonderful vistas of Magnuson Park, Lake Washington and the Cascades—northward to Mount Baker and south to Mount Rainier. Views from the "Panorama Room" on the top floor of Sand Point's clubhouse are among the most arresting in Northwest golf. Hayes owned the course—which at times was open to the public—until 1939, when the members bought the layout and formed Sand Point Country Club, Inc. An Olympic-sized swimming pool and tennis courts have since been built.

The original course was sparsely wooded, with deep gullies and creeks entering play. Old photos taken just after it opened reveal fairways virtually bereft of trees. Today, there are no streams and the only ravine is off the tee at the 7th, an uphill par-3 of 200 yards. And trees have grown to be an integral part of these golfing grounds, stymieing any golfer who strays off the path. The most significant modern-day upgrade occurred in the mid-1980s, when architect Robert Muir Graves redesigned the 1st, 2nd, 6th and 10th holes, adding bunkers and rebuilding those greens. Recent improvements include a sanding program that has improved drainage, new bunker sand, and two bunkers along the 14th fairway. The clubhouse was remodeled in 1994.

Despite its 6,000-yard length, Sand Point plays tough. Ranking among the region's hilliest layouts, Sand Point forces players to be very adept at negotiating odd-angled lies; it's rare to get a normal stance anywhere on this track. Fairways are narrow and, with 40-plus bunkers around the course and trees always a concern, accuracy is a must. Besides the 7th, which requires a well-placed drive to find its wavy and very slick green, the 8th is a tough front-nine hole. The 565-yard par-5 contains a right-curling, tree-lined fairway with three different levels along its descending route. Lined along the left by OB and on the right by dense woods, the 8th eventually concludes at a rolling and fast green trapped left-front. A hole representative of the hillier back nine is the 12th, a difficult 390-yard par-4 that rises steeply to a hill-cut, very quick front-tilting green guarded by four bunkers. Playing this hole is a Sisyphean feat, particularly in winter when there's no roll.

The course record of 62 is held by PGA Tour pro and honorary member, Rick Fehr. Fehr got his start in golf through his father, Gerald, a long-time Sand Point member and now the executive director of the Washington Junior Golf Association. Another notable golf administrator and member is Dr. John Wagner, 1996-97 president of the Washington Golf Association. Other golfers who learned the game at Sand Point include Albert "Scotty" Campbell, a fine amateur and former Walker Cup team member; Eddie Draper, winner of Washington State and Northwest opens; and Mike Gove, currently the head pro at Astoria Golf & Country Club and past Player of the Year for the Pacific Northwest Section of the PGA. Another outstanding player is Ann Swanson, a winner of numerous Washington State Women's amateurs, Seattle City championships, two Oregon Coast events, seven Southern Oregon championships, and a three-time U.S. Open entrant. Judy Hoetmer, daughter of Sand Point's longtime pro, John Hoetmer, won an NCAA title while at the University of Washington and is in the Husky Hall-of-Fame. Sand Point is the "home course" for the University of Washington women's golf team.

Seattle Golf Club

18

210 NW 145th, Seattle, WA 98177. (206) 363-8811. Doug Doxsie, pro. 18 holes. 6,645 yards. Par 72. Grass tees. Course ratings: men—B72.4/128, M70.1/123; women—M75.4/130, F72.3/125. Year Opened: 1908 (current site). Architects: John Ball & Bob Johnstone; Arnold Palmer (remodel). Members & guests.

Located high above Puget Sound in the Shoreline district northwest of the city, Seattle Golf Club's roots stretch back to the mid-1890s, when a golf-loving Scotsman, Alexander Bailee, arrayed three holes and erected a tent in a cow pasture at Lake Union's north end near the current Gas Works Park. The club's first official meeting was held August 20, 1900, when Josiah Collins invited 102 of Seattle's leading citizens to help form the "Seattle Golf and Country Club." Fifty-three prospective members, including prominent businessmen, lawyers and a judge, accepted the invitation. Shortly thereafter, the founders hired John Ball of Minneapolis to lay out a nine-hole layout in Laurelhurst near Lake Washington, on land leased from David Ferguson.

By 1903, the membership, which originally was limited to 125, expanded to 250. Caddies were paid 50 cents plus carfare for an 18-hole loop. In 1907, the club grew interested in acquiring 350 acres four miles north of Ballard on Richmond Beach Road. After selling the Laurelhurst site for $100,000, the club bought 155 acres at the

Richmond location, with The Highlands, an exclusive neighborhood whose residents were all prominent in the Seattle Golf and Country Club, buying the remaining acreage. To help fund the new course, the membership was expanded to 300 and the initiation fee raised to $300.

The new layout—also designed by Ball, with help from the club's pro, Bob Johnstone—was finished in late-summer 1908. On November 2, 1912, the club officially became Seattle Golf Club, to avoid confusion with The Country Club of Seattle on Bainbridge Island. Travel from the city to the new course was over 11 miles of dirt and plank roads. A few members owned automobiles, but it was a rugged hour-long motorcar drive from Seattle. Many members rode the Everett Interurban Line to the station at 145th Street, then took an electric car over tracks that ran to the west and ended 250 yards from the clubhouse. Aside from renovations to the golf layout and the clubhouse, Seattle Golf Club has remained relatively unchanged over the decades. Indeed, many current members are second, third and fourth generations of the founders.

Between 1994 and 1997, the course underwent an extensive makeover by the legendary Arnold Palmer. In all, 15 holes were remodeled. The work included removing some trees, expanding the driving range, adding several new greens, and augmenting ponds. Palmer preserved the course's hallmarks—stately firs and ornamental specimens, an efficient and walkable layout and tremendous hole-after-hole variety—which have distinguished it over the years. Throughout its lengthy history (a centennial will be celebrated in the year 2000), Seattle Golf Club has sustained the longest-running caddie program in Northwest golf.

Among the luminaries who've brightened the golfing grounds at this exclusive club are former President William Taft, Chick Evans, Harry Vardon, Ted Ray, Walter Hagen, trickshot artist Joe Kirkwood, and the great Bobby Jones, who visited on November 18, 1934, at the height of his success. Seattle Golf Club has also spawned some notable golfers, including the inimitable Harry Givan, Frank Dolp and Jack Westland, who also played out of Everett Golf & Country Club. The course has hosted such events as the Western Golf Association Championship in 1927, Western Golf Association's Women's in 1940, the USGA Championship in 1952, and Walker Cup matches in 1961. An upcoming tournament is the 1999 Pacific Coast Amateur Championship.

Among Seattle's tougher holes is the 2nd, a 365-yard par-4 that starts off an elevated tee and then curls uphill to the right. Four bunkers guard the fairway along the left, with trees right, as the hole ascends to a skinny-but-deep, three-tiered green with traps on both sides. The 7th, a 521-yard par-5, goes straight and slightly uphill along a route that parallels Greenwood Avenue North. Three bunkers on the right squeeze the tee-shot landing area. Over its last 150 yards, the hole angles rightward to a raised, front-sloping green with bunkers right-front and right. A pond shimmers off to the left. Views of Seattle's clubhouse and the Olympic Mountains are available from the tee at the 8th, a 173-yard par-3. This lovely hole has a pond that runs from tee to green. Another pond is left of the right-sloping, undulating green, which is trapped left-front and rear. The 10th, a 421-yard par-4, is a beautiful downhiller that bisects trees over rolling terrain. A pond along the 11th hole may enter play for balls hit too far left. The final 75 yards of the hole wind up to a front-sloping, hill-cut green trapped twice at the left-front.

The tricky 12th, a 344-yard par-4, runs straight uphill off the tee; the hidden landing area is fairly wide. At the 100-yard mark, the fairway winds left around trees to a small green guarded closely on the right by a pond. The water is tucked behind a big trap, and two other bunkers squeeze the putting surface. There's lots of trouble to be found at the 15th, a 394-yard par-4 that winds leftward around trees off a raised tee. Three bunkers line the fairway's left edge once around the corner. Two big bunkers lie 75 yards from the right-front edge of a two-tiered, left-front sloping green with a deep trap right-front. The remodeled 18th, a 518-yard par-5, features a great elevated tee and a descending fairway that heads down to a tight landing area guarded left by a pond and right by two bunkers. Here, the hole reverses itself and goes uphill to the left, passing a huge trap on the right. The route is gradually squeezed by coniferous sentinels as it reaches a skinny-but-deep green trapped right-front. The ascending 18th tests the stamina of players, and is a fine home hole.

Snoqualmie Ridge TPC Golf Course

18

8008 356th Avenue SE, Snoqualmie, WA 98065. Call (425) information for phone number. 18 holes. 7,000 yards. Par 72. Grass tees. Course ratings not available. Year Opened: 1998. Architect: Jack Nicklaus. Members, guests & reciprocates.

Like The Golf Club of Newcastle, this is another of those courses that wasn't open before this book went to press. Yet, with a financially-secure backer (Weyerhaeuser Real Estate Company), a famed designer who won't put his name on a potential flop (Jack Nicklaus), and affiliation with one of the sport's preeminent powers (the PGA Tour), Snoqualmie Ridge looks like a sure thing. After visiting the site in late 1996 and seeing two fairways shaped and seeded, construction on the course—unless nature intervenes with a major calamity—should be completed in time for its projected July 1998 opening. Weyerhaeuser's contract with the PGA stipulates that Snoqualmie Ridge host a Senior Tour event, and it may do so as early as the year 2000. In February 1997, Weyerhaeuser decided to make Snoqualmie Ridge a private course; the company had previously considered semiprivate status.

The genesis of Snoqualmie Ridge dates back to 1985 when former PGA commissioner Deane Beman gave Weyerhaeuser the go-ahead to build a PGA-sanctioned, TPC (Tournament Players Championship) track. In the meantime, the developer jumped through a decade's worth of local-, county- and state-imposed hoops to obtain permits and proceed with the project. The town of Snoqualmie—into which the 1,343-acre site was eventually annexed—was particularly fussy about approving it because of the project's 2,000 single- and multi-family houses. Such concern is justifiable; once Snoqualmie Ridge is filled with residents, the town's population will double. Besides a 220-acre course and large subdivision, the project includes a 40,000-square-foot clubhouse, schools and commericial/business areas. In its contract with Weyerhaeuser the PGA Tour mandated that a massive double-ended driving range be built to allow pros to practice there any time free of charge. Before opening the course, Weyerhaeuser paved a four-lane, multi-million-dollar parkway into the site, which lies about a half-mile north of Interstate 90 off the Highway 18 exit. The company also was required to build a sewage treatment plant; the permit calls for the course to be irrigated with treated effluent by the year 2003.

The course was built by Fairway Construction of Temecula, California, a firm that has built 11 other Nicklaus designs. One of the local construction supervisors was Joe Howe, who worked on the Mill Creek, Bear Creek and Battle Creek layouts. Aptly-named Snoqualmie Ridge roosts atop a promontory with an elevation of 600 feet. Many points offer incredible views of the Cascades to the east and expansive vistas in nearly every other direction. Considerable expense went into raising the 12th hole so that Snoqualmie Falls—a well-known local tourist spot—is observable from the course. Due to the site's hilliness, many holes begin at panoramic elevated tees, with fairways sweeping across side- and downhill terrain. Upon seeing the site, Redmond (Washington) resident and PGA Senior Tour player, Al Geiberger, commented, "It will take players awhile to play the course because of the views." Nicklaus also lauded Snoqualmie Ridge's "spectacular setting."

About a million yards of dirt were moved during shaping. Wide concrete cart paths were paved throughout the layout; Nicklaus won't do a golf course if asphalt is spec'ed for the cart paths—they must be curbed and concrete. About the only flaw in the site is power cabling along the 11th hole. During construction, deer, bears and elk were seen. The fairways were planted with rye, the rough fescue, and greens Providence bentgrass. The Rainbird irrigation system was fitted with nearly 2,000 sprinklers, a considerable amount of heads for a west-of-the-Cascades course. The 18th green sits in a hill-cut depression, providing a natural amphitheater for tournament spectators.

After playing a couple of Nicklaus courses in Cabo San Lucas, Mexico, I see some similarities with those and Snoqualmie Ridge. Among them are broad, meandering fairways that don't require exacting precision off the tee. The courses also employ multiple sets of tees cut out of hillsides, which provide aesthetics while letting players eyeball the challenge ahead. Huge, dramatic bunkers guard fairways and greensides. Grandiose water hazards appeal visually while giving a verisimilitude of a lakeside venue. Nicklaus specializes in epic courses, probably like no other designer extant. With the endemic and human-engineered features of Snoqualmie Ridge, and a magnificent setting, this course—Nicklaus' first championship track in the Northwest—may well emerge as one of the Golden Bear's greats.

Tam O'Shanter Golf & Country Club

9

1313 183rd NE, Bellevue, WA 98008. (425) 746-3502. John Thorsnes, pro. 9 holes. 3,084 yards. Par 36. Grass tees. Course ratings: men—B70.1/123, M68.7/121; women F70.8/124. Year Opened: 1966. Architect: Jack Reimer. Homeowning members, guests & limited reciprocates.

Tam O'Shanter's dual-tee nine opened in 1966 and is an integral part of a Bellevue housing development. The course is played by about 200 of the neighborhood's 497 homeowners. Purchase of a Tam O'Shanter home automatically entitles membership in the golf club, which enjoys a well-conditioned layout, a full-service clubhouse and an iron-only practice range. The course crosses parts of a steep hill and valley floor. The dual-tee track, which extends 6,168 yards over two circuits from the back tees, was designed by Jack Reimer and built by Ray Coleman.

New greens have been constructed since Tam O'Shanter opened. Greens superintendent Tom Corlett initiated a topdressing program for greens and a drainage-improvement project for holes on the lower valley level. Tam O'Shanter's large greens are equipped with two flags. The different flags serve as targets for front- and back-nine rounds, which can be played using one of the three tees per hole. The course is imperiled by five ponds and over 20 sand traps. Particularly tough are the hillside holes, some of which have severely tilting fairways. Perhaps Tam O'Shanter's sternest test is the 5th, a 200-plus-yard par-3 with a pond left-front of a slick, bi-trapped green.

Tam O'Shanter has developed a fine junior program, and hosts district-level Washington Junior Golf championships every three years (with 1997 being the latest). Since 1970, the big club event has been the 75-team, three-day Tam O'Shanter

Invitational. The club is overseen by head pro John Thorsnes, a fine tournament player who was previously an assistant at Sahalee.

Par-3 Courses

Crossroads Park Golf Course

16000 NE 10th, Bellevue, WA 98005. (425) 453-4875. 9 holes. 753 yards. Par 27. Mat tees. No course ratings. Economical, jr./sr. rates. No reservations.

Par-3 Crossroads is operated by the Bellevue Parks and Recreation Department as part of their Crossroads Community Center. The 26-acre complex (nine of which are used for the golf course) is a recreational outlet for troubled youth. The facility, staffed by counselors who conduct crime-prevention programs, also contains a gym, weight rooms, lockers and showers.

The course, played primarily by youngsters and older golfers, is open from March to November. Built in 1981, it was originally the site of an 18-hole par-3 course called Village Greens. Portions of the old Village Greens layout are now used in this short track. Group lessons and clinics for kids are conducted by local golf pros.

Green Lake Golf Course

5701 West Green Lake Way, Seattle, WA 98103. (206) 632-2280. 9 holes. 705 yards. Par 27. Grass tees & mats. No course ratings. Economical, jr./sr. rates. No reservations.

Operated by Seattle's parks department and leased to manager Marlene Taitch, Green Lake Golf Course lies on the southeast end of its namesake lake, the city's busiest park. The course is a popular haunt for beginning golfers of all ages. Somewhat buffered from the nearby hustle and bustle by tall evergreens, the 700-yard track is less an athletic challenge than a grandstand for watching passersby on the 3.2-mile trail that winds around the lake. Green Lake's nine holes run straight toward postage-stamp greens.

Lobo Country Club

8324 121st SE, Snohomish, WA 98290. (360) 568-1638. 9 holes. 1,005 yards. Par 27. Grass tees. No course ratings. Economical, sr. rates. No reservations.

Par-3 Lobo lies in forested environs northeast of Snohomish, off the 88th Street exit of Highway 2. The family-operated facility was begun in 1990 by Gordon Loth, designer of the course. Gordon and his wife, Fedora, manage the facility. If no one is in the "clubhouse," golfers pay green fees on the honor system. Lobo's holes are tree pinched and narrow, and end at small and elusive greens. The venue is easy to walk onto, and is not widely known to golfers in the Puget Sound area.

DRIVING RANGES

EagleQuest at Golf Park

9116 212th Street, Kent, WA 98032.
(253) 850-8300. Five pros on staff.

Gold Creek Tennis & Sports Club

15327 140th Place NE, Woodinville, WA 98072.
(425) 487-1090. Juanita Reinhardt, pro.

Iron Eagle Sport Center

16651 Currie Road, Monroe, WA 98272.
(360) 794-0933. Chris Aoki, pro.

Kaddyshack Golf Center

4003 204th SW, Lynnwood, WA 98036.
(425) 775-8911. Pete Dixon, pro.

Longshots Driving Range

1215 80th Street SW, Everett, WA 98203.
(425) 355-2133. Bob Osgood, pro.

Marysville Golf Center

7431 64th Drive NE, Marysville, WA 98270.
(360) 653-2000. Gary Nicholson, pro.

Puetz Evergreen Golf Range

11762 Aurora North, Seattle, WA 98133.
(206) 362-2272. Six pros on staff.

Red Wood Golf Center

13029 Redmond-Woodinville Road NE, Redmond, WA 98052.
(425) 869-8814. Scott Williams, pro.

South Center Golf

18791 Southcenter Parkway, Tukwila, WA 98188.
(206) 575-7797 or 1-800-293-4621. Jim Bennett, pro.

Super Range

511 128th SE, Everett, WA 98204.
(425) 742-5790 or 338-2424. Kevin Mackay, pro.

University of Washington Driving Range

Next to Graves Baseball Field off Union Bay Place NE, one-quarter mile north of Husky
Stadium (Mail Stop GF10), Seattle, WA 98195. (206) 543-8759. John Krebs, pro.

Upcoming Courses

Duvall — Conifer Ridge Golf Club (1999). This project off Lake Joy Loop Road has received permits. In early 1995, a New Jersey resident bought the 165-acre site and hired Peter Thompson to design an 18-hole course. The following year, after repositioning a planned clubhouse to a newly-acquired 15-acre parcel, some permits had to be requested again.

Fall City — Aldarra Farm Golf Club (1999). In April 1997, a group of investors had an option to buy this 650-acre site owned by the Boeing family. Their plan was to built a private Tom Fazio-designed course. Previous plans involved a public Arnold Palmer layout and 300 homes.

Lake Stevens — Woodland Greens Golf Course (1999). Plans for this 297-acre site include two 18-hole courses. The layouts will be designed and developed by Evergreen Golf Design, overseen by golf pro Fred Jacobson. Acquiring water permits from the state has been the biggest stumbling block. A conditional-use permit for the course has been issued.

Marysville — Tulalip Indian Project (1999). The Tulalips included a nine-hole course in their plans for a destination-type resort on tribal property west of Interstate 5.

Redmond — Ames Lake (1999). A public 27-hole golf course with 100 lots has been proposed for a 454-acre site between NE Tolt Hill Road and Ames Lake-Carnation Road NE In 1996, the owner was in the process of selling the site, which still lacked a few permits.

Redmond — Blakely Ridge (1999). In late 1996, a Snohomish County Superior Court upheld the approval of this large-scale development. Besides an 18-hole golf course and over 2,000 single- and multi-family homes, the project includes a 125,000-square-foot commercial area, tennis courts, a swimming pool, shuttle bus system, clubhouse and 533 acres of open space.

TACOMA
& VICINITY

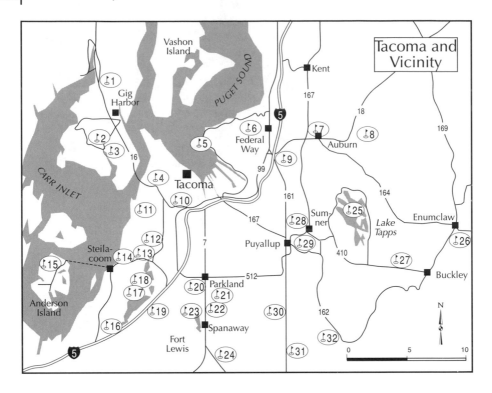

Tacoma and Vicinity

1. **Canterwood Golf & Country Club** — private 18
2. **Gig Harbor Golf & Country Club** — semiprivate 9 & driving range
3. **Madrona Links Golf Course** — public 18
4. **Highlands Golf & Racquet Club** — public 9
5. **North Shore Golf & Country Club** — public 18 & driving range
6. **Twin Lakes Golf & Country Club** — private 18
7. **Auburn Golf Course** — public 18
8. **Jade Greens Golf Course** — public 9 & driving range
9. **Christy's Golf Course & Driving Range** — public 9 (par-3) & driving range
10. **Allenmore Public Golf Club** — public 18
11. **Fircrest Golf Club** — private 18
12. **Meadow Park Golf Course** — public 18, par-3 9 & driving range
13. **Oakbrook Golf & Country Club** — private 18
14. **Fort Steilacoom Golf Course** — public 9
15. **Lake Josephine Riviera Golf & Country Club** — private 9
16. **Fort Lewis Golf Course** (military) — private 27
17. **American Lake VA Golf Course** — private 9
18. **Tacoma Country & Golf Club** — private 18
19. **Whispering Firs Golf Course** (military) — private 18
20. **University Golf Club** — public 9
21. **EagleQuest at Linksman Golf Center** — driving range & 18-hole putting course
22. **Brookdale Golf Course** — public 18 & driving range
23. **Lake Spanaway Golf Course** — public 18 & driving range
24. **Classic Country Club** — public 18 & driving range
25. **Tapps Island Golf Course** — public 9
26. **Enumclaw Golf Course** — public 18
27. **Emerald Links Driving Range**
28. **Sumner Meadows Golf Links** — public 18 & driving range
29. **Linden Golf & Country Club** — private 9
30. **Meridian Greens** — public 9 & driving range
31. **Lipoma Firs Public Golf Course** — public 27 & driving range
32. **High Cedars Golf & Country Club** — public 18, executive 9, driving range & 18-hole putting course

This area south of Puget Sound includes south King and Pierce counties. The state's second most-populated city, Tacoma—like Seattle to the north—is in a boom period. The once-sleepy town of Dupont south of Tacoma is in the midst of unprecedented growth; it's already drawn two major industries with more to follow. This part of the Northwest is in the mild, marine air-influenced climate zones of 4 and 5. Well-endowed with quality golf facilities, the "City of Destiny" also enjoys a central location that allows linksters access to dozens of courses between Seattle and Olympia, as well as those on the Kitsap and Olympic peninsulas. And the area has plans for even more courses.

Public Courses

Allenmore Public Golf Club

18

2125 South Cedar, Tacoma, WA 98405. (253) 627-7211. Don Mojean, pro. 18 holes. 6,064 yards. Par 71. Grass tees. Course ratings: men—B68.5/118, F67.4/116; women—B73.8/125, F72.9/123. Year Opened: 1931 (original nine); 1935 (original second nine); 1970s (rebuilt second nine). Architect: Ray Ball. Moderate, jr./sr. rates. Reservations: Call a week ahead for weekends & holidays. Walk-on chances: Ok for singles. Walkability: Good. Playability: Enjoyable course near Tacoma's downtown.

Allenmore is often overlooked as a choice for linksters visiting the City of Destiny. Handily located off South Cedar Street just north of Highway 16 (it's visible from this busy state route), Allenmore began with nine holes in 1931. Originally owned by Sam Allen—*ergo* Allenmore—it is currently run by the Tacoma Elks, which keeps it open to the public. In the 1970s, the Elks converted Allenmore's 1935-built back nine into an Elks lodge, rebuilding the current back nine on a plot to the south.

Allenmore's traditional layout boasts considerable variety. The enjoyable track crosses bowl-shaped terrain, so there are a few flat holes along with those generating off-kilter lies. Most fairways are tree-lined, with some on the narrow side. Allenmore is known for its rolling greens which, when mowed low during the dry summer months, are quick. Generally, the throats of Allenmore's greens are bunkerless, so those who prefer pitch and run play should do well here.

Notable holes include the tree-lined 3rd, a tight, 364-yard par-4. This gradual dogleg-right ends at a steeply-graded green fronted by bunkers. The 11th, a 517-yard par-5, follows a wildly rolling, left-curling route, and has a green flanked by two traps. Allenmore's 16th is a quaint 149-yard par-3. The hole contains a fairway-wide pond—filled with ducks and lily pads—that golfers cross via a footbridge. Two traps guard the right edge of the small, front-sloping green. Allenmore's 18th, a 419-yard par-4, is a good closer. The sidehill fairway parallels the Allenmore Ridge condominiums en route to a laterally-trapped, tilting green.

Auburn Golf Course

29630 Green River Road, Auburn, WA 98092. (253) 833-2350. Doug Campbell, pro. 18 holes. 6,265 yards. Par 71. Grass tees. Course ratings: men—B69.5/111, M68.3/109, F66.2/105; women—M72.0/124, F70.4/114. Year Opened: 1952. Architect: Auburn Parks & Recreation Department. Moderate, jr./sr. rates. Reservations: Call a week ahead. Walk-on chances: Ok for singles. Walkability: Good, despite a couple of hills. Playability: New tees and greens have enhanced challenge of popular muni course.

This layout flanks the Green River on the east edge of Auburn, a rapidly expanding town filling up with new commercial enterprises and citizens. The municipal venue is like an enclosed city park, though the Cobble Creek housing development lines the layout's 11th and 12th holes. The 1952-built course was built by Auburn's Parks and Recreation Department; the busy facility hosts over 65,000 rounds a year. Auburn's head pro is Doug Campbell, a former PGA tourer who's won his share of regional events, including two Oregon Opens, two Pacific Northwest PGA Championships and Spokane's Lilac Open.

Many improvements have been made to Auburn's course over the last couple of years. The renovations—implemented by the city through golf proceeds—include new tees, a dozen new greens, ponds and bunkers and paved cart paths throughout. In 1997 the 16th green was rebuilt, and two holes reconfigured. Upcoming plans include a much-needed automatic irrigation system, further improvements to drainage, and an all-new clubhouse. Long-time superintendent Kevin Van has overseen the on-course work. In winter, the course is somewhat boggy because of its proximity to the Green River. Hopefully, the drainage-enhancement program will fix that problem.

The challenge of Auburn's generally flat, mid-length course has been heightened by all the upgrades. A tough hole is the 6th, a 402-yard par-4 lined by the Green River along the left. Evergreen sentries tower 75 yards off the tee, and the rolling, left-bending fairway ends at a slick, undulating green. The 9th, a 492-yard par-5, is a yawning dogleg-left with a fir tree in mid-fairway 100 yards off the tee. Another large tree—and a pond 100 yards farther down—impede progress to the steeply tilting, bi-trapped green. The top-rated 10th, a par-5 of 567 yards, starts at a raised tee then doglegs left between trees. The hole winds past a pond outside the turn en route to a saddle-shaped green. At the promontory-perched 12th, golfers glimpse an industrious Auburn Valley to the west. This slightly uphill, 475-yard par-5 gradually tapers as it curls leftward to a green squeezed by two traps.

Brookdale Golf Course

802 Brookdale Road East, Tacoma, WA 98445. (253) 537-4400 or 1-800-281-2428. Tom Parkhurst, director of golf; Craig Wilcox, pro. 18 holes. 6,425 yards. Par 71. Grass tees. Course ratings: men—B69.6/112, M68.4/110; women F70.0/111. Year Opened: 1931. Architect: Christopher Mahan. Moderate, jr./sr. rates, credit cards. Reservations: Call a week ahead. Walk-on chances: Fair. Walkability: Efficient routing is pedestrian-friendly. Playability: Quite good, particularly in spring and fall when the course is one of western Washington's driest.

Brookdale is one of the best-draining venues on the west (or wet) side of the Cascades, either in Washington or Oregon. The course's underlayment is the same porous amalgam of sand, pebbles and topsoil that extends from Tacoma south to Olympia. The only other Puget Sound-area courses of equivalent wintertime playability are Capitol City in Olympia and Classic in Spanaway. Brookdale's playlist is comprised mainly of locals who view the place as a home away from home.

Brookdale was originally owned, designed and built by Christopher Mahan. The layout in southeast Tacoma has been owned by Chuck Brown since 1960; Brown took over the lease in 1952. He's also the proprietor of Yelm's Nisqually Valley course. Director of golf Tom Parkhurst has been here since 1978. Parkhurst's stepson, Craig Wilcox, is the head pro. In 1997, Brown began plans for a driving range. Brookdale is a popular place for private tournaments. The layout spans meadows east of Pacific Avenue amid an established neighborhood, and offers southeasterly vistas of Mount Rainier on clear days.

The walker-friendly track crosses generally flat terrain. Its hazards include a small stream that enters play on four holes, with a few bunkers imperiling some fairways and greens. Overall though, the layout is uncomplicated by manmade hazards. Tougher holes include the 3rd, a 414-yarder. The tee shot at this par-4 is made to a mound-obscured fairway, which can be reconnoitered through a periscope by the tee. A creek runs off the tee, and the fairway ends at a small green. The 9th, a 250-yard par-3, heads straight to a small green behind the clubhouse. The 16th, a par-4 of 340 yards, requires an accurate drive over a creek and reservoir to reach a left-curling fairway. And the 17th, a 405-yard par-4, requires two well-struck shots to find a mid-sized putting surface.

Classic Country Club

18 *4908 208th Street East, Spanaway, WA 98387. (253) 847-4440 or 1-800-924-9557. Lorie Isaac, pro. 18 holes. 6,793 yards. Par 72. Grass tees. Course ratings: men— B73.6/133, M71.6/130, FF69.6/124; women F73.3/135. Year Opened: 1991. Architect: Bill Overdorf. Moderate (expensive on weekends), jr./sr. rates, credit cards. Reservations: Call a week ahead. Walk-on chances: Fair. Walkability: Excellent. Playability: One of the best public courses in western Washington.*

Located at the south end of Spanaway off Highway 7, Classic is often included among the Northwest's top golf tests. In *Golf Digest's* 1996-97 "Places to Play" guide, the tough Classic track received three-and-a-half stars. The facility was developed by Curtis LeMay, who named it after his antique car collection. LeMay sold the 125-acre course in 1992 to Otaka Inc., a subsidiary of Takao Group of Japan. Otaka also runs Riverside Country Club in Chehalis; the company always appends "Country Club" to its courses, seeking to connote a place of poshness. The public course opened on September 21, 1991, along with a modest clubhouse and grass-teed driving range.

Lynden architect Bill Overdorf gave the 6,800-yard layout an efficient, walker-amenable routing. Also abetting bag toters is gently rolling terrain with only 40 feet of elevation change. When it debuted, the course was remarkably mature as the fairways, tees and greens grew a full year before golfers set foot on them. The former tree farm had porous, gravelly soil to begin with, and the site was further enhanced by a deep deposit of sand and topsoil, resulting in exceptional drainage and dry winter play. Classic's holes are defined by 30-year-old firs, with a few oaks dotting the premises. Mount Rainier looms southeast of the course, which is occasionally visited by deer, porcupines, foxes and birds. After earning her Class A card from the PGA's Northwest section in 1996, Classic's head pro Lorie Isaac became the only woman in the state to earn such status.

Overdorf endowed the course with over 70 sand traps and four ponds. Besides its signature amoeba-like greens, which allow tough pin placements, Classic is imperiled by many grass bunkers. The bunker grass is often allowed to grow as high as six inches, thus enabling the turfed pits to more than adequately meet the definition of "trap." Another major concern are water hazards lurking invisibly along some fairways.

Tougher tests include the 1st, a 395-yard par-4 that winds leftward between a hidden pond left and bunker right. The hole rises to a diminutive, hill-cut green trapped front-right, left and rear; a pond also squats at the right-front. The 7th, a 530-yard par-5, is a dogleg-left that bypasses homes and OB left and a squadron of grass bunkers right en route to a raised, trap-ringed green. The top-rated 9th, a 563-yard par-5, is a long dogleg-left that bisects a pond right and huge bunker left. The fairway curls along a tree-tapered path to a wide-but-shallow green engirded by four sand bunkers.

Classic's back nine is highlighted by such holes as the 13th, a left-turning 429-yard par-4 that skirts trees and OB. A good-sized landing area is available to the right of the fairway, but watch for bunkers inside the turn. From here, the 13th ascends leftward to a tree-fronted, hill-perched, boomerang-shaped green that is well-trapped. Another dandy is the 581-yard, par-5 18th. The fairway heads straight off an elevated tee. Beware here: a pond sits along the left, driving distance out. Over its last 125 yards, the home hole curls rightward between trees and sundry bunkers to a slick, front-sloping green linked to the 12th green. The 18th green is fronted and backed by a representative sampling of Classic's ubiquitous sand and grass bunkers.

Enumclaw Golf Course

45220 288th SE, Enumclaw, WA 98002. (360) 825-2827. John McGregor, pro. 18 holes. 5,629 yards. Par 70. Grass tees & mats. Course ratings: men 66.0/106, women 68.8/110. Year Opened: 1949 (original six) holes; 1950 (three holes); 1975 (second nine). Architects: Local golfers (original nine); Bill Teufel (second nine). Moderate, jr./sr. rates. Reservations: Call on Wednesday for weekends. Walk-on chances: Fair. Walkability: Good, but watch out for tree roots. Playability: Some challenges to be found on shorter course.

The 80-acre venue here sits on the northern doorstep of Mount Rainier National Park off Highway 410, at Enumclaw's east end. Hosting about 40,000 rounds a year, the facility is owned by King County, which was deeded the site by the White River Lumber Company. Head pro John McGregor has run Enumclaw's golf operations since 1982. The course is frequented by folks from Puget Sound and environs, with golfers from Yakima and other points east finding their way here. Over the past decade, over a million dollars have been invested in improvements to the course.

The relatively short track crosses rolling Cascade foothills and a meadow, and adjoins Pete's Pool, a local landmark. Designed and built by local golfers, Enumclaw opened with six holes in 1949. Three holes were added in 1950, and a Bill Teufel-designed back nine was appended in the mid-'70s. The course features many old-growth evergreens, offers nice mountain vistas on clear days, and has salmon-bearing Boise Creek winding through it. The widespread flooding that wracked the Puget Sound area in February 1996 put seven Enumclaw holes completely underwater; the 10th and 18th fairways had to be replanted. Future renovations include a new tee and bunker at the par-3 13th hole.

Enumclaw is a popular site for private tournaments, with post-event barbecues held at an outdoor deck off the clubhouse. Among its tougher holes is the 473-yard, par-5 4th. A deep swale precedes the wavy, dogleg-right fairway, and the hillside-cut 4th green is engirded by trees. A par-4 of 420 yards, the runway-like 11th hole ends at a tree-ringed green backed by Boise Creek. The tee at the 16th, a par-5 of 511 yards, offers a view of a fairway that rises and runs between a massive set of goalpost-like firs. The tilting 16th green is fronted by the meandering creek, which has a knack for snagging underclubbed second shots.

Fort Steilacoom Golf Course

8202 Elwood Drive SW, Tacoma, WA 98497. (253) 588-0613. Keith Johnson, pro. 9 holes. 2,518 yards. Par 34. Grass tees. Course ratings: men 62.8/98, women 66.8/105. Year Opened: 1951. Architect: Ray Ball. Economical, jr./sr. rates. Call for reservations. Walk-on chances: Good. Walkability: No problems at short layout. Playability: Good place for youngsters and beginners to learn the game.

Nine-hole Fort Steilacoom lies next to Western State Hospital, Washington's largest mental institution. The course was designed and built by Ray Ball in 1951 as a rehabilitation facility for patients. Ball operated the course for the state until 1970, at which time Pierce County Parks inked a 50-year lease with the state's Department of Social and Health Services and opened it for public play. In 1994, Sikma Enterprises, Inc. signed on as the concessionaire. Headed by former NBA star, Jack Sikma, the firm has made some improvements to the venue, but not as many as they'd have liked. Permits were issued in mid-1994 to build a 2,800-square-foot clubhouse, but construction has yet to commence. Consideration has also been given to building a John Steidel-designed back nine on a baseball field next to the existing course. The county and the city of Lakewood would like to see these holes come to fruition (at which time the clubhouse would likely be expanded), but issues related to the county's lease with the state have not been resolved.

The course occupies a ridge above a Boise Cascade mill and a railroad yard on Puget Sound, a sometimes noisy proposition. Fort Steilacoom's waterside locale brings regular visits from raccoons, deer and sea otters. Though it has recently received a few sand traps, the course remains a facile layout with six short and birdieable par-4s, two par-3s and a par-5. Some greens at the par-4s can be driven, but overhanging fir and madrona branches will block misplaced shots. The January 1997 storm knocked down some trees, but not enough to affect play. The dual-tee track extends 4,820 yards over two circuits.

Interesting holes include the top-rated 7th, a 343-yard par-4 that doglegs left around woodlands. A long and high, corner-cutting drive can reach the small 7th green. The 9th, a 260-yard par-4, winds rightward. This hole tempts golfers to drive the green for an eagle or birdie. Hit too far left or through the fairway, however, and you're on the aforementioned baseball diamond. Go too far to the right, and you're in a greenside bunker or, worse, a well-treed jail.

Gig Harbor Golf & Country Club - semiprivate

9

6909 Artondale Drive NW, Gig Harbor, WA 98335. (253) 851-2378. Jeff Mehlert, pro. 9 holes. 2,702 yards. Par 35. Grass tees. Course ratings: men 65.6/109, women 68.8/114. Year Opened: 1956. Architect: Ken Tyson; Robert Muir Graves (remodel). Moderate, jr./sr. rates, credit cards. Call for reservations. Walk-on chances: Fair. Walkability: Some tall hills, but this is a tight, walkable layout. Playability: Moderate test for low- and mid-handicappers getting steady improvements.

Gig Harbor's nine-hole course sprawls across a hillside south of its namesake town. The layout was built on an old apple orchard and originally called Artondale Golf Course. The semiprivate facility is owned by its members, but public play is allowed (call ahead in case club events are planned). Besides an enjoyable place to golf, the 80-acre venue has a banquet facility, clubhouse and driving range. In recent years, members have discussed acquiring neighboring acreage for a back nine. Robert Muir Graves—who renovated some holes in the late-1980s—has drawn up a design for this site.

Before considering any nine-hole expansion, the club's 250 members have been supporting a plan that overhauls the current nine. Superintendent Russ Price has concentrated on upgrading drainage to enable year-round play, and built new tees. The 4th hole has been "dried out," and a new bunker was added beside the 9th green. Also improved was the range, which may soon be equipped with lights. Price has been enlarging every green on the course in an effort to better facilitate the course's two-flag system.

Gig Harbor's golfers enjoy nice views of Mount Rainier on clear days. The "18-on-9" layout, which extends 5,420 yards over two circuits, will more adequately simulate an 18-hole track once Price expands all the greens. Besides tipped topography, golfers should be concerned with several bunkers and a spring-fed creek—also the course's primary irrigation source—on the 8th and 9th holes. Interesting holes include the 1st, a narrow 425-yard par-4 that skirts a fairway bunker along the left. The hole tapers 100 yards from a large green backed by a berm. The 7th, a 496-yard par-5, has a pond off the tee and a tree-pinched fairway. The route widens as it descends to a trapped-right green with a steep rear end. The uphill 9th plays much longer than its 307 yards. The creek crosses the par-4 100 yards off the tee, then the fairway climbs to a bunker-guarded green lined left by trees.

High Cedars Golf Club

27

14604 149th Street Court East, Orting, WA 98360. (360) 893-3171. Regulation Course: 18 holes, 6,303 yards, par 72, grass tees; course ratings: men—B70.2/116, M68.7/113, F67.2/110; women—M73.8/122, F72.0/118. Executive Course: 9 holes, 1,566 yards, par 28, grass tees; course ratings—men 53.8/78, women 56.4/83. Years Opened: 1970 (regulation course); 1990 (executive nine). Architects: Glen Proctor & Roy Goss (regulation course); Bill Stowe (executive nine). Moderate for both courses, credit cards. Reservations: Call a week ahead. Walk-On Chances: Fair. Walkability: Good on both courses. Playability: All clubs in the bag will be used on challenging 18-holer. Executive track and putting course also fun.

Located between Sumner and Orting, High Cedars is owned by Wally Staatz, whose family operated Staatz Bulb Farms at the site before converting it into a full-service golfing outlet. The regulation layout is etched within groves of ancient cedars, while a 1990-opened executive nine is treeless and links-like. On clear days, impressive views of Mount Rainier are available from both courses. Besides 27 holes, High Cedars has a driving range, clubhouse-restaurant and 18-hole putting course. Around 200 homesites are being developed around the executive course.

The Glen Proctor and Roy Goss-designed layout, located just north of the Puyallup River, is greatly enhanced by the thousands of daffodils, tulips and irises that bloom in spring. In July and August, the resident annuals—geraniums, marigolds and petunias—sustain the colorful display. The grounds are frequented by Canada geese, which feed near a lake between the 9th and 10th holes. Because of its river-side locale, High Cedars was particularly hard hit by the winter of 1996 floods. A nearby dike broke, damaging four holes. To allow golf to continue, Statz incorporated holes that were not harmed with some on the executive course and charged players $12, calling it a "disaster rate." By summer 1996, High Cedars was back to normal.

Both the regulation and executive courses are flat and easy to walk. On the 6,300-yard 18, the primary obstacles are old-growth cedars looming menacingly in target zones and a goodly number of sand and water hazards. Good holes include the top-rated 7th, a par-4 of 405 yards with a tight, cedar-paneled route. The hole passes a heart-shaped lake along the left before ending at a contoured green. Beginning at an elevated, pond-fronted tee, the 9th, a 539-yard par-5, is defined by red-skinned timber left and the goose lake right. The last leg of this pretty hole bends rightward to a rockeried pond in front of a trapped-right green. The 14th, a 524-yard par-5, runs long and straight, passing a cornfield along the left en route to a raised, hogbacked green. The best Rainier views at High Cedars are from the 14th fairway.

Highlands Golf & Racquet Club

9

1400 Highland Parkway North, Tacoma, WA 98406. (253) 759-3622. 9 holes. 1,279 yards. Par 28. Grass tees. No course ratings. Year Opened: 1931. Architects: Founding members; Highlands' developer (remodel). Economical, credit cards. No reservations. Walkability: No problems. Playability: Quite good for a short course.

Par-28 Highlands curls between homes and townhouses near downtown Tacoma. The course boasts manicured greens, tees and fairways, well-placed ponds, and white-sand bunkers. It wasn't always in such good shape, however. In the mid-'70s, a local group calling itself Highlands Twenty, Inc. purchased the rundown facility for $88,000 and immediately began renovations. A member of this group, Doug McArthur—former chairman of the Safeco Classic, an annual LPGA event held at Meridian Valley Country Club, recalls finding the course overrun with weeds, dying fish in the ponds (local kids made headlines when they tried to rescue them), and broomsticks holding flags on the greens.

With help from Wayne Thronson, McArthur tried to convince Tacoma's Metropolitan Park District to buy the course, but the district wasn't interested. The duo then solicited financial pledges from friends; the Highlands Twenty soon owned a golf course. The group is now down to 17 members. The "Racquet Club" part of the Highlands alludes to the two outdoor tennis courts near the course entrance. The course, tennis courts and housing occupy what used to be the site of Highlands Golf Course, a 1931-opened regulation-length track that lacked irrigation water.

Despite its position amid housing (the layout was designed and built by the subdivision's developer), the course is quiet, though holes adjoining Highway 16 on its southern edge are a bit noisy. Ponds at the 3rd and 5th holes are occupied by ducks and Canada geese, and attractive flower gardens decorate some of the well-tended grass tees. If timed correctly, a weekday round can take about an hour. Eight of Highlands' holes range from 100 to 180 yards, with the only par-4 being the 250-yard 4th. The course is a good test for iron play, and its small, trap-guarded greens mandate accuracy. Interesting holes include the 3rd, a 165-yarder. A pond fronts a saddle-shaped green squeezed by trees left and a bunker right-front. The top-rated 4th bisects trees en route to a front-sloping, kidney-shaped putting surface. Also tough is the 7th, a 180-yard par-3 with a tree-hemmed fairway and a large, saucerlike green trapped along the right.

Jade Greens Golf Course   9

18330 SE Lake Holm Road, Auburn, WA 98002. (253) 931-8562. Doug MacDonald, pro. 9 holes. 2,656 yards. Par 34. Grass tees. Course ratings: men—B66.1/112, M65.0/110; women—B71.0/120, M69.7/117, F65.5/108. Year Opened: 1990. Architects: Jim Hawk & Bob Soushek. Moderate, jr./sr. rates, credit cards. Reservations: Call a week ahead. Walk-on chances: Fair. Walkability: Good. Playability: Fun for all ability levels.

Jade Greens Golf Course, which lies in the Covington district northeast of Auburn, is owned by Jim and Mary Jo Hawk. Their holdings totaled 88 acres but, because of wetlands on the property, a significant slice of the parcel was left in its native state. The course was named after the Hawks' jade-collecting hobby; non-gem-quality jade stones may one day be used as tee markers. The course was designed by Jim Hawk and Bob Soushek of Fore, Inc., who also built it. A driving range and a 2,800-square-foot clubhouse with a restaurant and pro shop have been added since the course opened in 1990.

Because of the wetlands, King County made the Hawks follow strict guidelines during construction of the course, including limiting the chemicals used in maintenance after it opened. The owners' patience with the process paid off, as the 20 acres of wetlands in the layout's midsection sustain frogs, raccoons, blue herons, red-tailed hawks, songbirds, various blackbirds, sandpipers, ducks and woodpeckers. Jade Greens is an entertaining layout, with 18-hole rounds encouraged. The layout features widely disparate tee blocks, and seven of the greens contain two flags on separate tiers; the 1st/10th and 9th/18th holes each have two greens. Over two circuits, the track extends 5,348 yards.

Only a few sand traps are found here, but ponds enter play on four holes. Despite its arrayal around the wetlands, Jade Greens drains fairly well and is a good choice for winter play. Interesting holes include the 2nd, a 442-yard par-4 that runs straight over rolling terrain. Out-of-bounds lines the left edge of the fairway, which ends at a swale-fronted, horseshoe-shaped green trapped left. The 5th, a 259-yard par-4, is an extremely narrow hole that stretches out to a rolling, pond-fronted green. The garden spot for drives at the top-rated 9th, a 407-yard par-4, is the crest of a hill. From here, the skinny 9th green can be viewed along the right at the base of the hill. The small and squarish 18th green is up off to the left.

Lake Spanaway Golf Course

18 *15602 Pacific Avenue, Tacoma, WA 98444. (253) 531-3660. Keith Johnson, pro. 18 holes. 6,835 yards. Par 72. Grass tees. Course ratings: men—B72.4/124, M70.2/ 118, F69.1/114; women—M76.0/128, F73.4/123. Year Opened: 1967. Architect: Arthur Vernon Macan. Moderate, credit cards. Reservations: Call five days ahead. Walk-on chances: Fair. Walkability: Good. Playability: One of the Puget Sound area's most enduring challenges.*

Located southeast of Tacoma, Lake Spanaway often ranks among the state's top-20 courses. The 1967-opened, Pierce County-owned facility is leased to Sikma Enterprises, Inc., which also runs Fort Steilacoom Golf Course for the county. Sikma is also involved at Harbour Pointe in Mukilteo and Holmes Harbor on Whidbey Island. Shortly after taking over "Spanaway's" operations, Sikma's firm improved the venue's rather dated clubhouse. The popular course hosts, on average, over 60,000 rounds a year, and is frequently used for state, regional and prep tournaments.

Lake Spanaway is etched within woodlands just south of the county-operated Henry Sprinker Recreational Center. The layout, one of the final designs of PNGA Hall-of-Fame architect, Arthur Vernon Macan, is bordered by Pacific Avenue South on the east, a neighborhood to the south, and Lake Spanaway on the west. These peripheral areas shouldn't enter play, though Pacific Avenue is but a wild slice away from the 1st tee and a duck-hook drive from the 10th. The course sits under the flight patterns of planes taking off and landing at nearby McChord Air Force Base, so golfers may be subjected to periodic parades of droning, low-flying military aircraft.

Towering fir trees dominate this track, looming inside doglegs, near green fronts and within target zones. Bunkers and ponds also abound. The course drains reasonably well, though in winter plays much longer because of less roll. Andy Soden, the county's director of golf, will pursue a more aggressive topdressing and aerification program to help extend Lake Spanaway's "dry" season. A new irrigation system was recently installed. Pierce County officials have been in discussions with the USGA for a national event for Lake Spanaway; the national Publinx or the Mid-Amateur may be held here. Before the course's 30th Anniversary in 1997, the county renovated the tees and completely rebuilt the bunkers.

Among the toughest holes is the 5th, a dogleg-right par-5 of 501 yards. The generally flat hole ends at a raised, tree-ringed green guarded by three bunkers. The 10th, a par-5 of 452 yards, may be Lake Spanaway's signature hole. A depression in mid-fairway second-shot distance out harbors a hidden pond. The elevated 10th green is guarded right-front by a large trap. Another good test is the 15th, a 429-yard par-4 that snakes leftward between Titleist-caroming conifers to a front-sloping, laterally-trapped green.

Lipoma Firs Public Golf Course

18615 110th Avenue East, Puyallup, WA 98374. (253) 841-4396 or 1-800-649-4396. Jim Cayton, pro. 27 holes. Course ratings: Blue/Green (6,687 yards, par 72) men—B72.4/125, M70.1/121, F66.9/114; women—M75.2/126, F71.3/118. Gold/Blue (6,805 yards, par 72) men—B72.5/124, M69.5/118, F67.2/ 112; women—M74.5/124, F71.0/117. Gold/Green (6,722 yards, par 72) men— B72.5/124, M70.2/120, F66.8/113; women—M75.3/126, F71.1/117. Years Opened: 1989-90 (Gold/Blue); 1994 (Green). Architect: Bill Stowe. Moderate, jr./sr.rates. Reservations: Call a week ahead. Walk-on chances: Fair. Walkability: Good overall, with a few lengthy between-hole hikes. Playability: Stay out of its name-sake trees, and you may score well on lengthy track.

Perched atop Puyallup's South Hill, Lipoma Firs has evolved from a semi-rural 18-hole facility into a full-blown 27-holer in the midst of peripheral suburbanization. Though the course retains a forested ambience, civilization has moved into the neighborhood as the owners, the Lipoma family, are developing 66 single-and multi-family residences near its entrance. The facility—readily accessible off Puyallup's primary north-south thoroughfare, Meridian Avenue—was originated by Tony Lipoma, who once operated a Christmas tree farm at the site. The senior Lipoma died in 1994, and his son Sam Lipoma now runs the course.

The Bill Stowe-designed 27-holer crosses a mixture of terrain, with some hills but mostly flat ground encountered along the way. Since the three nines—Green, Gold and Blue—are etched within evergreen trees of uniform height, there's a nagging sameness to the design. But that doesn't mean the course is a pushover. It's of paramount importance to stay within the tree-paneled corridors of Lipoma Firs, as the rough is dense and rocky and recoverability is chancy at best. A primary feature of this course is the periodic glimpses it affords of Mount Rainier, which crops up over the tree tops in some startling places. When the original 18 holes debuted in 1989-90, many fairways were bare in places. Golf ball-sized rocks hadn't been screened and

The 2nd hole on Lipoma Firs' Green 9 is a 328-yard par-4.

often came in contact with clubs. During a later visit in fall 1995, I found the turf of the recently-opened Green nine much thicker than its predecessors.

Lipoma Firs, which hosts over 60,000 rounds a year, offers a quiet round of golf, with its fairways appearing as self-contained "islands" because of the thick woodlands. Among the best Gold holes is the 5th, a 396-yard par-4 that follows a rolling, dogleg-right path to a fast, trapped-right green. The 9th, a 515-yard par-5, is a fir-squeezed, straight-running hole that ends at a bi-bunkered green guarded left by a pond. The Blue 3rd, a 417-yard par-4, features a fir-lined fairway that curls right-ward to a green trapped laterally. Blue's 531-yard, par-5 9th runs fairly straight over undulating terrain en route to a sloping green protected by two traps.

The top-rated hole on the Green side is the 4th, a 547-yard par-5 with a long, direct fairway that concludes at a raised and rolling green trapped twice left and once right. The 4th fairway provides a perfect frame for Mount Rainier, which looms behind the green. The Gold 7th may be the prettiest hole at Lipoma Firs. The right-bending, 392-yard par-4 skirts a glimmering pond 100 yards from a small, domed, front-sloping green trapped left-front and right-rear.

Madrona Links Golf Course

18

3604 22nd Avenue NW, Gig Harbor, WA 98335. (253) 851-5193. Rob Edwards, pro. 18 holes. 5,590 yards. Par 71. Grass tees. Course ratings: men—B65.5/110, M63.7/107; women—M68.1/115, F65.6/110. Year Opened: 1977. Architect: Ken Tyson. Moderate, jr./sr. rates, credit cards. Reservations: Call a week ahead. Walk-on chances: Fair. Walkability: Good. Playability: Good choice for high and mid-handicappers.

Madrona Links is owned by the city of Tacoma; Lillian Urbauer, owns 15 of its acres. The tight track winds through 100 wooded acres south of Gig Harbor. Houses have been built around the course, and more are on the way. Madrona Links is named after the red-skinned arboreal specimens that line its fairways and serve as the course's primary obstacle to par. The layout has received various upgrades in recent years and, according to the players who frequent it, has developed into an enjoyable place to play.

Though its length is abbreviated, the course features adequate bunkering, rolling fairways and tight target zones. Four ponds fill its midsection. Interesting holes include the par-4 1st, a 435-yarder that winds rightward and skirts a small lake along the left. The rolling hole ends at a thin green trapped left-front. The 8th, a par-5 of 485 yards, descends slightly along a narrow route. Rated the toughest hole, the 8th is concluded by a heart-shaped green trapped twice along the right. Deep depressions dot the fairway at the 16th, a 385-yard par-4 that bends slightly right toward a very steep rise. The wide but shallow 16th green is trapped right-front.

Meadow Park Golf Course

7108 Lakewood Drive West, Tacoma, WA 98467. (253) 473-3033. Lynn Rautio, **27**
pro. Regulation course: 18 holes, 6,093 yards, par 71. Par-3 Nine: 1,275 yards, par
27. Grass tees. Course ratings: men—B69.9/116, M67.3/113; women—B74.8/121,
M72.9/119, F70.2/115. Opened: 1917. Architects: Founding members (original
course); John Steidel (remodel). Moderate, jr./sr. rates, credit cards. Reservations:
Call a week ahead. Walk-on chances: Fair. Walkability: Very good. Playability: Much
improved after major remodel.

Meadow Park—which includes 18-hole regulation-length and par-3 courses—appears as a lovely green belt amid car traffic, homes and a strip mall in Tacoma's south end. Owned and operated by the Metropolitan Park District of Tacoma, the facility was closed between the summer of 1992 through May '93 for a massive renovation. The 1917-built layout received extensive changes by architect John Steidel; the $2.8-million project was built by Portland's Teufel/Leahy Golf. About 400 yards were added to the regulation course, and 200 yards subtracted from the short nine. Holes were rerouted and lengthened, a new driving range was built, signage was replaced, and an automatic sprinkler system installed. Additionally, an all-new clubhouse with a restaurant and pro shop was constructed. All the rehabilitation, completed by 1994, was needed as Meadow Park is Tacoma's busiest golf facility, hosting 90,000 rounds annually over its 27 holes.

Bunkers were replaced and repositioned, and the 1st hole—for safety reasons—was moved away from Lakewood Drive, thus halting the hundreds of balls annually launched toward the busy thoroughfare. Four new holes were built, mounding was added to define some fairways, new back tees helped lengthen several holes, and a pond now adds beauty and peril to the 5th, a 254-yard par-4. A new lake between the 16th and 17th holes shrinks both fairways. Improvements were also made to Meadow Park's short course, renamed the Ralph Williams Nine after a former park board commissioner. Meadow Park is part of the rota of local venues used for the Tacoma City Amateur. In 1996, the course hosted the Washington State High School Girls and the Washington State Women's Golf Association championships.

Among the better holes at the revamped regulation track is the 3rd, a 433-yard par-4 with a dogleg-right fairway that winds between trees to a small, front-sloping green trapped left. The 4th, a 171-yard par-3, has an elevated tee and a kidney-shaped, front-leaning green guarded by a tree right-front and bunkers left and right-rear. The top-rated 7th, a 565-yard par-5, runs slightly downhill along an S-shaped, tree-lined path. The hole initially winds right around a fat tree, then goes left. The mid-sized 7th green tilts steeply toward a bunker in front and has a steep back side. The 9th, a 398-yard par-4, heads slightly uphill on a path that skirts big bunkers left. The fairway rises to a trapped-right green protected left-front by a tree.

The 10th, a 538-yard par-5, is a long right-curling hole between trees. At the 200-yard mark, the hole rises to a small green bunkered left and rear. The 11th, a 418-yard par-4, descends off the tee, then goes uphill over its last 200 yards to a small and flat, tree-ringed green trapped on the right. The flattish 12th, a 343-yard par-4, drops steeply at the 150-yard mark en route to a plateaued green bunkered left and right-front. A raised tee starts the 14th, a 348-yard par-4 that requires an accurate drive to circumvent a canyon and reach a severely right-sloping fairway. (From below it, the tee looks like the prow of a battleship.) The hole ends at a steeply right-sloping green guarded right-front by a pesky grass bunker. The 16th, a 470-yard par-5, follows a left-bending path squeezed by a bunker driving distance out along the left. The last part of the fairway descends to a hill-cut green with a pond right-front and trap left-front.

Meridian Greens Golf Club

9705 136th Street East, Puyallup, WA 98373. (253) 845-7504. Rusty Fancher, pro. 9 holes. 1,450 yards. Par 30. Grass tees. Course ratings: men 56.4/84, women 59.6/92. Year Opened: 1986. Architects: Harry Benton, Mike Bauman & John Cochran. Economical, jr./sr. rates, credit cards. Reservations: Call a week ahead. Walk-on chances: Good. Walkability: No problems. Playability: Good training course.

Meridian Greens lies on Puyallup's South Hill. The course is owned by Brian Patton, who's also the proprietor of Willows Run in Redmond. Meridian Greens opened with an executive-length track and driving range in March 1986. The layout occupies 28 acres of former pastureland bordered by a residential neighborhood. With its benign demeanor, Meridian Greens is a popular place for beginning and intermediate golfers.

The course is virtually treeless, with four ponds serving as the predominant impediments to par. The dual-tee set-up utilizes an "18-on-9" configuration that reaches 3,358 yards over two circuits. There are six par-3s and three par-4s in the 260- to 270-yard range, with the toughest hole the 9th, a 270-yard par-4 that curls leftward to a pond-fronted green.

North Shore Golf & Country Club

4101 North Shore Boulevard, Tacoma, WA 98422. (253) 927-1375 or 1-800-447-1375. Director of golf, Jim Bourne; Dave Wetli, pro. 18 holes. 6,305 yards. Par 71. Grass tees. Course ratings: men—B69.9/120, M68.6/118; women F70.7/119. Year Opened: 1961 (original nine), 1978 (second nine). Architects: Al Smith (original nine); Glen Proctor (second nine). Moderate, credit cards. Reservations: Call a week ahead. Walk-on chances: Ok for singles. Walkability: Good overall. Playability: Interesting course with water, sand and trees—in no particular order—of concern.

North Shore is a full-service venue near Brown's Point northeast of Tacoma and about five miles west of Federal Way. The place has a spacious driving range, a clubhouse restaurant, an "at-the-turn" grill, motorized snack purveyors that feed golfers on the course, and over 80 power carts. North Shore is owned by its director of golf, Jim Bourne, a north Seattle native who has developed the course into one of the Puget Sound area's most popular golf facilities. Besides a course that generates over 60,000 of rounds and hosts 140 private tournaments annually, Bourne oversees a pro shop which has been a fixture in *Golf Shop Operations* magazine's listing of the nation's top-100 retail outlets. He's also repped Ping clubs since 1961.

The course began with nine holes in a then-remote part of Pierce County in 1961. The founders, members of Rainier Golf & Country Club, owned 450 acres. Bourne began leasing the course from them in 1962, and bought North Shore in 1978 when the second nine was built. At that time, the founders began developing residences on acreage around the 115-acre course. Today, North Shore's once-isolated locale is a thing of the past as houses now engird the course. In the early '90s, an extension of Highway 18 was completed to the north, thus directly linking Brown's Point to the rest of the world.

Though the majority of fairways are lined by timber, townhouses enter play along the 12th hole. North Shore is imperiled by bunkers and five ponds, with its tight tree-lined fairways also a concern. Holes 10 through 18 are noted for well-forested, hilly terrain—making them more challenging than the front nine, which crosses flattish ground and involves fairways with mid-height trees.

North Shore's tougher holes include the 497-yard 3rd, a par-5 with a left-turning, tree-pinched fairway stretching out to a raised green backed by a pond. The 9th, a 515-yard par-5, contains a fairway pond reachable from the tee. Once past this juncture, the hole climbs to a laterally-trapped green. Tough back nine holes include the 17th, a 225-yard par-3 with an elevated tee. From here, golfers must execute an accurate drive into prevailing winds slightly downhill to a severely front-sloping green ringed by three bunkers. The 18th is a tough 554-yard par-5 with a fairway curling rightward along a tree-cut route. Golfers may opt to loft drives over the evergreens to bite some of the distance from the home hole, but mishit balls will land in jail. The 18th green is engirded by four bunkers.

Sumner Meadows Golf Course

14802 Eighth Street East, Sumner, WA 98390. (253) 863-8198 or 1-800-959-4344. Ron Hagen, director of golf; Stuart Ward, pro. 18 holes. 6,669 yards. Par 72. Grass Tees. Course Ratings: men—B72.2/128, M69.0/116; women—M75.2/133, F71.3/125. Year Opened: 1995. Architects: John Harbottle III & Lynn William Horn. Moderate, jr./sr. rates, credit cards. Reservations: Call a week ahead. Walk-on Chances: Fair. Walkability: Good. Playability: Quality test for low- and mid-handicappers.

This newer course occupies part of a 288-acre site and lies conveniently about a mile from Highway 167; take the Eight Street exit and go east. The facility includes a small clubhouse and driving range, and is owned by the city of Sumner, which may be adding a full-sized clubhouse in the future. Sumner Meadows is operated by Golf Resources, Inc., headed by director of golf, Ron Hagen, and Ron Coleman. The 1995-opened layout was designed by Tacoma-based architects, John Harbottle III and Lynn William Horn.

The topography of this course is decidedly flat; the triangular site is hemmed in by the White Stuck River and railroad tracks. The city paid about $5.4 million for the land and spent another $3 million to design and build the course. At first glance, Sumner Meadows reminded me of Trysting Tree. During my round, however, I found it not as compelling as the Corvallis course nor as entertaining or safe. Admittedly, the layout had been open only a couple of months; next-hole signs hadn't been installed, the drainage was still unsettled, and the turf wasn't fully knitted. But these are common, readily fixable problems often encountered with some new courses.

The safety issues are worth noting, however, and players should be alert for neighboring ball-strikers as some tees and greens are too close to parallel holes. And, while walking down the 10th fairway, it's a good idea to watch activities on the driving range, which is back-left and but a wild slice away. With 288 acres at its disposal, more between-fairway space should have been allotted, particularly since the layout lacks protective trees. Adding to the safety questions are the mounds which, though useful in defining fairways, block the views of players who might otherwise spot incoming golf balls. As part of an environmental plan, 500 trees will be planted over the next few years. The trees may ultimately change the course's links-like demeanor, but it'll be years before they'll be big enough to knock down misdirected shots.

That bitching out of the way, I enjoyed Sumner Meadows, which boasts a plenitude of traps and water hazards as well as considerable length. Though the layout seemed compressed and oddly arrayed in places (with two par-3s in a row at the 6th and 7th), there's a goodly amount of challenges to be had. The entries to the greens are relatively trap-free—thus enabling a pitch-and-run approach, and the putting surfaces have lots of fun-filled wows in them. Good tests include the 549-yard 3rd, a par-5 rated the course's toughest hole. The slight dogleg-left has a pond left of the tee, and another pond farther down on the left at the 150-yard mark. The hole winds up to a large, ridge-perched green trapped laterally. The 9th, a par-4 that stretches a whopping 490 yards, has a wide fairway guarded left by a pond. The right-bender curls between mounds to a hill-roosting green protected right-front by wetlands and along the right by a bunker.

Two holes on the back nine are memorable. The 15th is a 628-yard par-5 for men and a par-6 for women. The White Stuck River lines the left side of the 15th's mildly rolling fairway; a pond sits over to the right. The hole eventually curls left around alder trees and a bend in the river to a raised and steeply front-sloping, terraced green trapped left and right-front. The 16th is a dandy 232-yard par-3. The hole begins at a slightly raised tee from which one must rip a lengthy shot over a pond. The smallish green is trapped left, and has a ridge running through it.

9 Tapps Island Golf Course

20818 Island Parkway East, Sumner, WA 98390. (253) 862-7011. Chris Lofthus, pro. 9 holes. 2,643 yards. Par 35. Grass tees. Course ratings: men—B66.5/117, M64.2/113; women—B70.9/125, M68.1/120. Year Opened: 1979. Architect: Ron Fream. Moderate, jr./sr. rates, credit cards. Reservations: Call a week ahead. Walk-on chances: Fair. Walkability: Fine, with several treks over bridges. Playability: Expect an aqueous experience if erratic with your shots.

Tapps Island follows the shoreline of a vast reservoir that supplies the hydroelectric fuel for the Puget Power utility company. In winter, Tapps Lake is one-quarter full; in mid-May, water sluiced from the White River fills the basin. Either filled or empty, the reservoir is the dominant feature of Tapps Island's course, as eight of the nine holes either skirt it or cross channels radiating off the lake. The island contains a rather sizable neighborhood, with most residents enjoying water-front homes and views of Mount Rainier when the sun's out. This popular nine-hole layout hosts upwards of 40,000 rounds a year, and is occasionally visited by deer, raccoons, pheasants, geese and ducks.

The layout—stretching 5,343 yards over two circuits—features two disparate sets of tees over its "18-on-9" configuration. Each of its bentgrass greens is equipped with two different-colored flags. Tapps Island's signature features include tight doglegs, lots of water hazards, and a relative plethora of sand traps. The venue also has a sizable clubhouse with food and beverage services.

Particularly memorable holes include the top-rated 5th, a 456-yard par-5 that doglegs right after the fairway is crossed by a canal. The V-shaped and quick 5th green is ringed by shot-blocking trees and a sand trap, and bears a steep back edge. The penalizing 9th, a 314-yard par-4, is a narrow, tree-pinched tester. Two traps along the fairway's left side lead players to push drives into trees along the right. Over its last 100 yards, the fairway slopes to the right and toward a pond. Many approach shots to the 9th's large, right-front-sloping green end up in this water hazard.

University Golf Club

754 South 124th, Tacoma, WA 98444. (243) 535-7393. Gary Cinotto, pro. 9 holes. 2,732 yards. Par 35. Grass tees. Course ratings: men 64.4/100, women 69.4/112. Year Opened: 1926. Architects: Founding members. Moderate, jr./sr. rates. Reservations: Call a week ahead for weekends. Walk-on chances: Fair. Walkability: Piece of cake. Playability: Rather perfunctory layout serves students and local players.

A traditional nine-holer on the campus of Pacific Lutheran University in southeast Tacoma, this course has always been owned and operated by the college. Once containing 18 holes, nine holes were eliminated in the 1950s to allow for Keithley Junior High as well as PLU's Olson Auditorium and running track. University is played mainly by students and senior citizens, both of whom receive discounts on green fees. This is one of the driest and least busy of Tacoma's courses, hosting roughly 20,000 rounds a year.

Characterized by flat terrain and tall evergreens, the layout skirts homes on the south. Airplanes from McChord periodically sweep overhead but, generally, University is a quiet suburban-type course. Interesting holes include the top-rated 1st, a par-4 of 344 yards that reaches out to a slick green. Also tough are the 4th, a par-5 of 519 yards, and the 9th, a 506-yard par-5.

Private Courses

American Lake VA Golf Course

Department of Veteran's Affairs, VA Medical Center, Tacoma, 98493. (253) 582-8440, extension 6762. 9 holes. 2,862 yards. Par 35. Grass tees. No course ratings. Year Opened: 1957. Architects: Volunteer founders. VA Hospital patients, outpatients, employees, volunteers & guests.

Located on a former vegetable farm, this dual-tee nine beside Tacoma's VA Medical Center opened for play in 1957. VA Hospital patients, outpatients, employees, volunteers and their guests are eligible to play it. The course is conditioned and run by about 30 volunteers, with its operations overseen by Marty Blackburn. All the golf equipment is donated, and various veterans' organizations—including AmVets and the VFW—chip in cash contributions. This VA course is the busiest of the region's three VA golf facilities (the others are in Roseburg and White City, Oregon), hosting about 27,000 rounds a year despite being closed from mid-December through January.

The well-tended American Lake course is somewhat hilly, with its generally wide, tree-lined fairways ending at small, rolling greens. Ten sand traps—most at green-sides—add to the challenge. Wildlife includes coyotes, deer, eagles, Canada geese and rabbits. The 18-hole course record of 59 was set in 1958 by a patient named Calvin Coolidge. These lush fairways beside American Lake, a lovely water body in south Tacoma, are nurtured by a caring group of local citizens who provide a relaxing, therapeutic outing for veterans in need.

Canterwood Golf & Country Club

18

4026 Canterwood Drive NW, Gig Harbor, WA 98335. (253) 851-1745. Doug Gullickson, pro. 18 holes. 7,175 yards. Par 72. Grass tees. Course ratings: men—T76.5/ 141, B74.4/138, M72.1/134, F68.8/125; women—M78.3/145, F74.5/130. Year Opened: 1988. Architect: Robert Muir Graves. Members, guests & reciprocates.

Situated southwest of Gig Harbor, Canterwood Golf & Country Club is part of a 700-acre residential and recreational enclave with 750 homesites. As of 1996, over 400 of the lots were sold. Canterwood's "vacation every day" philosophy certainly seems to be working; the club enjoys a full roster of 362 golfing members and 240 social members. In February 1996, the club was sold by its developer, Lorigon Corp., to the clubmembers for an amount equal to the cost of construction of all club facilities, which include an 18-hole championship golf course, a 25,000-square-foot clubhouse, swimming pool and tennis complex. Lorigan retained ownership of the subdivision.

When the members bought Canterwood, they acquired a course rated among the Northwest's toughest. It's also a regular entry in the "top-5" lists of various magazines (including *Golf Digest*) ranking the state's best courses. The forest-etched layout contains nearly 80 bunkers, with water hazards entering play on 11 holes. Its multi-terraced greens are slick and fast. There are upwards of nine tees per hole, and the layout's hilly terrain must always be taken into account when evaluating stances and shot selections.

Canterwood's relentless difficulty has caused some golfers to view it as too penalizing. Perhaps that is sour grapes, because the layout certainly presents one of the region's sternest tests of golf. That fact has been borne out by the many tournaments held here, including the 1996 Pacific Northwest Mid-Amateur Championship and 1997 Hudson Cup Matches. Contestants in tournaments encounter many fairways leaning away from doglegs and toward ponds, traps or trees, with rear-sloping greens on ridges creating blind approaches.

Some holes have been "softened" in recent years. Plans are also afoot to correct the 9th hole, a 388-yard par-3 with a 90-degree dogleg-right fairway that winds around a pond. Trees weren't planted along the right side of the tee when the hole was built, so golfers could easily cut the corner and go over the pond to reach the hill-cut 9th green. Most of Canterwood's other bentgrass putting surfaces have exaggerated contours, and all can be equipped with difficult pin placements. A typically tough Canterwood hole is the 18th, a 540-yard par-5 that doglegs right—and slopes left, away from the turn—over an uphill route. Skirting woods along the right, the fairway is guarded left by a pond, mere driving distance out. The hole then ascends between three fairway bunkers to a 30-yard-deep, tri-trapped green that cants toward the left-front.

Fircrest Golf Club

18

6520 Regents Boulevard, Tacoma, WA 98466. (253) 564-5792 or 564-6756. Glenn Malm, pro. 18 holes. 6,605 yards. Par 71. Grass tees. Course ratings: men—B72.0/126, M71.2/125; women F74.8/129. Year Opened: 1923. Architect: Arthur Vernon Macan; John Harbottle III (remodel). Members, guests & reciprocates.

This magnificent course lies in the Fircrest neighborhood in west Tacoma. The Macan-designed layout ranks among the region's premier private tracks, sharing rarified company with such epic venues as Eugene Country Club, Royal Oaks, Seattle Golf Club, Sahalee, Columbia-Edgewater and Oswego Lake. The 1924-founded club has received steady improvements over the years. Tacoma designer John Harbottle has overseen ongoing, course-wide improvements which have included a $1-million irrigation system, new tees, a modification of some greens, and overall lengthening of the course. Bunkers have been added, existing traps were rebuilt, and landscaping enhanced. More tees will be updated in the years ahead.

In early 1997, a new 35,000-square-foot, $5-million clubhouse opened for member use. The structure—patterned after a Pacific Northwest lodge—contains dining areas, locker rooms, banquet facilities, fitness center and sports bar. This is actually Fircrest's third clubhouse; the first was built in 1925 and the second in 1960. Also new in 1995 was a 7,500-square-foot maintenance facility; the club renovated its outdoor pool in 1997.

Fircrest has all the attributes that make classic parkland courses so alluring. It enjoys fastidious care; huge, now-modernized tees; dense, ancient timber for secluding fairways; hole-after-hole variety; an efficient and walkable layout; no fairway-side houses; decent drainage for wintertime play; an attentive staff led by longtime pro, Glen Malm; and a wonderful practice facility. There's even a club-provided ball retriever beside the pond in front of the 5th tee. About the only quibble one could find at Fircrest is traffic noise along the front nine. But that vanishes as one marches toward the course's densely-forested interior.

The layout winds over up-and-down terrain, with trees—deciduous, coniferous and other specimens—squeezing fairways. Though the course is over 70 years old, the greens are contemporary in scope and contour, with sundry humps, hollows and tiers requiring players to be constantly vigilant. Fircrest has proven itself through tournaments such as the 1960 Carling World Championship, two National Left-Handers, the Washington State Open and Northwest Pro-Am. The Washington Junior Golf Association was originated at Fircrest, which has long espoused one of the region's most dedicated junior golf programs.

A sampling of outstanding holes includes the 1st, a 500-yard par-5 that runs straight up a narrowish, concave path. Over its last 150 yards, the fairway slopes steeply rightward as it ascends to a deep-but-slender green trapped right-front. The top-rated 2nd, a 450-yard par-4, heads uphill for its first 175 yards, then drops down a rolling, tree-lined route. The large 2nd green tilts right-front toward a bunker, and is trapped left-rear. The 3rd, a 200-yard par-3, ascends to a ridge-perched, right-front-sloping green trapped twice right and once left. The 5th, a 425-yard par-4, heads uphill once off its pond-fronted tee. At the 150-yard mark, the fairway flattens and goes up to a small, front-tilting green trapped laterally.

The narrow 7th, a 495-yard par-5, follows a downhill, left-turning path bunkered along the right. At the 100-yard mark, the hole rises to a hill-cut green trapped twice left-front and once right-front. A pronounced hogback through the huge 7th green enables malicious pin placements. The 8th, a 195-yard par-3, goes steeply uphill to a hill-perched, steeply front-canted green trapped left-front and right. The green is narrow but deep, and has a midriff bulge. The 8th hole is ranked Fircrest's 17th toughest, a clear indication that the course offers no respites.

On the back nine, the 420-yard, par-4 11th stands out. The fairway descends for 220 yards off a raised tee, then goes 45 degrees leftward to a large and round, humped-in-the-middle green trapped left, right-front and right-rear. The 14th, a 400-yard par-4, goes downhill to the 125-yard mark, where it curls sharply rightward around trees to a small and rolling, laterally-trapped putting surface. The 15th, a 425-yard par-4, has bunkers along both sides of its narrow, left-turning fairway. The hole ends at a domed, right-front-sloping green trapped left and right. The tight 17th, a 390-yard par-4, has a greatly undulating, right-leaning fairway lined by jail on both sides. A swale lurks before its front-tilting green, which is bunkered right and left and bears a steep left-rear flank. The 18th, a 365-yard par-4, houses a canyon-like fairway that bends leftward over wavy terrain. The radical 18th green tilts steeply right-front toward a bunker. This humps and hollows in this slick putting surface serve to stymie par on Fircrest's home hole.

Fort Lewis Golf Course (military)

27

P.O. Box 33175, Fort Lewis Army Base, Fort Lewis, WA 98433. (253) 967-6522. Jim Barnhouse, pro. 27 holes. Grass tees. Course ratings: Blue/Green (6,823 yards, par 74) men—B72.3/125, M70.9/121, F68.4/116; women F73.4/122. Red/Blue (6,855 yards, par 72) men—B72.8/125, M70.6/120; women F73.3/122. Red/Green (6,878 yards, par 74) men—B72.9/126, M71.5/123, F69.2/119; women F74.9/126. Years Opened: 1937 (original 18) & 1979 (third nine). Architects: Works Progress Administration (original 18); Bill Teufel (third nine). Military personnel & guests.

The 27-hole course at Fort Lewis continues to fulfill the U.S. Army's original mission that it give soldiers a diversion from their military regimens. The course also helps slake the recreational needs of the military retirees who live in Lakewood and other nearby burgs. Appropriately, Fort Lewis's original "pro shop" was a guard shack. A clubhouse later built by the WPA had two entrances—one for enlisted men and another for officers. In May 1996, a new $3.5-million, 16,000-square-foot clubhouse opened, thus moving the historic course—one of the nation's oldest on a military reserve—closer to the 21st Century. The structure contains a pro shop, lounge, snack bar and banquet areas. The clubhouse and golf course have been overseen by Jim Barnhouse, a civilian, since 1979.

Because of an irrigation water agreement with the nearby Dupont Water Department that ran from 1938 to 1952, the Army allowed workers at the utility to play the course for perpetuity. The "Dupont Originals," none of whom are still living, received permission to golf only after the commanding general gave his blessing each year. According to Ross Fue, a staffmember at the facility for a couple of decades, a "Dupont Original," the late Walter Shinnell, was of considerable help as a course historian. Over 1995-96, a $1.4-million irrigation system was installed, and a new lake and maintenance building were built. Future plans include replacing the Green nine's bunker sand. Play levels were down during the construction period; it usually hosts 70,000 rounds a year.

Fort Lewis—unlike the military courses at Whispering Firs and Gallery—often hosts "outside" tournaments, such as the PNGA Junior Boys, PGA Pro Members, Washington State Open, Washington State Amateur, National Publinx and 1997 U.S. Open Qualifying. The PNGA Washington State Men's Amateur will be played here in 1999. The course record, a 64, is held by Walter Morgan, the facility's manager from 1977 to 1980. The cigar-smoking Morgan—an Army "lifer" who retired out of Fort Lewis—is now one of the PGA Senior Tour's up-and-coming stars. Morgan broke his Tour "maiden" by winning the 1995 GTE Northwest Classic at Inglewood Golf Club in Kenmore.

Fort Lewis's 27 holes are divided into the Red, Blue and Green nines, with the Red-Blue sides combined for 18-hole rounds. The Green side is set aside for nine-hole rounds. With all the recent changes, the Red-Blue layout is quite contemporary, with bunkers filled with high-quality Ravensdale sand, lovely ponds, gardens, large tees and paved cart paths. Fort Lewis has fair drainage during the wet season, and most fairways are lined by mature firs, oaks and maples. The course enjoys a park-like ambiance, though traffic from nearby Interstate 5 (the course is right off Exit 116) is audible along southern holes.

Among the top tests on the Red side—played as the front—is the 3rd, a 505-yard par-5. This mid-width left-bender has a deep swale off the tee and then runs over rolling ground past trees, OB and I-5 along the right. The hole eventually reaches an undulating green trapped both sides. The 4th, a 433-yard par-4, bends rightward over a slightly ascending route to a rolling green trapped twice in front. The top-rated 5th, a 439-yard par-4, heads narrowly between trees along an uphill, right-turning route, and slopes steeply to the left toward jail. Over its final 100 yards, the fairway rises to a skinny-but-deep, two-tiered green trapped left. Another Red dandy is the 7th, a 457-yard par-4. The first part of this long left-bender is wide open, but at the 200-yard mark, firs left and oaks right shrink its path. A deep swale fronts the squarish, trapped-right-front 7th green.

On the Blue nine (numbered in back-nine fashion), the 13th, a 448-yard par-4, stands out. From a raised tee, the fairway goes rightward around trees, sloping left toward jail. At the 150-yard mark, the hole curls around to a mid-sized and raised, saddle-shaped green bunkered right-front and left-rear. The 17th, a 422-yard par-4, goes straight for 250 yards or so before winding around trees 90 degrees to the left. The last 150 yards rise up to a rolling green that leans toward a big trap right-front. The 18th, a 598-yard par-5, runs over corrugated terrain toward the 200-yard mark. Here, the hole descends leftward over left-leaning ground to a front-tilting green trapped right-front.

Fort Lewis's Green nine is a throwback to 1930's golf architecture; its generally small greens are guarded closely by nasty, upwardly-angled bunkers. A tough hole here is the 2nd, a 230-yard par-3 that rises slightly to a rounded, laterally-trapped green. The straight 4th, a 445-yard par-4, is gradually tapered by trees en route to a small, front-sloping green. The 5th, a 510-yard par-5, has a big fir in mid-fairway about 150 yards out. Once past this narrow seam, the fairway widens before bearing rightward to a wide-but-shallow, two-tiered green trapped left-front. The 6th, a 515-yard par-5, is a tree-squeezed left-bender needing a 225-yard tee shot to reach the corner. Once around the bend, the fairway tapers as it crosses wavy, ascending ground en route to a tidy, left-sloping green trapped left.

Lake Josephine Riviera Golf & Country Club

9

11019 Country Club Drive, Anderson Island, WA 98303. (253) 884-9634. 9 holes. 1,610 yards. Par 29. Grass tees. Course ratings: men 56.1/88, women 59.6/95. Opened: early 1970s. Architect: Heritage Properties. Members, guests & reciprocates.

Alternatively called Lake Josephine Riviera Golf & Country Club or simply "Riviera," this private facility adjoins Lake Josephine on Anderson Island, Puget Sound's southernmost isle. The course is the exclusive domain of folks living in the Lake Josephine Riviera neighborhood, which contains 3,200 lots. The subdivision—whose lots are now all sold—was initiated by Heritage Properties of Seattle as a retirement community. In recent times, however, younger couples with children have gradually moved in. Year-round residents now total 400, with many mainlanders retreating here on weekends to stay in summer cabins. A ferry out of Steilacoom makes the 20-minute passage to Anderson Island each day.

Overseen by manager Al Hundis and greens superintendent Ron Hall, the dual-tee layout is playable year-round, but the pro shop is open only Friday through Monday. If playing the short nine over two circuits, it extends 3,311 yards. Members and guests are challenged by the course's rolling topography and small greens, and often spot deer and raccoons on the course.

Linden Golf & Country Club

9

2519 Main Avenue East, Puyallup, WA 98371. (253) 845-2056. David Leon, Jr., pro. 9 holes. 3,095 yards. Par 36. Grass tees. Course ratings: men—B/M69.7/120, M//68.1/117; women—B/M75.9/127, M/F74.1/123. Year Opened: 1927. Architects: Founding members. Members, guests & reciprocates.

Linden's tricky nine-holer occupies 50 acres along busy Main Avenue east of Puyallup. About 125 yards north of the private course is the Puyallup River. During the wet winter of 1996, Linden's 5th and 7th holes were flooded. According to head pro David Leon, the flooding was the worst it's ever been. The soft-spoken Leon, an Arizona native, has overseen the golf goings-on here since 1972. He's been helped since the early '80's by Tony Fatica, a veteran Tacoma-area pro who's previously worked at Fircrest, Tacoma Country & Golf Club and the now-defunct Renton Driving Range. Dean Hansen is the superintendent.

Linden's first two holes offer nice views of Mount Rainier and, with its riverside locale, the course is visited by deer, skunks, badgers, coyotes, muskrats, geese and ducks. Bears have been spotted on occasion. A raspberry farm lines the western border. The fairways have gradually been squeezed over the years by firs, lindens (the European cottonwood after which the club is named), hemlocks, mountain ashes and birches.

Featuring three tees per hole, the layout was designed by an unknown Scotsman and the founding members. The fairways cross wildly undulating terrain marked by depressions and humps; it's quite apparent the course has settled over its 70-plus years. Linden's wavy terrain disallows flat lies, once beyond the tees. The greens—diminutive and wrapped by gray-sand bunkers—are often concave in contour. These swards can be mowed low, stimping out at an ultra-slick 11. The 18-hole course record is a 62, shot by venerable Northwest pro, Ockie Eliason. In 1997, Eliason, two-time winner of the Pacific Northwest Open, was named to the Pacific Northwest Section of the PGA's Hall of Fame.

Linden's tougher holes include the par-4 1st, a 406-yarder with a canyon-like fairway that descends between trees to a mid-sized, inverted green trapped right-front and left. The top-rated 5th, a 381-yard par-4, starts at a raised, pond-fronted tee. The rolling hole then winds rightward between fat trees. The last 125 yards of the hole curl up to a two-tiered, right-front-sloping green guarded at the right-front by a hidden pond, and bunkered twice on the rear. The 6th, a 203-yard par-3, runs slightly uphill to a severely terraced green that leans precipitously to the left-front. This slippery target is trapped left-front and right and is treed closely behind. The 7th, a 522-yard par-5, heads a bit uphill over corrugated, tree-lined ground. The straight-running fairway crosses various humped and hollowed hills and dales to a tiny front-canted green trapped twice on the right.

Oakbrook Golf & Country Club

8102 Zircon Drive SW, Tacoma, WA 98498. (253) 584-8770. Tad Davis, pro. 18 holes. 6,658 yards. Par 71. Grass tees. Course ratings: men—B71.6/125, M69.8/121, FF67.6/116; women—FF73.3/124, F70.2/117. Year Opened: 1967. Architects: Robert Brout & Jack Reimer; John Steidel (remodel). Members, guests & reciprocates.

Oakbrook Golf & Country Club lies within a sprawling residential district southwest of Tacoma. The Oakbrook course and community were built in 1966-67 by a joint venture of Chambers Creek Associates, United Homes Corporation and Oakbrook Realty. The club was incorporated in 1966, and in 1969 the members bought it from the developers. Robert Brout of Tolucca Lake, California, layed out the holes, and Jack Reimer of Vancouver, B.C. designed the greens. Oakbrook's first superintendent, Larry Proctor, oversaw construction of the course. Mike Brownfield was the club's initial golf pro.

This 6,658-yard track is tight, tree-lined and well tended. Tricky greens, over 50 sand traps, and two ponds challenge the club's 450 members. Seemingly par-able holes can quickly turn into ego-deflating triple-bogeys. The course record—an amazing 60—was shot by one-time Oakbrook member, noted left-hander and former PGA Senior Tourer, the late George Lanning.

In 1994, Oakbrook's clubhouse underwent a $1.3-million remodel. Also that year the course completed a 10-year master plan overseen by architect, John Steidel. The project included improved drainage, new tees and a rebuilt 6th green. A fairway trap and greenside bunker were added to the 10th hole, and a bunker by the 5th green was reshaped. A trap was also built alongside the 16th green. Though not one of the region's most illustrious layouts, Oakbrook has a deserved reputation as a fine golf course, one that presents a stiff test for all the players who participate in a variety of Northwest and state tournaments held at the south Tacoma venue.

Tacoma Country & Golf Club

18 *Country Club Drive SW, Tacoma, WA 98498. (253) 588-0404. Rich Friend, pro. 18 holes. 6,590 yards. Par 72. Grass tees. Course ratings: men—B71.6/124, M70.1/ 121; women F72.7/124. Year Opened: 1905 (current site). Architect: Stanley Thompson; John Steidel (remodel). Members, guests & limited reciprocates.*

Founded in 1894, Tacoma Country & Golf Club is the oldest continuously operated American golf club west of the Mississippi River. On August 6, 1994, the club celebrated its centennial with bagpipes and lanterns, ragtime music and newsreels. The 785 members in attendance paid homage to a Tacoma institution that began generations ago.

Originally named the "Tacoma Golf Club," its activities began in 1894 on a rough-hewn course in Edison, in south Tacoma. The club's initiation fee was $2.50, with monthly dues of 25 cents. Tacoma's members, through the efforts of one of its co-founders, Alexander Baillie, imported the first golf clubs—built by the St. Andrews clubmaker, Forgan—and gutta-percha golf balls to the region. The original Edison layout had nine holes. By the turn of the century the 160-member club expanded the course to 18 holes, with a total yardage of 5,522 yards.

When the club outgrew the Edison site, the members acquired the R. B. Lehman farm and an adjoining parcel by American Lake. The new course, designed by Stanley Thompson, opened on June 29, 1905. Over its 100-plus years of existence, the club has been visited by dignitaries from various fields: Chick Evans, Harry Vardon, Ted Ray, Walter Hagen, Willie Leith, Babe Dedrikson Zaharias, Byron Nelson, Lou Worsham, Lloyd Mangrum, Bing Crosby, Dwight D. Eisenhower, Dinah Shore, Sandy Koufax, Arnold Palmer, the Scottish clubmaker Laurie Auchterlonie, and Hale Irwin.

Tournaments hosted here have included the first-ever PNGA Championship in 1899; 1961 U.S. Women's Amateur; 1984 U.S. Senior Women's Amateur; 1910, 1915, 1925, 1931, 1966 and 1979 Northwest Opens; 1992 PNGA Junior Girls; 1993 Senior Northwest Golf Association Championships; 1993 Northwest Pro-Am (co-hosted with Fircrest); 1994 U.S. Women's Mid-Amateur; 1997 Washington State Open; and 1997 Pacific-10 Conference women's championship. The club's most accomplished golf pro was the Englishman, James Barnes. Shortly after leaving Tacoma, Barnes won the first-ever PGA Championship in 1916 and repeated in 1919. He won the U.S. Open by nine strokes in 1921 and won the 1925 British Open.

Other historical tidbits: The Balfour Medal—named after Sir Robert Balfour, a Tacoma-based dealer in wheat and lumber—has been presented to the club champion every year since 1897. The oldest team tournament in North America is the annual match between Tacoma and Victoria (B.C.) Golf Club. The two clubs have competed for the Gunderson trophy since 1895. Among Tacoma's most accomplished golfers are Pat Lesser Harbottle and her husband, Dr. John Harbottle. In 1955, Pat Lesser won the U.S. Amateur and became the first woman ever to win the *Seattle P-I* Man of the Year award. She's also won 19 club championships. Her husband has won 15 club titles along with several national and regional events.

Tacoma Country & Golf Club is bordered on the west by American Lake and east by Interstate 5. A cedar fence about a mile long buffers the course from the freeway. Though traffic is heard on the eastern holes, the course is quite tranquil. The layout was updated in the late-1980s with three new holes (14-16) designed by John Steidel. The club's prettiest hole may be the 15th, a 171-yard par-3 garnished with a pond, fountain and flower gardens. The renovation opened up the original holes and made room for a new grass-teed driving range.

Most holes are old-style in nature, with the greens well-bunkered. And except for the newer holes, the close-cropped *poa* putting surfaces are straightforward but slick. The newer greens have some tiers and undulations. Tacoma's toughest hole is the 438-yard 8th, a par-4 requiring two long shots for any hope at par. Often considered one of the top par-4s in the Northwest, this slightly ascending dogleg-right requires a good drive along the left edge of the fir- and oak-lined fairway to get a glimpse of a laterally-trapped green.

Tacoma Country & Golf Club has one of the Northwest's stateliest clubhouses. Besides elegant furnishings and lovely interiors, it offers great views of American Lake. Photos of past presidents adorn walls, with one showing Baillie in turn-of-the-century golf regalia. Also shown are clubs once used by such visiting luminaries as Tom Watson and Ted Ray. Displays honor Ray and Chuck Congdon, the latter of whom was very popular during his tenure as Tacoma's head pro from 1935 to 1965. Congdon memorabilia includes testimonials and photos in the clubhouse, while a plaque beside the 10th tee hails him as "our friend and teacher."

Twin Lakes Golf & Country Club

18

3583 SW 320th Street, Federal Way, WA 98023. (253) 838-0345. Joe Trembly, pro. 18 holes. 6,196 yards. Par 72. Grass tees. Course ratings: men—B70.6/123, M68.3/ 120; women—M73.5/124, F69.4/118. Year Opened: 1967. Architects: Bill Teufel (original nine), Jack Reimer (second nine). Members, guests & limited reciprocates.

Twin Lakes' private track winds through a sprawling Federal Way neighborhood. Now member-owned, Twin Lakes and the surrounding residences were developed by Quadrant Corporation, an arm of Weyerhaeuser. All but one hole (the wonderful 15th) are lined by homes. Because of the adjoining houses, golfers here must be aware of OB on nearly every hole. Some of the white-staked areas are interior—not peripheral as is normally the case. One example of Twin Lakes' interior OB is the 7th, a 454-yard par-5 that winds around poplar trees and the adjoining 6th hole. The white stakes are intended to prevent corner-cutters from using the 6th fairway, a potentially dangerous situation for players on that par-4.

Twin Lakes' considerable bunkering lends difficulty to the already tight track. The layout also boasts excellent yardage markers, nice gardens and landscaping, and a couple of Puget Sound viewpoints. In winter, there are a few wet places in lower sections of the course. Walking the layout is a bit of a test as golfers must cross several roads to get to subsequent holes. Future plans include lengthening the driving range. Among the tournaments held here over the years are the Ladies' State Amateur, PNGA Junior Boys and Girls, and Seattle City Amateur.

Each Twin Lakes hole bears a name, such as "Lone Tree" and "Boulder." Good tests include the 4th, a 501-yard par-5 that rises narrowly off the tee, passing Southwest 320th Street along the left and houses and OB right. The mid-width, tree-lined fairway winds rightward to a small, left-front-sloping green trapped right-front, left-front, left and left-rear. The top-rated 5th, a 377-yard par-4, is a rolling right-bender that goes between houses and OB. The hole curls about 70 degrees to the right, skirting bunkers and trees inside the turn. It then rises uphill—narrowly passing firs on the right—to a bi-trapped green that leans frontwards. The 6th, a 369-yard par-4, features an elevated tee and a downhill, left-curling fairway with homes and OB left, and poplars right. Over its final 75 yards, the right-leaning hole curls sharply uphill leftward to a front-left-sloping green fronted by two big traps.

The 8th, a 211-yard par-3, heads down to a V-shaped, front-tilting green guarded right-front by a trap which must be among the Northwest's biggest. The 9th, a neat 286-yard par-4, is a downhiller squeezed by OB left and a pond right. Over its last 75 yards, the hole ascends to a slippery, right-front-tilting green trapped left-front and right-front; a creek on the right also is a factor. The 13th, a 386-yard par-4, curls leftward over slightly rising, right-sloping terrain. Bunkers lurk left (at the 165-yard mark) and right (outside the turn at the 140-yard mark) as the fairway winds up to a rolling green bunkered left-front.

The 14th and 15th are both gems. The 14th, a 387-yard par-4 called "The View," offers Puget Sound vistas and a tight, right-sloping fairway bunkered left. At the 125-yard mark, the hole ventures uphill to the right to a right-sloping green guarded left-front by two deep bunkers. The houseless 15th, a 503-yard par-5, features an elevated tee and unobstructed Sound views. From here, the fairway descends steeply, passing three bunkers on the left. The narrow, chute-like route curls to the right, passing jail left and a steep hill right. The last 150 yards ascend steeply to a hill-cut green trapped twice at the left-front. The 18th, a 392-yard par-4 that shoots off a raised tee, is a good home hole. Bunkers line both sides of the turn, which goes 90 degrees to the right but slopes left. The 18th green is large and front-sloping, and is amply trapped left-front and left. OB is close to the green's left edge.

Whispering Firs Golf Course (military)

18 *McChord AFB, WA 98438. (253) 984-4947 or 984-4948. 18 holes. 6,628 yards. Par 72. Grass tees. Course ratings: men—B71.8/122, M70.5/119, F68.1/114; women F73.3/120. Years Opened: 1962 (original nine), 1972 (second nine). Architects: Local players (original nine); Manny Proctor (second nine). Military personnel & guests.*

Entertaining Whispering Firs—which hosts over 50,000 rounds a year—is in McChord Air Force Base, southeast of Tacoma, and is played by active-duty military personnel, Department of Defense workers and retirees. The layout occupies 160 acres, though superintendent Terry Beck and his crew are required to maintain 278 acres of wetlands and woodlands in and around the fairways. The facility has been run by manager James ("Tommy") Tompkins since 1987, though his McChord roots date back to 1965. Unlike Fort Lewis, Whispering Firs doesn't entertain "outside" tournaments. It's major yearly event is the Whispering Firs Amateur, a popular "haggle" run by the men's club.

Course improvements—including an all-new irrigation system that, according to Tompkins, took "21 years to get done"—are performed by the greens staff. The course was built by the U.S. Army Corps of Engineers, with the front nine opening in 1962 and the back a decade later. The forest-etched is appropriately named, with stately firs (none of which I heard whispering) defining the holes. Oaks and deciduous trees also dot the well-tended grounds. As might be expected, taking-off and landing aircraft are heard, with an occasional muffled explosion also lending aural variety. Despite these possible distractions, Whispering Firs is a tough parkland track with outstanding greens, ample trouble and fine conditioning.

A noteworthy hole is the 2nd, a 426-yard par-4. The fairly wide dogleg-left bears a pond off the tee, then crosses flat ground before being tapered by trees over its concluding 100 yards. The 2nd ends at a ridge-perched green guarded by a big trap right-front. The top-rated 6th, a 468-yard par-4, begins with a pond-fronted tee and a gradually rising fairway. At the 200-yard mark, the hole curls leftward between trees, narrowing over its last 100 yards en route to a large, rolling, left-sloping green trapped left. The tree-squeezed 7th, a 402-yard par-4, goes straight before curling sharply left at the 150-yard mark. The hole's last leg ascends to a slick, hill-perched putting surface bunkered right-front. The 8th is a dandy 200-yard par-3 with an elevated tee and a smallish, tree-ringed green squeezed by traps on both sides.

Back-nine tests include the 11th, a 531-yard that winds downhill before doglegging left around deep jail 200 yards out. Teers may opt to cut the corner, but a towering tree swats inadequate shots into unrecoverable scrub. Once around this perilous juncture, the 11th follows the straight and narrow—skirting more jail on both sides—to a raised, hill-cut green guarded right-front by a hidden bunker. The lovely 13th, a 410-yard par-4, winds between firs to a small, greatly undulating green trapped right-front. The 16th, a 357-yard par-4, winds rightward around firs; a sizable landing area is out to the left. Here, the fairway fishhooks back to the right and descends slightly to a front-right-sloping, high-backed green trapped on both sides. The 17th, a 408-yard par-4, heads over undulating ground into the prevailing wind. A pocket of oaks lurks along the right, 300 yards out. Over its final 100 yards, the 17th rises up to a huge, rolling green guarded by a vast hidden bunker in front.

Par-3 Courses

Christy's Golf Course & Driving Range

9

37712 28th Avenue South, Federal Way, WA 98003. (253) 927-0644. George Christy, pro. 9 holes. 905 yards. Par 27. Grass tees. No course ratings. Economical, sr. rates. No reservations. Driving Range.

Christy's par-3 nine and driving range lie a mile south of Enchanted Village, the amusement park on the east side of Interstate 5 in Federal Way. The facility is owned by George Christy, who's also its teaching pro. The driving range has been operating since 1978; the par-3 opened in 1990.

The facility certainly meets the definition of "family-run" enterprise. George, a teaching pro for 37 years at Puetz Driving Range, and his wife Arlene brought their family (sons Bruce, David and Robert, and daughter Karen) from their north Seattle home to Federal Way on weekends to construct the course. Outside of a shaper used to move dirt around, the Christys built the layout themselves, installing the irrigation system and hand-raking rocks from fairways. Over the four years it took them to complete the par-3 track, the family slept in pup tents and ate out of coolers during their weekend work parties. Talk about a labor of love.

Today, David and Robert help their father with the teaching. Arlene still manages the books, and Karen runs the pro shop. Bruce, a Class A pro who followed in his father's footsteps for 11 years as a teaching pro at Puetz, is now an assistant at Sand Point Country Club. Things are running so smoothly that the Christys may acquire an adjacent 10-acre parcel for another nine holes.

The current course and range occupy 20 acres of forestland. The practice facility is equipped with 27 covered and lighted tee stalls and several target greens.

The par-3 track winds through towering firs and cedars; its postage-stamp greens will test golfers of all skills. Holes range in length from 65 to 145 yards. The course's major hazard is a pond on the 95-yard 2nd hole.

Driving Ranges

EagleQuest at Linksman Golf Center

708 122nd Street East, Tacoma, WA 98445.
(253) 537-3037. Keith Sanden, Joe Beach & Carl Conzatti, pro. 18-hole putting course.

Emerald Links Driving Range

22719 State Highway 410, Buckley, WA 98321.
(253) 862-8496.

Upcoming Courses

Auburn — Washington National Golf Club (1999). In early 1997, OB Sports of Portland, owner of Langdon Farms Golf Club south of Portland, had a purchase agreement with the owner of this 510-acre site. Hanging up the deal was a transfer of the water rights. If OB Sports proceeds with the purchase, work may begin in summer 1997 on a 36-hole public facility. The University of Washington men's golf team may use this new venue for its home course. Also planned is a driving range and clubhouse.

Black Diamond — Black Diamond Associates Project (2000). On and off the back burner for several years, this 783-acre project still plans nearly 800 houses and an 18-hole course.

Bonney Lake — Bonney Lake Golf & Country Club (1999). The backers of the 567-acre project on historic Connell's Prairie east of the city are gradually moving forward in the permit process for a golf course and over 1,300 homes.

Bonney Lake — Fennel Creek GC (1999). The 449-acre project was being closely scrutinized by Bonney Lake officials, who fear groundwater contamination. The developer proposes a sewage septic-tank system which, when combined with chemicals used on the golf course, causes local officials to be worried about harm to Bonney Lake's drinking water. Project also includes nearly 1,000 single- and multi-family homes.

Dupont — Northwest Landing (1999/2000). Included in this massive 3,000-acre project backed by Weyerhaeuser Real Estate Company are 4,600 housing units and an 18-hole golf course. The site, west of Fort Lewis, already has a State Farm Insurance regional center and an Intel manufacturing plant.

Gig Harbor — Tacoma Airport Project (2000/2001). In September 1996, the Federal Aviation Administration requested that the city of Tacoma back away from a proposal for an 18-hole golf course, 1,000-foot runway extension to the Tacoma Airport, a hotel and convention center, office buildings and 70 homes. The project could still happen, but not until the city, which owns the airport, completes a master plan which maps out the airport's future.

Graham — Mountainview Dairy Project (1999/2000). This project has been in the works for several years. Tacoma architect Lynn Horn has come up with a design for an 18-hole course; also planned are 70 houses.

Sumner — Matlock Farms Project (1999/2000). Once considered dead in the water, this project may have re-emerged when the farmsite was sold in summer 1995. All permits must still be acquired before work can commence on the planned 18-hole course.

Tacoma — Chambers Creek Project (1999/2000). In 1996, Pierce County officials were evaluating various uses for a 900-acre county-owned site northwest of Lakewood. An 18-hole course has been proposed for land beside a wastewater treatment plant.

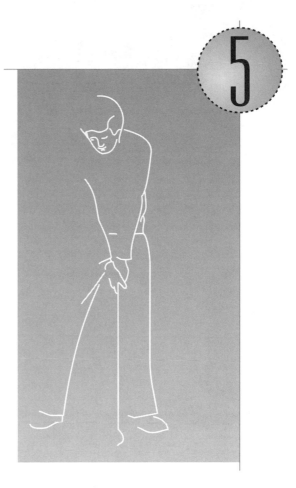

5

OLYMPIC PENINSULA

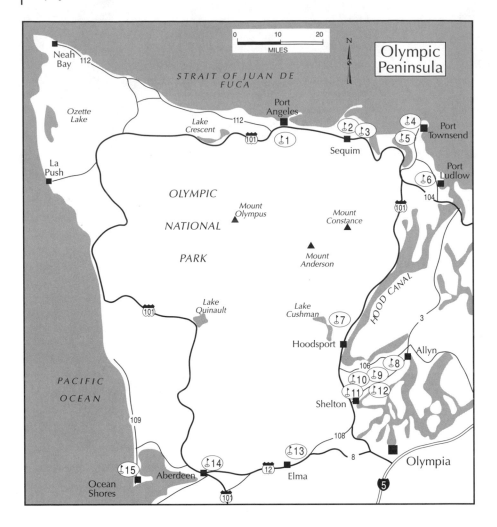

1. **Peninsula Golf Club** — private 18
2. **Dungeness Golf Course** — public 18 & driving range
3. **Sunland Golf & Country Club** — semiprivate 18 & driving range
4. **Port Townsend Municipal Golf Course** — public 9 & driving range
5. **Chevy Chase Golf Club** — public 18 & driving range
6. **Port Ludlow Golf & Meeting Retreat** — semiprivate 27 & driving range
7. **Lake Cushman Golf Course** — public 9
8. **LakeLand Village Golf & Country Club** — semiprivate 27 & driving range
9. **Alderbrook Golf & Yacht Club** — semiprivate 18 & driving range
10. **Lake Limerick Country Club** — semiprivate 9
11. **Batstone Hill Practice Golf** — driving range
12. **Shelton Bayshore Golf Club** — semiprivate 9
13. **Oaksridge Golf Course** — public 18 & driving range
14. **Grays Harbor Country Club** — private 9
15. **Ocean Shores Golf Course** — public 18

The upper left-hand corner of Washington contains some of the state's most pristine and least populated areas. The majority of residents live near Grays Harbor and at the peninsula's north end near Sequim and Port Angeles. Pacific Ocean beaches, Hood Canal and the Strait of Juan de Fuca define the region. Except for the Olympic Mountains, the area enjoys a mild zone 4 climate. Inland areas occupy temperate zone 5, while Sequim and Port Angeles are in banana belts. In summers, the courses on the Olympic Peninsula are bursting with vacationing golfers. It's hoped that the proposed new facilities will enhance the golf scene in this growing area.

Public Courses

Alderbrook Golf and Yacht Club - semiprivate

18 *East 300 Country Club Drive East, Union, WA 98592. (360) 898-2560. Mike Fields, pro. 18 holes. 6,336 yards. Par 72. Grass tees. Course ratings: men—B70.1/118, M68.9/116; women—M74.0/123, F71.0/117. Year Opened: 1967. Architects: Ray Coleman, Roy Goss & Glen Proctor. Moderate, sr. rates, credit cards. Reservations: Call up to a week ahead; three weeks if staying at the Inn. Walk-on chances: Fair. Walkability: Not bad, with a few hills. Playability: Tight layout is enjoyable for all golfers, with nice scenery a bonus.*

Alderbrook's course spans the crest of a hill overlooking Hood Canal. The venue is part of Alderbrook Estates, a 500-acre enclave with residential lots up to a half-acre in size, four rubberized tennis courts and a party area. A 1,200-foot-long pier for boat moorings juts into Hood Canal beside Alderbrook Inn. The 1967-built course was developed by the late Wesley M. Johnson; it is now owned by Johnson's daughter, Nancy Lynch, and her husband Joe. It was built by co-designer, Ray Coleman. Alderbrook is the site of many tournaments, both private and those associated with golf associations. In 1996, it hosted the Frank Rodia Pacific Northwest Junior Championship, an event that has youngsters competing in six divisions.

Fairways on the longer holes are virtual tree-lined corridors as Alderbrook winds through dense woodlands. The tight, well-conditioned layout is dotted with sundry bunkers, and a pond borders the 10th and 18th holes. But overall, Alderbrook's forested surroundings predominate the challenge. Despite some hilly jaunts, the course is generally easy to walk. Over the years, Alderbrook's 8th hole has received much notoriety. Once picked by *Golf Digest* as one of the Northwest's toughest holes, the 8th is a sinuous, chute-like 536-yard par-5. Nearly 175 yards off the tee, the serpentine "S-shaped" fairway turns 90 degrees to the right. Down another 100 yards or so, the hole abruptly angles left to a tree-ringed green. OB lurks behind the untrapped green, and swirling winds also raise havoc with approach shots.

Other good tests include the 4th, a 429-yard par-4 that slopes sharply right before bending left. After the turn, the fairway reaches out to a narrowly-entered and small, trapped-left green. The 18th, a par-5 of 496 yards, winds rightward around a fairway bunker about 200 yards off the tee. The last 275 yards of the hole descend to a green fortified in front by two traps and by a pond on the left. Alderbrook's 18th hole affords wonderful views of Hood Canal and the Olympic Mountains. Also on display at this enjoyable course are deer, raccoons, and both flicker and pileated woodpeckers.

Chevy Chase Golf Club   18

7401 Cape George Road, Port Townsend, WA 98368. (360) 385-0704 or 1-800-385-8722 (in Washington). Ryan Wilson, pro. 18 holes. 6,745 yards. Par 73. Grass tees. Course ratings: men—B71.5/120, M68.1/113, F64.7/106; women—B77.6/129, M73.4/120, F69.2/111. Year Opened: 1925 (original nine); 1997 (second nine). Architects: M. Nagel (original nine); Michael Asmundson (second nine). Moderate, sr. rates, credit cards. Reservations: Call a week ahead. Walk-on chances: Fair. Walkability: Good on original nine; fair on newer back nine with some hilly treks. Playability: Much improved since new second nine opened.

Seven-decades-old Chevy Chase has undergone a significant transformation of late. The brother-and-sister proprietors, Bruce and Barbara Bailey, decided in 1994 to proceed with a long-awaited nine-hole expansion. With the course's newfound status as an 18-holer, the owners are taking this once-antiquated nine into the big time. The Baileys own 200 acres, with the new holes crossing 40 of those. Tree-clearing took place over fall and winter of 1995-96, with construction by John Kruty commencing on the Michael Asmundson-designed, $1.3-million holes in March '96. A Northwest native, Asmundson worked with Scott Miller Design in Arizona, and was involved in laying out the Coeur d'Alene Resort course. Superintendent Scott Westwood, formerly with Kitsap Golf & Country Club, came on board in early 1997 for the grow-in.

The place has great possibilities. Chevy Chase's locale is one of the Northwest's most scenic, stretching along a promontory above Discovery Bay about five miles south of Port Townsend, an artsy, laid-back city with plenty of fun things to do. The totally revised course opened in May 1997, a date that coincided with the centennial of the Chevy Chase Inn. This Victorian-era hostelry on the Bailey property has also been renovated. Once the new nine is open awhile, the original holes will be upgraded and the course will be fully reborn. Future plans include the development of homesites, but that project still needs permits. In an effort to increase play, the Baileys have retrofitted the driving range, expanded food service, added events for members and public golfers, and begun promoting tournaments for groups outside Jefferson County. "Stay-and-play" packages may in the offing (call for details).

Chevy Chase Golf Club and its site enjoy a colorful history. On the property is a house built by the Tukeys—one of Port Townsend's first families; the 1851-built home is Jefferson County's oldest building. Another anecdote stems from an incident in 1864, when a thief supposedly buried $60,000 in gold coins stolen from a British Columbia railway (the 250-pound haul would be valued today at over a million dollars). An Indian witnessed the man bury the gold in the deserted beach below the Tukey farm. Over the decades, treasure hunters have come to Chevy Chase searching for the "Port Discovery Gold." A Tukey granddaughter, Mary Chase, eventually took over the inn, which was originally called Saints Rest. Mary renamed the inn Chevy Chase—after the Cheviot hills in England where her maternal grandparents had lived, and had the course built. In 1945, Mary Chase sold the property to four Seattle investors. Philip Bailey, publisher of the *Seattle Argus*, soon bought out his three partners and turned the inn into a family resort with horses, a swimming pool and tennis court. For 30 years Bailey hosted the Chevy Chase Invitational, a 60-player tournament whose entrants included Harry Givan—a wonderful player who won nearly every Northwest tournament in his prime—and some of Seattle's leading citizens.

Bruce and Barbara Bailey and their siblings (who are no longer involved) used the inn for get-togethers after their father's passing. In the early '90s, the two decided to convert Chevy Chase into a full-service golf facility. The original par-37 layout—now called the Farm Nine—traverses a gently sloping hill. The new holes—called Forest and played as the back nine—is north and east of the originals and more heavily treed. Views from the course take in Mount Baker, the Olympics and Discovery Bay. Play on both nines is affected by the site's southward tilt toward the bay. Wildflowers border fairways and deer and bald eagles live in the neighborhood. Chevy Chase lies in a banana belt, averaging a mere 19 inches of rain a year.

Several sand bunkers guard greensides but, overall, Chevy Chase's challenge stems from its tipped topography, the wood-paneled fairways, and some radical greens. A tough Farm hole is the top-rated 6th, a 424-yard par-4 that bends rightward over rolling terrain to a trapped-right green. The Forest Nine features such testers as the 11th, a 507-yard par-5 that rises over rolling ground. Mount Baker looms in the background of the tree-lined route, which ends at a large front-sloping green guarded on the right by a bunker. The narrow 13th, a 410-yard par-4, runs uphill over right-leaning ground, skirting deep jail left. The fairway eventually reaches a hill-cut, left-rear-tilting green trapped right. The 200-yard, par-3 16th heads off an elevated tee into the prevailing wind. A big bunker lurks right-front—with trees and another trap left—of the course's largest green.

Dungeness Golf & Country Club

18 *491-A Woodcock Road, Sequim, WA 98382. (360) 683-6344 or 1-800-447-6826. Robert Bourns, pro. 18 holes. 6,372 yards. Par 72. Grass tees. Course ratings: men—B70.1/123, M68.5/120; women—M74.1/128, F70.3/119. Years Opened: 1969 (original nine) 1970 (second nine). Architect: Jack Reimer. Moderate, credit cards. Call for reservations. Walk-on chances: Fair. Walkability: Pretty good overall. Playability: One of the most enjoyable places to golf in Western Washington.*

Dungeness is the Olympic Peninsula's most popular place to golf. A favorite course for tourists and residents alike, the facility hosts about 70,000 rounds a year. Designed by Canadian architect Jack Reimer, Dungeness was built by Ray Coleman. Its front nine opened in 1969; the back nine was ready the following year. The course is owned by golf professionals Ron Hagen (Sumner Meadows) and Rick Adell (Inglewood Golf Club) along with four partners. The entertaining course lies off the road that leads to the famous Dungeness Spit—a sandy finger jutting into the Strait of Juan de Fuca. Also nearby is John Wayne Marina.

Both old-growth and younger trees line the fairways at this attractive layout. Though the spit and strait are not visible from the course, local shorebirds and great blue herons are. One of the most prominent features at Dungeness is the quantity and dimensions of its sand traps, among the amplest in Northwest golf. The bunkers are also well-placed between parallel fairways to maximize use. A meandering creek enters play on half the holes, while some homes line parts of the course. A family who lives in a house by the 5th green, the Galles, began decorating a short pine tree with golf bag tags in Christmas 1989. Since they initiated this custom, golfers from around the world have contributed dozens of "ornaments" while passing by.

Players must use all clubs in the bag at Dungeness. The signature hole is the 3rd, a 483-yard par-5. The narrow, rolling hole bends rightward around a huge mound containing bunkers shaped like a crab claw. The left-front edge of the sunken 3rd green is well-trapped. The 7th, a 581-yard par-5, heads slightly downhill off the tee. There's ample bail-out area to the right for tee shots, and the fairway skirts a trap along the right en route to a mid-sized green ringed by three traps.

From the tee at the 14th hole, a 523-yard par-5, there are great views of the surrounding countryside. About 75 yards out, the fairway is crossed by the creek. The hole skirts two fairway bunkers along the right and fenced-in OB left. The 14th is tapered by trees once it nears the green; wooded "jail" along the right contains the creek. The hill-cut, front-sloping green is bunkered right-front and left-rear. The home hole, a 392-yard par-4, requires a 250-yard tee shot to reach the bottom of a hill. The putting surface at the 18th is deep and ringed closely by trees.

Lake Cushman Golf Course   9

North 210 West Fairway Drive, Hoodsport, WA 98548. (360) 877-5505. 9 holes. 2,957 yards. Par 35. Grass tees. Course ratings: men 68.0/117, women 71.5/122. Year Opened: 1967. Architects: Sid Anderson, Manny Proctor & Roy Goss. Moderate. Reservations: Call two weeks ahead. Walk-on chances: Good. Walkability: Good, overall. Playability: Excellent choice for vacationers.

Lake Cushman Golf Course lies in a lush valley at 800 feet above sea level on the southeastern edge of Olympic National Park. The lake is a popular spot for skiing, swimming, boating and other water sports. The well-conditioned layout is owned by Lake Cushman Management Company, which oversees the development of nearby homesites, and it's managed by Brad Brush. The venue is regularly visited by elk, deer, raccoons, coyotes, woodpeckers and many birds.

Lake Cushman's golf course and the surrounding residential community were developed in the late-1960s by Seattle-based Lake Cushman Properties, headed by Ben Clifford. The course was built by co-designer, Sid Anderson; well-known superintendents Roy Goss and Manny Proctor were also involved in the design. Over the years, the property has continued to be popular with out-of-towners who use their cabins and homes mainly during summers.

The dual-tee, 60-acre venue has red, white and blue tee markers, and spans 5,843 yards over two circuits. Its large greens are noted for their undulations and multiple tiers. Sufficient challenges are found on the par-4s, which range in length from 322 to 401 yards. Good tests include the top-rated 7th, a 401-yard par-4 that doglegs right, around trees. A creek fronts the domed 7th green, which is further guarded along the right by a pond. At 495 yards, the par-5 8th is Lake Cushman's longest hole. The ascending left-bender is bordered along the left by a ditch before ending at a multi-tiered green.

9 Lake Limerick Country Club - semiprivate

East 790 St. Andrews Drive, Shelton, WA 98584. (360) 426-6290. Terry O'Hara, pro. 9 holes. 2,898 yards. Par 36. Grass tees. Course ratings: men—B67.0/111, F65.4/107; women—B72.2/121, F70.2/117. Year Opened: 1968. Architect: Mark Antoncich. Moderate, credit cards. Reservations: Call a week ahead. Walk-on chances: Fair. Walkability: Not bad, with a few lengthy between-hole jaunts. Playability: Two disparate sets of tees offer enjoyable 18-hole rounds.

Lake Limerick's course is the centerpiece of a 820-acre residential and recreational reserve occupied by retirees and younger families. Lake Limerick's neighborhood spreads over forested hills and valleys along the Kitsap Peninsula's scenic south end. The fully-developed community has a regular newspaper and a volunteer fire department. It even holds a 4th of July parade every year. The site is split by Cranberry Creek, a salmon- and trout-bearing stream. The club's namesake lake is to the east. Though owned by over 300 members, the course is open to the public.

Lake Limerick's course and like-named community were founded and developed by Mark Antoncich, who designed and built the course. A former state patrolman who did police work at Grand Coulee Dam during its construction between 1936-41, Antoncich also played football and basketball for the University of Washington from 1930-33. Antonicich says that Lake Limerick's site was just "dense forest and a swamp" before he began the development in 1965. The course opened in 1968; Antoncich sold the course to the homeowners in 1970.

The 63-acre layout is characterized by tree-squeezed target zones and sundry man-made hazards. Cabins and homes border some holes, and infrequently used railroad tracks run between the 3rd and 4th, and 8th and 9th holes. Lake Limerick is known for its well-separated sets of tees. The course extends 5,779 yards over two rounds, and golfers will be surprised by the different looks afforded by the tee blocks. Good tests include the top-rated 2nd, a 521-yard par-5 that heads straight along a tree-lined path. The fairway slopes left over its initial two-thirds, then leans rightward en route to a fir-ringed green. The 5th, a 325-yard par-4, has a conifer-lined fairway that initially rises, then descends to a trapped-left, hillside-perched green. The 7th is a 158-yard par-3 on the front nine and a 249-yard par-4 on the back. A pond runs along the fairway's left flank, and the dome-shaped, front-sloping 7th/16th green is trapped laterally and rear.

27 LakeLand Village Golf & Country Club - semiprivate

East 200 Old Ranch Road, Allyn, WA 98524. (360) 275-6100. Randy Jensen, pro. 27 holes. Grass tees. Original 18 (5,752 yards, par 71) course ratings: men—B68.5/ 117, M67.7/114; women F69.6/119. Third nine: 3,300 yards, par 36 (course ratings not available). Years Opened: 1972 (original nine); 1986 (second nine); 1997 (third nine). Architects: Virgil Anderson (original nine) & Gene "Bunny" Mason (second & third nines). Moderate, sr. rates. Call for reservations. Walk-on chances: Fair. Walkability: Fair, with some between-hole length and hills. Playability: Shortish original 18 plays tough while newer nine offers a variety of interesting tests.

LakeLand Village Golf & Country Club lies off Highway 3 atop a hillside above the small town of Allyn. The course is part of a housing development inhabited mainly by retirees. The village's initial nine holes were designed and built in 1972 by the development's founder, Virgil Anderson. The second set of holes were done by architect Bunny Mason, who also designed the 1997-opened third nine. This newer part of LakeLand Village lies on a 100-acre parcel to the west; these holes will eventually be lined by upwards of 100 homes.

The once-private course opened to the public in 1986, and is now operated by Virgil's sons, Bob and Don Anderson. Bob's son, Rick Anderson, is the superintendent. Head pro Randy Jensen has run LakeLand Village's golf operations for several years. Though measuring just under 5,800 yards from the tips, the original 18 plays tough, with the 1986-built front nine 500 yards longer than the original back. These well-tended grounds are dotted with many water and sand hazards. Hand-carved wooden ducks serve as tee markers, fountains adorn ponds, and flower beds brighten the verdure.

Stern tests on these holes include the 1st, a 500-yard par-5 with a narrow dogleg-left fairway off an elevated tee. The fairway leans toward a series of ponds along the right, with trees, OB and houses left. The long and skinny 1st green is guarded left-front by a tree, and has a steep right edge that tilts toward another water hazard. LakeLand Village's top-rated hole is the 8th, a 511-yard par-5 with a mid-width fairway that leans toward ponds along the right. Bypassing OB left and running straight for 350 yards or so, the 8th eventually ascends leftward along a tree-squeezed path to a hill-cut green guarded left by a grass bunker. Perhaps the best hole on the old-style back nine is the 11th, a 394-yard, dogleg-left par-4 with a large pond inside the turn. The heart-shaped green has a steep left flank that leans toward the pond.

Just before this book went to press, a contest—involving the 165 men's club members and 140-member ladies club—was underway to name the three nines. All three of the sides will be used simultaneously; if one of the hole-sets shows wear and tear, it'll be closed and only 18 holes will be played. The newer "west" nine should be drier in winter than its alter-egos as the fairway edges were contoured to better facilitate run-off. These new holes are quite nice. Though not dotted with a ton of bunkers, the layout crosses varied terrain, features several water hazards, and has trees in strategic spots.

Good holes here include the 1st, a tree-lined, 386-yard par-4 that winds uphill over rolling ground before eventually rising up to a ridge-perched, front-sloping green trapped left-front. The 3rd, a 352-yard par-4, runs slightly downhill off the tee. Over its final 150 yards, the hole curls tightly rightward around trees down to a large, trapped-right green. Trees are quite close to its right-front entry. The pretty 5th, a 463-yard par-5, ascends off the tee over right-tilting ground to a sunken area at a hilltop. Here, at about the 200-yard mark, the fairway winds downhill to the right, skirting a pond along the left of the 75-yard mark. The hogbacked 5th green is wide-but-shallow, and is trapped front and left. The 8th, a 169-yard par-3, goes up to a ridged green guarded left by a pond and a trap, with trees right. The 9th, a 358-yard par-4, winds rightward, passing a bunker, OB and homes on the left. The fairway is squeezed at the 150-yard mark, then descends rightward between trees left and two ponds right to a narrow-but-deep, right-tilting green.

Oaksridge Golf Course

18 *207 Elma-Monte Road, Elma, WA 98541. (360) 482-3511. Rich Walker, pro. 18 holes. 5,643 yards. Par 70. Grass tees. Course ratings: men B65.3/100; women— B70.1/111, F68.9/108. Years Opened: 1926 (original nine); 1975 (second nine). Architects: Hiram Mouncer (original nine); members (second nine). Moderate, jr./ sr. rates, credit cards. Reservations: Call for weekends & holidays. Walk-on chances: Good. Walkability: Very good. Playability: Nice place to stop and play on the way to the beach.*

Eighteen-hole Oaksridge lies west of Elma, just off Highway 12. The facility is visible from the highway, one of the primary westbound routes to Washington's Pacific Ocean. Fronting Oaksridge is a place called The Links Restaurant and Lounge, a popular local eatery. Just to the south are the mothballed cooling towers of the Satsop Nuclear Plant, a reminder of the WPSSS fiasco in the 1980s.

Oaksridge was purchased in the mid-1980s by Rich Walker, son of Ray Walker, the former pro at Shelton Bayshore and the Riverside courses in Chehalis and Ferndale. With help from his parents, Rich has upgraded the course during his proprietorship. The venue was originally owned by the Mouncer brothers—Hiram, Homer, and George, who built it on their family farm. Hiram quit what's now called Washington State University in mid-semester and used his college tuition to plot nine fairways and greens on the family's cow pasture. During World War II, the course's grass was grown into pasturelands for cattle used to feed soldiers.

High tides and spillover from the banks of the Chehalis and Satsop rivers flood Oaksridge in the fall and spring. Because the course is relatively short and flat with minimal hazards, it's ideal for all players. Much play is generated by golfers who stop on their way to the beach. Among Oaksridge's top holes is the 6th, a 433-yard par-4 with a ravine-fronted tee and a narrow fairway that leads to a small green backed by a few houses. The 10th is a 486-yard par-5. Over its last 150 yards, the hole veers left to a sizable green fronted by a tall evergreen. The 11th, a par-3 of 194 yards, heads straight into the teeth of prevailing westerlies to a small green trapped left.

Ocean Shores Golf Course

18 *500 Canal Drive, Ocean Shores, WA 98569. (360) 289-3357. Ronnie Espedal & Curt Zander, pros. 18 holes. 6,252 yards. Par 71. Grass tees. Course ratings: men 70.2/115, women 69.6/115. Years Opened: 1962 (original nine); 1965 (second nine). Architect: Gene Gabler. Moderate, sr. rates, credit cards. Call for reservations. Walk-on chances: Fair. Walkability: No problems. Playability: Reasonably priced golf outings at the beach.*

Ocean Shores Golf Course began with nine holes in 1962. A 10th hole followed soon after. The unique 10th was called "5 1/2" by players. It was used for hole-in-one tournaments and as a turn-around point for fatigued golfers. In 1965, the second nine was added. The Gene Gabler-designed layout lies within Ocean Shores, an incorporated town with year-round and seasonal residents. The course was the site of the Pat Boone Classic, an LPGA Tour stop in the 1960s. Among the stars who played in the pro-am were actors Chuck Connors, William Demarest and Forrest Tucker, and University of Washington football coach, Jim Owens. In 1970, the ladies' tour came back for the Wendell-West Invitation Tournament. Future LPGA Hall-of-Famer and Kirkland, Washington, native JoAnne (Gunderson) Carner won her first professional tournament here. In 1996, the Celebrity Golf Classic returned with 19 NFL players. The corridors in the original clubhouse were lined with photos of celebrities-past. In 1996, that structure was torn down for a new 2,600-square-foot clubhouse with a pro shop, restaurant and enclosed deck.

Ocean Shores Golf Course has endured its share of down times, primarily due to financial problems. But the course has survived and become one of the most popular on Washington's coast. Besides vacationers and local players, it hosts many privately-sponsored tournaments. A big annual event is the Golden Gull Classic, a June tourney played by 120 women.

The layout contains two different nines, each of which is numbered in a nine-hole manner. The older front, called the North Course, is similar to a links, with treeless, windswept fairways stretching out to domed, untrapped greens. Some holes are crossed by Grand Canal, a slender waterway that belies its name. A North Course hole of note is the 5th, a 440-yard par-4 that bends slightly right to a heart-shaped green fronted by a ditch. The fairways on the South Course are flat and lined by pine trees. On this more restrictive side, the 434-yard, par-4 3rd stands out. The hole winds over rolling terrain en route to a raised green trapped twice on the left. The tee at the 419-yard par-4 8th is ringed by colorful flowers. From here, one must launch a drive over a roadway to a landing area dotted with ball-knocking trees. The rolling 8th green is slippery.

Port Ludlow Golf & Meeting Retreat - semiprivate

27

751 Highland Drive, Port Ludlow, WA 98365. (360) 437-0272 or 1-800-455-0272 (within Washington). Mike Buss, Director of Golf; Al Salvi, pro. 27 holes. Grass tees. Course ratings: Trail/Timber (6,756 yards, par 72): men—B73.6/138, M71.4/128, FF69.2/123; women—FF74.6/136, F70.8/124, Short F69.8/124. Trail/Tide (6,683 yards, par 72): men—B73.1/138, M70.7/128, FF69.2/123; women—FF74.7/136, F71.3/124, Short F70.3/124. Tide/Timber: (6,787 yards, par 72): men—B72.7/130, M70.3/124, FF68.8/121; women—FF74.3/130, F72.9/126. Years Opened: 1974-75 (Tide & Timber); 1992-94 (Trail). Architect: Robert Muir Graves. Expensive, credit cards. Reservations: Call a week ahead unless a resort guest. Walk-on chances: Fair. Walkability: Take a cart and save your legs for another day. Playability: Original 18 far superior to Trail nine.

For years, Port Ludlow was ranked among the state's top courses. The original 18's position among old-growth timber and its sublime design, length and difficulty made travel writers from around the world gush over the golfing experience at the Olympic Peninsula enclave. At one time or another, Port Ludlow Golf & Meeting Retreat was ranked by *Esquire* magazine as one of the world's top-six golfing destinations, and placed among the nation's top-10 resort courses by *Golf Digest*. So in the early '90s when news leaked that another nine was being built at Port Ludlow, there was considerable anticipation from golfers near and far.

But, alas, the third "Trail" nine was widely panned when opened in 1992. The newest link in Robert Muir Graves' troika of hole-sets was criticized by players, who carped, "there's no room for error," "you lose too many balls," and "you need to hit too many 7-irons off the tees of long par-4s." In response, Port Ludlow's owner, Pope Resources, closed Trail and commenced a major renovation. But in this writer's opinion, no amount of money could make Trail work. The site involves over 250 feet of elevation change and is just too severe for golf. (The holes are actually closed in

The 3rd hole on Port Ludlow's Trail 9 is a 493-yard par-5.

winter because the steep cart paths are rain-slicked and unsafe for walking or riding.) Additionally, deep ravines cross fairways in wrong places to prevent the use of woods, and interior OB is overly used on many holes. I'm not alone in this belief. In his book, *The Confidential Guide to Golf Courses*, golf architect Tom Doak writes that "they (Port Ludlow's owners) were nuts to build a course here. . . Six of the holes are serious candidates for the worst-hole honors." Out of his 0-10 rating system, Doak gave Trail a "0."

Maybe the best Trail hole is the 1st, a 372-yard par-4 with an elevated tee fronted by a deep canyon. Drives (off the back blues) must cross that chasm to reach a ribbonish fairway lined left by two traps. The last 175 yards of the hole run steeply up to a skinny two-tiered green trapped right-rear and left-front. The 4th, a 412-yard par-4, runs straight uphill over its initial two-thirds. Unbeknownst to first-time Trail-ers, the last 150 yards of the 4th go blindly 70 degrees uphill to the right to a mid-sized, front-sloping green trapped twice in front. The 8th, a 551-yard par-5, contains a deep barranca off its elevated tee. The narrow hole passes a bunker along the left on the other side of this stuff, then descends along an OB-lined path. The small, right-front-sloping 8th green has a stump (!) in its back-right corner, and two traps in front.

The public outcry over Trail probably stemmed from the disappointment of golfers who loved the original course, now broken into the Timber and Tide nines. Timber and Tide house considerable water and sand hazards, and the forested surroundings gave foursomes a feeling they were the only people on the course. But that former solitude is gradually changing as peripheral forests are being cleared for new townhouses and single-family homes. Ludlow's traditional wetness—mitigated in recent years through considerable expense—is returning as the removal of the woodlands, once again, has increased runoff onto fairways and overtaxed drainage systems.

Among the best holes on Tide is the top-rated 4th, a 512-yard par-5. A swale off its raised tee is followed by a tree-lined fairway rise. The hole initially doglegs right, then curls left to a small, steeply front-sloping green protected by a creek (75 yards in front), large pond (left-front), and three bunkers (left-front, left and rear). The 7th, a 415-yard par-4, curls to the right along a tree-pinched route to a creek 230 yards out. The 7th green is trapped right and rear, and has a stump off the right-front that muddies the mental yardage gauge without actually blocking approach shots (like Trail's 8th). Timber's 3rd, a 537-yard par-5, stands out. The fairway bends sharply right 190 yards out, mandating a precise tee shot. The fairway bears a ditch and trap along the left before ending at a concave, tri-trapped green. The uphill 9th, a 497-yard par-5, has a sinuous pond along the right of the tees. The hole then curls rightward along a moguled ascent to a crescent-shaped, front-tilting green bunkered right, rear and left-front.

Besides adding residences along the original 18, Pope Resources has cleared woodlands around Trail in preparation for hundreds of housing lots. What this infiltration of civilization bodes for Port Ludlow's golf course is anyone's guess, but drainage across these 27 up-and-down fairways will change. The resort now includes rentable condos, restaurants, an expanded clubhouse, docking facilities, the Inn at Ludlow Bay, hundreds of residents, and 300-plus members who have changed the course's public status to semiprivate. Port Ludlow has pretty much shed its former "destination resort" designation, developing into a community unto itself.

Port Townsend Municipal Golf Course

9

1948 Blaine Street, Port Townsend, WA 98368. (360) 385-0752. Mike Early, pro. 9 holes. 2,763 yards. Par 35. Grass tees. Course ratings: men—B66.2/110, F66.1/110, women—B71.6/116, F71.5/116. Year Opened: 1904. Architects: Founding members. Moderate, jr. rates. Reservations: Call a week ahead. Walk-on chances: Fair. Walkability: Good, with a few uphill climbs. Playability: Quick rounds meet some challenges.

This course at the south end of historic Port Townsend sprawls over a hill, offering views of the marine activities on Admiralty Inlet to the east from its higher points. Founded in 1904, the layout occupies city-owned property which is deeded to forever remain a golf course. Recent changes include the installment of a statue of Chief Chetzemoka on Sentinel Rock, a large boulder on the site. Chetzemoka was a Klallam Indian chief who served as a peacemaker for white settlers in the 1850s.

A less attractive change arose in late 1995 and carried into 1997 when course manager Steve McPherson and his wife Carol faced trial for writing thousands of dollars worth of bad checks (they were later found guilty). The couple had purchased the lease from previous operator, Mike Early, in mid-1994 but had failed to repay Early as well as other creditors. A settlement with the city eventually found Early back in charge of the course. While the McPhersons were in charge, the pro shop operations and restaurant trade went downhill. Some local players reacted by moving on to greener pastures. Early's task is to rebuild the trust of local golfers and restore the customer-service amenities he'd worked so hard to establish during his previous tenure.

Port Townsend's dual-tee track enjoys fairly separate tee blocks over its pair of "nines," which stretch 5,604 yards over two go-rounds. Because of the course's exposed location, golf shots can be flailed by winds. On the plus side, Port Townsend's hilly site affords decent drainage—except for the lower holes—to make it a good winter venue. The course's predominant characteristic is its tilted topography and several fairways horizontally traverse the slope, making for ungainly stances. Among

"PT's" best holes is the 1st, a rolling 504-yard par-5 with an elevated tee, a right-sloping and dogleg-right fairway, and a trapped-left green lined closely left by poplars. The top-rated 4th, a par-4 of 370 yards, starts at a tee fronted by a view-blocking knoll. The fairway then rises to a hill-cut, right-sloping green ringed by three bunkers. The straight-running fairway at the 8th, a 330-yard par-4, leans to the right toward a trap. It then rises to a nasty two-tiered green trapped twice along the left.

Shelton Bayshore Golf Club - semiprivate

9 *East 3800 Highway 3, Shelton, WA 98564. (360) 426-1271. Brian Davis, pro. 9 holes. 2,945 yards. Par 36. Grass tees. Course ratings: men 69.2/116, women 72.6/121. Year Opened: 1948. Architect: Phil Bailey. Moderate, sr. rates. Reservations: Call for weekends and holidays. Walk-on chances: Fair. Walkability: Good, but watch for tree roots. Playability: Enjoyable layout alongside Lake Spencer.*

Member-owned Shelton Bayshore Golf Club opened in July 1948. The course was originated by a local family, which later sold it to the members. The nine-holer sits north of Shelton on the western banks of Lake Spencer, a V-shaped body of water that skirts the southern borders of the Kitsap and Olympic peninsulas. Members have exclusive use of the course on Tuesdays (women), Wednesdays (men) and Sunday mornings (both). Over its five decades, Shelton Bayshore has changed very little. The 60-acre course looks flat, but its corrugated, uneven fairways caused by subterranean tree roots create ungainly lies. The greens are in outstanding shape, and the mostly tree-lined fairways show fine care. A stream winds through two holes on the layout's southern end, and Lake Spencer looms as a hazard only at the 5th.

The layout uses a dual-tee arrangement for 18-hole rounds, which play a total of 5,982 yards. The 2nd is the only hole with two greens. Good tests include the 1st, a 426-yard par-5 that doglegs right, around and through trees. The washboard-like fairway harbors a depression, then the hole is crossed by a creek before ending at a small, front-sloping green. The 4th, a 387-yard par-4, ventures straight between evergreens to a spacious but well-canted green. The 5th, a 458-yard par-5, has a rolling fairway bordered left by the lake. Its wavy and trapped-right green bears a narrow entry.

Sunland Golf & Country Club - semiprivate

18 *109 Hilltop Drive, Sequim, WA 98382. (360) 683-6800. Kelly O'Mera, pro. 18 holes. 6,319 yards. Par 72. Grass tees. Course ratings: men—B70.4/120, M69.2/118; women—M74.2/123, F71.5/120. Years Opened: 1971 (original nine); 1976 (second nine). Architect: Ken Putnam. Moderate, credit cards. Call for reservations. Walk-on chances: Ok for singles. Walkability: Flat and efficient layout quite walker-friendly. Playability: Well-conditioned track with short-cropped turf affords easy-to-pick lies and moderate challenge.*

Located on the northwest edge of Sequim (pronounced "Skwim"), this course is part of an upscale neighborhood inhabited mainly be retirees. Owned by its members, the course retains semiprivate status. Tuesday is the only day the course is fully reserved for members. On the remaining weekdays, public players may use the course after 2:00 p.m. They may also play Saturday after 12:00 a.m. and after 10:30 a.m. on Sunday. If member-blocked times are not filled, the public has access to the course. In any event, call the pro shop for a tee time.

All 18 holes were designed by Ken Putnam. A parcel north of the course contains Sunland's driving range. In May 1994, the members celebrated the opening of a new 12,000-square-foot, $1-million clubhouse. The structure contains the pro shop and an expanded restaurant and lounge. Nearby is a sizable swimming pool, a popular place during Sequim's sunny summers. Kelly O'Mera was hired as the head pro in February 1997.

Sunland is etched within a dense stand of trees, with homes along the edges of most holes. The fairways and greens are well-manicured, and many tees are graced with lovely gardens. Because the course lies within an Olympic Peninsula banana belt that receives 17 inches of annual rainfall (less than half of Seattle's total), this is one of the driest courses in western Washington. Senior PGA tourer and native Seattleite, Don Bies, holds Sunland's record, a 64. This fine score was achieved on a course with midwidth fairways and generally small, well-trapped greens. Sunland's top-rated hole is the 3rd, a par-4 of 440 yards. The straight fairway leads to a left-sloping green ringed by grassy mounds.

Private Courses

Grays Harbor Country Club

9

5300 Central Park Drive, Aberdeen, WA 98520. (360) 532-1931. Keith Liedes, pro. 9 holes. 2,915 yards. Par 35. Grass tees. Course ratings: men B67.0/111; women— B72.4/121, F71.6/119. Year Opened: 1912. Architects: Walter Fovargue & Ray Ball. Members, guests & reciprocates.

Grays Harbor Country Club lies between Montesano and Aberdeen off Highway 12. The par-35, dual-tee layout, which plays to 5,758 yards over two circuits, contains two par-5s, three par-3s and four par-4s. The historic course was designed by Walter Fovargue and Ray Ball, and opened in 1912. It features tree-pinched fairways and small and slick, well-trapped greens. Recent upgrades to the nicely-kept layout include paved cart paths. The club owns adjoining property. Over the past 30 years, the members have intermittently discussed adding nine holes, but no expansion plans are imminent.

Besides an enjoyable course, 350-member Grays Harbor has a nice clubhouse adjoined by a swimming pool. Located in the Central Park area of Aberdeen, the course is surrounded by dense forests and lovely residences. Included on the club's yearly tournament docket is the Smiles & Frowns—a couples event—in late-May, the Earley Tire Best-Ball in July, Grays Harbor Pro-Am in August, and Bank of Grays Harbor Scramble in September.

Among the better holes is the 1st, a 529-yard par-5 with a right-turning route guarded by a big bunker on the left, 250 yards out. Here, the hole rises over a tree-tapered path to a round green trapped on both sides. Two fat trees impede entry to the green from the left-front. The top-rated 3rd, a 413-yard par-4, is a rolling dogleg-left whose back tee sits in trees. Drives from this point must be hooked or drawn to make initial progress on the lengthy hole. The last 100 yards descend slightly to a squarish, laterally-trapped green with a steep back end.

The idiosyncratic 6th, a par-4 of 264 yards, has a 70-degree dogleg-right fairway that requires a short-iron tee shot. The hole climbs a hill, passing a fairway bunker along the right, before winding downhill leftward to a hill-cut green trapped front and left-front. This putting surface also has a steep rear flank. Grays Harbor's 9th, a 192-yard par-3, involves an accurate shot over a gully to reach a humped-in-the-rear, steeply front-tilted green protected by a huge bunker left, a trap right, and yet another steep rear edge.

Peninsula Golf Club

18 *824 South Lindberg Road, Port Angeles, WA 98362. (360) 457-6501. Chris Repass, pro. 18 holes. 6,334 yards. Par 72. Grass tees. Course ratings: men—B70.3/122, M69.1/119; women—M74.5/125, F70.3/120. Years Opened: 1924 (original nine); 1978 (second nine). Architects: Francis L. James (original nine); Jack Reimer (second nine). Members, guests & reciprocates.*

Peninsula Golf Club overlooks the Strait of Juan de Fuca and Vancouver Island—20 miles distant—from its hilltop vantage. The club, founded in 1924, was originally a members-only facility but, for financial reasons, opened its doors to the public in 1984. On February 1, 1993, Peninsula Golf Club's membership grew to the point where it once again turned private. The three major events on the club's calendar are the Spring Shotgun on Memorial Day Weekend, Peninsula Chapman Invitational in July, and Fall Shotgun over Labor Day Weekend.

The newer back nine was designed by Jack Reimer and built by Ray Coleman. The legendary Byron Nelson played Peninsula whenever he visited Port Angeles during the 1940s. Despite many trees around the course, Peninsula resembles a links venue, with view-blocking mounds and grassy swales strewn about the layout. Peninsula's predominant characteristic is the northward descent of its tilted site, with winds off the nearby strait also a factor. Where fairways traverse the slope horizontally, a flat lie is impossible to find. The layout is dotted with a couple dozen bunkers.

Tough holes include the top-rated 5th, a left-bending, 484-yard par-5 that slopes toward OB. The hole is lined left by trees, and it ends at a fir-ringed green. On clear days, Vancouver Island is quite viewable from Peninsula's 12th, a 354-yard par-4. The hole doglegs right around trees and a trap in a depression to a round, trapped-left green in a hollow. The 489-yard, par-5 15th begins at a tee where the view is blocked, so it's difficult to know where the fairway is heading. Running astride a hill, the fairway eventually bends left to a front-sloping green trapped twice along the right.

DRIVING RANGES

Batstone Hill Practice Golf

321 Mason Lake Road, Shelton, WA 98584.
(360) 426-4276. Jeff Jackson, pro.

UPCOMING COURSES

Brennan — Pleasant Harbor Golf Course (1999). In early 1997, a local couple was lining up financing for an 18-hole, Peter Thompson-designed course and 19 houses on a 191-acre site near this town on Hood Canal. The 6,400-yard resort-type course will be located beside an existing campground.

LaPush — James Island Resort (1999). Architect Jim Williams has designed a 30-acre resort with a par-3 nine, 150-room lodge, convention facilities, casino, bingo parlor, pool, exercise room, RV park, two restaurants and retail shops near LaPush.

Port Angeles — Juan de Fuca Golf Course (2000). This 275-acre project has been on hold since the state Fish and Wildlife department required an extensive Environmental Impact Statement. The plan, which includes a Jack Frei-designed 18 and 130 townhouses, may never materialize as the site contains eagle nests and spawning salmon.

Port Angeles — Municipal Golf Course (2000). In June 1996, the city of Port Angeles received the results of a feasibility study that concluded a municipal-type golf course would succeed at a 110-acre site near Fairchild International Airport.

Sequim — Skyridge Golf Course (1999/2000). Bill Overdorf has designed an 18-hole, par-69 golf course for 110 acres owned by the Pedersen family. Plans for the site, which occupies the Pedersen's former dairy farm at Cays and Woodcock roads, also includes a driving range.

Sequim — Sikma/LeGolf Project (2000). After some well-publicized activity when announced, this 27-hole proposal has slowed of late. The reason? The developers—Sikma Enterprises and LeGolf—must build the course in conjunction with the city's proposed wastewater treatment plant. The course would be irrigated by treated wastewater.

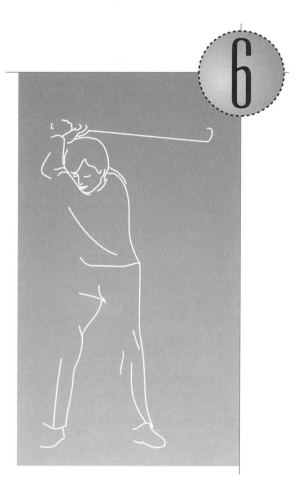

6

OLYMPIA &
SOUTHWEST WASHINGTON

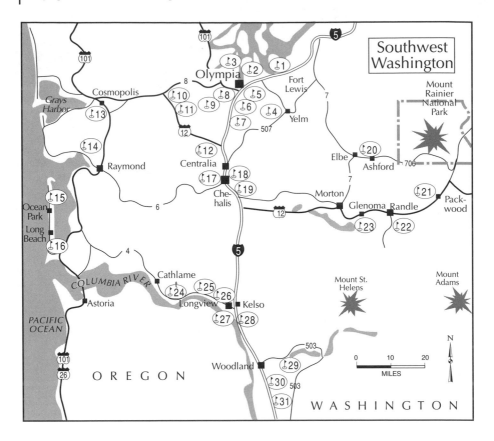

1. **Meriwood Golf Course** — public 18, driving range & 9-hole putting course
2. **Olympia Country & Golf Club** — private 18
3. **Steamboat Golf** — driving range
4. **Nisqually Valley Golf Course** — public 18
5. **Tumwater Valley Golf Club** — public 18 & driving range
6. **Scott Lake Golf Course** — public 9
7. **Pacific Golf Center** — public 9 & driving range
8. **Delphi Golf Course** — public 9
9. **Eagle View Golf Center** — public 3 & driving range
10. **Capitol City Golf Club** — public 18 & driving range
11. **Indian Summer Golf & Country Club** — private 18
12. **Grand Mound Driving Range**
13. **Highland Golf Course** — public 18 & driving range
14. **Willapa Harbor Golf Club** — public 9 & driving range
15. **Surfside Golf Course** — public 9 & driving range
16. **Peninsula Golf** — public 9
17. **Riverside Country Club** — public 18 & driving range
18. **Centralia Public Golf Course** — public 9
19. **Newaukum Valley Golf Course** — public 27 & driving range
20. **Ashford Driving Range**
21. **High Valley Country Club** — private 9
22. **Maple Grove Golf** — public 9
23. **Ironwood Green Golf Course** — public 9
24. **Skyline Golf Course** — public 9
25. **Mint Valley Golf Course** — public 18 & driving range
26. **Longview Country Club** — private 18
27. **Golfgreen Golf Center** — public 9 (par-3)
28. **Three Rivers Golf Course** — public 18 & driving range
29. **Lewis River Golf Course** — public 18 & driving range
30. **Par IV Golf Learning Center** — driving range
31. **Tri-Mountain Golf Course** — public 18, 18-hole putting course & driving range

This corner of the Evergreen State is bordered by the Cascade Mountains on the east, the Pacific Ocean to the west, Washington's capital of Olympia on the north, and the town of Woodland on the south. Bring your umbrellas when golfing in this area, which involves climate zones 4 and 5. Greater Olympia is growing rapidly, with residential and industrial developments cropping up here and there. Property both north and south of Olympia along the Interstate 5 corridor is particularly active, with several new golf-related projects proposed for this increasingly populated stretch.

Public Courses

Capitol City Golf Club

18 *5225 Yelm Highway SE, Olympia, WA 98503. (360) 491-5111. Tim Walsh, pro. 18 holes. 6,536 yards. Par 72. Grass tees. Course ratings: men—B70.6/121, M69.2/118; women—M75.2/124, F71.2/116. Year Opened: 1962. Architect: Norman Wood. Moderate, jr./sr. rates, credit cards. Reservations: Call a week ahead. Walk-on chances: Fair. Walkability: Good. Playability: One of the Northwest's better choices for winter golf.*

In mid-1994, the nation's largest golf course-management firm, American Golf Corp. (AGC), purchased this south Olympia course for a reported $2.9 million from Joe Thiel. Thiel sold Capitol City to concentrate on his Eagle View Golf Center, located about a half mile away. Designed by Canadian architect Norman Wood and opened in 1962, Capitol City is bordered by a quiet residential neighborhood. The layout was originated by Jim Carlson and Arizonan Lyle Anderson, the latter of whom has become a big-time developer of world-class resorts in Hawaii and Arizona. As an AGC course, Capitol City—for an annual fee of $229—offers a program giving participants discounts on green fees, power carts, equipment and apparel here. AGC also does this at its courses in Arlington (Gleneagle) and Maple Valley (Lake Wilderness).

Capitol City is widely considered to be among the region's best places for winter golf. Perched on flat meadows, the layout features well-draining turf as well as wonderful views of Mount Rainier and the Cascades. Over 50 Scottish-style bunkers and sundry water hazards dot the layout, and assorted evergreens line fairways. Excellent conditioning helps make the experience an enjoyable one. Some of Capitol City's holes are fairly close to homes, so it's not uncommon for golf balls to clank off siding and rooftops. The facility is augmented by a large clubhouse with a full-service restaurant and lounge.

Among Capitol City's best holes is the 7th, a 504-yard par-5 with a bumpy, tree-lined fairway bordered along the right by a huge bunker. Another trap looms along the fairway's left edge, 30 yards from a small green trapped left and rear. On the back nine, the 11th stands out. This 194-yard par-3 houses a sizable pond along the right and two large traps around its slippery green. The 458-yard par-4 13th—rated the second-toughest hole—doglegs slightly left around a large bunker. The rolling 13th green is squeezed by lateral traps.

Centralia Public Golf Course

1012 Duffy, Centralia, WA 98531. (360) 736-5967. 9 holes. 2,851 yards. Par 36. Grass tees. Course ratings: men 67.3/121, women 70.8/125. Opened: 1930s. Architect: Works Progress Administration. Economical, jr. rates. Call for reservations. Walk-on chances: Good. Walkability: Get a workout at sidehill layout. Playability: Note ratings, this is no stroll in the park.

9

This 40-acre course, previously called Armory Hills before reverting to its original name (minus the "Elks" identifier), is owned by the city of Centralia. After some disagreements with the previous operators, the city entered into a lease with Michel and Renee Rey. The Reys, Switzerland natives who moved to Washington in 1991, have improved the course by adding cart paths and a much-needed irrigation system. As a result of these changes, play levels have increased at the 60-year-old course.

Designed and built in the 1930s by Works Progress Administration labor, Centralia's layout once consisted of 18 regulation-length holes. Nine of these holes later became a neighborhood. The existing course crosses the edge of Seminary Hill on Centralia's east edge; the first seven holes gradually climb the hill to its crest. These side-slope holes have long been a bone of contention to players. Even well-placed tee shots tend to roll off fairways into trees or a ditch. The dual-tee layout, which plays to 5,674 yards over two circuits, punishes the errant.

Good tests include the top-rated 4th, a 449-yard par-5 with a narrow and rolling fairway bearing two humps. Before bending left, the route skirts OB left and an evergreen grove right. After the turn, players encounter "The Canyon," which eats up second shots into a slick, hill-cut green. The 373-yard, par-4 7th bends slightly right around trees. Recent modifications have taken some of the leftward tilt out of the fairway. The 8th, a 440-yard par-5, bends upward to the left, while sloping right toward a ditch. (Players get a free drop from the ditch.) A pond lurks 50 yards before the right front of the small 8th green, which is bunkered at the left and front.

Delphi Golf Course

6340 Neylon Drive SW, Olympia, WA 98512. (360) 357-6437. Rich Williams, pro. 9 holes. 1,937 yards. Par 32. Grass tees. Course ratings: men—M61.4/102, F60.6/101; women—M63.4/106, F61.8/102. Year Opened: 1972. Architect: Glenn Correa. Moderate, jr./sr. rates, credit cards. Call for reservations. Walk-on chances: Good. Walkability: No problems. Playability: Quick rounds found at Black Hills layout.

9

Delphi's short nine winds between the backyards of ranch-style homes in the Black Hills area of Olympia. The residents of Delphi Park—under the auspices of a nonprofit association—own the course. The homeowners' group acquired Delphi from the founder and course's designer, Glenn Correa. All green fees are placed into a fund to maintain the fairways and greens, and much of the maintenance work is performed by volunteers. Recent projects have included drainage improvements, new tees and landscaping upgrades.

The 2,000-yard layout occupies 37 acres of a former Christmas tree farm, and can be termed "executive-length." It has two sets of tees, and a few ponds and bunkers squeeze target zones. Perhaps Delphi's prettiest hole is the 5th, a 137-yard par-3. A pond with a fountain fronts the tee and extends to the front of a large and undulating green, which is trapped right. The tree-lined 6th, a 328-yard par-4, curls rightward to a midsized green ringed by three traps. Delphi's 9th, a 333-yard par-4, is pinched by firs and pines along its uphill, left-turning route. At the 100-yard mark, a fat cedar squeezes the entry to a right-sloping green ringed by trees and trapped left-front and right-rear.

Highland Golf Course

18 *300 Yard Drive, Cosmopolis, WA 98537. (360) 533-2455. Joe Golia, pro. 18 holes. 5,992 yards. Par 70. Grass tees. Course ratings: men—B67.4/108, M65.7/105; women—B72.9/120, M70.9/116, F67.5/109. Year Opened: 1930 (original nine); 1994 (second nine). Architects: Francis L. James & Walter Fovargue (original nine); Bill Overdorf (second nine). Moderate, credit cards. Call for reservations. Walk-on chances: Good. Walkability: Fair, with many hills and dales along the way. Playability: Considerably better with recently-added holes.*

Highland's recently-expanded course is off Highway 101 at the the south end of Cosmopolis, a timber town near Aberdeen. The layout is owned by Mike Strada, who's also the greens superintendent. A Bill Overdorf-designed back nine opened in 1994, although it was conceived in the mid-1970s. The two-decade delay was due to Strada being unable to acquire adjacent privately-owned parcels for the expansion. These holes are slightly longer than the original front side, which was built by horse-drawn scrapers and opened in 1930. Upcoming plans include replacing the original "push-up" greens with USGA-spec putting surfaces.

Highland lies across Highway 101 from a Weyerhaeuser mill, but noise from the plant is muted by the dense stands of trees around the course. Indeed, Highland's forestry is one its primary impediments to par. Strada is gradually adding bunkers to the peripheries of greens and fairways, and as these hazards come along, Highland's difficulty will increase. The Stradas (led by Mike's mother Phyllis) bought the course in the early-1950s from Tom Swenson and Pete Oseng, builders of the original nine. In 1931, a back nine was built, but financial problems created by the Depression prevented it from ever opening. Head pro Joe Golia, here since 1985, conducts lessons at a grass-teed driving range. Mike Strada's daughter, Vicky, is one of the Northwest's premier players, recently starring on Stanford University's golf team.

Highland's 200-acre site ranges from gently rolling to steep, and some of its turf is patchy in places. Among the more interesting holes is the top-rated 1st, a 515-yard par-5 that runs downhill off a raised tee over left-tilting terrain. Over its last 200 yards, the 1st bends slightly left over rolling ground to a large, V-shaped green with tough pin possibilities. The tree-lined 7th, a 350-yard par-4, starts at a chute-like tee in trees, then follows a steeply right-banked path. Over its last 125 yards the hole descends to a hill-cut, right-front-sloping green with a very steep right flank that leans toward jail. The 9th, a 409-yard par-4, is long and narrow and bends slightly left. The hole eventually tapers as it descends to a small, front-sloping green guarded left-front by trees.

A standout among the newer holes is the 11th, a 405-yard par-4 with a slightly uphill, right-turning fairway. The deep and rolling, front-sloping 11th green is surrounded by evergreens. Over its initial 300 yards, the 14th, a 570-yard par-5, runs uphill and slopes steeply left. The hole curls leftward before winding back up around to the right. The 14th ends at a long and skinny green carved out of a hillside. After dropping off a towering elevated tee, the 17th, a par-5 of 490 yards, takes off on a left-bending path. Dense woods shadow both sides of the hole, which rises steeply over its last 125 yards to a front-right-sloping green guarded in front by a grass bunker and behind by trees.

Ironwood Green Golf Course   9

8138 U.S. Highway 12, Glenoma, WA 98336. (360) 498-5425. 9 holes. 1,435 yards. Par 30. Grass tees. No course ratings. Year Opened: 1983. Architect: Jim Redmon. Economical, sr. rates, credit cards. No reservations. Walkability: No problems. Playability: Short course contains a few challenges.

Ironwood Green borders the south side of Highway 12 in the small hamlet of Glenoma. The course is owned by the husband-and-wife team of Jim and Alice Redmon. Jim designed and built the course on 10 acres of former pasture. The site is on the floor of a scenic Cascade valley. According to Jim, Ironwood Green's 8- by-10-foot pro shop is the world's smallest. If the Redmons aren't in attendance, pay green fees to the clerk in the convenience store next door to the course.

Ironwood Green's fairways are generally flat, but its postage-stamp greens can be elusive targets. The 1st and 2nd fairways parallel Highway 12. A creek winds past the 80-yard 5th hole and through the top-rated 115-yard 8th. Other hazards include ponds along the par-4s at the 245-yard 4th and 212-yard 6th. Bunkers dot a few greensides. Young trees line most fairways, with a few taller species impeding play on the creek holes.

Lewis River Golf Course   18

3209 Lewis River Road, Woodland, WA 98674. (360) 225-8254. Dick Smith, pro. 18 holes. 6,247 yards. Par 72. Grass tees. Course ratings: men—B69.5/124, M67.5/ 117; women—M72.5/125, F68.9/118. Year Opened: 1967 (original nine); 1969 (second nine). Architects: Gail Wellwood (original nine); Ralph Stading (second nine). Moderate, sr. rates, credit cards. Reservations: Call a week ahead. Walk-on chances: Fair. Walkability: Good. Playability: Upgrades to front nine now match difficulty of back.

Eighteen-hole Lewis River lies five miles east of Woodland in an area called Clover Valley, and is the closest course to Mount Saint Helens. Owner Ralph Stading— along with friends and family—was at the course on May 18, 1980, and watched the volcano 25 miles to the northeast vent its spleen. Another, more sedate natural trait of this forested layout is that it is within one of the world's finest steelhead fishing zones. Lewis River and various forks of the Clark and Cowlitz rivers are all nearby. Indeed, the course occupies a V-shaped parcel defined by a jog in the Lewis.

The layout arose in 1967 with Gail Wellwood's front side; Stading's entertaining back nine followed two years later. The course, previously a farm, has been in the Stading family since 1960. In 1995, Stading, with help from his son, Ralph Jr., began remodeling the back nine. A pond fronting the par-3 17th hole was expanded and bunkers were added. The upgrades were nearly finished in February 1996 when the Lewis spilled over its banks and washed out the work. A new split-level home on the east side of the course was literally tipped over by the flood. The storm blew over a barn that had been a fixture on the 150-acre property since 1900. The Stadings regrouped and, by summer 1996, the remodeling was finally complete. Stading has water permits pending with the state Department of Ecology to allow development of 200 single- and multi-family homes on land beside the 12th and 13th holes. Additional plans include a conference center, a 150- to 250-room lodge, office space and remodeled pro shop. The 6th and 9th holes may also be extended.

All the recent work has resulted in a much more refined Lewis River Golf Course, with Wellwood's once-featureless front nine maturing nicely. Good holes here include the 1st, a 314-yard par-4 that doglegs right between trees. A large pond crosses before the front-sloping green, which is further guarded left-front by a bunker. The right-turning 5th, a 452-yard par-5, is narrowed by trees over its last 150 yards. Its small, tilted green is trapped twice in front. The 7th, a 189-yard par-3, requires a drive over a creek off an elevated tee. This pretty hole ends at a large, round green trapped on the left.

Holes 12-17 on Stading's back nine are all outstanding. The top-rated 12th, one of the Northwest's longest par-5s at 649 yards, follows a slightly left-bending and narrowish path. At the 225-yard mark, the fairway descends past a pond en route to a trapped-left-front, wildly-sloping putting surface. The straightahead 13th, a 429-yard par-4, skirts a large bunker at the 150-yard post along the right. Two bunkers (left and right-front) and trees (right-front) protect its mid-sized, right-front-sloping green. The tree-squeezed 14th, a 362-yard par-4, is a narrow right-turner that requires a lofted tee shot to carry trees along the right and avoid a pond left. Another pond crosses the fairway 50 yards from a left-leaning green trapped left-front, with fat maples pinching the right-front entry.

Another behemoth par-5 is the 15th, a 582-yard affair with a pond off the tee, a narrow and "S"-shaped fairway (going right, then left), and a big left-leaning green trapped right-front. The idiosyncratic 16th, a 313-yard par-4, goes out about 225 yards, then turns 90 degrees to the right. Shots into its small, steeply right-front sloping green must evade a new pond guarding it along the right, a fat tree right-front, and two cedars left. The 131-yard 17th, Lewis River's most photogenic hole, descends slightly to a wide-but-shallow, water-engirded green garnished by a lovely flower garden.

Maple Grove Golf

9 *Highway 12 & Cispus Road, Randle, WA 98377. (360) 497-2741. 9 holes. 1,653 yards. Par 29. Grass tees. Course ratings: men 56.8/90, women 56.8/80. Year Opened: 1987. Architect: Roy McCain. Economical, jr./sr. rates, credit cards. No reservations. Walkability: Good. Playability: Facile golf near the north entrance to Mount Saint Helens.*

Maple Grove Golf borders the western banks of the Cowlitz River near Randle and the northern entrance to Mount Saint Helens National Park. The course is part of Maple Grove Resort, an RV-oriented oasis which opened in 1985. After doing the groundwork for the resort, owner Roy McCain built the golf course in 1987. RVers often stay for up to a week in this scenic west-Cascades area, enjoying the private forested camping sites, recreational facilities and proximity to a spectacular park that has recently been upgraded with a magnificent visitor's center.

The resort sits at 900 feet above sea level. With its riverside locale, the venue is frequented by deer and elk. Since opening the 15-acre track McCain has added a water hazard and a few bunkers. He's tried to acquire a 40-acre parcel across the Cowlitz for another nine holes, but has yet to clinch a deal with the landowner. Maple

Grove's rudimentary course is kept in good shape, and the 2,000-square-foot greens are lusher than the fairways. It contains five par-3s and four par-4s, the shortest being 211 yards and the longest 245. Par-3s range from 114 to 180 yards. All holes are straightforward and unfettered by hazards.

Meriwood Golf Course - semiprivate

4550 Golf Course Road NE, Lacey, WA 98516. 1-360-412-0495 or 1-800-558-3348. Ron Coleman, director of golf; Joe Creager, head pro. 18 holes. 7,170 yards. Par 72. Grass tees. Course Rratings: men—B75.1/135, M71.4/126; F67.7/120; women— M77.5/142, F73.0/127. Year Opened: 1995. Architect: Bill Overdorf. Expensive, credit cards. Reservations: Call up to 30 days ahead. Walk-on chances: Fair. Walkability: Cart part of greens fee for good reason. Playability: Plenty of difficulty, with course involving lots of topographical changes, length and abundance of hazards.

Opened in April 1995, this 18-hole course north of Olympia is part of a 1,153-acre master-planned community called Meridian Campus. The project is a joint development of Weyerhaeuser Real Estate Company and Hong Kong-based Vicwood Development Corporation. Meriwood's course is managed by Golf Resources, Inc., an operation headed by long-time Northwest pros, Ron Coleman and Ron Hagen. The course is regarded as semiprivate; memberships are sold, but Meriwood plans to always allow public play.

Besides the construction of over 1,000 single-family homes and 1,400 townhouses, Meridian Campus will include business and light-industrial areas, shops, open spaces, trails, parks and schools. Future plans include another 18-hole golf course on the adjacent, 720-acre Hawks Prairie site owned by Vicwood. Work on the Peter Thompson-designed layout may be completed by 1999. Upwards of 1,700 homes are in Vicwood's plan. Located about a mile west of Interstate 5 (off exit 111), this area has long been known as Hawk's Prairie. Local Indians used the site above the southwestern end of Puget Sound for trade with other tribes. Nearby are the Nisqually National Wildlife Refuge and Nisqually Reach Nature Center, federally-protected places with abundant wildlife.

Because of its sprawling layout, length and hills, Meriwood has a cart-mandatory policy. The cart requirement usually means that golf is an expensive proposition; though identified as such above, Meriwood's green fees are between $37 (weekdays) and $42 (weekends). Lower rates are available in the off-season. Besides a huge grass-teed driving range, the venue has a clubhouse with food service. Meriwood hosted 43,000 rounds in its first year of business, 1995. Still in its infancy, the course is etched within dense forests; until the housing is built, golf will remain a quiet experience. The Bill Overdorf-designed course is reminiscent of McCormick Woods in Port Orchard, Kayak Point in Stanwood and Indian Summer in south Olympia. Each has an epic scope, with considerable acreage, native old-growth evergreens, tilted topography and plenty of hazards.

Meriwood's challenge begins right away at the 1st, a 415-yard par-4 that winds slightly uphill to the left. Huge bunkers lurk along the right, 150 yards from a large, amoeba-shaped green trapped right-front and rear. The top-rated 4th, a 542-yard par-5, doglegs uphill to the right. The right-tilting route bears a series of gravity-fed ponds—with lovely waterfalls—and bunkers along the right. The 4th is wide initially, then narrows over its last 150 yards before reaching a right-sloping green guarded by a pond right and grass bunkers in front. The tough-driving 5th, a 407-yard par-4, is a tight, right-sloping dogleg-left that curls downhill to a two-tiered green trapped twice left and once right-rear. The 453-yard, par-4 7th ascends slightly as it curls past grass bunkers along the left; its mid-sized putting surface is trapped right-rear.

The 9th, a 573-yard par-5, has a pond off the tee, then veers 70 degrees to the right 225 yards out. A big bunker inside the turn narrows the landing zone. Once around the bend, the hole winds downhill toward a fairway-wide wetlands at the 130-yard mark. This impenetrable, 40-yard-deep jail fronts a small, left-sloping green bunkered right-front and rear. The 12th, a 440-yard par-4, winds leftward along a downhill path that passes a pond on the right. The ridge-perched 12th green is bunkered on the back. The 570-yard 14th is a fairly narrow, left-sloping par-5 lined on the right by trees. The serpentine hole curls rightward about 250 yards out, eventually winding leftward to a mid-sized, front-left-tilting green. The broad fairway at the 15th, a 464-yard par-4, is squeezed along the left by three bunkers. Its front-sloping green is trapped laterally. Meriwood's best par-3 is the 16th, a pretty 202-yarder that starts at an elevated tee and drops down to a huge, two-tiered green fronted closely by two ponds.

Mint Valley Golf Course

18 *4002 Pennsylvania Street, Longview, WA 98632. (360) 577-3395. Mahlon Moe, pro. 18 holes. 6,379 yards. Par 71. Grass tees. Course ratings: men—B69.4/114, M67.2/109; women—M72.4/117, F69.0/109. Year Opened: 1976. Architect: Ron Fream. Moderate, jr./sr. rates. Reservations: Call a week ahead. Walk-on chances: Fair. Walkability: Good. Playability: A bit wet in the winter, but otherwise, an enjoyable course.*

Owned by the city of Longview and opened for play in 1976, Mint Valley is a fine course situated within an established neighborhood on the city's west side. The contemporary venue is blessed with a goodly number of hazards—including fairway and greenside bunkers—and many water hazards. The on-course ponds and ditches

Mint Valley's 4th hole is a 173-yard par-3.

and offshoots of the nearby Cowlitz and Columbia rivers. Mint Valley has traditionally been a poor-draining layout, but a sanding and topdressing program over the past 15 years has made the course much drier in spring and fall. Recent improvements include a new bridge on the 17th hole; the tees at the 4th and 6th holes will be revamped soon.

The municipal course hosts upwards of 50,000 rounds a year, and is the site of many privately-sponsored tournaments. The venue also holds the Columbia Ford Open, a popular event that draws its 160-player field from throughout southwest Washington and the Portland area. The tournament, which celebrated its 20th go-round in 1996, has a purse totaling $9,500, making it one of the more lucrative events of its kind in the Northwest.

Tournament contestants and other golfers will be challenged by such Mint Valley holes as the top-rated 5th, a 394-yard par-4 that doglegs sharply right. A pond lurks right of the tee, the fairway's left edge is well-trapped and lined by a culvert, and the small 5th green is bunkered in front. Most of the par-3 17th is pond. A lofted shot is needed at this 177-yarder to carry the water for a safe landing on a front-tilting green trapped back-left. The narrow fairway at the 18th, a par-4 of 407 yards, curls rightward. Large bunkers along the right and two ponds left create a tight "garden spot" for drives. The sloped and slick 18th green is trapped right-front and left-rear.

Newaukum Valley Golf Course 27

3024 Jackson Highway, Chehalis, WA 98532. (360) 748-0461. Scott Date, pro. 27 holes. Grass tees. Course ratings: South/East (6,168 yards, par 72): men—B68.5/ 109, M66.8/105; women—M72.2/116, F68.3/108. West/East (6,213 yards, par 72): men—B68.4/109, M67.0/105; women—M72.2/117, F68.9/110. West/South (6,491 yards, par 72): men—B69.9/113, M68.0/108; women—M73.6/119, F70.6/112. Years Opened: 1979 (West & South nines); 1996 (East Nine). Architects: Henry Date & John Date (West & South); John Date (East). Moderate, sr. rates, credit cards. Call for reservations. Walk-on chances: Fair. Walkability: Good. Playability: Three nines may lead to full day on the links.

Located east of Chehalis, Newaukum Valley was developed by Henry Date. Before his passing in 1995, the senior Date ceded management of the course to his son John, who's also the superintendent. Henry's daughter Mary Jane Matthews oversees the snack bar, and grandson Scott runs the pro shop. Henry and John Date designed and built the facility's initial 18 holes (now called the West and South nines), which opened in 1979. A third nine designed by John debuted in March 1996. Newaukum Valley is bordered by the Chehalis River, and the flood of February 1996 spread silt from this waterway across the course. Some bridges across feeder ditches off the river were also wiped out. By summer '96, all systems were go for the 27-holer, which also has a full-service clubhouse and driving range.

Besides its proximity to the river, where many local anglers fish for fall-run Chinook salmon, Newaukum Valley contains nice views of mounts Saint Helens and Rainier. Players find some tough holes, with the newer East nine containing greens of more contemporary scope and contour than their predecessors. Among the more interesting South holes is the tree-lined 2nd, a 430-yard par-4 with a narrowish, right-bending fairway that rises over its last 150 yards to a hogbacked green trapped at the left-front. The top-rated 6th, a 512-yard par-5, curls rightward around two ponds. At the 250-yard mark, the hole veers sharply right to a very slick, two-tiered green.

A West nine toughie is the 2nd, a 575-yard par-5. This lengthy left-turner eventually straightens out before reaching a mid-sized, trapped-left green with a big hump in its back. A nice par-3 is the 3rd, a 145-yarder with an undulating, good-sized green protected by a pond behind and a trap on the right. The 6th, a 430-yard par-4, runs straight past OB along the left en route to a rolling green guarded by trees and a fat bunker left and a pond right.

A notable East hole is the 2nd, a 340-yard par-4 with an elevated tee fronted by a pond. The fairway curls rightward around another pond which runs up to guard the right-front edge of a green that tilts toward it. The top-rated 4th, a 514-yard par-5, has a wide landing area lined on the left by a water hazard. At the 160-yard mark, a pond crosses the fairway, which then bears slightly left. The 4th ends at a shallow-but-wide green shadowed left-front by a tree. The 8th, a 462-yard par-5, has white OB stakes along both sides of its dogleg-left path. The last 100 yards ascend to a hill-cut, front-sloping green fronted by a pond.

18 Nisqually Valley Golf Course

15425 Mosman Street, Yelm, WA 98597. (360) 458-3332 or 1-800-352-2645. Eric Olsen, pro. 18 holes. 6,007 yards. Par 72. Grass tees. Course ratings: men—B68.0/113, M67.1/111; women—M72.6/118, F71.4/115. Years Opened: 1967-70 (1967 (original nine); 1973 (second nine). Architect: Archie Ferguson. Moderate, jr./sr. rates. Reservations: Call a week ahead. Walk-on chances: Good. Walkability: Very good. Playability: Enjoyable layout in Yelm.

Originally called Yelm Country Club, Nisqually Valley lies within the growing town of Yelm. Once a snarly blackberry and raspberry patch, the course brought civilization to the site through the efforts of its designer and builder, the late Archie Ferguson. Ferguson put the first six holes together in 1967, the next three in 1970, and the back nine in 1973. He let friends play for free, and enjoyed smacking a ball or two whenever the urge struck. But Archie's contrariness came to the fore whenever strangers asked to play his course. According to local legend, Archie actually waved a shotgun at unwelcome guests if he didn't like the looks of them. In slightly warmer moods, he'd charge a dollar a hole.

Current owner Chuck Brown acquired the course in 1979. He found that the greens were spiral-cut (not mowed in the usual linear manner), and the grass around holes hand-clipped. Brown, who also owns Brookdale Golf Course in Tacoma, has since installed an automatic sprinkler system, added ponds at the 4th, 5th and 14th holes, and built new tees. Nisqually Valley enjoys good drainage with an underpinning of porous soil, so it's a good winter venue. The course also offers outstanding vistas of nearby Mount Rainier.

Nisqually Valley is varied topographically by ridges and depressions. Its greens are generally small and there's quite a bit of slope in them. Among the tougher tests is the 1st, a 476-yard par-5 with a wide, rolling fairway that stretches out to a flat green in a hollow. The 13th, a 211-yard par-3, features a green that leans toward a steep bank. The 17th, a par-5 of 536 yards, requires a blind tee shot to reach a right-bending fairway lined by OB along the left. The 17th ends at a front-sloping green.

Pacific Golf Center

8080 Center Street SW, Tumwater, WA 98502. (360) 786-8626. Jeff Parsons, pro.
9 holes. 1,721 yards. Par 29. Grass tees. Course ratings not available. Year Opened:
1996. Designers: Owners & Bill Overdorf. Economical, jr./sr. rates, credit cards.
Reservations: Call a week ahead. Walk-on chances: Good. Walkability: Good.
Playability: Quick, challenging rounds at new executive track off I-5.

9

Previously a driving range-only facility, Pacific Golf Center added a par-29 executive track in late-1996 to its list of amenities. The course was designed and built by its owners: head pro Jeff Parsons, general manager Eric Rowe, Eric's father Ron Rowe, and Neil Lupkes. Lupkes is the former manager of the Chehalis Elks course, now called Armory Hills, and Parsons previously plied his trade at Indian Summer. Bill Overdorf, creator of such fine layouts as Meriwood and Classic Country Club, designed the bentgrass greens. To get to this 36-acre venue, take the Airdustrial Way exit (#101) and go east; at the first light, turn right.

During its first few months of operation, players were enjoying hour-and-10-minute spins around the course. Many workers in the area come here during lunch breaks for a round of golf. Besides the course, Pacific Golf Center has a 32-stall, lighted and heated range and a pro shop. The owners have a 30-year lease with the property's owner, the Port of Olympia. Prior to construction, they hired superintendent Rusty Sauls to help with shaping. The course crosses Olympia's well-draining soil, and is made verdant by an automatic, 144-head irrigation system. Pacific Golf Center offers outstanding vistas of Mount Rainier.

Shortly after it opened, the nine-hole course record was established, a 25. This is a good score on a track that can play tough. Three stormwater retention ponds dot the layout, providing water hazards in spring and winter. In drier weather, the water lowers and isn't as much a factor. The two par-4s are 260 and 360 yards, with the shorter of the two—called "the shelf," containing an OB-lined, 30-yard-wide fairway. Perhaps the toughest holes are back-to-back 200-plus-yard par-3s. Pacific Golf Center's greens—medium-sized overall—are quite interesting, with assorted slopes and undulations to test flat-blade wielders. The course's shortest hole—a 105-yarder—sports a hogbacked putting surface. Besides the ponds, seven greenside bunkers add to the challenge.

Peninsula Golf Course

Off Highway 103, Long Beach, WA 98631. (360) 642-2828. Bev McCallister, pro.
9 holes. 2,148 yards. Par 33. Grass tees. Course ratings: men 59.9/90, women
64.2/100. Year Opened: 1947. Architect: Earl Edmunds. Economical, credit cards.
Reservations: Call a week ahead. Walk-on chances: Fair. Walkability: No
problems. Playability: Low-key layout ideal for laid-back rounds at the beach.

9

Peninsula Golf Course lies on the east side of Highway 103, just north of Long Beach. Measuring 28 miles from tip to tip, Long Beach Peninsula is the longest natural beach in the United States, and the world's longest unbroken beach. Engirded by the Pacific Ocean on the west and Willapa Bay to the east, the peninsula ranges from two to five miles in width. The spit's hub is Long Beach, which has a permanent population of about 2,000. The area is a haven for tourists who flock here for the sandy beaches, cottages with views of crashing surf, fresh seafood, and saltwater taffy. The Kite Festival held in mid-August draws high-flyers from around the world.

Peninsula Golf Course fits the mold of the low-key Long Beach Peninsula, which isn't as trendy as Seaside or Cannon Beach in Oregon. Built in 1947 by Earl Edmunds, the course was purchased in 1965 by D.H. Thompson and family, who operated it until 1986. The course was closed at that time and was for sale for several months until Jerry Zorich began leasing it. Zorich has made several improvements during his tenure.

The 2,148-yard track stretches across generally flat ground involving woodlands and a meadow. A few ditches cross the layout, which, for the most part, is wide open. The venue has a modest clubhouse to go along with a course unfettered by hazards. Peninsula is dominated by tourists, many of whom don't play golf on a regular basis. Be sure to set aside some extra time when playing Peninsula.

18 Riverside Country Club

1451 NW Airport Road, Chehalis, WA 98532. (360) 748-8182 or 1-800-242-9486. David Conzatti, pro. 18 holes. 6,155 yards. Par 71. Grass tees. Course ratings: men—B69.3/118, M67.6/112; women—M73.0/120, F71.2/116. Opened: early 1970s. Architect: Ray Schmidt & Joe Mehelich (original nine); Roy Goss (second nine). Moderate, credit cards. Reservations: Call a week ahead. Walk-on chances: Fair. Walkability: Quite good. Playability: When the Chehalis is inside its banks, Riverside is quite enjoyable.

Aptly-named Riverside borders the Chehalis River on the west side of Interstate 5, near the Chehalis Airport. After heavy rains, the Chehalis floods its banks and closes Riverside Country Club. In February 1996, when the combination of record rainfalls and mountain snowpack melt deluged the golf courses in western Washington and western Oregon, Riverside was out of commission for several months. The water rose to record levels, rising so high as to inundate the clubhouse, which sits about three feet off the ground. Riverside returns to being an enjoyable course once the water goes away.

The proprietor of the 18-holer is Otaka Corporation, a Japanese firm that also owns Classic Country Club south of Tacoma. After acquiring the course in 1990, Otaka built new bunkers and tees, paved the cart paths, planted new trees, and made other landscaping improvements. The course was begun by Ray Schmidt and Joe Mehelich, who designed and built the front nine. The newer back side was designed by well-known greens superintendent, Roy Goss. The layout is dotted with full-grown alders and firs; its low-cut, rolling greens putt very true.

Tough holes include the 5th, a 380-yard par-4 that requires a tee shot over a leg of the Chehalis. A huge fir on the other side of the river squeezes the target zone. Once across the river, the fairway curls rightward to a small, bi-trapped green bordered left by OB. The top-rated 14th, a 527-yard par-5, is a wide dogleg-left that skirts the river along the right en route to a small, front-sloping green trapped right-front. The 16th, a 491-yard par-5, winds rightward. Though the fairway is wide and seemingly benign, a hidden pond in front of the raised 16th green is a catch basin for many golf balls.

Scott Lake Golf Course

11746 Scott Creek Drive SW, Olympia, WA 98502. (360) 352-4838. 9 holes. 2,555 yards. Par 35. Grass tees. Course ratings: men—B62.9/94, M61.5/90; women— B66.9/103, F64.4/97. Year Opened: 1964. Architect: Howard Larson. Economical, jr./sr. rates. Reservations: Call 10 days ahead. Walk-on chances: Good. Walkability: Flat and easy to walk. Playability: Suitable starter's course.

9

The layout here abuts Scott Lake, a 100-acre body of water that provides viewing pleasure for nearby homeowners. The course was built in 1964 by Howard Larson and his firm, Scott Lake Development Company. It was intended to be a recreational centerpiece for a large community of retirees from Seattle and Tacoma. The layout originally consisted of three holes; six more were added later. By the mid-1970s, the course had grown into an 18-holer. In the mid-'80s when the retirement community didn't reach fruition, Larson sold the course to Trudie and Fred Tuengel, who closed the boggy back nine and rerouted the remaining holes. In 1989, the Tuengels sold the facility to Joel and Karen Boede. During the Tuengel and Boede eras, Scott Lake Golf Course has grown in popularity with local players.

The 44-acre course spans 4,878 yards over two circuits. The holes cross an old peat bog so, after heavy rains, the lake creeps across the 1st fairway. Big Creek— fed by runoff from hills to the west—also runs through the layout. The course is flat and easy to walk, with deer and geese making occasional visits. The toughest hole is the 2nd, a 330-yard par-4. Players might consider using an iron from this tee, as the tree-pinched, dogleg-left fairway is guarded along the left by a pond. Its small, rolling green is backed by a trap.

Skyline Golf Course

20 Randall Drive, Cathlamet, WA 98612. (360) 795-8785. 9 holes. 2,255 yards. Par 35. Grass tees & mats. Course ratings: men 62.7/106, women 63.2/102. Years Opened: 1965 (original three holes); 1968 (final six holes). Architect: Ralph Rodahl. Economical. Reservations: Call a day ahead. Walk-on chances: Very good. Walkability: Okay overall, with some hills. Playability: Course gradually receiving upgrades.

9

Skyline sits high above the Columbia River's northern banks and the small town of Cathlamet. The 65-acre course is readily accessible off Highway 4. Owners Ralph and Juanita Rodahl began Skyline as a three-holer in 1965. The course was later enlarged to five holes and, in 1968, assumed its current nine-hole configuration. Skyline's hilltop locale affords great panoramas of the Columbia River to the south and west. Elk and deer are also seen at this rural layout.

The Rodahls began leasing Skyline to their friend, Wayne Cochran, in 1990. Cochran has since installed new sprinklers, upgraded the irrigation system, built new tees, added bunkers and remodeled the clubhouse. The work has resulted in increased play, especially among locals who participate in all manner of weekly competitions. Skyline's "18-on-9" setup spans 5,739 yards over two circuits. Featuring large and rolling greens, Skyline gains difficulty from its tilted topography. Good scoring opportunities abound, however; some of the par-4s are slightly over 200 yards long and the par-5s are definitely birdieable. Perhaps the toughest hole is the 1st, a 431-yard par-5 that winds downhill to the right along a tree-lined route that concludes at a rolling green.

Surfside Golf Course

9 *31508 J Place, Ocean Park, WA 98640. (360) 665-4148. Louis Runge & Scott Basse, pros. 9 holes. 2,960 yards. Par 36. Grass tees. Course ratings: men—B/M68.6/119, M/F67.5/117; women—B/M74.0/127, M/F72.5/124. Year Opened: 1968. Architect: Gene Neva. Moderate, jr./sr. rates, credit cards. Reservations: Call a week ahead. Walk-on chances: Good. Walkability: Quite suitable for bag-packers. Playability: Surprisingly tough course near the crashing Pacific.*

Nine-hole Surfside sits in Long Beach Peninsula's midsection near several ocean-view hotels. Owned by the state of Washington's Parks and Recreation Department, Surfside is leased to co-head pro, Louis Runge; Louis' father Henry, ran Willapa Harbor Golf Course for years. Surfside's immediate operations are handled by Scott Basse as Runge is still based at Willapa Harbor. Runge and Basse have made several improvements to Surfside since taking it over in 1990, including the installation of a computerized irrigation system. Work on a new clubhouse may commence soon. A second nine, briefly mulled over in the early 1990s, is on hold.

Surfside was built by local golfers off a design from a local surveyor, Gene Neva. The course occupies part of a 352-acre parcel that was willed to the state with one proviso: the property be retained for recreational use only. Besides a nice nine-hole course that hosts upwards of 20,000 rounds a year, Surfside contains an irons-only driving range. The venue is a popular spot for privately-sponsored tournaments. Off-season play is quite low, but call for tee times during the busy summer months at this vacation mecca.

Over two nine-hole rounds the layout plays to a par of 72 and extends 5,955 yards. As noted by its relatively high ratings, the course plays tough. Water hazards vie for errant shots on several holes, and narrow, tree-lined fairways require accuracy. Stiffer tests include the dogleg-right 4th, a 519-yard par-5 that skirts a pond along the left en route to a slippery green. The 5th, a 320-yard par-4, swings 90 degrees to the left off a pond-fronted tee. A water hazard lines most of the fairway's left edge and runs up to guard the green's flank. The 7th, a 436-yard par-4, contains a roller coaster-like, tree-squeezed fairway that leads to a small, undulating green backed by a pond.

Three Rivers Golf Course

18 *2222 South River Road, Kelso, WA 98626. (360) 423-4653. Chris Smith, pro. 18 holes. 6,707 yards. Par 72. Grass tees. Course ratings: men—B70.8/117, M68.3/112; women—M73.6/120, F69.8/112. Year Opened: 1982. Architect: Robert Muir Graves. Moderate, jr./sr. rates. Reservations: Call a week ahead. Walk-on chances: Fair. Walkability: Quite good. Playability: One of southwest Washington's more enjoyable courses.*

Three Rivers was built upon the thousands of tons of dust, ash and mud that clogged the Cowlitz River following the eruption of Mount Saint Helens on May 18, 1980. Named for the Columbia, Cowlitz and Toutle rivers, the Robert Muir Graves-designed layout opened in 1982. Three Rivers arose through the efforts of local citizens, the U.S. Army Corp of Engineers and the Kelso Elks Lodge, the latter of which operates it. Three Rivers occupies a promontory beside the Cowlitz; on the opposite (south) side of the river are steaming pulp mills.

Because of its porous volcanic underlayment, Three Rivers is one of the Northwest's driest winter courses. The facility hosts over 50,000 rounds a year, making it among southwest Washington's most popular. Besides length, the layout features three tees per hole, dozens of sand bunkers, and a creek that crosses several holes. Three Rivers spans gently rolling terrain, and some fairways are tree-lined.

Tough holes include the 1st, a 531-yard par-5 with a wavy fairway that ascends past a trap along the right to a large, trapped-right green. The 14th, a par-4 of 453 yards, is a narrow dogleg-left beside railroad tracks. A deep swale inside the turn contains a fairway-squeezing lake. The small 14th green is ringed by traps. The par-5 18th is trapped on both sides of its 550-yard route. A pond fronts the heart-shaped green, which is trapped laterally.

Tri-Mountain Golf Course

1701 NW 299th Street, Ridgefield, WA 98642. (360) 887-3004. Chuck DaSilva, pro. 18 holes. 6,580 yards. Par 72. Grass tees. Course Ratings: men—B70.5/120, M68.4/116, FF65.8/111; women—M74.0/127, FF71.3/121, F69.6/117. Year Opened: 1994. Architect: William Robinson. Moderate, sr. rates, credit cards. Reservations: Call five days ahead. Walk-on chances: Fair. Walkability: Good. Playability: Fun course with water and sand galore.

18

Daily-fee Tri-Mountain opened in July 1994. The $6.4-million layout lies on the east side of Interstate 5, directly behind a weigh station north of Ridgefield Junction. Take exit 14 to get to the course. Besides a driving range where golfers launch lighter-than-water balls into a pond, Tri-Mountain contains a fun 18-hole putting course. The 130-acre site was farmland owned by a local man, Gene Lampson, before being converted into an entertaining, Bill Robinson-designed course. Tri-Mountain is named after its vistas of mounts Saint Helens, Adams and Hood, with the volcanic cone of Saint Helens particularly impressive on cloudless days.

In 1997, Clark County purchased the facility from its developer, the Port of Ridgefield, and immediately proceeded to finish a partially-completed $750,000 clubhouse. The county signed a 10-year lease with the port. The lease terms allow the county to sell Tri-Mountain to a private party, or hire a private operator to run and maintain it. These developments clarify Tri-Mountain's once-clouded picture. The port encountered financial problems when Tri-Mountain didn't meet its forecasts for annual rounds. The port hoped the course would generate 50,000 rounds a year, but it averaged less than 40,000 each of its first few years. The situation was complicated by a lawsuit filed by the port against the course's builder, Atlantic Golf Construction of Bangor, Maine. At press time, the suit—which claims Atlantic didn't lay enough sand under fairways to address drainage—remained unsettled.

The layout traverses gently rolling ground. Though 500 trees were planted before the course opened, Tri-Mountain will retain a links demeanor. Nearly half a million yards of dirt were moved during shaping, resulting in many fairways lined by tall mounds. Golfers should be alert when hitting over these mounds as their shots may end up in one of the 11 lakes involved on 12 holes. Also of concern are 84 sand traps and prevailing westerlies that average 10-15 miles per hour.

The longer holes are relatively wide, but those darned ponds always seem to crop up at the worst times. Among Tri-Mountain's sterner tests is the 436-yard 3rd, a par-4 that heads leftward—into the wind. A pond along the right can be reached by longer hitters, as might two big bunkers on the left. The water hazard runs up to guard the right-front edge of a humped-in-the-middle, shallow-but-deep green bunkered left and right-front. The 10th, a 377-yard par-4, has bunkers squeezing both sides of the garden spot for drives. The hole then descends to a trapped-left-front, ridge-perched green with steep rear and left flanks.

The 13th, a 488-yard par-5, has a pond left-front of the tee and bunkers in the landing area. The mound-lined route is marked by sundry bumps and swales before curling rightward. A 100-yard-long pond appears along the left at the 150-yard mark. A very long bunker looms—with another trap behind it—right-front of a mound-ringed, small green backed by a pond. The 17th, a 196-yard par-3, has a raised tee fronted by a pond that runs up to protect a large and rolling green trapped right- and left-rear. Tri-Mountain's home hole is a dogleg-left, 555-yard par-5 that skirts the driving range pond and the course's tallest trees along the left. Bunkers lie outside the fairway's wide turn, with more traps farther down. The 18th descends over its last 180 yards to a wide-but-shallow, two-tiered green bunkered twice in front.

Tumwater Valley Golf Club

18 *4611 Tumwater Valley Drive, Tumwater, WA 98501. (360) 943-9500. Chris Mitchell, pro. 18 holes. 7,004 yards. Par 72. Grass tees. Course ratings: men—T73.1/120, B70.7/115, M68.8/111, F65.9/105; women—M74.0/122, F70.4/114. Year Opened: 1968. Architects: Gus Bowman, Roy Goss & Glen Proctor. Moderate, jr./sr. rates. Reservations: Call up to eight days ahead. Walk-On Chances: Fair. Walkability: Good. Playability: Be sure to hit the ball on the screws at this lengthy track.*

At just over 7,000 yards from the tips, Tumwater Valley Golf Club ranks among western Washington's longest courses. This is particularly evident in spring and fall when the ball loses its roll and getting around the course becomes a more demanding task. Its location in a valley east of Interstate 5 allows golfers splendid vistas of Mount Rainier. Besides an enjoyable layout with 20 greens and 20 tees (more on that later), Tumwater Valley features a full-service restaurant and driving range.

The facility underwent a big upheaval in April 1996 when the city of Tumwater purchased it from Pabst Brewing Company for $2.7 million. Along with the new owners came the departure of Tumwater Valley's long-time pro, Gary Parker. Parker was replaced by Chris Mitchell, one of the Northwest's top tournament players and a former teammate of Fred Couples at the University of Houston. Shortly after buying it, officials said the city would spend $600,000 on improving parking lots, roads, culverts, a bridge and parts of the irrigation and drainage system. The latter two items have been long overdue. Tumwater Valley crosses real estate next to the Deschutes River (no relation to the like-named Oregon waterway), and has traditionally suffered from poor drainage.

The course was built by the Olympia Brewery (purchased by Pabst in the 1980s) on the site where its beer's key ingredient was obtained. Over a million gallons of pure artesian water are still pumped daily from wells situated along fairways. Tumwater Valley is imperiled by dozens of sand traps, and the river enters play on several holes. Other water hazards—presumably of the artesian variety—further complicate play.

Noteworthy holes include the top-rated 4th, a 456-yard par-4 with a creek 50 yards off the tee, and a flattish fairway that stretches out to a rolling green. Another toughie is the 5th, a 552-yard par-5 that follows a left-turning route to a trapped-right green. The 14th, a 568-yard par-5, contains a pond-fronted tee and a winding fairway concluding at a trapped-right green. Tumwater Valley's 2nd and 17th holes—both par-3s—have two tees and two greens. At the 2nd, golfers have the choice of firing at a green 161 yards out, or taking a chance with a much more difficult 218-yard shot over a pond. At the 17th, the choice is a 155-yard shot over the corner of a lake or a 213-yard blast over the water hazard's fattest section.

Willapa Harbor Golf Club   9

Route 3, Box 441, Raymond, WA 98577. (360) 942-2392. Louis Runge, pro. 9 holes. 3,004 yards. Par 36. Grass tees. Course ratings: men 68.8/119, women 72.7/123. Year Opened: 1926. Architect: Walter Fovargue. Moderate, credit cards. Reservations: Call a week ahead. Walk-on chances: Good. Walkability: Good. Playability: One of the best nine-holers in the state.

Seventy-year-old Willapa Harbor Golf Club is accessed by Fowler Road from Highway 101. The layout is lined by the south fork of the Willapa (pronounced "Will-ah-pah") River, which also enters play at the 3rd and 5th holes. Deer, hawks, bald eagles and cranes are regular visitors, while bears and bobcats inhabit the area. Elk occasionally stomp across the putting greens, wreaking havoc on this nine-hole layout, a Raymond landmark since the 1920s.

Willapa Harbor—designed and built by Walter Fovargue—was originally conceived as a private country club by the local mill owners who founded it. Soon after its 1926 grand opening, PGA Hall-of-Famer Horton Smith, winner of the first-ever Masters Tournament in 1934 (which he won again in 1936) played the course. A sepia-toned photo in the clubhouse captures Smith's visit. The facility was acquired in the 1940s by Bill Leher, who opened it to the public. Henry and Leah Runge (Leher was Leah's father) took over Willapa Harbor in 1957.

After retiring in the late 1980s, Henry and Leah ceded management of the course to their son Louis, a Class A pro who also runs Surfside in Long Beach. Another son, Kris, is an assistant pro at North Shore in Tacoma. The Runges have made several improvements over the years, such as adding 20 full-service RV slips for traveling golfers (RVers get discounts on rounds); upgrading maintenance and topdressing standards; and installing a practice bunker on Willapa Harbor's 300-yard-deep driving range.

The difficulty of the course owes to sundry water hazards, tight fairways, and small, tilted greens ringed by grass bunkers. The dual-tee course—extending 6,002 yards over two circuits—is noted for its raised, steep-sided putting surfaces. The top-rated 5th hole, a 402-yard par-4 and one of the state's premier tests, can be grueling. The river crosses in front of the tee, and the rolling fairway winds tightly between firs and cedars. Another fork of the river passes about 100 yards from a slippery green that sits in a depression and is invisible from the fairway-side of the river.

PRIVATE COURSES

High Valley Country Club

9 *Off Cannon Road (Box 427), Packwood, WA 98361. (360) 494-8431. 9 holes. 1,728 yards. Par 31. Grass tees. Course ratings: men 58.2/83, women 59.1/87. Year Opened: 1964. Architects: Founding members. Members, guests & reciprocates.*

High Valley was designed and built in 1963-64 by its founders. High Valley's 120 members from as far away as the Tri-Cities, Seattle, Longview, Anacortes and Puyallup migrate to this club in the Cascades during summers. The course lies east of Packwood on Cannon Road, a thoroughfare off Highway 12 that leads to residences. The course is augmented by a modest clubhouse with a pool beside it. Cabins and larger homes ring the shortish layout.

The flat High Valley track occupies about 30 acres and curls between tall evergreen trees. When I visited it in October 1995, its greens were surrounded by yellow rope laced through steel poles. These "barriers" help keep a roving 50-head herd of elk off the putting surfaces. The members recently tried to buy 75 acres from a neighboring landowner for another nine holes, but the deal fell through.

The dual-tee track extends 3,456 yards over two circuits and has several holes skirting OB. The course is crossed by a snow-fed creek in spring and summer; the 3rd, 4th, 5th and 7th holes are imperiled by the stream. Recent improvements include an automatic irrigation system. The club has a full-time greenskeeper, with day-to-day operations overseen by manager Mike Christiansen.

Indian Summer Golf & Country Club

18 *5900 Troon Lane SE, Olympia, WA 98501. (360) 459-3772. Kevin Bishop, pro. 18 holes. 7,216 yards. Par 72. Grass tees. Course ratings: men—C74.5/133, B72.5/128, M70.8/124, FF68.4/118; women—FF74.5/130, F70.4/123. Year Opened: 1992. Architect: Peter Thompson. Members, guest & reciprocates.*

Opened in 1992 as a public facility, this Peter Thompson-designed venue turned private in 1995; the club has room for 450 members. Indian Summer's course is an important part of a like-named 453-acre development, one which eventually may contain 300 single-family homes, 150 townhouses, a swimming pool and tennis courts. A 31,000-square-foot clubhouse opened in 1995 with a restaurant, lounge, banquet facilities and outdoor deck. The structure also serves as the home of the Pacific Northwest Section of the PGA. The course hosted the inaugural Olympia Open in October 1996; the Nike Tour event had a 144-player field. Indian Summer also hosted the tourney—whose name was changed to Puget Sound Open—in 1997.

Indian Summer is one of the finest courses to recently open in the region. Despite initial ownership conflicts, the layout, now owned by Aoki Corporation, made a smooth transition to private status. Indian Summer was co-developed by Aoki—led by Norikazu Aoki—and Hiroshi Tanaka. After buying Tanaka's share in early 1993, Aoki completed the remaining infrastructure. During Indian Summer's development, Aoki had to preserve an area on the site that contained the Chambers Homestead, established in 1848. After settling in the area, Andrew and Thomas Chambers erected a 10,000-square-foot stockade that sheltered 32 local families during the Puget Sound Indian Wars of 1855-57. As part of Indian Summer's conditional-use permit the three-quarter-acre homestead was donated for archaeological research.

Prior to its purchase by Aoki and Tanaka in January 1991 from Arizona-based golf-development tycoon Lyle Anderson, the property was a Christmas tree farm. Due to that previous usage and a magnificent stand of old-growth fir, cedar, hemlock and alder, this is a forested course, though a few holes cross open meadows. Great views of Mount Rainier are on tap from several junctures, and a dazzling array of wildlife (deer, beavers, shrews, rabbits, squirrels, skunks, and birds ranging from owls to hawks to hummingbirds) are on display.

Consisting of the Lakes and Forest nines—numbered 1 through 9 and 10 through 18, respectively—the dry-in-winter venue involves dozens of traps, several ponds and streams. Prevailing westerlies are a factor on nearly every hole. The only aesthetic detriment are power lines above the 6th fairway and along a few back-nine holes. Top tests include the 3rd, a 561-yard par-5 with a tee fronted by a creek that feeds into a pond along the right. Two big bunkers also lurk along the right of the fairway, with trees and OB left. The hole runs straight and slightly uphill, with another pond appearing later along the right. The small, ridge-perched 3rd green is bunkered laterally and rear.

The top-rated 5th, a 593-yard par-5, is an intimidating hole. Towering firs and a trap along the right and two bunkers left tightly compress the landing area. The pretty, well-framed 5th stretches out to a long and skinny, front-sloping green trapped on the sides and rear. Despite the toughest-rating enjoyed by the 5th, the 558-yard, par-5 10th may be Indian Summer's nastiest hole. This is a three-shot par-5 as there's no way to carry the towering trees before the green. The serpentine 10th initially winds rightward around trees and an expansive wetland. A big bunker sits outside the "second turn." The toughest pin placement on the V-shaped 10th green is back-left. At 256 yards from the tips, Indian Summer's 11th is one of the region's lengthiest par-3s. The hole runs straight along a tree-lined chute to a mound-ringed, rolling green bunkered left.

Longview Country Club

18

41 Country Club Drive, Longview, WA 98632. (360) 425-3132. Jeff Bartleson, pro. 18 holes. 6,004 yards. Par 70. Grass tees. Course ratings: men—B68.2/120, F66.2/ 115; women—B74.0/120, 71.6/117. Year Opened: 1926 (original nine); 1946 (second nine). Architect: Francis L. James; William Robinson (remodel). Members, guests & reciprocates.

Most of the 525 members of this club hail from the Longview-Kelso area, with others from Portland, Kalama and Cathlamet. Longview has hosted several important tournaments over the years, most recently the 1993 Washington State Amateur. Its big annual event is the Lumberjack & Jill each summer. The course occupies a southwest-facing hillside on the northeast edge of town. Club facilities include an iron-only driving range and a nice clubhouse with a swimming pool and large deck. Longview's course is well-appointed, with asphalt cart paths throughout. Jeff Bartleson, son of Coos Country Club's long-time pro, Jim Bartleson, oversees the golf activities at Longview.

The course has undergone three major transformations, including the openings of the original nine in 1926 and a second nine in 1946. The club is currently

Longview's 148-yard, par-3 7th hole is known by members as the "Mickey Mouse hole" because of the grass-bunkered "ears" in front of the green.

in the midst of its third makeover. In spring 1996, three new William Robinson-designed holes (the 4th, 5th and 6th) came into play. In July of '96, the remaining front-nine holes were shut down to strip the topsoil and install drain tile. Further alterations were made to these traditionally poor-draining holes, including remodeling the severest greens. The front-nine work—which cost $2 million—was completed by spring 1997. Next up for member consideration is a master plan for the back nine.

Longview's front side traverses tipped terrain, while the back splays over a generally flat, wooded parcel. The park-like layout is old-style at heart but, with all of the upgrades, has a much more contemporary demeanor. Having been "seasoned" for over 70 years is a decided plus, as its trees are truly grand (appropriate since Longview is a community with deep roots in the timber business). Golfers must come to grips with towering firs, maples, willows and other titans in many target zones. The challenge begins right away at the opener, a 456-yard par-5 with a right-turning fairway that slopes left. The hole curls rightward over tilted terrain to a skinny, bi-trapped green angled 45 degrees to the fairway. The right-sloping 2nd, a 406-yard par-4, skirts trees along the right. Over its last 150-yards, the fairway narrows as it rises steeply to a small, round green trapped right.

The 4th, a 325-yard par-4, features an uphill and mogulled route that tilts left toward a bunker. At the 150-yard mark, the hole ascends to a rolling, left-leaning green trapped right-front and left-rear. The 6th, a 375-yard par-4 called "Hungry Hollow," follows a dogleg-right path with a fat bunker outside the turn. The fairway has a deep dip about 250 yards out, and its three-tiered green is bunkered left-front and rear. The 7th, a 148-yard par-3, has a ravine-fronted tee and a newly expanded green, one which is much flatter than its predecessor. The hole—dubbed "Mickey Mouse" for the three green-fronting grass bunkers that look like Disney's famous ears—was recently stretched 50 yards by a new tee.

The 8th, a 291-yard par-4 ("Longview"), has a 150-foot-high elevated tee, three tall firs in mid-fairway that must be carried, a pond along the right, and an old-style "push-up" green trapped laterally. A good back-nine hole is the 11th ("Big Bend"), a 500-yard par-5 that winds 60 degrees to the right between trees and OB left. A creek crosses before its oval, tree-guarded green. The 403-yard, par-4 13th, is a slight left-bender intersected by a creek 200 yards out. Appropriately called "Hidden Green," the 13th ends at diminutive putting surface shielded by a mound 80 yards in front. Longview's top-rated hole 14th, a 431-yard par-4, is called "Coffin Rock" as the uphill dogleg-left winds around three chubby boulders. In between the first two rocks and the third is a hidden creek. All this trouble lies about 125 yards from a raised, left-sloping green.

Olympia Country & Golf Club

3636 Country Club Drive NW, Olympia, WA 98502. (360) 866-9777. Scott Smith, pro. 18 holes. 6,048 yards. Par 71. Grass tees. Course ratings: men—B69.6/116, M68.6/114; women—B74.9/132, M73.5/128, F70.7/123. Year Opened: 1926 (original nine); 1958 (second nine). Architects: John Ball & Walter Fovargue. Members, guests & reciprocates.

The members of this historic club in the state's capital originally played a rough-hewn, 1914-built nine-holer in Lacey, called Mountain View. The club moved to its present location near Butler Cove in 1926, calling it "Olympia Golf & Country Club." Things were going smoothly until the early 1940s, when the club went bankrupt. After a reorganization, the second-generation founders renamed it Olympia Country & Golf Club to disassociate themselves from the previous operation. Since this transitional period the club has prospered and, in recent years, has enjoyed a full membership. One Olympia member of note is Dick Kanda, the 1996-97 PNGA president and director of the Washington State Golf Association.

The course sprawls across a promontory overlooking Budd Inlet, a southern finger off Puget Sound. Due to its hilly site, Olympia's layout vies with Seattle's Sand Point, Oswego Lake and Oregon Golf Club in West Linn for the region's mountain-goat award. The up-and-down terrain results in a few idiosyncratic holes, including the 243-yard 1st and 317-yard 10th—straight-uphill par-4s both, and the 18th, which takes the "elevator" down to the clubhouse. Also adding interest are a few greens that sit in hollows. These putting surfaces are guarded by deep bunkers not observable from the fairway. Two holes (the 15th and 16th) are split from the rest of the course by Cooper Point Road; the 483-yard par-5 and 424-yard par-4 add distance to the mid-length layout. The nicely-appointed venue enjoys good signage, cart paths throughout, and beautiful vistas of the inlet from many holes.

Among Olympia's more interesting tests is the aforementioned 1st, which rises steeply off the tee. The last 75 yards climb straight uphill to a round, front-sloping green trapped left-front. The 4th, a 384-yard par-4, has a canyon off the tee and a narrow, left-curling fairway skirted by OB left and trees right. At the 150-yard mark, the hole curls 80 degrees to the left to a domed and slick, left-tilting green trapped left-front, right, and left-rear. The tough-driving 6th, a 469-yard par-5, is a downhill dogleg-left that leans steeply to the right. About 200 yards out, the fairway straightens out and runs narrowly down to a skinny-but-deep green with a huge trap left-front and two more bunkers right-front and left. A 180-yard drive should carry the canyon fronting the tips at the 7th, a 482-yard par-5. The hole then descends along a right-curling path before rising up to a front-sloping green trapped twice in front.

The 448-yard, par-4 18th hole at Olympia Country & Golf Club descends steeply over its last leg.

Getting to the men's 10th tee from the 9th green involves hiking down a steep descent, teeing off, then reversing the trek back uphill. A blind drive from the tee may find the 10th fairway, which curls left around towering trees at the 150-yard mark. The hole ends at a good-sized green bunkered right and left-front. The top-rated 12th, a 422-yard par-4, follows a rolling, downhill and narrow route lined by trees. Carrying the canyon that crosses the hole at the 100-yard mark involves executing a tough shot off a downhill lie. The trapped-right-front 12th green is domed, quick and canted to the right. The 15th and 16th are side-by-side testers lined along the left by homes. Olympia's home hole, a 448-yard par-4, runs slightly downhill off the tee and skirts homes and OB left. At the 135-yard mark, the fairway drops off the face of the earth on a steep descent to a small, front-sloping green backed by a long, sinuous trap whose main purpose is to snag mishit shots.

PAR-3 COURSES

Golfgreen Golf Center

9 *561 7th Avenue, Longview, WA 98632. (360) 425-0450. 9 holes. 1,175 yards. Par 27. Grass tees & mats. No course ratings. Economical.*

Par-3 Golfgreen lies on Longview's southeast end. Residences and small businesses ring the course, which opened in 1963. Golfgreen was designed and built by original owner, Arthur G. Manke, who operated it until he passed away in 1987. It's now run by Skip Manke, Art's son. Golfgreen was equipped with a driving range, but it was closed in 1980 because too many windows in nearby homes were assaulted by errant shots.

Since this is the only par-3 course in the greater Kelso-Longview area, as many as 300 players may circuit it over a summer weekend. Golfgreen is considered a "living memorial." A local bank owns the course, but it cannot change Golfgreen's status while Manke's the manager. The layout sports small, well-kept greens and has holes ranging from 55 to 198 yards. The course does not have an abundance of hazards, but it's a good practice venue, providing linksters a quick round without exacting stiff financial, physical or mental tolls.

Driving Ranges

Ashford Driving Range

29716 State Route 706 East, Ashford, WA 98304.
No phone. Rich Mulholland, pro.

Eagle View Golf Center

8000 72nd Lane SE, Olympia, WA 98513.
(360) 493-1000. Joe Thiel, pro. 3-hole practice course.

Grand Mound Driving Range

20525 Old Highway 9, Grand Mound, WA 98531.
(360) 273-9335. Denny Densmore, pro.

Par IV Golf Learning Center

500 Robinson Road, Woodland, WA 98674.
(360) 225-8869. Jim Howard, pro.

Rainbow Golf Driving Range

2723 Harrison Avenue, Centralia, WA 98531.
(360) 330-0585.

Steamboat Golf

3605 Steamboat Island Road, Olympia, WA 98502.
(360) 866-4653. Scott Geroux, pro.

Upcoming Courses

Centralia — Mayfield Lake Project (1999/2000). The Lewis County Commission has approved a preliminary plat for this development, which proposed a nine-hole executive course and 12 condominiums. The backer of the project needs a Class A water permit from the state before proceeding.

Elbe — Park Junction Project (1999/2000). The backers of this 400-acre, $30-million resort project would like to build an 18-hole course along with a 300-room hotel, 200 townhouses, a 300-slip RV park, 70,000-square-foot shopping mall, interpretive center and railroad terminus linked to Tacoma. The site is off Highway 706 at the entrance to Mount Rainier. Neighbors have opposed the project, saying they don't want their rural way of life threatened by such a large development.

Kelso — Anchor Point Project (1999/2000). In mid-1996, the city of Kelso rezoned a 350-acre site on the Longview Wye at the confluence of the Cowlitz River and Carrolls Channel. Once permits are in hand from the Army Corps of Engineers, developer Wasser and Winters of Longview may proceed with plans to build an 18-hole golf course, 168 homes and 60 condominiums on the former Collins Estate.

Lacey — Vicwood Golf Links (1998/1999). In early 1997, the owner of this 720-acre site next to Meriwood—Vicwood Chong of Hong Kong—was moving forward with plans to build a Peter Thompson-designed 18-hole course. Upwards of 1,700 homes may follow after the course opens.

Olympia — Prairie Glen Estates (1999). In August 1996, George Heidgerken announced plans for an 18-hole golf course and 459 houses on a 1,224-acre tract he owns near Olympia.

Rosburg — Seal River Golf Course (1998). A nine-hole, 3,000-yard golf course is gradually being built on Robbie Johnson's former dairy farm in Wahkiakum County.

Seaview — Columbia Heights Project (1999/2000). This project, in planning for nearly a decade, has received support from Ilwaco city officials and local businesses and may soon proceed with an 18-hole golf course (designed by Ron Fream), a hotel and upwards of 400 homes. Developer Joe Nelles has asked that the 350-acre site near Seaview be annexed into Ilwaco.

Tokeland — Tokeland Golf Club (1998/1999). This public 3,153-yard nine is being resurrected on land next to the Tokeland Hotel. Dormant since 1929, the layout is gradually being brought to life by two Tokeland residents.

Westport — Port of Grays Harbor Project (1999/2000). In May 1996, officials of the Port of Grays Harbor began a request-for-proposal process that could lead to the purchase by a private concern of a 330-acre port-owned site east of Highway 105. The port would like to see an independent firm develop an 18-hole golf course, hotel and restaurant on the property.

Winlock — Skye Village (1999/2000). Announced in 1994, this slow-moving project in Lewis County would occupy both sides of Interstate 5 at the Winlock interchange. Besides a William Robinson-designed 18-hole course, the 368-acre site would also be home to a Scottish-style village, hotel, restaurants, shops, parks, paths, picnic areas, tennis courts, swimming pool, health club and condominiums.

Yelm — Thurston Highlands (1999/2000). This 1,200-acre project may ultimately contain 36 holes and upwards of 1,600 single-family dwellings. The developers have gotten the site annexed into the city of Yelm, and construction continues on the infrastructure.

7

NORTH-CENTRAL WASHINGTON

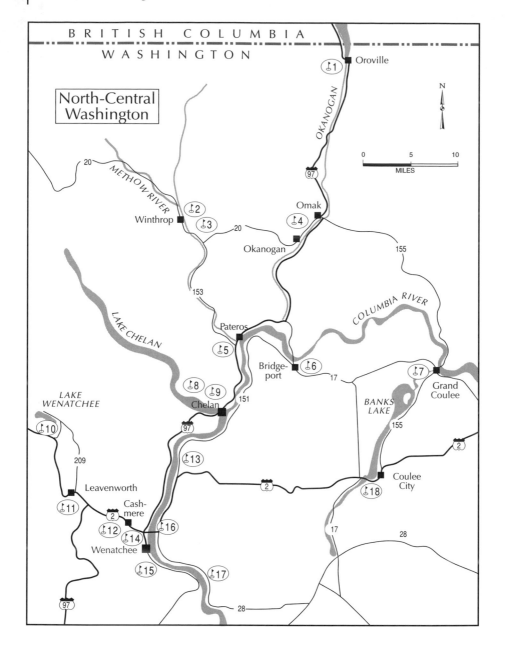

BRITISH COLUMBIA

WASHINGTON

North-Central
Washington

N

OKANOGAN

🛗1 Oroville

0   5   10
MILES

20

METHOW RIVER

97

🛗2
Winthrop
🛗3
20

Omak
🛗4
Okanogan

155

153

COLUMBIA RIVER

LAKE CHELAN

Pateros
🛗5

Bridge-
port
🛗6
17

🛗7
Grand
Coulee

🛗8 🛗9
Chelan

LAKE
WENATCHEE

151

BANKS
LAKE

155

🛗10

97

209

🛗13

2

Coulee
City
🛗18

2

Leavenworth
🛗11
Cash-
mere
🛗12
🛗14
Wenatchee
🛗15

2
🛗16

17

28

🛗17

97

28

1. **Oroville Golf Club** — public 9
2. **Sunny Meadows Golf & Four Seasons Resort** — private 9 (par-3)
3. **Bear Creek Golf Course** — public 9
4. **Okanogan Valley Golf Club** — semiprivate 9
5. **Alta Lake Golf Course** — public 18 & driving range
6. **Lake Woods Golf Course** — public 9 & driving range
7. **Banks Lake Golf Club** — public 9 & driving range
8. **MA-8 + 1 Golf** — public 9 & driving range
9. **Lake Chelan Golf Course** — public 18 & driving range
10. **Kahler Glen Golf Course** — public 18 & driving range
11. **Leavenworth Golf Club** — public 18
12. **Home Place Golf Course** — public 9 & driving range
13. **Desert Canyon Golf Resort** — public 18, driving range & 18-hole putting course
14. **Crystal Springs Golf Center** — driving range & 18-hole putting course
15. **Three Lakes Golf Course** — public 18 & driving range
16. **Wenatchee Golf & Country Club** — private 18
17. **Rock Island Golf Course** — public 9 & driving range
18. **Vic Meyers Golf Course** — public 9

This beautiful part of the Pacific Northwest—Washington's version of "Big Sky Country"—runs from the Canadian border down through the eastern foothills of the Cascades to Wenatchee, then east to Grand Coulee Dam and Banks Lake. Located in the mountainous climate zones 1 and 2, north-central Washington experiences frigid, snowy winters and sun-baked summers. Frozen ground limits the golf season to seven or, perhaps, eight months a year. Given the relatively short season and sparse permanent population, the courses rely on tourists to make ends meet. Canadians and "wetsiders" seem particularly smitten with the area, which continues its mission of broadening the tourism base with destination resorts.

PUBLIC COURSES

Alta Lake Golf Course

Alta Lake Road, Pateros, WA 98846. (509) 923-2359. John Roberts, pro. 18 holes. 6,497 yards. Par 72. Grass tees. Course ratings: men—B71.3/125, M69.5/121; women F69.9/118. Year Opened: 1976 (original nine); 1993 (second nine). Architects: Vaughn T. Wolfe (original nine); Don Barth (second nine). Moderate, credit cards. Call for reservations. Walk-on chances: Fair. Walkability: Hilly topography and hot temperatures in summer can make for a grueling walk. Playability: Challenging desert track contains surprises around nearly very bend.

This 18-hole course by Alta Lake State Park offers a fine golfing experience. The venue lies east of the Billy Goat Mountains in picturesque foothills above the confluence of the Methow and Columbia rivers. Owners Don and Susan Barth purchased the course, clubhouse, restaurant and a small hotel in 1983 from the facility's originator, Vaughn T. Wolfe. Alta Lake was a nine-holer when opened in 1976; Don Barth designed and built the back nine in 1993 on part of the couple's 215-acre plot. Besides upgrading some holes on the front side, the Barths plan to double the size of the hotel while adding 20 RV slips and 40 homesites. A driving range and practice green were finished in 1996.

The expanded course has generated much more play, such that summer weekends now require a tee time. Alta Lake is a good alternative to Desert Canyon, which lies about 20 miles to the south on the Columbia's east side. Alta Lake is cheaper than Desert Canyon and has almost as much challenge, particularly in its sloping and slick greens. Alta Lake's original nine has some of the Northwest's wildest putting surfaces. Barth retained that characteristic with the new holes which, in lieu of sand traps, are guarded by grass bunkers. In my notes I described some of the putting surfaces as "too cute." Following that summation, I wrote "what the hell," figuring that some element was needed to give the course a personality. And these greens make Alta Lake's positively bubbly.

Tough holes on the original front nine include the top-rated 1st, a 543-yard par-5 that winds downhill past OB on the left. At the 150-yard mark, the hole goes steeply uphill to a front-sloping green with two tiers. (Most front-nine holes have multiple tiers; its original nine featured two pins per green, with each tier sporting a different-colored flag.) The fairway at the 395-yard, par-4 9th is almost impossible to hit. Starting at an elevated tee, the route follows severely right-sloping ground. OB lines the left side of the hole, with the right defined by desert detritus. The fairway eventually ascends to a radically right-sloping, bi-level green guarded in front by trees. The second shot at Alta Lake's 9th hole may be the round's nastiest.

Unlike the front nine, which sprawls over a valley, the back nine crosses generally flat, plateau-like ground. The two sides are split by Alta Lake Road, and getting to holes 10-18 involves crossing the road. Interesting holes include the 477-yard, par-5 10th, which ascends and winds leftward around a rocky hill. From 150 yards out, the grass trap-fronted, undulating green cannot be seen as it abuts a rocky scree along its left. The 12th is a tough 192-yard par-3 that rises to a large two-tiered green. The putting surface is squeezed on both sides by sagebrush and has a very steep rear end. The 17th, a 545-yard par-5 ranked the second-toughest hole, traverses a long and winding path. From 75 yards on in, the green is veiled by a berm. The diminutive, terraced putting surface is ringed by sagebrush and guarded on the right by a grass bunker. The 18th, a 387-yard par-4, is a ribbon-like dogleg-left through sage and rocks, with OB right. Over its final 150 yards, the hole rises steeply to a heart-shaped green that slopes rear-left.

Banks Lake Golf Club

Off Highway 155, Grand Coulee, WA 99133. (509) 633-0163. John Combs, Jr., pro. 9 holes. 3,055 yards. Par 36. Grass tees. Course ratings: men M69.3/115; women—M74.5/126, F70.4/119. Year Opened: 1985. Architect: Keith Hellstrom. Moderate, credit cards. Call for reservations. Walk-on chances: Good. Walkability: No problems. Playability: Course plays tough when the wind picks up.

Banks Lake Golf Club is situated on a mesa above Banks Lake, a massive reservoir created by Grand Coulee Dam. The course occupies part of a 160-acre parcel owned by the Grant County Port District, which it leases to the club member-operators. Designer Keith Hellstrom designed a back nine, and land is available. In mid-March 1997, the club members approved a proposal to double the size of the course. Work on the new back nine will begin in 1998 and be open for play in 1999. The existing dual-tee nine now stretches 6,134 yards over two circuits, and offers wonderful vistas of prehistoric canyons and rugged environs. The virtually treeless track resembles a links, with tall land heaves hiding greens and swales causing ungainly lies.

The venue at Banks Lake is a credit to the local golfers who—over a 50-year period—had tried to build a place to play. After four unsuccessful stabs at building a course, the fifth try worked. The course was financed by 100 founders who spent $2,600 each for collateral on a Coulee Dam Federal Credit Union loan. Course construction began in February 1984, and the volunteer builders—most of whom were farmers—implemented Hellstrom's design. The same construction work force will be used for the second nine; most of its estimated cost of $200,000 will be for the irrigation system. The facility currently hosts about 9,000 rounds a year; when the second nine is built, play levels should double.

Banks Lake owes much of its difficulty to par-4s and par-5s that cross wavy terrain. Sometimes-powerful winds are also a concern. Many greens sit in depressions: difficult targets for players unfamiliar with the layout. Tough holes include the 446-yard, par-5 2nd, a deceptively long dogleg-left that winds between

OB and ball-eating scrub to a bi-trapped green. The 3rd, a 383-yard par-4, contains a narrow, ridged fairway with steep edges. Bending rightward, the 3rd skirts a rugged canyon and swale 75 yards from a round green atop a rise.

Bear Creek Golf Course

9 *Off Highway 20 & Eastside County Road (Route 1, Box 275), Winthrop, WA 98862. (509) 996-2284. 9 holes. 3,114 yards. Par 36. Grass tees. Course ratings: men 68.9/117, women 69.4/113. Year Opened: 1969. Architect: Herm Court. Moderate. Reservations: Call ahead for weekends and holidays. Walk-on chances: Fair. Walkability: Some hills but, overall, not bad for bag-packers. Playability: Laid-back, enjoyable course with stunning surroundings.*

Situated in the beautiful Methow Valley, Bear Creek Golf Course lies north of Twisp and east of Winthrop. In summer, hang-gliders jump off Studhorse Mountain—located to the east—and occasionally land on the course. The layout occupies part of the former Ortell cattle ranch, a 480-acre spread with roots dating back to 1892. Bear Creek's course was originated by Herm Court, a former Seattle firefighter who bought the ranch in 1948. Court began mulling a public golfing grounds in 1952, but didn't proceed because the local population wasn't big enough to support it. Despite that, in the 1960s he began building the course and, by 1969, completed a regulation-length nine. When the North Cascades Highway opened in 1972, connecting north-central Washington with population centers in the west, Court's concerns about getting golfers to play it dissipated. The venue, which hosts an average of 20,000 rounds a year, is now operated by Court's son, Ashley, and Ashley's wife Linda.

Ashley Court has improved the course with new tees, traps and an automatic sprinkler system. The new tees—many of which offer wonderful vistas of Okanogan National Forest, Pasayten Wilderness Area and Sawtooth Ridge—give Bear Creek's holes significantly different looks over two circuits. Besides the occasional hang-glider, deer, bears, moose, mountain lions and upland birds visit the pastoral venue, where leisurely rounds are enjoyed. The Courts recently acquired a 265-acre parcel beside Pearrygin State Park where they'd like to build another nine. Though Idaho architect, Jim Kraus, has drawn up a design for·the site, realization of the plan is not in the immediate offing.

The course stretches 6,155 yards over two nines. Water hazards enter play on the 2nd, 4th, 8th and 9th holes. The primary obstacle to par is Bear Creek's tipped topography. Good holes include the 3rd, a 390-yard par-4 that starts at an elevated tee, then bends leftward over a right-sloping path to a ridge-perched green. The 4th, a 538-yard par-5, sports a wavy fairway lined along the left by scraggly rough and a hill. A pond guards the right-front edge of the bi-level, left-sloping 4th green. The top-rated 5th, a 419-yard par-4, ventures off an elevated tee and concludes at a left-rear sloping green fronted by a depression.

Desert Canyon Golf Resort

114 Brays Road, Orondo, WA 98843. (509) 784-1111 or 1-800-258-4173. Jack **18**
Frei, director of golf; Brad Dally, pro. 18 holes. 7,293 yards. Par 72. Grass tees.
Course ratings: men—C73.9/134, B72.1/125, M69.1/114; women—FF70.6/115,
F67.2/106. Year Opened: 1993. Architect: Jack Frei. Expensive, credit cards.
Reservations: Call a week ahead. Walk-on chances: Fair. Walkability: Cart required
for good reason. Playability: Washington's well-executed answer to Arizona golf.

Located by Daroga State Park, Desert Canyon overlooks a fat part of the Columbia River called Lake Entiat. Besides a course that ranks second in the state (to Sahalee Country Club) and one that received four stars ("outstanding") in *Golf Digest's* 1996-97 "Places to Play" guide, this golf resort contains homesites and rentable townhouses, swimming pools, spas, biking and jogging trails, tennis courts, a children's playground, RV park and boat storage. Desert Canyon has a natural-turf 18-hole putting course replete with waterfalls, sand traps and tilted putting surfaces. The first Jim McLean Golf Learning Center in the Northwest debuted here in 1995. Future plans include a 120-seat restaurant and another 18-hole golf course which, at 6,200 yards, will be more "walker-friendly" and economically-priced than this one. Desert Canyon's designer and builder, Jack Frei, who's also the resort's director of golf and co-owner, may complete the second course by 1999.

Well aware of the popularity of Arizona's target-style tracks, Frei knew he could succeed with a similar desert layout in Washington after seeing this seared, sagebrush-covered property. Abetting the development were supportive Douglas County officials, and existing wells and an irrigation system slated to be used on a never-developed apple orchard. Frei's co-developers were Luke Lueckenotte and Wen Golf, Inc., a Wenatchee real estate firm. After opening in 1993, the course hosted the Northwest Open and generated much acclaim from the tournament players. Desert Canyon held the event again in 1994 when the course record, a 65, was set by PGA Tourer and Northwest native, Rick Fehr. Fehr is Desert Canyon's PGA Tour representative.

The longest hole in the Northwest is Desert Canyon's 6th, a 690-yard par-5.

The course is accessible from Highway 97 off the Brays Road exit, and is split into the Lakes Nine and Desert Nine. The lush fairways wind past sagebrush, a few pines and scrub growth; in spring, desert wildflowers are ablaze in a riot of color. Pine trees enter play on several holes, with ample water and sand hazards guarding fairways and greens. Desert Canyon is not a flat course; there's about 200 feet of elevation change. Green-to-next-tee distances are long, so carts are part of the green fees. Players have views of Mission Ridge, Stormy Mountain, Lake Chelan, Chelan Butte and Earthquake Point on the opposite side of the Columbia. Wildlife visitors include coyotes, deer, pheasants, quails, and bull and king snakes.

Remarkably, Desert Canyon finished second (behind Augusta National Golf Club) in Conditioning, one of the seven criteria used by *Golf Digest* when it came up with its 1997 list of America's 100 Greatest Golf Courses. Top holes on the Desert Nine, which is played as the front, include the 1st, a 534-yard par-5 that winds downhill to the left between a huge waste bunker right and two traps left. Scrub pines lurk in the fairway, which ends at a huge trapped-rear and -left green (linked to the Lakes' 1st) protected right-front by a pond. The 429-yard, par-4 4th has a vast waste area along the right beneath the crackling BPA power lines that bisect the layout. There's a big landing area to the left, with another barranca across the hole 125 yards from a mid-sized green guarded by pot bunkers right-front and grass bunkers right. The top-rated 6th, a 690-yard par-5 (the Northwest's longest hole) spills off multiple tees, skirting a 600-foot-high canyon left and pot bunker right. A fat rock lies in mid-fairway, 250 yards from a front-tilting green with two bunkers right and a trouble-some tree right-front. Another notable hole is the dogleg-right 9th, a 500-yard par-4 (yes, that's a par-4) that descends past pot bunkers left and a vast bunker at the turn to a boomerang-shaped green trapped right, right-rear and rear-left.

Lakes Nine holes of note include the 5th, another beyond-regulation par-4 of 512 yards. The downhill hole crosses moguled ground and skirts traps right. The fairway narrows over its last 125 yards before ending at a heart-shaped green trapped rear and left-front; a pond lurks right-front. Desert Canyon's second-toughest hole is the Lakes 7th, a 574-yard par-5 with an uphill fairway dotted by pine trees. At the 150-yard mark, players can glimpse two greens, one on the fairway-side of a deep chasm and the other on the opposite side of the trouble. The farther green is trapped left and backed by a hill and grass bunkers. It's wide but very shallow.

Home Place Golf Course

9 *6404 Kimber Road, Cashmere, WA 98815. (509) 782-3498. 9 holes. 2,600 yards. Par 35. Grass tees. No course ratings. Year Opened: 1997. Architect: Paul Hansen. Economical. Call for reservations. Walk-on chances: good. Walkability: No major problems. Playability: Mid-length course winds through fruit orchards.*

The new Home Place layout winds through an orchard once harvested by its owners, Paul and Edna Hansen. Home Place sits behind the Chelan County Fairgrounds at Cashmere's west end. The course's unique name traces back to how farmers identified various parcels acquired over the years. An original farm site is called the "Home Place," and that's what this was when Edna's parents began the orchard several decades ago. Besides nine holes that opened in 1997, the facility includes a small pro shop and driving range, the latter of which debuted in 1995.

The Hansens endured an arduous road to see their course come to fruition.

Originally proposed in 1991, the golf plan was fought by a neighboring orchardist who feared that wind-drift from chemicals sprayed on his orchard would become airborne and sicken golfers. After Chelan County denied them a conditional-use permit to build the course, the Hansens filed with the state Court of Appeals in Spokane and got the denial overturned. Work began on the course in 1995; Paul Hansen designed and built the layout.

The 38-acre venue—Cashmere's first golf course—spans gently rolling ground through the Hansen's apple and cherry trees. Players enjoy views of Icicle Ridge, Brender Canyon, Wedge Mountain and peripheral fruit orchards. Wildlife visitors include coyotes, deer and a few elk in winter. Home Place involves one pond (which is both irrigation storage and a hazard) and two par-5s. Its greens are generally flat and average around 3,000-square-feet in size. The primary impediments to par are the trees along fairways. Now popular with local players—who previously had to travel to Leavenworth or Wenatchee to golf—Home Place serves as the training ground for Cashmere's high school golf teams.

Kahler Glen Golf Course

20890 Kahler Drive, Leavenworth, WA 98826. (509) 763-3785. Ed Paine, pro. **18**
18 holes. 5,963 yards. Par 70. Grass tees. Course ratings: men—B67.6/118, M65.7/ 115; women—M71.0/121, F67.1/114. Year Opened: 1989 (original nine); 1995 (second nine). Architect: Randy Pelton. Moderate. Reservations: Call three weeks ahead. Walk-on chances: Fair. Walkability: Fair, with some hilly terrain and some between-hole hikes. Playability: Better have your swing in order as this course demands accuracy.

Located off Highway 2, Kahler (pronounced "Kay-ler") Glen Golf Course is the brainchild of its two owners, Randy Pelton and Glen Week. The golfing got underway at this course beside Lake Wenatchee State Park in 1989. After several

The 2nd hole at Kahler Glen is a nifty 190-yard par-3.

delays caused by opposition from local residents and Chelan County officials, the second nine was finished in 1995. Between the time the front and back sides opened, Pelton and Week began developing 75 single-family lots around their 240-acre parcel. A new 3,000-square-foot clubhouse opened in mid-1996. Also planned are a convention facility, driving range and putting course.

With guidance from turfgrass expert and golf architect, Roy Goss, Pelton designed all 18 holes at Kahler Glen. The new holes were mixed and matched with the original nine to create the current configuration. The bowl-shaped site, once forestland, results in fairways winding over severe terrain. The older holes are noted for their generally small, dome-like greens; the newer holes have considerably larger putting surfaces. The golfing experience is quite pastoral, with players enjoying views of Entiat Ridge and Dirty Face Mountain and occasional visits from deer. Forested foothills to the west were blackened by the damaging fire that raced through Chelan County in 1994.

After Kahler Glen was expanded, play increased upwards of 75 percent. Linksters who come to the course better have a goodly amount of golf balls as some of the fairway peripheries—particularly along the newer holes—are dense underbrush. Staying in the beaten path can be a demanding task as doglegging fairways tilt away from turns and many holes are quite narrow. There are also a few long walks, particularly the arduous uphill hike between the 14th and 15th holes. Good tests include the 1st, a par-4 that plays much longer than its 320 yards as it runs straight uphill along a right-sloping route. OB lines the hole on the right, and the hill-cut 1st green has a very steep left side. The 3rd, a 454-yard par-4, is a downhill dogleg-right through trees. The fairway slopes left over its initial leg, then flattens at the 150-yard mark. The large 3rd green bears a diagonal tier about two feet high.

The top-rated hole is the 8th, a 450-yard par-4 that bends sharply left around alders about 180 yards out. You can cut the corner, but a big trap lies on the other side of the trees. The small and round 8th green is fronted by a sizable, sunken pond. The 12th, a 625-yard par-5, begins at an elevated tee then descends along a right-curling path lined by a pond on the left. The fairway narrows here, then bends left between trees (left) and two bunkers (right) en route to a small, raised green trapped twice on the right. Another back-nine test is the 17th, a 355-yard par-4 with a narrow, uphill fairway that goes between OB and condos right and trees left. The hole concludes at a mid-sized, prow-shaped green with a six-foot-high front end.

Lake Chelan Municipal Golf Course

18 *1501 Golf Course Drive, Chelan, WA 98816. (509) 682-5421. Jim Oscarson, pro. 18 holes. 6,365 yards. Par 72. Grass tees. Course ratings: men—B70.3/119, M68.7/ 116; women—M74.6/124, F70.9/113. Year Opened: 1970. Architects: Eddie Joseph & Ron Sloan; John Steidel (remodel). Moderate, credit cards. Reservations: Call a week ahead. Walk-on chances: Fair. Walkability: Good, except during high noon in summer. Playability: Quite satisfactory for all concerned.*

Lake Chelan lies just north of Chelan on a bluff overlooking its 55-mile-long namesake lake. The venue was initiated by a group of local golfers who not only helped finance the $285,000 course, but built it using donated equipment and labor. The course was designed by its first pro Eddie Joseph, and Ron Sloan, then a foreman for Green Lawns, a landscaping company based in Kalispell. Local businessmen donated $100 apiece to get the project going in 1968; in 1970 the course opened. The city of Chelan acquired it in 1975.

The layout occupies land long owned by three local couples. In fall 1995 when the contract was paid off, the mayor and dozens of long-time Chelan golfers participated in a mortgage-burning ceremony. At that event, a plaque with the names of the course's early-day contributors was placed at the site. Today, Lake Chelan's course is one of Eastern Washington's busiest, hosting about 50,000 rounds annually. Blessed with large and active men's and women's clubs, the facility is also popular with vacationers who come by the thousands to this summertime mecca. Parts of the layout winds through apple orchards, and nearly every hole offers arresting panoramas of the lake and town below.

The course is irrigated by water from Lake Chelan and remains verdant during Chelan's searing summer months. Pure-white Idaho sand fills strategically-placed bunkers. Each hole has a name, such as "Cascade," "Sweet-It-Is," "O.B. Careful" and "Living End." Recent improvements have been made to the course as part of a five-year master plan overseen by John Steidel. (In a related move, Chelan's Parks and Recreation Department built an 18-hole putting course at nearby Don Morse Memorial Park. The putting layout was designed by John Fought of Portland.) Lake Chelan has one of the best-looking driving ranges in the Northwest; the grass-teed practice facility offers 180-degree views of the sparkling lake below.

Good tests include the 3rd, a 400-yard par-4 dubbed "Coyote Canyon." The uphill dogleg-right ends at a small and raised green. From the elevated tee of Lake Chelan's 10th ("Groundhog Hollow"), a par-4 of 406 yards, golfers peer into a rugged canyon. The fairway starts on the far side of this crevice and curls uphill to the left. A lengthwise ridge splits the 10th, and a swale fronts its green, which perches on a hillock butted against a sagebrush-covered hill.

Lake Woods Golf Course

9

240 State Park Road, Bridgeport, WA 98813. (509) 686-5721. 9 holes. 2,836 yards. Par 35. Grass tees. Course ratings: men B/M66.7/115, women—B/M73.4/123, M/ F69.3/114. Year Opened: 1962. Architects: Founding members. Moderate, jr./sr., credit cards. No reservations. Walkability: Good. Playability: Suitable challenge, especially when the winds pick up.

Lake Woods lies next to the Columbia River in Bridgeport State Park. The member-operated venue is leased from the state's Corps of Engineers, which owns the site. Besides local and visiting golfers, deer, doves, Chinese pheasants and quails frequent the course. Full-grown maples and evergreens line most fairways. The 50-acre, member-designed layout was built in 1962 with all-volunteer labor. An adjoining 75 acres may be available for a back nine, but expansion plans are not on tap.

Despite residing in arid climes, Lake Woods' track is lush, quite a contrast to the tawny-colored foothills around it. Some time ago, the course was re-layed out, a move that results in its small greens sloping disconcertingly toward the rear. Approach shots to these swards must be carefully executed. The dual-tee layout plays to 5,642 yards over two circuits. Noteworthy holes include the top-rated 4th, a 386-yard par-4 that bends slightly left. The fairway runs narrowly between poplars over its initial leg, then widens before concluding at a two-tiered green trapped in front. The 344-yard, par-4 9th ascends between maples and the Columbia River to a two-tiered green.

Leavenworth Golf Club

18 *9101 Icicle Road, Leavenworth, WA 98826. (509) 548-7267. Jim Van Tuyl, pro. 18 holes. 5,711 yards. Par 71. Grass tees. Course ratings: men—B66.6/110, F64.6/ 106; women—B71.8/118, F69.4/112. Year Opened: 1927 (original nine); 1969 (second nine). Architects: C.F. Russell & Jock Wood (original nine); members (second nine). Moderate, credit cards. Reservations: Call for the following week on Mondays. Walk-on chances: Fair. Walkability: Good. Playability: Though not long, course plays tough with corridor-like fairways and squeezed target zones.*

Situated off Highway 2 (take the Icicle Road exit and go about half a mile to reach it), this forested course borders the Wenatchee River, and offers views of the spectacular crags ringing its namesake town. Homes line some fairways, while the river curls around the eastern edge. The layout is one of the region's best-landscaped tracks, with vibrant flower gardens throughout. With its Alpine-Bavarian motif, Leavenworth is one of the Northwest's most-popular tourist destinations. Among its many seasonal events are Oktoberfest in fall and a Christmas tree-lighting ceremony. The year-round recreational mecca offers stream fishing, horseback-riding excursions, camping, whitewater rafting, cross-country skiing and sleigh rides. A putting course was recently built next to the Enzian Motor Inn. This part of Washington has four distinct seasons, with golf played six or seven months of the year.

The course started with six holes and sand greens in 1927. Three holes were built later. The course occupies land which was once the site of the Chelan County Fair; it was also a city landfill, baseball diamond and loading dock for Great Northern Lumber Company. Oldtimers recall that after hitting off the sand and oil tees, they'd jump into the river by the 5th hole to wash off the goo. During the course's formative years members picked up rocks from fairways and formed regular work parties. In 1966, the club built the back nine after acquiring an alfalfa field from Leavenworth State Bank founder R.B. Field and another four acres. Construction began on these holes in 1967, and the new holes opened two years later.

Despite its 5,700-yard length, Leavenworth plays tough as it crosses hilly terrain—which leads to ungainly lies, and involves many tree-pinched fairways. (The 2nd hole, a tight 265-yard par-4, is named "Kuch's Alley" after charter member, Ted Kuch.) The venue is known for its small and slick putting surfaces, many of which are bunker-ringed. But perhaps Leavenworth's signature trait is a series of tough par-3s. All sorts of wildlife reside on and around the course. In 1996, golfers watched as state wildlife agents shot a young black bear with a tranquilizer gun, later capturing the bruin along with its mother and another cub and relocating them to greener pastures.

Top holes include the 6th, a right-bending, 384-yard par-4 with Wenatchee River off the tee and along its right edge. The upsloping hole leans toward the river en route to a raised, right-tilting green with a hill close by its left side. The top-rated 7th, a 501-yard par-5, winds rightward around a tree-covered hill. At the 125-yard mark, the fairway curls sharply right to a mid-sized, front-sloping green with a tree towering over its right-front entry. The 155-yard 9th is a mind-boggling par-3 that runs straight uphill along treed, chute-like terrain. Picking the right club to hit into the steeply front-banked 9th green is the key.

The 10th, a 450-yard par-5, has a mid-width fairway that tilts toward a steep dropoff along the right. The hole tapers over its last 100 yards before ending at a bowl-shaped green. The 11th, a 346-yard par-4, has the river and OB right, tall trees on both sides of a bi-level landing zone, and a humped-in-the-middle, trapped-right green. The 12th, a 193-yard par-3, starts at an elevated tee, then drops into a depression before climbing up to a steeply front-leaning green. The 14th, a 321-yard par-4, curls uphill to the right along a path that skirts a pond left. Second shots into the two-tiered 14th green are blind, as a hill blocks the view. The 18th is another long (192 yards) par-3, and it ends at perhaps Leavenworth's largest putting surface.

MA-8 + 1 Golf

455 Wapato Lake Road, Manson, WA 98831. (509) 687-6338. 9 holes. 2,138 yards. **9**
Par 31. Grass tees. No course ratings. Year Opened: 1993. Architect: Don Sibold.
Moderate, jr. rates. Reservations: Call three days ahead. Walk-on chances: Good.
Walkability: No problems. Playability: Good beginner's course.

Located northwest of Chelan off Highway 150, this executive-length nine crosses a hillside above Lake Chelan. The 1993-opened layout is generally facile with some shortish trees defining fairways. MA-8 + 1 is owned by Bill Evans, who also happens to be the reigning chief of the Wapato Point tribe. The course's odd name stems from its parcel designation: Moses Agreement Number 8. The original owner of the land—which had previously been the site of a sawmill—was Wapato John, Evans' great-grandfather. Wapato John was part of a group of Native Americans who roamed the area between Entiat and Chelan in the late 1800s.

Golfers enjoy nice views of the lake; a small clubhouse serves as the starting point. Evans owns about 100 acres, so there's room for another nine holes. The course adjoins Mill Bay RV Resort, a members-only facility with 33 full-service slips. Also nearby is Mill Bay Casino, a gambling operation owned by the Colville Confederated Tribes. The course and casino were hit hard financially in August 1994 when the great Chelan fire blocked off access to the area.

MA-8 + 1's most difficult holes are a trio of par-3s that each stretch upwards of 200 yards. Its greens are generally big, and some sand and water hazards enter play. When I visited the course in September 1995, the wind was howling about 40 miles an hour and some players were having a tough time beating golf shots into the gale. In summer, conditions are considerably more user-friendly. Top holes include the 2nd, a 200-yard par-3 with a pond right of the tee. Tee shots need to be placed between trees to reach the huge 2nd green. The 6th, a 193-yard par-3, runs uphill (with the prevailing wind coming from the left) to another sizable putting surface trapped right.

Okanogan Valley Golf Club - semiprivate

Golf Course Drive, Omak, WA 98841. (509) 826-9902. Bill Sproule, pro. 9 holes. **9**
3,010 yards. Par 35. Grass tees. Course ratings: men—B70.5/119, M69.1/117;
women—M74.9/124, F71.9/119. Year Opened: 1946. Architects: Founding
members. Moderate. Reservations: Call four days ahead. Walk-on chances: Fair.
Walkability: Pleasant jaunt for bag-packers. Playability: Course ranked among state's
top-five toughest nines may soon receive a long-missing back side.

Semiprivate Okanogan Valley is set amid orchards between Omak and Okanogan. Okanogan Valley Golf Club was built in 1946, and has served as a sporting and social center for the two towns ever since. About 175 proprietary members own the course, with its day-to-day operations overseen by Texas-born Bill Sproule, a friendly Class A pro who's been here since 1974. Fruit orchards engird the layout to the east;

rock-strewn, sagebrush-covered hills lie to the west. A large groundhog contingent emerges from lairs between mid-April and June, and deer, quails, pheasants and bull snakes occasionally make appearances on the course. Okanogan Valley once had the Northwest's only "Cayman" driving range, but it was closed because neighborhood kids kept stealing the expensive balls.

Another driving range may be built, however, along with nine more holes and a new irrigation system. In 1996, the clubmembers were awaiting approval of a lease of neighboring land with the federal Bureau of Land Reclamation. The members need this lease in order to access an irrigation source for the new holes. If and when the expansion proceeds, perhaps as early as 1997 (with it opening in 1998 or 1999), the revised 100-acre course will involve more doglegs. Sproule and the former head of Washington State University's turfgrass program, Roy Goss—who now lives next to Okanogan Valley—have come up with a design for the all-new 18-hole layout.

The National Golf Foundation once ranked Okanogan Valley among the state's top-five nine-holers. The tricky dual-tee track extends 6,417 yards over two circuits. Interesting holes include the top-rated 5th, a rolling 395-yard par-4 that doglegs right. The fairway is crossed by a creek twice before concluding at a squarish green. The 9th, a 550-yard par-5, features a perched tee that offers excellent territorial views. The 9th runs straight before bending rightward around a large grove of trees to a front-sloping green.

Oroville Golf Club

9 *Off Nighthawk Road, Oroville, WA 98844. (509) 476-2390. 9 holes. 2,897 yards. Par 36. Grass tees. Course ratings: men 67.8/113, women 74.0/126. Year Opened: 1960. Architects: Founding members. Moderate, credit cards. Reservations: Call a week ahead. Walk-on chances: Fair. Walkability: Fine, though expect some hilly hikes. Playability: Enjoyable golf above the city of Oroville.*

Located west of its namesake town, Oroville Golf Club lies amid apple orchards off Nighthawk Road. The course is owned by its members, many of whom participate as volunteers in work parties. Oroville is overseen by manager Jerry Sneve, who's assisted by his wife Dolly. Other Sneve family members involved at the facility include daughters Cindy Boyer, the greens superintendent, and Mary Thornton, who works in the pro shop and gives lessons. Son J.B. Sneve is a competitive golf pro who has played California's Golden State Mini-Tour and the Canadian Tour. In 1987, J.B. set Oroville's 18-hole course record, a 62. The Sneves became involved through Jerry's father, Sid (better known as "Pappy"), who started working here as the manager in 1966.

Arrayed over 45 acres of hilly terrain, Oroville crosses a ridge overlooking the Similkameen River, offering spectacular views of downtown and the Similkameen Canyon. The lush layout is irrigated from the river. Golfers might spot deer, pheasant and quail. A sizable population of marmots (also called groundhogs or woodchucks) comes out of hibernation in June, and remain until August. Though no one has ever been bitten while golfing, rattlesnakes, blue racers and bull snakes dwell in rocky outcrops around the course. Recent improvements include a renovated green, pond, new tee and paved cart paths. The member-owners have discussed acquiring a 100-acre parcel across Nighthawk Road for another nine holes and a driving range. But the Bureau of Land Management, owners of the parcel, has been slow in responding to the members' proposal.

Oroville's dual-tee layout extends 5,937 yards over two circuits. Many holes sport panoramic tees and greens backed by steep cliffs. Tough holes include the 1st, a 465-yard par-5 that begins at a raised tee. The narrow, rolling fairway contains a deep swale 250 yards out at a juncture squeezed by boulders. The severely right-sloping green sits on a knoll. The 4th, a 351-yard par-4, bends rightward after passing a depression off the tee. The route ascends to a green perched atop a towering promontory.

Rock Island Golf Course   9

314 Saunders Road, Rock Island, WA 98850. (509) 884-2806. 9 holes. 3,396 yards. Par 36. Grass tees. Course ratings: men—M69.7/111, F67.4/106; women—M75.8/ 120, F73.0/114. Year Opened: 1978. Architect: Munson & Associates. Economical, jr./sr. rates, credit cards. Call for reservations. Walk-on chances: Good. Walkability: No problems. Playability: Hit the ball far and you should do well at one of Washington's longest nine-hole courses.

The 1978-built Rock Island layout is a replacement for the neighboring town's original course, which was flooded when Rock Island Dam was finished in 1973. The current track was constructed as part of the mitigation requirements for the dam, and the Chelan PUD continues to hold title to some of the land occupied by it. The city of Rock Island owns the course itself, which is leased to Don Barth, owner of Alta Lake up north in Pateros. In January 1996, Barth made an offer to buy Rock Island Golf Course from the city, but the city council said it didn't want to sell. If Barth had proceeded with his purchase he probably would have added another nine holes.

At nearly 3,400 yards, this lush layout above Highway 28 ranks among the state's longest nine-holers. Over two circuits the course stretches 6,467 yards. Spanning a gently sloping hill that leans toward the nearby Columbia River, the layout gains difficulty from its length as well as some well-placed water and sand hazards. The ponds and sloughs along Rock Island's south edge are favorite haunts for thousands of Canada geese in spring, also providing irrigation for the fairways and nearby fruit orchards.

Tough holes include the 5th, a 572-yard par-5 that runs straight over slightly left-tilting ground. The fairway ends at a small green trapped laterally. The par-5 8th is a double-dogleg that turns left, then right, over its 545 yards. A lake looms along the left of the latter portion of the hole, which finishes at a wavy green ringed by grassy mounds. The 9th, a 343-yard par-4, has the steepest fairway on the course. The hole heads straight uphill to a wavy, slick green beside Rock Island's clubhouse.

Three Lakes Golf Course   18

2695 Golf Drive, Wenatchee, WA 98828. (509) 663-5448. John Christensen, pro. 18 holes. 5,298 yards. Par 69. Grass tees. Course ratings: men B65.2/104; women— B69.3/115, F68.8/114. Year Opened: 1953 (original nine); 1972 (second nine). Architects: Local players & the men's club. Moderate, jr. rates. Reservations: Call a week ahead. Walk-on chances: Fair. Walkability: Pretty good with some uphill hikes. Playability: Short track features tight fairways and tipped topography.

The 5,300-yard, par-69 Three Lakes course crosses a hillside above the Columbia River and the fruit-rich Wenatchee Valley. Surrounded by orchards, Three Lakes is a tight, knoll-strewn course with compressed target zones. Its 18 holes were designed by local players and members of the men's club. Three Lakes is owned by stockholders who operate it on a nonprofit basis. The course occupies 90 acres, and hosts upwards of 45,000 rounds a year.

Three Lakes is a well-maintained course, with its automatic sprinkler system keeping fairways and greens verdant during Wenatchee's sun-baked summers. Because of its abbreviated length and squeezed configuration, Three Lakes appears like a quaint golf park. But its compressed nature penalizes the misguided. A hole representative of Three Lakes' restrictiveness is the 6th, a 267-yard par-4 that follows an extremely narrow route (an adjoining cart path is nearly as wide as the fairway) to a small, raised green. Sporting a tight, roller-coaster fairway that slopes toward a pond along the right, the 326-yard, par-4 15th ends at a hilltop-roosting green.

Vic Meyers Golf Course

9 *34228 Park Lake Road NE, Coulee City, WA 99115. (509) 632-5738. 9 holes. 3,123 yards. Par 35. Grass tees. Course ratings: men 67.9/102, women 70.8/108. Year Opened: 1949. Architect: state of Washington. Economical, credit cards. Call for reservations. Walk-on chances: Good. Walkability: Good, except during summer's hottest days. Playability: Wide-open fairways make it a good beginner's course.*

This course is named after a former lieutenant governor of the state of Washington. Vic Meyers lobbied to establish a state park in the Sun Lakes area; one of the requirements for the park's creation was a golf course. The facility lies at the entrance to Sun Lakes State Park Resort, an area with rental cabins, tenting and RV spaces, horseback riding and trout-stocked lakes. The 4,000-acre resort lies in one of the Northwest's hottest areas; in summer, temperatures over 100 degrees are common. Perched along an escarpment, the nine-hole track offers views of the resort and its rugged, prehistoric environs. The hazard-less venue, ideal for vacationers who golf infrequently, is generally open from March 1 through November.

Opened in 1949, the course is about the same as it was when built. Over two nine-hole rounds, Vic Meyers plays to a total of 6,001 yards. Ruddy rocks and sagebrush-covered foothills ring the course, and rocky underpinnings have made washboards of fairway surfaces. Wildlife include Canada geese, coyotes, raccoons and marmots. In winter, a 250-head herd of deer grazes the course, a state-protected sanctuary. In early 1997, a consultant hired by the state recommended building another 18 holes along with a driving range and lodge with a restaurant at the south end of Park Lake. The state is looking at ways to broaden the appeal of the resort. The existing nine holes involve severe, rocky slopes, with fairways splaying over a promontory. Good holes include the top-rated 1st, a 511-yard par-5 that follows a narrow, uphill route to a small, domed green. The 5th, a par-4 of 434 yards, begins at an elevated tee. After bending to the right, the hole ends at a humped-in-the-middle green.

Private Courses

Sunny Meadows Golf & Four Seasons Resort

280 West Chewuch Road, Winthrop, WA 98862. (509) 996-3103 or 1-800-433-3121. 9 holes. 1,134 yards. Par 27. Grass tees. No course ratings. Year Opened: 1995. Architects: Bob Odenthal & Bob Spiwak. Guests of the bed and breakfast.

9

Sunny Meadows' short nine graces the grounds of a like-named bed and breakfast run by Lani and Bob Odenthal. The overnight accommodations are fully-appointed apartments in a large house. The home was designed by Dr. Kelley, a famed alternative cancer-treatment specialist who built self-contained areas in the house for patients. The Odenthals moved to Winthrop from Northern California in 1989, and converted the home into a comfortable place for paying guests. The venue lies north of Highway 20 off Chewuch Road in a pastoral canyon.

The par-3 track was built and designed by Bob Odenthal, a former developer and contractor, with help from local golf writer Bob Spiwak. It can be played by guests at Sunny Meadows or those staying at other hostels in the Methow Valley. I played the course a month after it opened, and found its fairways and greens thickly turfed. The bentgrass greens are quite small and—with any wind through the valley—elusive. Some parts of the layout are a bit strange. For example, the tee shot at the 3rd hole must be lofted over the 2nd tee. But since this isn't a high-traffic facility, safety shouldn't be an issue. Besides, players can see everyone on the course and will have plenty of time to holler.

A pond that provides lovely morning wake-up viewing for guests enters play on a few holes. The 230-yard par-3 at the 6th is legitimately tough, requiring a left-bending tee shot over tall fescue grasses to reach a teardrop-shaped green. The prettiest hole is the 95-yard 7th, which has a tiny green fronted closely by the pond. Odenthal was building a new elevated "black" tee that will stretch this little dandy out to 150 yards.

Wenatchee Golf & Country Club

1600 Country Club Drive, East Wenatchee, WA 98802. (509) 884-7050. Pat Welch, pro. 18 holes. 6,347 yards. Par 72. Grass tees. Course ratings: men—B70.1/123, M68.9/120; women—M74.3/124, F71.3/120. Years Opened: 1923 (original nine); 1958 (second nine). Architects: Founding members (original nine); Arthur Vernon Macan (second nine). Members, guests & reciprocates.

18

The lovely course here lies in East Wenatchee, across the Columbia River from its namesake city. The golf course was begun in 1923 when founding members designed and built the first nine holes (played now as the front). The back nine, designed by PNGA Hall-of-Fame architect Arthur Vernon Macan, opened in 1958. The club has a total of 475 members, 350 of whom golf. The mature layout spans a hillside that not only provides great vistas of the Wenatchee Valley, but also complicates the quest for par. The course is a centerpiece of a 354-acre residential reserve with 167 houses. In late 1994, the homes and the country club were annexed into the city of East Wenatchee; previously, the area was considered part of Chelan County.

Wenatchee's layout receives water from an irrigation canal and is kept in great shape during its eight- or nine-month season. Fairways wind between ornamental,

Wenatchee's 13th hole is a 486-yard par-5.

deciduous and conifer trees of various heights. The walkable track enjoys excellent signage and colorful flower gardens. An elementary school borders the 8th hole; in fall, kids playing outdoors at recess give the place a friendly, down-home ambience. As might be expected, the original front-nine greens are small and slippery. On the other hand, Macan's back-nine greens are larger and more tilted. When mowed low during the season, all of Wenatchee's putting surfaces are slick.

The course record of 62 is held by Kene Bensel, now the pro at Lake Padden in Bellingham. That's a nice score for a track with some tough holes. These include the top-rated 3rd, a 392-yard par-4 with a narrow, right-tilting fairway that ends at a diminutive, laterally trapped green backed by a wood-planked garden. The 7th, a 570-yard par-5, follows a long and rolling path which is flat over its initial leg, then descends over its final 300 yards. The latter part of the hole is tapered by trees before reaching a round green bunkered at the left-front. The 8th, a 400-yard par-4, heads steeply uphill and straight past OB and a road along the right. The fairway gradually narrows en route to a small, round green.

Wenatchee's 10th, a 483-yard par-5, starts at an elevated tee that offers great vistas of the valley. A good-sized landing area for drives is banked into a left-sloping hillside. Trees at the 200-yard mark pinch the fairway, which then curls rightward over left-sloping ground. Two traps left and one right guard the tiny, two-tiered 10th green. The 11th, a 443-yard par-4, contains a long and tight fairway that rises up to the 175-yard mark. Here, the hole drops into a canyon and then climbs steeply back uphill to a mesa-mounted putting surface trapped at the right-front. The 201-yard 14th is a dandy par-3. Guarded by OB left, the hole ascends to a hill-cut, front-tilting green trapped at the left-front.

DRIVING RANGES

Crystal Springs Golf Center

405 Ohme Gardens Road, Wenatchee, WA 98801.
(509) 663-6300. Greg Knight, pro. 18-hole putting course.

UPCOMING COURSES

Chelan — Snowcreek Resort (1999/2000). In 1996, the backers of this 400-acre project on the south side of Lake Chelan came up with a revised proposal that includes a Hale Irwin-designed 18-hole course, homes, a tennis center, conference facilities, pool, spa, putting course, restaurants and lounges.

Mazama — Arrowleaf Resort (1999/2000). The developers of this 1,100-acre project, R.D. Merrill Co. of Seattle and Lowe Development Co. of Los Angeles, have done some site preparation for an 18-hole, 7,400-yard course designed by Robert Cupp. In early 1997, the project was appealed by a small but zealous group of opponents who live in Twisp, way at the other end of the Methow Valley. It's possible that once this legal issue is addressed, construction on the initial nine holes could commence in 1997, which could open as early as late-summer 1998. The second nine could follow the next year. Besides the course, the resort (called Early Winters in a previous incarnation) includes a 12-room inn, 100-room lodge, tennis and swim club, equestrian center, shops, clubhouse, 250 homesites, cabins and 750 acres of open space.

Waterville — Wheat Farm Project (1999/2000). In early 1997, plans were being formulated for an 18-hole course and 120-room hotel on part of a 700-acre wheat farm. The site is about 12 miles northeast of Orondo, home of the popular Desert Canyon golf resort. The project may be developed in tandem with Waterville's plan to beautify the town and make it a more attractive destination for tourists.

8

SOUTH-CENTRAL WASHINGTON

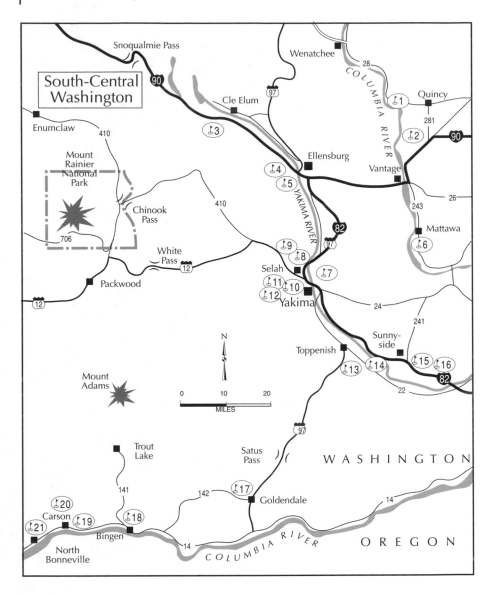

South-Central Washington

Snoqualmie Pass

Wenatchee

28

90

Quincy

Cle Elum

97

281

Enumclaw

410

Mount
Rainier
National
Park

Chinook
Pass

706

White
Pass

12

Packwood

12

Mount
Adams

N

0   10   20
MILES

Ellensburg

Vantage

Yakima River

90

26

243

Mattawa

82

97

24

241

Sunny-
side

Toppenish

22

Goldendale

141

142

97

Satus
Pass

W A S H I N G T O N

14

O R E G O N

Trout
Lake

Carson

Bingen

North
Bonneville

14

COLUMBIA RIVER

COLUMBIA RIVER

Selah

Yakima

Cle Elum

1. **Crescent Bar Resort** — public 9, driving range & 18-hole putting course
2. **Quincy Valley Golf Course** — public 18
3. **Sun Country Golf Resort** — public 9
4. **Ellensburg Golf Club** — semiprivate 9 & driving range
5. **Carey Lakes Golf Course** — public 18 & driving range
6. **Desert Aire Golf & Country Club** — semiprivate 18 & driving range
7. **Yakima Country Club** — private 18
8. **Yakima Elks Golf & Country Club** — private 18
9. **Suntides Golf Course** — public 18, driving range & 18-hole putting course
10. **Fisher Park Golf Course** — public 9 (par-3)
11. **Westwood West** — public 9 & driving range
12. **Apple Tree Golf Course** — public 18 & driving range
13. **Mount Adams Country Club** — semiprivate 18 & driving range
14. **Harvest Valley Golf Center** — driving range
15. **Lower Valley Golf Club** — semiprivate 18 & driving range
16. **Straight Arrow Driving Range**
17. **Goldendale Country Club** — semiprivate 9
18. **Husum Hills Golf Course** — public 9
19. **Hot Springs Golf Course** — public 18 & driving range
20. **Skamania Lodge Golf Course** — public 18 & driving range
21. **Beacon Rock Public Golf Course** — public 9

This southern slice of Washington is defined on the north by Quincy, the Columbia River on the south, and Sunnyside on the east. To the west stretch the Cascades, and at its core is the fertile Yakima Valley. Occupying climate zones 1 and 2, the area experiences brisk winters with moderate snowfall and high winds in spring and fall, particularly in the Kittitas Valley and along the Columbia River Gorge. The golf season runs from March 15 to November 15, weather permitting. Along with north-central Washington, this area may attempt to become the Evergreen State's equivalent of Bend, Oregon. If more courses like Apple Tree in Yakima emerge during the 1990s and in the next century, it may indeed rival central Oregon's golf-happy hunting grounds.

PUBLIC COURSES

Apple Tree Golf Course

18 *8804 Occidental Avenue, Yakima, WA 98903. (509) 966-5877. George Price, Jr., pro. 18 holes. 6,892 yards. Par 72. Grass tees. Course ratings: men—T73.3/129, B72.0/127, M70.7/124, FF68.0/118; women—FF74.2/129, F72.0/124. Year Opened: 1992. Architects: John Steidel & Owners. Moderate. Reservations: Call up to 30 days ahead. Walk-on chances: Fair. Walkability: Fair, with some hilly terrain and long walks between holes. Playability: Lots of variety will challenge mid-handicappers and scratch golfers.*

With an apple-shaped green that's been photographically featured in magazines as diverse as *Golf Digest* and *Good Fruit Grower*, this course has quickly become one of the Northwest's best-known layouts. And well it should be, since the island green at the par-3 17th is not so much an attention-grabbing gimmick as an indicator of the variety found at this course in Yakima's fruit-rich West Valley. *Golf Digest's* "Places to Play 1996-'97" agreed, giving Apple Tree exalted four-star status. The site, a former apple orchard operated by the Hull family since the late-1800s, involves all sorts of terrain—from flat to ridge-perched to up- and downhill. And, with a plethora of water and sand hazards, Apple Tree will test anyone's game.

John Steidel designed the course and, during construction, members of the ownership group (Apple Tree Partnership, comprised of local orchardists and businessmen) made changes along the way. When conceived, the project was to have 300 to 400 housing lots along fairways. But sewer permits have been difficult to obtain, and Apple Tree's homes have not come to fruition. The course, the Hull family's former home, and a turreted clubhouse now occupy the 275-acre site. Apple Tree has a no-nonsense slow-play policy that requires each group to average 15 minutes a hole. Those too slow at front-nine checkpoints are asked to speed it up; in extreme cases, particularly laggard players may be denied back nine play. The course—with its center-of-the-state location and high regard—has hosted some significant tournaments, including the 1995 Washington State Men's Amateur.

Among the tougher tests is the 2nd, a 196-yard par-3 that runs along a ridge. The trapped-left-front green sits in a depression so, from the tee, it's hard to assess the size of the putting surface. The triple-tiered target is huge and deep, and has OB close

The famous apple-shaped hole at Apple Tree Golf Course is the 17th, a 180-yard par-3

to its left edge. The top-rated 4th, a 461-yard par-4, doglegs right around two bunkers. Once past the bend, the mid-width hole drops down before rising up to a wide-but-shallow green trapped right-front and left-rear. Another good front-nine hole is the 7th, a 362-yard par-4 with water galore. The fairway descends slightly between a big bunker right and pond left. The water hazard crosses before the 7th's skinny, elongated green, mandating a precise second shot.

Players must cross Occidental Avenue to get to the 10th through the 15th. These holes cross flat terrain and weave between orchards. The best hole here is the 15th, a 423-yard par-4 that doglegs left around a bunker. Apple Tree's builder-owners fashioned a grass "coffin" bunker outside the turn of the 15th fairway. Originally containing sand, this rectangular-shaped, above-ground receptacle looks like a giant coffin: about four feet high and 20 feet long. The latter part of the 15th curls between mounds to a steeply front-sloping green trapped left.

Often considered the *state's* signature hole, the famed 17th has nine tees that stagger-step down a steep slope, enabling it to be played from 90 to 180 yards. The colorful par-3—with its sky-blue lake, green grass, white leaf-shaped bunker and brown branch-like bridge—is very striking when viewed from above. Fortunately, the green is about 10,000-square-feet in size and, unless there are strong winds aloft, is quite reachable. The fairway at Apple Tree's 506-yard, par-5 18th slopes left toward a lake, located about 250 yards off the tee. A fairway "finger" across the lake can be reached—to shorten the hole considerably—but only with a powerful, well-placed drive. A bunker 280 yards out along the right side of the lake is a safer target. From here, the route ascends leftward to a ridge-perched, ribbon-like putting surface linked to the 9th green. At the base of the ridge is an array of gravity-fed pools. The green, bunkered front and back, also has an apple-shaped trap. Sprawling over the slope before the green, this bunker is filled with fine-grained, ruddy-colored lava to make it look like a Red Delicious apple. Yet another reminder of this course's location in "The Fruit Bowl of the Nation."

Beacon Rock Public Golf Course

9 *Off Highway 14, North Bonneville, WA 98639. (509) 427-5730 or 1-800-428-5730. 9 holes. 2,746 yards. Par 36. Grass tees. Course ratings: men 67.5/115, women 69.7/ 109. Year Opened: 1971. Architects: Local golfers. Moderate, sr. rates, credit cards. Call for reservations. Walk-on chances: Good. Walkability: Good. Playability: Fairly wide open, but wind howling down the Gorge can wreak havoc.*

North Bonneville's Beacon Rock course offers players great views of the Columbia Gorge. The course's namesake monolith, the world's second-largest—after the Rock of Gibraltar and before Haystack Rock in Cannon Beach, Oregon—looms impressively to the west. The layout is near one of the nation's oldest hydroelectric projects, Bonneville Dam. It was designed and built by volunteers on land donated by the Bonneville Power Admininstration to the Port of Skamania. A club member-comprised board of directors oversees the non-profit facility, and Jim and Linda Borup are the managers.

A member of the Oregon Golf Association, Beacon Rock is a dual-tee nine that stretches 5,580 yards over two circuits. Though a few traps guard its large greens, the course is generally facile with wide and flat fairways. Several bunkers and two water hazards enter play. Strong winds occasionally wash across the track, skewing shots from their intended flights. Trees line several holes, and neighborhoods lie to the east and south. The toughest hole is the 5th, a 491-yarder. The par-5 runs straight between a water hazard left and bunkers right to a small green backed by trees.

Carey Lakes Golf Course

18 *1201 Umptanum Road, Ellensburg, WA 98926. (509) 962-5256. Desmond Cooley, pro. 18 holes. 4,000 yards. Par 59. Grass tees. Course ratings not available. Year Opened: 1997. Architect: John Casey. Economical, credit cards. Call for reservations. Walk-on chances: Good. Walkability: Good. Playability: Though short, water hazards spell problems.*

Carey Lakes is a new executive track along Interstate 90 just west of Ellensburg near Irene Reinhart Park. The facility—visible from the freeway and closed from November through March—also contains a driving range and a modular clubhouse with a pro shop and food service. Carey Lakes is the brainchild of John and Cheryl Casey. John, a retired Seattle fireman, designed and built the course. The Caseys were supported in the endeavor by six other investors; the ownership group is called Par Five Inc. When he graduates from the turfgrass management program at Walla Walla Community College in 1998, their nephew, Travis Pike, will be the greens superintendent.

The project was started in February 1995. After waiting seven months to get permits from Kittitas County, site preparation, irrigation installation, shaping and seeding occurred in 1996. The Caseys acquired the property from Pautzke Bait Company; it had previously been a hay field. Near the course is one of Ellensburg's famed stockyards, Washington Beef. The 65-acre venue lies on a 100-year floodplain of the Yakima River, but the course should remain unscathed. During the floods of February 1996, which resulted in two feet of water rushing down Ellensburg's down-town streets, Carey Lakes was dry save for some seepage. The pie-shaped parcel is hemmed in by three elevated thoroughfares—Dike Road, Umptanum Road and I-90—and is well protected.

Though safe from the threat of flooding, Carey Lakes (named after some popular recreational ponds nearby) has an aqueous personality as 13 of its 18 holes involve water hazards. These hazards include a creek—which was restored by Casey during construction—as well as ponds and Bull Ditch, an irrigation canal. The track, a par 59 for men and par 67 for women, crosses rolling terrain and involves a few hills. Surprisingly, Ellensburg's prevailing winds are a factor on only four front-nine holes as other parts of the course are shielded by trees.

The Caseys sold 25 lifetime passes about a year before the course opened. A wife of one of the lifetime "members" was attracted to the offer because the Caseys set aside a shaded space for picnic tables. This could be a popular spot for other non-golfing spouses who can relax while their mates make the rounds. For I-90 wayfarers, 18 holes should take only two-and-a-half hours to complete. Those who par the course earn a free round, and children under 12 play for free when accompanied by an adult. The Caseys feel that getting youngsters interested in golf at an early age will pay off down the road.

Crescent Bar Resort

864 Crescent Bar Road #29, Quincy, WA 98848. (509) 787-1511 or 1-800-824-7090. 9 holes. 3,034 yards. Par 35. Grass tees. Course ratings: men— B68.8/108, M68.4/107; women—M73.5/120, F72.4/118. Opened: 1960s. Architect: Arnold Palmer. Moderate, sr. rates, credit cards. Reservations: Call a week ahead. Walk-on chances: Fair. Walkability: Good, except during the dog days of summer. Playability: A reasonable test for all linksters.

This nine-hole course located seven miles west of Quincy is an integral part of Crescent Bar Resort, a recreational haven along the banks of the Columbia River. Situated along a wide, slow-moving section of the river, the resort is ringed by sheer cliffs that are occasionally used by hang-gliders who land on the course. The popular recreational facility contains summer homes, RV and trailer parks, boat-launching pads and playgrounds. A scattering of fruit orchards fronts Crescent Bar's entrance; eagles, hawks and rattlesnakes frequent the area.

Seattle's Richard Hadley and Associates owns Crescent Bar's resort and golf course, which crosses a ledge-like riverbank. Though not endowed with a great deal of man-made hazards, the flat track can play tough, particularly when winds are aloft. The venue is decidedly laid-back, with barefoot, shirtless teens hacking golf balls alongside prim and proper seniors. The dual-tee track plays to a total of 6,068 yards over two go-rounds. Challenges include the top-rated 4th, a 447-yard, par-4 that winds down a long and narrow lane toward a small, well-canted green. The 7th, a par-4 of 388 yards, doglegs right while skirting poplar trees left. The 8th, a 414-yard par-4, bends slightly left en route to a small, front-sloping green trapped left-front and rear.

Desert Aire Golf & Country Club - semiprivate

18

505 Clubhouse Way, Mattawa, WA 99344. (509) 932-4439. Brad Eakman, pro. 18 holes. 6,479 yards. Par 72. Grass tees. Course ratings: men—B69.9/111, F66.9/104; women—B75.7/120, F71.9/111. Years Opened: 1970 (original nine); 1992 (second nine). Architects: Harry Davidson (original nine); Jim Kraus (second nine). Moderate. Reservations: Call a week ahead. Walk-on chances: Fair. Walkability: Good overall. Playability: Few trees at links-type layout, which means wind can destroy scores.

Because its location by the Columbia River helps avert the freezing snaps found elsewhere east of the Cascades, Desert Aire's course enjoys one of the longest playing seasons in eastern Washington. On occasion, golf has been a year-round activity here. The 18-hole layout winds through a growing, 1,000-acre community five miles from the small town of Mattawa. Desert Aire was originated in 1970 by Harry Davidson, an Everett real estate developer. Though homesite sales in its first decade were sluggish, they've taken off in recent years; over 80 percent of the 1,650 lots have been sold. The community now boasts a shopping mall, fire station, RV park and two restaurants. Working with the Grant County Sheriff's Office, a voluntary police force patrols the community.

Nine holes were built soon after Davidson began Desert Aire. In 1992, a Jim Kraus-designed back nine opened for play. All holes wind over tabletop ground overlooking the Columbia; vistas include the river and foothills to the west. Most days are sunny in these arid environs but, with the planar terrain virtually bereft of trees, wind does all sorts of wild things to golf shots. It's recommended to play in the morning when the wind is reasonably calm.

Tough holes on the original nine include the top-rated 4th, a 415-yard par-4 that follows a narrow route to a knoll-perched green. The back nine is 120 yards longer but topographically similar to its alter ego, albeit with more traps and a lake (involved at the 12th and 16th holes). The contemporary side also features sizable bentgrass greens with peripheral mounding. Perhaps the most challenging back-side hole is the 18th, a 541-yard par-5 that winds leftward over a narrow, rolling path to a tri-trapped green.

Ellensburg Golf Club - semiprivate

9

3231 Thorp Road, Ellensburg, WA 98926. (509) 962-2984. Rich Farrell, pro. 9 holes. 2,988 yards. Par 35. Grass tees. Course ratings: men—B68.8/114, F66.9/109; women—B74.6/125, F72.3/120. Year Opened: 1925. Architects: Founding members. Moderate. Call for reservations. Walk-on chances: Fair. Walkability: Good. Playability: Can be tough if the Kittitas Valley's notorious winds are blustering.

Semiprivate Ellensburg Golf Club lies south of Interstate 90 off Thorp Road. It crosses a generally flat 80-acre parcel bordering the Yakima River. Ellensburg Golf Club, now owned by twin brothers, Frank and Keith Crimp, originated in 1925 on farm land donated by Malcolm Moe. It replaced Ellensburg's original golf course, which sat on a hill above the town. The course was closed during World War II. After the war, local golfers restarted it as a private club. In 1962, the Elks Club operated the facility until the Crimps bought it in 1985. Recent improvements include an upgraded irrigation system and a rock wall along the Yakima River that should help deter the flooding that occurred in late 1996. One tee and 450 yards of banks were lost in two floods that year. Also helping to mitigate future erosion are fresh plantings of alder, aspen, birch, pine and willow trees.

The Yakima river should—barring a very wild tee shot at the 4th—enter play only on the 5th hole. The dual-tee nine stretches 6,093 yards over two trips. Golf shots will be altered by winds that howl off the Cascades down through the Kittitas Valley. Painted horseshoes (appropriate for a course in horse and cattle country) are used as tee markers. Some tees are quite far apart and give varying looks to fairways and greens over front- and back-nine rounds. A series of ditches wind through the layout, and golfers will encounter an occasional greenside bunker. A notable hole is the 429-yard, par-4 3rd, which skirts willows, creeks and a sand trap on a dogleg-right path that concludes at a slick green. When played as the 12th, the hole becomes a 482-yard par-5. The 4th, a 295-yard par-4, bends 90 degrees to the right en route to a bunkered, two-tiered green.

Goldendale Country Club - semiprivate

9

1901 North Columbus, Goldendale, WA 98620. (509) 773-4705. Joel Crocker, pro. 9 holes. 2,789 yards. Par 36. Grass tees. Course ratings: men 66.2/107, women 69.4/114. Year Opened: 1923. Architects: Founding members. Moderate. No reservations. Walkability: Good. Playability: Nice quiet rounds, adequate challenge, and good views of nearby mountains.

Located at Goldendale's north end, this course crosses rolling terrain. Trout-laden Bloodgood Creek intersects the site, which is visited by quail, pheasants and ducks. The course's western holes border grasslands, and offer golfers great views of Mount Adams and the Simcoe Mountains. Goldendale's only golf course began with nine holes equipped with sand greens in 1923. In 1955, the greens were converted to grass. Today, the 52-acre layout is well-tended and a popular local gathering spot. Its semiprivate status stems from being owned by Goldendale's members, whose events during the April-to-October season may close the course to the general public.

Though not adorned with an abundance of man-made hazards, this track can play tough, particularly when Goldendale's famed winds are in full throat. Among the more interesting tests is the top-rated 1st, a 496-yard par-5 that bends slightly right. The rolling fairway is crossed by the entry road, and trees line the route as it ventures to an undulating green. The fairway at the 6th, a 452-yard par-5, runs straight and slopes left on its way to a trapped-right putting surface. Goldendale's prettiest hole is the dogleg-right 7th, a 306-yard par-4 that winds around trees and a fairway bunker to a laterally-trapped green. The 9th, a 158-yard par-3, crosses a fat part of the creek; its smallish, tree-ringed green can be elusive.

Hot Springs Golf Course

18 *Saint Martin Road, Carson, WA 98610. (509) 427-5150. 18 holes. 6,407 yards. Par 72. Grass tees. Course ratings: men—B69.8/113, M68.0/109; women—M73.3/119, F69.1/110. Years Opened: 1990 (original nine); 1991 (second nine). Architect: Rudy Hegewald; John Spencer (remodel). Moderate, sr. rates. Reservations: Call for weekends. Walk-on chances: Good. Walkability: Overall good, with some steep hills. Playability: Appropriate for beginning to intermediate "sticks."*

Hot Springs Golf Course is an integral part of Carson Hot Mineral Springs Resort, a health spa established in 1896. According to early records, the springs were used by local pioneers and Indians as early as 1876. Rudy Hegewald bought the resort (then called Saint Martin's Hot Springs) in the 1970s. He was the architect and builder of the course, opening the front nine in 1990 and the back the next year. Hegewald's son-in-law, John Spencer, fine-tuned the design over the next couple of years. Hegewald died in mid-1994; in fall of that year his survivors sold the 280-acre facility to a Korean, Gapdo Park, for $3 million. Park announced plans for a 100-room hotel and a restaurant; he's also planning improvements to the course.

Lined by a few homes, the layout sweeps across a promontory above the hot springs and Columbia Gorge. There are nice views of Wind Mountain to the east. The site was once a dense forest, but all the trees were removed prior to construction. Since opening, over 1,000 trees have been planted along fairways, with bunkers and water hazards also added. An irrigation pond on the back nine has a fountain that spews 105-degree naturally-heated water, the same as produced by the spa. The water is cooled to 60 degrees before being piped through the irrigation system. Rich in minerals, the water makes the turfgrass strong and wiry, resulting in great lies.

Interesting holes include the 1st, a 527-yard par-5 that runs uphill past the driving range along the right. A small bunker lurks along the right edge of the fairway, which rises to a raised, dome-shaped green. The 1st green is typical of the old-style putting surfaces at Hot Springs. These two-foot-high, toadstool-like affairs crest in their midsections, then slope toward the aprons. The 10th, a 480-yard par-5, runs straight and uphill along a well-bunkered path to a small, bi-trapped green. The 11th, a 542-yard par-5, skirts fairway traps along the right en route to a rolling green bunkered laterally. The 13th, a 267-yard par-4, has water off the tee and a small pond left-front of its bi-trapped green. Though straight and minus many hazards, the top-rated 15th, a 415-yard par-4, is tough because it plays into a head wind.

Husum Hills Golf Course

9 *820 Highway 141, Bingen, WA 98605. (509) 493-1211 or 1-800-487-4537. Gary Tamietti, pro. 9 holes. 2,631 yards. Par 35. Grass tees. Course ratings: men 63.7/96, women 67.6/104. Year Opened: 1964. Architect: Bob Meresse. Economical, credit cards. Reservations: Call a week ahead. Walk-on chances: Good. Walkability: Some hills, but walker-friendly overall. Playability: Fun course enjoyed by all golfers.*

Public Husum Hills overlooks the Columbia River six miles north of Highway 141, and offers striking views of Mount Adams. The 56-acre course is partly owned by its golf pro, Gary Tamietti, a resident of San Clemente, California. Tamietti tried to sell the course in 1994. A local developer interested in buying it wanted to shut down the golf operations and convert Husum Hills into a subdivision. When that deal fell through, Rick and Jamie Graves of Husum and Don and Heidi Struck of

THE NORTHWEST GOLF GALLERY

The Columbia River skirts Lake Woods Golf Course in north-central Washington.

The downhill, dogleg-right 16th hole at Spokane Country Club, a 561-yard par-5, ends at a rolling green ringed by bunkers and trees.

Previous Page: *Early-morning fog shrouds Madrona Links in Gig Harbor.*

Located in Eastern Washington wheat country, Harrington Golf & Country Club offers such holes as the 7th, a 140-yard par-3 with a pond- and bunker-guarded green.

A rainbow arcs behind Crosswater's 9th hole, a 456-yard par-4.

The verdant route of Eagle Ridge's 337-yard, par-4 3rd is lined by lava outcrops and colorful desert flora.

A good-sized pond protects the green at Bend Country Club's 3rd, a 186-yard par-3.

A glimpse down one of the corridor-like fairways at Laurel Hill Golf Course in Gold Hill, Oregon.

A view across the sporty putting course at Desert Canyon Golf Resort.

Golfers encounter an assortment of hurdles at Stoneridge Golf Club in Eagle Point, Oregon. Water is the major concern at the 7th hole, a 400-yard par-4.

The green at Pleasant Valley's 6th, a 376-yard par-4, is fronted by a pond.

Flathead Lake and mountains loom north of Polson Country Club. Shown here is Polson's 10th, a 495-yard par-5.

Prineville Golf & Country Club sports such holes as the water-lined 7th, a 155-yard par-3.

Fall color brightens the scene at Yakima Country Club. Shown here is the 17th, a 190-yard par-3.

One of the many tough holes encountered on McCormick Woods' front nine is the 4th, a 227-yard par-3.

Creekside in Salem features such challenges as the 4th hole, a 480-yard par-5.

An early-morning storm heads toward Trysting Tree Golf Club in Corvallis, Oregon.

Seattle's skyscrapers soar behind West Seattle's 12th, a narrow and rolling, 515-yard par-5.

Lake Washington is on full view from Sand Point Country Club's 18th green.

Though known for its rampant water hazards, Homestead also has plenty of bunkers, as evidenced by the 421-yard, par-4 10th hole.

Useless Bay's opener, a 531-yard par-5, angles uphill to the right.

Maple leaves dot the 347-yard, par-4 4th hole at Bellingham Golf & Country Club.

The 16th hole at Spokane's Creek at Qualchan course is a difficult 472-yard par-5.

One of Meriwood's prettier tests is the 2nd, a 197-yard par-3.

Big Sky Country is in its full glory at Eagle Bend in Bigfork, Montana.

The park-like Oswego Lake Country Club has many beautiful holes. Shown here is the 183-yard, par-3 3rd.

Western views from Gallery Golf Course on Whidbey Island take in Puget Sound and the Strait of Juan de Fuca. Shown here is Gallery's 152-yard, par-3 6th.

Quail Ridge's 9th, a 328-yard par-4, typifies the hilly Clarkston layout.

The lush Lewis River Golf Course in Woodland, Washington, boasts such lovely holes as the 7th, a 189-yard par-3.

Towering above Caledon's sylvan setting is snow-capped Mount Pilchuk.

White Salmon purchased a 50-percent share (with Tamietti owning the other half), thus ensuring that the site remains dedicated to golf. The Strucks, the Graveses and Tamietti have made several improvements since the ownership change, including paving the parking lot, entry road and cart paths. They've also added some drainage ditches and bridges. Upcoming plans include redoing the ladies' tees.

The nine-hole venue lies near a Columbia Gorge area considered one of the best places in the world to windsurf. Sailboarders from around the globe flock to this corner of the U.S., with some finding their way to Husum Hills, boards mounted to car roofs. Most mornings are calm at the course, with the wind picking up in the afternoons. Other local outdoor activities include camping and hunting, and steelhead, salmon and trout fishing. The course is frequented by deer, rabbits, and wild turkeys, with black bears and coyotes inhabiting peripheral forests.

As its name implies, the track spans up-and-down topography, with many fairways proferring awkward lies. The dual-tee nine extends 5,136 yards over two circuits. Particularly tough holes include the 1st, a 498-yard par-5 that runs straight over rolling ground to a small green. The 2th, a 453-yard par-5, heads directly to a long, skinny green with steep sides.

Lower Valley Golf Club - semiprivate

18

31 Ray Road, Sunnyside, WA 98944. (509) 837-5340. Craig Thomas, pro. 18 holes. 6,635 yards. Par 72. Grass tees. Course ratings: men—B70.2/112, M68.4/108, women—M74.2/118, F70.6/111. Years Opened: 1950s (original nine); 1995 (second nine). Architects: Founding members (original nine); Rambo Construction (second nine). Moderate, credit cards. Reservations: Call a week ahead. Walk-on chances: Fair. Walkability: Flat course is easy to walk. Playability: Well-treed original holes mixed in with wide-open newer nine.

Recently-expanded Lower Valley lies on the edge of Sunnyside by an Elks Club and Interstate 82. For years a nine-hole venue, Lower Valley received another set of holes in May 1995. The member-owners of the course hired Rambo Construction of Yakima to design and build the addition. Besides a full-blown 18-holer, semiprivate Lower Valley Golf Club enjoys a nice driving range and a full-service restaurant and bar. The venue is overseen by head pro, Craig Thomas, who's helped in the pro shop by his wife, Kathy. The Thomases have observed increased play since the course was expanded.

New and old holes were intermingled, with Rambo's nine—located on flat and treeless rangeland to the east—readily differentiated from the originals. Though seedlings have been planted here, they're a long way from impeding play. Power lines cross the new holes, which end at mostly contourless greens. Among the better tests is the new 6th, a 525-yard par-5 that runs straight. A pond sits right of the tee, and a road and OB line the hole along the left. Over its last 100 yards, the 6th curls rightward around a pond to a large, right-rear-sloping green. The 9th, a 186-yard par-3 from the original course, is a pretty hole that involves a tee shot over a pond to a steeply front-sloping green trapped on the left.

The 13th, a 555-yard par-5, is a wide dogleg-left; a pond lurks 50 yards from the right-front edge of another steeply front-tilting putting surface. Lower Valley's top-rated hole is the 573-yard, par-5 14th, a descending dogleg-left that winds around a pond. At the turn, the fairway stretches toward a mid-sized green with two tiers. The

15th, a 436-yard par-4 and one of the best-designed of the new holes, has a wide fairway that skirts a pond along the left. The pond runs up to the left-front edge of a planar, raised green. The 16th, a 460-yard par-4, completes Lower Valley's triad of back-nine monsters. The straight and flat 16th is lined by a trench along the left, and has a large green backed by a berm.

Mount Adams Country Club - semiprivate

18 *1250 Rocky Ford Road, (Off Highway 97), Toppenish, WA 98948. (509) 865-4440. Scott Galbraith, pro. 18 holes. 6,341 yards. Par 72. Grass tees. Course ratings: men 70.6/121, women 73.6/126. Year Opened: 1926 (original nine); 1967 (second nine). Architects: Members. Moderate, jr. rates, credit cards. Call for reservations. Walk-on chances: Fair. Walkability: Good. Playability: Length and some tight fairways create honest challenge.*

Historic Mount Adams Country Club lies south of Toppenish off Highway 97. Golf in the Lower Yakima Valley began in 1923 when this club was founded by Horace Woodard Sr., Dr. George Wimberley and Len Dornan. For the first three years the 50 or so members golfed on a parcel just east of the Seigel Packing Plant on nearby La Rue Road. The salt grass fairways ended at sand greens; the sand was treated with oil to make it smooth and prevent it from blowing away. Cattle were loosed on the course in summer to keep the grass low, causing locals to refer to the sport of golf as "Cow Pasture Pool." Acreage for the current site was acquired in 1925, and a nine-hole course was built by members the next year. Animals were an integral part of Mount Adams course in its early years. Besides the fairway-grazing cows, there were cats and dogs as well as chickens, which were sold to the golfers by one of the caretakers.

In the years before grass putting surfaces were planted in 1952, Mount Adams hosted the Washington State Sand Greens Tournament. Ken Fields of Yakima, the winner in 1951, holds the distinction as being the state's last "sand greens champion." The grass putting surfaces became feasible when an irrigation system was installed by the farmer-members. In the early 1950s, green fees were 75 cents on weekdays and $1 weekends. Dues for a married couple were $24 a year. In 1966, the members bought 70 acres of sagebrush land east of the course and built another nine holes.

When the full 18 came into play in 1967, the members began looking forward to the day when a new clubhouse could be built. Those dreams came to fruition in early 1996 when a $310,000 clubhouse was completed. Funding for the structure was raised through the sale of 21 homesites, which are being developed along the 6th and 17th holes. With the newly expanded clubhouse, the lots and an enlarged parking lot taking up portions of the original course, a new 9th hole was built. The revised hole—once a straightaway 316-yard par-4—is now a 290-yard dogleg-right.

Surrounding the semiprivate venue are the row crops and fruit orchards endemic to the Toppenish, Wapato and Zilla area. Mount Adams generally enjoys more moderate weather and a longer golf season than nearby courses. Its primary challenge comes from lengthy fairways lined by willows, maples, poplars, fruit trees, Russian olives, locusts (also called trees of Paradise), and blue, mountain and green ashes. Siberian elms that were on the property before the original nine was built were hand-irrigated by members, who kept the trees alive in broiling summers by hauling water to them with teams of horses. Quails, deer, great horned owls and pheasants often alight on these lush fairways.

Among the tougher tests at Mount Adams is the 2nd hole, a par-5 of 465 yards that runs past a billowing willow to a trapped-right green fronted by a swale. The top-rated 11th, a 415-yard par-4, is a rolling dogleg-left that follows a tree-lined path to a ditch-fronted green. The 12th, a 581-yard par-5, ventures over ridges and swales en route to a front-sloping green. The 13th, a 539-yard par-5, is a virtual mirror-image of the 12th: a lengthy and straight hole punctuated by rises and falls before reaching a raised, bi-level green.

Quincy Valley Golf Course

1705 5 NW, Quincy, WA 98848. (509) 787-3244. Bill Porter, pro. 18 holes. 5,979 yards. Par 70. Grass tees. Course ratings: men—B67.3/101, M67.0/100; women— M74.0/117, F69.0/107. Years Opened: 1989 (original nine); 1996 (second nine). Architects: Charles & Rob Anabel (original nine); Rob Anabel & Ed Paine (second nine). Moderate, jr./sr. rates, credit cards. No reservations. Walkability: Good. Playability: Wide-open fairways have some sneaky water hazards.

Family-run Quincy Valley is five miles south of Quincy, off Highway 281 at White Trail Road (also called 5 NW). The course is owned and operated by the Annabels—Charles and Lenora, and their son Rob, who serves as the greens superintendent. After purchasing the 140-acre site in 1988, the family immediately began work on a nine-hole golf course. It went so well that by June 1996, the Annabels opened another nine holes. The family saw an immediate jump in rounds with the expanded course.

The Annabels are also developing 95 lots along White Trail. The small lots are designed for "park model" homes, which range from 400- to 1,300-square-feet in size. Quincy Valley head pro, Bill Porter, was a regular on the Nike Tour in the early and mid-'90s. The Quincy native fell short in his efforts to qualify for the PGA Tour in 1995 and '96, and will play the Nike Tour part-time while giving lessons at his home course when his schedule permits.

Quincy Valley lies in an area that gets less wind and rain than Quincy proper. It's occasionally washed by breezes off the nearby Colockum Range, the only mountain chain in the Cascades that runs east to west. The long and skinny site is 300 to 500 yards wide and a mile long; the new holes occupy the western end. Unlike the original nine, which is watered by an above-ground pivot irrigation system (that will be replaced in the future), the newer side has computerized underground sprinklers. The new and old nines will be separated if and when a new clubhouse is built at the center of the Annabel's parcel. As it now stands, the front nine contains three new holes and six originals, with the back having six of the new holes. Rob Anabel and Ed Paine co-designed the new 4,000-square-feet bentgrass greens. Scrub growth and sagebrush separates the bluegrass fairways, each of which contains three tees. Players should be concerned with ponds on several holes.

Skamania Lodge Golf Course

18 *Skamania Lodge Way, Stevenson, WA 98648. (509) 427-2541 or 1-800-293-0418. Guy Puddefoot, pro. 18 holes. 5,776 yards. Par 70. Grass tees. Course ratings: men— B68.9/127, M66.7/122; women—M70.7/126, F65.2/115. Year Opened: 1993. Architect: Gene "Bunny" Mason. Moderate, jr. rates, credit cards. Reservations: Call two weeks ahead. Walk-on chances: Fair. Walkability: Though carts are not required, they're recommended because of some long green-to-next-tee distances and hills. Playability: Shortness of course belies its difficulty.*

Etched within dense woodlands beside upscale Skamania Lodge, this course sits on a bluff above the Columbia River near Stevenson, off Highway 14. The lodge contains 195 rooms, a 12,000-square-foot conference center, restaurant, tennis courts and fitness center. Also on the premises are equestrian facilities and hiking trails, which wind throughout the grounds, including parts of the golf course. The $24.5-million project was co-developed by the U.S. Forest Service—which operates an interpretive center in the lodge, Skamania County and Grayco Resources. In August 1996, the resort was sold to Yarmouth Group, Inc., a New York-based real estate investment company.

The course at Skamania Lodge was previously named Bridge of the Gods after a historic steel bridge over the nearby Columbia. It caters to overnight guests and the business types attending seminars at the conference center. The 100-acre layout encompasses a 240-foot elevation change, so players here might want to ride a motorized chariot. Wildlife visitors include deer, elk, beavers, herons and eagles. Nice touches include 10-minutes-apart starting times, clean and modern on-course bathrooms, plentiful water fountains, and fully-equipped carts. Benches along the way serve as viewing areas for the Columbia River and Red Bluff, a precipice to the northwest.

The narrow fairways are lined by feral rough and have fat trees in target zones. You'd better hit the ball straight—or into intended spots—for any chance of success at the restrictive track. Since much of the play is by infrequent golfers staying at the lodge, the course may be the "lost-ball capital of the Northwest." Among its tougher holes is the 3rd, a 371-yard par-4. From the elevated tee, drives should be placed to the right side of a wee tee-shot landing area pinched by trees on the left. The hole then descends toward a large left-sloping green perched on a stone base and guarded right by a pond. The corridor-like 4th, a 477-yard par-5, runs steeply uphill over a left-curling, left-tilting route. The hole tightens considerably over its last 75 yards before reaching a deep-but-narrow, trapped-left green. The top-rated 8th, a 410-yard par-4, harbors a dogleg-right fairway that's just a bit wider than the adjoining cart path. The wood-paneled hole concludes at a small green that leans left toward a bunker.

The 13th, a 330-yard par-4, features a beautiful elevated tee that offers vistas of the Columbia River. The tiny landing area at the 13th is squeezed by detritus and pot bunkers, and its large, saddle-shaped green is trapped left-front. The 16th, a 463-yard par-5, starts at a canyon-fronted tee. The narrow path rises slightly as it passes dense jail along the right. At the 150-yard mark, the route bends leftward to a good-sized, tree-ringed green positioned behind a hillock. A tree at the right-front makes the 16th green an elusive target. The lodge sits off to the left of the 18th, a 370-yard par-4 whose descending fairway skirts rocks and trees right and OB left. A bunker squats in mounds along the right of the home hole which, over its final 100 yards, curls leftward to a kidney-shaped green trapped left-rear.

Sun Country Golf Resort

9

Golf Course Road, Cle Elum, WA 98922. (509) 674-2226. 9 holes. 2,861 yards. Par 36. Grass tees. Course ratings: men 68.8/119, women 70.9/124. Year Opened: 1970. Architects: Course founders; Gaylord Riach (remodel). Economical. Reservations: Call a week ahead. Walk-on chances: Good. Walkability: Fair, with some steep between-hole hills. Playability: A bit rough around the edges, course involves plenty of trouble along the way.

Nine-hole Sun Country is off Interstate 90's Golf Course Road exit (once called East Nelson Siding Road), west of Cle Elum. Closed from October to mid-April each year, the course spreads over a portion of a 200-acre resort which has been owned by Gaylord and Ella Riach since 1974. Their son, Ken Riach, manages the place. Besides the course, Sun Country has an RV park and cabins. In early 1996, the Riachs announced plans to open an inner-tubing hill for winter use when the course is covered in snow.

The dual-tee layout stretches 5,671 yards over two circuits, crossing a valley floor and a hill that creates some impressive elevated tees. Though on the short side, Sun Country can play tough, with westerly winds off the Cascades skewing shots into peripheral peril. Flat lies are hard to find, and the greens are small. While playing this up-and-down track, golfers might espy elk, deer, an occasional bear and Canada geese. Tough holes include the par-5 1st, a 460-yard dogleg-left that winds around the clubhouse and a grove of trees. Water and OB line the fairway along the right before it ascends to a green cut into a berm. The 6th, a 115-yard par-3, sports an elevated tee and a small putting surface backed by two ponds. The 7th, a 455-yard par-5, runs long and straight after passing a pond off the tee. Out-of-bounds and dense woods line the left edge of the 7th, and telephone wires cross the hole diagonally.

Suntides Golf Course

18

231 Pence Road, Yakima, WA 98908. (509) 966-9065. Paul Cobleigh, pro. 18 holes. 5,934 yards. Par 70. Grass tees. Course ratings: men—B66.4/110, F63.7/105; women—B72.4/116, F69.2/112. Year Opened: 1965. Architect: Joe Grier. Moderate, jr. rates, credit cards. Reservations: Call Wednesday for Fridays & weekends. Walk-on chances: Fair. Walkability: Quite good, except during Yakima's hot spells. Playability: Suitable for all skills.

Well-tended Suntides, located northwest of Yakima off Highway 12, butts against the rocky base of Selah Heights. The popular facility is owned by Wally Johnson, under the auspices of his company, Suntides, Inc. In recent years, Johnson has installed RV sites along Pence Road, a move that has attracted more traveling linksters. Other improvements include a new ladies' tee at the 9th hole. In summer 1997, a new 18-hole grass putting course came on line. The putting layout, designed by head pro Paul Cobleigh, lies on a two-acre parcel between the RV park and a grocery store. Future plans include an updated irrigation system and perhaps an all-new clubhouse.

Suntides was designed by Joe Grier, a long-time head pro at Yakima Country Club who retired in 1961. While I was growing up in Yakima in the mid-1960s, Suntides quickly became one of my favorite haunts soon after it opened. Since that time, the course's pine trees have grown considerably, though the fairways are still amply girthed to generally forgive bad shots. Irrigated by water from the Roza Irrigation District, this lush layout vividly counters its arid surroundings.

Among the more interesting holes at Suntides is the 8th, a 540-yard par-5 that winds yawningly between a fenced-in cow pasture and a creek. The creek winds across the hole about 125 yards from a front-sloping, laterally-trapped green. The 12th, a par-4 of 364 yards, doglegs left off an elevated tee at the base of Selah Heights. The landing area is squeezed along the left by a creek and tall grass, with trees right. Traps guard both sides of the small 12th green. The 17th, a slightly uphill par-3 of 232 yards, has a raised green bordered along the right by water. With any headwind, this hole should be a par-4.

Westwood West

9 *6408 Tieton Drive, Yakima, WA 98908. (509) 966-0890. 9 holes. 2,691 yards. Par 35. Grass tees. Course ratings: men 64.9/107, women 69.1/110. Year Opened: 1964. Architect: M.F. "Curley" Hueston. Moderate, sr. rates. Reservations: Call a week ahead. Walk-on chances: Fair. Walkability: Like a stroll through an apple orchard. Playability: Great place for beginners.*

Situated on the south side of Tieton Drive, this course is in Yakima's ever-expanding West Valley. While a kid growing up in a neighborhood on Westwood West's east side, I'd sneak onto the course and play a few holes before being shooed off by the cantankerous Curley Hueston, Westwood West's designer and first pro. When opened in 1964, the course was touted as only the second golf course in America built within an apple orchard. Though that distinction no longer applies, it was fun golfing here in the fall, smacking apples that had fallen on the ground.

The course was developed by Westwood West Corporation—headed by Bob Schultz, which still owns it. The site was part of Congdon Orchard's once-vast apple empire, most of which has since been sold off and converted into housing tracts. Westwood West spans 5,378 yards over two circuits, and is a good training ground for juniors and beginners. Among its more entertaining holes is the 284-yard 4th, a downhill par-4 with a reachable green ringed by apple trees. Perhaps the toughest test is the 395-yard, par-4 7th. The tree-lined hole has a straight fairway that runs past houses and OB along the left to a raised and slick green.

Private Courses

Yakima Country Club

18 *500 Country Club Drive, Yakima, WA 98901. (509) 452-2266. Jim Gilbert, pro. 18 holes. 6,477 yards. Par 71. Grass tees. Course ratings: men—B70.7/123, M69.4/120; women F72.6/126. Year Opened: 1915 (original nine); 1956 (second nine). Architects: Francis L. James (original nine); members (second nine); Ted Robinson & John Steidel (remodels). Members, guests & reciprocates.*

Yakima Country Club sits atop a promontory, providing outstanding vistas of the Yakima Valley. The 18-hole layout is positioned amid houses, hop fields and fruit orchards in the Terrace Heights section of east Yakima. Rivaling Spokane Country Club in terms of maturity, conditioning and amenities, the 180-acre club has a nice driving range, a clubhouse with a restaurant and bar, tennis courts and a swimming pool.

The original Francis James-designed nine was built in 1915, with the second set of member-designed holes coming on line four decades later. Ted Robinson oversaw some remodeling work in 1974 and, in the 1990s, architect John Steidel did further renovations. When I visited Yakima Country Club in October 1995, I was struck by the wonderful condition of its turf and the ample size of the bunkers. Due to the course's lofty perch, golfers encounter many odd-angled lies, with target lines requiring compensation on some of the more tilted routes.

Among Yakima's top tests is the 2nd, a 517-yard par-5 that doglegs right around a pond. The fairway curls harder to the right once past the water hazard, while passing OB along the left. A fat bunker sits 40 yards from the right-front edge of the small, left-sloping 2nd green, which is trapped twice. The top-rated 3rd, a 440-yard par-4, runs straight and slightly uphill between trees and a bunker along the left. The fairway eventually ascends to a hill-cut, steeply front-tilting green trapped on the right. An interesting hole is the uphill 6th, a 152-yard par-3 with a large, rolling green trapped on the right.

The 7th, a 380-yard par-4, winds left around a pond, skirting a series of bunkers outside the turn. The corner can be cut, but a tall tree on the far side of the pond grabs inferior tee shots. The steeply front-sloping 7th green has a tier in its forward third, and is trapped left and right-front. The 10th, a 390-yard par-4, starts with a beautiful elevated tee that offers western panoramas of Yakima and environs. The narrow and tree-lined fairway slopes severely left. A deep depression lies at the base of the hill-perched, prow-shaped and very slick 10th green, which tilts steeply toward the left-front. The 18th, a 433-yard par-4, has a swale-fronted tee and a fairway that ascends over a right-curling route to a two-tiered, laterally-trapped green. From here, players can glimpse the snow-capped peak of Mount Adams to the southwest.

Yakima Elks Golf & Country Club

Golf Course Road, Selah, WA 98942. (509) 697-7177. Stuart Kitzmiller, pro. 18 holes. 6,586 yards. Par 71. Grass tees. Course ratings: men—B70.8/120, F68.4/ 115; women F74.1/120. Opened: 1930s (original nine); 1940s (second nine). Architects: Members. Elks Club members, guests & reciprocates. **18**

Located on the east edge of Selah off Interstate 82, this private club is for Elks Club members and their guests. The club has been joined by more and more younger golfers in recent years. Recent course upgrades include cart paths, fairway renovations, new bunkers and attractive granite tee signs. Because of its location beside the Yakima River, the Elks layout occasionally floods. Recent inundations came in the winter of 1995-1996, when the pro shop had two feet of water and the course was covered in silt. Though many bunkers were damaged, the tees and greens were left intact. The flooding in February 1996 was particularly damaging, but the course was open for play by March. By June, the members were playing a course with all-new bunkers. Long-range plans include adding more tees.

The 180-acre layout crosses generally flat ground, with most fairways tree-lined. A feeder ditch off the Yakima enters play on five holes, with "Lake Grabenstein" creating havoc at the 14th, the course's second-toughest hole. Nice touches include a wishing well behind the 15th green; other tributes to past members are sprinkled throughout the course. Perhaps the signature features of the Yakima Elks is its small, domed greens, which are mowed low and very quick in the summer. The club's big annual tournament is the Elks Seniors, an event that draws contestants from throughout the state.

Top holes include the 3rd, a 420-yard par-4 that curls leftward past OB along the right. The hole winds around trees to a good-sized green trapped twice in front. The top-rated 4th, a 428-yard par-4, has a long and wide fairway lined on the right by OB. The fairway curls left over its last 125 yards to a raised, trapped-left green. The 5th, a 202-yard par-3, ends at a very small green guarded left by a grass bunker. The right-bending 10th, a 429-yard par-4, is tree-lined and narrow. The fairway dips down over its last 100 yards to a small, tree-ringed green bunkered at the left.

The 14th, a 452-yard par-4, is a very tough hole. The pond fronts the tee, then the fairway crosses a flat and generally wide route lined by water along its entire right edge. The 14th concludes at a steeply front-sloping green trapped laterally. The 17th, a 530-yard par-5, runs slightly uphill off the tee. The feeder creek crosses the fairway which, about 320 yards out, winds rightward to a swale-fronted, domed green trapped on both sides.

Par-3 Courses

Fisher Park Golf Course

9 *South 40th Avenue at West Arlington, Yakima, WA 98902. (509) 575-6075. Bob Hoag, pro. 9 holes. 1,354 yards. Par 27. Grass tees & mats. No course ratings. Economical, jr./sr. rates. No reservations.*

Par-3 Fisher Park is across South 40th Avenue from Eisenhower High School. Owned and operated by the city of Yakima, Fisher Park opened in June 1962. Its well-tended fairways are lined by fat 30-foot-high pines. In summer, the course is the site of the Moonlight Golf program on Saturday nights. During these evening rounds—which begin at 9:30 p.m. and end at midnight, golfers aim day-glow golf balls at flagsticks affixed with the same type of magnesium cylinder used in the balls.

As one of the state's major convention cities, Yakima draws people from throughout the United States. Those who find their way to Fisher Park often leave impressed with the course. Visiting and local golfers alike laud the venue's close-cropped bentgrass greens and lush fairways. They also enjoy the colorful flower gardens beside the tees and around the greens. The course's toughest hole is the 9th, a 191-yarder lined by South 40th Avenue along the left and trees right en route to a small, front-sloping green.

DRIVING RANGES

Harvest Valley Golf Center

530 Cherry Hills Road, Granger, WA 98932.
(509) 854-1800. Randy DuFord, pro.

Straight Arrow Driving Range

6303 East Allen Road, Sunnyside, WA 98944,
(509) 836-2270.

UPCOMING COURSES

Cle Elum — Indian John Project (1999/2000). In 1996, a Bellevue family was evaluating the feasibility of a destination-type resort on its former farm. The 1,300-acre site, located along Interstate 90 near the Indian John rest area, would include an 18-hole course and other amenities.

Dallesport — Columbia River Gorge Municipal Golf Course (1999/2000). The city of The Dalles, Oregon, which lies across the Columbia River from this small Washington town, has had serious discussions about building an 18-hole course beside the Dallesport airport. In late 1996, a feasibility study concluded that a golf course could be successful. Well-known architect, Michael Hurdzan, has drawn up a preliminary design.

Ellensburg — Stone River Project (1999/2000). In the summer of 1996, Florida golf architect Gene Bates visited this 300-acre site, which lies west of Interstate 82 on a Yakima River floodplain. Other interested parties, including Jack Nicklaus' Golden Bear International, have also talked about designing an 18-hole course for a developer who has been trying to buy the property from ranch's current owner, the Mouer family.

Moxee — Red Tail Golf Course (1999). In August 1996, two local men announced plans to build a 7,363-yard 18-hole course and 123 homes on Konnowac Pass between Moxee and Wapato. One of the proponents, Cliff James, designed the course. At the time they made known their plans, they had yet to file for permits with Yakima County.

Quincy — Monument Hill Golf & Country Club (1999/2000). The backers of this 560-acre project, who once slated a 1995 opening, encountered financial difficulties and construction was halted. Some fairways on the Jim Kraus-designed 18-hole course were routed, shaped and seeded, but the remainder of the project needs to be completed.

Quincy — Sun Valley Estates (1999). A nine-hole golf course is part of a residential-type proposal for 160 acres off Road 13 NW. Also planned are over 580 housing units and a 100-slip RV park.

Roslyn — Trendwest Project (1999/2000). In October 1996, Jeld-Wen of Klamath Falls acquired a 7,400-acre parcel from Plum Creek Timber Company for $15 million. The site between Interstate 90 and Highway 903 is south of Roslyn. A

Jeld-Wen subsidiary, Trendwest Resorts, developer of Oregon's Eagle Crest and Running Y resorts, plans a $350-million resort with at least 36 holes, hotels, restaurants, condos, chalet houses, vacation homes and recreational facilities. Trendwest submitted a permit application in March 1997 to the Kittitas County Planning Department.

Toppenish — Yakima Indian Tribe Project (1999/2000). A public 18-holer has been mentioned as a possible tourist attraction for land beside a tribal-owned casino and resort.

9

Spokane & Northeast Washington

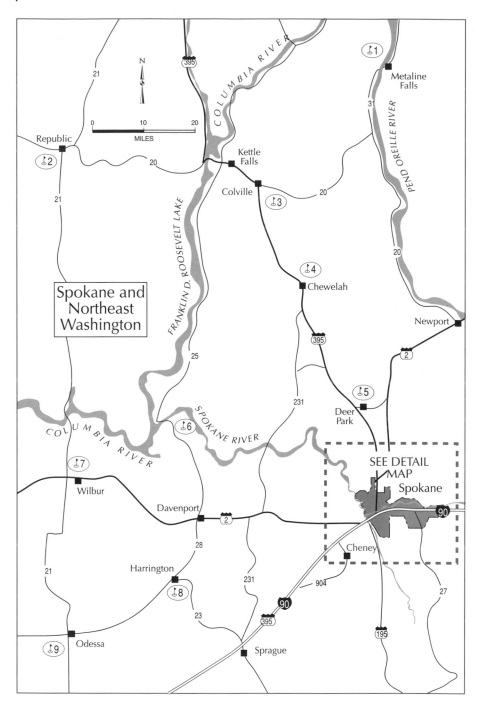

N

21

395

COLUMBIA RIVER

♨1
Metaline
Falls

31

0   10   20
MILES

Republic

♨2

20

21

Kettle
Falls

Colville

♨3

20

PEND OREILLE RIVER

FRANKLIN D. ROOSEVELT LAKE

Spokane and
Northeast
Washington

25

♨4
Chewelah

395

20

Newport

2

231

♨6

SPOKANE RIVER

♨5
Deer
Park

COLUMBIA RIVER

♨7

Wilbur

Davenport

2

SEE DETAIL
MAP
Spokane

90

28

21

Harrington

♨8

231

90

395

Cheney

904

195

27

♨9

Odessa

23

Sprague

1. **Pend Oreille Golf & Country Club** — public 9
2. **Sheridan Greens Golf Course** — public 6
3. **Colville Elks Golf Course** — public 9 & driving range
4. **Chewelah Golf & Country Club** — semiprivate 18 & driving range
5. **Deer Park Golf & Country Club** — semiprivate 18 & driving range
6. **Deer Meadows Golf Course** — public 9 & driving range
7. **Big Bend Golf & Country Club** — semiprivate 9 & driving range
8. **Harrington Golf & Country Club** — semiprivate 9 & driving range
9. **Odessa Golf Club** — public 9
10. **Wandermere Golf Course** — public 18 & driving range
11. **Pineacres Par-3 Golf Course** — public 9 (par-3) & driving range
12. **Spokane Country Club** — private 18
13. **Birdies Golf Place** — driving range
14. **Sundance Golf Course** — public 18 & driving range
15. **Esmeralda Golf Course** — public 18 & driving range
16. **Beacon Hill Golf Center** — driving range
17. **Downriver Golf Course** — public 18 & driving range
18. **Indian Canyon Golf Course** — public 18 & driving range
19. **Buckhorn Par-3** — public 9 (par-3) & driving range
20. **The Fairways at West Terrace Golf Course** — public 18 & driving range
21. **Manito Golf & Country Club** — private 18
22. **The Creek at Qualchan** — public 18 & driving range
23. **Hangman Valley Golf Club** — public 18 & driving range
24. **Painted Hills Golf Club** — public 9 & driving range
25. **Valley View Golf Course** — public 9 & driving range
26. **MeadowWood Golf Course** — public 18 & driving range
27. **Liberty Lake Golf Course** — public 18 & driving range

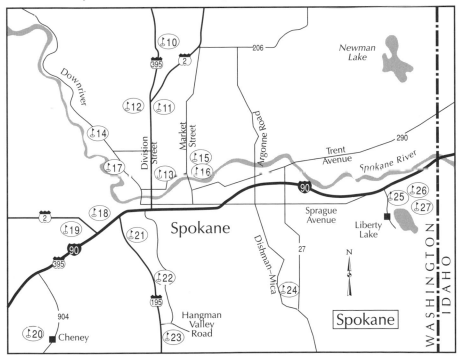

The area north of Spokane is one of Washington's most remote and least populated. Stevens, Pend Oreille and Ferry counties combined are known as Panoramaland, a region of mountainous terrain and dense forests. Spokane, the capital of the Inland Empire, has recently experienced considerable growth in new industries and population. Located in climate zones 1 and 2 and situated at approximately 2,400 above sea level, Spokane and northeast Washington enjoy four distinct seasons. The area averages 16 inches of annual precipitation, half falling as rain and half as snow. The golf season typically stretches from March 15 to November 15. Along with Portland, Spokane has the region's highest per-capita percentages of golfers. And the linksters of the Lilac City enjoy reasonably priced green fees. In 1995, *Golf Digest* gave Spokane a fifth-place rating in "America's Cities/Areas for Best Values" category. And in March 1997, the magazine extolled Spokane's many affordable golf courses in a feature article.

PUBLIC COURSES

Big Bend Golf & Country Club - semiprivate

9 *Off Highway 21 & Golf Course Road, Wilbur, WA 99185. (509) 647-5664. Kevin Wheeler, pro. 9 holes. 2,985 yards. Par 36. Grass tees. Course Ratings: men—B68.5/109, M67.4/107; women—M73.6/120, F72.5/115. Year Opened: 1964. Architects: Founding members. Economical, credit cards. Call for reservations. Walk-on chances: Good. Walkability: No problems. Playability: One of the state's best rural courses.*

Semiprivate Big Bend lies on the edge of Wilbur, a farming center in sparsely-populated Lincoln County. Appropriately, the dual-tee layout, which stretches 6,117 yards over two circuits, occupies a former farm. Nearby wheat fields reflect the area's primary industry. Most of the 120 members are farmers who often volunteer their labor and equipment to maintain the course. Big Bend opened in 1964 and, with its full-service clubhouse, remains one of Wilbur's more popular sporting and social centers. In 1997, the members hired Big Bend's second golf pro, Kevin Wheeler, a Eugene native.

I consider Big Bend one of the state's outstanding nine-hole layouts. It boasts lush close-cropped fairways watered by an automatic sprinkler system, outstanding directional signs, lovely flower gardens, and some slippery greens. The raised, radical putting surfaces have high sides and steep slopes; most greens are guarded by sand traps. Ornamental trees line most fairways, and deer and game fowl grace peripheries.

Tough holes include the 2nd, a 437-yard par-4 with a rolling, right-bending fairway leading to a wavy green. The top-rated 5th, a 468-yard par-5, has many ridges and swales along its way. After curling around a bunker, the fairway ascends to a front-sloping green trapped right-front. The 7th, a 475-yard par-5, features a left-turning route that skirts Big Bend's driving range. Once around the corner, the hole ends at a fat, trapped-left green. A pond enters play at the 8th, a 150-yard par-3 with a sizable, steep-sided green.

Chewelah Golf & Country Club - semiprivate

Sand Canyon Road, Chewelah, WA 99109. (509) 935-6807. Kim Walker, pro. **18**
*18 holes. 6,486 yards. Par 72. Grass tees. Course ratings: men—B70.9/125, M69.9/
123; women—M75.4/126, F72.7/120. Years Opened: 1976 (original nine); 1983
(second nine). Architect: Keith Hellstrom. Grass tees. Moderate, jr./sr. rates. Reservations: Call a week ahead. Walk-on chances: Fair. Walkability: Generally good
for bag-packers, with some hilly terrain. Playability: Keep the "big dog" in the bag
and you may escape (relatively) unscathed.*

This semiprivate venue north of Chewelah has undergone considerable changes
of late. Owned for years by the U.S. Department of Natural Resources, the course and
adjoining property (640 acres total) were sold to the club members in September
1995. Prior to their acquisition, the member-owners began developing 260 housing
lots on peripheral acreage; nearly 100 were sold before the end of 1996. Lot buyers
have included folks from throughout the U.S., Canada, and such distant places as
Guam. One Hawaiian bought 12 lots sight unseen after viewing a videotape of the
project. Future plans include platting another 150 lots and building a third nine. This
Jim Kraus-designed hole-set may be ready for play by 1999.

Despite its isolated locale and a small local population, Chewelah's course
gets quite a bit of play, primarily from walk-on visitors. A nearby casino has helped
bring in players, while many Spokaners wander north to northeast Washington's parks,
lakes, and this golf course off Highway 395. The layout has received several recent
improvements, including the widening of some fairways (for the sake of accelerating
play and platting housing lots), seven new tees, a new pond at the 16th hole, and
more sand traps (now totaling 30). Head pro Kim Walker, the son of MeadowWood's
Kaye Walker, says that all the improvements have helped double Chewelah's annual
rounds—from 16,000 to over 30,000.

Chewelah has a distinct Northwest flavor. Though the arrayal of homesites
has led to extensive tree-thinning, the course's claustrophobic, piney character
remains. Overhanging branches serve as canopies over sharp doglegging fairways,
and lodgepole pines in the middle or edges of target zones impede play. Tough holes
include the 3rd, a 367-yard, par-4 dogleg-left that demands an accurate drive over a
ravine. A deep swale and ball-grabbing conifers boggle second shots into a rolling
green. The 6th, a 475-yard par-5, is a tight dogleg-left, and its large green is ringed
with more ball-batting sentinels. A 433-yard par-4, the top-rated 9th is a left-bending
hole lined by a fairway bunker along the right. A pond guards the left edge of its
laterally-trapped green. The 15th, a par-5 of 520 yards, doglegs left toward a ridge in
mid-fairway. A depression fronts the 15th green, whose entry is squeezed by pines
and whose back edge bears a water hazard. A 412-yard par-4, the 18th features a long
and, for Chewelah, reasonably wide fairway. A pond along the left and a bunker right
protect the green.

Colville Elks Golf Course

9 *1861 East Hawthorne Road, Colville, WA 99114. (509) 684-5508. Andy Hite, pro. 9 holes. 3,125 yards. Par 36. Grass tees. Course ratings: men 69.5/112, women 73.1/122. Year Opened: 1950. Architects: Founding members. Economical. No reservations. Walkability: Good. Playability: Sidehill-type course offers intermediate challenge and lovely views of surrounding valley.*

The nine-hole Colville (pronounced "Cawl-vill") Elks course has been owned by the Elks Club since it opened in 1950. The venue has a charter which stipulates it remain open to the public. The layout crosses a hillside that offers golfers arresting vistas of Washington's Kettle River Range, and the Bonnington Range and Rosslan Mountains in Canada. Besides golfers, regular visitors include deer, ducks and muskrats. The deer, apparently enraptured by the sweet crabapple trees on the course, sometimes dance a damaging four-step on the greens. Occupying around 50 acres, the layout is generally quiet, though the sounds of planes from a nearby airport occasionally pierce the calm.

Colville Elks boasts short-cut greens and well-conditioned fairways. The dual-tee affair plays to a total of 6,310 yards over two circuits. There was talk about adding a back nine a few years ago, but a feasibility study concluded the bond-backed project wouldn't pan out financially. Top holes include the 6th, a 530-yard par-5 that runs over rolling terrain to a large, swale-fronted green guarded left-front by a pond. The 7th, a 175-yard par-3, is Colville Elks' prettiest hole. A sizable pond fills the space between the 7th tee and a knoll-perched, trapped-front green. A cart cul-de-sac around the tee is made of fancy brickwork, and a nearby water fountain inlaid with golf balls is home to ducks fed bread crumbs by golfers.

The Creek at Qualchan

18 *301 East Meadow Lane Road, Spokane, WA 99204. (509) 448-9317. Mark Gardner, pro. 18 holes. 6,596 yards. Par 72. Grass tees. Course ratings: men—B71.6/127, M69.9/123; women—M75.7/133, F72.3/126. Year Opened: 1993. Architect: William Robinson. Moderate, jr./sr. rates, credit cards. Reservations: Call a day ahead for weekdays & a week ahead for weekends. Walk-on chances: Fair. Walkability: Fair, with some hills and lengthy green-to-tee distances. Playability: Very challenging 17 holes plus an odd par-4.*

The Creek at Qualchan sits off Highway 195, about four miles south of the Lilac City. The facility—complete with a grass-teed driving range and a 5,800-square-foot clubhouse—occupies 225 acres in an area known as Vinegar Flats. The layout is named for Latah Creek, which crosses it, and Qualchan, a Native American warrior who was hanged nearby in 1858. The site was once a farm run by the Bruel family, and is now home for deer, blue herons, badgers, squirrels, chipmunks, waterfowl, and fish in Latah Creek. Parts of the course skirt sensitive wildlife areas, places golfers are forbade to enter.

Though a city-owned, $6-million venue, The Creek at Qualchan differs from its sister courses (Indian Canyon, Esmeralda, and Downriver) in that it boasts resort-like amenities, including tee times spaced 10 minutes apart and a stronger service orientation. It also has a two-tiered green-fees system: county residents pay less than players from outside the area. Two floods, in February 1996 and January '97, deluged the course when the Latah came over its banks, but it was restored shortly after. Besides the creek, hundreds of pine trees, 65 bunkers and five ponds impede play. Each hole has multiple tees and the ryegrass-bluegrass-fescue fairways are on the narrow side. The bentgrass greens—averaging 6,500 square feet—are generally straight-forward. In a 1997 *Golf Digest* article about Spokane's public courses, an unidentified local pro called "Qualchan" as a "six-six-six course," saying "six holes are nightmares, six are so-so, and six are outstanding." I'm not quite that skeptical; it's more like a "17-and-one layout."

Challenging holes include the 3rd, a 533-yard par-5 with a pine-dotted fairway lined on both sides by ponds. The green is concave and guarded left by a pond, with traps right and rear. The 9th, a 361-yard par-4, requires a tee shot over Latah Creek. The left-sloping fairway is flanked along the right by a jailed hillside. The 9th has Qualchan's smallest green, a mound-ringed affair trapped at the left-front. A bit shorter and with less water hazards than the front, the 3,213-yard back nine has tighter fairways and hillier terrain. Good tests include the top-rated 12th, a 451-yard par-4 with a pond-fronted tee. The narrow, ascending fairway winds between ponds. The hole is squeezed by a huge bunker 100 yards from a small, right-sloping green, which is trapped right and backed by a pine-dotted hill.

The 13th, a 334-yard par-4, is an odd hole and totally out of character from the rest of the course. The 90-degree dogleg-left falls off a promontory-perched tee, and its sheer fairway slopes steeply toward trees along the right. First-time players may aim left and drive over the trees to land on the next hole, a 171-yard par-3. A 190-yard iron shot should find a tiny landing area and be just short of the three pot bunkers outside the turn. The two-tiered 13th green has a steep right edge; along the left is a tree-covered hill. There's been talk of fixing Qualchan's 13th; let's hope it gets done.

The home hole, a 497-yard par-5, has a bunker and jail left of its right-turning route, with a bushy tree along the right. The fairway then descends to a flat and open area before arriving at a 100-foot-wide section of Latah Creek. Once here, players may opt to lay up or go over the creek. Going for the green can be a tough proposition since the fairway on the far side of the creek is 30 feet higher than the tee-shot landing area. The large, front-sloping 18th green has a knob in its right-center section, and is bunkered laterally.

Deer Meadows Golf & Country Club

9

Off Highway 28 (Route 1, Box 203), Davenport, WA 99122. (509) 725-8488. 9 holes, 3,115 yards. Par 36. Grass tees. Course ratings: men B60.0/112, F64.0/ 103; women—B73.9/125, F68.1/113. Year Opened: 1995. Architects: George Livingston & Charlie Spencer. Economical. Reservations: Call a day ahead. Walk-on chances: Very good. Walkability: Aside from the steep hill back up to the clubhouse, not bad. Playability: Good for beginners & intermediate players.

Overlooking Roosevelt Lake, nine-hole Deer Meadows lies two miles from Two Rivers Casino, a gambling concern operated by the Spokane Tribe. The course was developed by Charlie and Gloria Spencer, and George and Lura Livingston. The original site included 640 acres, but it's less now that the Livingstons left the partner-ship in September 1995. Besides nine additional holes, which may be open by 1999, the Spencers want to build a 5,000-square-foot clubhouse, 16-unit hotel, RV park and 180 homesites. As of 1996, about 100 lots had been sold to folks from Spokane, the Tri-Cities and the Washington coast.

Because of its locale at 1,500 feet above sea level and its proximity to Lake Roosevelt, rural Deer Meadows hosts all sorts of wildlife, including its namesake ruminants (which ate many seedlings after they were planted along fairways), turkeys, Chinese pheasants, quails, ducks and geese. The ducks and geese called this home when the site was an alfalfa field. The Spencers had owned the property for years before proceeding with the self-built course. Gloria owns Turf Realty, a local firm through which she's marketing the lots. Charlie, a U.S. Army vet who was part of "Merrill's Marauders" in Burma during World War II, has been a truck driver and realtor over the years. Son, Chuck E., helps with course maintenance.

Deer Meadows' golf season runs from March to October. The layout sprawls over tableland at the south end of Lake Roosevelt, and offers magnificent views of the huge basin and surrounding foothills. After visiting the course in September 1995, I concluded that the rudimentary track should improve with time as a few of the greens had not yet matured. A quirk of the course—which cannot be improved without repositioning—is the oddly-placed white-sand bunkers. These traps are away from target zones and quite far from greens.

Interesting tests include the 1st, a 335-yard par-4 with a towering hill-perched tee. The fairway curls rightward along a route paralleling the hill. Once past the mid-sized landing area, the hole rises to a severe left-sloping green with a two-foot-high tier through it. The 5th, a 540-yard par-5, is a wide dogleg-right that ends at a right-front-sloping green trapped laterally. The top-rated 6th, a 445-yard par-4, bends slightly left along a treeless path. The fairway is crossed by a small creek about 130 yards from a large green, which sits on a mesa and leans frontward.

Deer Park Golf Club

18 *1201 Country Club Drive, Deer Park, WA 99001. (509) 276-5912 or 1-800-334-6443. Craig Schuh, pro. 18 holes. 6,690 yards. Par 72. Grass tees. Course ratings: men—B71.2/114, M69.0/110, F65.2/103; women—M76.6/122, F70.0/113. Year Opened: 1996. Architect: Keith Hellstrom. Moderate, credit cards. Reservations: Call a day ahead for weekdays and Sunday for following weekend. Walk-on chances: Fair. Walkability: Good—efficient layout crosses flat ground. Playability: Plenty of hazards makes this a fine addition to the Spokane-area golf scene.*

Though open for a few days in fall 1995, this 18-hole facility officially debuted in spring 1996. The layout north of Deer Park (go east on Crawford Road from Highway 395) is part of a master-planned community that will ultimately contain 400 single- and multi-family residences. The Keith Hellstrom-designed course was built by Johnson Pacific on the site of a one-time agricultural field and fruit orchard. Odessa native, Craig Schuh, was hired as the head pro about a year before Deer Park opened. He operates out of a 4,000-square-foot clubhouse with a restaurant and lounge, and teaches on a 300-yard-deep, grass-teed driving range. Chehalis-based Warren Development purchased the project from Quantum V in September 1995, and immediately began marketing the homesites, which are suitably away from the field of play.

Deer Park sits on an underlayment of sandy loam. Unlike other courses in the area, the layout has several fairways bordered by huge waste areas. Water hazards enter play on nearly half the holes; the greens, ranging from 4,500 to 8,000-square-feet in size, are generally straightforward. When I visited Deer Park Golf Club in September 1995, the turf (bentgrass for greens, bluegrass for tees) on some holes hadn't fully knitted. However, because the project was stalled before Warren Development bought it, some of the greens had been allowed to grow for three years. In time, all the putting turf will be equal in thickness and pace.

This is Deer Park's first golf course, and it's one the 3,500 townspeople should enjoy. It's got length, plenty of hazards, and some tightness because of the waste areas. Particularly attractive is its amenability for walking. Play on the mostly flat course can be affected by wind, which comes from the south in summer and out of the north in winter. Among the more interesting holes is the 4th, a 178-yard par-3 that requires a tee shot over water to reach a mid-sized, creek-backed green. The 6th, a 538-yard par-5, winds uphill along a left-bending route to a trapped-left green. The top-rated 9th is a 424-yard par-4 that stretches out to a tri-trapped green.

Like the 4th and 8th holes, the 149-yard 13th is a water-laden par-3 that demands a well-placed tee shot to avoid a ball-drenching. The 14th, a 416-yard par-4, doglegs sharply left. A canal crosses the fairway at the turn, then a pond lines the last portion of the hole's right edge as well as the trapped-left green's right flank. Perhaps Deer Park's toughest hole is the 18th, a rolling 450-yard par-4 that runs straight to a laterally-bunkered green.

Downriver Golf Course   18

North 3225 Columbia Circle, Spokane, WA 99205. (509) 327-5269. Steve Conner, pro. 18 holes. 6,130 yards. Par 71. Grass tees. Course ratings: men B68.8/115, women—B73.7/120, M72.4/118, F70.5/114. Year Opened: 1916 (original nine); 1922 (second nine). Architect: John W. Duncan. Economical (county residents), moderate (outside of county), jr./sr. rates. Reservations: Call a day ahead for weekdays and Saturday for next weekend. Walk-on chances: Fair. Walkability: Good, except for hikes up to 9th and 18th greens. Playability: Traditional challenges—trees, tilting topography and some length—at Spokane's oldest public course.

Owned by the city of Spokane, this municipal course lies on the north side of the Spokane River within a well-established neighborhood. Indian Canyon is nearby, as is Riverside State Park (the layout's original name was Riverside Golf Course). When opened with nine holes in 1916, Downriver acted as a successor to the old Upriver Golf Links, located on the present site of Felts Field Flying Strip. Spokane's park superintendent at the time, John Duncan, layed out Downriver. Over the years the course has remained pretty much unchanged, with the bull pine trees around it growing taller. Once away from the hustle and bustle of a full-service clubhouse and driving range, the golf at Downriver is quiet and unhurried. One might hear periodic interruptions to the calm from airplanes out of nearby Spokane International Airport.

Along with the dense stands of pines and other trees, Downriver's position along a side-slope beside the Spokane lends it difficulty. Many of the par-3s are quite long, and some of the greens slope disconcertingly from front to rear. Doglegging fairways wind over sometimes-hilly terrain and between full-grown trees, which truly resemble "jails," with the trunks serving as the "bars." It doesn't have the epic scope of Indian Canyon, but Downriver is a good choice for linksters looking for an intermediate challenge while visiting the Lilac City. One of Spokane's favorite all-time golfers, Rod Funseth, grew up playing golf at Downriver.

Downriver's nines are reversed every four years or so, and most of the sand traps have been rebuilt. The course received three stars in *Golf Digest's* 1996-97 "Places to Play" guide. Notable holes include the 219-yard 3rd, a par-3 that heads straight to a green with a tree-pinched entry. The top-rated 4th is a 481-yard par-5 guarded by OB along the right. The fairway ultimately ends at a small, untrapped green. The 14th, a par-4 of 439 yards, is a long dogleg-left that knifes through trees to another rolling, unbunkered green. The 16th, a par-5 of 510 yards, has a right-bending fairway and a tilted green guarded along the right by traps.

Esmeralda Golf Course

18 *East 3933 Courtland, Spokane, WA 99207. (509) 487-6291. Bill Warner, pro. 18 holes. 6,249 yards. Par 70. Grass tees. Course ratings: men—B69.2/114, M68.2/ 112; women—M73.5/118, F71.0/112. Year Opened: 1957. Architect: Francis L. James. Economical (county residents), moderate (outside of county), jr./sr. rates. Reservations: Call a day ahead for weekdays and Saturday for next weekend. Walk-on chances: Fair. Walkability: Good. Playability: Good place for all golfers to tune up their games.*

Situated in Spokane's Hilyard neighborhood, Esmeralda is owned by the city. It was built primarily through the efforts of the Athletic Round Table, a civic- and sports-minded group in Spokane. The Round Table members—along with the Spokane park board and city council—were encouraged to build a golf course by Laurence Hamblen, president of the park commission from 1931 to 1956. The Round Table helped finance the facility with money won through a race horse named Esmeralda, as well as through slot machines scattered about the city.

Called "Essie" by locals, Esmeralda hosted the U.S. Senior Open in its first year of operation, 1957. At an opening-day ceremony attended by local dignataries and Round Table members, a mock live volcano helped make a blast of the proceedings. During the U.S. Senior Open tournament Olin Dutra set the course's competitive record of 62, a score later tied by Spokane's late, great Rod Funseth. Funseth subsequently shot Essie's unofficial record, a 60. Another feather in Esmeralda's cap was its hosting of one of the first Ladies Professional Golf Association tournaments in 1961. Esmeralda has been headed nearly since its inception by head pro, Bill Warner.

Esmeralda crosses 164 acres; the layout is flat and easy-to-walk. It offers some challenging holes and enjoyable rounds. Steady winds and the course's southern exposure result in Esmeralda having a milder climate and a longer golf season than other Lilac City courses. With its longer season, close-in location and popularity among golfers, the facility hosts about 70,000 rounds a year. Among its better holes is the 7th, a 448-yard par-4 that curls leftward to a knoll-perched green. The 16th, a par-4 of 417 yards, ends at an undulating green.

The Fairways at West Terrace Golf Course

18 *West 9810 Melville Road, Cheney, WA 99004. (509) 747-8418. Jerry Zink, pro. 18 holes. 6,398 yards. Par 72. Grass tees. Course ratings: men—B69.2/114, M67.7/ 111; women—M73.4/121, F68.4/113. Year Opened: 1987. Architect: Keith Hellstrom. Moderate, jr./sr. rates, credit cards. Reservations: Call a week ahead. Walk-on chances: Fair. Walkability: Good. Playability: Suitable for all abilities, just make sure the putting stroke is in order.*

Located west of Spokane in Cheney (take the Medical Lake exit off Interstate 90 and go east), this course is part of a planned-unit development called The Fairways, which was originated by a Canadian, Charles Klar. In addition to the

18-hole course, the community contains houses, tennis courts, and jogging and hiking trails. Residents have access to nearby lakes for all manner of water sports, and enjoy nice mountain vistas from the sloping site. The Fairways co-hosts the annual Lilac City Invitational with Downriver.

The course was designed by Spokane's Keith Hellstrom, and it was built Randy Carne of R&M Golf, a Wisconsin-based firm. Recent improvements include enhancements to the irrigation system and drainage. Fairways cross generally flat ground, with very few trees defining routes. Man-made hazards—six ponds and dozens of bunkers—are constant factors, as are powerful winds which sweep across the course in spring and fall. The Fairways boasts a local reputation for having the fastest greens in the Inland Empire. During my last visit in June 1994, some members of my foursome were aghast after three- and four-putting these slick swards.

Tough holes include the top-rated 5th, a 525-yard par-5 that bends rightward around a pond to a trapped-right green. That same pond invades the narrow 6th, a par-4 of 370 yards whose small green lies on the far side of the water hazard. The 14th, a 493-yard par-5, is a triple-dogleg (going right, left, then right again) strewn with traps of varying magnitude, including a couple around its slippery green. A par-4 of 413 yards, the dogleg-right 18th descends to a green fronted by a fat lake.

Hangman Valley Golf Club

East 12210 Hangman Valley Road, Spokane, WA 99203. (509) 448-1212. Steve Nelke, pro. 18 holes. 6,901 yards. Par 71. Grass tees. Course ratings: men—B71.9/ 126, M69.5/119; women—M76.0/125, F71.6/118. Year Opened: 1969. Architect: Bob Baldock & Son. Economical (residents), moderate (non-residents), jr./sr. rates, credit cards. Reservations: Call up to a week ahead. Walk-on chances: Fair. Walkability: Ok, with some steep hills and lengthy between-hole distances. Playability: New back tees have added yardage and challenge to course.

Hangman Valley Golf Club sprawls across 200-plus acres south of the Lilac City. Take the Hatch Road exit off Highway 195 and go five miles to find it. Hangman Valley was named for its locale, the site of the Battle of Steptoe. This 1858 clash saw U.S. soldiers trap Native Americans and hang 13 chiefs. The parched, pine-covered terrain of the area has been victimized by forest fires over the years. Though there have always been a few homes in the Hangman Hills neighborhood, more have recently popped up on a ridge west of the course.

The Spokane County-owned layout is a cut above other muni facilities. A tee-building program in the early '90s increased the course's yardage, and new cart paths have been added. The course arose through the largesse of local landowner, John Peterson Jr., who donated property for the layout in 1964. Bob Baldock & Son, an architectural firm from California, designed the track, which winds along ledge-like promontories and a valley floor crossed by Hangman Creek. The creek, ponds and dozens of bunkers vie for errant shots along the 6,900-yard track. Two floods—in February 1996 and New Year's Day '97—spread mud all over the course. The Spokane County Commissioners initially predicted Hangman Valley would be closed throughout 1997, but later said it hoped to get the course in shape by late spring of that year, just as it had in 1996.

I found Hangman Valley in excellent shape during a recent round. One problem I had, however, was being smacked by an errant drive while walking down the 1st fairway. It seems that a golfer on the tee at the 2nd hole—which parallels the 1st and runs in the opposite direction—didn't see his low slicing drive heading for me. No verbal warning was uttered. Fortunately, the ball caromed off a non-vital body part (my leg). Beware of slices while playing Hangman Valley's opener. Since the course occupies considerable acreage with adequate setbacks from adjoining holes, safety problems elsewhere are negligible.

The course's signature characteristics are its lengthy par-5s and greens invariably pinched by lateral traps. Good holes include the top-rated 5th, a 625-yard par-5 that starts at an elevated tee. A bunker sits inside the turn of the dogleg-left, which descends to a small, laterally-trapped green with jail close behind. The 8th, a par-5 of 526 yards, is lined along the right by the creek. The hole runs straight and gradually tapers before arriving at a skinny and slick green trapped on both sides.

The 10th, a 549-yard par-5, requires a tee shot that must cross the creek diagonally to reach a fairway squeezed on the left by trees. The creek lines the hole along the right. Halfway through, the 10th curls leftward between trees left and the creek and OB right. The hole then drops slightly to a domed, rolling green trapped left and right. The 12th, a 423-yard par-4, is wide and flat until the 300-yard mark; it then rises and bends to the right, while sloping left. The mid-sized 12th green is guarded in front by two bunkers and has a steep rear end. The 16th, a 606-yard par-5, starts at an elevated, pine-framed tee. The fairway descends for 250 yards, then bends rightward along a route that skirts a jailed hillside right and a bunker left. The hill-cut green is trapped twice in front and is guarded by trees left.

Harrington Golf & Country Club - semiprivate

9 *700 South 2nd, Harrington, WA 99134. (509) 253-4308. George Winn, pro. 9 holes. 3,240 yards. Par 36. Grass tees. Course ratings: men 70.1/119, women 74.6/126. Year Opened: 1962. Architect: Robert Putnam. Moderate, sr. rates, credit cards. Call for reservations. Walk-on chances: Fair. Walkability: No problems. Playability: A plenitude of hazards and excellent conditioning make this one of the Northwest's best nines.*

This course on the south end of Harrington is often mentioned as one of the region's top nine-holers. Designed by Robert Putnam, it was built in 1962 by local farmers who volunteered their labor and equipment. According to Putnam, the volunteers constructed the course closer to his specifications than many of the professional construction companies with which he'd worked. Harrington's layout was the first in the country to be funded by a farm association loan, appropriate for a golf course smack dab in the middle of wheat country.

The semiprivate venue occupies 64 acres of a former wheat farm; pheasants and quails scoot across the fairways. A few homes occupy the course's northeast edge. Most greens are surrounded by grassy mounds, and the fairways are lined by pines and willows. There are also 26 bunkers and three ponds encountered along the way. The members have considered acquiring neighboring acreage for another nine holes, but these plans are long range. The full-service clubhouse hosts many member events, and Harrington boasts a grass-teed driving range.

The dual-tee nine plays to 6,348 yards over two circuits, and is kept quite verdant by an automatic sprinkler system. The conditioning of the course is a joy to behold. Good tests include the 2nd, a 396-yard par-4 that doglegs left to a rolling green which is trapped laterally and backed by a pond. The 9th, a 158-yard par-3, has a small green squeezed by ample water and sand hazards.

Indian Canyon Golf Course

18

West 4304 West Drive, Spokane, WA 99204. (509) 747-5353. Gary Lindeblad, pro. 18 holes. 6,255 yards. Par 72. Grass tees. Course ratings: men—B70.7/126, M69.3/123; women—M74.6/130, F71.3/126. Year Opened: 1935. Architect: H. Chandler Egan. Moderate, jr./sr. rates. Reservations: Call a day ahead for weekdays and Saturday for next weekend. Walk-on chances: Fair. Walkability: Though efficiently layed out, hilly site can make for an arduous workout. Playability: Still one of the top tests in Northwest golf.

Regularly ranked in the first 25 of *Golf Digest's* "75 Best Public Golf Courses," this track continually passes the test of time, overcoming each titanium club, long-distance ball, and new-and-improved swing technique thrown at it by players. H. Chandler Egan's design for the hilly site is still inspired. Modern turfgrass maintenance practices and a supportive budget from its city of Spokane owners ensure Indian Canyon will stay that way. During a recent visit, I found the course in spectacular shape. The virtually weedless greens had just been verti-cut, so putting was exceptionally true. More significantly, I was again impressed at the course's variety of holes, its interest-piquing short and long par-4s, the many up- and downhill lies which must be mastered, and the mind-boggling shot options found on every hole. Egan's gift to Spokane will endure.

The course was built by Works Progress Administration labor between 1932-35. The site had previously been used for powwows by the Colville Confederated Tribes, thus its name. Indian Canyon opened with a red-brick clubhouse, since renovated with a fully-stocked pro shop overseen by long-time head pro, Gary Lindblad. From its perch atop a promontory, the clubhouse overlooks a lovely Spokane River valley. Hung on its walls are photos taken at the grand opening, including a neat shot of a ceremonial match between the Nespelem Indian tribe and U.S. Army officers.

The course has been the site of several prominent tournaments, including three U.S. Public Links championships. Indian Canyon hosted the PGA Tour in 1947 with the Esmeralda Open. During that event, Ben Hogan got his second Tour hole in one on the 4th hole, a 160-yard par-3. Affirming its status as one of the country's top courses, *Golf Digest* gave Indian Canyon three and a half stars in its "Places to Play, 1996-97" guide. In 1996, *Golf Digest* again recognized the course, ranking the venue sixth in its listing of the nation's "Top-75 Affordable Courses." Also that year, the course hosted the Pro Classic, a shootout involving 18 PGA Senior Tour players.

The rectangular-shaped layout is densely wooded. Its primary source of difficulty stems from narrow, tilted fairways and irregular terrain. Sundry hazards impede play, while Egan's endorsement of the risk-reward school of design is evident on nearly every hole. It's difficult to pinpoint particularly difficult holes at Indian Canyon, since so many of them are. But, if having to do so I would include the 5th, a 403-yard par-4 that runs uphill, then winds left to a rolling and tilted green. A long left-bender, the 535-yard, par-5 12th threads between woodlands to a teacup-shaped green bunkered left. The 14th, a par-4 of 443 yards, is a ditchlike dogleg-left. Rated Indian Canyon's third-toughest hole, the 14th concludes at a tiny, trapped-right green.

Liberty Lake Golf Course

18 *24403 East Sprague Avenue, Liberty Lake, WA 99019. (509) 255-6233. Bob Scott, pro. 18 holes. 6,398 yards. Par 70. Grass tees. Course ratings: men—B69.8/121, M68.7/118; women—M74.4/127, F73.0/124. Years Opened: 1930s (original nine); 1959 (second nine). Architect: M.F. "Curley" Hueston; John Steidel (remodel). Economical (residents), moderate (non-residents), jr./sr. rates, credit cards. Reservations: Call on Tuesdays for next-week tee times. Walk-on chances: Fair. Walkability: Good overall. Playability: Gradually improving with various upgrades.*

Liberty Lake's course sits next to another Spokane County-owned venue, MeadowWood, east of Spokane. Both layouts are accessible off I-90's Exit 296. Built in 1959 from a design by golf pro, M.F. "Curley" Hueston, Liberty Lake occupies a flat 112-acre parcel. An Elks Club-operated nine-holer had previously been at the site. Always a staple of Spokane's active golfing population, the track has seen its former "simple" personality complicated by the addition of ponds and bunkers, a $250,000 clubhouse remodel, and eight new greens designed by John Steidel between 1993 and 1997. Though it will probably always lack the epic scope of its neighbor, Liberty Lake has arrived as a true "player" on the local scene.

Liberty Lake's course is easy to walk and, with all the improvements, now contains an assortment of trouble spots. It also boasts two of the longest par-4s in the Northwest, the 2nd and the 5th. The 2nd, a 475-yarder that is a par-5 for women, runs straight to a mound-ringed, untrapped green. The 5th's gently rolling 463-yard fairway stretches out to a raised, trapped-right green. With MeadowWood's course bordering it along the left, the 12th, a 513-yard par-5, runs directly to a small green. The 13th, a par-4 of 386 yards, curls uphill along a right-bending route lined by three traps. A giant bunker guards the right edge of its two-tiered green. The 17th, a 432-yard par-4 rated Liberty Lake's second-toughest hole, has a big rise off the tee. Once past this juncture, the fairway expands onto a wide plateau to offer players a clear view of the green.

MeadowWood Golf Course

18 *East 24501 Valley Way, Liberty Lake, WA 99019. (509) 255-9539. Kaye Walker, pro. 18 holes. 6,874 yards. Par 72. Grass tees. Course ratings: men—B72.1/126, M70.0/122; women F73.5/131. Year Opened: 1988. Architect: Robert Muir Graves. Moderate, credit cards. Reservations: Call on Tuesday for following week. Walk-on chances: Fair. Walkability: Not bad overall, with one steep uphill hike at round's end. Playability: Tough but fair course among region's best public venues.*

Located in Liberty Lake, Spokane County-owned MeadowWood spans 150 acres of mostly flat ground, with the 17th and 18th holes going up and down a tall hill along the property's eastern edge. Known for its length and excellent conditioning, MeadowWood ranks among the Northwest's best public courses. It has all the accoutrements of top-flight facilities, with an expansive driving range (where golfers shoot lighter-than-water balls into a 10-acre pond) and a contemporary clubhouse set up to handle golfers. For all these features, MeadowWood was given a four-star— "outstanding; plan your next vacation around it"—rating in *Golf Digest's* "Places to Play 1996-'97" guide.

The course boasts over 70 bunkers and 20 acres of ponds, ample hazards by any measure. Though dotted by 750 deciduous and evergreen trees, the links-like

MeadowWood's 15th is a 377-yard par-4.

venue is dominated by hulking, fairway-bordering mounds. I last played the course in a wet and windy June storm that howled through Spokane. After temporarily escaping the sideways-moving rain at the turn, we played the back nine during a lull in the weather. On that wild day MeadowWood may have more closely met the Scottish links specifications envisioned by Graves than perhaps at any other time. Certainly golfers with "Scottish" chip-and-run skills will enjoy rolling the ball toward the pins on the big greens here.

Good tests include the 2nd, a rolling 561-yard par-5. The fairway curls between a large trap and a pair of bunkers outside the turn to a bi-trapped, bowl-shaped green. The 7th, a 524-yard par-5, doglegs sharply left around a bunker. A protozoa-shaped trap looms 40 yards from a trapped-left, front-sloping putting surface. The 11th, a 196-yard par-3, has a lake off the tee with a bunker behind it, and a shallow, trapped-right-front green backed closely by a hillock.

The top-rated 16th, a 607-yard par-5, is MeadowWood's signature hole. The behemoth goes fairly straight for nearly 525 yards before making a sharp left turn around a billowing tree and venturing up a hill. Along the first leg of the hole are mounds, traps and a lake. A large bunker lurks near the tree inside the turn, and a pond sits outside the dogleg. The terraced, cut-in-a-hillside 16th green is trapped right-front and slopes steeply to the front. The 17th and 18th, a par-3 and par-4, respectively, differ greatly from the previous 16 holes as they're hilly and set amid a dense stand of bull pines. The 17th requires an accurate shot to reach its deep and hidden green, while the right-bending, recently-redesigned 18th slides downhill to a tri-trapped putting surface.

Odessa Golf Club

Off Highway 28, Odessa, WA 99159. (509) 982-0093. 9 holes. 3,178 yards. Par 36. Grass tees. Course ratings: men B68.8/113; women—B74.8/117, F72.3/ 112. Year Opened: 1964. Architects: Local farmers. Economical, credit cards. Call for reservations. Walk-on chances: Good. Walkability: Other than a moderate hill, no problems. Playability: Quite appropriate for all golfers.

Odessa Golf Club lies on the eastern edge of its namesake town, off Highway 28. The facility is owned by Gary Valenta, who purchased it from Pete and Tracy Frigard in 1992. The Frigards got the course from Wally Hoback, who had bought it from Louis Kagele. Opened in 1964, Odessa Golf Club was built by local golfers using their own farm equipment. The city originally owned the 60-acre course, which is appended by a small clubhouse and 15 full-service RV spaces. The civic role of Odessa's course is felt during the town's Deutsches Fest, when a golf tournament is held in conjunction with other activities.

Odessa Golf Club was a replacement to Odessa's original 1920s-built course. It sits in the middle of Washington's prime wheat and bluegrass country. After moving here from Fall City, Washington, Valenta improved the clubhouse and cart storage area, in addition to planting more trees and adding fairway bunkers. Odessa's layout is generally flat, with a few hillside holes generating odd-angled stances. Odessa native Craig Schuh— winner of Spokane's 1987 Lilac City Invitational and now the head pro at Deer Park's course—holds the course's 18-hole record, a 67. Such a relatively high record tally indicates the challenge of this dual-tee track, which stretches 6,248 yards over two circuits. The course features several tough par-5s and a 200-yard par-3, and offers lovely views of Odessa Valley.

Painted Hills Golf Club

South 4403 Dishman-Mica, Spokane, WA 99206. (509) 928-4653. Scot Shagool, pro. 9 holes. 3,239 yards. Par 36. Grass tees. Course ratings: men—B/M70.2/113, M/F64.2/ 101; women—-B/M76.3/125, FF/F69.0/110. Year Opened: 1989. Architects: Mike Senske & Keith Hellstrom. Moderate, jr./sr. rates. Call for reservations. Walk-on chances: Fair. Walkability: Good. Playability: Though equipped with some wide-open fairways, course contains sundry water and sand hazards.

Painted Hills is southeast of Spokane near Liberty Lake. Surrounded by suburban neighborhoods, Painted Hills is owned by Mike Senske, who designed it with help from Keith Hellstrom. The course opened in 1989 along with a full-service clubhouse and driving range. The layout involves over a dozen sand traps and three ponds, with Chester Creek entering play at the 1st and 9th holes. Fairways are lined by pines and deciduous trees, and the greens are dome-shaped. The dual-tee track extends 6,532 yards over 18 holes.

The layout is fairly wide open, with most greens guarded by bunkers or ponds, the latter of which often lurk invisibly from afar. Good tests include the top-rated 3rd, a 421-yard par-4 with a dogleg-right fairway and a small, flat green trapped twice on the right. The 482-yard, par-5 6th winds rightward between trees to a small tee-shot landing area. The 6th green sits in a swale and is fronted by a sodded hump; from the fairway, only the top of the flagstick is visible. The 8th, a 468-yard par-5, is the women's top handicap hole as the front tee is near the tips. The dogleg-left hole curls around a hidden pond 300 yards out en route to a raised, mid-sized green with steep sides. The 9th, a 329-yard par-4, winds past OB along the left before arriving at a pond-fronted, bunker-backed green.

Pend Oreille Golf & Country Club

Off Highway 31, Metaline Falls, WA 99153. No phone. 9 holes. 2,183 yards. Par 31. Grass tees & mats. No course ratings. Opened: 1960s. Architect: Local golfers. Economical. No reservations. Walkability: Good, just don't expect much company. Playability: Cheapest green fees in the Northwest ($1 a round, $1.50 all day) priced just about right.

9

A former six-hole layout, Pend Oreille Golf & Country Club stretches over a bowl-shaped meadow off Highway 31, about a mile north of Metaline Falls. The course is one of the region's most rugged and remote places to golf. Upgraded to nine holes in the late-1980s, the track has holes ranging from a 71-yard par-3 to a 541-yard par-5. It's one of only two public venues in the Northwest—Woodburn Golf Club in Oregon is the other—with sand greens. (Don't forget to "sweep" the putting surface upon completing a hole.)

The course lies near Colville National Forest and is five miles from the Canadian border. Wildlife visitors dwelling in the surrounding forests include deer, bears and foxes. Local activities center around the great outdoors; Sullivan Lake and the reservoir behind Box Canyon Dam on the East Pend Oreille River are prime trout-fishing spots. The above green fees are paid on the honor system. Just insert a buck in the box on the outside of the quonset-hut clubhouse and go for it. The greens and fairways may be brown, but if you have the urge to golf while in this out-of-the-way corner of the state, Pend Oreille Golf & Country Club is the only place to do so.

Sheridan Greens Golf Course

380 Sheridan Road, Republic, WA 99166. (509) 775-3899. 9 holes. 2,185 yards. Par 32. Grass tees. No course ratings. Opened: 1980s. Architects: Local players. Economical. No reservations. Walkability: Good. Playability: Rough-hewn course is Republic's only golfing grounds.

9

This erstwhile six-holer was upgraded in the early '90s with three more holes. The layout borders residences and summer cabins west of the small town of Republic in the Colville National Forest. Local points of interest include a gold mine. Republic is also where the fossil imprint of a 50-million-year-old apple tree was found. The course is appended with a modest wood-paneled clubhouse with an open deck, snack bar and lounge. When no one is present in the clubhouse—which is most of the time, players insert the good-for-all-day green fees ($6 for 9, $8 for 18) in a pay box near the front door.

Sheridan Greens crosses generally flat ground, with a creek winding through or alongside four fairways. It contains holes ranging from two 110-yard par-3s to a 430-yard par-5. The layout's top test is probably the 8th, a 415-yard par-4 that winds over rolling ground to a smallish green. Despite its nearness to houses, this venue atop a forested-in meadow is decidedly quiet.

Sundance Golf Course

18 *9725 Nine Mile Road, Nine Mile Falls, WA 99026. (509) 466-4040. Ken Johnston, director of golf; Denny Johnston, pro. 18 holes. 5,960 yards. Par 70. Grass tees. Course ratings: men M67.9/112; women—FF72.9/116, F71.5/113. Years Opened: 1965 (original nine); 1966 (second nine). Architect: Del Knott. Economical, jr./sr. rates. Call for reservations. Walk-on chances: Fair. Walkability: Flat track is easy to walk. Playability: Suitable for beginners who want to graduate to intermediate challenge.*

Del Knott-designed Sundance Golf Course is owned by its director of golf, Ken Johnston. The layout began with nine holes (now used as the back) in 1965; the second set of holes opened the next year. Sundance lies about eight miles northwest of Spokane near the burg of Nine Mile Falls. Because of its locale, getting a tee time here is often easier than at Spokane's busier close-in courses.

Spokane River flows west of the course, but these waters don't enter play. Though some fairways are lined by houses, the pine tree-lined and flat track offers a quiet and relaxing round. The only water hazard enters play on two holes, and about a dozen bunkers guard greensides. Because of its generous fairways and minimal hazards, Sundance is a good place for beginning players who want to take on a mid-level course before graduating to stiffer tests.

Among Sundance's better holes is the 2nd, a 382-yard par-4 that doglegs left through trees to a large green trapped at the left-front. The fairway on the 403-yard, par-4 12th bends 90 degrees to the right around trees en route to a slick putting surface. Another right-angled hole is the 15th, a par-5 of 451 yards. After making the turn, the fairway ascends to a green bunkered left-front.

Valley View Golf Course

9 *Off Liberty Lake Road, Liberty Lake, WA 99019. (509) 928-3484. Dennis Reger, pro. 9 holes. 2,072 yards. Par 32. Grass tees. Course ratings (for local use): men 58.0, women 62.0 (no slope). Year Opened: 1973. Architects: Austin Reger & Dennis Reger. Economical, jr./sr. rates. No reservations. Walkability: Good. Playability: Though short, amply-hazardized course plays tough when winds are aloft.*

Valley View is an executive-length track designed and built by its owner and pro, Dennis Reger, and his late father, Austin. It lies off the same I-90 interchange as the Liberty Lake and MeadowWood facilities. Billed as "Spokane's only executive course," Valley View is a good choice for golfers seeking a quick fix. Though a tad over 2,000 yards long, it offers suitable challenge through an assortment of sand and water hazards. It also boasts a full-service clubhouse and a covered driving range. The course gets its name from the green hills that form a verdant valley to the south.

The loop-type Valley View layout has its first four holes going out from—and the latter five returning to—the clubhouse. With a pair of tees at each hole, the course stretches 4,095 yards over two circuits. The five par-4s on the front side (the 1st, 2nd, 4th, 8th and 9th) become three on the back side, with the 11th (220 yards) and 18th (215) transformed into difficult par-3s. Among the sterner tests is the top-rated 1st, a par-4 of 326 yards; when played as the 336-yard 10th, it's Valley View's longest hole. The 1st/10th runs straight and slightly downhill to a tilted green. The 3rd, a 148-yard par-3, has a slick green fronted by a pond. The moved-up tees at the 11th and 18th holes result in nasty par-3s. Swirling winds can make finding these greens in regulation a dicey proposition.

Wandermere Golf Course

18

North 13700 Division Street, Spokane, WA 99208. (509) 466-8023. Robert C. Ross, pro. 18 holes. 6,108 yards. Par 70. Grass tees. Course ratings: men—B68.9/109, M68.0/ 108; women—M73.5/116, F70.7/111. Years Opened: 1931 (original nine); 1948 (second nine). Architects: Robert Charles Ross (original nine); Cliff Everhart (second nine); Herb Brown & Scott Dartha (remodel). Moderate, jr./sr. rates, credit cards. Reservations: Call a week ahead for weekends and a day ahead for weekdays. Walk-on chances: Ok for singles. Walkability: Not bad overall. Playability: Redesigned holes lend contemporary scope to traditional Spokane facility.

One of Spokane's busiest courses, Wandermere crosses rolling terrain beside the Little Spokane River. The course has been operated by a member of the Ross family ever since its first nine holes opened in 1931. The original nine was designed and built by Robert Charles Ross, the grandfather of its current owner and head pro, Bob Ross. Herb Brown—Wandermere's former superintendent—is now a partner. The duo owned a total of 387 acres before the state Department of Transportation condemned 70 acres of their property to build a new Highway 395 bridge over the river. Once a financial settlement over the condemnation has been reached with the state, Ross and Brown may develop homesites and a 140-room hotel by the course.

In its early years, Wandermere was used for ice skating, tobogaing, and ski jumping in winter. In more modern times, some fairways have been converted into snowmobile tracks. At one time, the Little Spokane River was a popular summer spot for swimming and fishing. While those activities have ceased, Wandermere remains a regular haunt for many Spokaners. Combined, there are over 1,000 members in its men's and women's clubs and the course hosts over 70,000 rounds annually. Recent improvements to the 110-acre venue include expanded tees, a lengthening of the par-4 10th, and a new 17th hole. The work was overseen by Brown and greens superintendent, Scott Dartha.

The gently rolling, par-70 track contains over a dozen sand traps and several water hazards, including ponds and the Little Spokane. Tough holes include the recently lengthened 10th, now a 410-yarder with a large green backed by a pond. The 175-yard, par-3 17th requires an accurate shot over the river to reach a well-bunkered, 10,000-square-foot putting surface. The home hole, a 475-yard par-5, starts at a tree-ringed tee before going straight out for 230 yards and turning 90 degrees to the left. Tall trees lurk inside the turn, and thin creeks wander through the landing area. The 18th green is small and slick.

Private Courses

Manito Golf & Country Club

18 *4502 Hatch Road, Spokane, WA 99203. (509) 448-5829. Steve Prugh, pro. 18 holes. 6,378 yards. Par 71. Grass tees. Course ratings: men—B70.0/123, M69.2/ 120, FF66.9/116; women—FF72.3/125, F69.2/118. Year Opened: 1917. Architect: Arthur Vernon Macan. Members, guests & reciprocates.*

Located in Spokane's south end, Manito Golf & Country Club opened in 1917. The Arthur Vernon Macan-designed layout lies amid upscale homes. Sixteen holes lie east of Hatch Road, with the 14th and 15th west of the street and accessible via a tunnel. Manito's 120-acre course is appointed with a 1987-built clubhouse containing a full-service restaurant, lounge and health club. Members also have access to a grass-teed driving range. Before being named Manito's head pro in 1981, Steve Prugh was a neighborhood kid who first began working here in 1967.

The layout is noted for its large, cavernous bunkers. These old-style, greenside traps have high lips that make escaping from them difficult. Fairway bunkering is also creative, with adjoining holes sharing the same sand hazards. Manito's 9th and 18th greens are linked together; a pond virtually encircles these putting surfaces. Manito was the site of the 1945 PGA Championship, where Byron Nelson was vanquished by Jack Fleck in 36-hole match-play. After the contest Nelson said Manito's greens were the toughest he'd ever played. Other big-time events have included Hudson Cup matches, the Pacific Northwest Pro-Am, PNGA Master-40, U.S. Open Qualifying, Ladies State Championship and Washington Juniors.

Good holes include the 395-yard 1st, a narrow right-bending par-4 that curls between trees right and two large bunkers left, driving distance out. The rolling and

Manito's 18th is a difficult 351-yard par-4.

skinny 1st green is trapped right-front and left-rear, and sits at a 45-degree angle to the fairway. The 6th, a 423-yard par-4, is a classic Northwest hole that winds slightly uphill between towering pines. Mounds engird the rear and left flanks of its two-tiered, trapped-left green, which is large and slick. The 9th, a 384-yard par-4, doglegs slightly left toward a pond-fronted and steeply front-sloping green. The trapped-right-front putting surface is garnished with pretty gardens. The dogleg-right 11th, a 415-yard par-4, runs slightly uphill. A bunker lurks outside the turn at the 150-yard mark, but two towering pines at the inside corner may cause more problems. The last leg of the hole is tapered by trees as it rises to a steeply front-sloping green trapped laterally.

The 12th, a 182-yard par-3, is a lovely hole with a pond at the left-front of a massive, "L-shaped" green bunkered right-rear and rear. The putting surface has a pronounced tier in its front half, and a pot bunker lurks hidden from the tee at its right-front. The top-rated 13th, a 570-yard par-5, winds somewhat downhill along a tree-lined path. The entry to the mid-sized, front-left-sloping 13th green is squeezed by bunkers and pines left-front. The 14th and 15th—427- and 392-yard par-4s respectively—follow tight fairways squeezed by Hatch Road on the left and OB and homes right. Manito's signature hole is the 18th, a 351-yard par-4 that winds sharply right around trees. A huge bunker in a mound sits out along the left, 100 yards from a steeply front-tilting, trapped-right green. The putting surface is guarded in front and along the left by the same pond that swings around the 9th green. A severe tier runs through the 18th green, a target that can be set up for some perilous pin placements. Perhaps the toughest on this beautiful but treacherous finishing hole is on the back quarter, which tilts precipitously toward the pond.

Spokane Country Club

West 2010 Waikiki Road, Spokane, WA 99218. (509) 466-9813. Les Blakley, pro. 18 holes. 6,679 yards. Par 72. Grass tees. Course ratings: men—B71.2/126, M69.6/ 122, FF67.3/118; women—FF74.0/129, F72.0/127. Year Opened: 1911 (current course). Architects: James Barnes; Robert Muir Graves (remodel). Members, guests & reciprocates.

Spokane is the Northwest's third-oldest golf club (after Tacoma Country & Golf Club and Portland's Waverley Country Club). It was organized in 1898 and incorporated in 1904. Over its long life the club has had three different golf courses. The first, a rough nine-holer with sand greens, was near what is now 14th Avenue in the Liberty Park addition. The second was a par-36 nine on 52 acres at the present site of Lewis and Clark High School. The current course, which occupies 162 acres near the Little Spokane River, was completed in 1911.

Spokane Country Club has been home to several illustrious golf pros over the years. Its first head pro, and the designer of the current course, was James M. Barnes. Barnes won the 1921 U.S. Open, beating Walter Hagen by nine strokes, as well as the 1925 British Open. After Barnes left in 1911 to become Tacoma's golf pro, Tom Hughes, Jack Findlay, Joe Novak and Martin Watson followed. In 1932, Roy Moe began a 40-year stint at the club near Whitworth College. Gene Carbery became Spokane's pro in 1963, and the likable Les Blakley is the current head professional.

Among the more prominent golfers from Spokane Country Club are Al Mengert (National Junior Champion in 1946 and 1947, and Walker Cup member); Marvin

"Bud" Ward (U.S. Amateur champion from 1939 to 1941, Western Amateur winner in 1940, 1941, and 1947, and Walker Cup member 1938-1947); the inimitable Rod Funseth; top women players Bess Riegel, Betty Jean Rucker, Connie Guthrie (the first woman ever to earn a letter on Gonzaga's men's varsity golf team) and Peggy Conley (Curtis Cup member 1964-68).

Big tournaments at Spokane have included the first-ever U.S. Women's Open in 1946 (won by Patty Berg), several PNGA championships, and the U.S. Juniors. Annual events include a senior tournament the weekend after the Fourth of July, and the gala Spokane Country Club Invitational also in July. Every four years the course hosts the Spokane Junior League Golf Clinic and Exhibition. The highlights of this event occur when youngsters receive lessons from PGA stars such as Arnold Palmer, Jack Nicklaus, Lee Trevino and Tom Watson, the latter of whom holds the course record of 64.

Spokane's course enjoys a wonderful variety of holes and exceptional conditioning. The Barnes' design benefited from a major remodel by Robert Muir Graves in 1988. Its locale beside the Little Spokane lends it a quiet serenity, and enables visits from sundry wildlife. During a visit in September 1995, I observed a fox cross nonchalantly before me on the first fairway. Spokane has wonderful greens which, though slick, putt very true. The care given the place is evidenced at every turn, with colorful flower gardens, huge ornamental trees and other landscaping enhancements. Members dedicated the 9th hole, a lovely 187-yard par-3, to Norris R. Beardsley, Spokane's greens superintendent from 1936 to 1989 and the man who set the standard for the course's manicured state.

Among Spokane's toughest holes is the 3rd, a 501-yard par-5 that runs uphill and straight; the last 150 yards are squeezed by trees. Access to the green is pinched along the left by a towering vine-covered pine. The V-shaped putting surface is trapped right-front and left-rear. The 4th, a 446-yard par-4, heads downhill past bunkers along the right. A fat olive tree—with a branch-veiled pond behind it—pinches the right-hand entry to a large green, which sits in a hollow and is trapped right and rear. The top-rated 8th, a 524-yard par-5, starts at a pond-fronted tee and then rises between trees and a bunker along the right. Towering pines gradually narrow the hole, with trees on the left squeezing access to the saddle-shaped, ridge-perched 8th green, a laterally trapped affair fronted by a depression.

Most of the back nine crosses a promontory above the clubhouse; a tram takes ambulating golfers up to the 10th tee. This hole, a 516-yard par-5, is a sharp dogleg-right that winds around trees and a duck-filled pond about 175 yards out. Traps guard both sides of its small, front-tilting green. The 215-yard, par-3 11th has a tough target in its deep-but-skinny, laterally-trapped green. The 12th, a 554-yard par-5, ascends over a right-turning path that passes bunkers right. More traps are found along the right and center of the fairway, 125 yards from a bunker-ringed green. The pretty 14th, a 420-yard par-4, winds leftward around trees; a bunker squats on the far side of these woods. The large, kidney-shaped green is trapped both sides.

Special mention goes to the 16th, a 561-yarder rated Spokane's second-toughest hole. The par-5 features an elevated tee where drives must be lofted over the club's entry road. The hole demands a decent opening shot to be able to peek around trees at the corner of the right-turning route. A fat bunker along the left shrinks the landing area. The fairway then descends steeply between trees and OB right and homes (the only houses on the course) and OB left. Downhill stances are the norm for approach shots to the tree-ringed 16th green, a bi-level affair trapped twice in front and once left. One of the region's handsomest par-3s is Spokane's 17th, a 196-yarder with nine tees stepping down a hillside. Tee shots must find a rolling green guarded closely at the left-front by a pond, with a bunker and a trap along the right. Views from the green back up to the tees find waterfalls spilling into small ponds, with flower gardens also adding beauty to the setting.

Par-3 Courses

Buckhorn Par-3

West 13404 Highway 2, Airway Heights, WA 99010. (509) 244-3650. 9 holes. 907 yards. Par 27. Grass tees. No course ratings. Economical. No reservations. Driving Range.

This par-3 layout lies west of Spokane on the south side of Highway 2 near Fairchild Air Force Base. Besides a tidy nine-hole track, the facility has a small pro shop and lighted driving range. Buckhorn's plot is less than 10 acres, and it's a good choice for families and youngsters learning the game.

Pineacres Par-3 Golf Course

11912 North Division, Spokane, WA 99218. (509) 466-9984. Jim Tucker, pro. 9 holes. 760 yards. Par 27. Mat tees. No course ratings. Economical, jr./sr. rates. No reservations. Driving Range.

Opened in 1960, Pineacres is owned by golf pro Jim Tucker, who bought it from Ed Coture in 1974. A driving range was added in 1965. One of Spokane's more popular practice venues, the range has trees that simulate fairways, and several target greens. The course occupies 20 acres of a dense stand of Ponderosa pines, and is generally open from April through October. Although it was once equipped with lights and open until 11:30 at night, the par-3 track is now open only during daylight hours.

Tucker, a Class A PGA professional, conducts lessons at the range. When he first took over Pineacres, the facility was dangerously close to bankruptcy. Since then, Tucker has turned Pineacres into a profitable business. The course has hosted the Pineacres Open each autumn since 1978. At this event local pros and top amateurs compete for a $2,500 purse on a tight par-3 nine with holes from 62 to 115 yards in length, and postage-stamp greens.

Driving Ranges

Beacon Hill Golf Center
4848 Valley Spring Road, Spokane, WA 99207.
(509) 482-0622. Ken Gustafson, pro.

Birdie's Golf Place
1111 E. Westview Court, Spokane, WA 99218.
(509) 468-5000. Clint Wallman, pro.

Upcoming Courses

Cheney — McClurg Project (1999). In 1996, Jack McClurg of Mill Creek contacted Bill Overdorf about designing a 36-hole course on 500 acres near Cheney. McClurg's family has owned the parcel for over 120 years. It's possible that the city of Chelan will run a pipe from its sewage treatment plant to the site and provide treated effluent for irrigating the course.

Davenport — Seven Bays Resort (1999). In 1996, the backers of this project were still awaiting permits for a project that includes an 18-hole, William Robinson-designed course, a driving range, general store, marina, boat moorage on Lake Roosevelt, clubhouse and 300 housing units.

Newman Lake — Newman Lake Project (1999/2000). In early 1997, Ed Adair, owner of Post Falls-based golf contruction firm, AdairCo, had permits to build an 18-hole course and 64 homes on a 303-acre parcel four miles north of Interstate 90. Adair needs to finalize a purchase agreement with the site's landowner for the project to reach fruition.

Spokane — Woodland Hills Golf Course (1998/1999). In 1997, developer Michael Zink had received permits for an 18-hole, Keith Hellstrom-designed course and 38 homes. Financing was being arranged as this book went to press. The venue will be built on a 250-acre site in the old Otis Orchards at Trent and Campbell roads in east Spokane. The project also includes a clubhouse and driving range.

Wellpinit — Two Rivers Resort (1999/2000). To enhance an existing gambling casino, the Spokane Tribe says it wants to build a 36-hole golf complex and destination resort. The site is between the towns of Wellpinit and Ford on the Spokane Indian Reservation in Stevens County.

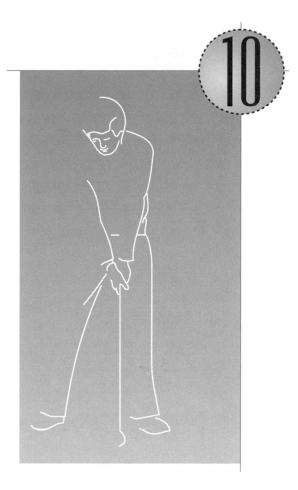

SOUTHEAST
WASHINGTON

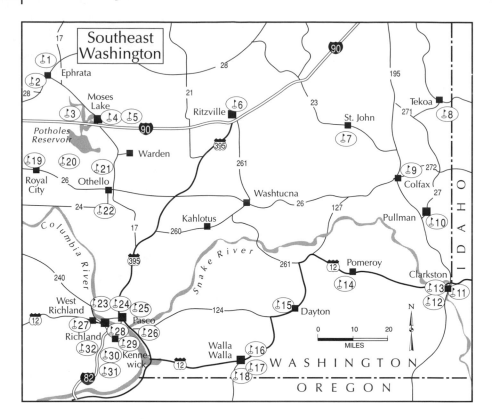

Southeast
Washington

17
1
Ephrata
2
28
Moses
Lake
3
4 5
90
Potholes
Reservoir
Warden
19 20
21
Royal
City
26 Othello
24
22
17
260
395

28
21
Ritzville
6
395
261
Kahlotus
Washtucna
26
261

23
St. John
7
195
127
Pomeroy
12
14
Snake River

195
Tekoa
271
8
272
9
Colfax
27
Pullman
10
Clarkston
13 11
N
12

240
West
Richland
23 24 25
12
27 28 Pasco
Richland 26
29
32 30 Kenne-
wick
82 31

124
15 Dayton

Walla
Walla
12
16
17
18
WASHINGTON

0   10   20
MILES

OREGON

Columbia River

1. **Lakeview Golf & Country Club** — private 18
2. **Oasis Park** — public 9 (par-3)
3. **Moses Lake Golf & Country Club** — private 18
4. **Desert Lakes Driving Range**
5. **South Campus Public Golf Course** — public 9 & driving range
6. **Ritzville Municipal Golf Course** — public 9
7. **St. John Golf & Country Club** — semiprivate 9
8. **Tekoa Golf Club** — public 9
9. **Colfax Golf Club** — public 9
10. **WSU Golf Course** — public 9 & driving range
11. **Gateway Golf Center** — driving range & 18-hole putting course
12. **Quail Ridge Golf Course** — public 18 & driving range
13. **Clarkston Golf & Country Club** — private 18
14. **Pomeroy Golf Course** — public 9
15. **Touchet Valley Golf Course** — public 9
16. **Veteran's Memorial Golf Course** — public 18 & driving range
17. **Walla Walla Country Club** — private 18
18. **Tour Fairways Golf Range** — driving range
19. **Royal City Golf Course** — public 9 & driving range
20. **Potholes Golf Course** — public 9
21. **Sage Hills Golf Club** — public 18 & driving range
22. **Othello Golf Club** — public 9 & driving range
23. **West Richland Municipal Golf Course** — public 18 & driving range
24. **Columbia Point Golf Course** — public 18 & driving range
25. **Sun Willows** — public 18 & driving range
26. **Pasco Golfland** — public 9 (par-3) & driving range
27. **Columbia Park Golf Course** — public 18 & driving range
28. **Longest Drive** — driving range
29. **Meadow Springs Country Club** — private 18
30. **Tri-City Country Club** — semiprivate 18
31. **Canyon Lakes Golf Course** — public 18, driving range & 18-hole putting course
32. **Horn Rapids Golf & Country Club** — public 18, driving range & 18-hole putting course

Southeast Washington stretches south from Ephrata through the Tri-Cities and Walla Walla to Oregon, then east to Idaho's border. The Snake River runs through the region, joining the Columbia River south of Pasco. This lower right-hand corner of the state encompasses Grant, Adams, Whitman, Franklin, Benton, Walla Walla, Columbia, Garfield and Asotin counties, whose landscapes are tinged by colorful fields of row crops, wheat, alfalfa and barley. The Palouse Hills of southeastern Washington were created by loess-blown soil from Ice Age lakes, resulting in the richest wheat land in the world.

The climate of southeast Washington encompasses zones 1 and 2, as well as the more moderate zone 3. Thanks to nearby rivers, banana belts in the Tri-Cities and Walla Walla occasionally allow golf courses to stay open year-round. Though most of the courses in the area are well established, new facilities on the horizon herald a change in the local golf scenes.

Public Courses

Canyon Lakes Golf Course

18 *3700 West Canyon Lakes Drive, Kennewick, WA 99337. (509) 582-3736. Terry Graff & Brad Graff, pros. 18 holes. 6,973 yards. Par 72. Grass tees. Course ratings: men—B73.4/127, M71.2/124, FF69.2/120; women—FF75.3/133, F72.0/124. Year Opened: 1980. Architect: John Steidel. Moderate. Reservations: Call a week ahead. Walk-on chances: Fair. Walkability: Not bad for such a spawling layout. Playability: Can play quite tough, particularly when the wind is blowing.*

Canyon Lakes' tough and lengthy 18-hole track is accessible from the West 27th exit off Highway 395. The course is owned by Mike Lundgren and Terry Graff. It had been owned by Terry and his brother Brad Graff, but Brad recently sold his share to Lundgren. Brad will spend more time teaching golf at Canyon Lakes and following the progress of his daughter, Heather, a former state golf champion at Kamiakin High School and outstanding player for the University of Arizona. Heather's amateur career reached a high point when she won the 1996 U.S. Women's Amateur Public Links Championship.

Originated by Bend-based Brooks Resources, this course is one of the Tri-Cities' most popular. The holes wind along and through desert arroyos and Columbia Basin scablands northeast of Horseheaven Hills, and are home to various desert varmints. Since the Graffs bought Canyon Lakes in 1991, they've improved playability and built a new clubhouse. Recent plantings on the course have included pampas grass, mountain ash and oak. An effort has been made to clean up the weeds in the ponds and plant ornamental grasses around the course to give Canyon Lakes a Palms Springs-like feel. Also, in 1997 an 18-hole, natural-turf putting course opened for play.

The venue is known for its vast sand traps—filled with white Idaho sand—which loom at strategic junctures. The lush fairways are separated by sagebrush, which allow recoverability if the lie is unfettered. Among Canyon Lakes' better holes is the top-rated 3rd, a winding 584-yard par-5 guarded left by a lengthy pond and right by poplar trees. A canal lurks in an elevated ditch beyond the poplars. The fairway bends left, then right—with telephone poles and cables above—en route to a trapped-right-front green. The narrow 527-yard, par-5 9th winds downhill off an elevated tee. Pine trees line the right flank of the fairway, and a steep hill shadows its left edge. A large pond fronts an hourglass-shaped green trapped rear-left. The 10th, a 458-yard par-5, begins at a 75-foot-high tee. The left-turning hole has three fairway-squeezing traps driving distance out, and its canted green is narrowed by bunkers.

Colfax Golf Club

Off Cedar Street (Route 1, Box 46-A), Colfax, WA 99111. (509) 397-2122. Craig Gronning, pro. 9 holes. 3,010 yards. Par 35. Grass tees. Course ratings: men B/M67.9/117; women—B/M72.9/120, M/F70.9/115. Year Opened: 1927. Architects: Founding members. Moderate. Reservations: Call for weekends & holidays. Walk-on chances: Good. Walkability: Good, but watch out for tree roots. Playability: Suitable choice for beginners and intermediate players.

This nine hole layout has been a Colfax sporting fixture since it opened in 1927. The layout occupies 40 acres about a quarter-mile from town. It sits next to the Palouse River, which usually is a harmless stream, especially in summer when it's nearly dry. But in the January 1996 storm that raced across the Northwest, the Palouse flooded its banks and deluged this golf course, depositing silt and other debris. By October of that year, city officials were completing plans for $62,000 worth of repairs to the 3rd tee, 5th green and 8th fairway.

Colfax sits in a banana belt of sorts; while neighboring areas are pelted by heavy snowfall, the town often goes unscathed. For local golfers, this means a longer season at the dual-tee layout, which extends 5,907 yards over two circuits. Players here might spot deer, geese, ducks, marmots and coyotes. The club was originally a members-only facility, but the town of Colfax now owns it. Plans for a new $250,000 clubhouse were put on hold in 1995 after a survey of members failed to generate sufficient financial pledges to support the project.

The old-style layout features washboard fairways lined by full-grown trees. Over 10 traps ring the venue's small, sloping greens, and a feeder ditch off the Palouse crosses the 538 yard 7th hole. Good tests include the 2nd, a 298 yard par 4 that curls sharply left around conifers to a right-sloping, trapped-left green. The 6th, a 437-yard par-4 where players are usually aided by a tailwind, ends at a nasty two-tiered green trapped in front. The par-5 7th curls rightward along a tree-lined route. The ditch crosses the hole diagonally, 175 yards from a large round green. The river also skirts the left edge of this putting surface, while a trap lurks along the right.

Columbia Park Golf Course

18 *2701 West Columbia Drive, Richland, WA 99352. (509) 586-4423. Dale Schoner, pro. 18 holes. 2.722 yards. Par 55. Grass tees. Course rating: 51.1/71 (for local use). Opened: 1960's. Architect: Army Corps of Engineers. Economical, jr./sr. rates. Reservation: Call for weekends. Walk-on chances: Good. Walkability: No problems. Playability: Fun short course enjoyable for whole family.*

This par-55 18-holer lies next to the Columbia River. Designed, built and owned by the Army Corps of Engineers, the course is leased to Benton County. Columbia Park is a low-key place where may kids swing their first clubs on a real golf course. Dale Schoner has run Columbia Park since 1986, giving lessons at a small driving range behind the chalet-like clubhouse. The facility hosts about 30,00 rounds a year.

The rectangular layout contains 17 par-3s and a short par-4, and presents a good test for the short game. Complicating matters are assorted water and sand hazards, and westerly winds that inhibit shots to postage-stamp greens enveloped by overhanging limbs. Aces are attainable, however. The course is conditioned by a county maintenance crew, and its small greens hold approach shots well. With the Columbia River right next door, ample irrigation sustains the venue's verdure. Par-3 holes range from 95 to 202 yards in length, with the 14th, a par-4 of 254 yards, rated the course's toughest.

Columbia Point Golf Course

18 *Off George Washington Way, Richland, WA 99352. Call (509) Information for phone number. 18 holes. 6,700 yards. Par 72. Grass tees. Course ratings not available. Year Opened: 1997. Architect: Jim Engh. Moderate, credit cards. Call for reservations. Walk-on chances: Fair. Walkability: Good. Playability: Complete makeover of old Sham-Na-Pum enjoys close-in locale.*

Columbia Park Golf Course represents a major metamorphosis of the old Sham-Na-Pum track, which was completely graded over for the new venue. Columbia Point's $7-million layout is an important element in a redevelopment plan for the 270-acre site (130 for the course) alongside the Columbia River. The project is slated to contain townhouses, a retail complex, a 125-room hotel, office buildings, cultural center, museum, theater and a "river walk" hiking and biking path. Sham-Na-Pum's clubhouse was torn down in preparation for a new 6,000-square-foot structure, and a new grass-teed driving range and maintenance facility were built. Premium Golf of Colorado was hired to manage the course; the firm will hire a head pro and superintendent to oversee the operations and maintenance.

The all-new course was designed by Colorado-based architect, Jim Engh of Global Golf. Engh's other design projects have included several in Asia and Europe as well as the Sanctuary course in Denver and a new municipal facility in Castle Rock, Colorado. Engh honed his golf-architect skills while serving as the lead designer for IMG, the company that handles high-profile clients like Tiger Woods and Arnold Palmer.

Engh assisted such IMG clients as Bernhard Langer and Nick Faldo in various European golf projects.

Work on Columbia Point's layout began in early 1996. Hundreds of years ago the site was a gathering spot for a now-extinct Indian tribe. Burial grounds and artifacts (including arrowheads) were unearthed during construction. The project—backed by the city of Richland—was temporarily halted in the summer of 1996 when a lawsuit was filed against the course's builder, Valley Crest Landscape Inc. of Phoenix, by Benton County Clear Air Authority. The agency cited the company for wind-drift problems caused by dust. The contractor countersued in November 1996, and the project became embroiled in litigation. At that time, all but four holes were seeded. Though the legal action stalled the project, it was back on track in spring '97. A "soft" opening was planned for late-summer '97 (after this book went to press).

Columbia Point bears no resemblance to Sham-Na-Pum, which sacrificed its popular par-3 nine to the redevelopment. Engh routed many fairways in the opposite direction as their predecessors, thus making the site's full-grown Russian olive, birch and cottonwood trees a factor on nearly every hole. Roughly a half-million yards of dirt were shaped into fairway-bordering mounds. Four ponds dot the track, entering play on the 3rd, 7th, 9th, 12th, 14th, 15th and 18th holes. Dozens of bunkers—filled with Emmett, Idaho sand—occupy the sides of fairways and greens.

The easy-to-walk track has seven holes split by a new entry road off George Washington Way. Columbia Point was built for a wide variety of public players, so there are up to five tees per hole. Golfers will encounter generally wide landing zones, with other strategic areas squeezed by trees, ponds and bunkers. Fairways and roughs are a bluegrass/rye blend, with the tees and greens bentgrass. I wasn't able to get to Columbia Point before it was completed. But the layout—in conjunction with the redevelopment at Columbia Point—should be a boon to Tri-Cities' linksters as well as the local economy.

Horn Rapids Golf Club   18

2800 Clubhouse Lane, Richland, WA 99352. (509) 375-4714. Matt Mandel, pro. 18 holes. 6,945 yards. Par 72. Grass tees. Course ratings: men—B73.6/130, M71.0/122, FF69.0/118; women—FF74.7/130, F70.4/117. Year Opened: 1994. Architects: Bob Soushek & Keith Foster. Moderate, jr./sr. rates. Reservations: Call a week ahead. Walk-on chances: Fair. Walkability: Fair—some holes are far apart and there's plenty of hills. Playability: Ribbon-like fairways, blind shots, rugged terrain and radical weather throws a hefty gauntlet at golfers.

Located about two miles west of Highway 240, this target-style, desert layout is part of an 800-acre project which may ultimately contain upwards of 1,500 homes. The Horn Rapids community is backed by Columbia Triangle Ventures L.P., in affiliation with Bellevue-based Murray Franklyn Family of Companies. The golf course was co-developed by Bob Soushek of Fore, Inc., and Hiroshi Tanaka. Soushek has built several Washington courses, while Tanaka helped develop such venues as Harbour Pointe and Indian Summer before exiting the regional golf scene. Featuring a clubhouse with food service, a driving range and this golf course, Horn Rapids was appointed with an 18-hole putting course in 1997.

The name "Horn Rapids" is taken from the course's site above the Yakima River, which winds below holes 12-14. This section of the layout—along with most of

Horn Rapids' 8th hole is a 203-yard par-3.

the back nine—is deprived of civilization, while the front nine has homes along some fairways. When I visited Horn Rapids in October 1995, a howling wind drove the wind chill down to near zero. Extreme weather is common in this part of the state; in summer, it's not unusual to encounter 100-degree temperatures. These multi-part fairways are bordered by sagebrush and scrub. You can hit balls from these areas, but trying to hack through sagebrush is not advised. In sum, Horn Rapids has many factors that can spoil a round: severe up-and-down terrain, routine wind buffetings, very tight fairways, and considerable length from the back tees (it plays 6,400 yards from the regular whites). This is not a negative assessment of the place. It's just an advisory that golfers should anticipate experiencing some agony while playing the difficult course.

Noteworthy holes include the 1st, a 380-yard par-4 that heads uphill toward a barranca about 150 yards out. Here, the fairway ascends past OB right and rocks left. Another scrub area, bunkered on both sides, crosses the hole 100 yards from a small green trapped twice at the left-front. The 3rd, a 579-yard par-5, doglegs left between scrub, OB and bunkers. Once around the bend, the hole rises to a steeply front-leaning green on a hill. The 4th, a 196-yard par-3, descends to a large, two-tiered green with a precipitous back side. With any wind, this trapped-right-front target is very elusive. The top-rated 7th, a 419-yard par-4, starts with a blind tee shot as the fairway climbs narrowly to a hilltop. The hole then drops down to a small, left-sloping green bunkered right. The downhill 8th, a 203-yard par-3, has a barranca in mid-fairway and a large, left-leaning and greatly undulating green trapped in front. The 9th, a 497-yard par-5, has a huge bunker in the left half of the fairway at the 225-yard mark. Adjoining the trap is scrub. The hole then rises leftward to a sunken green trapped right-front and guarded rear by a pond.

Holes 11-14 are all tough. The 11th, a left-turning 453-yard par-4, runs uphill along a narrow path before descending over its last 150 yards to a sizable and slick, front-sloping green trapped right-front. The 12th, a 537-yard par-5, requires a long carry over barranca to reach an upsloping fairway. A patch of desert detritus crosses the hole at the 175-yard mark. A hill in the 12th fairway crests about 100 yards from the green, so you can't see the mid-sized, front-sloping green trapped at the right-front. The left-sloping 13th, a 421-yard par-4, is a sharp dogleg-right with a huge trap beyond the turn. Two fat traps guard the right edge of the skinny 13th green, which is rolling and has a steep left flank. The 14th, a 512-yard par-5, starts at a lovely elevated tee where you can shot for another fairway crossing desert terrain. The fairway is split off the tee by barranca and is narrow on both sides of this rough stuff. The slick 14th green is trapped left-front. Another challenger is the 16th, a 429-yard par-4 with a left-leaning fairway that descends between sagebrush. Mounds along the left push misdirected shots toward the fairway (or into deeper trouble on the other side), while the undulating 16th green is trapped right.

Othello Golf Club

9

West Bench Road, Othello, WA 99344. (509) 488-2376. Doug Buck, pro. 9 holes. 3,066 yards. Par 35. Grass tees. Course ratings: men 68.5/110, women 74.2/123. Year Opened: 1964. Architect: Jack Reimer. Economical. Reservations: Call two days ahead. Walk-on chances: Good. Walkability: No problems. Playability: Can play quite tough, particularly when winds howl through the Othello Valley.

Nine-hole Othello Golf Club lies off West Bench Road southwest of its namesake town. The facility is owned by head pro Doug Buck, whose plans for another nine holes have simmered on the back burner for several years. The dual-tee nine extends 6,187 yards over two circuits, and was designed by Jack Reimer, a Canadian architect who did quite a bit of work in western Washington during the 1960s and '70s. The course spans 42 acres of former farmland; along its east and south flanks are rows of vegetable crops. Othello's clubhouse has a restaurant, banquet room and bar, while the course enjoys such embellishments as white-sand bunkers, paved cart paths and good conditioning. Water hazards enter play on two holes.

Othello's flat layout is tree-lined, with apricot and cherry trees adding color in spring. Play at the course can be affected by winds that blow through the Othello Valley, particularly in spring and fall. Tough holes include the 3rd, a 464-yarder that ranks among the Northwest's longest par-4s. This straight-running hole goes between trees—and into the teeth of the valley's prevailing westerlies—to Othello's smallest green. Another tester is the 9th, a 352-yard par-4 that curls rightward along a route that skirts a pond on the left. The putting surface at the 9th is wavy and slick.

Pomeroy Golf Course

9

1610 Arlington Street, Pomeroy, WA 99347. (509) 843-1197. 9 holes. 2,042 yards. Par 31. Grass tees. Course ratings: men B60.2/92, women—B63.7/98, F63.3/96. Year Opened: 1933. Architect: Works Progress Administration. Economical, jr./sr. rates. No reservations. Walkability: Good, save for one tall hill. Playability: Though short in length, course sports small, elusive greens.

Pomeroy's layout was financed and built in 1933 by the U.S. Government's now-defunct Works Progress Administration. The layout at the southeast edge of town is now owned by the city of Pomeroy, which lies in the fertile Pataha Valley, a trading center for area farmers whose crops include wheat and barley. The valley's steep walls shadow the town and the golf course; it receives irrigatation water from three reservoirs perched atop the rims. Pomeroy's only course is a source of community pride. Pretty flower beds grace many tees; it boasts a volunteer-installed automatic sprinkler system; and sheds by the modest clubhouse store about 60 carts owned by the regulars.

Benjamin Gulch Creek lines the venue's western flank. Golfers here might spot birds, squirrels and bull snakes. The layout has undergone several changes over the years. Two of its holes once occupied the current site of Pomeroy High School, located across Arlington Street. Those holes were repositioned at the course's south end. The short dual-tee track—which plays to an 18-hole total of 4,066 yards—has a few nondescript holes. But six fairways traverse a steep hill. From these higher points, views of the Pataha Valley are on tap. Pomeroy's signature hole is the 6th, a 121-yard par-3 with a hillside-carved green that sits about 60 feet above the tee. Shots hit short of this steeply front-tilting target roll almost all the way back to the tee.

Potholes Golf Course

9

6897 O'Sullivan Dam Road (SR 262), Othello, WA 99344. (509) 346-9491. John Erwin, pro. 9 holes. 2,269 yards. Par 33. Grass tees. Course ratings: men—B60.2/90, F59.5/88; women—B63.7/97, F62.4/93. Year Opened: 1994. Architects: Fred Barker & Gary Santo. Economical, jr./sr. rates. Reservations: Call a week ahead. Walk-on chances: Good. Walkability: No problems. Playability: Suitable for the whole family.

Located at the entrance to Potholes State Park and beside O'Sullivan Sportsman Resort, a full-service RV oasis, this course is in a banana belt of sorts; in its first year of operation, golf was played until December 15. The dual-tee layout, driving range and clubhouse were built by the resort's proprietor, Fred Barker, with design assistance on the course from Gary Santo.

The par-33 track is wide open, with now-short trees lining fairways. There's adequate bunkering, and the traps are filled with good-quality sand. Potholes is less a nerve-wracking challenge than a place where its primary users—the RV guests and park visitors—can stretch their legs. Decent holes include the 2nd, a 193-yard par-3 that runs slightly uphill to a domed, front-tilting green trapped right-front. The 3rd, a 333-yard par-4, has a rolling, right-sloping fairway with bunkers along both sides. The hill-cut, right-sloping 3rd green is trapped right. The top-rated 5th, a 365-yard par-4, runs straight and slightly downhill. A bunker sits along the fairway's right edge about 100 yards from a steeply front-leaning green that looks like a mushroom.

Quail Ridge Golf Course

18

3600 Swallow's Nest Drive, Clarkston, WA 99403. (509) 758-8501. Peter Goes, pro. 18 holes. 5,861 yards. Par 71. Grass tees. Course ratings: men—B68.1/114, M66.9/113; women—B72.6/121, M71.1/119, F66.2/107. Year Opened: 1968 (original nine); 1993 (second nine). Architects: Al Herniak (original nine); Don & Mark Poe (second nine). Economical, sr. rates, credit cards. Reservations: Call a week ahead. Walk-on chances: Fair. Walkability: Be sure to have your cleats sharpened for this billy goat track. Playability: Plays tough as there's not a flat lie to be found.

Quail Ridge lies south of Clarkston on a hill overlooking Highway 129 and the Snake River. From the lofty site, golfers have wonderful vistas of the river and Lewiston, Idaho, on the other side of the Snake. Besides its namesake bird, pheasants, chukars, deer, rabbits and rock chucks inhabit the grounds. Quail Ridge is owned by Don Poe, who, with help from son Mark, designed and built a second nine on a hill by the original side. The first course, named Swallow's Nest, was owned and built by Al Herniak. Besides expanding the course, the Poes built a new clubhouse, driving range and parking lot. They're also developing about 70 houses on their 400-acre parcel.

Quail Ridge's clubhouse is a popular spot for tournament festivities, corporate outings and parties, with barbeques held on an outdoor deck. Overseeing the operation is Peter Goes, a Coloradan who has helped boost the annual round total. The layout—especially the new holes—traverses some severe hills and dales. Odd-angled lies are the norm at Quail Ridge, which derives much of its difficulty from the tilted site. Make sure your legs are in good working order if you plan to walk, or be sure there's decent rubber on the cart tires so they won't spin out while chugging up the steep hills.

When I visited here in October 1995, I found the greens and tees in great shape. Flower beds enlivened tees and, since my last trip back in 1989, more peripheral homes had popped up. Good holes include the 1st, a 481-yard par-5 that runs steeply uphill (expect to find the adjectives "steep" and "hilly" frequently in these descriptions) past OB on the left. Over its last 150 yards, the fairway curls leftward to a hill-cut green guarded by a big bunker along the right. The 4th, a 362-yard par-4, heads straight uphill before winding rightward around mounds at the 150-yard mark. The steeply front-tilting 4th green is backed by a grass trap.

The 7th, a 334-yard par-4, rises along a path lined left by OB. A pond-filled depression fronts a knoll-perched green with a steep left edge. The 8th, a 379-yard par-4, is a downhill dogleg-left with a tiny landing area. Bordered by the driving range on the left, the hole ends at a right-front-sloping green with steep left and rear edges and a trap on the right. The top-rated 12th, a 354-yard par-4, has a tight fairway that leans severely left toward OB and a canyon. Its very small green slopes left toward yet more trouble. A tee shot over a canyon is needed at the par-3 13th, a 178-yarder. The 13th green is hill-cut and tree-ringed, and slopes precipitously toward the left-front.

The 16th, a 516-yard par-5, contains a narrow, chute-like fairway lined by escarpments along both sides. Deep jail lurks along the left. The small 16th green tilts sharply left, a configuration exacerbated by a tier running through its left half. The right-turning, a 364-yard par-4 18th is, shall we say, interesting. Going downhill off the tee past OB on the right, the hole requires a 200-yard drive to safely cross Critchfield Road and find the fairway's second leg. A bunker lurks right of the landing area, then the hole rises up to a severely front-sloping green trapped right-front.

Ritzville Municipal Golf Course   9

104 East 10th Street, Ritzville, WA 99169. (509) 659-9868. Ron Barker, pro. 9 holes. 2,812 yards. Par 35. Grass tees. Course ratings: men 67.1/112, women 72.7/122. Years Opened: 1938 (first six holes); 1943 (remaining three holes). Architects: Local players. Economical, jr./sr. rates. No reservations. Walkability: Good. Playability: Bushy, full-grown trees primary impediments to par.

Crossing well-treed terrain beneath Ritzville's water tower, north of Interstate 90 off Exit 221, this venue, a replacement to the original 1927-built Ritzville course, opened with six holes in 1938. It was financed by winnings generated through slot machines in what later became the clubhouse. Three holes completed the layout in

1943. The dual-tee nine, which extends 5,617 yards over two circuits, sits like a fenced-in park within an established neighborhood. Ritzville Muni has been overseen since 1982 by head pro Ron Barker and his wife, Amy. The Barkers maintain a low-key ambience appropriate for Ritzville, a sleepy agricultural burg in east-central Washington. It's not uncommon to see neighborhood kids walk or bicycle up to the pro shop and dicker over candy bars and green fees.

Barker is also Ritzville's superintendent, and he does this job well. The verdant grounds are kept in good shape during the course's seven- or eight-month season. The primary obstacles to par are towering, bushy trees along fairways. The holes are lined by pines, willows, maples, locusts and Russian olives. The easy-to-walk track is bisected by East 10th Street, and golfers reach the 3rd, 4th, and 5th holes via a crosswalk.

There was a considerable discussion over 1994 and 1995 regarding another nine holes at Ritzville; the plan has since been on hold. The proposal involved a joint public-private partnership (with the city and a local couple) for building new holes on a 50-acre plot donated by the neighboring landowners. The project actually involved 12 holes on a parcel to the south, with only three holes retained from the part of course north of East 10th Street. If this project comes to fruition, Ritzville's course might become more attractive to wayfaring golfers traveling on I-90.

Royal City Golf Course

9 *13702 Dodson Road South, Royal City, WA 99357. (509) 346-2052. 9 holes. 3,106 yards. Par 36. Grass tees. Course ratings: men B68.4/110; women—B74.0/118, F71.3/112. Year Opened: 1991. Architect: Keith Hellstrom. Economical. Reservations: Call a day ahead. Walk-on chances: Good. Walkability: No problems. Playability: Fun course crosses rolling ground near huge farming operations.*

Located about four miles east of Royal City, this rural layout off Highway 26 crosses a plateau. In the vicinity are the agricultural operations of the Crab Creek area of the Columbia Basin. Views from the course include the Saddle Mountains to the south; lush fields of wheat, beans, peas, apples, corn, cherries and potatoes ring the facility. Golfers plying these fairways often hear the drone of cropduster planes in spring and summer. Wildlife visitors include muskrats, ducks, geese, pheasants and coyote. For RVers, there are 33 slots across Dodson Road from the course.

The nine-hole layout arose through the efforts of a cadre of local farmer-golfers. The 80 acres of scrublands had been owned by the state's Fish and Wildlife Department, which donated it to the city in 1986 for the purpose of building the course. The city now leases the layout to the Royal City Golf Association. Association founders built the Keith Hellstrom-designed course using their own equipment and muscle. They employed considerable moxie to obtain—at discounted costs—the irrigation system, signage, and used mowers and equipment. In mid-1996, some members of the golf association had become so smitten with the course that they submitted a proposal to the city for eight homesites along some fairways.

The rolling layout spans 6,127 yards over two circuits. Westerly winds can be a factor but, in general, this is a wide-open course with good scoring chances. The straightforward bentgrass greens are in good shape, with the turf now fully knitted. Power lines cross over some fairways, and hazards include an occasional sand trap, pond and Crab Creek. With their steep perimeters, Royal City's dome-shaped putting surfaces can be slick, particularly in summer when they tend to dry out. A good test is the 3rd, a 406-yard par-4 that skirts State Route 26. Crossing wavy ground into the prevailing wind, the hole heads to a small, undulating green. The top-rated 5th, a 527-yard par-5, runs straight for 400 yards or so before turning abruptly left to a mushroom-shaped green.

Sage Hills Golf Club

10400 Sage Hills Road SE, Warden, WA 98857. (509) 349-7794. Mark Fancher, pro. 18 holes. 6,772 yards. Par 72. Grass tees. Course ratings: men—B72.2/124, M70.0/120; women—M76.0/123, F72.0/117. Year Opened: 1965. Architect: Founders; Dan Thomas & Jim Smith (remodel). Moderate, jr./sr. rates, credit cards. Reservations: Call a week ahead. Walk-on chances: Fair. Walkability: Good, overall. Playability: Lengthy course can play tough.

18

Eighteen-hole Sage Hills lies south of Warden on the west side of Highway 17. From the course, players enjoy vistas of a rugged Columbia Basin valley. Over the years, the course has evolved from a private facility (also called Sage Hills), to a public venue (renamed Warden Golf Course), to a revitalized track which is gradually seeing its peripheries developed. A group of Spokane investors began the course in 1965, using a loan from the Farmers Home Association. In 1972, John Graham, former owner of the now-defunct Redmond Golf Course near Seattle, bought the property after the founders encountered financial problems. Then in 1982, Spokane-native Dan Thomas acquired the venue and set about making it a viable alternative for golfing travelers in Eastern Washington. Sage Hills came after an earlier Warden course built in the late-1920s.

The improvements included the planting of hundreds of shrubs and ornamental trees along fairways; a restoration of the greens and tees; many new bunkers; a 150-acre, 43-home development called Sage Hills Estates; and a camping area with 35 full-service RV hookups. The venue is one of the region's most popular places for RVers, who often head to this place near the Pothills Recreation Area. Named after Sage Lake in the Potholes, the facility has a thriving full-service clubhouse. In recent years Thomas has turned over operations of the facility to his daughter Ann Smith, and her husband Jim Smith, who's also the superintendent and co-designer of many of the renovations.

The RV park is full when the annual 100-player Washington State VFW tournament is held. Sage Hills also hosts the Eastern Washington State Open, an event with a field of PGA members and sub-5-handicap amateurs. The players in these tourneys are challenged by such holes as the 1st, a par-4 of 372 yards that runs downhill along a dogleg-left route to a creek-fronted green. The par-4, 459-yard 8th has a narrow, left-tilting fairway bordered by a slender pond over its last 220 yards. A 427-yard par-4, the 14th winds rightward around poplar trees to an oval green. Beginning at a raised tee, the 606-yard, par-5 18th makes a wide right-turning path. The fairway slopes left—away from the turn—through most of its length before ascending to a bunkered green.

South Campus Public Golf Course

9 *1475 East Nelson Road, Moses Lake, WA 98837. (509) 766-1228. 1,800 yards. Par 31. Grass tees. No course ratings. Year Opened: 1990. Architect: Dan Thomas. Economical. No reservations. Walkability: Good. Playability: Horizons expanding at former par-3 layout.*

Opened in 1990, this course lies on the former campus of Big Bend Community College, which closed in 1975. Dan Thomas—proprietor of Sage Hills Golf Club in Warden—bought the college property and built the golf layout and a driving range. Next to it is the South Campus Athletic Club, which has racquetball and handball courts, a swimming pool and weight rooms. Big Bend's former gymnasium now houses the athletic club as well as the South Campus pro shop.

In 1996-97, Thomas began extending the former par-3 layout, adding two par-4s and a par-5 to bump the par total to 31. As this book was going to press, Thomas was contemplating stretching South Campus even more, so the above length and par may change. The current course crosses relatively flat ground, and features some tree-lined fairways.

St. John Golf & Country Club - semiprivate

9 *Off Highway 23, St. John, WA 99171. (509) 648-3259. 9 holes. 2,876 yards. Par 35. Grass tees. Course ratings: men—B67.0/111, B/M66.5/109, M66.0/106, M/F64.9/105; women—B72.2/115, B/M71.6/114, M71.0/113, M/F69.7/111, F68.4/109. Year Opened: 1935 (original six); 1995 (four new holes). Architects: Founding members (original course); Curt White & local players (newer holes & remodel). Moderate. No reservations. Walkability: Good. Playability: Surprisingly challenging golf amid the "wilds" of the Palouse.*

St. John's pastoral course is on the northwest side of a farming town in eastern Washington's Palouse country. The semiprivate course, owned by 265 members, began in 1935 when local farmers purchased the site and built six holes with their own equipment. The course was closed during World War II and remained out of service until the mid-1950s. When it reopened, a small clubhouse was added. In 1994, the members began work on four new holes. The holes include par-4s of 408 and 412 yards (the 4th and 6th, respectively), a 152-yard par-3 (5th), and a 500-yard par-5 (3rd). The old number 2, a 140-yard par-3, was eliminated.

As with all construction projects at St. John Golf & Country Club, the work was donated. The members raised $80,000 among themselves (a process that follows a club rule to "not borrow money from the government") for the project. Construction of the new holes became feasible after the members installed a $15,000 well in 1993, thus enabling enough water pressure to irrigate an expanded course. An all-new St. John Golf & Country Club debuted in 1995. Other recent changes include the development of a 16-lot housing tract beside the new holes.

St. John's members have plenty to be proud of, for this is a well-maintained, enjoyable venue. Offering all-day green fees of $10 and annual membership dues of $225, the sport of golf is definitely not an elite affair in this part of the Northwest. Instead, the game provides a social and recreational outlet for the wheat ranchers in the nearby towns of Pine City, Sunset, Ewan, Thornton, Steptoe and Willada. When played over two circuits, St. John stretches to a total of 5,752 yards. Among its better tests is the 3rd, the new 500-yard par-5. This double-dogleg goes left, right, then left again en route to an angular green. The 6th, the 412-yarder, runs in a rightward direction to a rolling, slippery green. Perhaps the best original hole is the 7th, a 371-yard par-4 with a bi-trapped putting surface.

Sun Willows

2035 20th Avenue, Pasco, WA 99301. (509) 545-3440. Joe Dubsky, pro. 18 holes. 6,799 yards. Par 72. Grass tees. Course ratings: men—B72.0/120, M69.8/116; women F71.6/119. Year Opened: 1959. Architects: Founders (original course); Robert Muir Graves (remodel). Economical, jr. rates, credit cards. Reservations: Call a week ahead. Walk-on chances: Fair. Walkability: Good overall. Playability: Length and variety of holes make this one of the region's better public facilities.

Sun Willows lies off Interstate 182 in the northeast part of Pasco. Originally named Pasco Municipal Golf Course, the venue underwent a name change in the late-1980s. The layout was rather perfunctory when built by the founding owners in 1959, but a thorough remodel in 1982 by architect Robert Muir Graves completely transformed the playing field. The result is a course which rivals the best public tracks in the region. Now owned by the city of Pasco, Sun Willows has been overseen by head pro Joe Dubsky since 1973. It serves as the site for the annual Sun Willows Tri-Cities Amateur, which, with a field of 525 players, ranks as the largest amateur tourney in the western U.S. The course is appended by a full-service clubhouse and driving range.

The layout, a replacement for an earlier Pasco course built in 1925, is well-conditioned during its eight-month season. Sun Willows contains plenty of hazards: five lakes and 37 bunkers vie for errant shots. The topography is gently rolling, but tall mounds lend fairway definition while obscuring views to greens. The routes are further squeezed by mature trees. Most greens feature multi-trapped front entries, with their back edges lined by mounds. Outstanding holes include the 6th, a 580-yard par-5 with a dogleg-left fairway that winds around a pond. A bunker lurks 100 yards from a small green bunkered left and rear.

The dogleg-left 10th, a 410-yard par-4, boasts danger galore: many trees, a pond with a fountain along the left, and wavy, uphill terrain. Another fountain adorns a pond that guards the front entrance to the well-canted and sand-ringed 10th green. The 15th, a 505-yard par-5, curls slightly right between trees. The pond squeezing the 6th hole enters play on the 15th along the port side of its final jog. The green is squeezed by traps right-front and rear, and by the pond on the left.

Tekoa Golf Club

Off Highway 27, Tekoa, WA 99033. (509) 284-5607. 9 holes. 2,550 yards. Par 35. Grass tees. Course ratings: men B/M64.5/109; women—B/M68.9/111, M/F67.6/108. Year Opened: 1960. Architect: Waldo Hay. Economical. No reservations. Walkability: Good. Playability: Rural golf set amid lovely fields.

Tekoa's nine-hole course lies just south of its namesake town along Highway 27. The layout is a popular spot for residents of the Latah Valley, which includes the townships of Tekoa (pronounced "Tee-koe"), Latah, Oakesdale and Farmington. Set amid multi-hued wheat and alfalfa fields, the course was built in 1960 on a 40-acre parcel that Waldo Hay leased from his father. Hay, with help from his golfing buddies, designed and built the layout, which barely squeaked through its early years. When grain prices rose in the 1970s, Tekoa Golf Club was temporarily converted to a wheat field.

The city of Tekoa applied for a state grant and bought Hay's lease after the course was returned to its original purpose. Shortly thereafter, the city installed an automatic sprinkler system fed by a nearby creek. Today, the course serves local golfers and other linksters who happen through this town, located about an hour from Spokane. In October 1996, the course was annexed into the city limits.

Tekoa's dual-tee layout extends 5,164 yards over two circuits. The virtually treeless track traverses the side of a rolling hill, and plays very similar to a Scottish-style links. Besides an occasional coyote or deer that ventures down from Tekoa Mountain, stray cows may cross these fairways. Notable holes include the 3rd, a 454-yard par-5 that runs long and straight past a ball-gulping wheat field to a large green. The 6th, a 315-yard par-4, heads over rolling terrain to a small putting surface. And the 9th, a 332-yard par-4, has hills and depressions in a fairway that eventually arrives at a steeply right-sloping green.

Touchet Valley Golf Course

9 *North Pine Street, Dayton, WA 99328. (509) 382-4851. 9 holes. 2,931 yards. Par 36. Grass tees. Course ratings: men 67.8/114, women 71.0/122. Year Opened: 1925. Architects: Founding members. Economical. No reservations. Walkability: Good. Playability: Well-tended course has two holes running through the infield of a horseracing track.*

The 1925-built Touchet Valley layout is on the northwest corner of Dayton by the Columbia County Fairgrounds. Two holes at Touchet (pronounced "Tooshie") Valley occupy the infield of a horseracing track at the fairgrounds. Other than the nine holes at Portland Meadows, this is the only Northwest course whose configuration more than meets the definition of the golf colloquialism, "track." Oldtimers recall teeing off towers to fairways along the track's perimeter in the early days. The layout, closed during fair week and converted into a parking lot, also adjoins the Touchet River. The course had previously flooded after heavy rains or snow runoffs, but a dike now stems the flow.

New managers took over Touchet Valley in April 1996. Merle and Pearl Bickelhaupt have spiffed up the place, and Pearl's Place restaurant serves hearty fare. Touchet Valley began with six holes; three were added later. The dual-tee course, which extends 5,772 yards over two circuits, has always gotten support from local golfers for maintenance projects. Crossing flat ground, the layout is embellished by flower gardens, short-cropped greens and assorted sand and water hazards.

Top holes include the 3rd, a 570-yard par-5 bordered along the right by the dike. The fairway is quite wide for its first 370 yards, then a tree and pond shrink it considerably. A creek meanders along the last 200 yards of its left edge before the hole ends at a small green. The 5th, a 473-yard par-5, has a right-bending fairway that skirts a flower bed en route to a front-sloping, trapped-right-front green. Signs warning golfers to look both ways for galloping horses precede Touchet Valley's infield holes which, at one time, were also the site of a football field. Mirror-image 316- and 319-yard par-4s, the side-by-side 7th and 8th head through the center of Columbia County's largest stadium to greens placed against the track's inside railings.

Tri-City Country Club - semiprivate

314 North Underwood Street, Kennewick, WA 99336. (509) 783-6014. Chris Isaacson, pro. 18 holes. 4,693 yards. Par 65. Grass tees. Course ratings: men 62.5/ 112, women 65.2/115. Year Opened: 1938 (original nine); 1959 (second nine). Architects: Founding members (original nine); Forest Bishop, Bill Welch & Russell Brown (second nine). Moderate. Reservations: Call two days ahead. Walk-on chances: Fair. Walkability: Good. Playability: Though short, there's plenty of trouble to get into at this fine course.

Tri-City Country Club is a secluded sanctuary in a well-developed part of Kennewick. The fenced-in, 75-acre layout is immaculately tended and a joy to play. Dubbed Twin City Golf Club when it opened with nine holes in 1938, the course received its current name in 1948. The back nine was designed by Russell Brown and two of the Tri-Cities' most notable golfers, Bill Welch and Forest "Forie" Bishop. Welch, the father of golf pro Pat Welch (now at Veteran's Memorial in Walla Walla), was a longtime golf pro who taught many of the area's best "sticks." Before his death in 1995 (which happened while working at the old Sham-Na-Pum course), Bishop set maintenance standards lauded by players around the region. Still a 9 handicap from the back tees at Meadow Springs at the age of 78, Bishop was seemingly always thinking about golf. He invented a lawnmower to verti-cut greens, a device used to cut cups, and gear to help weak-wristed golfers.

Partly owned by its 685 club members (the city of Kennewick has controlling interest in part of the back nine), Tri-City Country Club is a "semi-civic" operation whose doors must remain open to non-stockholders. The course is not one of the most difficult in central Washington. But for all its shortness and apparent ease, there's plenty of trouble to be found. Full-grown trees and mounds squeeze fairways, and two well-placed ponds and dozens of bunkers penalize errant play. Tri-City has slick and rolling, mostly diminutive greens. The course contains eight par-3s, and is a shotmaker's delight.

Top holes include the 308-yard, par-4 5th, a very narrow dogleg-left. A cluster of tries occupy the inside corner while a pond squeezes the outside of the turn. The 5th green is ringed by three traps. The 7th, a 491-yarder, is Tri-City's only par-5. Bordering Kennewick Avenue, this straight-running hole bypasses OB left and a bunker right along a gradual ascent to a trap-ringed green. From the 100-foot-high tee at the 165-yard par-3 14th, one's shot must be carefully directed to a small green protected by trees left, two lateral traps, and a pond at the rear.

Veteran's Memorial Golf Course

201 East Rees, Walla Walla, WA 99362. (509) 527-4507. Pat Welch & Nick Manolopoulos, pros. 18 holes. 6,650 yards. Par 72. Grass tees. Course ratings: men—B70.7/115, M69.2/111; women F69.5/111. Year Opened: 1948. Architects: Local golfers. Moderate, jr./sr. rates, credit cards. Reservations: Call for weekends. Walk-on chances: Fair. Walkability: Good. Playability: Better have the "big dog" in working order to score at this lengthy track.

Located off Highway 12 east of Walla Walla amid rolling wheat fields., this 120-acre course was named after World War II veterans and is a fine municipal venue. The operation of the course underwent a major change when Pat Welch—longtime pro/manager of Richland's now-defunct Sham-Na-Pum—signed an 18-year lease in

March 1996. Welch replaced Ken Haak, who'd been here since 1984. On May 31, 1997, Welch and co-head pro Nick Manolopoulos hosted the first annual Forey Bishop Memorial Sham-Na-Pum Best-Ball, a two-day event honoring Forest Bishop, the late Tri-Cities' superintendent, and Sham-Na-Pum, the late Richland golf course.

Besides managing the pro shop, Welch will oversee the golf course as well as the restaurant and lounge. Immediate changes by Welch include remodeling the interior of the clubhouse. No major changes are planned for the course, which will continue to be maintained by superintendent, Bill Griffith, a past-president of the Northwest Turfgrass Association.

A set of infrequently used railroad tracks runs through Veteran's Memorial, which is kept lush even in these arid climes. Pine, poplar, hawthorn and fir trees line the fairways, which run over gently rolling terrain. Though ample bunkers guard the greensides, distance is the primary obstacle to par here. Among the lengthier holes is the top-rated 5th, a 445-yard par-4 with a yawning dogleg-right fairway that splits trees and a wheat field en route to a raised green. At 471 yards, the 10th is among the region's longest par-4s. Over its initial stretch, the 10th goes slightly downhill before bending rightward to a knoll-perched green that tilts left toward a trap.

The 13th, a par-4 of 372 yards, runs straight uphill to a small, tree-tucked green skirted on both sides by grass bunkers. The dogleg-right 14th, a 578-yard par-5, slopes decidedly left after the turn. Various ridges and swales precede its small green, which is ridge-perched and fronted by a depression. A 403-yard par-4, the flat 15th is bordered by trees and ball-eating rows of wheat. Grass and sand bunkers guard its tidy putting surface. The 16th, a 528-yard par-5, is a narrow left-bender that descends to a left-leaning green trapped twice in front.

Washington State University Golf Course

9

North Fairway Drive, Pullman, WA 99163. (509) 335-4342. Dan Koesters, pro. 9 holes. 2,880 yards. Par 36. Grass tees. Course ratings: men 67.9/117, women 69.5/115. Year Opened: 1926. Architects: Founding members; Robert Muir Graves (remodel). Economical, credit cards. Reservations: Call two weeks ahead. Walk-on chances: Good (especially in summer). Walkability: No problems. Playability: Can play quite tough, with tilted topography and ample bunkering.

This nine-hole course at the east edge of the Washington State University campus is a fine recreational outlet for students and Pullman residents alike. The layout, originated in 1926, received a Robert Muir Graves-designed remodel of the 5th and 6th holes and a new driving range in 1970. In mid-1996, local realtor Daryl Roberts was spearheading a move to add another nine holes. A WSU alum, Ted Locke, designer of the North Bellingham course in northwest Washington, has drawn up plans for the expansion. Before construction can begin, a feasibility study must be completed and financing arranged. There's plenty of land east of the existing course for the new holes.

WSU's course is played primarily by students and retirees who live in the greater Pullman area, and is a good value. Holes traverse gently sloping ravines and ridges, with several tees atop knolls affording panoramic views of golden wheatfields and the campus. The park-like track is conditioned by students in the summer. Pheasants and quails inhabit the well-tended grounds. Quite unexpectedly, a moose wandered across the fairways in November 1988. The course is now overseen by Dan

Koesters, who's also WSU's men's and women's golf coach. Taking over for former coach and head pro, Christine Burkhart, Koesters had been the golf coach at the nearby University of Idaho.

The dual-tee layout extends 5,785 yards over two circuits. Good tests include the 4th, a 170-yard par-3 with a two-tiered green trapped on both sides. Beginning at an elevated tee, the canyon-like, 492-yard, par-5 5th bends rightward to a large green trapped laterally. The uphill fairway of the top-rated 6th, a 473-yard par-5, curls to the right while sloping left. Its clover-shaped green sits on a ridge and is trapped right-front and left. The elevated tee at the 9th, a 329-yard par-4, offers sweeping vistas of the university. This narrow hole is dented with a deep swale 200 yards off the tee; a pair of traps guard its large and squarish green along the right.

West Richland Municipal Golf Course

18

4000 Fallon Drive, West Richland, WA 99352. (509) 967-2165. Rod Marcum, pro. 18 holes. 5,826 yards. Par 70. Grass tees. Course ratings: men 67.7/114, women 70.3/114. Year Opened: 1952. Architects: Founding members. Economical, jr./sr. rates, credit cards. Reservations: Call a week ahead. Walk-on chances: Good. Walkability: Good, just be sure to have water available on hot summer days. Playability: Beginners can hack away with relative impunity on these wide-open fairways.

West Richland is a 5,800-yard course on the northeast end of its namesake city. The layout borders the Yakima River, a location that caused it to be flooded during the horrendously wet months of January and February 1996. The course has since been restored. West Richland is run by Rod Marcum, a local pro who's reinvigorated the facility with various improvements (including a much-needed irrigation system) and more user-friendly operations. West Richland has long been a training ground for budding Tri-City linksters. Affordable fees—still under $10 a round—along with a facile demeanor let beginners whale away at the ball without undue penalty. Its place in local golfdom seems assured.

The course—previously called Tapteal and West Richland Elks—is owned by the city of West Richland and leased to Marcum. Its fairways cross generally flat ground; short trees line some of these broad holes. The turf conditions have improved dramatically since the introduction of the modern sprinklers, as has the condition of the greens. Tough holes include the top-rated 2nd, a 495-yard par-5 with a wide dogleg-right fairway. The hole turns abruptly to the right 150 yards from a trapped-left green. The 11th, a 180-yard par-3, requires a tee shot over a creek to find the green. Another good test is the 545-yard 15th, a par-5 with a right-curling fairway and a rolling putting surface.

Private Courses

Clarkston Golf & Country Club

18 *1676 Elm Street, Clarkston, WA 99403. (509) 758-7911. Vicki Mallea, pro. 18 holes. 6,650 yards. Par 72. Grass tees. Course ratings: men—B72.3/122, M71.5/ 121; women—M77.6/135, F74.4/124. Years Opened: 1937 (original nine); 1948 (second nine). Architects: Members; Keith Hellstrom (remodel). Members, guests & reciprocates.*

Clarkston Golf & Country Club spreads across a generally flat 100-acre parcel west of Clarkston. The club is off Highway 12; a wide section of the Snake River is visible on the other side of this major arterial. Members designed and built all 18 holes, and Spokane architect Keith Hellstrom oversaw a major remodel of the course. Hellstrom's work involved moving 900,000 yards of soil to fill the course above the water level of the nearby Snake. The Spokane architect rebuilt 13 holes, dug five lakes, and installed an automatic irrigation system. The club is a popular place for residents in the Clarkston-Lewiston area. It has a total membership of 565, 400 of which are golfers. The golf portion of the operation has been overseen by head pro, Vicki Mallea, since 1987. Superintendent Bill Barkshire tends the well-conditioned grounds.

The park-like layout boasts flower gardens on many holes, tall trees along fairways, a grass-teed driving range, and paved cart paths. The highway borders parts of the course, while houses and condominiums dot other perimeters. Besides length, play on Clarkston is affected by seasonal winds that steam down the Snake River Canyon. The small, slick greens—most of which are well-bunkered—are another concern. The fairways are occasionally crossed by deer, which travel down from a draw above the course. Among the club's bigger tournaments are the 8-Man Invitational at the end of March; the Firecracker Open around the 4th of July; a two-man best-ball which has been held in both June and September; the Banana Belt Seniors; and the Ladies Harvest Fest in late September.

Among Clarkston's toughest holes is the 1st, a 532-yard par-5 with a dogleg-left fairway that winds around a fence and a road; trees and OB are along the left. The hole rises slightly over its final 100 yards to a hill-cut and severely right-sloping green trapped left-front. The straight-running 6th, a 420-yard par-4, has mounds in the middle of the fairway. A pond begins along the left at the 150-yard mark and runs up to guard the port side of the diminutive, left-tilting 6th green. The 380-yard, par-4 7th doglegs uphill to the left; a pond lurks right of the tee. The fairway starts narrowing at the 150-yard mark, then concludes at a steeply front-sloping, trapped-left green with a depression at the right-front.

The 8th, a 162-yarder, is a tough par-3 that ascends to a small, hill-perched green guarded by deep bunkers right-front, with OB left and rear. The 9th, a 299-yard par-4, runs straight downhill to a miniscule landing area that tilts toward trees. The slick 9th green—tucked back to the left—leans rightward and is bunkered in front. Running into the teeth of the prevailing wind, the top-rated 10th, a 435-yard par-4, has a narrow, tree-lined and right-sloping route lined on the left by OB and Elm Street. A sign beside a house on the other side of the road reads: "Hookers welcome — others kaput!" At the 100-yard mark, the 10th descends to a small, trapped-left green. The

17th, a 540-yard par-5, requires a tee shot that must be placed between Highway 12 on the left and a pond right, driving distance out. The pond continues up the right side, squeezing the hole over its last 150 yards. The left-sloping and fast 17th green is trapped left-front; the pond sits about 30 yards from its right-front edge.

Lakeview Golf & Country Club

18

52 Golf Club Road, Soap Lake, WA 98851. (509) 246-0336. Don Tracy, pro. 18 holes. 6,614 yards. Par 71. Grass tees. Course ratings: men—B70.9/114, M69.5/111; women—M76.3/126, F72.5/116. Years Opened: 1951 (original nine); 1982 (second nine). Architects: Founding members (original nine); Gene Gabler & Rich Paulson (second nine). Members, guests & reciprocates.

Lakeview lies south of Ephrata off Highway 28 at the 19th Street Northwest exit. Activities at the private club began in 1951, when a member-designed nine holes opened for play. A second nine came on line in 1982; Gene Gabler and Lakeview's former pro, Rich Paulson, designed these holes. Besides a 6,600-yard layout, the club is appointed with a swimming pool and modest clubhouse. The 125-acre course spans generally flat ground; it's lined by homes and undeveloped lots. The presence of a feedlot on the course's eastern edge may explain why some of the droller members refer to Lakeview as a "country" country club. Pheasants, quails and an occasional coyote cross these fairways.

Recent improvements include a redesigned 12th green (with new ponds on both sides), and a grass-teed driving range. The club's 350 members hail from Soap Lake, Ephrata, Moses Lake, Quincy, Coulee City and Seattle. Nice touches on the walkable course include sprinkler head yardage readings. A restroom by the 11th green bears a sign that says, "Donated by the Sagebrush Tournament Committee of 1983 & 1984." Perhaps Lakeview's signature characteristic is its greens; these radical, multi-tiered affairs are among the Northwest's most severe. The members may redo the 14th and 16th greens, the latter of which is so dome-shaped as to appear like an upside-down teacup.

Tough holes include the 2nd, a straight-running, 427-yard par-4 with a pond off the tee. The fairway winds between trees en route to a raised, front-tilting green. The top-rated 3rd, a 420-yard par-4, is a lengthy right-bender that passes OB along the right on its way to a left-sloping green guarded left-front by a grass bunker and tree. The 6th, a 420-yard par-4, bends rightward along a slight descent. Its severely front-leaning putting surface has a one-foot-high shelf in its back third and a trap left-front. The 430-yard, par-4 10th rises on a straight, tree-lined path to a peanut-shaped, front-right-sloping green with a steep left side and two grass bunkers in back.

The 11th, a 500-yard par-5, curls rightward on a route that skirts a drive-in theater and the feedlot on the left. The 11th ends at another radical putting surface. The terraced green is trapped in front and has a steep back side. The 13th, a 183-yard par-3, ends at a wild, tri-level green. The 14th, a 415-yard par-4, bends leftward between trees to a steeply front-sloping green with a bunker along the right. And the home hole, a 520-yard par-5, goes straight for 370 yards or so before curling 70 degrees to the right between trees. The 18th ends at a ridge-perched green trapped at the right-front.

Meadow Springs Country Club

18 *700 Country Club Place, Richland, WA 99352. (509) 627-2321. Greg Moore, pro. 18 holes. 6,944 yards. Par 72. Grass tees. Course ratings: men—T73.3/132, B71.3/ 127, M68.9/123; women—M75.4/135, FF72.6/129, F69.2/120. Year Opened: 1968. Architect: Jack Reimer; Robert Muir Graves (remodel). Members, guests & reciprocates.*

Ringed by upscale homes, the course at Meadow Springs Country Club is one of the region's most well-respected, having hosted such significant events as the Pacific Northwest PGA Championships, Sandvik Washington State Open, Washington State Amateur and PNGA Men's Championship. Each September the Nike Tour stops for the Tri-Cities Open. The tournament draws crowd of 10,000 and generates $30,000 a year for local charities. Upcoming tournaments include the Washington State Women's Golf Association Match Play in 1999. Club events include the Meadow Springs Best-Ball in March and Meadow Springs Amateur in June.

The 17th hole at Meadow Springs is a 228-yard par-3.

Besides a top-flight layout, the club boasts tennis courts and a swimming pool. The Jack Reimer-designed course opened in 1968. In 1973, Robert Muir Graves oversaw an extensive remodel that represents the course played today. The layout spans a bowl-shaped site, with Leslie Avenue separating the 12th and 13th from the other 16 holes. In 1995, the members had an automatic sprinkler system installed, a much-needed upgrade. The popular course hosts 30,000 rounds annually, and has stayed open virtually year-round during particularly mild Tri-Cities' winters. Wildlife visitors include blue herons, raccoons, ducks, geese and pheasants. The course record is a 63, set by former Hogan Tour player, Kelly Gibson.

Top holes include the 1st, a 532-yard par-5 that begins at an elevated tee, then heads leftward around two huge bunkers and a pond, with OB right. Once completing its 80-degree left turn, the hole rises up to a big front-sloping green trapped left-front. The top-rated 4th, a 536-yard par-5, runs slightly uphill on a right-bending route. Homes line the right edge of the hole, which ascends to a slick, knoll-perched green trapped once right and twice left. The 5th, a 437-yard par-4, is a rising dogleg-right around houses. Tall, bushy trees guard the right-front entry to its mid-sized, right-tilting green. The 8th, a 216-yard par-3, has an elevated tee and a vast and rolling, front-canted green trapped twice right-front and once left. This becomes a very tough par-3 when played in any kind of wind.

The 10th is a 555-yard par-5 that winds downhill to the left. A creek sits at the base of the hill-fronted tee, then the fairway ascends along a route that passes a bunker left at the 100-yard mark. The V-shaped 10th green is trapped laterally. The 11th, a 409-yard par-4, has an uphill, right-leaning fairway lined on both sides by traps. The hole narrows over its last leg before concluding at a mid-sized, bi-trapped putting surface. The 13th, a 425-yard par-4, is a downhill dogleg-left with houses right and two ponds inside the turn. The large and greatly rolling 13th green is trapped laterally.

Meadow Springs' 16th, 17th and 18th holes rank among the top three finishing holes in the Northwest. The 16th, a 579-yard par-5, curls to the right around a pond. Another pond farther down along the left results in a small landing area for drives. Wetlands and a fat bunker lurk along the left at the 150-yard mark, with another bunker on the right 25 yards farther down. The steeply front-tilting 16th green is crossed in front by a creek and bunkered right. The par-3 17th is a bear from the tips, where it stretches 228 yards. A huge tee-to-green pond occupies the "fairway" at the 17th, which features a wide-but-shallow, rear-trapped green. The 18th, a 451-yard par-4, is a steeply uphill dogleg-right lined by water left and houses right. The ascending route eventually reaches a severe, two-tiered green trapped at the left-front.

Moses Lake Golf & Country Club   18

Off Interstate 90 (Box 328), Moses Lake, WA 98837. (509) 765-5049. Mike Eslick, pro. 18 holes. 6,436 yards. Par 71. Grass tees. Course ratings: men—B69.5/111, M68.5/109; women F72.5/120. Years Opened: 1956 (original nine); 1961 (second nine). Architects: Founding members. Members, guests & reciprocates.

Moses Lake Golf & Country Club lies west of its namesake city, directly off Interstate 90 at exit 174. Besides an enjoyable course, the club boasts a full-service clubhouse, swimming pool and driving range. New practice putting and chipping greens were built in 1995. Located about two and a half hours from Issaquah, east of Seattle, the club's roster lists many out-of-town members. It's also the home club for many Japan Air Lines instructors, who teach budding JAL pilots how to fly 747 airplanes at a training facility north of Moses Lake. A few homes line the course on its north and east perimeters, with fairways defined by evergreens, elms, Russian olives, cottonwoods, poplars and fruit trees. Wind is a decided factor at this track, particularly in the afternoons when it averages 10-15 miles per hour.

Fed by irrigation water from Grand Coulee Dam, the course stays quite green during its (weather-permitting) year-long season. Though without a particularly high slope rating, Moses Lake provides a good test, primarily because of its very slick greens. In summer these putting surfaces can measure upwards of 11 on the Stimp meter, making them as fast as glass. Tougher holes include the 1st, a 501-yard par-5 that curls left between trees. The fairway is squeezed about 100 yards from the green by trees on the right. The right-front-sloping putting surface at the 1st is trapped left-front. The 3rd, a 338-yard par-4, is a sharp dogleg-left around poplars. After the turn, the fairway ascends to a right-tilting, tree-veiled green. The top-rated 8th, a 462-yard par-4, heads slightly downhill toward a swale (observable from the tee through a periscope). Once past the dip, this hole bordering I-90 flattens and bends slightly leftward into the prevailing wind. The small, front-tilting 8th green has a tall back side.

The 11th, a 324-yard par-4, begins with another blind tee shot mitigated by a periscope. The fairway curls uphill to the right around trees to a trap-fronted green that tilts precipitously toward the front. The 444-yard, par-4 12th is a long dogleg-right that winds between trees, scrub growth and houses to a round, trapped-right green. The 13th, a 518-yard par-5, skirts trees, rough and homes along the left. The fairway ascends over its last 100 yards to another fast, domed green. The 14th, a 427-yard par-4, winds leftward to a diminutive and slick, front-leaning green trapped left-front. The 18th, a 548-yard par-5, is a fairly narrow dogleg-left around scrub and the driving range, with olive trees along the right. The hole ends at a sizable hill-perched green.

Walla Walla Country Club

18 *1390 Country Club Road, Walla Walla, WA 99362. (509) 525-1562. Steve Stull, pro. 18 holes. 6,434 yards. Par 72. Grass tees. Course ratings: men—B71.0/123, M68.1/118; women—M73.3/124, F71.5/120. Years Opened: 1917 (original nine); 1946 (second nine). Architect: W. W. Baker. Members, guests & reciprocates.*

Walla Walla Country Club is a parkland-style course set amid homes in the southern part of Walla Walla. An elegant Victorian mansion stands beside the 4th hole. The golf course arose with nine holes in 1917; a second nine followed in 1946. Both sets of holes were designed by a local banker and golf-club builder, W. W. Baker. A sad moment in club history occurred in July 1996 when Walla Walla's stately 73-year-old clubhouse burned to the ground. The fire, which caused an estimated $3.5 million in damage, occurred just after the structure had undergone a $700,000 renovation. Faced with hosting the Washington State Women's Golf Association Championship a couple of days after the fire, the members scrambled to set up tents and outdoor facilities for the tournament, which went off without a hitch. The fire also caused damage to the pro shop and swimming pool, but the golf course was unaffected by the inferno. In early 1997, the members selected Seattle's The Bumgardner Architects to design a new 22,000-square-foot clubhouse.

Walla Walla's members hail from a 50-mile radius of the city. Golf is usually a 10-months-a-year activity, though the season has occasionally encompassed a full year. Other tournaments hosted by the club over the years have included Hudson Cup matches, the 1985 PAC-10 Championship, 1993 Women's Pac-10 Championship, and Washington Junior Invitational (co-hosted with Veteran's Memorial). PGA stars Lee Trevino and Dan Pohl once played an exhibition here. Walla Walla is overseen by head pro Steve Stull, a fine tournament player and the younger brother of Ron Stull, head pro at Sand Point Country Club in Seattle.

The course record is a 63, set in 1951 by Jim Russell, Walla Walla's head pro for 30 years. The course gains difficulty from fairways squeezed by locust, fir, pine, maple, oak, sweetgum, cottonwood, pear and crabapple trees. Also of concern are over 30 sand traps and many grass bunkers; Stone Creek winds through the target zones of several holes. Top tests include the straight-running 6th, a 420-yard par-4 crossed by the creek about 200 yards out. A fat tree farther down along the right narrows the hole before it runs over rolling ground to a small green guarded by a hidden bunker at the left. The slightly uphill 9th, a 419-yard par-4, is a wide dogleg-right that stretches out to a steeply front-sloping green bunkered twice on the right. The 11th, a 402-yard par-4, is a sharp dogleg-left that ascends past interior OB on the left. The hole climbs to a humped-in-front green trapped along the left.

The par-4 12th is a pretty dogleg-right of 357 yards. Stone Creek crosses at the base of the tee, then runs along the right edge of the hole all the way up to a willow-veiled, two-tiered green bunkered left. The 15th, a 357-yard par-4, is an unusual hole. It begins at a raised tee, then descends along a tree-lined route interrupted by an irrigation shed in its midsection. The entry to the 15th green is squeezed by trees; the small, laterally-trapped putting surface has a deep grass bunker at its right-front edge. The 16th, a 396-yard par-4, bears a mid-width fairway lined by trees right and a bunker left. At the bunker, the fairway descends to a large, two-tiered green that leans toward the creek in front. A huge trap on the right makes the shot into the 16th green a difficult one. The 17th, a 202-yard par-3, heads slightly uphill past a big willow tree on the right to a small, front-right-sloping green trapped left and right-front.

Par-3 Courses

Oasis Park

2541 Basin SW, Ephrata, WA 98823. (509) 754-5102. 9 holes. 930 yards. Par 27. Grass tees. No course ratings. Economical, jr./sr. rates. No reservations. **9**

Owned by Mike and Patti Donovan, this par-3 track is in Oasis Park Resort. The 33-acre resort contains a miniature putt-putt course, RV slips, a children's fishing pond, nature trails, picnic areas, tent sites and a swimming pool. An office and convenience store sit at the entrance. The 1972-built course occupies land leased from the city of Ephrata by the resort's owners. The short track winds around RV and tent-camping sites. Two ponds serve as hazards, and its postage-stamp greens wreak minor havoc. Short fairways run beneath overhanging tree branches.

Pasco Golfland

2901 Road 40, Pasco, WA 99301. (509) 544-9291. Tony Beck, pro. 9 holes. 1,000 yards. Grass tees. Economical, jr. rates. No course ratings. No reservations. Driving range. **9**

A short course and driving range southwest of the city, Pasco Golfland is accessible from the 20th Avenue exit off Interstate 182. Originally called the Academy at Sun Willows after the like-named regulation course located a mile-and-a-half away, the facility was started by local golf pro, Jeff Hendler. Hendler built the driving range and three par-4 practice holes on the 27-acre site, which is owned by the Port of Pasco.

When Hendler encountered financial difficulties, Bill McIntyre stepped in and built the par-3 layout. A fully-stocked pro shop opened in 1997. Chipping and putting greens are available in addition to the 165-yard-wide, grass-teed range. The course is dotted by a few bunkers and a pond; McIntyre hopes to add two more ponds in the future. Holes range from 70 to 170 yards, and there are two sets of tees for 18-hole forays.

DRIVING RANGES

Desert Lakes Driving Range

610 Yakima Avenue, Moses Lake, WA 98837.
(509) 766-1553. Two pros on staff.

Gateway Golf Center

725 Port Way, Clarkston, WA 99403.
(509) 758-4366. Rick Eisele, pro.

Longest Drive

6311 West Clearwater Avenue, Kennewick, WA 99336.
(509) 735-6072. Three pros on staff.

Tour Fairways Golf Range

1150 Abadie, Walla Walla, WA 99362.
(509) 529-5810. Jim Henderson, pro.

Upcoming Courses

Ephrata — Port of Ephrata Project (1999). The Port of Ephrata and the city of Ephrata may team up to build an 18-hole public course on some of the port's 2,000 undeveloped acres.

Ephrata — Myrick Project (1999). As of 1996, work still hadn't begun on this public nine, which is planned along with over 820 RV sites and 732 single- and multi-family dwellings. Though Grant County has approved the project, a lawsuit by a neighboring orchardist who feared the effects of chemical wind-drift on golfers must be settled.

LaCrosse — Winona Road Project (1999/2000). A nine-hole course has been proposed for a 91-acre site north of LaCrosse, in Whitman County.

Moses Lake — Moses Pointe (1999/2000). Though approved in May 1992 by Grant County commissioners, work on this 391-acre residential community resort on Lakeshore Drive hasn't begun. The backers would like to develop an 18-hole golf course, hotel, 91 RV hookups, tennis courts, restaurant, 168 lots and 550 townhouses.

Palouse — Spencer Project (1999). In 1996, the city of Palouse was still considering a offer from a private developer who wanted to buy a 160-acre, city-owned site to develop a par-3, 18-hole golf course and 100 homes.

Pasco — Badger Mountain (1998/1999). After seeing their partially-built nine holes go to seed over 1994 and 1995, the backers of this 27-hole project returned with a new infusion of cash and began work on the course in late 1996. The 1,000-acre project includes upwards of 1,200 housing units, a putting course, driving range, hotel and conference center.

Richland — Buckskin Ranch Golf Course (1998). In 1996, the Port of Benton was moving ahead with a plan to build an executive-length nine on 51 port-owned acres near the Tri-Cities Airport. The port leased the site to Jerry Asher and Ed Hunnicutt, who will design, build and operate the facility, which will include a driving range.

West Richland — Marcum Project (1999/2000). As of 1996, the head pro at West Richland Golf Course, Rod Marcum, still hadn't begun work on an 18-hole layout to be located on 200 acres of Yakima River floodplain.

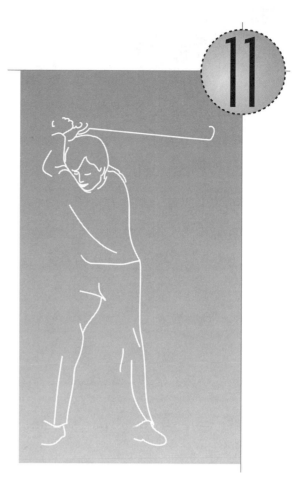

PORTLAND, VANCOUVER & VICINITY

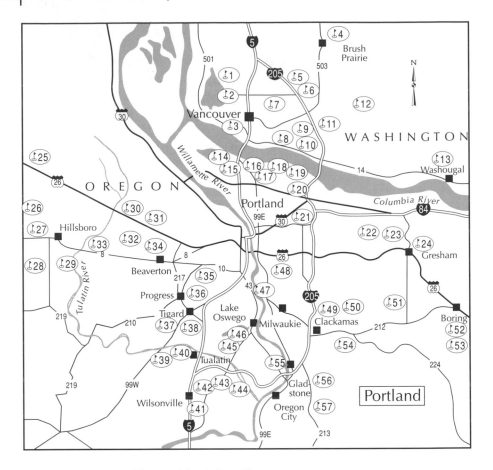

1. **Pine Crest Golf** — public 9 (par-3)
2. **Lakeview Golf Challenge** — public 9 (par-3)
3. **Westside Golf Range** — driving range
4. **The Cedars Golf Club** — public 18 & driving range
5. **H & H Driving Range**
6. **Bowyer's Par 3 Golf** — public 9 (par-3)
7. **Club Green Meadows** — private 18
8. **Vanco Driving Range**
9. **Royal Oaks Country Club** — private 18
10. **Fairway Village Golf Course** — semiprivate 9
11. **Evergreen Golf Center** — driving range
12. **Hartwood Golf Course** — public 9
13. **Orchard Hills Country Club** — private 18
14. **Heron Lakes Golf Course** — public 36 & driving range
15. **Portland Meadows Golf Course** — public 9 & driving range
16. **Columbia-Edgewater Country Club** — private 18
17. **Riverside Golf & Country Club** — private 18
18. **Broadmoor Golf Course** — public 18 & driving range
19. **Colwood National Golf Club** — public 18
20. **Chuck Milne's 82nd Avenue Golf Range** — driving range
21. **Rose City Golf Course** — public 18

22. **Glendoveer Golf Course** — public 36 & driving range
23. **Jim Colbert's Hound Hollow Golf Center** — public 9, driving range & 18-hole putting course
24. **Gresham Golf Course** — public 18 & driving range
25. **Pumpkin Ridge Golf Club** — Witch Hollow (private 18) & Ghost Creek (semiprivate 18 & driving range)
26. **Quail Valley Golf Course** — public 18 & driving range
27. **Killarney West Golf Club** — public 9
28. **The Reserve Vineyards Golf Club** — public 18 & private 18 & driving range
29. **Meriwether National Golf Club** — public 27, executive 9, driving range & 18-hole putting course
30. **Rock Creek Country Club** — private 18
31. **Claremont Golf Club** — semiprivate 9 & 18-hole putting course
32. **Orenco Woods Golf Club** — semiprivate 9 & driving range
33. **McKay Creek Golf Course** — public 9 & driving range
34. **Golden Bear Golf Center at Sunset** — driving range
35. **Portland Golf Club** — private 18
36. **Progress Downs Municipal Golf Course** — public 18 & driving range
37. **King City Golf Course** — semiprivate 9
38. **Summerfield Golf & Country Club** — semiprivate 9
39. **Tualatin Country Club** — private 18
40. **Tualatin Island Greens** — driving range & 18-hole putting course
41. **Langdon Farms Golf Club** — public 18, driving range & 9-hole putting course
42. **Charbonneau Golf & Country Club** — public 27 & driving range
43. **Sandelie Golf** — public 27 & driving range
44. **The Oregon Golf Club** — private 18
45. **Lake Oswego Golf Course** — public 18 & driving range
46. **Oswego Lake Country Club** — private 18
47. **Waverley Country Club** — private 18
48. **Eastmoreland Golf Course** — public 18 & driving range
49. **Top O'Scott Public Golf Course** — public 18
50. **Pleasant Valley Golf Club** — private 18
51. **Persimmon Country Club** — semiprivate 18 & driving range
52. **Mountain View Golf Club** — public 18 & driving range
53. **Greenlea Golf Course** — public 9
54. **Sah-Hah-Lee Golf Course** — public 18 (par-3) & driving range
55. **The Children's Course** — public 9
56. **Oregon City Golf Club** — public 18
57. **Dino's Driving Range**

This part of the Northwest is region's second most-populated. Geographically, it's defined by two major rivers—the east-west running Columbia and the north-south Willamette, with greater Vancouver in Washington's southwest corner. Portland and environs enjoy dramatic views of mounts Saint Helens and Hood and the Coast Range Mountains, as well as year-round golf in moderate climate zone 6. With new industry and an increased population, Vancouver is rapidly emerging from the shadow of neighboring Portland.

Like Spokane, the Rose City has an outstanding municipal golf program, with affordable, top-of-the-line public courses. Portland's many stately private clubs further reinforces its status as a Northwest golf mecca. But troubles may be on the horizon for the city-owned golf courses, which are run on an enterprise system similar to Spokane's. A surcharge for non-resident golfers in 1994 turned off many out-of-towners (including those from Vancouver) to the municipal courses—Rose City, Eastmoreland, Heron Lakes and Progress Downs. Because of decreased play and lost revenue needed for course upgrades, the city discontinued the surcharge in summer 1996.

Now the golf program must meet a challenge posed by Measure 47—a tax initiative which cuts property taxes as well as caps taxable income—approved by voters in 1996. Measure 47 maintains 1995 tax levels and limits tax boosts to 3%, thus straining the income of Portland's government such that the city could turn to its profitable golf courses for financial help. (The same goes for Lake Oswego and its 18-hole muni.) Though the jury was still out on this issue in 1997, Measure 47 could limit capital improvements to Portland-owned golf courses in the years ahead.

PUBLIC COURSES

Broadmoor Golf Course

18 *3509 NE Columbia Boulevard, Portland, OR 97211. (503) 281-1337. Scott Krieger, pro. 18 holes. 6,404 yards. Par 72. Grass tees. Course ratings: men—B70.2/122, M68.2/116; women—M73.6/117, F69.9/110. Year Opened: 1931. Architect: George Junor. Moderate, credit cards. Reservations: Call a week ahead. Walk-on chances: Ok for singles. Walkability: Good. Playability: One of Portland's most popular courses has something for everyone.*

Hosting upwards of 70,000 rounds a year, this popular facility features a nice golf course, driving range, full-service clubhouse, three teaching pros, and discounted green fees in winter. The venue lies off Columbia Boulevard in the same neighborhood as Colwood and the country clubs at Columbia-Edgewater and Riverside. Portland International Airport is also nearby. From its higher points are views of mounts Saint Helens and Hood. Broadmoor occupies land once used as a dairy farm, and has been owned for years by members of the Schneider family. Only one of the six Schneider sisters originally involved with the course is still alive. She's the grandmother of Broadmoor's head pro, Scott Kreiger.

The 220-acre layout, designed by George Junor, opened during the Depression. The course crosses gently rolling terrain above the Columbia River. The 1st and 10th holes descend off a knoll bordering Columbia Boulevard, while the 9th and 18th run back up the hill toward the clubhouse. Broadmoor has undergone several renovations in recent years, including a new back tee at the 16th and a new 13th green which added 50 yards to the hole.

Though there isn't a plethora of sand traps, various water hazards—including Broadmoor Lake at the 9th and sloughs winding through the 8th and 17th holes—interrupt play. Over 20,000 golf balls a year are removed by scuba divers from these waters. When balls are dredged from the 9th's "Lake of Despond," a name taken from Hogarth's classic book, *Pilgrim's Progress*, assorted clubs and bags are also brought up.

Broadmoor's original green fees were 30 cents; as a result of its low fare and opening during the Depression, the course initially experienced tough times. It stayed afloat, however, by holding dances, crab feeds, pheasant hunts and other paying activities. Historical footnotes include the 1948 Vanport Flood, which buried the course under 15 feet of water and six feet of mud. Greenskeeper Charlie Beauford saved the greens, thus allowing the course to survive a potentially ruinous situation. Interestingly, Broadmoor was not among the local courses heavily damaged by the floods between 1995 and 1997.

Good golf tests include the top-rated 3rd, a 437-yard par-4 with a narrow and rolling fairway that stretches out to a round, tree-ringed green. The 9th, a 358-yard par-4, starts at an elevated tee fronted by Broadmoor Lake. An accurate drive must cross this waterway as well as a cluster of trees on the hazard's opposite side. The 9th green tilts steeply frontwards. The 17th, a par-4 of 344 yards, requires a diagonal tee shot over a slough for a safe landing. The small and slick 17th green perches atop a hillock.

The Cedars Golf Club

15001 NE 181st Street, Brush Prairie, WA 98606. (360) 687-4233. Ron Blum, pro. 18 holes. 6,423 yards. Par 72. Grass tees. Course ratings: men—B71.2/129, M69.6/125; women—M75.0/129, F70.2/119. Year Opened: 1977. Architect: Jerry James. Moderate, jr. rates. Reservations: Call a week ahead. Walk-on chances: Fair. Walkability: Fair. Playability: Lots of watery graves along this Brush Prairie course. **18**

The Cedars is in Brush Prairie, a growing town north of Vancouver. Now owned by National Golf—which is also the proprietor of Meriwether National in Hillsboro and Colwood in Portland, The Cedars began in 1977 as a private club for residents living in an adjacent subdivision. When it failed as a members-only facility, the course was opened to the public.

The Cedars is etched within forests east of Brush Prairie. The layout winds through a dense stand of old-growth firs and its namesake trees. Though homes line the peripheries of some holes, many fairways are forested and secluded from civilization. Players can spot a variety of birds and deer at the pastoral layout. Work continues on upgrading the drainage of the course, which is traditionally wet during the rainy seasons. New drain tile and French-type drains have helped alleviate the course's sogginess.

Salmon Creek as well as ponds and well springs cross several holes. Among the better tests is the top-rated 2nd, a 435-yard par-4 that winds rightward over wavy ground to a laterally-trapped green. The entry to the green is squeezed by trees. The 7th, a 189-yard par-3, requires a lofted tee shot over a cattail-filled pond to reach a green trapped twice in front. A par-4 of 395 yards, the 16th features a narrow fairway that skirts water right and trees left. The hole runs up to a deep and slender green lined along the right by yet more water.

The Cedars' immediate operations are overseen by head pro Ron Blum. When he's not teaching lessons or performing a golf pro's myriad other duties, Blum is an official in the National Football League. One noteworthy game in Blum's officiating career, which began in 1969, was the notorious "ice bowl" game in 1995 which found fans throwing snowballs onto the field, including one that knocked out a trainer for the San Diego Chargers. Another memorable game was while Blum worked as a Pac-10 official. That was the 1982 Stanford-California game that begat the "The Play," the hilarious multi-lateral kickoff return which resulted in a Cal win and an upended tuba player in the end zone. Due to his NFL commitments, Blum is gone most weekends between mid-July through early January.

Charbonneau Golf & Country Club

27 *32020 Charbonneau Drive, Wilsonville, OR 97070. (503) 694-1246. Bob McAllister, pro. 27 holes. Course ratings: Yellow/Green (4,248 yards, par 62): men—B60.6/ 94, M59.8/92; women—M61.9/92, F59.8/92. Green/Red (4,146 yards, par 62): men—B60.0/94, M59.3/93; women—M61.3/95, F59.5/94. Red/Yellow (4,108 yards, par 62): men—B60.0/93, M59.3/90; women—M61.0/94, F59.1/92. Years Opened: 1973 (Red Nine), 1976 (Yellow) & 1979 (Green). Architect: Ted Robinson. Moderate, credit cards. Reservations: Call a week ahead. Walk-on chances: Fair. Walkability: Good; be ready to share the paths with ducks. Playability: Tight track amid homes requires patience and accuracy.*

This 27-hole facility east of Interstate 5 off the Charbonneau exit is an integral part of a 477-acre subdivision developed by Willamette Factors. In 1991, the developer sold the course to a group of homeowners, who call themselves Charbonneau Golf Club, Inc. The purchase was financed by a $3-million loan, an amount quickly repaid by the sale of 554 stock certificates.

Conditioned by greens superintendent Mary Rock, one of a handful of women superintendents in the region, Charbonneau's course winds between nicely-kept homes. Overall, the houses are discreetly apart from the field of play. The three nines are rotated in a clockwise direction every week, and can play tough. Considerable quantities of sand and water hazards complicate par; the fairways, though of executive-length, are tight. The 120-acre course has no par-5s, but its par-4s, which stretch upwards of 350 yards, lend difficulty to the testy track. Charbonneau's greens are quick and multi-tiered. Vistas include the Willamette Valley, Mount Hood and the Cascades.

Among the stiffer tests on the Yellow side is the 3rd hole, a 205-yard par-3 with a large bunker left-front of its right-sloping green. The 215-yard, par-3 5th has a fairway pond along the right; its green is bunkered left. The top-rated Green hole is the 1st, a 345-yard par-4. A bunker lurks along the right of its rolling fairway, while two traps guard the green's right flank. The Red Nine starts with a 292-yard par-4. Bunkers line this fairway and three traps ring its slick green. The 3rd, a par-4 of 286 yards, features another bunker-squeezed fairway and well-trapped green.

The Children's Course

19825 River Road, Gladstone, OR 97027. (503) 722-1530. 9 holes. 1,480 yards. Par 28. Grass tees. No course ratings. Year Opened: 1961. Architect: John Junor. Economical, jr./sr. rates. No reservations. Walkability: Good. Playability: Once expanded with new facilities, course should be an ideal training ground for junior golfers.

9

A short course at the fork of the Clackamas and Willamette rivers, this venue has undergone several transformations over the years. Prior to becoming a golf course it was the site of the first Oregon State Fair. The property's second owner, Judge Rye, built a few holes for the enjoyment of family and friends. Then in 1961, a John Junor-designed 18-holer opened for public play. The course—at that time called Rivergreens—was owned by Chuck Thomas II. In 1990, Minnesota developer CSM acquired the facility from Thomas and converted the acreage into an apartment complex for retirees. As part of the deal, nine holes were retained but were played only by residents of the adjoining apartments.

In early 1996, the course was purchased by Duncan Campbell. Campbell formed a non-profit corporation, Youth Resources; hired longtime Portland pro Larry Aspenson to be the director of operations; and renamed the facility The Children's Course. Working through schools and area youth programs, the operators immediately generated interest among budding linksters. During its first year, over 22 junior tournaments took place. Though the course is open to the general public, with seniors accounting for much of the play (particularly off-season), many kids are finding their way here. In the summer of 1996 juniors accounted for about 60 percent of the rounds, a number the operators hope will increase in the years ahead. Families are an integral part of the plan as well, with fathers and sons, and mothers and daughters playing golf together.

During its first year, the course received a few tees. The rough was allowed to grow and delineate fairways. In late 1996, the owner was seeking a grant from the USGA to help fund a new driving range where kids can practice. If the project goes through, a few holes will be realigned on currently unused property. Also in the works is another par-4 to make the course a par-29 layout. The only current par-4 is a 265-yarder, with the par-3s ranging from 130 to 170 yards. Here's hoping The Children's Course succeeds, and that it serves as a model for other short tracks around the Northwest.

Claremont Golf Course - semiprivate

15955 NW West Union Road, Portland, OR 97229. (503) 690-4589. Steve Morrison, pro. 9 holes. 3,000 yards. Par 36. Grass tees. Course ratings: men B68.6/116; women—B73.8/120, F70.4/114. Year Opened: 1990. Architect: ROMA Design Group. Moderate, credit cards. Reservations: Call a week ahead. Walk-on chances: Fair. Walkability: Good. Playability: Water hazards and rooftops vie for errant shots.

9

Claremont's nine holes wind between the 500-plus houses in a like-named subdivision in west Portland. The final, seventh phase of homesite development in 1997 included an 18-hole putting course. Claremont was developed by Claremont L.P., an investment group led by George Marshall Development Company. The neighborhood is near the massive Rock Creek subdivision. Because of the popularity of Claremont's houses, there's no room for a back nine.

The course was designed by ROMA Design Group of San Francisco. Located on the old Purvis Horse Farm, the layout crosses a ridge that allows westward views of Oregon's Coast Range. Geese occasionally alight on ponds and other birds frequent the grounds. Recent upgrades include a pond situated about 170 yards off the 4th tee, and another pond along the right side of the 5th hole.

The course occupies about 40 acres of Claremont's 193-acre site. Its fairways are lined by young trees; a stand of oaks towers over the course's western edge. In some cases, Claremont's houses are too close to fairways, as demonstrated by the breaking of several windows since the course's debut in 1990. The original fairways enjoyed adequate setbacks to the houses, but because of booming lot sales were later redesigned and placed closer to residences. Another safety concern is found at the 1st hole, a narrow 327-yard par-4 where golfers can hit snap hooks into car traffic on NW West Union Road.

Perhaps Claremont's toughest hole is the par-5 2nd, a 587-yarder that winds rightward to a slick green. Its prettiest hole is the 8th, a 95-yard par-3 with a tee-to-green pond and a small, slippery green.

Colwood National Golf Club

18 *7313 NE Columbia Boulevard, Portland, OR 97218. (503) 254-5515. Dave Miller, pro. 18 holes. 5,978 yards. Par 72. Grass tees. Course ratings: men—B68.1/113, M66.2/108; women—M71.7/112, F70.3/109. Year Opened: 1929. Architect: Arthur Vernon Macan. Moderate, jr. rates. Reservations: Call a week ahead. Walk-on chances: Fair. Walkability: Good, overall. Playability: Macan design not up to high standards of his private clubs, but Colwood presents a good, enduring test.*

Originally called Meadowbrook Golf Course when it opened in 1929, Colwood was built by A. Larrowe, a real-estate developer. Larrowe and Meadowbrook went bankrupt in 1932. Soon after, 250 shares were sold to 200 golfers, who purchased the course and initiated Colwood Golf Club. Cecil Saunders and his son, William Saunders of Hawaii, bought the course from the stockholders in 1955. Saunders' portfolio as owner of National Golf has since grown to include Meriwether National in Hillsboro and The Cedars across the Columbia River in Brush Prairie, Washington.

The course is topographically similar to Broadmoor, which lies about a mile to the west. Both layouts feature clubhouses perched on knolls alongside Columbia Boulevard, starting holes that descend from elevated tees, and some fairways traversing side slopes. Colwood's white, plantation-like clubhouse has a restaurant, lounge and banquet space, and is a popular place for social and post-tournament gatherings. Planes in and out of nearby Portland International Airport occasionally split the calm at the well-treed venue. Colwood is one of the few remaining Northwest golf facilities using a totally manual sprinkler system. Two night watermen set the manual sprinklers and hand-water the course from 8 p.m. to 5:30 a.m.

The layout is bisected by Alderwood Drive; signs warn golfers to look both ways before crossing the road. Colwood is kept in good year-round shape, and has fair drainage during the rainy months. Though close to the Columbia River, the fairways were unaffected by the floods of 1995-1997. Colwood has remained unchanged in recent years, with no major revisions or upgrades planned. Good tests include the 2nd, a par-4 of 397 yards that rises up to a small, tree-ringed green trapped on both sides. The 7th, a 360-yard par-4, has a rolling fairway lined by OB left. Bunkers guard the right and rear flanks of its undulating putting surface. The 333-yard 11th is an interesting hole with a pond-fronted tee and a front-tilting, tree-ringed green.

Eastmoreland Golf Course

2425 SE Bybee Boulevard, Portland, OR 97202. (503) 292-8570 or 775-2900. Clark Cumpston, pro. 18 holes. 6,529 yards. Par 72. Grass tees. Course ratings: men—B71.7/123, M70.0/119; women—M74.6/125, F71.4/117. Years Opened: 1918 (original nine); 1921 (second nine). Architects: H. Chandler Egan & John Junor. Moderate, jr./sr. rates. Reservations: Call a week ahead. Walk-on chances: Ok for singles. Walkability: Efficient layout quite suitable for bag-packers. Playability: One of the Northwest's premier public facilities.

18

Golf began at this 200-acre plot in southeast Portland in 1918, when Eastmoreland's original nine debuted. By the time the second nine opened three years later, a greens fee-fed savings account had raised $26,000 to build a clubhouse. This amount was accumulated when golfers were charged 25 cents a round. The course has undergone several upgrades over the years, the most recent being a modification of the 10th green. The original clubhouse has since been replaced by a modern structure, with a double-decker driving range adjoining it. In the summer of 1995, all of the bunkers were rebuilt and resanded. The course is in demand as a tournament venue; the last major event here was the 1990 National Publinx. In 1996, a local golfer, David Hull, shot an incredible two-under-par 70 in the Doug LaMear One-Club Championship. Hull, who used a 6-iron, was told by *Golf Digest* that his 70 tied for the lowest one-club round ever played on a regulation course.

Often ranked among the top-25 of America's 75 Best Public Golf Courses by *Golf Digest*, Eastmoreland received three stars in the magazine's "Places to Play 1996-'97" guide. Another kudo dates back to the 1920s when the legendary Walter Hagen, during a tournament, said the par-5 13th hole was one of the best holes he'd ever played. That's not surprising considering Eastmoreland's co-designer, H. Chandler Egan. Winner of the 1902 U.S. Amateur and several regional events, the Medford native oversaw the original remodel of Pebble Beach and also designed several sterling Northwest courses. Egan was assisted in Eastmoreland's design by Oregon Golf Hall-of-Famer, John Junor.

Eastmoreland's well-treed fairways cross gently rolling terrain. In the middle of the back nine is Crystal Springs Lake. Fed by wells originating near Mount Hood, the lake is a hazard for golfers and a refuge for ducks and geese. On the east side of the lake—across the tee from the par-3 12th hole—lies the city of Portland's Rhododendron Test Garden. A unique feature of Eastmoreland is that its four par-5s point northward, so players usually have prevailing winds at their backs. The back nine is also 200 yards longer than the front.

Good tests include the 7th, a tight, tree-lined 416-yard par-4 that winds leftward along a snaky route to a slick green. The scenic 12th, a 165-yard par-3, has Crystal Springs Lake from tee to green. Two traps guard the peripheries of its small putting surface. The 462-yard 13th begins at a hill-fronted tee, then winds sharply left around trees, skirting OB the length of the hole along the right. At about the 200-yard mark, a creek in a ravine crosses the fairway. The latter leg of the wavy 13th slopes left toward jail before ending at a slippery, trapped-right green.

Fairway Village Golf Course - semiprivate

9

15503 SE Fernwood, Vancouver, WA 98684. (360) 254-9325. 9 holes. 2,500 yards. Par 34. Grass tees. Course ratings: men—B64.3/106, M63.6/105; women—M69.0/ 108, 67.1/106. Year Opened: 1981. Architect: Gene "Bunny" Mason. Moderate, sr. rates, credit cards. Reservations: Call a week ahead. Walk-on chances: Fair. Walkability: Good. Playability: Contemporary nine nestled amid retirement suites.

Fairway Village's course winds through an over-55 community east of Vancouver. The subdivision now has upwards of 1,400 residents. Houses line all the holes; in late-1996, only two open lots remained in the neighborhood, a development of Portland's Hillman Properties. Though the semiprivate course—which was bought from Hillman by the homeowners' association in 1995—is aimed at local players and homeowners, it allows public play. The public is advised to use discretion—both in dress and deportment—when golfing at Fairway Village.

The members enjoy priority tee times and exclusive use of a restaurant and outdoor swimming pool. They also have access to a fine course designed by Bunny Mason. The dual-tee nine plays to 2,500 yards on the front nine, with 2,633 yards on the back. Some holes offer views of the Columbia River and Portland's skyline; Mount Hood looms to the southeast. Impinged by homes on some fairways, Mason's contemporary layout boasts big bunkers, sizable greens with lots of roll, and some dicey water hazards.

Good tests include the 2nd, a 210-yard par-3 that drops down to a saddle-shaped green ringed by three bunkers. The top-rated 3rd, a 446-yard par-5, contains a straight fairway squeezed by a pond 250 yards out along the right. A smaller pond crops up just beyond this first water hazard, and borders the right flank of the trapped-right 3rd green. The 8th, a 277-yard par-4, bends leftward between residences. A large bunker sits 225 yards out along the left. The hole ends at a raised green guarded right-front by a "doughnut" bunker (sand around a grassed "hole"), with another trap left.

Glendoveer Golf Course

36

14015 NE Glisan Street, Portland, OR 97230. (503) 292-8570 or 253-7507. Daran Dauble, director of golf; Jim Chianello, pro. 36 holes. Grass tees. Course ratings: East Course (6,296 yards, par 73): men—B69.4/120, M67.3/114; women F71.2/115. West Course (5,922 yards, par 71): men—B67.4/110, M65.8/105; women F68.2/106. Year Opened: 1924. Architect: John Junor. Moderate, jr./sr. rates. Reservations: Call for weekends & holidays. Walk-on chances: Fair. Walkability: Good. Playability: Regular upgrades sustain interest in Northwest's first 36-hole facility.

Located on the site of an old potato farm, Glendoveer was the region's first golfing venue with 36 holes when it debuted in 1924. It wasn't until 1981 when Sunriver North (now called the Woodlands) opened that another Northwest site had as many holes. Almost from its inception, Glendoveer has been a popular track; it now averages upwards of 220,000 rounds annually on its two layouts. Besides golf, the 230-acre facility offers tennis and racquetball courts, a double-decker driving range, and jogging paths that go around two-thirds of the East and West courses.

Glendoveer has been overseen by several owners over the years; at one time, its survival was doubtful as one owner had plans to build a hospital on the site. Eventually, Glisan Street Recreation, Inc. (GSR) obtained a lease on the property, with the provision that it build a new clubhouse, restaurant, lounge, pro shop, driving range and indoor tennis courts within 20 months. GSR met the challenge, and the company continues to run a highly successful venue. Joe Hickey manages Glendoveer, and director of golf, Daran Dauble, runs the golf operations.

The courses were designed by Oregon golf pioneer John Junor, and built by Glendoveer's original owner, Frank Stenzel. Though the East and West courses are not particularly long, they contain some good golf holes. Fairways are narrow and tree-lined, with both layouts secluded amid towering firs. West 18 is a bit more open, and a residential neighborhood borders its southern edge. GSR is constantly upgrading the courses; in the past few years the company has rebuilt all the bunkers and added ponds.

Challenging East holes include the top-rated 7th, a straight-ahead 565-yard par-5 shadowed by trees en route to a small, slick green. The 17th, a 560-yard par-5, bends rightward along a yawning path to a tree-ringed green. The toughest hole on West is the 9th, a par-4 of 444 yards that curls left toward Glendoveer's imposing, warehouse-like clubhouse. The 16th, another 444-yard par-4, doglegs left to a well-trapped green surrounded by evergreens.

Greenlea Golf Course   9

26736 SE Kelso Road, Boring, OR 97009. (503) 663-3934. 9 holes. 1,510 yards. Par 30. Grass tees. No course ratings. Year Opened: 1978. Architect: Walt Markham. Moderate. No reservations. Walkability: Good. Playability: Like a stroll through a park.

Though short in yardage, this 27-acre nine is enjoyable thanks to its proprietors, Walt and Muriel Markham. The couple built Greenlea on the site of their former wholesale business, Markham Nursery. The layout winds through such arboreal species as deodar cedar, black spruce, white fir, Norway spruce, Ponderosa pine, cypress, redwood, Scotch pine, Irish yew, assorted hollies and dwarf hinoki trees. A planting of Meyer junipers and smoke trees abut the 8th green, while rhododendrons and azaleas lend spring color.

Executive-length Greenlea lies just south of Mountain View Golf Club, and contains six par-3s and three short par-4s. The course is quite conventional, with short and straight fairways ending at small, well-tended greens. In recent years, Greenlea's conditioning has improved thanks to superintendent, Phil Emerson, who's concentrated on upgrading the fairways. A new mower has helped Emerson's cause. The course received a big boost in play in 1996 when nine holes at nearby Sah-Hah-Lee were underwater. The Markhams hope the added exposure will increase play levels in the years ahead.

Gresham Golf Course

18 *2155 NE Division, Gresham, OR 97030. (503) 665-3352. Stuart Smart, pro. 18 holes. 5,814 yards. Par 72. Grass tees. Course ratings: men—B68.1/109, M67.2/ 107; women—M72.0/112, F69.0/107. Year Opened: 1965. Architects: Eddie Hogan & Sam Wolsborn. Moderate, jr. rates, credit cards. Reservations: Call for weekends. Walk-on chances: Fair. Walkability: Very good. Playability: Moderate challenge found at suburban-type course in Gresham.*

Gresham Golf Course lies off NE Division, about 12 miles east of Portland. The fairways curl between fruit and nut trees, vestiges of its orchard-past, and are surrounded by houses and apartments. The course is owned by co-designer, Sam Wolsborn, who now leases it as well as Gresham's full-service clubhouse-restaurant to his sons, Chuck and Bob. The venue was originally known as Gresham Golf & Country Club; Wolsborn was helped in the design by longtime Portland pro, Eddie Hogan. Great views of Mount Hood are available from the course on clear days.

The layout is mostly straightforward, with a few holes imperiled by ponds and creeks. Long a source of unwanted fairway water, the creeks were recently dredged to prevent future flooding. Upcoming plans include elevating the 9th tee. Some of Gresham's mid-sized putting surfaces are trapped, with many in the form of pot bunkers. Good tests include the pretty 3rd, a par-3 of 115 yards that requires a well-placed shot to span a fairway-long pond and reach its small green. The top-rated 5th, a 469-yard par-5, bends slightly right. A bunker sits 225 yards out, then the hole heads to a green that tilts toward two traps in front. The 16th, a 456-yard par-5, is lined along the right by filbert (also called hazelnut) trees. The rolling fairway concludes at an undulating green.

Hartwood Golf Course

9 *12506 NE 152nd Avenue, Brush Prairie, WA 98606. (360) 896-6041. 9 holes. 1,588 yards. Par 29. Grass tees. No course ratings. Year Opened: 1996. Architects: Pat & Jim Hart. Economical, sr. rates. Call for reservations. Walk-on chances: Good. Walkability: Very good. Playability: New executive-length track added to Vancouver- area golfing menu.*

Located northeast of Vancouver, this executive-length layout is owned and operated by Jim and Sue Hart, and Jim's parents, Pat and Mary Hart. The senior Harts run Pine Crest, a par-3 track northwest of Vancouver. The course, whose name reflects the ownership, opened on October 13, 1996, along with a clubhouse. The Harts plan to keep the green fees low to encourage play from families, seniors and juniors.

The Harts own about 60 acres at the above address—a former pasture for cattle, with 35 acres used for the course. Besides some towering Douglas fir, oak, Oregon ash and quaking aspen trees, the property had a few wetlands. The site contained "dollar loam," a soil that has a few rocks but, in general, is fine for golf courses. An automatic irrigation system keeps the course green year-round.

The Harts planted ryegrass for tees and fairways; the greens, built with a sandy base, were sown with Providence bentgrass. Ducks and coyotes visit the site, which is in a still-rural part of Clark County. Offering nice views of mounts Saint Helens and Hood, Hartwood involves two par-4s (335 and 274 yards) and par-3s ranging from 105 to 170 yards. Besides some slick greens and three ponds on several holes, golfers must overcome prevailing winds out of the northwest.

Hartwood's better tests include the 3rd, the 335-yard par-4. The fairway passes a pond right of the tee en route to a rolling green. Perhaps the toughest hole is the 274-yard 6th, a dogleg-right. It may be tempting to carry the trees inside the fairway's turn; but a bunker sits right-front of the raised, pond-backed 6th green. The 130-yard 8th features a two-tiered putting surface guarded along the right by a water hazard.

Heron Lakes Golf Course

36

3500 North Victory Road, Portland, OR 97217. (503) 292-8570 or 289-1818. Byron Wood, pro. 36 holes. Grass tees. Course ratings: Great Blue Course (6,916 yards, par 72): men—T73.6/132, B71.3/128, M69.4/122; women—M74.2/130, F69.8/ 120. Greenback Course (6,595 yards, par 72): men—B71.6/123, M68.7/118; women—M73.5/122. F69.8/120. Years Opened: 1971 (Greenback), 1988 (Great Blue original nine), 1992 (Great Blue second nine). Architect: Robert Trent Jones, Jr. Moderate, jr./sr. rates (Greenback only). Reservations: Call a week ahead. Walk-on chances: Ok for singles. Walkability: Generally good for both courses. Playability: Length, water and sand merge to create two tough courses.

The 36 holes here represent one of the Northwest's busiest golf facilities, hosting over 200,000 rounds a year on its Great Blue and Greenback courses. The municipal venue—owned and operated by the city of Portland—began with Greenback in 1971; it was then known as West Delta Park. In 1988, the name was changed to reflect the type of birds that nest in the area. By then, the first nine holes of Great Blue had opened; when the second nine was finished in 1992, its success was assured. Visitors should note that the green fees are a bit steeper for the tougher Great Blue layout.

West Delta's original course got off to a whimpering start. It experienced bad drainage and, because it was opened too soon, debuted with poor turf; these conditions initially kept players away. Under Portland director of golf John Zoller Jr.'s guidance, however, Greenback was upgraded and is now much more playable. Heron Lakes' popularity really took off when Great Blue opened. Robert Trent Jones Jr. fashioned a goodly number of sand and water hazards for both courses, with watery graves particularly prevalent on Great Blue. This course is the site of the G.I. Joe's Northwest Open in mid-September. Featuring top Northwest sticks as well as some PGA tourers, the event is one of the largest regional PGA tournaments in the country, attracting nearly 10,000 spectators. A past winner is Seattle native and 1992 Masters Champion, Fred Couples.

A good Greenback test is the 1st, a 536-yard par-5 that winds rightward around a bunker. Another trap lurks 75 yards from its tri-trapped green. Five bunkers ring the green at the 3rd, a 165-yard par-3 with a pond-fronted tee. The 503-yard, par-5 13th is a tight dogleg-right that curls around a large bunker to a small, pond-fronted green protected by lateral traps. Water shimmers along the left of the 205-yard, par-3 14th, and three bunkers engird its deep-but-slender green.

Great Blue's fairways cross gently rolling terrain, and encompass an impressive array of water and sand hazards. This side also involves more fairway mounding than its sister layout. Challenging holes include the 2nd, a 515-yard par-5 with a wide, straight and rolling fairway squeezed by a pair of bunkers along the right. A pond on the right starts at the 160-yard mark and curls around the right flank of a mesa-like green, which is bunkered left, front and rear. The 4th, a 168-yard par-3, has water from tee to green and a two-tiered, bi-trapped putting surface fronted by the pond. The top-rated 5th, a 566-yard par-5, rises slightly along a route skirted by two pot bunkers left and a trap right, driving distance out. Bunkers sit at the left and right-front edges of the boomerang-shaped, pond-backed 5th green.

The 205-yard 6th is a tough par-3, with a narrow-but-deep, two-tiered green trapped front and right. The dogleg-left 8th, a 466-yard par-4, is lined by a slough along the left. While trees and a bunker occupy the inside of the turn, traps lurk along the right. The hole then winds up to a ridge-perched, terraced green with a steep left side and traps left-front and right. The 525-yard, par-5 12th winds sinuously rightward around a pond en route to a rolling green guarded on the right by water. The 16th, a 390-yard par-4, is squeezed by lakes on both sides of its slender path. Great Blue's home hole, a par-4 of 413 yards, crosses ridge-like terrain lined by more water on the right. The 18th green has bumps and hollows, and is quite slick.

Jim Colbert's Hound Hollow Golf Center

9 *23010 West Arata Road, Wood Village, OR 97030. (503) 669-2290. Dode Forrester, pro. 9 holes. 1,501 yards. Par 30. Grass tees. Course ratings: men 57.4/90, women 57.4/94. Year Opened: 1992. Architect: Lee Brune. Economical, jr./sr. rates, credit cards. Call for reservations. Walk-on chances: Good. Walkability: Good. Playability: Lots of trouble to be found on short track.*

Hound Hollow's executive nine and driving range/teaching center sit at the northeast end of the Multnomah Greyhound Track in Wood Village, east of Portland. The facility is owned by the Multnomah Kennel Club and Senior PGA Tour pro, Jim Colbert, the tour's leading money winner in 1996. Named after the nearby dog track, Hound Hollow is run by head pro Dode Forrester, a longtime associate of Colbert.

The layout was built by Portland's Leonard Bernhardt Landscaping on 44 acres purchased by the kennel club in 1956. The holes cross rolling ground and are amply threatened by water and sand hazards. The site was once popular with duck hunters; wetlands and native grasses were there prior to the course. When the project was completed in 1992, Wood Village officials gave the proprietors an award for sensitivity to the environment. The overgrown property was not only transformed into something useful, but the course recycles irrigation water.

The nine-holer bears three par-4s (275, 315 and 360 yards) and six par-3s (from 90 to 145 yards). Its teaching center features a driving range with both grass and covered-mat tees, three target greens, an "all-turf" 18-hole putting course with a par of 44, and a 2,000-square-foot clubhouse with swing computers, video gear and exercise equipment. Since opening, the course has been planted with various trees. Over a dozen sand traps dot Hound Hollow's 1,500 yards, and four ponds and a stream enter play. Though designed for beginning and intermediate golfers—who will hopefully see improved scores after visiting the learning center, Hound Hollow also challenges better sticks. The USGA-specified greens are mowed low and can be quite slick.

Killarney West Golf Club

1275 NW 334th, Hillsboro, OR 97124. (503) 648-7634. 9 holes. 2,544 yards. Par 36. Grass tees. Course rating: 64.4/108 (for men & women). Year Opened: 1979. Architect: Hank VanGrunsven. Moderate. Reservations: Call for weekends. Walk-on chances: Fair. Walkability: Good. Playability: Straightforward layout has a few twists and turns.

A nine-hole track off Highway 8 between Cornelius and Hillsboro, Killarney West is owned by Joe and Vera O'Meara, who, for years, ran the local O'Meara Dairy. When the course opened in the late-1970s, the couple devoted their energies exclusively to golf. And their children have followed suit. Five of the O'Meara's six children—Cathy Tarpley (Cross Creek), Pat (Springwater), Kevin (Nine Peaks), Bill (Wildwood), and Jane Reding (McKay Creek)—own and operate Oregon golf courses.

Fifty-acre Killarney West is crossed by the Council and Dairy creeks. The layout was severely affected by the floods of 1995-1996. Three inches of water crept into the clubhouse, and the course was closed for six months while the water receded and repairs were made. The O'Mearas had to rebuild a washed-out 6th green. Locals claim the flooding—which also caused considerable damage to nearby Meriwether National—was the worst in 100 years. By fall of 1996, Killarney West was, for the most part, back to normal playing conditions.

The easy-to-walk, bunkerless layout winds through forests harboring deer, squirrels, chipmunks, raccoons, possums, geese, swans and fish cranes. Ideal for beginning-intermediate players, Killarney West has five par-4s (from 252 to 360 yards), a pair of par-5s (435 and 410 yards), and par-3s of 95 and 110 yards. The first three holes lie east of 334th, with the remainder of the course to the west. Good tests include the top-rated 2nd, a 275-yard par-4 that goes between trees before doglegging 90 degrees to the right over its final 75 yards. A creek lines the fairway's left edge, with the small and raised 2nd green backed closely by evergreens. The 6th, a 310-yard par-4, is noteworthy for a sunken, two-tiered green guarded behind by a creek. A 360-yard par-4, the 9th doglegs sharply left around a pond to Killarney West's biggest putting surface.

King City Golf Course - semiprivate

15355 SW Royalty Parkway, Tigard, OR 97224. (503) 639-7986. Bob Gasper, pro. 9 holes. 2,428 yards. Par 33. Grass tees. Course ratings: men 62.4/100; women— M65.8/97, F64.6/96. Year Opened: 1963. Architect: George Marshall Development Company. Moderate. Reservations: Call a week ahead. Walk-on chances: Fair. Walkability: Overall, good. Playability: Though short, there's trouble to be had on this course.

King City's nine lies off Highway 99W and winds through a retiree-oriented community in Tigard. Residents in the neighborhood have access to a swimming pool and a town hall where social events are held. King City has an English-royalty theme; the dual-tee layout (stretching 4,839 yards over two circuits) is split by King Charles and Queen Elizabeth roads. The golfing grounds are overseen by longtime Class A pro, Bob Gasper, the head pro at Astoria Golf & Country Club for 20 years before moving to Tigard.

Recent course improvements include a new and enlarged 4th green, shaped by Arnie Saari. The putting surface was replaced after the previous green was destroyed by a freeze in the winter of 1995-1996. A few trees have also been added. The course occupies 52 acres of gently rolling terrain, and is visited by ducks and geese. King City's par-3s are quite long, extending 217, 217 and 179 yards. Greens are guarded by a few sand traps, with a pond in play at the 7th. Seasonal winds can create havoc, and the greens housing some tricky undulations. Good tests include the 2nd, a 217-yard par-3, and the 7th, a 385-yard par-4 rated the toughest hole. Heading straight across a fairway lined by homes, the 7th ends at a raised, laterally-trapped green fronted by the pond.

Lake Oswego Golf Course

18 *17525 SW Stafford Road, Lake Oswego, OR 97034. (503) 636-8228. Patty Miller, pro. 18 holes. 2,724 yards. Par 61. Grass tees (one mat). No course ratings. Year Opened: 1967. Architects: Cliff & Arnie Schmautz. Economical, jr./sr. rates. Reservations: Call for weekends. Walk-on chances: Fair. Walkability: No problems. Playability: Good short-iron test.*

This 18-hole, par-61 course is owned and operated by the city of Lake Oswego. In 1996, the city council agreed to make $1.4-million worth of improvements to the facility. The first phase includes redoing the hitting areas of the 21-tee driving range and adding lighting for nighttime use. Other work involves building a new 17th hole. The original 17th was too close to the driving range and the new hole will make better use of a creek running through the property. Recent improvements include a new clubhouse and enlarged tees. Drainage upgrades are ongoing. Like the city of Portland's, Lake Oswego's golf program may be affected by Measure 47, a statewide referendum passed in 1996 that limits taxes. Measure 47 may ultimately strain a local government's ability to fund capital improvements to city facilities, such as this golf course.

The facility runs one of the region's busiest junior golf programs. In summers, upwards of 140 kids are allowed to block off tee times. Among the juniors who participated in the 1996 program were the children of PGA Tour pro, Peter Jacobsen, a Lake Oswego resident. Former LPGA touring pro Cindy Lincoln runs the course with help from fellow pro, Patty Miller. Sadly, a longtime Oregon teaching pro who was instrumental in developing Lake Oswego's junior program, Paul Kaskinen, passed away in 1994.

Though hosting as many as 84,000 rounds annually, Lake Oswego only had 63,000 rounds in 1996 because of unusually wet weather. Designed and built by the then-owners of the Portland Buckaroos hockey team, Cliff and Arnie Schmautz, Lake Oswego's 42-acre track spans gently rolling, hilltop terrain. A creek enters play on several holes. The course has seven par-4s—the longest a mere 192 yards, an ideal setup for neophytes. With the water hazards and a goodly number of greenside bunkers, Lake Oswego also provides a decent test for more proficient golfers.

Langdon Farms Golf Club

24377 NE Airport Road, Aurora, OR 97002. (503) 678-4653. Jeff Fought, pro. 18 holes. 6,935 yards. Par 71. Grass tees. Course ratings: men—B73.3/125, M71.2/ 121, I68.9/116, F64.8/108; women—I74.0/126, F69.4/114. Year Opened: 1995. Architects: Robert Cupp & John Fought. Expensive, credit cards. Reservations: Call up to 30 days ahead. Walk-on chances: Fair. Walkability: Good. Playability: Lots of challenges to be found at newer course south of Portland.

Langdon Farms occupies a former seed and sod operation between Interstate 5 and Highway 99. Named after Harold and Emma Langdon's farm, the course sustains the agricultural theme with a 25,000-square-foot, barnlike clubhouse. The structure was named by *Crittenden Golf Inc* magazine in 1996 as the nation's best in the daily-fee, over 6,000-square-foot category. Inside the structure—designed by Portland's GBD Architects—is the Big Red Barn Restaurant, an eatery popular with golfing and non-playing diners. Outside is a patio with picnic tables and benches carved and built by a local farmer. The pro shop was named 1995's best by the Oregon PGA. Other praise came in 1995 when Langdon Farms was nominated by *Golf Digest* as being among America's Best New Public Courses.

Also on the site are administration offices for Langdon Farms' proprietor, O.B. Sports, Inc., which also owns and operates the Legacy and Angel Park courses in Nevada. Headed by Orrin Vincent, a Northwest native who played collegiate golf at Seattle University, the firm manages Stevinson Ranch in California and the new Reserve Vineyards Golf Club in Hillsboro. Orrin's son, O.D., is the coach of the men's golf team at the University of Washington. Hosting about 50,000 rounds a year, Langdon Farms serves as the site of a John Jacobs golf school from April through October. As a strong supporter of junior golf, Vincent offers Langdon Farms as the site of the annual Ralph Lauren Polo American Junior Golf Association tournament, an event played by ten dozen young golfers from around the country.

The green at Langdon Farms' 18th, a 514-yard par-5, is linked to the putting surface at the 9th.

The full-service facility boasts one of the region's largest driving ranges and a nine-hole putting course, and is a popular site for private tournaments. In its first year, 120 such events were held. In an effort to encourage local play, Langdon Farms sells two types of annual passes to help discount the facility's rather steep green fees. In 1996, the $395 Red Barn card allowed $15 off the price of admission and unlimited use of the range, while the $245 Farm Card offered the fee discount only.

The gently rolling course cost $10.5 million to build; the high price was because the course was sodded and has concrete cart paths. The yardages on sprinkler heads may be a bit confusing for first-timers. The distances are color-coded to match the pin positions—red (front), white (middle) and blue (back), but once understood, are very helpful. The course is walkable, with the path between the 7th and 8th holes through an old barn. Langdon Farms is surrounded by nurseries, small farms and quiet neighborhoods to the east. But I-5 car traffic is audible, as are planes out of a nearby airport.

Towering mounds define most holes on the track, whose links-like personality is complicated by westerly winds. For the most part, the mounds help golfers by redirecting shots hit along the edges of holes back toward short grass. But in a few instances, the taller mounds cause safety problems as they block views of neighboring tees. Players should be mindful of this and shout "Fore!" whenever shots are hit over greens. Another quibble could be made over the severity of some of the putting surfaces. Moguls, tiers and wild undulations mark some of them, with perhaps the "best" example of this found at the 18th, where two pronounced knobs rise out of the green's right side. Contrarily, an appealing aspect of the course is the low-mowed areas at the "throat" of the greens. Though some of these aprons sit in swales, players can still putt from them.

Notable holes include the 1st, a 405-yard par-4 whose straight-running fairway passes a bunker along the left. Another trap sits 30 yards from the right-front edge of a promontory-perched, front-left-tilting green fronted by a swale. The 4th, a 356-yard par-4, is a narrow left-bender with a steep lower ledge along the left. A bunker sits at the end of this area, which has higher grass than the fairway's right half. A target helps direct approaches to the mound-ringed green, which has a tall tier through its midsection that causes the back half to tilt rearward. The 440-yard 5th is a straight-running par-4 into the prevailing winds. The fairway—littered with bunkers along the left and mounds right—is squeezed by a bunker along the right, 75 yards from a radical two-tiered green trapped on the right.

The 552-yard, par-5 7th has an open driving area, but second shots are muddied by a stream that merges into the fairway from the left. The water hazard crosses the hole diagonally; huge, rough-covered mounds line the hole to the right. The creek winds in front of the 7th green, which has a hump that tips it both right and left. The top-rated 8th, a 464-yard par-4, bears a 70-yard-long church-pew bunker (a la Oakmont in Pennsylvania) driving distance out. The latter part of the hole is narrowed by the circa 1915 "Langdon Red Barn" left and mounds right. A bunker lurks 80 yards from the large, humped-in-the-middle 8th green.

Tough back-nine tests include the par-5 11th, a winding and left-bending 629-yarder. A triad of bunkers cross the hole 325 yards out, where the fairway is also narrowed by trees. The last section of the hole descends to a small, left-sloping green trapped left. The 12th, a 446-yard par-4, rises past a bunker along the left. The long and skinny 12th green is boomerang-shaped, and has two bunkers right, one of which is doughnut-shaped (sand around a "turfed hole"). Perhaps the toughest par-3 at Langdon Farms is the 17th, a 224-yarder with a concave green lined on the left by seven bunkers. A prominent ridge runs vertically through this massive putting surface.

McKay Creek Golf Course

1416 NW Jackson Street, Hillsboro, OR 97124. (503) 693-7612. 9 holes. 2,727 yards. Par 36. Grass tees. Course ratings: men M64.4/101, women—M68.4/105, F66.6/100. Year Opened: 1996. Architects: Bill O'Meara & Jeremy Reding. Moderate, credit cards. Call for reservations. Walk-on chances: Good. Walkability: No major problems. Playability: Players use all clubs in the bag at course designed for average golfer.

Opened on June 20, 1996, McKay Creek Golf Course is owned by yet another member of Oregon's O'Meara family. Jane Reding, daughter of Joe and Vera O'Meara, proprietors of Killarney West about a half-mile to the west, and her husband John own the nine-hole venue. All but one of Joe and Vera's children own Oregon golf courses. These include daughter Cathy Tarpley (Cross Creek) and sons Pat (Springwater), Kevin (Nine Peaks) and Bill (Wildwood, and co-designer of this course).

John and Jane Reding had operated a carpet-cleaning and restoration business for 20 years before following her parents and siblings into the golf business. Sons Jeremy (McKay Creek's co-designer) and Jason—students at Oregon State University when this was written in 1996, and daughter Michelle—a student at Hillsboro's Glencoe High School—helped build the layout. Before entering OSU, the brothers played golf on Glencoe's boys team. Jeremy directed Jason where to move dirt while shaping the greens as Jason operated an old Caterpillar. Though John Reding had no previous experience in conditioning a course, he maintains McKay Creek. Michelle, a member of Glencoe's girls golf team, helps in the pro shop.

The nine-holer was built on the old Naught Dairy Farm. The site is split by McKay Creek; part of the 50-acre property is in Hillsboro, with the remainder in unincorporated Washington County. The Redings had a relatively smooth permit process thanks to their close study of the pitfalls experienced by other recent Washington County courses, particularly Quail Valley. The creek floods each year in January and February, so the course is closed then. McKay Creek's 22-stall driving range sits on higher ground and is open year-round. The clubhouse is a renovated farmhouse, and has a pro shop and snack bar; the facility has a liquor license.

Located just north of Fir Lawn Cemetery, the layout spans flat terrain beside the creek. Tall trees line most fairways, which are visited by deer, squirrels, nutria, geese and other birds. The course is made up of three par-3s, three par-4s and three par-5s, and has a couple of ponds that squeeze a few holes. Because of the flooding, the Redings built a bunker in 1997 to see how it survives future inundations before adding more traps. McKay Creek's bentgrass greens are mostly straightforward, with the exceptions being the hogbacked putting surface at the 4th and the two-tiered 9th green.

Meriwether National Golf Club

36 *5200 SW Roodbridge Road, Hillsboro, OR 97123. (503) 648-4143. Jim Petersen, pro. 27 holes & Executive Nine. Grass tees. Course ratings: Executive Nine (1,789 yards, par 30)—men 57.6/84, women 56.6/82. South/North (6,779 yards, par 72): men—B71.2/117, M69.0/114; women F71.9/113. West/North (6,719 yards, par 72): men—B71.3/121, M69.5/118; women F72.3/113. West/South (6,752 yards, par 72): men—B71.3/115, M69.1/111; women F71.2/112. Years Opened: 1960 (North), 1962 (West), 1994 (South) & 1996 (Executive Nine). Architects: Course founders (North/West) & Dave Powers (South & Executive Nine). Moderate, jr./sr. rates. Reservations: Call for weekends. Walk-on chances: Fair. Walkability: Good. Playability: Three regulation nines, an executive track, 18-hole putting layout and driving range generate lots of swings at golf balls.*

When Meriwether National opened in the early 1960s with a lengthy 18-hole course, head pro Jim Petersen worked out of a utilitarian cinderblock clubhouse. Today, Petersen, Meriwether's overseer since 1962, enjoys an 11,000-square-foot "office" with a restaurant, bar and pro shop. Outside, Petersen observes such additions as another regulation-length nine, an executive course, an 18-hole putting layout, and a driving range. Unfortunately, just before the new Executive Nine opened in February 1996 the original West and North sides were flooded when a dike that walled off the nearby Tualatin River broke. It took seven months to clean up the mess. Roughly 35,000 gallons of water a day were pumped off West and North. Petersen and his staff were nearly marooned; the water rushed through the dike's breach so fast they barely escaped.

By fall 1996, Meriwether's operations were back on track, but not before the 6th hole on the West nine was rebuilt. While all the work was underway on West and North, play continued on South. Neither that side nor the Executive Nine were damaged. The costly repairs made to Meriwether National were borne by its owner William W. Saunders. The dike was repaired, so the course should not be inundated again by another of those "100-year floods." The previous natural calamity occurred in February 1974 when the Tualatin washed over the dike. When all of Meriwether is in operation, a triple-tee system and all 27 regulation holes are used. Golfers seeking a quick fix play the Executive Nine.

The layout on Hillsboro's southwest edge crosses flat, unremarkable land. Because the newer South nine was zoned as Exclusive Farm Use by Washington County, designer Dave Powers could not raise the tee boxes. Though it's uncertain how flat tee boxes relate to farming, the result is a featureless course with holes bearing perfunctory starting and ending points. The greens look okay, but there's a real sameness to their construction. Among South's best holes is the 4th, a 435-yard par-4 with a slight left-bending fairway lined by jail along the right. A big bunker sits farther down along the right, 125 yards from a rolling, trapped-left green. The 9th, a 394-yard par-4, winds narrowly rightward around a pond to a slick, front-tilting green trapped on the right.

A good North test is the 2nd, a par-4 of 447 yards that bends rightward around trees. A creek crossing the fairway 250 yards out is often found by longer hitters. The left edge of the large 2nd green is guarded by a bunker. West's 2nd, a 418-yard par-4, curls slightly leftward en route to a raised, laterally trapped green. A pond looms off the elevated tee at the 215-yard, par-3 4th, whose green is laterally trapped.

Perhaps the most fun to be had at Meriwether National is at its 18-hole putting course. The mini-track just beyond the windows in the clubhouse lounge features "fairways" lined by tiny bunkers, sloping holes curling off a knoll, and lights for nighttime play.

Mountain View Golf Club

27195 SE Kelso Road, Boring, OR 97009. (503) 663-4869. Toby Tommaso, pro. **18**
18 holes. 5,920 yards. Par 71. Grass tees. Course ratings: men—B68.0/118, M66.0/
113; women—M71.0/110, F69.8/109. Year Opened: 1963. Architects: Jack
Beaudoin & Jack Waltmire. Moderate, jr./sr. rates, credit cards. Reservations: Call
a week ahead. Walk-on chances: Fair. Walkability: Pretty good on the front with
some hilly traverses along the back. Playability: Though located in the town of
Boring, this course has variety.

This aptly-named course lies within sight of four mountains—Adams, Rainier, Saint Helens and Hood. Thanks to porous soil and a pocketed locale to protect it from rain-bearing westerlies, the 130-acre layout is one of western Oregon's driest courses in winter and spring. Mountain View's longtime pro and owner, Jack Beaudoin, and his former partner, Jack Waltmire, designed and built the course. In August 1990, Beaudoin sold Mountain View to Ed Jarrett and Jerry McKay. Beaudoin, who passed away in early 1997 at age 59, set the course record, a 60, during his tenure here.

The current proprietors have made several improvements during their tenure, the most recent being a rebuilt 13th hole. The par-3 went from a 125-yarder to a considerably more challenging 170 yards. Upcoming plans include the addition of some ponds to the front nine which will lend character and difficulty to the flattish side. Though not a nerve-wracker with a plethora of sand or water hazards, well-tended Mountain View offers an enjoyable golf round and a variety of holes.

The front side is conventional, with holes winding through evergreens. Its stiffest test is the 2nd, a 455-yard par-5 with a 90-degree, dogleg-right fairway and a wavy green. Mountain View's back is very hilly, with tilting fairways lined by maples and firs, tricky greens, a few water hazards, some towering elevated tees, and occasional deer sightings. The 12th, a 184-yard par-3, drops 180 feet down from its perched tee to a large green. (A sign nearby says, "This hole may be hazardous to your health.") Deep Creek—a tributary of the Clackamas River—trickles behind the trapped-left putting surface. Another good hole is the 14th, a 528-yard par-5 with a rolling, narrow fairway crossed by a creek and a mid-sized, trapped-right green.

Oregon City Golf Club

20124 South Beavercreek Road, Oregon City, OR 97045. (503) 656-2846. Bill **18**
Hagedorn, pro. 18 holes. 5,864 yards. Par 71. Grass tees. Course ratings: men—
B67.3/107, M65.6/103; women—M70.8/116, F69.4/113. Years Opened: 1925
(original nine), 1960 (second nine). Architects: George Junor (original nine); Joe
Herberger (second nine). Moderate, sr. rates, credit cards. Reservations: Call two
weeks ahead. Walk-on chances: Fair. Walkability: Good, overall. Playability:
Continuing improvements enhance challenge.

Many recent renovations have greatly aided the condition and difficulty of this 18-hole course. Owned since 1950 by Rose and the late Joe Herberger, Oregon City's course is now operated by the Herberger's children: son John—who's the superintendent, and daughters Rosemary Holden and Teresa Cornella. The siblings have reinvested in the facility by adding bunkers to greensides and routing paved cart paths through much of the layout. A new irrigation system was installed, and barrancas were added to give fairways more character and difficulty. A newly-expanded clubhouse—now 5,000-square-feet in size—contains a banquet room that augments a popular dining area. Recently, the nines were switched and an upgraded irrigation system allowed the construction of three ponds. Though some nearby courses have experienced downturns in total rounds, Oregon City has held steady at 60,000 rounds a year.

Oregon City's original George Junor-designed nine was built in 1925 on an old farmstead. The Herbergers waited 10 years after buying the course before building the second nine in 1960. Joe Herberger, who passed away in November 1996, came to Oregon City with quite a background in golf, apprenticing as a greenskeeper at Salem Golf Club and working under his superintendent father, John Herberger, at Oswego Lake Country Club.

The rural area surrounding Oregon City's 126-acre course has gradually become developed with subdivisions. On clear days, golfers enjoy views of mounts Hood, Adams and Saint Helens. Players might also spot deer, skunks, brown bears and foxes, though wildlife visitations have decreased with the peripheral suburbanization. The course crosses gently rolling terrain, with most fairways tree-lined. The course's toughest hole may be the 3rd, a double-dogleg, 595-yard par-5 that initially goes sharply left, then backtracks rightward to a trapped-right green. Perhaps the prettiest hole is the 9th, a 175-yard par-3 featuring a pond-fronted, rolling green.

Orenco Woods Golf Club - semiprivate

9

22000 NW Birch Street, Hillsboro, OR 97123. (503) 648-1836. Rich Haaland, pro. 9 holes. 2,626 yards. Par 35. Grass tees. Course ratings: men—B65.8/114, M65.3/111; women F67.3/109. Year Opened: 1952. Architect: Darrell Brown. Moderate, jr./sr. rates, credit cards. Reservations: Call a week ahead. Walk-on chances: Fair. Walkability: Good overall, with some exercise involved. Playability: Quick rounds available at one of the few Elks-owned courses left in the Northwest.

Orenco Woods was originated in 1952 by its designer, builder and owner, Darrell Brown. It's been owned by the Elks Club since 1970. The venue—one of the few Elks courses left in the region—was named after the Oregon Nursery Company ("Ore-n-co") which, before the Depression, was the largest plant supplier west of the Mississippi River. Alongside the 3rd hole stands an ornate brick home built in 1909 by the company's president. Rich Haaland has been the head pro since 1980. There have been no significant course modifications in recent years, though a few new tees may be built in the future.

The 49-acre track crosses well-wooded hills and valleys, with Rock Creek a factor on nearly all the holes. The course's up-and-down terrain results in tricky doglegging fairways and greens often unobservable from afar. The double-tee layout is comprised of a 2,626-yard, par-35 front and a par-36, 2,750-yard back. Good tests include the 1st, a 472-yard par-5 that crosses flat ground before dropping leftward to a rolling green backed by Rock Creek. The 2nd, a 298-yard par-4, starts at a creek-fronted tee, then winds narrowly rightward to a small, undulating green. The top-rated 9th, a 402-yard par-4, becomes a 444-yard par-5 when played as the 18th. Once off a creek-fronted tee, the 9th/18th rises over steep ground—past trees and OB left—to a large, right-tilting putting surface.

Persimmon Country Club - semiprivate

500 SE Butler Road, Gresham, OR 97080. (503) 661-1800. Larry Skreen, pro. **18**
*18 holes. 6,435 yards. Par 72. Grass tees. Course ratings: men—B71.2/125, M69.5/
122, I66.9/113; women—M73.9/126, I70.3/122, F66.1/122. Year Opened: 1993.
Architect: Gene "Bunny" Mason. Expensive, credit cards. Call for reservations.
Walk-on chances: Fair. Walkability: Okay on the front nine except for two hills;
carts recommended for the steeper back. Playability: Up-and-down topography,
considerable hazards, and tricky design features make for challenging golf.*

Located east of Portland off Hogan Road, this upscale course sprawls across a
hillside, offering unimpeded views of Mount Hood. Complemented by a full-service,
16,000-square-foot clubhouse and a driving range near the facility's entrance, Persimmon features a fine Bunny Mason-designed layout. The Persimmon development—
named for the wood used in golf clubs—was called Crystal Springs when originally
proposed by Quincorp Investment Group in 1988. When Quincorp pulled out of the
project in 1992, CGC Inc.—owned by Vancouver (Washington) developer Hiroshi
Morihara—bought it for $5.4 million and finished the course. CGC is developing
houses to the west and multi-family units east of the course. The 375-acre site is on
the Multnomah County line and borders Clackamas County. The site was homesteaded
by the Shiiki family, who grew berries and vegetables after settling here in the early
1900s.

Persimmon boasts many accoutrements of a first-class golf facility, with wide
concrete cart paths, exemplary turf, pretty gardens, and excellent signage. Save for two
steep hills, the front nine is reasonable for ambulating golfers. Conversely, the
up-and-down back nine is quite arduous, with long, uncomfortable hikes over pavement.
Persimmon allows relaxing rounds, with the only perimeter noise emanating from traffic
on Hogan, a fairly busy north-south two-laner. Persimmon is almost links-like; when the
fairway-side trees mature, its personality will change. Perhaps the course's signature trait is
its tough par-3s, two of which appear consecutively at the 3rd and 4th.

Notable holes include the top-rated 2nd, a 601-yard par-5 that runs uphill to
the right. A bunker sits along the left at the 175-yard mark. The fairway then rises to
a large, front-sloping green with a hump in its right half and traps left-front and right.
The 3rd, a 201-yard par-3, gets its third-toughest ranking from a severely right-front-
sloping green trapped left-front and right. The 7th, a par-3 of 210 yards, ascends to a
steeply front-tilting, wildly undulating green that leans to the right-front. The
interesting 8th, a narrow 259-yard par-4, runs uphill past a gnarly drop-off along the
right. Once past a big bunker along the right at the 100-yard mark, the hole curls
slightly rightward to a hill-cut green trapped left-front; it also has a precipitous right
side. The 404-yard, par-4 9th drops off an elevated tee down a chute-like fairway. The
last 75 yards of the hole are filled with a jailed gully and creek. Second shots must be
lofted over this detritus to reach a wide-but-shallow, trapped-left-front green riven
with rises and swales.

The 10th, a 375-yard par-4, ventures off a towering tee along a 90-degree,
dogleg-right path around bunkers. The fairway passes a trap left of the 150-yard mark
before ending at a two-tiered, hill-carved green trapped left-front and left-rear.
Persimmon's fourth-toughest hole is the 12th, a 170-yard par-3 that offers superb
Mount Hood vistas. Its big and rolling green tilts right-front, and is bunkered twice in
front. Persimmon's 18th is a fine closer. The 433-yard par-4 begins at another scenic
tee, then descends to a mid-sized landing area squeezed on the right by jail. Over its

concluding 100 yards, the fairway rises toward an overgrown canyon. The chasm crosses before the steeply front-leaning 18th green, which is backed by three pot bunkers. Don't overshoot this putting surface as you'll face Persimmon's toughest shot: a downhiller out of a trap to a sloping-away green perilously close to inextricable trouble.

9 Portland Meadows Golf Course

901 North Schmeer Road, Portland, OR 97217. (503) 289-3405. 9 holes. 1,983 yards. Par 31. Grass tees. No course ratings. Year Opened: 1951. Architects: Stan Terry & Eddie Hogan. Economical. No reservations. Walkability: Good. Playability: Ideal for quick golf fixes, as long the urge hits between May and September.

The nine-hole "track" here covers the infield of the Portland Meadows horse-racing oval. The layout is the only one—other than Touchet Valley in Dayton, Washington—featuring golf holes in and around a horseracing facility. Its entrance is at the Meadows' south end; golfers must cross the oval to reach a small clubhouse. The course is open only from May to September. It opens at 10:00 a.m. weekdays to allow the ponies to exercise during early morning hours, and opens at 7:00 a.m. on weekends. Golf is taboo while the horses run from October through April. Another reason for the short season is that the layout has poor drainage in winter and early spring.

Opened in 1951, the nine was patterned after the layout at San Francisco's Bay Meadows. The executive-length course contains five par-3s and four short par-4s. A small pond enters play on the first three holes, and several traps dot the the sides of generally small greens. This venue can be circuited in just over an hour if there aren't many golfers around. One of its busiest times is during weekday lunch hours, when businessmen doff coats and ties to chase the white pea around.

18 Progress Downs Municipal Golf Course

8200 SW Scholls Ferry Road, Progress, OR 97005. (503) 646-5166. Jerry Minor, pro. 18 holes. 6,426 yards. Par 71. Grass tees. Course ratings: men—B69.8/112, M68.4/110; women—M74.8/123, F71.7/115. Year Opened: 1965. Architect: Ervin Thoreson. Moderate, jr./sr. rates. Reservations: Call a week ahead. Walk-on chances: Ok for singles. Walkability: Good. Playability: Though well-worn, holes here have variety and challenge.

Progress Downs is equipped with a pro shop rated among the nation's top-100 golf-equipment retailers by *Golf Shop Operations* magazine, a double-decker driving range, and a restaurant with lounge and banquet space. It is owned by the city of Portland, whose director of golf is John Zoller, Jr. Zoller has been sitting on a plan for a $3-million remodel of Progress Downs. Unfortunately, reserve funds have not been available to begin the project, which involves stretching the course out to 6,800 yards and building new tees, greens, and sand and water hazards.

The year 1996 wasn't kind to Portland's municipal courses, with annual rounds down and revenue below once-healthy levels. A surcharge on green fees begun in 1994 deterred out-of-towners. Though the two-tiered rate system was ditched in the summer of 1996, it effectively altered the patterns of the regular patrons of Progress Downs, Eastmoreland, Rose City and Heron Lakes. Making matters potentially worse, a voter-approved tax initiative called Measure 47 may serve to throttle the funding of golf projects. The 1996 measure cuts property taxes and caps taxable income, maintains 1995 tax levels, and limits tax boosts to three percent. It may eventually strain local governmental purse strings such that Portland may turn to its profitable golf courses for financial help. Instead of reusing revenues generated by the courses through an innovative Enterprise system, Portland's golf program may become a fat cow tapped by officials whenever funds are needed.

It's too bad if that turns out to be the case. Portland's courses are vital public holdings. But due to frequent use, they will need capital improvements to stay tied with Spokane as the Northwest's premier municipal golf program.

Perhaps the busiest of all Portland courses, Progress Downs crosses forested, rolling ground near the intersection of highways 217 and 210. In other words, the locale is ideally suited for hosting hordes of golfers. The site is also quite good for a golf course. Though it doesn't drain particularly well, Progress Downs manages to make it through Portland's wet winters relatively unscathed. The master plan, which will retrofit fairways with much-needed drain tile, would greatly help Progress Downs' year-round shape. Until the renovations are made, players must be entertained by such holes as the 2nd, a 388-yard par-4 that winds leftward around a fairway pond. The water hazard stretches up to guard the green's left edge. The 12th, a par-5 of 457 yards, has a wide, left-tilting fairway and a bi-trapped green with a tree-squeezed throat. The second-toughest hole, the 15th, is a 436-yard par-4 with OB left of its up-angled fairway. The knoll-perched 15th green is laterally trapped.

Pumpkin Ridge Golf Club - Ghost Creek - semiprivate

18

12930 Old Pumpkin Ridge Road, Cornelius, OR 97113-6147. (503) 647-4747 or 647-9977. Jerry Mowlds, director of golf. 18 holes. 6,839 yards. Par 71. Grass tees. Course ratings: men—T73.6/134, B71.4/132, M69.0/130; women—M69.0/130, F71.4/117. Year Opened: 1992. Architects: Robert Cupp & John Fought. Expensive, credit cards. Reservations: Call a week ahead. Walk-on chances: Ok for singles. Walkability: Quite good for such an expansive layout. Playability: One of the Northwest's best public or private tests.

Ghost Creek, the public half of Pumpkin Ridge's 36-hole facility, is one of the region's best all-round courses. Its players must overcome all manner of hazards and length, which work in tandem with a timeless design recalling works of the legendary golf course architects. Pumpkin Ridge was initiated in 1986 with the purchase of land by its founders—Portland businessmen Gaylord Davis, Marvin French, Barney Hyde, and Shigero Ito of the Japanese investment company, Aiko Group. All these men are avid golfers, with Davis a two-time winner of the Oregon Amateur. Atlanta-based designer Robert Cupp was hired to fulfull the owners' desire that Pumpkin Ridge's courses reflect the "Golden Era" of golf architecture, a period led by such masters as MacDonald, Tillinghast, Thompson, MacKenzie and Ross. Cupp was aided by John Fought, a native Portlander and former PGA Tour pro.

The 36-hole facility (see also Witch Hollow in this chapter's Private Courses section) spans 340 acres of one-time farm- and timberlands. Pumpkin Ridge will forever be a golf-only concern; there will never be homesites along fairways. Holes are lined by fir, maple, oak, ash and fruit trees, with wetlands and its namesake Ghost Creek routinely affecting play. The course offers views of the Coast Range, Cascades, Tualatin Hills and fertile Willamette Valley. Ghost Creek was named *Golf Digest's* Best New Public Course in 1992, the same year Witch Hollow was awarded the second-best private course. The conditioning of this venue is overseen by superintendent Bill Webster, and director of golf Jerry Mowlds runs the golf operations.

The 36 holes at Pumpkin Ridge are all-bentgrass. Four years after the courses' debuts, bent remains the predominant strain, with *poa annua* (so far) successfully excluded. Keeping *poa*—a bluegrass native to the Northwest—out is a diligent process. Webster and crew do this by mowing the grass low; picking up grass clippings; and "stressing" the bentgrass turf at certain times of the year to kill off the *poa*. An optional soft-spikes policy was begun in 1996 with good results and near-unanimous participation. (*Poa* often "invades" bentgrass when the seedhead attaches itself to clubs and metal spikes; cleaning clubs before use and wearing the soft, plastic spikes helps minimize *poa's* introduction.)

Ghost Creek is the annual site of the Nike Tour Championship, the culmination of the pro tour sponsored by Beaverton's shoe manufacturer. With Witch Hollow, Ghost Creek co-hosted the 1996 U.S. Amateur Championships at which Tiger Woods electrified the golf world by winning his third straight title and springing into stardom on the PGA Tour. Witch Hollow was the primary venue for the 1997 U.S. Women's Open, with Ghost Creek used as the practice site. Other events held at Pumpkin Ridge have included the 1993 Oregon Amateur. In the year 2000, the 36-hole facility will host the U.S. Junior Boys and U.S. Junior Girls tournaments, making it only the second venue to hold two USGA championships at the same time. It's likely that a U.S. Open or PGA Championship will be played here in the future.

Members of Witch Hollow have access to Ghost Creek as part of their privileges, and each layout has its own clubhouse. Visiting players use one end—with the members on the other—of a massive grass-teed driving range. Like its sister course, Ghost Creek is efficiently arranged, with no long walks between holes. The 6,800-yard layout is not cheap to play, but it affords golfers a rare opportunity to test their abilities against a genuinely tough, exquisitely maintained track.

Particularly memorable holes include the top-rated 4th, a 515-yard par-5 that rises steeply off the tee. There's a sizable landing area atop a ridge, but pulled tee shots will die in a steep, jailed hillside. At the 150-yard mark, the hole is squeezed by trees before ending at a three-tiered green lined left by pot bunkers. The 7th, a 409-yard par-4, winds uphill to the left around a bunker. Two traps left of the landing area prevent balls from rolling into more serious trouble, and a pair of pot bunkers guard the the broad-but-shallow, left-tilting green. The beautifully-framed 8th, a 562-yard par-5, has two bunkers right and trees left of the tee-shot garden spot. Here, golfers can glimpse nice vistas of a green valley to the south before the hole winds downhill. A bunker along the right sits 100 yards from a mid-sized, rolling green trapped right-front. The 9th, a 443-yard par-4, has a wide fairway lined left by two bunkers and OB, with Ghost Creek trickling along the right. The stream crosses the hole 140 yards from a right-front-sloping, trapped-right green. A pond sits closely by the left edge of this putting surface, which is further imperiled along the rear by the creek.

The 12th is a 406-yard par-4 with a panoramic tee and a fairway that curls rightward around two bunker-fronted evergreens. Golfers might try carrying these trees with drives, but they may find bunkers outside the turn. Four traps line the fairway's left edge en route to a severely front-sloping, trapped-right-rear green with a tall spur along its rear quarter. The 17th, a fun-filled 301-yard par-4, has the creek running along its left edge, with bunkers right. The stream crosses the fairway in the driving zone, 100 yards from a radical, two-tiered green bunkered left. The 18th, a 428-yard par-4, is defined by a tree-enclosed, right-leaning fairway bordered along the right by the creek. The rill eventually feeds into a pond that pinches the right and front edges of a front-left-sloping, two-tiered green protected by a grass bunker left.

Quail Valley Golf Course

12565 NW Aerts Road, Banks, OR 97106. (503) 324-4444. Doug Hixson, pro. 18 holes. 6,603 yards. Par 72. Grass tees. Course ratings: men—C71.6/122, B70.2/ 118, M68.9/114; women—M74.4/127, F71.5/117. Year Opened: 1994. Architect: John Zoller, Jr. Moderate. Reservations: Call a week ahead. Walk-on chances: Fair. Walkability: Good. Playability: Interesting, entertaining layout is one of Portland area's best all-round choices.

Quail Valley Golf Course lies west of Portland near the town of Banks; head west on Highway 26 and follow the signs to Highway 6. Quail Valley is near two pricier 36-hole venues, Pumpkin Ridge and Reserve Vineyards. Thanks to its valley location, Quail Valley is usually open when Pumpkin Ridge is closed by frost. Though not quite as epic (and expensive) as Pumpkin and Reserve, Quail Valley can hold its own in many regards. The attractions of the course, designed by Portland's director of golf, leave a strong impression. Looking at the flattish layout from ground level does not do justice to the nooks and crannies and humps and hollows encountered while playing the entertaining and surprisingly varied holes.

The course, which averaged 40,000 annual rounds in each of its first few years, was begun by Ron Mack and two brothers, Kenneth and Forest Bump. The trio originally wanted a 36-holer, but Washington County officials stopped that plan through its byzantine regulations. Mack, an expatriate of the computer business, serves as the general manager. The owners wisely directed their financial resources toward the course, opting for a modest clubhouse with a snack bar and pro shop instead of a dollar-draining behemoth structure. An outdoor pavilion for barbeques is in the works, as are more bunkers and trees along the course. The venue has a 14-acre grass-teed driving range, with lessons overseen by Class A PGA pro Doug Hixson. Hixson, whose father Harvey was a longtime Oregon pro before retiring in 1993, is a fine tournament player, most recently winning the 1996 Northwest Open. His brother Dan is the head pro at Columbia-Edgewater in Portland.

Built by Bernhardt Golf of Portland, Quail Valley is blessed with a naturally draining site. Before being converted into a golf course the 160 acres were farmed by David Vandehey, who grew beans, corn, strawberries and grass seed. Though upwards of 50 trees will be planted in each of the next few years, Quail Valley will remain a links-style layout, with westerly winds sweeping across the course and water entering play on 14 holes. Lovely views of the Coast Range and surrounding valley are on tap. During the 1996 U.S. Amateur at Pumpkin Ridge, employees of ESPN and NBC as well as players in the tournament came to Quail Valley, leaving glowing compliments in their wake.

Equipped with paved cart paths throughout, Quail Valley is efficiently arrayed and very walkable. Fairway peripheries were planted with fescue, which is cut short and therefore escapable. The greens were built with plenty of undulations, but are not overly tricky. Tough holes include the top-rated 5th, a 526-yard par-5 that runs straight and slightly uphill past wetlands along the left. The fairway narrows over its last 100 yards before ending at a right-sloping green guarded right by a pond; three traps lurk left and left-rear. The 6th, a 165-yard par-3, requires a well-placed shot over a large pond to reach a wide-but-shallow green trapped right-front and rear. The 8th, a 402-yard par-4, has a big pond off the tee that goes along the left side of the fairway. The slightly descending 8th eventually reaches a kidney-shaped, right-front-sloping green trapped in front and bearing wetlands on the right. The 9th, a 431-yard par-4, follows a straight-ahead, rising route defined by mounds along the right. Over its final 160 yards, a pond lines the fairway's left side, then curls up to front a large, rolling green.

Quail Valley's "Amen Corner" comes at the 12th through 14th holes. The slightly downhill 12th, a 474-yard par-4, is lined by a fence and OB left. Two big bunkers sit along the left at the 235- and 185-yard marks, respectively. The rather small, right-front-tilting 12th green is trapped left, with jail close behind and a grass bunker in front. The 13th, a 239-yard par-3, starts at an elevated tee and ends at a big wavy green trapped right-front. The 14th, a 412-yard par-4, has an oak-ringed tee and a fairway that winds around a pond. The hole—quite tight at this point—curls leftward to a wide-but-shallow, front-tilting green protected by a pond and pot bunker left-front and a trap left. The 440-yard par-4 18th has a wide, rising fairway that doglegs left between scrub growth left and bunkers right. The hole skirts a pond along the right en route to a mid-sized, right-front-leaning green trapped twice left and once right.

The Reserve Vineyards Golf Club

36 *4747 SW 229th, Aloha, OR 97007. (503) 649-2345. Andy Heinly, pro. 36 holes. Grass tees. Course ratings not available. Fought Course: 18 holes, 7,200 yards, par 72; Cupp Course: 18 holes, 6,900 yards, par 72. Grass tees. Year Opened: 1997. Architects: John Fought; Robert Cupp. Expensive, credit cards. Call for reservations. Walk-on chances: Fair. Walkability: Good. Playability: Public/private facility newest to come on line in booming Hillsboro area west of Portland.*

Scheduled to open in fall 1997 with all 36 holes, this new venue (hereafter called The Reserve) is the latest to join greater Portland's thriving golf scene. Because the courses weren't open before this book went to press, I didn't visit or play them. So this writeup is based on conversations with co-designer, John Fought. Fought and The Reserve's other architect, Robert Cupp, previously worked together at nearby Pumpkin Ridge and Langdon Farms, south of Portland. In the case of this track, the two courses are eponymously named after the designers (they may be named after grapes in the future).

A golf course was planned at this site for years, with the previous proposal, called The Legends, also to contain 36 holes. PGA Tour veteran Tom Kite and Cupp were to design those layouts. The 329-acre parcel lies about a mile south of Highway 26 off SW 229th. It was purchased in 1995 by D.S. Parklane Development Company, a Korean firm owned by D.S. Park. The Reserve is managed by O.B. Sports, a concern headed by Orrin Vincent, the proprietor of Langdon Farms. Park financed the $20-million project, which includes a massive driving range with a golf learning center and a 40,000-square-foot clubhouse. The name of the course stems from the vineyards—some of which previously existed and others newly-planted—around it. The clubhouse will have fine-dining facilities and serve wines with Reserve Vineyards labels.

Unlike the public/private 18s at Pumpkin Ridge, the courses at The Reserve will be rotated daily, allowing public players and members regular access to each course. When initially offered in fall 1996, the non-proprietary memberships were selling for $21,000 for individuals and $28,000 for families. Wadsworth Golf Construction built the courses. The Reserve was designed with tournaments in mind. The scuttlebutt in late-1996 was that the Fred Meyer Challenge may move from The Oregon Golf Club to here, perhaps as soon as 1998. D.S. Park owns 50 undeveloped acres nearby, so there's ample parking for large-scale events.

According to Fought, The Reserve has less wetlands and elevation changes than Pumpkin Ridge—50 feet versus 150 feet. Several creeks were built, with Cupp's track involving more water hazards, including an 11-acre lake and two smaller ponds. A stream runs through Fought's layout, which is considerably longer and more heavily bunkered (110 traps in all) than Cupp's. The tighter Cupp track features more terrestrial "movement," along with 25 sand traps. While Fought's course has more trees and larger greens, Cupp's involves more mounds and smaller putting surfaces. Both layouts were sown with ryegrass for fairways and tees, with all-bentgrass greens. The site, previously an agricultural operation, has good drainage and is easy to walk, according to Fought. I'm looking forward to playing The Reserve Vineyards which, with its well-heeled backers and skilled designers, promises to be one of the Northwest's more exciting new courses.

Rose City Golf Course   18

2200 NE 71st Avenue, Portland, OR 97213. (503) 292-8570 or 253-4744. Hank Childs, pro. 18 holes. 6,520 yards. Par 72. Grass tees. Course ratings: men—B70.0/ 118, M69.2/115; women—M74.4/122, F71.6/117. Year Opened: 1922. Architect: George Otten. Moderate, jr./sr. rates. Reservations: Call five days ahead. Walk-on chances: Fair. Walkability: Good. Playability: Steady improvements over the years have given older course contemporary scope.

Rose City's course, the second built by the city of Portland (following Eastmoreland), lies in an established neighborhood off NE 71st Avenue. Prior to becoming a golf course, the site was home to the old Rose City Speedway. The layout would never have come to fruition without the efforts of A. H. "Jay" Gould. In 1921, after getting permission from the city's park bureau, Gould burned the speedway's tall infield grass and built a rough-hewn nine-holer. He equipped greens with tin cans for holes and used packing cases for tees, iron rods for pins and cloth rags for flags. Golfers policed fairways for rocks and other debris before starting their rounds.

The main hazards—located off the 7th tee at that time—were two wrecked steam engines left from a head-on collision event staged that year. The course was temporarily reconverted into an auto and motorcycle racetrack, but a flood permanently closed the raceway. In 1922 the site permanently became a golf course, with design credit going to George Otten. Gould bought the first green fee and drove the first ball at Rose City's grand opening.

The facility has received several facelifts over the years, making it now a thoroughly modern golfing grounds. The projects have included adding goodly volumes of sand and water hazards, expansive grass tees, and USGA-spec greens. Most recently, new back tees bumped up the yardage. Jay Gould would be proud with how Rose City has turned out.

Noteworthy holes include the 3rd, a 511-yard par-5 that passes OB along the left en route to a trapped-right green. The 9th, a 436-yard par-4, curls rightward to a saddle-shaped, tree-ringed green. Rose City's 18th is a 443-yard par-4. The tee shot must split a set of goal post-like firs to find the landing area. Here, the hole bends slightly left, while tilting steeply rightward away from the turn. A bunker guards the right edge of its domed green.

Sandelie Golf

27

28333 SW Mountain Road, West Linn, OR 97068. (503) 655-1461 (original 18) or 682-2022 (West Nine). 27 holes. Grass tees. Course ratings: Original 18 (5,890 yards, par 70): men M66.6/99; women—M72.0/109, F69.3/103; West Nine (3,150 yards, par 36): no ratings. Years Opened: 1964 (original nine); 1974 (second nine); 1996 (West Nine). Architects: Harvey Junor (original nine); Bill Kaiser (second nine); Keith Kaiser (West Nine). Moderate, sr. rates. Reservations: Call two weeks ahead. Walk-on chances: Good. Walkability: Good. Playability: Wide fairways and limited hazards make this a good training ground.

Situated south of Interstate 205 off Stafford Road, Sandelie Golf (there's no "course" in its name) is a good choice for golfers who can't get tee times on Portland's closer-in courses. For years, the facility was comprised of a straightforward 18-hole course that offered relatively unfettered rounds and wonderful views of a lush Tualatin Valley. In 1996, a driving range and a third nine of equivalent scope were added. The new nine and range are west of the original course. Though only about three-quarters of a mile away from the original course, the West Nine is actually in Wilsonville (address: 3030 SW Advance, Wilsonville, OR 97070) and has a separate phone number (see above).

West Nine's "clubhouse" is an old water tower that's been converted into a cozy space. Designed by Keith Kaiser, the son of Sandelie's founders, Jan and Bill Kaiser, the West Nine is rather perfunctory. Its wide and flat fairways wind across untreed meadows and through dense, second-growth evergreens and oaks to flattish greens. This set of holes—which took the Kaisers five years to get permitted due to a solitary neighbor's protests—should improve as it matures.

Sandelie's original 18 occupies 100 acres of ex-farmland. The front nine was designed by Harvey Junor, kin of Oregon golf notable John Junor. Bill Kaiser designed and built the second set of holes. Sandelie is easy to walk and offers pastoral rounds. Its wide-open, generally hazardless character allows golfers to use all clubs with minimum penalty. Better tests include the 3rd, a 416-yard par-4 that runs to a small green guarded by trees right-front and rear. The 12th, a 471-yard par-5, starts at a tee fronted left by a pond with a fountain. A corn field along the right and trees left squeeze the entrance to a mid-sized green. The top-rated 18th, a 456-yard par-4, is a yawning dogleg-left that requires two accurate shots to reach its small front-tilting green.

Summerfield Golf & Country Club - semiprivate

9

10650 SW Summerfield Road, Tigard, OR 97224. (503) 620-1200. Bill Houston, pro. 9 holes. 2,353 yards. Par 33. Grass tees. Course ratings: men—B61.6/97, M61.4/96; women F65.0/103. Year Opened: 1975. Architect: Gene "Bunny" Mason. Moderate. Call for reservations. Walk-on chances: Fair. Walkability: Not bad for a layout amid housing. Playability: Goodly number of hazards encountered along shortish course.

The course at Summerfield winds through a Tigard retirement community. Owned by the Summerfield Civic Association, a homeowner group with approximately 1,300 residents, the course is augmented by a big clubhouse with a swimming pool, spa, restaurant and lounge, and weight room. Tualatin Development Company built the Bunny Mason-designed layout in 1975. Portland's Hillman Properties now oversees it. The semiprivate venue is played mainly by Summerfielders, but is open to the public.

Golfers are tested by sundry water hazards, including a lake at the 9th hole; two ponds invade the 5th fairway. Each hole is sprinkled with bunkers. With an 18-hole par of 66—33 per side—the dual-tee course has 2,320 yards on the front nine and 2,353 on the back. Good holes include the 1st, a 321-yard par-4 that, at 341 yards, is Summerfield's longest when played as the 10th. The 1st/10th bends slightly leftward over rolling terrain to a crescent-shaped, well-trapped green. The 5th, a 296-yard par-4, bears two ponds along its dogleg-left route before reaching a rolling green. The pretty 9th, a 116-yard par-3, involves a tee-to-green pond and a knoll-perched, trapped-rear green.

Top O'Scott Public Golf Course

12000 SE Stevens Road, Portland, OR 97266. (503) 654-5050. Scott Nash, pro. 18 holes. 5,254 yards. Par 69. Grass tees. Course ratings: men 63.9/99, women 62.3/96. Years Opened: 1928 (original nine); 1931 (second nine). Architect: A. Miller. Moderate, jr./sr. rates, credit cards. Reservations: Call a week ahead. Walk-on chances: Fair. Walkability: Good overall, with some uphill hikes. Playability: Short 18-holer may become a par-3 or executive-length track.

Perched atop Mount Scott, this course offers great westward views of Portland and an ever-developing valley. When its full 18 holes opened in 1931, Top O'Scott became one of Portland's most popular courses, hosting many players and various tournaments, including the 1953 Oregon Open. Over the intervening years, sections of the course were sold off to the nearby New Hope Church and the local Catholic archdiocese, which built parking lots and office buildings (a multistory brick building now occupies the original 2nd green). In 1996, Top O'Scott embarked on another chapter in its history.

Local developers Neil Nedelisky and James Osterman bought the layout from New Hope and the archdiocese, and began pursuing plans to convert it into a nine- or 18-hole par-3 or executive course. Shortly after buying Top O'Scott (which may be renamed Eagle's Landing), Nedelisky and Osterman built a 32-stall driving range on the old 9th hole. A cinderblock clubhouse was extensively remodeled and offers food service in the expanded space. Besides a completely revised course, Nedelisky and Osterman may develop housing units on the property, depending on the permit applications. All the work—not to mention the future of Top O'Scott—may be finalized by the year 1999.

Because of the driving range's placement on the old 9th, a short par-3 was built as a replacement. While the new owners sort out their development options, improvements will be made to a course that failed to draw players in recent years because of poor maintenance practices. Until an all-new layout is built, Top O'Scott's golfers must overcome a shortish course with tilted topography, small and sloping greens, a half-dozen traps, and a creek that winds through some holes.

PRIVATE COURSES

Club Green Meadows

18 *7703 NE 72nd, Vancouver, WA 98661. (360) 256-1510 or (503) 230-1461. Ross Thurick, pro. 18 holes. 6,465 yards. Par 72. Grass tees. Course Ratings: men—B70.9/119, M70.0/117; women—M76.0/130, F73.1/124. Year Opened: 1960. Architect: Leo Frank. Members, guests & reciprocates.*

The course at Club Green Meadows curls tightly through a housing development on Vancouver's east end. A public facility called Green Meadows Golf Course when it debuted in 1960, the venue received a new name when it went private in 1987. The pro shop is on the ground floor of a cavernous fitness center with basketball and tennis courts, swimming pools, weight rooms, aerobics studio, and a bar and restaurant. Club Green Meadows has 450 golfing members, with an astonishing 4,500 belonging to the athletic club.

The first nine holes—designed along with the second nine by course founder Leo Frank—were built by Jim Walling and Pat Hart; Hart owns the par-3 course at Pine Crest in Vancouver and served as co-designer and builder of the new Hartwood facility in Brush Prairie. Frank sold the course and, after several owners, it was purchased by Vancouverite Don Grimm, who's still the proprietor.

The flattish track has experienced poor drainage over the years but recent efforts have mitigated the wetness of fairways during rainy months. The greens have a sameness about them: small, raised and dome-like, though quite slick when mowed low. Club Green Meadows' primary feature is the close proximity of homes and yards, several of which are guarded by nets to protect them from mishit golf balls. The layout is easy to walk, except for a long hike between the 10th and 11th holes.

Good tests include the 3rd, a 441-yard par-4. The lengthy dogleg-left is initially lined by a pond, with mounds farther down outside the turn. The fairway runs narrowly between trees to a right-front-sloping green. The 5th, a 528-yard par-5, follows a right-curling path squeezed by trees and houses. A pond lurks along the right of the landing zone. The big 5th green is raised and has steep sides. The top-rated 9th, a 408-yard par-4, is squeezed by trees off the tee before opening up. At the 180-yard mark, the fairway curls leftward and descends to a trapped-right green.

The 10th, a 419-yard par-4, is a mirror image of the 9th. The left-bending fairway goes around poplars to a raised, two-tiered and right-sloping green. The 13th, a 361-yard par-4, rises slightly on a left-turning path around OB and houses. Its wide-but-shallow green is guarded right-front by trees, with bunkers front and left. The 16th, a 195-yard par-3, crosses wavy ground en route to a large, concave green ringed by three traps. The 514-yard par-5 18th, starts at a pond-fronted tee then winds rightward, passing a big bunker along the right at the 200-yard mark, with OB and homes left. The small, front-tilting 18th green is trapped rear and left, and is backed by Club Green Meadows' gigantic athletic building.

Columbia-Edgewater Country Club

2220 NE Marine Drive, Portland, OR 97211. (503) 285-8354. Dan Hixson, pro.
18 holes. 6,702 yards. Par 71. Grass tees. Course ratings: men—B71.1/128, M69.6/
124, I68.3/122; women—M75.3/132, I73.7/129, F71.5/125. Year Opened: 1925.
Architect: Arthur Vernon Macan; Robert Muir Graves, William F. Bell, & Robert
Cupp (remodels). Members, guests & reciprocates.

Featuring a classic Northwest parkland course, this private club lies above the Columbia River in north Portland. Outside of noise from nearby Portland International Airport, the golfing environment at Columbia-Edgewater (known by members and locals as C-E) is truly sublime. Not a group that stands on its laurels—and C-E has garnered quite a few over its long life, the membership has implemented several modernization projects over the years. The most recent came in 1992, when architect Robert Cupp fine-tuned some holes and upgraded the driving range.

When I visited C-E in September 1996, the temporary bleachers used for the Ping-Cellular One Championship were being dismantled. The tournament, which has been held here since 1990, is well-attended and, because of C-E's Macan-designed course, one of the most popular among LPGA players. In a 1996 poll by *Golf Course News* of 60 LPGA players, C-E finished second (to Mission Hills Country Club in Palm Springs) as the Tour's Best Conditioned Course. The 1996 Ping-Cellular One was won by Dottie Pepper, who set a tournament record of 14 under par. Other competitions held at C-E have included the Al C. Giusti Memorial, Payless Drug Stores Celebrity Classic, Portland Open, Payless Golf Classic, and an embryonic professional touring competition, the 1933 Equitable Savings Northwest Open.

The course is fronted by NE Marine Drive, with a few homes on its southeast corner and farm operations along other peripheries. C-E has no cart paths beside fairways; instead, holes are lined by towering firs and cedars, fat deciduous trees, and ornamentals which lend the place a stateliness. The tees and greens are so well-established and fit so well with the site that they seem to have been in place for centuries. Pretty flower gardens, outstanding conditioning, ponds garnished with lily pads, and cavernous bunkers alongside slick *poa* greens are other hallmarks. The course, which hosts upwards of 50,000 rounds a year, is visited by wildlife such as deer, coyotes, raccoons, rabbits, red-tailed hawks, owls, ospreys, goldfinches and assorted waterfowl.

C-E's front nine winds around interior holes 10-18. Among the more memorable holes is the 1st, a right-bending, 512-yard par-5 that heads slightly downhill over rolling terrain. A pond appearing along the right at the 130-yard mark runs up to guard a trapped-left-front, wide-but-shallow green with a steep tier through its left half. The 2nd, a 317-yard par-4, has a rolling fairway that winds upward to the right around bunkers. The hole curls up to a ridge-perched, terraced green with a steep back side and traps right-front and left. The 3rd, a 532-yard par-5, involves a trench-like fairway with tall sides and humps and hollows along the way. At the 150-yard post, the fairway's midsection has a tall ridge that forces balls left (to safety) or right (into trees). The mid-sized 3rd green leans frontward and is trapped both sides.

Perhaps C-E's best par-3 is the 7th, a 204-yarder that rises up to a smallish and slick green. This ridged-in-the-middle putting surface tilts both front and back, and is trapped laterally. The top-rated 8th, a 401-yard par-4, runs straight over very wavy ground for 275 yards or so. Then it curls rightward to a precipitously left-front-leaning green trapped right and left-front. Trees engird this slick, bi-level sward. The 9th, a 407-yard par-4, features a beautiful set of staggered tees. The broad fairway descends along a route bunkered along the right. Over its concluding 120 yards, the hole drops down to a wide and steeply front-sloping green guarded by a pond left-front and traps right and left-rear.

The 424-yard par-4 12th follows a rolling path off a raised tee. The right-bender leans left as it traverses undulating ground. The knoll-perched 12th green has a huge bunker right-front and two traps left. The 13th, a 440-yard par-4, is lined by OB and trees left and two bunkers right. A trap sits left-front of a small, trapped-left green with a billowing tree at the left-front. The 16th is a dandy 460-yard par-4. This uphiller is lined by OB left and trees right. Over its final 200 yards, the 16th descends slightly to a diminutive green trapped right and left-front; OB is quite close along the left.

Orchard Hills Country Club

18 *605 39th Street, Washougal, WA 98671. (360) 835-5444. Rick Edwards, pro. 18 holes. 5,896 yards. Par 70. Grass tees. Course ratings: men—B68.4/115, M67.5/ 114; women—M72.4/123, F71.0/119. Years Opened: 1930 (original nine); 1966 (second nine). Architects: George Junor (original nine); Bill Sanders (second nine); William Robinson (remodel). Members, guests & reciprocates.*

Orchard Hills lies just north of Washougal amid established and newer homes. Besides a rather short course with several interesting holes, Orchard Hills contains a cozy clubhouse and small practice area. The front and back nines are separated by 39th Street; getting from one side to the other involves crossing the road. The course has undergone several renovations of late, including eight new greens on the front nine, a rebuilt 14th tee, new bunker sand and improved drainage. Much of the work was done in-house by superintendent Scott Coogan. Head pro Rick Edwards has overseen the golf operations at Orchard Hills since the mid-1970s.

The club was named for a plum orchard run by the course's founder, Billy Wood. When Wood's farming operation ceased to be profitable in 1929, he decided to build a public nine-holer. George Junor—groundskeeper at the now-defunct Alderwood course in Portland—designed the layout. The course opened July 4, 1930, with green fees of 25 cents. During its initial decade, Orchard Hill barely scraped by as winter maintenance costs outstripped the profits made the previous summer. Because of a poor bottom line, Woods announced he was closing the course. In an attempt to keep it open and provide a stable revenue stream, the Crown Willamette Golf Association was formed by residents of Camas and Washougal. With dues of $2 per month, 120 people soon joined. Some members were civic-minded non-golfers who worked at the Camas paper mill; they made automatic payroll deductions to pay dues. An old newspaper article covering an early-day tournament shows the event's winner accepting prized live chickens.

World War II created a whole new set of financial roadblocks. Association memberships dropped as men went off to war. Wood went to work in Salem, and Orchard Hills was managed by several husband-and-wife teams. In 1943, Wood decided to sell the 39-acre course for $20,000. The remaining members of the association wanted to keep it open; they decided the best way to do this was to form a private club. At $100 apiece, 200 memberships were needed to be sold to meet Wood's asking price. After several months, 185 stock certificates had been bought, with only $18,500 raised. A few founding members approached Wood and offered that amount. He accepted, and private Orchard Hills Country Club was launched in 1945.

Members built the current clubhouse in the 1950s. Orchard Hills remained a nine-hole layout until 1966, when a second nine was built on a 76-acre parcel east of 39th Street. The original (front) nine is short, with tight tree-lined fairways. About 400 yards longer, the back nine is considerably more spread out; posh new homes on a hillside overlook these holes. Oddities of the layout include a 7th green that sits behind the 8th tee; the tee is fenced in to protect players from errant shots. Holes 14 through 16 are called "The Triangle," as they sit within a wooded area apart from the rest of the course.

Interesting tests include the 2nd, a 234-yard par-4 that runs uphill and straight for 200 yards. Here, the narrow hole veers 90 degrees rightward to a raised green trapped thrice right and once left-front. The top-rated 4th, a 392-yard par-4, winds leftward between treees en route to a steeply front-tilting green trapped left, right-front and rear. The 389-yard par-4 6th has a straight-running fairway that leans to the right toward OB. The sizable, severely right-front-sloping 6th green has a tier through it, and is trapped right-rear and left-front. The 8th, a 410-yard par-4, is a downhill dogleg-left that eventually reaches a mid-sized, trapped-left green with a steep back side.

The 11th, a 396-yard par-4, runs slightly uphill along a right-tilting path crossed by a creek. The large 11th green is bunkered right-front. The 13th, a 579-yard par-5, is a long and sweeping hole that, over its final 200 yards, winds rightward and slopes sharply right. The slick, hill-cut green leans decidedly to the right. The 407-yard par-4 15th starts at an elevated tee, then winds leftward across up-and-down terrain. Its round and domed green sits in a hollow. The 17th, a 205-yard par-3, is Orchard Hills' prettiest hole. A pond runs from tee to green, with trees close to the left side of a steeply front-sloping, two-tiered putting surface guarded in front by a creek.

The Oregon Golf Club   18

2152-A SW Pete's Mountain Road, West Linn, OR 97068. (503) 650-7805. Craig Griswold, pro. 18 holes. 7,034 yards. Par 72. Grass tees. Course ratings: men—T74.4/ 135, B72.1/132, M69.8/123; women—M74.8/131, F71.1/125. Year Opened: 1992. Architects: Peter Jacobsen & Ken Kavanaugh. Members, guests & reciprocates.

Perched upon Pete's Mountain south of Portland, this private venue was spearheaded by PGA touring pro and Portland native, Peter Jacobsen. The 200-acre layout was purchased by National Golf Properties in December 1995, and is run by NGP's operating arm, American Golf. The towering site—a former Christmas tree farm and working cattle ranch—offers spectacular vistas of the Cascades and Mount Hood. The Willamette curls around the eastern base of Pete's Mountain, which lies at the confluence of the Willamette and Tualatin rivers.

The site was settled in 1868 by Peter Weiss, who staked a donation land claim on 360 acres. In the early days, the forests were logged off to feed a pulp and paper mill at Willamette Falls. As the forests thinned, farms cropped up on Pete's Mountain even though its soil was not particularly good for agriculture. In 1986, local residents halted plans for a huge, metropolitan garbage dump that the state wanted to put where Oregon Golf Club's clubhouse now sits. The locals said they'd rather have a golf course, and sold parcels of land to the club's founders. Near the course are large and expensive homes, which take advantage of the mountain's panoramic views.

The club—including an all-bentgrass course, 10-acre driving range, swimming pool, two tennis courts, and 32,500-square-foot clubhouse—cost $24-million to build. It's hosted the Fred Meyer Challenge since 1992. Known also as "Peter's Party" in tribute to the personable Jacobsen, the star-studded event has raised more than $5 million for local charities since beginning in 1986. Other big-time tournaments held here have included the 1994 NCAA Women's Championship.

The course sprawls across up-and-down terrain. Each hole has four sets of tees, so the layout is player-adaptable. Due to some steep and lengthy between-hole hikes, however, it is not particularly friendly to bag-packing golfers. On the plus side, the tilted topography allows fairways to drain well during wet weather. Tough holes include the 1st, a 560-yard par-5 with a swale-fronted, raised tee and an uphill, right-sloping fairway along a ridge. A pair of bunkers on the left tightens the landing area. Three traps guard the right side of a long and skinny, rear-sloping green. The 437-yard par-4 3rd has six bunkers in the left half of its wide, left-leaning fairway. These traps may be carried by long hitters. Once past this point, the hole curls leftward to a large green trapped thrice in front. The 5th, a 555-yard par-5, has a scenic elevated tee and a fairway lined along the right by the remnants of the Christmas tree farm. The hole later slopes rightward toward full-grown trees, then winds sharply uphill to the left. The wavy, two-tiered 5th green has a troublesome tree at its right-front entry. Two fairway bunkers lurk 75 yards from it along the right.

The 8th, a pretty 204-yard par-3, has a tee fronted by a pond, which feeds into a series of smaller ponds and a creek that eventually becomes a large lake. The oval green, guarded by four bunkers left and the lake right, has a spur running through its back-left quarter. The 15th, a 549-yard par-5, doglegs 70 degrees to the right around trees and a creek. A mammoth drive may reach the corner and allow players to peek around the firs to see a tree-ringed, creek-fronted green squeezed by bunkers right and rear. The 440-yard par-4 16th has 13 bunkers along its dogleg-left route. The uphiller goes between traps (most are along the left) to a two-tiered green guarded on the right by five bunkers. The 18th is an uphill, 449-yard par-4 that winds between a creek left and five hidden bunkers right. Once beyond the bunkers, the tree-pinched route rises steeply to a trapped-front green lined by the creek on its left and rear edges. Oregon Golf Club's 18th has rightly been called one of the toughest finishing holes in golf.

Oswego Lake Country Club

18 *20 Iron Mountain Boulevard, Lake Oswego, OR 97034. (503) 635-3659. John Welsh, pro. 18 holes. 6,557 yards. Par 71. Grass tees. Course ratings: men—B70.6/127, M68.7/123; women—M74.4/129, F71.5/126. Year Opened: 1925. Architect: H. Chandler Egan; Robert Muir Graves & William Robinson (remodels). Members, guests & reciprocates.*

A beautiful layout crossing hilly ground on top of Iron Mountain, this private club is located above downtown Lake Oswego. The site had been used for mining, but those operations ceased in 1894. The property's owner, Ladd Estate Company, decided to convert the area into a golf course, hiring Medford's H. Chandler Egan to design a 6,700-yard, par-73 layout. Interesting aspects of the original course include a tunnel running underneath the 15th green, and an old mine building beside the 14th green. Since its 1925 opening, Oswego Lake has undergone major remodels by Robert

Muir Graves and William Robinson. The course's length has been shortened three different times, reaching a low of 5,623 yards in 1949 when its par was reduced to 68.

Today, Oswego Lake is among the elite in the region's pantheon of championship-caliber tracks. With fairways sweeping over hills and dales; considerable sand and water hazards; a quiet, forested setting abridged by only a few houses; lovely views of mounts Hood, Saint Helens and Adams; and an exquisite variety of holes, the course is very well-endowed. Members have access to a clubhouse of classical architecture, with a separate pro shop near the first tee. Other hallmarks include superb conditioning by greens superintendent Dick Fluter—widely regarded as among the Northwest's best turf tenders—and an efficient layout that, despite some steep hikes, is quite walkable.

Oswego Lake's challenge begins immediately at the 539-yard 1st. The par-5 follows a ravine-like route that bends uphill to the right at the 250-yard mark, where a slender pond lurks along the left. Big bunkers lie along the right 75 yards from a front-banked green trapped right, right-rear and left-front. The 2nd, a 419-yard par-4, ascends along a path that skirts OB and some houses on the right. The right-sloping fairway runs up to a left-front-leaning green trapped right-front and left-rear. The troublesome 5th, a 482-yard par-5, has a chute-like fairway that curls narrowly to the right. A bunker sits along the left, 100 yards from a pear-shaped, two-tiered green trapped twice in front and once rear.

Once off the elevated tee at the top-rated, 436-yard 6th, the par-4 bends downhill to the left, skirting four pot bunkers along the right. Once around the corner, the hole rises up to a big, front-left-sloping green trapped left-front and right. The 8th, a 200-yard par-3, features a 200-foot-high tee with commanding views. The 8th green is large and round, and is ringed by four traps. The 447-yard par-5 10th bears a pond right of the tee. The fairway goes out for 225 yards or so, then winds 90 degrees to the right, skirting three bunkers outside the turn. The 10th passes a pond along the right before steeply rising to a hill-cut, front-tilting green imperiled by five bunkers. The 12th, a 426-yard par-4, is a slightly uphill left-bender. Two fat traps sit along the right, 150 yards from a right-sloping, wavy green trapped left, rear and right.

The 15th, a 442-yard par-4, boasts another towering tee. A large bunker lies in mid-fairway, with two traps along the right of the landing area. Another skinny trap lines the left edge of the hole, which drops down to a big green with a hump along its left edge and two traps in front. The 417-yard par-4 16th runs off a raised tee down a wide, left-sloping path. The fairway crosses channel-like terrain en route to a diminutive, right-leaning green with traps front and left; a deep grass bunker guards the right side of this slick putting surface. The 18th, a 536-yard par-5, has a pond right-front of its tee. This hazard shouldn't be a problem, but another pond along the left will swallow hooked drives. The rolling and uphill home hole winds between trees while passing a hidden pool along the right. At the 150-yard mark, the route curls leftward. A 50-yard-long pond runs up and stops 25 yards from the right-front edge of a small, steeply front-tilting green trapped left-front and rear.

Pleasant Valley Golf Club

18 *12300 SE 162nd Avenue, Clackamas, OR 97015. (503) 658-3101. Jim Smith, pro. 18 holes. 6,593 yards. Par 72. Grass tees. Course ratings: men—B72.4/132, M67.1/ 128; women—M75.4/130, F71.1/119. Year Opened: 1968. Architects: Barney Lucas & Shirley Stone. Members, guests & reciprocates.*

Located off Sunnyside Road within Pleasant Valley Golf Estates, a good-sized subdivision, this private course is owned by George Beall. The club's 500 members have access to a recently-remodeled clubhouse and a fine course which has received several upgrades over the years. The most recent changes occurred in 1996 when new tees were built and a pond was added to the 6th hole. Pleasant Valley was re-rated that year and, as indicated above, plays tough. Recent events held here include U.S. Open Qualifying in May 1996.

This represents the third attempt to build a course by Pleasant Valley's builder and co-designer, Barney Lucas. Lucas came to the project with an extensive background in golf; he owned Gearhart Golf Links and the Gearhart Hotel in the early 1940s. In 1949, he designed and built the Neah-Kah-Nie course near Manzanita, which closed in the early 1980s. His first stab at building Pleasant Valley—on a parcel along the Willamette River near Wilsonville—was destroyed by the 1962 Columbus Day Storm, which ravaged trees on the property. Lucas then tried to construct a course along the Clackamas River on what is now McIver Park. But a flood totaled that layout. In 1966, he obtained the Donley farm—an agricultural operation originated in the late 1880s, and began work on the course. The original Donley farmhouse served as Pleasant Valley's clubhouse until 1970, when a new structure was built.

During its first two years of operation, Pleasant Valley was a public facility. On Labor Day 1970—with 50 charter members—it went private. Beall bought Pleasant Valley in 1972. The layout crosses 127 acres and is ringed by houses, none of which are within the course proper. The venue offers stunning views of Mount Hood,

The 11th at Pleasant Valley Country Club is a 159-yard par-3.

and is occasionally visited by deer, elk, foxes, quails and pheasants. Pleasant Valley has an old-style feel, with mature trees lining fairways and high-lipped bunkers around the greens. But it is also quite contemporary, with excellent turf conditioned by a computerized irrigation system, yardages on sprinkler heads, an expansive driving range, and colorful gardens. The front nine is enclosed by the back, which winds around the outer edges of the squarish layout.

Notable holes include the 4th, a 560-yard par-5 with an elevated tee and a descending fairway that skirts a huge trap along the right. The last 100 yards of the hole curl slightly left to a smallish, trapped-right green. The 376-yard par-4 6th is an uphill dogleg-left between trees. A hidden pond lurks along the left behind a mound, while another pond sits left-front of a tiny green backed by a pot bunker. The 8th, a 509-yard par-5, follows an ascending, right-turning path that leads to a left-tilting green trapped left. A pot bunker sits at the right-front of the mid-sized putting surface. The 473-yard 9th, the second consecutive par-5, is a risk-reward tester with an elevated tee and a sharp dogleg-right fairway around two firs and a fat pond. Players who can drive the pond and trees will alight safety on a ramping fairway, which runs up to a raised, front-tilting green bunkered on the right. Another water hazard guards the green's left-front flank.

The top-rated 14th, a 418-yard par-4, runs straight between trees over right-leaning terrain; OB and homes are off to the left. Over its final 140 yards, the hole descends to a hill-cut and severely front-sloping green. The 532-yard par-5 17th is a tough uphill right-bender. A creek off the tee runs along the right flank of the right-tilting hole, which curls rightward between trees. The creek crosses in front of a radically front-tilting, small green with a steep back edge. The 18th, a 340-yard par-4, is a dogleg-left on a left-leaning path skirted by a pond. A huge bunker and a pond fronts a shallow-but-wide green squeezed further by three traps right.

Portland Golf Club

5900 SW Scholls Ferry Road, Portland, OR 97225. (503) 292-2778. Larry Lamberger, Jr., pro. 18 holes. 6,683 yards. Par 72. Grass tees. Course ratings: men—B72.4/ 131, M70.8/127; women—M76.9/135, F74.0/127. Years Opened: 1914 (original nine); 1915 (second nine). Architects: Founding members (original nine); George Turnbull (second nine); Donald & John Junor, Robert Trent Jones, Robert Muir Graves & John Steidel (remodels). Members, guests & limited reciprocates.

Occupying 137 acres, this historic club is in the Raleigh Hills section west of Portland. While searching for a golf course site, the club's founders selected this one east of Beaverton in Washington County. Founding members built the original nine; George Trumbull, Waverley's pro at that time, designed the second set of holes. The founders had considerable foresight when building the course. They installed an extensive drain system that carried excess water away, and put in an irrigation system for the greens. Shortly after Portland's course opened, brothers Donald and John Junor were hired. The Junors grew up in a house beside the 10th hole at Waverley Country Club, and John—the first pro at both Tualatin Country Club and Eastmoreland—became Portland's head pro. Donald was hired as the superintendent. The Junors eventually rebuilt the original greens and fairways, providing the layout used today.

During more than 80 years of existence, Portland Golf Club has hosted many tournaments. Bigger ones include the 1931 Western Amateur, 1934 Women's Western Open, 1946 PGA Championship (won by Ben Hogan), 1947 Ryder Cup, 1955 Western Open (Cary Middlecoff), 1969 Alcan Open (Billy Casper), the LPGA's

Portland Ladies Classic from 1972 to 1976, and 1979, PNGA Women (1976 and 1985), Hudson Cup matches, and 1982 U.S. Senior Open (Miller Barber). The PGA Tour's Portland Open was held here seven times. Portland was the original host site of the Fred Meyer Challenge, and also held the USGA's Mid-Amateur Championship. In 1999, the club will host the prestigious U.S. Senior Men's Amateur.

Portland's original clubhouse burned down shortly after the course opened. A second clubhouse was erected in 1916, but became inadequate as the club grew. The third structure—in use today—opened to great fanfare in 1928. The clubhouse has undergone several remodels over the years, but remains a fine representation of 1920's architecture. Later on, the members added a swimming pool. Among the many fine players who perfected their games at Portland Golf Club include early-day Northwest greats Don Moe and Rudie Wilhelm, Oregon Sports Hall of Famer Marion McDougall Herron, Bob Atkinson, and multiple club champs Maude Borst, Patsy Duffy and Sybil O'Byrne. Bobby Jones did an exhibition here in 1934. Other well-known guests have been Sam Snead, Hogan, Middlecoff, Casper, Jack Nicklaus, Kathy Whitworth, Donna Caponi, Nancy Lopez, Chuck Congdon, and JoAnn Washam. Following John Junor's tenure, Larry Lamberger Sr. was Portland's pro from 1927 to 1974, at which time he turned over the reins to his son, Larry Jr.

Portland's course sprawls over hills and swales split by Fanno Creek, which is crossed by stone bridges at various junctures along the layout. A freak rainstorm in November 1996 caused Fanno Creek to flood, spewing water over several holes. The course was restored shortly thereafter. Recent improvements include some new tees, with more planned. The forested track is apart from peripheral housing and offers quiet rounds. Interesting touches include a plaque beside the 18th fairway that commemorates the founding—by Russ Newland and Charles Bartlett—of the Golf Writers Association of America during the PGA Championship in 1946. The GWAA's first meeting was held in an abandoned ice cream concession stand.

The traditional track features quick *poa* greens and considerable bunkering. A personal quibble are Portland's dirt cart paths which become dusty in dry weather. Each of the holes has a name that dates back to the club's early days. Good tests include the top-rated 2nd ("Long John"), a 436-yard par-4 with Fanno Creek off the tee and a right-bending fairway that rises past a bunker along the right. At the 150-yard mark, the route descends to a round, rolling green trapped laterally. The 524-yard par-5 5th ("Homestead") bisects bunkers right, with a road and OB left. The fairway goes down to a slick, high-backed green trapped twice in front. The 9th, a 361-yard par-4 called "Dickson," is an uphill right-bender with a huge bunker on the left. The radical, humped-in-the-middle 9th green tilts right-rear, and is trapped left-front, left-rear and right-front.

The 509-yard par-5 10th ("Beaver") heads straight over rolling ground, passing a large bunker on the right. The hole eventually curls leftward to a trapped-right green with a bunker 40 yards from its right-front edge. A sequoia tree towers over the green's left-front entry, while Fanno Creek is close behind. The 11th ("Mallard"), a 370-yard par-4, has a pond off the tee and an ascending fairway. At the 175-yard marker, the hole climbs even steeper up to a hill-perched, right-rear-sloping putting surface trapped right-front and left. The 384-yard par-4 13th, called "Fir," is a right-leaning hole narrowed by evergreens. A bunker sits 30 yards from the right-front edge of a large, front-tilting green, which is trapped right-front and left. The 15th is a 542-yard par-4 called "Firlock Station." The old Oregon Electric Railroad—the only way to get to the club prior to 1916—dropped off passengers at the current site of the 15th tee. The hole winds downhill to the left, passing OB left and a huge bunker right. The fairway ultimately ends at a right-sloping green trapped twice in front and once right-rear.

Pumpkin Ridge Golf Club - Witch Hollow

18

12930 Old Pumpkin Ridge Road, Cornelius, OR 97113-6147. (503) 647-4747 or 647-2500. Jerry Mowlds, director of golf. 18 holes. 7,017 yards. Par 72. Grass tees. Course ratings: men—T74.8/141, B72.3/138, M70.1/133, I69.6/124; women— M75.5/137, I73.0/126, F70.6/121. Year Opened: 1992. Architects: Robert Cupp & John Fought. Members, guests & reciprocates.

Witch Hollow is the private half of 36-hole Pumpkin Ridge Golf Club. Located west of the public Ghost Creek, Witch Hollow served as the site of the U.S. Women's Open in 1997. Shortly after opening, the club enjoyed a near-capacity roster of 400 members. Not many changes have been made during its relatively young life; it was that close to perfection when debuting. *Golf Digest* certainly thought so, ranking Witch Hollow America's second-best new private course in 1992. The few renovations made were requested by the USGA for the Women's Open and for the 1996 U.S. Men's Amateur won by Tiger Woods. A new tee at the 16th made the hole a 400-yarder into a headwind for the Open. Cross bunkers in the 7th fairway were also removed and replaced by grass.

Witch Hollow has 500 non-equity memberships available. Members have access to Ghost Creek as well as a clubhouse separate from the public facility's. Pumpkin Ridge's driving range is double-ended, with members practicing at one end and the public at the other. In 1996, the club instituted a spikeless-shoe policy from May through October. After initial concerns, most members ended up liking the softer shoes, which are easier on the feet. Going spikeless is one technique that aids superintendent Bill Webster's efforts to prevent *poa* from invading Witch Hollow's all-bentgrass turf. Other methods include keeping power carts off fairways, "stressing" (underwatering) the bentgrass, and picking up grass clippings.

Witch Hollow is similar in some ways to Ghost Creek, but it has eight dogleg-left fairways. The creek so involved on the public layout is not as incidious at the more forested private track. I also believe Witch Hollow's greens are a bit more severe, with assorted whorls, ridges, tiers, bowls, spurs and hogbacks marking the surfaces. Notable holes include the 3rd, a 414-yard par-4 that ascends rightward around two bunkers. The hole is tapered by trees before ending at a creek-fronted, trapped-right green. The 533-yard, par-5 4th has traps along the right of its left-bending route. The tree-ringed 4th green has a spur running through it, and is squeezed by three bunkers left and one right. The 211-yard, par-3 5th drops down to a wide-but-shallow green fronted by a pond and backed by three pot bunkers.

The 6th, a 453-yard par-4, winds leftward between trees and a bunker outside the dogleg. After the turn, a creek crosses the hole and then winds along the fairway's left edge. The 6th ends at a ridge-perched and rock-walled, two-tiered green. The top-rated 7th, a 623-yard par-5, begins at an elevated tee before venturing down a route squeezed by three bunkers left and another trap farther down. The second half of the hole descends past a bunker left and oaks right to the 100-yard mark, an area filled with tall grass, mounds and a cavernous bunker. The right-front-sloping 7th green is well-trapped. The 9th, a 467-yard par-4, has a left-curling fairway narrowed by bunkers 200 yards out. A pair of firs stand guard at the left entrance to the small green, which is protected by a bunker 50 yards in front.

The "S-shaped" 11th, a 553-yard par-5, initially descends between a fat bunker left and trees right. Once beyond this pinched juncture, the hole curls right. A bunker-backed fir blocks views to the laterally-trapped 11th green, which may be Witch Hollow's tiniest putting surface. The dogleg-left 17th, a 422-yard par-4, has a bunker along the left 180 yards out. Seven traps occupy both sides of the turn, with trees inside the bend. The undulating, left-leaning 17th green is trapped left-front and right-rear. The multi-part fairway at the 545-yard par-5 18th starts with a wetlands-fronted tee. The second section is pinched by trees and wetlands left, with three bunkers right. Another swampy area—fronted right by a bunker and backed by two traps—swallows inadequate second shots into the 18th green, a narrow-but-deep affair trapped left-front.

Riverside Golf & Country Club

18 *8105 NE 33rd Drive, Portland, OR 97211. (503) 282-7265. Pat Sutton, pro. 18 holes. 6,624 yards. Par 72. Grass tees. Course ratings: men—B72.3/130, M71.2/127, I69.9/ 123; women—I76.2/135, F74.1/130. Years Opened: 1926 (original nine); 1928 (second nine). Architects: Jim "Scotty" Henderson (original nine); H. Chandler Egan (second nine); John Steidel (remodel). Members, guests & reciprocates.*

Riverside lies just south of Columbia-Edgewater Country Club, off NE 33rd Drive. Portland International Airport is just to the east. Like C-E, Riverside is a mature layout with a remarkable variety of coniferous and deciduous trees. Over the years, these plants have not only grown into magnificent specimens, but have gotten fatter to squeeze the fairways. The course boasts colorful flower gardens and eye-catching landscaping in unexpected places, such as tree stumps. A long hedge veils a creek off the tee at the par-5 6th, and a mushroom sculpture graces an area by the 15th green.

Riverside is blessed with a very efficient, eminently walkable layout. This trait, common in early-day courses, leads me to ask: Why can't more new layouts be built like this? Though it now contains a challenging golf course and lovely clubhouse, Riverside endured its share of calamities to get where it is today. The club was founded after a group of local golfers got fed up with the crowded conditions at Portland's public courses. About 180 men signed up during the initial membership drive. With a source of funding, Jim "Scotty" Henderson was hired to design nine holes. During the first year the course was open, players found a bumper crop of potatoes and wild mustard growing in the 1st fairway. Riverside received a second nine holes, designed by Medford native H. Chandler Egan, in 1928.

In 1929, Riverside's clubhouse burned down, but the members soon erected a new one. After several years of financial strife spawned by the Depression, the club's financial situation improved such that the course was renovated in 1935. Then in 1948, the Columbia River washed over its banks and submerged the grounds. After three years of restoration work, the golf grounds and clubhouse were back to normal. Another natural disaster occurred in 1983 when a freeze caused an overhead sprinkler system in the clubhouse to burst, inundating it with six inches of water. Once again, the members regrouped, remodeling the clubhouse with vaulted ceilings and wood interiors.

Riverside has held its share of top-level tournaments, including the Cellular-One PING, an LPGA event now held at Columbia-Edgewater, and the 1993 PNGA Amateur

Championship. The club also hosts Hogan Cup Junior matches, a competition held in memory of the late Riverside head pro, Eddie Hogan. Its big annual event is the Riverside Best-Ball, a 140-player tournament. Riverside is the home course of Ray Chirgwin, a longtime member and former club president who made national headlines on July 26, 1978, when he aced the 11th hole. The hole-in-one capped an amazing feat: an 18-hole chain of eagles—one on every Riverside hole—plus a double eagle at the par-5 6th. If all of his eagles were totaled in a single round, Chirgwin's "eclectic" score of 35 would be 37 under par.

Riverside's well-maintained layout stays relatively dry following Portland's rains. Though the difference is probably negligible, the back nine seems tighter than the front. Noteworthy tests include the 4th, a 192-yard par-3 that involves a tee shot over a creek (called a "nature conservancy area") to a large, front-sloping, two-tiered green bunkered twice on the right. Traps at the 4th green's rear and left flanks create a nerve-wracking drive from the tips. The 5th, a 511-yard par-5, rises along a left-turning path lined by a huge bunker right. The fairway winds over rolling ground to a small, front-tilting green trapped right and left-front. The top-rated par-4 at the 8th is a 421-yard left-bender that curls around a large pond. The mid-width hole ends at a smallish, laterally-trapped green with a fat willow at its left-front.

The 405-yard par-4 9th requires a long tee shot (240 yards from the tips) to get around the poplar, fir and willow trees at the corner of its dogleg-left path. The 9th ends at a slick, front-sloping green with a tier in its rear-left quarter and bunkers on both sides. The 10th, a 510-yard par-5, is squeezed laterally by dense evergreens. The right-curling, left-tilting hole ends at a small, left-leaning green trapped once right and twice left, with trees close to its back edge. The 11th, a 166-yard par-3, features a tiny, well-trapped green with a tree-pinched entry. The fairway at the 413-yard par-4 14th is quite wide over its initial 250 yards. The hole eventually bends rightward along a tree-tapered route to a domed and very slick green. This radical putting surface is imperiled by a steep back-left edge and a deep bunker that encircles its right-front and right flanks. The 15th, a 500-yard par-5, bears a right-sloping, left-bending fairway that passes a vast trap along the left. A pond sits about 75 yards from a diminutive, right-sloping green trapped both sides and rear.

Rock Creek Country Club

18

5100 NW Neakahnie, Portland, OR 97213. (503) 645-1101. Rob Croskrey, pro. 18 holes. 6,634 yards. Par 72. Grass tees. Course ratings: men—B71.9/123, M71.0/ 122, women—M77.1/135, F72.5/125. Years Opened: 1964 (original nine); 1968 (second nine). Architects: George H. Otten & George W. Otten, Jr. Members, guests & reciprocates.

Rock Creek Country Club is west of Portland off the Sunset Highway. The club's fairways wind through a like-named subdivision originated by Park City Corporation in the 1960s. Park City sold the golf course to the Moschetti Corporation in 1976, at which time it went private. The non-equity club, with 500 members, has been owned by Paul Gabrillis since the early 1980s. Gabrillis announced plans to sell the course and clubhouse in 1992 but, as of 1997, still owned it. The course is overseen by its personable head pro, Rob Croskrey; Pat Hamlin is the superintendent.

Golfers enjoy nice views of Mount Hood's snowy cone from various junctures of the course. Though it winds through residences, Rock Creek is generally easy to walk, and the homes are suitably apart from play. The front nine spans hilly terrain, while the back sits on a floodplain bisected by the course's namesake waterway. Power lines run through, paralleling some holes from above. An ambitious master plan may be pursued some day. The proposal will add new tees to stretch the layout to 6,900 yards, and rehabilitate the bunkers and turf.

Many holes are arranged in a clockwise direction, which causes problems for golfers who hook, since 16 of Rock Creek's holes are bordered by OB. Good golf tests include the 2nd, a 425-yard par-4 that descends leftward between trees on the right, with houses and OB left. The fairway eventually arrives at a raised, trapped-left green. The 4th, a 368-yard par-4, is a narrow dogleg-right around a pond and willow tree, with houses and OB close by on the left. Once around the corner, the fairway rises up to a ridged, front-tilting green bunkered right-front. The 220-yard, par-3 11th runs up to a large, front-sloping green.

The top-rated 12th, a 421-yard par-4, crosses a straight and narrow route lined by OB and houses left, with trees right. Its rolling and slick green tilts toward the right-front. The 177-yard par-3 15th is Rock Creek's prettiest hole. A big pond with a fountain off the tee stretches out to guard a large, front-sloping green. The 16th, a 416-yard par-4, rises between trees before bending slightly right to a slick, front-tilted putting surface. The 17th, a 501-yard par-5, has OB and Rock Creek on the left of its downhill path. The creek crosses the fairway diagonally at the base of a hill between the 150- and 125-yard markers. The hole then rises up to a mid-sized, perched green.

Royal Oaks Country Club

18 *8917 NE Fourth Plain, Vancouver, WA 98662. (360) 256-1350. Steve Bowen, pro. 18 holes. 6,900 yards. Par 72. Grass tees. Course ratings: men—B71.2/125, M69.5/ 122, I67.8/116; women—M75.3/133, I72.6/127, F73.7/125. Years Opened: 1945 (original nine); 1947 (second nine). Architect: William Davies; Robert Muir Graves (remodel). Members, guests & reciprocates.*

Royal Oaks, a private club in Vancouver's east end, boasts one of the Northwest's premier golf courses. Completed in 1947, Royal Oaks was designed by William Davies, a brother of one of the founding members and an architect then serving in the U.S. Navy. Notable Oregon architect and greens superintendent, Fred Federspiel, built the course. Royal Oaks enjoys many salient attributes, including outstanding conditioning; concrete, curbed cart paths; a vast array of coniferous and ornamental trees; a garden-like setting with superb landscaping; stone bridges for creek passages; and a walkable layout with discreet holes. The landscaping is so fine that the edges of water hazards—normally neglected areas—are immaculately tended. The bases of trees, usually places where grass grows freely, are cleared for flowers and other plants.

The championship track is a frequent site for tournaments. Royal Oaks is in the regular rotation for major PNGA and OGA events. It hosts the Al Giusti Memorial tourney, a pro event with a purse of $90,000. At the 1994 PNGA Championship, Tiger Woods carded an unofficial record round of 63 (shot in match play with some putts conceded). Of the 108 holes he played at Royal Oaks, Woods fired a remarkable 33 birdies. The course has also been the site of the Northwest Open, LPGA Qualifying, U.S. Open (both Regional and Sectional) Qualifying, and the Pacific Northwest Pro Assistants Championship. Major club events include the 210-player Royal Oaks Invitational in June, the Lords & Ladies couples in August, and a member-guest also in August. The club enjoys a full membership of 450.

In 1997, Royal Oaks completed a five-year master plan designed by Robert Muir Graves. The final phase upgraded the 10th and 15th greens. The official course record, a 64 shot by Bob McKendrick in 1952, will probably hold up for awhile. McKendrick carded that number before the back tees were built and the course was stretched out to 6,900 yards. This is a golf-only reserve; homes lie along the perimeter but none are within it. Burnt Bridge Creek winds through the layout, snaking into hitting zones and billowing into ponds at crucial junctures. Among the arboreal species along fairways are the club's namesake giants, Douglas and noble firs, Ponderosa and western white pines, maples, cedars (incense, Port Orford and western red), dogwoods and giant sequoias.

Notable holes (each of which is named) include the 3rd, a 418-yard par-4 that winds slightly downhill to the left. The creek initially guards the mid-width fairway along the left, then crosses the hole at the 100-yard mark. The 3rd green tilts toward the right-front and is trapped both sides. The top-rated 4th ("Straight Arrow"), a 445-yard par-4, crosses a rolling path squeezed on the left over its final 100 yards by the creek. The small, front-tilting 4th green is trapped right and guarded by the creek left and left-rear. The meandering 6th, a 535-yard par-5, has a pond off the tee and OB and houses left. A big bunker sits at the 225-yard mark, where the hole then winds uphill leftward to a mound-backed, front-left-leaning green trapped left and right-front. The 427-yard par-4 9th rises slightly while bending left. Houses and OB skirt the fairway's left side, with trees right. Over its concluding 75 yards, the route narrows while going to a steeply front-sloping green trapped laterally.

The 11th, a 436-yard par-4, traverses wavy terrain while curling left around tall, densely packed firs. Its heart-shaped, front-leaning green is trapped on both sides. The 13th, a 555-yard par-5 called "The Monster," winds between wooded jail left and more trees right. A bunker lurks at the 100-yard mark left of the fairway, which then bends rightward to a small, trapped-right-front putting surface. The 451-yard, par-4 14th, called "The Gully," crosses rolling ground that narrows over its final 150 yards. The hole ends at a raised, wide-but-shallow green trapped left-front. The green sits at a 45-degree angle to the fairway, making it an elusive target for second shots. Perhaps the toughest par-3 at Royal Oaks is the 16th, a 217-yarder equipped with a big and undulating green pinched on both sides by bunkers.

Tualatin Country Club

9145 SW Tualatin Road, Tualatin, OR 97062. (503) 692-4620. Jon Peterson, pro. 18 holes. 6,601 yards. Par 72. Grass tees. Course ratings: men—B72.1/133, M69.8/ 125; women—M74.6/127, F71.2/120. Year Opened: 1912. Architect: H. Chandler Egan; Robert Cupp & John Fought (remodel). Members, guests & reciprocates.

Located along a scenic stretch of the Tualatin River south of Cook Park, this historic club has undergone several renovations in the Nineties. In 1992, six new holes arose from a design by Robert Cupp and John Fought. Though boasting modern construction techniques, these holes sustain the traditional feel of the 1912-built layout. In 1996, a massive $5-million remodel on the clubhouse began. Some repairs were performed on the course as well; the holes beside the river—the 7th, 8th and 9th—were 30 to 40 feet underwater following the winter of 1995-1996 floods. When I visited the course in September of 1996, these fairways and greens had been completely restored. To prevent future inundations, the club has been working with the Army Corps of Engineers to shore up the river bank.

Tualatin Country Club was founded in 1912 by Rabbi Jonah B. Wise, a Portland Jewish leader and member of Concordia Club #10688, a Portland gathering place for businessmen, card players and socialites. Rabbi Wise became interested in golf after playing the Metropolis Golf Club in New York City. Wise convinced some Concordia members to found a golf club, and a prominent group of Portland businessmen and community leaders soon joined in the effort. A 69-acre parcel owned by the Sweek family was leased for a golf course; subsequent land acquisitions upped the club's holdings to 110 acres. Rabbi Wise, Tualatin's original president Cecil Bauer and George "Scotty" Junor were the driving forces behind Tualatin Country Club, the first course to have Oregon bentgrass greens. The U.S. Department of Agriculture was so impressed with Tualatin's greens that they included them and their method of propagation in a study. John Junor was the club's first pro.

Medford's H. Chandler Egan, the 1902 U.S. Amateur Champion, designed a nine-hole layout and soon followed with a back-nine plan. Tualatin Country Club was on its way. A clubhouse was built; three slot machines—nicknamed Abe, Ike, and Jake—were early-day fundraisers. In Tualatin's early years, many of the caddies were girls as the young men worked on local farms. Since automobiles weren't prevalent in the early 1900s, members rode the "modern" Oregon Electric car from Portland to play their weekend rounds. The course has hosted its share of tournaments, including U.S. Open Qualifying, the Northwest Open, and several Oregon Opens and Oregon Amateurs.

The course stretches across meadows, rolling hills and dense forests alongside and above the Tualatin River. Towering trees line fairways which, like those on many older courses, are marked by heaves and falls that create ungainly lies. Tualatin's turf is outstanding—low-cropped and verdant—year-round. Lovely flower gardens grace many points, and paved cart paths wind throughout. The parkland track reminds me somewhat of Hayden Lake Country Club in northern Idaho, though Tualatin is tougher. Douglas firs and pines dominate the front nine, with deciduous trees—elms and cottonwoods—lining back-nine fairways. Deer, possums, foxes, nutrias and raccoons visit the layout.

Noteworthy holes include the 3rd, a 386-yard par-4 that runs between trees on a slightly uphill, left-curling route. A big bunker sits along the left at the 100-yard mark. The small and round 3rd green is trapped right-front and left, while grass bunkers line its back edge. The top-rated 6th, a 571-yard par-5, runs straight over rolling ground, passing OB and houses left. A bunker lurks along the right 275 yards out, then the fairway drops down before rising over wavy ground, skirting a trap left at the 75-yard mark. Another bunker on the right sits 50 yards before a slick, two-tiered green trapped twice in front. The shot from the 75-yard bunker to the 6th green may be Tualatin's most difficult.

The 7th and 8th are two of the better Cupp-Fought holes. Once off the elevated tee at the 7th, the 432-yard par-4 follows a right-bending path that skirts a bunker right of the landing area. The fairway then runs up to a mesa-like, high-backed green trapped left-front and right. The 380-yard par-4 8th is a slight left-bender that passes a lateral hazard and the Tualatin River along the left. The fairway goes 300 yards toward a bunker along the right, then bears leftward to a tiny, skinny green shadowed at the right-front by a towering oak. A creek crosses the fairway about 25 yards before this radical putting surface, which is also protected left by the river and behind by towering firs. The 9th, a 492-yard par-5, features a rolling fairway that winds between the river left and the driving range and trees right. Over its final 150 yards, the 9th drops off an embankment. A big fir sits 75 yards from a small, trapped-right green fronted closely by a pond.

The 489-yard par-5 11th traverses rolling, uphill terrain lined by OB left and a bunker right. Because the last 100 yards of the hole plateau following the ascent, an extra-tall pin aids visibility and direction to a sunken and small, steeply front-sloping green trapped in front. The 14th, a 347-yard par-4, rises slightly along a path skirted left by a bunker. Over its final 75 yards, the fairway goes straight downhill to another severely front-banked green. A blind second shot must be made to this target, which is bunkered both sides; the trap on the right is of the "doughnut" variety (sand around a turfed center). The 17th, a 382-yard par-4, requires a well-placed drives from the tips, as trees and a pond squeeze the landing area. The fairway runs uphill to the right toward a hill-cut, two-tiered green pinched laterally by cavernous bunkers. Tualatin's home hole, a 422-yard par-4, is a descending left-bender that passes a bunker along the left of the 230-yard mark. The fairway then flattens before reaching a front-left-tilting green protected on the right by a pond, and left by a pair of bunkers.

Waverley Country Club

18

1100 SE Waverley Drive, Portland, OR 97222. (503) 654-9509. John Wells, pro. 18 holes. 6,553 yards. Par 72. Grass tees. Course ratings: men—B71.6/126, M70.2/ 122; women—M76.1/131, F74.1/126. Year Opened: 1910 (current site). Architects: Jack Moffat, H. Chandler Egan & Arthur Vernon Macan. Members, guests & limited reciprocates.

Formed in 1896 by community leaders and a few Scotsmen who golfed before migrating to the Northwest, Waverley is one of the Northwest's oldest clubs. Its founders were H. E. Judge (then-president of the Multnomah Athletic Club, which formed in 1881 and is the nation's third-oldest athletic club) and Percy H. Blyth (members named the Blyth Medal after him in 1897). Waverley's original course was a links arrangement built in 1896. In 1898, the club moved to its current site along the Willamette River. After purchasing neighboring lots and waiting for the expiration of a lease held by the Italian gardeners who farmed the parcel, the members built a clubhouse and a new golf course in 1910.

Once settled in the new site, Waverley's membership initiated a philosophy still followed today. The club adheres to a belief that golf is a sport filled with tradition; its members endorse that belief to the extent that this golf course has been unchanged since its inception. With no major remodels or modernizing, Waverley's time-worn links feature tiny, tilting greens; greatly rolling fairways that continue to settle; and bunkers which get deeper and deeper after every sand-wedge use. There is no "modern" course record at Waverley; Dr. Oscar Willing's 63 is as remarkable a score today as it was when he shot it in the 1930s.

Because of its long history, Waverley's guest list reads like a "Who's Who" of golf. C. Harry Davis, Harry Vardon (six-time British Open winner), H. Chandler Egan (co-designer and 1902 U.S. Amateur champ), and Ted Ray (winner of the 1920 U.S. Open) played a match here in 1913. Chick Evans arrived with a group of golfers that included Jack Neville, Pebble Beach's designer. A prominent early-day mover and shaker in Northwest golf, A. S. Kerry, was an honorary member. The fabled Scotsman, J. Martin Watson, followed George Trumbull as the club pro from 1914 to 1919; and member Rudie Wilhelm developed into one of Oregon's most prolific tournament winners.

In 1904, Oregon's famed golfing family, the Junors—led by brothers William and George—arrived at Waverley from Scotland, moving into a house by what would later become the 10th hole. Lawson Little, Jr. honed his game at Waverley and then dominated play in the mid-1930s with wins in the U.S. Amateur, British Amateur and U.S. Open. Don Moe and Frank Dolp were top players, and Doc Willing won many events in the Twenties and Thirties. As a junior member, Dorothy "Sissy" Green played a few rounds at Waverley with the legendary Bobby Jones. Thus inspired, she became one of Oregon's top all-time women golfers. Bob Duden, who ruled Oregon golf in the 1950s and 1960s, got his start in golf as a junior member in 1938. Brothers Mickey and Tom Shaw, the latter now a Senior PGA Tourer, were Waverley pros. Marion McDougall Herron is a PNGA Hall-of-Famer, and PGA veteran Peter Jacobsen, along with his brother David, learned the game here.

Over the years Waverley has hosted many PNGA championships, over a dozen Oregon Amateurs, several USGA Women's Amateurs, the 1959 Western Amateur, the 1993 USGA Junior Amateur Championships, and the 1971 USGA Men's National Amateur. The latter event was won by Lanny Wadkins when the course played as a par-70 layout.

The club commemorated its 100th anniversary in 1996. The celebration took place in Waverley's stately white clubhouse, a colonial affair overlooking the Willamette. Earlier that winter, while many other Portland-area courses flooded, Waverley, too, suffered. Parts of the 17th and 18th fairways were awash, and its maintenance building had three inches of water running through it. The previous flood was in 1964. Though the course has pretty much stayed the same over its long life, there has been development activity on the opposite side of the Willamette. Work has been underway for several years on a remodel of the old Portland Waterworks building; its owner is converting the concrete structure into a five-story house. Elsewhere along the facing bank are spectacular homes.

Waverley's wavy fairways wind through towering coniferous and deciduous trees. The greens here may be the most severe in the Northwest and, because of the members' preservation principles, they'll only get tougher in the future. Particularly difficult holes include the 3rd, a 364-yard par-4 with a narrow, left-bending fairway that splits large bunkers on both sides. The steeply right-front-sloping 3rd green is trapped laterally. The 171-yard, par-3 6th descends to a greatly undulating, right-front-sloping green trapped twice left and once right-front. The 7th, a 381-yard par-4, winds uphill to the left around a bunker. The laterally-trapped 7th green leans toward a billowing tree at its left-front edge. The 605-yard, par-5 8th has a tree right of the tee and a downhill fairway. Big bunkers lie 225 yards out along the right. Another trap on the right lurks 150 yards from a round, front-tilting green trapped both sides.

The 10th, a 410-yard par-4, is rolling, straight and wide; a bunker on the 8th fairway enters play along the right, 200 yards out. Here, the hole rises slightly before ending at a slippery green that tilts toward the right-front and a deep bunker. The uphill 12th, a 414-yard par-4, has a pond left of the tee. The corrugated fairway flattens at the 230-yard mark, then goes to a tree-ringed green bunkered twice in front. The 148-yard, par-3 14th goes down to a small, right-front-sloping putting surface surrounded by deep bunkers in front, two traps right and another sand hazard right-rear. The 14th green has a prominent hump in its right half. The 16th, a 206-yard par-3, contains a large and wide, front-sloping green trapped right-front and right-rear. The trap at the right-front is truly cavernous. The straight-running 18th, a 578-yard par-5, tilts rightward toward the Willamette River en route to a mid-sized, front-left-sloping green guarded by two profound traps in front.

Par-3 Courses

Bowyer's Par 3 Golf

11608 NE 119th Street, Vancouver, WA 98662. (360) 892-3808. 9 holes. 1,015 yards. Par 27. Mat tees. No course ratings. Economical, sr. rates. No reservations.

The par-3 layout here has been owned and operated by the Bowyer family since 1968. Once the site of a chicken farm, the layout was begun by Gail Wellwood in 1958. Tall evergreens line the fairways, and the 10-acre course is generally in good shape. Bowyer's is a popular place for beginning players, juniors and seniors. Two of its regulars, Chuck Thurman and Morris Tiede, have played the course nearly every morning since 1974. Between them, Thurman and Tiede have achieved over 40 holes in one. Thurman alone has over 30 career hole in ones and has aced every hole on the Bowyer's course.

Lakeview Golf Challenge

2425 NW 69th Street, Vancouver, WA 98665. (360) 693-9116. 9 holes. 833 yards. Par 27. Mat tees. No course ratings. Economical, sr. rates. No reservations.

Lakeview's par-3 remains one of the region's most controversial golf courses. Occupying an 11-acre plot by Vancouver Lake, the short track—dubbed the "World's Toughest Par-3"—is not for everyone. The course was founded by Duke Wager, a Vancouverite who sold the facility to Doug and Janet Green of Beaverton in 1990. The Greens' son, Charlie, has trimmed trees, upgraded the landscaping and put to use new maintenance equipment.

Lakeview's layout has been lauded—and cursed—by such publications as *Star Magazine, The Oregonian, PGA Magazine,* and Vancouver's newspaper, *The Columbian.* ESPN once shot a video here. The devious Wager began building the course in 1976, finishing it five years later. The Greens continue Wager's tradition of changing the layout's "difficulty rating" every Thursday. On a scale of "1" to "10," the settings are determined by the pin placements on greens cut as low as 7/64th of an inch. Lakeview has 10 greens and 18 different tees. Except for holes 1 and 10, each green is equipped with two flagsticks.

When rated at its toughest, holes are cut in the peripheries of domed greens, mere inches from deep sand traps and ponds. Trees don't line these holes, they're *in* them; drives off mat tees must be lofted over the 20-foot-high obstacles. The grass on the fringes of greens is allowed to grow as tall as 7-1/2 inches. So if you miss the greens, or roll putts off them, expect to perform a flop shot of superior touch. In addition to zany pin placements, Lakeview has 10 bunkers, two grass traps, and 10 ponds. One green—the combined 8th and 17th—has a pond in its middle. Plum trees dot the track, and winds off Vancouver Lake cuff airborne shots off-line. The toughest holes are frequently the shortest. When set up to a "10," even the best golfers have a rugged time parring a hole. It's not uncommon to see players—including pros—get a 20 on a hole as short as 60 yards.

Pine Crest Golf Course

415 NW 143rd Street, Vancouver, WA 98685. (360) 573-2051. 9 holes. 1,206 yards. Par 27. Mat tees. No course ratings. Economical, sr. rates. No reservations.

9

Situated northwest of Vancouver, Pine Crest is owned by Pat and Mary Hart. The Harts recently teamed up with their son, Jim, and his wife Sue, to build the new Hartwood course in Brush Prairie. Pine Crest occupies 23 acres of rolling meadows; the site was a former chinchilla farm. The 1965-opened layout has holes ranging from 77 to 170 yards. The "pine" in the facility's name refers to the 120 trees planted by the Harts after the course had opened. Though all but one of the original trees died, the Harts persevered and seven varieties of pines, along with some pear trees, now line fairways.

Sand traps border a few greens, with a canyon on the 8th hole also eating up inadequate shots. Salmon Creek runs along the south edge of the site but is not involved in the field of play. Though one of the best-maintained par-3s in the Northwest, Pine Crest uses black rubber tee mats. A sternly worded sign outside the clubhouse admonishes, "Use the mats—violators will be barred from the course."

Sah-Hah-Lee Golf Course

17104 SE 130th Avenue, Clackamas, OR 97015. (503) 655-9249. Don Otto, pro. 18 holes. 2,477 yards. Par 54. Grass tees. No course ratings. Economical, jr./sr. rates. Reservations: call a week ahead. Walk-on chances: fair. Driving range.

18

Sah-Hah-Lee's par-3 layout, which opened on June 12, 1991, borders the Clackamas River. The location is scenic and involves considerable wildlife: Chinook salmon and steelhead in the river; quails, ospreys, herons, pheasants, rabbits and ground squirrels on shore. Unfortunately, the riverside site can also wreak havoc on the course. In February 1996, the river breached its dike and caused nearly $500,000 damage to Sah-Hah-Lee. The back nine holes nearest the river were closed for much of the year while repairs were made. Rocks, silt and trees were scattered about the grounds, and tons of mud covered many holes. Though four holes were wiped out, only two greens had to be rebuilt thanks to quick work by volunteers. Over three inches of water were inside the driving range building.

Sah-Hah-Lee is owned by two generations of the Lisac family; brothers John and Jerry funded the facility, and Jerry's sons, Steve and Bud, manage it. The Lisacs wanted to renovate the course with new bunkers, while adding a nine-hole putting course. But because of a reduction in 1996 rounds caused by the flood, the owners will wait awhile before proceeding with the upgrades. The owners received some financial assistance from FEMA, the federal government disaster-relief agency. Future floodings should be minimized as the dike was rebuilt taller than before.

Bud and Steve Lisac co-designed the fine short course, which occupies 40 acres of the family's 60-acre parcel. The 18 holes range from 98 to 187 yards. The site was once a rhubarb and potato farm; in an earlier life, Sah-Hah-Lee's clubhouse was a potato cellar. The driving range at Sah-Hah-Lee—a Clackamas Indian word for "heaven"—is the only practice facility in the Clackamas-Sunnyside area. Head pro Don Otto stays busy conducting lessons at the range, which features grass tees and mats.

The easy-to-walk track is separated from the river by full-grown oak and fir trees. Over 600 trees and rhododendrons were planted prior to its opening. Plants damaged by the flood will gradually be replaced. Sah-Hah-Lee's abbreviated layout involves a meandering creek, three gravity-fed ponds, and a handful of bunkers around the bentgrass greens, which average 3,500 square feet in size. There are some fun holes and, despite its travails in 1996, Sah-Hah-Lee remains a fine outlet for quick, enjoyable rounds.

DRIVING RANGES

Chuck Milne's 82nd Avenue Golf Range

2806 NE 82nd Avenue, Portland, OR 97220.
(503) 253-0902. Chuck Milne, pro.

Dino's Driving Range

21661 Beavercreek Road, Oregon City, OR 97045.
(503) 632-3986. Gary Rike, pro.

Evergreen Golf Center

16703 SE 1st, Vancouver, WA 98684.
(360) 253-3184. Jeff Marsh, pro.

H & H Driving Range

11405 NE 72nd Avenue, Vancouver, WA 98661.
(360) 573-3315. Jeff McRae, pro.

Golden Bear Golf Center at Sunset

16251 SW Jenkins Road, Beaverton, OR 97006.
(503) 626-2244. Brett James, pro.

Tualatin Island Greens

20400 SW Cipole Road, Tualatin, OR 97062.
(503) 691-8400. Todd Andrews, pro. 18-hole putting course.

Vanco Driving Range

703 North Devine Road, Vancouver, WA 98661.
(360) 693-8811 or (503) 253-0902. Chuck Milne & Scott Blake, pros.

Westside Golf Range

106 NW 139th Street, Vancouver, WA 98685.
(360) 573-2565.

Upcoming Courses

Portland Area:

Lake Oswego — Muni Project (1999/2000). In late-1996, a candidate for the Lake Oswego city council recommended building a golf course at the city-owned, 62-acre Luscher Farm on Stafford Road.

Oregon City — Stonegate Golf Course (1999). In February 1996, Clackamas County bought this partially-completed, 165-acre course for $2.4 million. With the purchase came permits to complete the course. As of late-fall 1996, however, the county was still determining how best to proceed. Peter Jacobsen has tentatively been named as course designer.

Troutdale — McMenamin Pubs Golf Course (1998/1999). Mike McMenamin may begin work soon on a par-3 18-hole course at his brewery and brandy distillery at Edgefield Manor. Portland's director of golf, John Zoller Jr., has done a preliminary design for the layout, which may adjoin a destination-style resort.

Greater Vancouver:

Camas — Camas Meadows (1999). A golf course has been planned for nearly a decade at this site on the edge of Camas. In September 1996, it was learned that the project backer, Vanport Realty, would soon proceed with the first nine holes, with another nine perhaps to follow. The star-crossed project has been delayed due to concerns about wetlands, American Indian artifacts, runoff into Lacamas Lake, and just about every other snag that could befall a golf developer.

Camas — Camp Bonneville Project (1999/2000). In November 1995, the U.S. Defense Department and Clark County officials announced a 36-hole golf course as one of several recreational uses under consideration for this 3,840-acre former military camp.

Orchards — Green Mountain Resort (1999/2000). After several years of delay, work may commence in 1997 on an 18-hole, Bunny Mason-designed course. Developed by Taiwanese investor, Sheng Chi Cheng, phase 1 of the project includes the course, a driving range, 13,000-square-foot clubhouse and maintenance building covering 177 acres of the 472-acre site northeast of Vancouver. Additional plans for the $85-million resort include 350 homesites, a 150-room hotel, conference center, commercial space, equestrian center and riding trails.

Vancouver — Vancouver Lake Project (1999/2000). This project has been bandied about by Port of Vancouver officials for several years as part of the port's Columbia Gateway development on lowland property by Vancouver Lake. Nearly 200 acres have been reserved for a public golf course. Skepticism remains, however, about golf at this site as it is replete with wetlands.

12

NORTHWEST OREGON

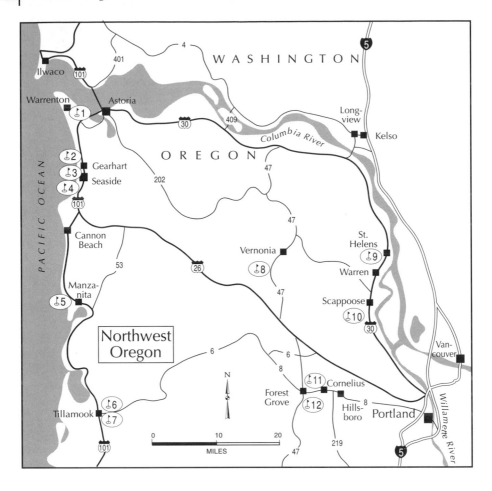

WASHINGTON

5

401

4

Ilwaco

101

Warrenton   Astoria   Long-
🚻1   view
                    30   409   Kelso
                                  Columbia River
                    O R E G O N

PACIFIC OCEAN

🚻2
    Gearhart   47
🚻3
    Seaside   202
🚻4
    101

Cannon
Beach   47

                                        St.
53   Vernonia   Helens
                    26   🚻8   🚻9
Manza-   Warren
nita
🚻5   47
                                        Scappoose
                                        🚻10
                                        30

Northwest
Oregon   6   6   Van-
                                                    couver
                                    8
            N   🚻11 Cornelius
                                  Forest   8
                        10   20 Grove   🚻12 Hills-   Portland
🚻6   boro
Tillamook 🚻7   Willamette River
    101
            0   10   20   219
                        MILES   47   5

1. **Astoria Golf & Country Club** — private 18
2. **The Highlands at Gearhart** — public 9
3. **Gearhart Golf Links** — public 18
4. **Seaside Golf Course** — public 9
5. **Manzanita Golf Course** — public 9 & driving range
6. **Alderbrook Golf Course** — public 18
7. **Bay Breeze Golf & Driving Range** — public 9 (par-3) & driving range
8. **Vernonia Golf Club** — public 18
9. **Saint Helens Golf Course** — public 9
10. **Wildwood Golf Course** — public 18
11. **Sunset Grove Golf Club** — public 9
12. **Forest Hills Golf Course** — semiprivate 18 & driving range

This wet and forested corner of Oregon is defined on the north and east by the Columbia River, west by the Pacific Ocean, and south by the area between Tillamook and Forest Grove. Most of Northwest Oregon enjoys moderate climate zones 5 and 6, but has some of the region's heaviest rainfall. Splitting the region is the Coast Range, which is in winter-cold zone 1. A few banana belts are also found. This part of Oregon has four of the Northwest's oldest courses—Gearhart Golf Links, Alderwood, Seaside and Astoria, and ocean beaches that draw plenty of tourists. But new golf developments—other than new nines attached to existing courses—are rare.

PUBLIC COURSES

Alderbrook Golf Course

18

7300 Alderbrook Road, Tillamook, OR 97141. (503) 842-6413. Steve Wilkes, pro. 18 holes. 5,692 yards. Par 69. Grass tees. Course ratings: men M66.8/105; women— M71.3/116, F69.3/108. Years Opened: 1923 (original nine); 1966 (second nine). Architects: Lee Smith (original nine); owner (second nine). Moderate, jr. rates, credit cards. Reservations: Call for summer weekends. Walk-on chances: Fair. Walkability: Good. Playability: Old-style course with small, slick greens and some water holes.

The first nine holes at Alderbrook opened for play in 1923, and were built by the Pangborn family on their dairy farm. While golfers smacked gutta-percha balls around the course, cows grazed the fairways. Over its first four decades of operation, Alderbrook changed hands more than a dozen times. And, from the late 1930s through 1967, the various owners continued Pangborn's dairy-and-golf operation. The facility has been owned by Neil Abrahamson since 1986.

The layout is north of Tillamook, about two miles from the city's famed cheese factory. Abrahamson has improved the facility during his proprietorship, upgrading the clubhouse and hiring Steve Wilkes as the head pro. The 100-acre course spans generally flat ground, with parts of the 15th and 16th holes curling alongside and up a forested hill on the site's eastern edge. This area is home for elk, deer, rabbits, coyotes and birds. Lakes and/or creeks enter play on five holes, while a few sand traps dot greensides.

As with most of Oregon's coastal courses, Alderbrook is busiest in summer. So call for weekend tee times. Due to a relatively lofty locale, a sandy base underneath fairways, and creeks that rarely flood, Alderbrook is a pretty good choice for winter play. Good tests include the 410-yard 4th, a par-4 with a gradually rising fairway and a fast front-sloping putting surface. The 7th, a 215-yard par-3, starts at a creek-fronted tee and ends at a small, slick green. The top-rated 13th, a 373-yard par-4, is a sharp dogleg-left lined along the left by trees and a creek. The fairway runs up to a front-tilting green backed by evergreens. The 128-yard, par-3 15th is dubbed by members as "The Fabulous 15th." This tough shorty goes straight uphill to a radical front-banked green. Not-so-fabulous drives at the 15th may roll back toward the tee.

Forest Hills Golf Club - semiprivate

36250 SW Tongue Lane, Cornelius, OR 97113. (503) 357-3347. Bruce Clark, pro.
18 holes. 6,173 yards. Par 72. Grass tees. Course ratings: men M69.7/122; women—
M74.5/131, F72.0/123. Years Opened: 1927 (original nine); 1954 (second nine).
Architect: William Martin. Moderate, credit cards. Reservations: Call a week ahead.
Walk-on chances: Fair. Walkability: Good. Playability: Wavy terrain and tight
target zones enhance flavor of rural track.

18

Forest Hills Golf Club is a full-service facility south of Cornelius in bucolic environs. Situated on 126 acres, the venue has been owned by Dick Speros—also the greens superintendent—since 1974. The semiprivate course offers two types of memberships: "country club" (175 of whom enjoy preferential tee times), and "regular" (500 total in the men's and ladies' clubs). Besides a tight 18-hole track designed by William Martin, Forest Hills boasts a clubhouse with a restaurant, bar, pro shop, club-repair room and a driving range. Recent upgrades include an expanded practice green and an automatic irrigation system over 1996-97. Future work may involve a redesign of the 16th and 17th greens, while plans to acquire a neighboring 70 acres for a third nine are on hold.

Forest Hills' founders, Martin of Tillamook and Lee Smith of Bay City, started with nine holes on the former Rehse Farm in 1927. The second nine was added in the mid-1950s. From its inception, the course has been a private club open for public play. Because the founders knew the course would draw players from Forest Grove and Hillsboro, they called it "Forest Hills." The traditional layout crosses rolling terrain, with fairways defined by fir, willow, maple, hazelnut and apple trees. Farms and plant nurseries ring the course. The layout is noted for its raised and steep-sided greens, targets invariably guarded by high-banked bunkers. A creek enters play— bulging into fat ponds on occasion—on nearly a third of the course. Each hole has a name, with some spelled phonetically in Scottish ("Mac Adam," "Loch Eala," "Oot Oboons," "Green Brae," and "Hameward Bend" for the 18th).

Good tests include the 2nd, a 467-yard par-5 with an elevated tee fronted by a pond in a swale. The hole bends rightward between fairway bunkers, then rises to a saddle-shaped green trapped twice in front. The 551-yard, par-5 6th is a canyonlike dogleg-right, with a bunker inside the turn. This narrow hole slopes left—away from the dogleg— en route to a left-sloping, trapped-right green. The top-rated 9th, a 410-yard par-4, starts in a tree-lined chute, with a pond right-front of the tee. The hole goes uphill and straight—skirting a bunker left—to a narrowly-entered, front-sloping green trapped in front. The pretty 11th, a 132-yard par-3, features a raised tee and a diminutive green protected by water and three traps. The 376-yard, par-4 16th traverses ravinelike, left-curling terrain. A broad pond lurks before its hill-cut, front-tilting green.

Gearhart Golf Links

North Marion Street, Gearhart, OR 97138. (503) 738-3538. Jim Smith, pro. 18 holes.
6,089 yards. Par 72. Grass tees. Course ratings: men—B68.7/114, M68.9/112; women
F70.5/112. Years Opened: 1892 (original nine); 1913 (second nine). Architect: Founders
Club. Moderate, credit cards. Call for reservations. Walk-on chances: Fair. Walkability:
Overall good, with some hills. Playability: Wonderful rendition of links golf.

18

Like Woodburn Golf Club and the country clubs at Waverley and Astoria, Gearhart Golf Links is a throwback to the golf courses built in the late 19th and early 20th centuries. With its first nine opening in 1892 and the second set of holes debuting 20 years later, Gearhart's links drew golfers from Spokane, Seattle, Tacoma and Portland soon after it opened. Except for a four-year period, the Oregon Coast Championship was held here from 1910 to 1951 before permanently moving to Astoria.

If the opening year of its original nine is accurate (golf historians have yet to find newspaper reports verifying the date), Gearhart Golf Links is the second-oldest course in western North America. It's been owned for several decades by Orson and Olive Kelley. The rectangular, 100-acre layout is one of the few in the Northwest meriting a "links" designation. The course sits about a long drive from the roaring Pacific, so wind, rain and other salty elements complicate the quest for par. Though its turf wasn't fertilized by birds as were the old Scottish links, nor its bunkers formed by herds of sheep huddling to get out of the wind, its contours were nonetheless shaped by natural forces. With no homes or other "civilization" within its interior, the course is visited by elk, deer and raccoons; seagulls hover overhead and alight on fairways, beaks to the wind.

About the only changes planned by the Kelleys are new ponds at the 5th and 7th holes. These water hazards, to be installed by 1997, occupy low areas which were always wet in winter. Other than the new ponds, Gearhart will stay the same, with its concave, chute-like fairways lined by grassed sand dunes and Scotch pines tipped to the leeward side. Tough holes include the 2nd, a 344-yard par-4 with a drainlike fairway that reaches its nadir midway to a wavy green trapped front and rear. The 3rd, a seemingly benign par-4 of 267 yards, heads straight. A sand trap sits about 40 yards from the left-front edge of a tiny, trapped-left green fronted by a deep, high-lipped bunker.

The 9th, a 348-yard par-4, crosses gnarled terrain halved by a ridge that causes golf balls to skitter either right and left. Large bunkers engird the left-front and right edges of the right-sloping 9th green. The 537-yard, par-5 13th traverses rolling, right-tilting terrain en route to a left-leaning green backed by driftwood. The top-rated 18th, a 580-yard par-5, is particularly tough when Pacific westerlies are aloft (which is almost every day in Gearhart). Gearhart's wildly undulating home hole houses myriad mounds and swales along its fairway, which is squeezed by trees left and a tall berm right. Over its last 80 yards, the 18th ascends leftward to a right-sloping, knoll-perched green.

9 The Highlands at Gearhart

#1 Highlands Road, Gearhart, OR 97138. (503) 738-5248. Dan Strite, pro. 9 holes. 1,776 yards. Par 31. Grass tees. Course ratings (men & women): 59.0/94. Year Opened: 1988. Architect: George Marshall. Moderate, credit cards. Reservations: Call for summer tee times. Walk-on chances: Good. Walkability: Good. Playability: Short-but-tight nine above the Pacific.

Originally slated to be an 18-hole championship track in a full-blown resort, this course was reduced to an executive-length nine by the silver-spot butterfly. The endangered insect was found to inhabit the 210-acre parcel, so the controversial resort idea was dropped. In 1990, the project's original backers—John Q. Hammons Industry and the George Marshall Development Company—sold the course to head pro, Dan Strite. Strite has since upgraded the well-designed short track, while building his pro shop into a mail-order golf-equipment retailer. Strite would like to add another nine holes but, because of the past butterfly problems, expansion is not imminent.

The existing 18-acre course winds between upscale homes and sand dunes; redwoods, ornamentals and dogwoods line some holes. The ryegrass fairways are short-cut, and the bentgrass greens are imbued with considerable break. Traps filled with white Idaho sand dot the grounds, which are visited by deer and elk in winter. Snowy plovers, blue herons and beavers are on year-round display.

The Pacific Ocean lies 500 yards west of The Highlands, so weather is a crucial factor at a layout with four short par-4s and five par-3s. Among the better holes is the 3rd, a 358-yard par-4 that winds over rolling ground to a small, wavy green. The 90-yard, par-3 5th features a panoramic tee and wonderful ocean vistas. Wildflowers bloom in spring and summer along the steep bank fronting the tee. The diminutive, tri-trapped 5th green sits 100 feet below. The 9th, a 189-yard par-3, requires a well-placed tee shot to find its well-bunkered green.

Manzanita Golf Course

Lakeview Drive, Manzanita, OR 97130. (503) 368-5744. 9 holes. 2,268 yards. Par 32. Grass tees. Course ratings: men M61.2/97; women—M65.0/106, F63.2/ 102. Year Opened: 1987. Architects: Ted & Steve Erickson. Moderate. Reservations: Call a week ahead. Walk-on chances: Fair. Walkability: Good. Playability: Fine set of holes with the par-3s among the Oregon coast's testiest.

This nine-hole venue lies just south of Manzanita, a once-secluded town along the Oregon coast that has been "discovered." The layout fills a void created when Neah-Kah-Nie Golf Course closed in the early 1980s. Ted Erickson began work on the Manzanita course in 1962, but business and personal responsibilities delayed progress. Erickson, with help from son Steve, finished it in 1987. Steve and his wife Penny now manage the place. The Ericksons have contiguous acreage for another nine but, as with the original set of holes, they'll move slowly. If and when expansion does occur a new clubhouse will be built and homesites developed on the property.

The existing nine is frequented by deer, elk, shorebirds and migratory waterfowl. Recent improvements include more bunkers. Manzanita's executive-length, single-tee track has five par-4s (242 to 320 yards) and four tough par-3s (160 to 225 yards). The course is bisected by Lakeview and Upland drives. Good holes include the 242-yard, par-4 2nd, which features a dogleg-right fairway and a well-canted green not observable from the tee. The 320-yard, par-4 4th runs narrowly uphill to the left toward a slick green. Nice Pacific vistas are found from the 4th's higher points. The top-rated 9th, a 225-yard par-3, has a small and flat green guarded closely at the right front by a big pond. Tee shots into the green are often swatted toward unintended places by winds off the ocean.

Saint Helens Golf Course

9

57246 Hazen Road, Warren, OR 97053. (503) 397-0358. Jeff Stirling, pro. 9 holes. 2,934 yards. Par 36. Grass tees. Course ratings: men 68.4/116, women 70.3/108. Year Opened: 1962. Architects: Clarence & Gordon Johnson; Jeff Stirling (remodel). Moderate, sr. rates. Reservations: Call a week ahead. Walk-on chances: Good. Walkability: Good. Playability: Some interesting holes on pastoral course, plus views of Mount Saint Helens.

Saint Helens Golf Course was designed and built by Clarence and Gordon Johnson, brothers who had operated a dairy farm at the site. The Johnsons' course was a replacement to the original Saint Helens layout, which was built in 1929. In 1986, Jeff and Angela Stirling bought the place and proceeded with many improvements. Major upgrades have been made to the drainage, irrigation system, bridges, pest control and overall conditioning. Jeff Stirling certainly has the background to maintain and operate a golf course. Once past the final interview in spring 1997, Stirling will have achieved a very rare double in the golf industry: he'll have a Class A card from the PGA and be a certified greens superintendent. Angela has also worked in golf; her parents, Joe and Rose Herberger, were the longtime owners of Oregon City Golf Club until Angela's siblings took over its operations.

Upcoming plans by the Stirlings include a new tee at the 4th hole and continued replacement of sprinkler heads. A much more ambitious project involves replacing the current 9th hole with a driving range. The double-ended practice and teaching facility may open by fall 1997. Long-range considerations include nine more holes on a portion of the Stirlings' 110-acre parcel. The couple may eventually replace the 50 or so trees lost during a December 1995 wind storm, which also damaged other courses in the area.

This layout south of Saint Helens lies just outside the small town of Warren, and offers nice vistas of its like-named mountain across the Columbia River in Washington. Also on display are deer, ducks, herons, beavers, gulls and coyotes. A creek running through is inhabited by beavers. In 1976, a seagull arrived at Saint Helens and showed a astonishing knack for swallowing golf balls. Fortunately, golfers were able to clear the bird's gullet of the potentially lethal objects.

Saint Helens crosses a few hills, a creek-cut valley and gently rolling meadows. The dual-tee nine features a par-36, 2,934-yard front side, and a par-35 back nine of 2,975 yards. Good tests include the par-5 1st, a 523-yard dogleg-left that slopes rightward over its initial half, then leans left after the turn. The fairway ends at a knoll-perched green guarded on the right by the creek. The 3rd, a 347-yard par-4, has a rolling fairway bordered left by the stream. Once past a rise in its midsection, the hole opens onto flat ground where golfers can view "The Wall," an imposing wood-planked fortress that holds up the 3rd green. The creek runs before this front-leaning putting surface, a skinny, two-tiered affair carved into a hillock.

Seaside Golf Course

9

451 Avenue U, Seaside, OR 97138. (503) 738-5261. Wayne Fulmer, pro. 9 holes. 2,593 yards. Par 35. Grass tees. Course ratings: men 64.2/102, women 69.6/106. Year Opened: 1920. Architect: H. Chandler Egan. Moderate. No reservations. Walkability: Good. Playability: Unfettered golf alongside Highway 101.

Seaside's nearly 80-year-old course sits at the south end of town, providing a greenbelt between busy Highway 101 and residences to the west. Necanicum Creek, filled with fat salmon in autumn, winds through the layout. A Clatsop Indian archaeological site—evidence of a 3,000-year-old settlement—lies in woods between the 7th and 8th holes. Deer, beavers and herons frequent the area, while a herd of elk migrating down a federally-protected trail near the coast occasionally tramp on Seaside's greens.

Seaside Golf Course was originated in 1920 by the Cartwright family. The H. Chandler Egan-designed layout has considerable history, being a prime recreational outlet in one of Oregon's most-popular resort areas. Old scorecards, photos and other memorabilia from Seaside's early days are displayed in the large, rambling clubhouse. Proprietor Fred Fulmer has 135 acres of land, with less than half of that devoted to golf. Fulmer plans to move the 1st green 60 yards to the left to make way for upwards of 22 housing lots. More than likely, Fulmer will sell these homesites to a builder who may proceed with duplexes or multi-family units.

In 1996, Seaside experienced the same flooding woes as did many other west-of-the-Cascades courses. It was inundated eight different times and was closed six months that year. Under normal conditions, Seaside drains merely adequately, with the 2nd hole and the cart paths particularly boggy. There are no sand traps here as the water table is too close to the surface. The course hosts many private summer tournaments, and is ideal for infrequent players on vacation. Decent tests include the top-rated 4th, a 485-yard par-5 with a wide left-bending fairway that curls around Necanicum to a small, flat green in trees. The 325-yard, par-4 8th runs straight, with the creek along its left edge, to a rolling green. The 9th, a 203-yard par-3, requires a lofted shot over Necanicum to reach an undulating putting surface.

Sunset Grove Golf Club

9

Off Highway 47, Forest Grove, OR 97116. (503) 357-6044. 9 holes. 2,875 yards. Par 36. Grass tees. Course ratings: men—B67.6/114, M67.2/111; women—M70.3/ 106, F69.4/104. Year Opened: 1965. Architect: Sohler Family. Moderate, jr./sr. rates, credit cards. Call for reservations. Walk-on chances: Good. Walkability: Good. Playability: Interesting course near Forest Grove.

Now owned by Joanne Abarno, this course lies on the east side of Highway 47 just north of Forest Grove. The 60-acre layout was built in 1965 by the Sohler family, who had operated a farm on the site. For the first dozen years, the length of Sunset Grove's holes was listed in meters. After hearing complaints from golfers continually hitting short of the greens, the signs and scorecards were converted to American-standard feet. Member-run Sunset Grove Corporation bought the course from the Sohlers in 1968, then sold it to Abarno in 1989. In recent years, vineyards in the surrounding area have developed a national reputation for high-quality grapes. From the course are nice easterly views of Mount Hood. Sunset Grove's rural locale makes it a habitat for ducks, muskrats and deer.

The dual-tee nine crosses gently rolling meadows, and over two circuits plays to 5,750 yards and a par of 72. The track is fairly straightforward, with its domed, toadstool-like greens presenting the biggest challenge. Well-drained and flat, the easy-to-walk course offers enjoyable rounds. Most fairways are wide and tree-lined, with a few traps and a water hazard complicating play. Good tests include the 3rd, a 304-yard par-4 that crosses flat terrain en route to a pond-fronted, tree-ringed green. The 459-yard, par-5 8th has a left-leaning fairway that stretches out to a left-leaning green. The top-rated 9th, a 392-yard par-4, winds leftward to a front-sloping green with a steep rear flank.

Vernonia Golf Club

18 *15961 Timber Road East, Vernonia, OR 97064. (503) 429-6811 or 1-800-644-6535. 18 holes. 6,100 yards. Par 71. Grass tees. Course ratings (original nine): men— M66.8/113; women—M71.4/116, F68.8/111. Years Opened: 1928 (original nine); 1997 (second nine). Architects: Founding members (original nine); Fred Fulmer III (second nine). Moderate, jr./sr. rates. Reservations: Call a week ahead. Walk-on chances: Good. Walkability: Good. Playability: Vistas of timbered course will broaden once second nine opens.*

In the winter of 1996, rough-grading and shaping took place on nine new holes at this course south of Vernonia. Designed and built by its proprietor, Fred Fulmer III, Vernonia's expanded layout—barring a major calamity—should be open for play by fall 1997 (after this book went to press). I'm usually leery of including unfinished courses or expansions to existing layouts before they open. But Fulmer, after taking five years to get the necessary permits, has the wherewithal to see the project through.

Getting permits for the project was delayed by a neighbor, who opposed nearly every move Fulmer made. However, the city of Vernonia has been supportive; it will extend sewer and water services out Timber Road. To lower costs on the expansion, Fulmer traded some lifetime memberships to local construction companies in exchange for their expertise. Like those on the original nine, several new holes will skirt the Nehalem River. In the winter of 1995-96, the river flooded its banks and washed out a new green. Fulmer moved the hole 20 yards away to ensure it won't be damaged in the future.

The new side is topographically similar to the original track, which crosses rolling meadows dotted with old-growth timber. Vernonia Golf Club was built in 1928 by a local farmer. It lies at 800 feet above sea level and enjoys a pocketed locale that protects it from coastal winds and rains. The facility is popular with RVers, who park their rigs in slips across Timber Road from the course or in full-service spots at nearby Airport and Anderson parks.

Vernonia's revamped track encompasses most of Fulmer's 130-acre plot. He may develop 20 homesites around the new nine, but must first get a zoning change and further permits before proceeding. The new par-36 back side stretches 3,200 yards, while the original par-35 front is 300 yards shorter. The older fairways are quite corrugated—with centuries-old tree roots underneath the turf, and they all conclude at steep-sided, slick greens. Vernonia's better original holes include the 5th, a 314-yard par-4 that bends leftward to a green with near-vertical back and left sides. The 149-yard, par-3 7th has a pond that runs from the tee to the foot of the hillock upon which a small, trapped-rear green is perched. The top-rated 9th, a 392-yard par-4, is a rolling dogleg-right bordered left by the Nehalem. It curls up to a tiny, berm-cut green trapped right-front. Perhaps the toughest of the new holes will be the 18th, a 450-yard par-4.

Wildwood Golf Course

21881 NW Saint Helens Road, Portland, OR 97231. (503) 621-3402. Nicholas **18**
Mabry, pro. 18 holes. 5,756 yards. Par 72. Grass tees. Course ratings: men 68.1/
111, women 72.4/120. Years Opened: 1991 (original nine); 1996 (second nine).
Architect: Bill O'Meara. Moderate, credit cards. Reservations: Call for weekends.
Walk-on chances: Fair. Walkability: Fair, with some steep hikes. Playability:
Exciting new back nine spices up hilly course west of Portland.

Wildwood's recently-expanded course lies off Highway 30, about a half-hour west of Portland near the Columbia River town of Scappoose. After the new back nine opened on July 4th, 1996, Wildwood's owner, designer and builder, Bill O'Meara, was thrilled to see the number of golf rounds triple. Upcoming work should draw even more players to the course. A driving range is scheduled to open in the winter of 1997 and, once the range is finished, the clubhouse will be expanded to include food service. Other plans for the currently trapless course include adding two bunkers per hole.

This course built by O'Meara, one of Oregon's golfing O'Mearas (see Killarney West in Chapter 11), is actually the second Wildwood course at the site. Opened in the spring of 1928, the original layout was mowed by horse-drawn cutters and had green fees of 50 cents. One of its early owners, Ted Otis, wanted to remake Wildwood into a glorious resort, but his dream never materialized. The original Wildwood was closed in 1968 when its then-owners, George and Mary Carter, couldn't get irrigation water pumped to three of the higher holes. The Carters also lost the clubhouse when the state widened Highway 30. The site eventually became an unofficial garbage dump and party area for local motorcyclists. Multnomah County then wanted to use the property as a landfill. But when its owners at that time, the Shriners Hospital, sold it to Bill and his wife Kay, locals were pleased to learn the land would again contain a golf course.

The all-new Wildwood occupies a bowl-shaped, 125-acre parcel intersected by Crab Apple, Peterson and Deer creeks. These streams wind through the layout and generate much consternation from golfers. O'Meara has done considerable drainage work, particularly on the back nine where the holes cross mesa-like terrain above the original front. The course involves about 300 feet of elevation change, with the par-3 3rd hole having a 150-foot drop from tee to green. Native redwoods, maples and oaks line several holes, and 400 saplings have been planted. The ryegrass fairways and bentgrass greens are conditioned by an automatic sprinkler system. Views of mountains—Adams, Rainier and Hood—are available from the higher holes, while elk, deer and coyotes occasionally visit the pastoral site.

Good tests include the top-rated 1st, a 541-yard par-5 that starts at a hill-cut tee then ventures downhill to the right around a tall tree and pond. The fairway concludes at a round, right-front-sloping green fronted by a creek and guarded closely at the right-front by a tree. The 4th, a 519-yard par-5, is a narrow dogleg-right between a creek right and trees left. At the 250-yard mark, the hole curls rightward to a rolling, creek-fronted green. The 315-yard, par-4 10th features a hill-cut tee and a right-bending fairway between trees and a large pond. Golfers need a solid drive to be able to peek around the corner and glimpse the small, mound-ringed 10th green, which sits behind a treed hillock.

The straight-running 13th, a 351-yard par-4, tilts toward a stream along the right; a steep hill shadows its route along the left. The hole concludes at a raised green that slopes right toward a creek. The 498-yard, par-5 16th is an uphill dogleg-right over rolling terrain. Deep jail lurks along the left. Over its final 150 yards, the fairway descends rightward to a knoll-perched, skinny-but-deep green with a steep drop-off along the right. The pretty 17th, a 323-yard par-4, has a gully-fronted tee and a generally wide, left-curling fairway lined by oaks. Its mid-sized putting surface is protected by sturdy oaks left-front and rear.

PRIVATE COURSES

Astoria Golf & Country Club

18 *Off Highway 101, Warrenton, OR 97146. (503) 861-2545. Mike Gove, pro. 18 holes. 6,494 yards. Par 72. Grass tees. Course ratings: men—B71.0/120, M70.4/118; women—M75.7/120, F72.8/115. Year Opened: 1924. Architects: Charles Halderman & George Junor. Members, guests & reciprocates.*

Considered a "hidden gem" by *GOLFWEEK's* architectural writer, Bradley Klein, the course at Astoria Golf & Country Club is a fine representation of Scottish-style linksland golf. Built on a deep strata of sand about a mile east of the Pacific Ocean, Astoria's holes are lined by towering dunes, some of which are 40 feet high. Klein, a nationally-recognized expert on such things, says this course "is unlike anything to be experienced in this hemisphere." Certainly it's the type of course that Northwesterners are lucky to have. For years, Astoria's course has been called the "St. Andrews of the Pacific" for its beach-side locale and links flavor.

The club, currently with 1,000 members—500 of whom are stockholding golfers, lies 85 miles west of Portland near Warrenton, between Highway 101 and the ocean. The 1924-built course was the brainchild of Astoria attorney Charles W. Halderman. Halderman and the other founders originally considered a design that called for a layout with holes running east-west, up and over the sand dunes paralleling the Pacific. Fortunately, this plan was nixed in favor of a design (by Halderman and greenskeeper George Junor) which placed fairways between the dunes. As a result of this wise decision, the course—virtually unchanged over the past 70-plus-years—features sunken holes lined by duned walls draped in native beach grasses.

The original clubhouse, leveled by a smoldering fire on June 2, 1968, has been replaced by a much larger building that better serves the members. About the only alteration to the course has been a gradual rebuilding of greenside traps. In late 1996, bunker work was completed on the 1st, 5th and 9th holes; more such work will occur over the next few years. Overseen by superintendent John Whisler, the reconfigured bunkers look and play more like traps found on a links. The course, which occupies an old cranberry bog, also received new sprinklers around greens and aprons. Other recent changes were attributed to Astoria's occasionally wild weather: the storms that battered the coast in December 1995 ripped out some trees.

The course record, a 65, is owned by member Ralph Dichter. Known locally as the "King of the Coast," Dichter is a 10-time winner of the Oregon Coast Invitational, an event originated in 1910 and held at Astoria since 1951. Also called

"The Coast," the tournament draws 400 players for an eight-day, Saturday-to-Saturday competition in July. Following a day of stroke-play qualifying, all subsequent rounds are match-play. Hundreds of volunteers—led by club manager John Mattingly, Whisler, and head pro Mike Gove (1992 Northwest PGA Player of the Year and past winner of the Oregon Open and PGA Sectional Championships)—spend a year planning the next tourney. The men and women participants fill up six divisions. Past winners have included such great sticks as Dr. Oscar Willing, Bob Duden, Don Krieger, John Schlee (U.S. Amateur champ), Mitch Mooney (former PGA Tour player) and Dichter. On the women's side, the victors include Gracie DeMoss Zwahlen, Edean Ihlanfeldt, Ann Swanson (multiple Washington Open winner) and Mary Lou Mulflur (the University of Washington's women's golf coach). The Mack family (father George, son George Jr., and daughters Lara Mack Tennant and Renee Mack Baumgartner) has won 11 titles.

Astoria's fairways were originally lined with Scotch broom, but the native plant was removed and replaced by coastal pines, now tilted eastward by oceanic breezes. The ravinelike holes conclude at tiny and tipped greens, generally bunkered in front. Astoria's three par-5s fall within a four-hole stretch: the 521-yard 9th, 540-yard 11th and 470-yard 12th. Par-3s range from 129 to 190 yards, with the former, the 10th, right beside the clubhouse patio. Depending on the winds, golfers use anything from a wedge to a 3-iron off the tee. And being adjacent to the clubhouse lounge, the 10th gets pretty rowdy during "The Coast." Only a couple of Astoria's channeled par-4s have any bend to them, with most heading straight over corrugated ground to remarkably quick *poa* greens.

Par-3 Courses

Bay Breeze Golf & Driving Range   9

2325 Latimer Road, Tillamook, OR 97141. (503) 842-1166. Mike Lehman, pro. 9 holes, 1,060 yards. Par 27. Grass tees. No course ratings. Economical. No reservations. Driving range.

With a driving range opened in November 1993 and a par-3 nine greeting players the following summer, Bay Breeze is Tillamook's newest place to golf. Indeed, it's the first course built in the dairy and timber city since Alderbrook in the 1920s. The course abuts the Tillamook Creamery on former pastures once used by that famed company. Bay Breeze is owned by Bud Gienger and Mike Lehman. The two designed and built the facility, which is fitted with a modest clubhouse and pro shop. Deli food service is available, as is a practice putting green. The course is closed during the winter, partly because its site is wet but also because Lehman is a commercial crab fisherman, and fall-winter is the prime time for that activity. The par-3 holes range from 75 to 140 yards, and the bentgrass greens are squeezed by sundry water and sand hazards.

UPCOMING COURSES

Scappoose — Paradise Lane Project (1999/2000). In late 1996, two local men were seeking approval from Columbia County officials for a nine-hole golf course, driving range and 30-space RV park off Paradise Lane in Scappoose.

Tillamook — Port of Tillamook Project (1999). Under consideration for several years, this proposal got off the back burner in late-1996 when Port of Tillamook officials moved the golf course site away from the planes coming in and out of Tillamook Airport, as recommended by the Federal Aviation Association. That summer the port received a grant from the Oregon Economic Development Department to continue studying a golf project.

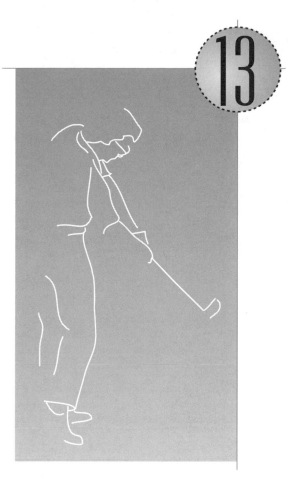

13

SALEM, CORVALLIS &
CENTRAL OREGON COAST

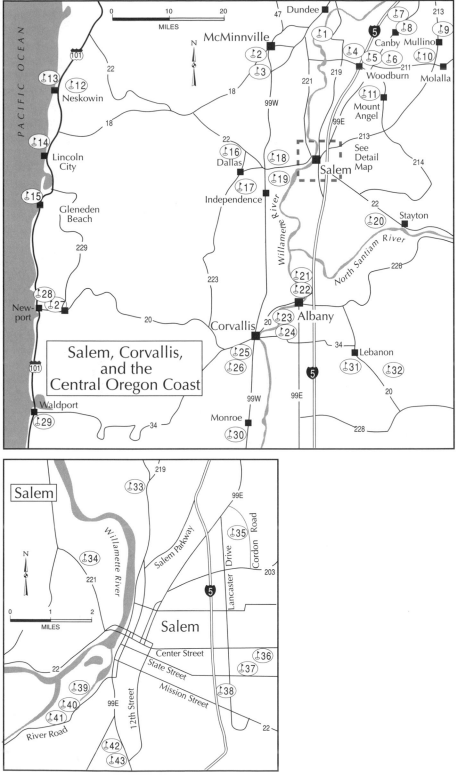

PACIFIC OCEAN

Dundee

McMinnville

Canby Mullino

Woodburn

Molalla

Neskowin

Mount Angel

Lincoln City

Dallas

See Detail Map

Salem

Independence

Gleneden Beach

Stayton

North Santiam River

Willamette River

Albany

Corvallis

Lebanon

Newport

Salem, Corvallis, and the Central Oregon Coast

Waldport

Monroe

Salem

Willamette River

Salem Parkway

Lancaster Drive

Cordon Road

Salem

Center Street

State Street

Mission Street

12th Street

River Road

1. **Riverwood Golf Course** — public 9 & driving range
2. **Michelbook Country Club** — private 18
3. **Bayou Golf Club** — public 9, par-3 9 & driving range
4. **Woodburn Golf Club** — public 9
5. **Senior Estates Golf & Country Club** — private 18
6. **OGA Members Course at Tukwila** — public 18 & driving range
7. **Frontier Golf Course** — public 9 (par-3)
8. **Willamette Valley Country Club** — private 18
9. **Ranch Hills Golf Club** — public 9
10. **Arrowhead Golf Club** — private 18
11. **Evergreen Golf Club** — public 9
12. **Hawk Creek Golf Course** — public 9
13. **Neskowin Beach Golf Course** — public 9
14. **Lakeside Golf & Racquet Club** — public 18
15. **Salishan Golf Links** — public 18, driving range
    & 18-hole putting course
16. **Cross Creek Golf Course** — public 18 & driving range
17. **Dallas Golf Course** — public 9 & driving range
18. **Oak Knoll Golf Course** — public 18 & driving range
19. **Westside Driving Range & Golf Center**
20. **Santiam Golf Club** — public 18 & driving range
21. **Spring Hill Country Club** — private 18
22. **The Golf Club of Oregon** — public 18
23. **Golf City** — public 9
24. **Trysting Tree Golf Club** — public 18 & driving range
25. **Corvallis Country Club** — private 18
26. **Marysville Golf Course** — public 9
27. **Olalla Valley Golf Course** — public 9
28. **Agate Beach Golf Course** — public 9 & driving range
29. **Crestview Hills Public Golf Course** — public 9
30. **Diamond Woods Golf Course** — public 18 & driving range
31. **Pineway Golf Course** — public 9 & driving range
32. **Mallard Creek Golf Course & RV Camp** — public 18
    & driving range
33. **McNary Golf Club** — semiprivate 18
34. **Salemtowne Golf Club** — private 9
35. **Cordon Road Driving Range**
36. **Auburn Center Golf Club** — public 9
37. **Caddieshack Driving Range**
38. **Meadowlawn Golf Club** — public 9
39. **Salem Golf Club** — semiprivate 18 & driving range
40. **Cottonwood Lakes Golf Course** — public 9 & driving range
41. **Illahe Hills Country Club** — private 18
42. **Creekside Golf Club** — semiprivate 18 & driving range
43. **Battle Creek Golf Course** — public 18

This part of Oregon is defined by Yamhill and Clackamas counties on the north and Corvallis to the south, the Pacific Ocean on the west and the Cascades to the east. The lush Willamette River Valley occupies much of the area. Temperate climate zones 5 and 6 are found along the coast and in the valley, with the Suislaw National Forest and the Coast Range in winter-cold zone 1. Golf is a year-round activity in the milder parts. Many lowland areas were deluged by flooding from the Willamette and its tributaries in 1995 and 1996, with several courses temporarily closed. All were restored to normal operations by 1997. On a more positive note, Salem and environs continue to boom, with new residents arriving daily. Several new golf courses will hopefully meet the demand from this growing part of the Northwest.

Public Courses

Agate Beach Golf Course

9

4100 North Coast Highway, Newport, OR 97365. (541) 265-7331. Terry Martin, pro. 9 holes. 2,777 yards. Par 36. Grass tees. Course ratings: men 65.8/109; women—B70.7/113, F68.7/109. Year Opened: 1931. Architect: Frank Stenzel. Moderate, credit cards. Reservations: Call a week ahead. Walk-on chances: Good. Walkability: Good. Playability: Great views of the Pacific from nine-holer.

Agate Beach Golf Course crosses a gradually sloping hill, offering wonderful vistas of the Pacific Ocean. The fairly straightforward track winds between coastal trees and is not too difficult. Following the death of William R. Martin in 1995, the course is now run by his widow Ramona Martinson, and their son Terry Martin, who's also the head pro. The late Martin had acquired Agate Beach from Ray Whiteside in 1960.

The 1931-built, Frank Stenzel-designed track has remained pretty unchanged over the years. The pro shop—remodeled in 1993—is amply stocked with equipment and clothing, and an eatery in the adjoining clubhouse serves breakfast and lunch. Agate Beach receives quite a bit of play in summer, so call ahead for tee times. During the rest of the year, demand drops considerably and players can generally walk on and readily tee off.

The well-conditioned layout is fun to play. Among the tougher holes is the par-4 4th, a 356-yarder that curls rightward to a round, untrapped green. The top-rated 6th, a 501-yard par-5, doglegs right along a tree-bordered path. Two spruces tower 75 yards in front of the right-tilting 6th green. A 474-yard par-5, the right-bending 9th skirts trees. Many rises and swales occupy the route, which ends at a tree-guarded green perched on a rise.

Auburn Center Golf Club

5220 Center Street NE, Salem, OR 97301. (503) 363-4404. 9 Holes. 1,338 yards. Par 29. Grass tees. No course ratings. Year Opened: 1962. Architect: Original owner. Economical, jr./sr. rates. No reservations. Walkability: No problems. Playability: Facile short course on Salem's east side.

9

This course lies in the Auburn-Center district of east Salem. Besides an abbreviated par-29 track, the venue has an 18-hole putt-putt layout sporting likenesses of Snow White and the Seven Dwarfs, a bear, lions, and a castle over a "water hazard." Open year-round, the short track is popular with day-care centers and church groups. Current owner, Gregg Smith, bought the course in 1993 from Ray and Peggy Low. Smith, formerly the proprietor of Ranch Hills in Mulino, runs the clubhouse, which serves snacks and has an arcade room popular with neighborhood kids.

When Auburn Center opened in 1959, it only had a driving range—closed by the Lows in 1987—and the putt-putt layout. The par-29 course was built in 1962 within an apple orchard. In addition to apple trees, firs line fairways. The layout has seven par 3s —ranging from 56 to 188 yards—and par-4s of 235 and 287 yards. The good beginners' course crosses flat ground, and its postage-stamp greens can be elusive targets.

Battle Creek Golf Course

6161 SE Commercial Street, Salem, OR 97306. (503) 585-1402. Lynn Baxter, pro. 18 holes. 6,015 yards. Par 72. Grass tees. Course rating: men—B68.8/117, M65.7/110; women—M69.5/112, F67.3/107. Years Opened: 1962 (original nine); 1971 (second nine). Architect: Bill Stevely. Moderate, jr./sr. rates, credit cards. Call for reservations. Walk-on chances: Good. Walkability: Good. Playability: Nice layout in south Salem.

18

Eighteen-hole Battle Creek is named after a Willamette River tributary that commemorates an 1846 battle fought between Native Americans and Willamette Valley settlers. The layout, owned by head pro Lynn Baxter, crosses about 100 acres in south Salem off Commercial Street (Highway 99). Battle Creek drains fairly well but, like other western Oregon courses, it was flooded in 1996. Recent improvements include the addition of 85 yards to the 10th hole. Previously a rugged 230-yard par-3 into a prevailing wind, the hole is now a 315-yard par-4 with a pond-fronted green. The revision at the 10th increased Battle Creek's par to 72. Future plans include adding new women's tees.

Beginning with a front nine in 1962, the layout was expanded with another nine in 1971. Baxter got the course in 1985 from Bill Stevely, the track's designer and developer. Besides the Battle Creek, a man made waterway runs through and three ponds enter play. Mostly flat in topography, the layout features tight fairways and, on perimeter holes, close out-of-bounds. Homes surround Battle Creek on three sides. With the various bodies of water crossing it, the course is a favorite landing strip for ducks. Golfers here might also spot deer.

Tough holes include the top-rated 3rd, a 385-yard par-4 with an evergreen squeezing drives off the tee. The rolling fairway leads to a mid-sized green guarded left-front by a fir. The 460-yard par-5 6th heads straight over corrugated ground. Both Battle Creek (250 yards off the tee) and the man-made stream (75 yards from the green) vie for errant shots. The 12th, a 400-yard par-4, has a tree-pinched fairway and a tiny, front-sloping green with a steep back edge.

Bayou Golf Club

18 *9301 SW Bayou Drive, McMinnville, OR 97128. (503) 472-4651. Sarah Bakefelt, pro. Regulation course: 9 holes, 3,166 yards, par 36. Par-3 course: 9 holes, 1,020 yards, par 27. Grass tees. Course ratings: men—B70.2/118, B/M69.4/117, M68.6/116; women—M73.8/128, M/F70.7/120, F67.6/109. Year Opened: 1964. Architect: B.A. White. Moderate (economical for par-3 course), jr./sr. rates. Reservations: Call for weekends. Walk-on chances: Fair. Walkability: Good. Playability: With a regulation nine and par-3 track, Bayou has a bit of everything.*

Despite being underwater for five months (February, March, May, November and December) in 1996, Bayou's regulation and par-3 nines were quickly brought into their best shape ever. Superintendent Mike Headrick has rejuvenated the fairways and greens, nursing the turfgrass after the floods and stepping up maintenance practices for the course's primary play periods. More golfers from beyond McMinnville have been finding Bayou, thanks in part to a casino 20 miles to the west that has drawn plenty of outsiders. Recent improvements include a fountain in the pond by the 3rd hole. Another fountain will be coming soon to a pond at the 6th, and a pond at the 7th may also receive a man-made geyser in the future.

Located south of McMinnville, Bayou has been co-owned by Jerry Claussen and head pro Sarah Bakefelt since 1983. The two courses were built in 1964 by their founder, B.A. White. White named the course "Bayou" for the Louisiana-like Spanish moss clinging to the native oak, weeping willow, ash and maple trees along the South Yamhill River, which flows through the course and is the source of the flooding. White's former 11,000-square-foot mansion, perched above the course, contains banquet space and a snack bar for golfers' enjoyment. A patio by the former residence is a popular place for barbecues following tournaments. The mansion is home to a friendly ghost called Charlie, who reportedly has caused many strange goings-on since the facility opened.

The par-3 track alongside Highway 99 West features contemporary mounding and postage-stamp greens. The regulation nine winds across a floodplain and a ridge along the northern portion of Bayou's 100-acre site. There are no bunkers on the course as the water table's too high. Good tests include the 2nd, a 427-yard par-4 that bends rightward between trees right and the Yamhill left to a slick, front-sloping green. The 356-yard par-4 5th doglegs right and tilts toward a pond. The top-rated 9th, a 504-yard par-5, has a rolling fairway guarded left by water. The latter part of the hole rises slightly to a tipped and fast putting surface.

Cottonwood Lakes Golf Course

9 *3225 River Road South, Salem, OR 97302. (503) 364-3673. 9 holes. 1,250 yards. Par 28. Grass & mat tees. No course ratings. Year Opened: 1991. Architect: Alan Olson. Economical, jr./sr. rates. No reservations. Walkability: Very good. Playability: Short course with tight fairways and wavy greens plays tough.*

Par-28 Cottonwood Lakes abuts the Salem Driving Range in southwest Salem. The 10-acre track and range are just south of Salem Golf Club and west of Minto-Brown Island Park in the Willamette River. The layout was designed by its original pro, Alan Olson, and is now owned solely by Gary Benson after Olson sold his interest to Benson in 1996. Benson has plans to expand the clubhouse and add a putt-putt course. He may also revise some holes. An interesting aspect of the driving range is its location on former horse stables; the concrete footings from old barns are still observable.

Cottonwood Lakes occupies reclaimed swampland along the Willamette. In 1996, the course was flooded and out of play for four weeks; the range, located on a lower parcel, was flooded three different times. The short track features small butte-like grass tees (where Astroturf mats are optional), large and occasionally-bunkered bentgrass greens, and rye-fescue fairways, some of which are mere tree-lined corridors. Water hazards—Willamette River sloughs, ponds and creeks—and well-treed jails further impede the quest for par. Cottonwood Lakes' par-3s range from 108 to 183 yards, with the only par-4, the 1st, a 239-yarder.

Creekside Golf Club - semiprivate

18

6250 Clubhouse Drive South, Salem, OR 97306. (503) 363-4653. Tom Carey, pro. 18 holes. 6,887 yards. Par 72. Grass tees. Course ratings: men—T73.6/131, B71.9/ 128, M69.5/120; women—M75.0/134, I72.6/130, F70.4/122. Years Opened: 1993 (original nine); 1994 (second nine). Architects: Peter Jacobsen & Jim Hardy. Expensive. Reservations: Call five days ahead (public play allowed only on weekdays). Walk-on chances: Fair. Walkability: Fair, with some lengthy between-hole hikes. Playability: Highly-refined golf course in south Salem.

Originally part of a 336-acre golf and housing development, Creekside Golf Club is now a separate entity. National Golf Properties bought the 150-acre layout in 1995; NGP's operational arm, American Golf, runs it. Creekside's original head pro, Tom Ferrin, is now the general manager. Though the course itself is no longer owned by Creekside's originator, Hawaii Northwest Ventures, the company continues to develop housing around it. Nearly 600 single-family homes are planned for these areas; in 1997, work commenced on an 80-home section above the 13th tee.

Creekside had nearly 300 members at the end of 1996. Once the membership totals 400, it will close to public play. Currently, non-members are allowed to play weekdays only, with members and guests having exclusive use on weekends. Besides a fine course that occupies a former Christmas tree farm, members have access to a 17,000-square-foot clubhouse with all the amenities. Creeksiders enjoy country club conditions that range from a manicured layout to immaculate, towel-equipped carts. This Salem course may have more signs—directional, informational and otherwise—than any in the Northwest. Informationals discuss the speed of the greens (by the 6th tee is news that, "There is a noticeable increase in putting speed through the remainder of the course"). Golfers are also advised to steer clear of wetlands and other areas (behind the 17th green is a steep cliff and a "danger falling rock" posting).

The course was co-designed by Portlander Peter Jacobsen and Houstonian Jim Hardy, and built over a three-year period by Wadsworth Construction. Jacobsen, who holds the course record from the tips (a 64), and Hardy created a very refined layout. Wetlands, creeks, ponds and terrific bunkering add difficulty to the track, whose 120 feet of elevation change lends it considerable hole-to-hole variety. Wetlands are more involved on the front nine, where multi-part fairways and dense trees are the norm. The back nine is hillier and lined by more housing. Three creeks—Powell, Jory and Battle—cross the field of play, and views of mounts Hood and Jefferson are on display. Wildlife include deer, nutrias, coyotes, hawks and geese. I saw a beaver lazily paddling across a pond at the 17th hole.

Particularly stern tests include the narrow 2nd, a 350-yard par-4 that doglegs left while tilting right toward jail. At the 225-yard mark, the hole winds 90 degrees left to a small, untrapped green guarded left-front by trees. The tree-lined 4th, a 480-yard par-5, is a rolling right-bender. At the 200-yard mark, three bunkers pinch the left side of the fairway, which then curls rightward to a raised and deep-but-narrow, steep-sided green. The top-rated 5th, a 417-yard par-4, has wetlands off the tee and bunkers squeezing the landing area. The fairway gradually rises to a heart-shaped, narrowly-entered green lined in front and left by a creek. The 442-yard, par-4 7th has a bog-fronted tee and three traps left of the landing zone. Once beyond this point, the fairway widens en route to a large, V-shaped putting surface trapped on the right.

The 447-yard, par-4 8th starts at a pond-fronted tee, then bends rightward around trees to a wide-but-shallow green trapped thrice right-front and twice left-front. The 10th, a 392-yard par-4, is made difficult by a forced carry over a creek and wetlands running diagonally across its left-sloping, left-turning path. Two deep bunkers sit out along the right. The creek runs up the left side of the hole which, at the 100-yard mark, is crossed by the creek before bending sharply left to a hill-cut, front-sloping green trapped left-front. The par-5 12th is dotted by over a dozen bunkers along its 524 yards. The hole descends off an elevated tee, passing houses and two traps right and six left. The hole ascends over its last 200 yards to a mid-sized, right-sloping green ringed by four traps left-front, three traps right-front, and two sandy ball-swallowers right-rear.

The 16th is a very narrow and severely right-sloping 521-yard par-5. From the tips, a well-placed drive should miss tree branches a mere 30 yards apart. Past this narrow seam is a fairly broad landing area. At the 150-yard mark, a creek crosses the fairway, which then rises past three traps to a right-front-sloping, humped-in-the-middle green bunkered twice left and once right. The 200-yard, par-3 17th descends to a water-fronted green which sits on the site of an old rock quarry. Vestiges of the quarry remain; the rock hillside was blasted out and the remaining scree backs the large, rolling 17th green, which is guarded by grass bunkers rear and a swale right-front. The 18th, a 462-yard par-4, skirts wetlands right and a hill left. At the 150-yard mark, a stream crosses the hole. The 18th's large and rolling putting surface has two pot bunkers left-front, two big traps right, another pot trap left, and two bunkers right-rear.

Crestview Hills Public Golf Course

9 *1680 SW Crestline Drive, Waldport, OR 97394. (541) 563-3020. 9 holes. 2,796 yards. Par 36. Grass tees. Course ratings: men 66.0/111, women 69.5/114. Year Opened: 1971. Architect: Willard Hall. Moderate, credit cards. Reservations: Call a week ahead. Walk-on chances: Fair. Walkability: Good. Playability: Nice nine-holer above the Pacific Ocean near Waldport.*

Nine-hole Crestview Hills was purchased in fall 1996 by Mark and Patti Campbell. The Campbells bought Crestview Hills from Tim and Kathee Tarpley, who went on to acquire the new Cross Creek layout in Dallas. The Campbells, who moved to the Oregon coast from Alaska, obtained a facility that has been a local fixture since 1971. Crestview Hills lies between the towns of Yachats (pronounced "yaw-hots") and Waldport, east of Highway 101. The generally flat layout is augmented by a clubhouse with food service and a lounge. While running Crestview Hills since 1988, the Tarpleys made many improvements, including an automatic irrigation system and landscaping enhancements. The Campbells plan to build a new driving range.

Fifty-acre Crestview Hills offers views of the Pacific Ocean. The site was originally owned by the city of Waldport, which donated it to area homeowners who, in turn, built the Willard Hall-designed course. The dual-tee track is visited by shorebirds and deer and is ringed by some homes. It has no sand traps, with a pond off the 5th green the most salient hazard. Interior fairways are fairly wide open, with perimeter holes lined by woods. Good tests include the 3rd, a 480-yard par-5 that runs straight to a tipped putting surface. The top-rated 5th, a 328-yard par-4, crosses rolling ground on a right-turning, tree-lined route. The 5th's tree-ringed green is guarded along the right by the pond. The serpentine 6th, a 495-yard par-5, skirts woodlands—going right, then back to the left—before concluding at a small, raised green.

Cross Creek Golf Course

18

13895 Highway 22, Dallas, OR 97338. (503) 623-6666. 18 holes. 6,830 yards. Par 72. Grass tees. Course ratings not available. Year Opened: 1997 (original nine); 1998 (second nine). Architect: Tim Tarpley. Moderate. Call for reservations. Walk-on chances: Good. Walkability: Good. Playability: New track near Dallas offers two different nines.

Located north of Dallas off Highway 22 about five miles west of Highway 99, Cross Creek Golf Course is one of western Oregon's newest places to golf. The project was initiated by Salem hotelier, Duncan Chaey, who envisioned 36 holes for the property. But a lack of finances foiled Chaey's plans and, in 1996, he sold a roughed-in 18-holes to Tim and Kathee Tarpley. The Tarpleys came to Cross Creek with a background in maintaining and operating a golf course; they previously owned Crestview Hills in Waldport, on the Oregon coast.

The couple basically started over with the layout, which was rough-graded—with tees, greens, mounding and bunkers barely observable to the naked eye. Tim Tarpley, who oversaw construction of Cross Creek, completed final shaping, irrigation system installation and seeding. The course was scheduled to open with the first nine holes in fall 1997 (after this book went to press), with the second nine to debut the following year. When all 18 holes are completed, the Tarpleys will start work on a clubhouse. The venue opened with a temporary clubhouse and a driving range.

The 210-acre site was previously used for farming; a 35-acre plum orchard occupies part of the land. Four creeks run through the property, which drains fairly well. One of the streams, Salt Creek (Chaey's original name for the course), is crossed four times by the layout (thus the Tarpley's new name for it). The track features four tees per hole, bentgrass greens and ryegrass fairways. The relatively flat original nine boasts two lakes and gentle mounding. The second (back) nine is hillier, and has four lakes in play. As the layout matures the Tarpleys will add at least two bunkers at greensides. Cross Creek is near the Basket Slough Wildlife Refuge, so it's regularly visited by deer, elk and ducks.

Dallas Golf Course

9 *11875 Orr's Corner Road, Dallas, OR 97338. (503) 623-6832. Brian Weaver, pro.
9 holes. 2,031 yards. Par 31. Grass tees. Course rating: 58.2/91 (for men & women).
Year Opened: 1990. Architect: Gary Christman. Economical, jr./sr. rates. Call for
reservations. Walk-on chances: Good. Walkability: Good. Playability: Good choice
for beginning and intermediate golfers.*

Formerly called Sandstrip, Dallas Golf Course lies two miles from its namesake town, near the Polk County Fairgrounds. The facility includes a clubhouse and driving range, and is owned by a group of Salem businessmen headed by Henry Beutler. One of the original partners, Gary Christman, designed the layout, which opened in March 1990. Class A pro Brian Weaver—previously at Willamette Valley Country Club—replaced former head pro Bruce Perisho in 1996.

The 44-acre course spans gently rolling, two-tiered terrain. Rickreall Creek skirts the layout, entering play at the 2nd hole, a 140-yard par-3. The course's original name stems from the old logging roads that cut across several holes; the roads have been filled with sand, and are now hazards. From the course are westerly views of the Coast Range on clear days. Wildlife visitors include ducks and geese.

Dallas Golf Course features rye-fescue fairways and Penncross bentgrass greens. The course, whose records are 26 (the nine-hole mark set by John Chase) and 55 (Perisho's 18-hole mark), is ideal for beginning to intermediate linksters. Other than the standstrip bunkers, three man-made ponds inhibit the quest for par. The site is halved by lower and upper tiers. Tee shots at the 9th, a 115-yard par-3, are made from the upper level down to a pond-backed green on the lower level. The top-rated hole, the 6th, is also the longest. This straight-running 355-yard par-4 skirts OB left before reaching a left-rear-sloping green.

Diamond Woods Golf Course

18 *96092 Territorial Road, Monroe, OR 97456. (541) 998-9707. 18 holes. 6,900 yards.
Par 72. Grass tees. Course ratings not available. Years Opened: 1997 (original nine);
1998 (second nine). Architect: Greg Doyle. Moderate, jr. rates, credit cards. Call
for reservations. Walk-on chances: Good. Walkability: Good, overall. Playability:
Length and ample hazards make for interesting and tough challenge.*

A new golf course located equidistant between Corvallis and Eugene, off Territorial Road, Diamond Woods is the brainchild of brothers Greg and Jeff Doyle. While youngsters growing up in Junction City playing Fiddler's Green (then called Country Place), the two dreamed of building and owning their own golf course. After high school, Jeff played baseball at Oregon State University and went on to become a professional ballplayer for the St. Louis Cardinals and the Nankai Hawks in Japan. Upon completing his baseball career, Jeff purchased this 168-acre site in the Willamette Valley.

While Jeff was pursuing baseball, Greg spent 15 years working in golf course maintenance and construction. During that time he earned a BA degree in landscape architecture. The idea for building Diamond Woods was hatched in 1989. The Doyles were helped in fulfilling their dream by their parents Gerry and Nancy Doyle, Jeff's wife Liz, and long-time friends, John Peterson and Ramon and Julian Gonzalez. The Doyles, their family and friends hope Diamond Woods becomes a popular place with golfers as well as tournament organizers.

Construction on the course began in 1994. The first nine was to open in June 1997 (after this book went to press), with the second nine ready the following year. The site involves 150 feet of elevation change, and stretches over foothills. Views of the Willamette Valley and the Cascades are on tap. The 6,900-yard track involves two streams (one of which is named Rattlesnake Creek—odd, since rattlesnakes aren't endemic to western Oregon), a lake, over 40 bunkers, four player-adaptable tees per hole, and mature stands of oaks, firs, pines and madronas. Diamond Woods opened with a driving range and temporary clubhouse; a permanent structure will be built once the full 18-holer is well underway.

Evergreen Golf Club

11694 West Church Road NE, Mount Angel, OR 97362. (503) 845-9911. Joe Druley, pro. 9 holes. 3,021 yards. Par 36. Grass tees. Course ratings: men—B68.6/114, B/M67.4/110, M67.2/104; women—B/F71.8/114, 70.8/111. Year Opened: 1962. Architect: Bill Schafer. Moderate, credit cards. Call for reservations. Walk-on chances: Fair. Walkability: Good. Playability: Nicely manicured track near Mount Angel.

Nine-hole Evergreen lies amid colorful farmlands west of Mount Angel. The course was purchased in 1993 by head pro Joe Druley and his wife, Maryann Mills. The duo bought Evergreen from the previous operators, Jim Hynds and Tom O'Neill, who'd operated the place since 1964. Sadly, Hynds, the head pro while here, passed away in November 1996.

Despite a slow start early in the year caused by wet weather, Evergreen enjoyed a gradually improving 1996, when it hosted 24,000 rounds. Druley and Mills have made several improvements to enhance play, including different cuts of rough, mowing the greens low to speed them up, new tees, improved conditioning, and installing automatic sprinklers at greensides. A deck was also added to Evergreen's popular restaurant, which has a sports-bar theme with big-screen TVs and a satellite dish.

The 63-acre course crosses gently rolling terrain. A slough and ditch flank one side of the 6th hole, while ponds in the 5th and 6th fairways are also a problem for golfers. Evergreen has no sand traps. Wildlife include deer, rabbits, ducks and geese. Other than water hazards, players must master fairways squeezed by their namesake conifers as well as flowering plums and gnarled filbert and cherry trees left from an old orchard. Good tests include the 2nd, a 428-yard par-4 that runs straight for most of its length. At the 75-yard mark, the hole veers sharply rightward to a tree-ringed green. Though not visible from the tee, a pond lies driving distance out at the 5th, a 462-yard par-5 that had been a tough par-4 before a new back tee was built. The 366-yard, par-4 9th heads directly to a small, front-tilting green with Evergreen's clubhouse close behind it.

Golf City

9 *2115 Highway 20, Corvallis, OR 97330. (541) 753-6213. Jim Hays, pro. 9 holes. 801 yards. Par 28. Grass tees. No course ratings. Year Opened: 1977. Architect: Original owner. Economical, credit cards. No reservations. Walkability: No problems. Playability: Abbreviated layout has the region's shortest par-4.*

Golf City was purchased in August 1996 by Jim Hays. Hays got the course from its previous owner and head pro, Dick Mason, now at The Greens at Redmond in central Oregon. Besides the diminutive track, Hays' acquisition included a pro shop, restaurant and bar. The 10-acre venue borders Highway 20 northeast of Corvallis, and is bound on the north by a nursery and east by a filbert orchard. It's popular with Oregon State University students and with seniors.

Originally a driving range, Golf City was converted to a short course in 1977. The layout has seen many holes-in-one; local player Tom Williams has aced all nine of its holes. The par-3 holes range from 53 to 110 yards; its 8th is an 85-yarder and the Northwest's shortest par-4. This "dogleg-right" around trees can be holed, but only if one scorches a low tee shot underneath the branches at the "corner."

The Golf Club of Oregon

18 *905 NW Spring Hill Drive, Albany, OR 97321. (541) 928-8338. 18 holes. 5,773 yards. Par 70. Grass tees. Course ratings: men—B67.1/107, M66.1/104; women—M71.1/115, F68.5/109. Years Opened: 1929 (original nine); 1949 (second nine). Architects: R.H. Dobell (original nine); Albert Fortier (second nine). Moderate, jr./ sr. rates. Reservations: Call a week ahead. Walk-on chances: Fair. Walkability: Good. Playability: Upgrades to older course have improved conditions.*

The Golf Club of Oregon began with nine holes in 1929; the second set of holes opened two decades later. Not to be confused with the private Oregon Golf Club in West Linn, this facility was founded by R. H. Dobell and originally called Albany Golf Club. Albert Fortier, who operated the layout with his brother Bud from 1945 to 1959, constructed the back nine in 1949. Dean Kingsbury and Jack True acquired the course in an estate sale and operated it until 1976, at which time Jerry Claussen— co-owner of McMinnville's Bayou Golf Club—and Richard Renn bought them out. Since 1991, The Golf Club of Oregon has hosted the annual KRKT Open, named after a local radio station.

The course occupies a squarish, 102-acre site bordered on the west by Spring Hill Drive, east by a farm, and south by the Willamette River. In February 1996, it was underwater after the Willamette flooded and closed for 50 days. One intrepid mariner was seen paddling across the submerged grounds in a boat. Later that spring, the layout was fully repaired and back to normal. Deer, rabbits, raccoons and possums visit the site, while bobcats and coyotes dwell in a forested buffer between the course and the river. Fairways are lined by black walnut, cedar, fir, cottonwood and maple trees. An elevated train trestle—still in use and the only such structure on a public Northwest course—lines the layout's western edge.

Though not generally considered a tough track—with no ponds and only a few greenside traps, The Golf Club of Oregon features tight fairways lined by jail and slippery putting surfaces. It averages about 50,000 rounds a year. Interesting holes include the 1st, a 397-yard par-4 (dubbed "Trestle") that bends rightward around trees right and the train tracks on the left. The 335-yard, par-4 5th ("Channel") is halved by upper and lower shelves running diagonally through the fairway. The top-rated 8th, a 430-yard par-4, follows a tree-tapered path en route to a crescent-shaped, tree-ringed green. The 298-yard, par-4 13th is called "Temptation," an apt name for the sharp left-bender. The heart-shaped 13th green can be reached with a well-placed drive, but shot-blocking trees inside the 90-degree dogleg swallow inadequate efforts.

Hawk Creek Golf Course

48405 Hawk Street (off Highway 101), Neskowin, OR 97149. (503) 392-4120. 9 holes. 2,343 yards. Par 34. Grass tees. Course ratings: 63.8/103 (men & women). Year Opened: 1969. Architect: Harold Schlichting. Moderate, credit cards. Call for reservations. Walk-on chances: Good. Walkability: Good. Playability: Lush setting for shortish nine-holer.

Hawk Creek lies on the opposite side of Highway 101 from Neskowin Beach Golf Course. Named after a creek that runs through it, the single-tee nine winds over a meadow and a forested hill. At 2,343 yards, the course contains three par-3s (109 to 144 yards), five par-4s (275 to 360 yards), and a 385-yard par-5. Hawk Creek was founded and built by Harold Schlichting in 1969. Darin Galle and his wife Judy now operate the facility. Wildlife include elk, deer and coastal birds.

Good tests include the 1st, a 360-yard par-4 that heads leftward off the tee—skirting evergreens left and Hawk Creek right—en route to a tree-ringed, front-sloping green. The 275-yard, par-4 3rd bends uphill to the left. The hole is crossed by the creek driving distance out, and features a small, slick green. The top-rated 5th, a pretty 300-yard par-4, slopes severely to the right, and ends at a right-tilting putting surface.

Lakeside Golf and Racquet Club

3245 Club House Drive, Lincoln City, OR 97367. (541) 994-8442. Todd Young, director of golf. 18 holes. 4,964 yards. Par 66. Grass tees. Course ratings: men—B62.0/102, M61.1/99; women—M65.0/106, F62.1/96. Years Opened: 1926 (original nine); 1992 (second nine). Architects: Founding members (original nine); Carl Mason (second nine). Moderate, jr./sr. rates, credit cards. Call for reservations. Walk-on chances: Fair. Walkability: Fair, with some steep hills. Playability: Despite abbreviated length, course can play tough thanks to tilted topography.

Lakeside Golf & Racquet Club lies on the west edge of Highway 101 at Lincoln City's north end, near the halfway point between the equator and North Pole. The course was previously known as Devil's Lake Golf and Racquet Club, in tribute to a like-named lake to the east. After a patron complained the name evoked satanic images, the course became Lakeside in January 1991. WDI Systems Inc. USA, a Japanese-owned firm with offices in California, owned the course from 1990 to 1995; the current proprietor is Lakeside Golf Club LLC, and Todd Young is the director of golf. Chris Burkhart came aboard as Lakeside's teaching pro in December 1996. Burkhart came from Washington State University, where she was the only woman in the nation to coach both the men's and women's golf teams at a university.

The course opened with nine holes in 1926. Carl Mason and Hal Fowler acquired Lakeside in the 1970s. In 1985, Mason built a 30,000-square-foot recreation facility on a ridge above the course, a move which created financial problems that led to the facility being placed in receivership. WDI rescued it, and the current owners have continued Lakeside's recent success. Lakeside's cavernous steel-walled athletic club contains tennis and racquetball courts, a restaurant, lounge, offices, banquet rooms, weight room, nursery and pro shop. In 1996, the course held a "beat the pro" contest hosted by PGA Tour star and Oregon native, Peter Jacobsen.

When its concluding five holes opened in 1992, Lakeside finally became an 18-hole track. Parts of the layout cross a fairly steep hillside, with the remainder of the holes traversing well-treed, gently sloping ground. On the hillier holes, flat lies are hard to find. Lakeside's tilted topography, smallish and slick greens, water hazards and goodly number of bunkers give the course its difficulty. A hole representative of the layout is the 9th, a 252-yard par-4 with a towering tee that offers lovely territorial views. The hole descends over a pond, which fronts a trapped-left green.

Mallard Creek Golf Course & RV Camp

18 *31894 Bellinger Scale Road, Lebanon, OR 97355. (541) 259-4653. 18 holes. 6,900 yards. Par 72. Grass tees. Course ratings not available. Year Opened: 1998. Architect: Mike Stark. Moderate, credit cards. Call for reservations. Walk-on chances: Good. Walkability: Good. Playability: New course caters to RVers and local golfers.*

Located three miles east of Lebanon off Highway 20 near the town of Waterloo, Mallard Creek Golf Course and RV Park was spawned by Karl Kaser and Vaughn Coffin. In 1996, the duo decided to convert their property into a recreational outlet for golfers and RVers. But obtaining approval to build the facility involved overcoming opposition from the Friends of Hamilton Creek, a group named after the waterway that winds through the site. The foes asserted that Linn County commissioners erred in 1996 when it issued a conditional-use permit for the project, and filed a lawsuit with Oregon's Land Use Board of Appeals (LUBA). In early 1997, LUBA ruled the lawsuit was frivolous and threw out the appeal.

Kaser and Vaughn also received stiff opposition from the owners of Pineway Golf Course, the Glassers, who fear Mallard Creek will take away their players. (I've never understood when an owner of an existing layout is threatened by a new nearby golf facility. Close analysis reveals that new courses actually increase play at neighboring layouts, which have often lacked play because of their isolation. I believe Mallard Creek will enhance Pineway's business if for no other reason than to bring more golfers to Lebanon.)

As of March 1997, Kaser, a businessman, and Vaughn, owner of a Salem machine shop, were completing financial arrangements for Mallard Creek. The two were also in the process of selecting a construction company, head pro and superintendent. The plan involved beginning work on all 18 holes in May 1997, with the course opening in spring 1998 (after this book went to press). I'm usually leery of including unbuilt courses in this book, but Mallard Creek looked solid with the legal entanglements out of the way. Besides a 6,900-yard, Mike Stark-designed course, the 203-acre project includes a 75-space RV park, a driving range (opened in July 1997) and a clubhouse with restaurant. Also planned is an 18-hole putting course. The RV area features a gazebo, a barbecue area and volleyball court. In an effort to make the RV facility environmentally-friendly by not digging septic systems at Mallard Creek, dump stations in Lebanon are used.

The site had previously been forested farmland, with a 60-head herd of cattle grazing it. Mallard Creek involves 160 feet of elevation change; ponderosa pines, firs, oaks and cottonwoods dominate the layout, which winds around wetlands. Wildlife includes elk, deer, wild turkeys, ducks and geese. Drainage on the lower fairways was addressed by placing down six inches of sand. Hamilton Creek invades one hole; golfers cross bridges over the stream twice during an 18-hole round. Stark specified bentgrass for greens and tees, with ryegrass for fairways. Tom Cook, the head of Oregon State University's respected turfgrass program, was consulted on the grasses. Over 55 traps were part of the design; some bunker pits dug during construction will be gradually filled in with sand. Kaser and Vaughn want Mallard Creek to take advantage of—but not despoil—its natural setting, making sure the course is aesthetically pleasing. Doesn't that coincide with the wishes of the Friends of Hamilton Creek?

Marysville Golf Course

9

2020 SW Allen Avenue, Corvallis, OR 97333. (541) 753-3421. 9 holes. 3,166 yards. Par 36. Grass tees. Course ratings: men 69.8, women 75.8 (no slope). Year Opened: 1958. Architect: Fred Federspiel. Economical. Call for reservations. Walk-on chances: Good. Walkability: Good. Playability: Mid-length layout near downtown Corvallis.

Nine-hole Marysville lies southwest of Corvallis behind Avery Park, at the end of a tree-lined road. The course bears the original name of Corvallis. Designed by Fred Federspiel, the course has been owned since its inception by the Hoselton family. Mode Hoselton built the layout and operated it until his death in 1984. His wife, Rozell, now operates Marysville along with son Doug, who attended Oregon State University on a golf scholarship. Doug holds both course records, a 31 for nine and the 18-hole mark of 6-under-par 66.

The 75-acre course crosses flat, easy-to-walk terrain. Once populated by deer, possums and raccoons, Marysville is now lined by homes which have diminished the wildlife visits. The layout has no sand traps, and a pond at the par-3 8th is its most threatening hazard. Challenging holes include the 1st, a 410-yard par-4 that skirts OB left en route to a small green. The 417-yard, par-4 3rd requires a pair of good shots to reach an oval putting surface. The top-rated 5th, a 525-yard par-5, sports a wide fairway and a rolling green. The 157-yard 8th calls for an accurate drive over water for safe landing on a tidy green.

McNary Golf Club - semiprivate

18

6255 River Road North, Salem, OR 97303. (503) 393-4653. Rich Brown, director of golf. 18 holes. 6,088 yards. Par 71. Grass tees. Course ratings: men—B69.3/117, M68.2/114; women—M73.5/120, F71.2/116. Year Opened: 1962. Architects: Howard Reed & Chuck Cross. Moderate, sr. rates, credit cards. Reservations: Call a week ahead. Walk-on chances: Fair. Walkability: Good. Playability: Fairways gradually squeezed by new homes.

McNary Golf Club lies north of Salem on land once farmed by the pioneering McNary family. The course was purchased in 1983 by Portland's Hillman Properties. In 1986, Hillman began developing homesites on the course's southern edge, paring 500 yards from its 6,700-yard length. Homesite development has continued in and around the 325-acre site; at the end of 1996, there were still 200 lots left. The push for housing has resulted in Hillman rebuilding several holes. McNary continues to move forward with plans to become a private golf club. The course currently has 250 members; once that number reaches 450, Hillman will sell it to the members and the facility will become private.

When opened in 1962, the course encompassed 210 acres. But the imposition of housing has shrunk the acreage. The mostly flat track is dotted by several dozen sand traps and three ponds; Claggett Creek crosses four holes. Along with residential backyards, the fairways are lined by oaks, firs, walnuts, redwoods and pines. McNary has a clay underlayment, resulting in poor drainage. Until all the residential development is completed, and the water runoff and drainage settles into a predictable and addressable pattern, the course will remain wet in spring and fall. McNary boasts a big, modern clubhouse with restaurant and banquet spaces, and is a popular site for private tournaments.

Tough holes include the narrow 6th, a 378-yard par-4 that runs rightward to a domed, steep-sided green. The 10th, a 144-yard par-3, requires a precise tee shot over Claggett Creek to find a small and slick green trapped thrice on the right. The 298-yard, par-4 16th is a dogleg-right between houses. The steep-sided fairway passes a large bunker at the corner before reaching a radical, three-tiered green trapped on the left. The top-rated 18th, a 567-yard par-5, skirts trees left while sloping toward a lake on the right. This water hazard is reachable in the summer when McNary's turf hardens and generates more roll. The huge, front-sloping 18th green tilts toward a moat-like leg of Claggett.

Meadowlawn Golf Club

9

3898 Meadowlawn Loop SE, Salem, OR 97301. (503) 363-7391. Greg Ganson, pro. 9 holes. 2,043 yards. Par 32. Grass tees. Course ratings: men—B58.8/93, M58.2/91; women—61.2/100, M/F60.8/99, F60.4/98. Year Opened: 1969. Architect: Bob Schafer. Moderate, credit cards. Reservations: Call a day ahead. Walk-on chances: Good. Walkability: Good. Playability: Nice executive course in east Salem.

The former site of Meadowlawn Dairy, this course was built in 1969—along with peripheral houses and apartments—by Salem's Ohmart and Calaba Realty. Bob Ohmart and Rudy Calaba hired Bob Schafer to design an executive-length course to wind between the homes. Meadowlawn residents are entitled to free golf with their rental payments. Besides a small pro shop, the facility has a snack bar.

The executive-length track contains five par-4s from 290 to 375 yards, and four par-3s from 95 to 150 yards. A few sand traps and two ponds enter play on the well-tended course, which has adequate drainage. Meadowlawn occasionally floods when a ditch that runs through it overflows after heavy rains. The fairways are lined by residential units as well as by spruce, redwood and pine trees. Top holes include the left-bending 1st, a 375-yard par-4 that heads between apartments to a skinny, undulating green. The 4th, a 335-yard par-4, goes straight over flat terrain to a kidney-shaped, gently sloping green. The 295-yard, par-4 7th has a pond right of the tee and a left-curling fairway.

Neskowin Beach Golf Course

9

*Hawk Creek Avenue, Neskowin, OR 97149. (503) 392-3377. Tom Clark, pro.
9 holes. 2,616 yards. Par 35. Grass tees & mats. Course ratings: men 65.3/103,
women 67.7/110. Year Opened: 1932. Architect: Graham Sharkey. Moderate, credit
cards. Call for reservations. Walk-on chances: Fair. Walkability: Good. Playability:
Historic course near the ocean gets new owner.*

Neskowin Beach Golf Course is north of Lincoln City, across Highway 101
from Hawk Creek Golf Course. In January 1996, Neskowin Beach was purchased by
Tom Clark, a Class A PGA member who was the head pro at Spring Hill Country Club
in Albany for 10 years before plunging into golf course ownership. Clark and his wife
Loretta bought the facility from William W. Martin, proprietor of Neskowin Beach
since 1977. Like Martin, the Clarks will have to find ways to succeed with a layout
that is fine from the first of May through the end of October, but is underwater the rest
of the year. Indeed, the problem with water at Neskowin Beach is so acute that
windsurfers have been spotted sailing across the course.

In an effort to extend the golf season, Clark has devised a unique plan to
convert the dry areas of the 50-acre course into a par-32, 1,800-yard executive track.
Most of the existing greens and tees can be used, with temporaries in effect where
needed. Other changes include reprising the old elevated 7th tee. The new-old back
tee at the 7th—which Clark remembers when he played Neskowin Beach as an
8-year-old—will stretch the hole out to 135 yards. Also planned are alternative ways
to get water off the course to extend the season. For years, old wooden flumes were
used to drain off the water. Those flumes are now plugged, so Clark has begun using
a pump that removes 16,000 gallons of water an hour. Several factors conspire to
make Neskowin Beach wet. it sits a mere six feet above sea level, it's subject to high
Pacific Ocean tides, and receives 100 inches of rain a year.

Opened in 1932, Neskowin Beach was designed by Graham Sharkey and
built by Billy Walton and Matt Sandige. The course is home for a great variety of
wildlife—elk, beavers, otters, swans, egrets, bald eagles, ducks, blue herons, deer and
geese. The layout involves two creeks—Kiwanda and Butte—which serve as hazards
on five holes. Neskowin Beach has no traps as the water table is too high. Top holes
include the 1st, a 387-yard par-4 that heads fairly straight over rolling ground to a
small green ringed by trees. The 351-yard, par-4 4th has a left-bending fairway crossed
by a creek driving distance out. The 5th, a dogleg-left, 301-yard par-4, is bisected by
both Kiwanda and Butte creeks—driving distance out and 50 yards before the green.
The 6th, a 456-yard par-5, is a 90-degree dogleg-right with a creek off the tee and a
small, slick green.

Oak Knoll Golf Course

18 *6335 Highway 22, Independence, OR 97351. (503) 378-0344. John McComish, pro. 18 holes. 6,208 yards. Par 72. Grass tees. Course ratings: men—B68.6/113, M67.1/111; women—M73.1/116, F69.2/113. Years Opened: 1924 (original nine); 1990 (second nine). Architects: Elbert Jones (original nine); Val & Tim Barnes (second nine). Moderate, credit cards. Reservations: Call three days ahead. Walk-on chances: Fair. Walkability: Good. Playability: Moderate challenge at course west of Salem.*

This popular, full-service facility lies on the north side of Highway 22 next to the Inn at Oak Knoll, an eatery with fairway views. Oak Knoll (one of two in Oregon, the other is in Ashland) is west of Salem in a scenic valley near Eola Hills, on the old Oak Knoll farm and granary. The course began in 1924, when Elbert Jones purchased the farm and carved out a rough-hewn six holes equipped with sand greens. From 1938 to 1959, Bill and Hazel Ashby ran the course. Oak Knoll changed hands a few more times before Val Barnes purchased it in 1979. With help from his son Tim, Barnes built another nine holes and a driving range. Recent upgrades include new tees and bunkers.

Oak Knoll's record of 64 is held its head pro, John McComish, one of the region's best players. The 6' 6", 255-pound giant was once legendary for his long-driving ability. He won the National Long Drive Championship in 1978, and finished second and fourth over the next two years. Three of the five years on the PGA Tour he averaged the longest drives, topping it off with a 286-yard average. A member of the PGA Tour from 1983 through 1990, McComish was forced to quit the Tour because of a bad back. The problem still flares up occasionally, but 1996 was relatively pain-free for the native of Santa Maria, California. McComish was named Oregon Player of the Year in 1994, 1995 and 1996. Among his accomplishments during that stellar run were wins at the 1993 Oregon Open, 1995 Northwest Open and 1996 Oregon Match Play, with a second in the 1996 Washington Open.

Oak Knoll's new holes were intermingled with those from the original course to create the existing layout. Four of the new holes are on the front side, with the remainder on the back. Except for the 14th, the newer holes are treeless and trapless and have modern-style, elevated greens. They contrast sharply to Oak Knoll's original holes, which are well-treed and feature small putting surfaces. Noteworthy tests include the top-rated 7th, a 511-yard par-5 that starts at a tee fronted by a pond with a fountain. The unbending fairway skirts trees along the right. A pond pinches the fairway 130 yards from a raised, squarish green ringed by mounds. Another good hole is the 377-yard, par-4 18th. The slightly ascending, tree-lined route runs straight to a small, undulating green trapped on both sides.

OGA Members Course at Tukwila

2990 Boones Ferry Road, Woodburn, OR 97071. (503) 981-6105. Chuck Siver, pro. 18 holes. 6,650 yards. Par 72. Grass tees. Course ratings: men—C72.1/132, B70.8/127, M69.0/123; women—M74.5/133, F72.2/125. Year Opened: 1994 (original nine); 1996 (second nine). Architect: William Robinson. Moderate (with discounts for OGA members). Reservations: Call five days ahead. Walk-on chances: Fair. Walkability: Good, but expect a workout. Playability: All members of state and regional golf associations should be so lucky as to have a course like this.

18

Besides having the distinction of being only the second state golf association-owned course in the country (the Northern California Golf Association's Poppy Hills is the other), the OGA Members Course at Tukwila is another stellar entry on Oregon's growing list of top-rate tracks. The Oregon Golf Association began considering having its own golf course back in 1976 when Dale Johnson was the executive director. The association looked at ways to build its own course after concluding how difficult it was to secure tournament venues. When Tukwila Partners offered to donate 170 acres of a 300-acre parcel for such a golf course in 1993, the OGA jumped at the opportunity. As part of the deal, Tukwila Partners will develop 600 homesites around the layout.

The OGA moved quickly on the project, opening a driving range in spring of 1994 and the first nine holes that August. The second nine followed in 1996. The operations are currently handled out of a temporary clubhouse. A permanent structure—to contain OGA administrative offices, a hall of fame and museum—may be built in 1999 or 2000. The first year the full 18 holes were opened proved the concept would succeed; upwards of 300 players made the rounds each weekend day. According to head pro Chuck Siver, an Oregonian who worked in Texas for 25 years before returning home, the OGA facility should average over 45,000 rounds a year. Roughly 70 percent of the players are OGA members, who receive discounts on green fees. The association didn't hesitate to begin holding tournaments; the course hosted the 1996 OGA Team Championship and three USGA qualifiers—for the Junior Amateur, Girls' Junior and Senior Amateur.

Built by Bernhardt Golf of Portland, the course sits on well-draining, sandy soil. The site was previously a filbert orchard (Tukwila is a Native American name for filbert, or hazelnut). Vestiges of its nutty background remain; dense rows of filbert trees line a few holes, but these will eventually be replaced by housing. Though the course crosses some up-and-down terrain, the holes are efficiently arrayed and easy to walk, with the longest hike between the 9th and 10th. Wide, paved cart paths wind throughout, and excellent signs mark the way. Wetlands are identified as "environmentally sensitive areas," with directional and yardage signs giving useful information.

To my thinking, this is Robinson's best work to date. The Florence, Oregon, architect made good use of the topographically varied site, realizing two different sides (the front nine is hillier than the back) and letting the course flow naturally over the land. Big bold mounds define the peripheries of fairways and greens, and the bunkering shows considerable creativity. But perhaps Robinson's greatest leap forward is found in the greens, which show tremendous diversity. Though containing many breaks, tiers and slopes, the putting surfaces are ultimately fair, a crucial element in a track destined to hold a wide variety of tournaments. The greens require much imagination from golfers, a trait that often separates the winners from the also-rans in competitive play. *Golf Digest* concurred with these assessments in December 1996 when it named the OGA track one of the nation's "Top 10 Best New Affordable Courses." OGA Members was tied for 8th. The course opened in 1994 but its back nine didn't come on line until 1996, thus making it eligible for the award.

Noteworthy holes—and there's a steady line-up of them—include the top-rated 2nd, a 425-yard par-4 lined along the left by a big lake and on the right by two bunkers. At the 150-yard mark, the hole curls leftward to a perched green trapped twice in front. The 516-yard, par-5 4th has a pond right of the tee and three pot bunkers in mounds along the left, driving distance out. At the 175-yard mark, a creek crosses the fairway. Once past this juncture, the hole angles sharply rightward along a right-sloping path lined by two bunkers left and a lateral hazard right. The humped-in-the-middle 4th green has a right-tilting front half and rear-sloping back. Traps guard its right-front, left-front and back edges. The 7th, a 394-yard par-4, is a downhill dogleg-left with a landing area squeezed by a bunker along the right. At the 125-yard mark, the hole is crossed by a creek-filled gully, then rises steeply to a knoll-roosting green trapped rear and left-front.

Some houses have been built along the back nine, with more to follow in the years ahead. Good tests here include the 11th, a 549-yard par-5 given additional length since it heads into the prevailing wind. The slightly uphill, right-turning fairway winds between a mound-veiled pond left and a bunker right. Another pond sits along the right about 175 yards from a domed putting surface bunkered left-front and rear. The 427-yard, par-4 12th has a pond right of the tee and a fairway squeezed by bunkers right and houses/OB left. A pond behind mounds on the left starts at about the 150-yard mark and runs up to guard the left-front edge of a deep, right-front sloping green angled 45 degrees to the fairway. Pot punkers further guard this target at its right-front and rear flanks.

The 14th, a neat 517-yard par-5, starts with a tee fronted by a creek which then winds along the left side of the left-sloping, left-bending fairway. Two big bunkers sit along the right. The hole follows a narrow path—sloping left all the way— toward a creek and wetlands. Two bunkers sit along the right at the 150-yard mark, a good lay-up point since the creek/wetlands cross the fairway, which goes hard to the left. The wide-but-shallow 14th green is a two-tiered affair ringed by traps left, left-rear and rear. The 437-yard, par-4 16th runs uphill and straight past two fat bunkers right of the landing zone. The concluding 150 yards of the hole ascend rather steeply to a small, two-tiered green trapped right-front and left. Incredibly, two players shot eagles at the 16th within a month of the course's opening. Perhaps the prettiest par-3 at the OGA Members Course is the 17th, a 161-yarder with a broad tee separated from a wide-but-shallow green by a stream and a ravine. A deep St. Andrews-style pot bunker swallows short tee balls hit at the right-front of the putting surface, which is further protected by three traps on the rear. The green has a bump in its midsection and slopes toward the left-front.

Olalla Valley Golf Course

1022 Olalla Road, Toledo, OR 97391. (541) 336-2121. 9 holes. 3,031 yards. Par 36. Grass tees. Course ratings: men B69.2/127; women—B75.2/130, F72.7/ 124. Year Opened: 1956. Architect: Mathew Gruber. Moderate, credit cards. Reservations: Call a week ahead. Walk-on chances: Fair. Walkability: Good. Play-ability: Surprisingly tough nine-holer in the wilds of Toledo.

Located east of Newport near the small town of Toledo, this course crosses forested hills in the Olalla Valley. ("Olalla" is an American Indian word for berry.) The course and adjoining restaurant were purchased by Gary Lau in 1994. Since buying the place from Fred Wolf, Guy Leech and R. L. Quillen, Lau has renovated the clubhouse, installing a full-service restaurant, lounge and banquet facilities. Lau's work has also extended to the course, where he's begun a program for topdressing greens, upgraded drainage, and built new tees. The fairways and roughs now receive different cuts, and Olalla Valley's overall conditioning has improved. Lau, a native of Longview, Washington, recently purchased an adjoining 40 acres. Another parcel would have to be acquired for him to proceed with plans for a back nine.

Occupying a former dairy and turkey farm, the course was built in 1956 by original owner Matthew Gruber. Elmer Hannigan, a Portland-area golf pro, took over the course in 1967; he then sold it in 1976 to Wolf, Leech and Quillen. The course is popular with players from Newport, Toledo, Corvallis and Eugene. Located at 300 feet above sea level, Olalla Valley is the habitat for many different species of birds as well as coyotes and deer. Olalla Creek runs through the grounds, serving as a source for irrigation and a hazard for golfers. Olalla Valley's up-and-down topography and tight fairways are the primary reasons the course plays tough. Other features include a canyonlike jail along the 7th hole and some slick greens with multiple tiers.

The dual-tee, 49-acre nine plays to 5,915 yards over two circuits. Interesting holes include the top-rated 5th, a slender, 420-yard par-4 that curls rightward over rolling ground to a tree-backed green. The 313-yard, par-4 7th is a tight dogleg-right that slopes steeply toward the aforementioned jail en route to a heart-shaped green. The 9th, a 462-yard par-5, has a wide fairway crossed by the creek. The hole heads over rolling ground to a slippery putting surface.

Pineway Golf Course

30949 Pineway Road, Lebanon, OR 97355. (541) 258-8815. Jim Glasser & Mickie Price, pros. 9 holes. 2,989 yards. Par 36. Grass tees. Course ratings: men 68.3/118, women 72.7/119. Year Opened: 1958. Architect: Fred Federspiel. Moderate, jr./sr. rates, credit cards. Reservations: Call a week ahead. Walk-on chances: Good. Walkability: Good. Playability: Hillside-crossing nine has easy access off Highway 20.

Pineway Golf Course occupies the side and foot of a maple- and pine-covered hillside, south of Lebanon off Highway 20. Besides a nice nine-hole course and driving range, the facility boasts a popular clubhouse restaurant. Designed by Fred Federspiel, the 44-acre layout was built in 1958 by Al and Marie Johnson. Once called Oakway, Pineway has been owned by the Glasser family since 1971. The course was originally intended to be an 18-holer, but wetlands waylaid the expansion.

Jim Glasser and his sister, Mickie Price, run the course. Both golfed on Oregon State University teams, and both attended the Billy Casper Golf Camp in San

Diego. The big annual event here is the Pineway Open in July. The tourney has four divisions, with 124 entrants vying for a variety of prizes. Recent improvements to Pineway include a new 1st tee, an elevated affair offering vistas of the course. The rural layout is occasionally visited by deer.

A dual-tee layout that stretches 5,967 yards over two circuits, Pineway has five holes crossing a steep, well-treed slope. Its remaining holes occupy a meadow. A few bunkers border the generally small and raised greens. Challenging holes include the top-rated 2nd, a 365-yard par-4 that runs straight between towering trees en route to a rolling green. The 480-yard, par-5 5th heads off an elevated tee and runs past OB along the left to another tilted putting surface. The 8th, a 382-yard par-4, traverses flat terrain on its way to a tree-ringed green.

Ranch Hills Golf Club

9

26710 South Ranch Hills Road, Mulino, OR 97042. (503) 632-6848. 9 holes. 2,601 yards. Par 36. Grass tees. Course ratings: men—B65.0/108, B/M64.7/106, M64.4/ 104; women—M/F66.5/109, F65.8/108. Year Opened: 1967. Architects: Bob Blaine & R. Joslin. Moderate. Reservations: Call a week ahead. Walk-on chances: Good. Playability: Enjoyable golf in bucolic setting.

A pastoral nine-holer east of Mulino, this course is on the former Enright Ellis Horse Ranch. The layout was begun in the mid-1960s by a group of five local men, led by Bob Blaine, who converted the ranch operation into one dealing with golfers. Jim and Pat Smith bought Ranch Hills from Blaine's group. In 1991, Dewey and Dinene Wyatt and Leon Poznanski purchased the course from the Smiths; the Wyatts bought out Poznanski's share in 1994. Dewey Wyatt is a longtime resident of the area; he attended the local high school and raised a family in Mulino.

Ranch Hills' owners had a difficult 1996. The course was flooded six different times, forcing it to be closed for nearly 120 days. Mill Creek runs through the 47-acre layout, and heavy rains caused the stream to wash over its banks. Debris and rock swept across fairways, and two concrete abutments attached to a covered New England-style bridge beside the 2nd tee were sunk. As a result of the flood damage, the Wyatts' plans for new tees and other upgrades were placed on hold until repairs were made. The couple recently hired superintendent Wyatt Bagley to help with turf care. Bagley, previously with The Knolls in Sutherlin and Springwater in Estacada, has greatly improved the course's conditioning—in between floods—and landscaping.

Ranch Hills' layout crosses a valley floor. Wildlife visitors include ducks and deer, with fish residing in Mill Creek. The well-tended fairways cross mostly flat terrain. There are a few greenside traps, and Mill Creek is a persistent factor. Though not overly daunting, Ranch Hills provides an enjoyable outing. Good tests include the par-3 2nd, a 150-yarder with the covered bridge left-front of its tee. Golfers must arc tee shots over the creek to reach a mid-sized green. The top-rated 5th, a 495-yard par-5, is crossed by the creek 150 yards out, just before the hole bends 90-degrees to the left. The stream lines the fairway's left edge after the turn, and two traps guard the green. The 470-yard, par-5 8th is another 90-degree dogleg-left, split diagonally at the turn by the creek. The hole requires a good drive to enable players to peek around the corner and glimpse a rolling putting surface.

Riverwood Golf Course

21050 SE Riverwood Road, Dundee, OR 97115. (503) 864-2667. Greg Brown, pro. 9 holes. 2,944 yards. Par 35. Grass tees. Course ratings: men 67.4/117, women 69.3/118. Year Opened: 1932. Architect: George Junor. Moderate, jr./sr. rates. Reservations: Call a week ahead. Walk-on chances: Good. Walkability: Good. Playability: Course could become a full-blown 18-holer in the years ahead.

In late 1996, Riverwood's owners, Greg and Irmi Brown, were setting up financial arrangements to fund a complete makeover of this 65-year-old course. The $4-million plan involves building nine new holes, a driving range with a teaching school, and retrofitting the original nine with all-new fairways and greens. The project, which the Browns hope to finish by 1998, will result in a 6,700-yard, par-72 track designed by Michael Stark. The facility will also be renamed Walkabout Creek Golf Course. Walkabout is an Australian aboriginal word meaning "going out and discovering things." The Browns have certainly had a walkabout while trying to get Riverwood up to snuff.

Work actually began on the project in 1993, but it was halted when the original owner of an adjoining 50-acre site the Browns had bought for the expansion was killed in a car accident. The property transfer went into lengthy probate, effectively stalling construction. Greg Brown, the son of Chuck Brown—who owns Tacoma's Brookdale and Yelm's Nisqually Valley courses, has amassed a total of 142 acres. Over the years, Brown had built new tees, reconditioned some greens, added ponds, planted deodoras, black pines, noble firs and blue spruces in place of course-damaging deciduous trees, and attempted to improve drainage. After all that, Riverwood continued to be wet during Dundee's rainy seasons. He figured it'd be just as cost-effective to start from scratch. Besides, growing Yamhill County could use an 18-hole facility.

Stark's design calls for moving 400,000 yards of dirt and topsoil during shaping. The new layout will feature USGA-spec bentgrass greens, five or six ponds, and upwards of 66 bunkers. (The bunkers will be cut but may not all be filled with sand initially.) The new property contains wetlands, so some fairways will circuit these sensitive areas. The existing 6,000-square-foot clubhouse was recently remodeled and will be used as Walkabout's new headquarters.

Riverwood/Walkabout occupies a picturesque plot bordered by a plant nursery, Riverwood Road, farms, orchards and the Yamhill River. Crops grown in the fields surrounding the course include filberts, walnuts, peaches, apples, cherries, strawberries, corn and soybeans. Also nearby are over a dozen wineries which have drawn tourists to the area. Local fauna includes deer, raccoons, possums and coyotes, as well as coastal and inland birds.

The expansion calls for the original George Junor-designed nine to be in play while the new holes are under construction. These holes were built by the Hirter family in 1932, making Riverwood Yamhill County's oldest course. The layout occupies 50 acres north of the Yamhill River. Good holes here include the top-rated 3rd, a 423-yard par-4 that bends slightly left over flat ground en route to a front-sloping green. The 520-yard, par-5 4th runs straight along a tree-lined path to a trapped-right green. The 6th, a 475-yard par-5, skirts a fairway bunker along the right as it heads to a trapped-left green backed by a pond.

Salem Golf Club - semiprivate

18 *2025 Golf Course Road, Salem, OR 97302. (503) 363-6652. Danny Moore, pro. 18 holes. 6,203 yards. Par 72. Grass tees. Course ratings: men—B69.6/118, M68.0/114; women F68.1/113. Years Opened: 1928 (original nine); 1929 (second nine). Architect: Ercel Kay. Moderate. Call for reservations. Walk-on chances: Ok for singles. Walkability: Good. Playability: Enduring, popular course along the banks of the Willamette River.*

Semiprivate Salem Golf Club lies southwest of the city on a Willamette River floodplain. The course is bordered on the north by Minto-Brown Island City Park and Wildlife Refuge, and on the west by the Willamette River. The course was founded, designed and built by Ercel Kay in 1928-29, and is still owned by the Kay family. Though Paul Sundin, Salem's pro for over 30 years, has handed the day-to-day operations over to protege, Danny Moore, he continues to work in the pro shop. The course superintendent is Mike O'Neil, who has overseen several upgrades in recent years. Salem Golf Club is the home course for Loren Lippert, the Northwest's most peripatetic golfer. (See Loren's story in this book.)

Salem's colonial-style clubhouse is the site of many members-only and public functions. Annual tourneys include the Capital City Amateur, Oregon State Father and Son, and Salem Women's Chapman. The 98-acre layout crosses gently rolling ground, with fairways lined by mature Douglas firs, Oregon white oaks, cottonwoods, mimosa silk trees and white ashes. A 350-tree apple orchard sits in its midsection. With the neighboring wildlife refuge, Salem is visited by deer, raccoons, foxes, nutrias, ducks and geese.

O'Neil has attempted to improve Salem's drainage, which can be poor along those parts of the course closest to the Willamette. Besides narrow fairways and some slick greens, golfers must beware of over 20 sand traps and a small creek crossing five holes. Among the better tests is the top-rated 4th, a 400-yard par-4 that winds between trees to a green fronted by a hidden water hazard. The 507-yard, par-5 9th heads leftward and skirts OB right en route to a trapped-right green. The 11th, a 379-yard par-4, curls to the right around a grove of trees that enveils a lake. After the turn, the fairway widens before reaching a sizable green bunkered right-front. The 405-yard, par-4 17th bypasses a treed slope along the right before ending at a round, front-sloping green ringed by trees.

Salishan Golf Links

18 *Highway 101, Gleneden Beach, OR 97388. (541) 764-3632, 1-800-452-2300 (resort), or 1-800-547-6500. Grant Rogers, pro. 18 holes. 6,390 yards. Par 73. Grass tees. Course ratings: men—B73.2/132, M70.4/130; women—M77.0/134, F72.3/128. Years Opened: 1963 (original nine); 1965 (second nine). Architect: Fred Federspiel; William Robinson (remodel). Expensive, credit cards. Reservations: Call two weeks ahead. Walk-on chances: Ok for singles. Walkability: Fair, with some steep hills and between-hole distances. Playability: Major remodel has reinvigorated longtime Northwest favorite.*

With a prime oceanside locale and a resort with all the amenities, Salishan is often included in "best of" lists for West Coast recreational facilities. But the resort hasn't rested on its laurels. Indeed, a $2.5-million remodel performed over 1995-96 has rejuvenated Salishan's primary attraction, its golf course. The 1960s-built layout was at a point where it needed infrastructural repair. The project, overseen by

Salishan's 15th hole is an uphill 121-yard par-3.

architect Bill Robinson, involved drainage improvements, a computerized irrigation system, fairway mounding, new water hazards, more bunkers, and changes to back-nine holes that gave them a stronger links feel. Upcoming plans include finishing the paved cart paths.

When the remodel was completed, Salishan's long-time owner, John Gray, sold the resort to New York-based Yarmouth Group for an undisclosed sum. The deal also involved another of Gray's properties, Skamania Lodge in south-central Washington. Before selling, however, Gray designed and built a natural-turf, 18-hole putting course beside the lodge. In 1996, Salishan was cited by *LINKS* Magazine as a "Best of Golf Award" winner in honor of its successful and ongoing commitment to "golf and the environment." The magazine named Salishan along with 40 other American courses as outstanding facilities which conserve natural resources.

Split by Highway 101, Salishan involves two distinctly different nines. Holes one through nine span a wooded hillside east of the highway. Though following the curvature of a forested promontory, the back nine is more like a links arrangement, with fairways burrowing through dense bushes and tall sand dunes. Housing is also more prominent on Salishan's back. Great views of Siletz Bay and the Pacific Ocean are on tap from various points along the course.

When I visited the remodeled layout in September 1996, the improvements were obvious, particularly on the back nine. Before that return, I felt that the course had become overrated. Its playing conditions simply didn't match the upper-end green fees. It seems that in some cases (Semiahmoo in Washington is another example), a resort's publicists can keep garnering high praise for a golf course even though the playing conditions may no longer justify lofty press. That's why I enjoyed finding Salishan getting a fresh coat of paint. Though many of the most significant changes made to the course were underground and invisible to the eye, players will get more bang for their buck at the renovated layout.

Best of all, Fred Federspiel's interesting design was retained, while some of the signature holes were enhanced and even strengthened. Among the better tests on the forested front is the 3rd, a 360-yard par-4 that runs uphill and straight past a bunker along the left to a steeply front-tilting, ridge-perched green trapped twice in front. The top-rated 7th, a 426-yard par-4, runs along a narrow and rolling, tree-lined path. At the 150-yard mark, the hole winds uphill leftward to a hill-cut, right-front-sloping green trapped left-front and right. The tree-lined 8th, a 547-yard par-5, crosses left-leaning, undulating ground for 225 yards or so, then curls 90 degrees to the right. The fairway tilts to the left as it runs up to a small, left-front-leaning green. A deep swale lurks before this putting surface, which is trapped twice at the left-front.

The 446-yard, par-5 10th has an elevated tee and a right-sloping fairway trapped on the right. A pond along the right starts at the 200-yard mark and runs up to guard the right-front edge of a diminutive, left-front-sloping green trapped right-front and left. The 12th, a 433-yard par-4 that really benefited from the remodel, bears westward into the prevailing wind. The fairway is lined by new "sand mounds" along the right. At the 175-yard mark, trees squeeze the fairway, which then bends to the right around a dune to a smallish, right-front-tilting green trapped left-front and rear.

The 14th, a 480-yard par-5, is an uphill right-bender lined by a creek and trees left and houses right. The hole plays much longer than its yardage as it makes a gradual ascent into prevailing winds. Gorse-covered dunes penetrate the right side of the fairway 150 yards from a rolling green guarded by huge bunkers left and front, and a smaller trap right. The 17th, a cool 291-yard par-4, has a raised tee where golfers launch drives toward a chute-like fairway trapped on the left. The severely front-sloping 17th green has a pot bunker right-front and a trap left. The 370-yard, par-4 18th winds leftward off an elevated tee along a route that tilts sharply rightward to jail. Over its final 100 yards, Salishan's home hole rises to a slick, knoll-perched putting surface fronted by two pot bunkers, with more traps right and left-front.

Santiam Golf Club

18 *Off Highway 22, Stayton, OR 97383. (503) 769-3485. Jack Coppedge, pro. 18 holes. 6,387 yards. Par 72. Grass tees. Course ratings: men—B69.9/123, M68.8/119; women—M74.9/128, F70.7/119. Years Opened: 1957 (original nine); 1967 (second nine). Architects: Ted Robinson (original nine); members (second nine). Moderate, jr./sr. rates. Reservations: Call a week ahead. Walk-on chances: Fair. Walkability: Good. Playability: Though flat in contour, course has plenty of hazards.*

Santiam Golf Club, a public 18-hole venue east of Salem off Highway 22, is owned by 300 member-stockholders on a for-profit basis. The stock cost $350 when originally offered in the mid-1950s; it's now worth over $4,000. According to Jack Coppedge, Santiam's head pro since 1970, some of the stockholders do not play golf. On average, the facility hosts upwards of 50,000 rounds annually. Play has increased of late thanks in part to non-member golfers buying 350 annual passes.

The course, clubhouse and adjoining lounge and Mexican restaurant occupy about 110 acres. Ever since Santiam opened with nine Ted Robinson-designed holes in 1957, shareholders have been required to work 80 hours a year to improve the playing conditions. The 1967-opened second nine was designed and built by members. The generally flat layout is made challenging by a balanced mix of natural and man-made hazards. Two ponds and 20 bunkers dot the grounds, and Mill Creek crosses several holes. Like many other western Oregon courses, Santiam experienced some flooding in 1996, with the front nine getting more unwanted water than the back. Cart paths were installed around the front nine in 1996; back-nine paths will be completed in 1997.

Full-grown maples, willows, evergreens, ash and oaks line Santiam's fairways. The greens, conditioned by greens superintendent Tim Halfman, are slick. Wildlife includes deer, raccoons and skunks. Mill Creek contains spawning steelhead, and the course offers choice views of the Santiam Valley. Good tests include the 5th, a 504-yard par-5 that winds rightward around a two-acre pond to a large green trapped right-front. The 424-yard, par-4 7th has a landing area crossed diagonally by Mill Creek. The hole then bends rightward to a slightly raised putting surface. The 16th, a 401-yard par-4, doglegs right along a tree-pinched route that stretches to a slick and rolling green. The 18th, a 338-yard par-4, skirts a large bunker along the left en route to a saddle-shaped green trapped laterally.

Trysting Tree Golf Club

34028 Electric Road, Corvallis, OR 97333. (541) 752-3332. Sean Arey, pro. 18 holes. 7,015 yards. Par 72. Grass tees. Course ratings: men—T73.1/127, B71.4/ 127, M69.2/119; women—M75.5/129, F71.3/118. Year Opened: 1988. Architect: Ted Robinson. Moderate, jr./student rates. Reservations: Call a week ahead. Walk-on chances: Fair. Walkability: Good. Playability: Length and some slick, undulating greens make this course enjoyable and tough. **18**

Trysting Tree is a difficult 7,000-yard layout operated by the Oregon State University Foundation. The for-profit facility occupies 165 acres of a university-owned, 200-acre plot purchased in 1952 from a local farmer. Trysting Tree's charter requires that it remain a recreational facility for students, support local golf, aid turf-management research, and be a practice venue for OSU's golf teams. The venue was named after a "trysting tree" on OSU's campus. The lawn under the tree was a meeting place for lovers; OSU's golf course, therefore, is a "meeting place for golf lovers."

The Ted Robinson-designed layout sprawls across generally flat land beside the Willamette River. Its riverside locale is a mixed blessing. In 1996, Trysting Tree was closed four different times when the Willamette backed up and spilled onto the course. About 5,000 rounds were lost because of the flooding. Channels radiating throughout the layout are generally dry in summer but, during Corvallis' rainy seasons, are filled with water. Unfortunately, when the river gets too high, the water surpasses the height of the channel walls and creeps over the fairways. Trysting Tree's operators plan to avoid future closures by arraying a nine-hole "winter" course. The par-36 layout will involve the 1st, 2nd, 7th, 8th, 9th, 11th, 15th, 16th and 17th holes. New bridges will be built so players can get around the abbreviated track. According to head pro Sean Arey, the winter course will feature "a lot of lakes."

For an inland layout, Trysting Tree is an excellent representation of a Scottish links. That was Robinson's mission when contracted to design the layout, a project spearheaded by Nat Giustina, proprietor of Tokatee Golf Club and a longtime OSU booster. Pacific westerlies whip over the grounds and western Oregon's often inclement weather is a regular influence. The course's flat topography is varied by plateaued tees, high-collared greens, and fairway-bordering mounds. Robinson injected considerable character into the putting surfaces, six of which are two-tiered and three with deep cavities. Other concerns are over two dozen bunkers and two permanent lakes. Trysting Tree is playable for all skills, with four tees per hole.

Because of its affiliation with a university (which has one of the nation's top turfgrass programs), Trysting Tree often hosts collegiate tournaments. The Men's and Women's Nike Tournament is an annual affair, and the course is on the regular rota for PAC-10 championships; it will hold the Men's Tournament in 2000. The PAC-10 women played here in 1995, when now-LPGA stalwarts Emilie Kline and Wendy Ward led Arizona State University to victory. Among the better holes is the 3rd, a 411-yard par-4 that winds rightward around a tree-ringed pond. The rolling fairway narrows before ending at a radical, trapped-right green, half of which has two tiers. The 552-yard, par-5 9th heads toward two fairway-pinching tree groves; a big depression fronts a two-tiered green trapped left-front.

The 10th, a 413-yard par-4, has a narrow landing area pinched even tighter when a diagonal ravine in the fairway is filled with water. After the turn, the hole runs up to a raised green with a steep back edge. The 154-yard, par-3 13th goes straight to a tiny green with a one-foot drop between tiers. Trapped left-front and right-rear, this front-banked putting surface is very slick. The 16th, a 455-yard par-4, stretches out along a wide route that skirts a pond along the right over its last 170 yards. The hole concludes at a raised, saddle-shaped green. The 224-yard, par-3 17th is endangered by ponds along both sides of its tight fairway. The 17th green is squarish, large and two-tiered, and is trapped rear and left-front.

Woodburn Golf Club

9 *Highway 214 West, Woodburn, OR 97071. No phone. 9 holes. 2,592 yards. Par 34. Grass tees. No course ratings. Year Opened: 1925. Architect: Gene Sharkey. Economical. No reservations. Walkability: Like strolling through an apple orchard. Playability: About as basic as golf gets.*

The Woodburn Golf Club is on the west side of I-5, off Highway 214. The layout is the polar opposite of the OGA Members Course at Tukwila, the highly cultured new track on Woodburn's east side. Indeed, Woodburn Golf Club is an atavistic relic when likened to almost any other North American golf course. The layout is just as it was when opened in 1925: straightforward, unfettered fairways ending at small and raised, sand greens. Sure, prices have risen. They're now two bucks instead of 25 cents for all-day play. There isn't a pro shop, just a starter's shed—erected in 1935— where golfers pay on the honor system.

Woodburn Golf Club arose through the efforts of local businessmen, who generated construction funds by selling 100 shares at 20 dollars each. A founder, Ted Hector, leveled the land and Salem pro Gene Sharkey designed the back-and-forth layout. The nine holes wind through a fruit orchard; the now-towering apple trees still bear fruit each fall. Since machinery to cut fairways wasn't available during Woodburn's early years, sheep were used to "mow" the grass. Chicken wire was erected around greens to keep the grazing animals off the putting surfaces. The barriers helped Woodburn's players perfect their chipping games as they had to loft shots over the fences to find the targets.

Early-day golfers shaped pedestals from wet sand scooped out of buckets to tee up balls. The sand greens at Woodburn represent one of only two Northwest courses so equipped; Pend Oreille in northeast Washington is the other. After putting on one of the "browns," a player—traditionally the loser of the hole—uses a rug attached to a broom handle to smooth the surface altered by ball or cleat marks. Oiled-sand greens can be very fast. An overstruck putt may run across the entire surface and roll off the other side. Woodburn's easy-to-walk, 2,600-yard layout plays to a par of 34. The sand greens still have the three-foot-tall wood flagsticks from yesteryear, and the ancient orchard remains the predominant threat to par.

Private Courses

Arrowhead Golf Club

28301 South Highway 213, Molalla, OR 97038. (503) 655-1441 or 829-8080. Joe Clarizio, director of golf; Rob Gibbons, pro. 18 holes. 6,324 yards. Par 72. Grass tees. Course ratings: men—B69.9/125, M68.6/122; women—M73.1/113, F69.4/106. YearsOpened: 1962 (original nine); 1965 (second nine). Architect: Kip Kappler; Craig Shriner (remodel). Members, guests & reciprocates. **18**

Arrowhead Golf Club was designed, built and developed by Kip Kappler, who conceived the idea for a golf course while looking across the street from his home and noticing how the neighbors' lawns rolled down to a little creek, then back up the other side. Next thing you know, Kappler acquired the former dairy beside Wright's Creek and built nine holes. Another nine followed two years later. Arrowhead was originally a public facility. After the course opened, Kappler hired a young Joe Clarizio as the pro. In 1972 when Kappler decided to retire, Joe and his wife Jean bought Arrowhead. By 1981, nearly 500 members had enlisted and the club went private. Over the years, the golf course has been augmented by a 16,000-square-foot athletic facility complete with racquetball courts, a weight and aerobics room, jacuzzi, sauna and swimming pool.

Prior to being appointed head pro in 1982, Rob Gibbons began playing Arrowhead as a six-year-old tyro. The Molalla native has enjoyed a stellar playing career, winning the Northwest PGA Championship in 1989 and the 1991 Rosauer's Open in Spokane. Gibbons was named the Oregon PGA's Player of the Year in both 1988 and '91.

The course has been in the midst of a long-term master plan. Overseen by Kansas City architect Craig Shriner and to be completed by the year 2000, the project involves a new irrigation system and three remodeled holes a year. Greens will be updated to USGA specifications. The project received a setback in February 1996 when the nearby Molalla River overflowed, washing out a riverbank. The course was back to normal by that fall.

Arrowhead's layout has Wright's Creek crossing it. The pleasant sounds of birds chirping and roosters crowing contribute to the place's pastoral hum. Shriner's new holes are considerably different from their predecessors. When compared to the remodeled holes, Kappler's seem rather pedestrian. And it's obvious that the new irrigation system has helped the turf. Particularly interesting holes include the 4th, a 361-yard par-4 that runs straight and slightly uphill between traps, driving distance out. The fairway rises to a rolling, front-sloping green trapped on the rear. The 399-yard, par-4 5th heads slightly left and passes OB left. A big pond guards the right edge of a right-front-sloping green trapped rear and left.

The left-curling, tree-lined 6th, a 341-yard par-4, has a pond right of the tee. A good drive is needed to have a shot at the saddle-shaped, mound-ringed 6th green, which is trapped twice in front. The top-rated 9th, a 394-yard par-4, is a lengthy and narrow left-bender through trees. A creek crosses the hole 50 yards from a small, front-banked putting surface. The 477-yard, par-5 10th is a wide dogleg-right with big bunkers outside the turn and a towering fir tree inside. The creek meanders across the hole 100 yards from a fir-ringed, left-sloping green protected by a trap 40 yards from its right-front entry. The 11th, a 410-yard par-4, runs long and straight along a path squeezed on the right by a bunker at the 170-yard mark. Here, the hole curls leftward to a rolling, tabletop-like green with a tall tier through it and a bunker in front.

The 403-yard, par-4 16th descends slightly as it bears rightward between trees to a right-sloping green bunkered at the right-front. The 17th, a 385-yard par-4, doglegs left around the river, with trees right. The fairway curls up to a steeply right-front-tilting green lined closely on the left by the Molalla. Arrowhead's home hole, a dandy 525-yard par-5, is bordered on the left by the river while Wright's Creek crosses the fairway 180 yards out. A fat bunker sits along the right 250 yards from the tee while another trap is on the left at the 150-yard mark. The 18th green is a wildly sloping, two-tiered affair protected by traps at the left-front, left, left-rear and right-rear. This putting surface contains several not-so-subtle humps and bumps; back-right is perhaps the toughest pin placement on this radical green.

Corvallis Country Club

18 *1850 SW Whiteside Drive, Corvallis, OR 97330. (541) 752-3484. Mark Tunstill, pro. 18 holes. 6,045 yards. Par 71. Grass tees. Course ratings: men—B69.0/121, M68.0/117; women—M73.3/122, F71.1/117. Years Opened: 1917 (original nine); 1956 (second nine). Architects: Founding members (original nine); Fred Federspiel (second nine). Members, guests & reciprocates.*

Historic Corvallis Country Club sprawls over a wooded hillside in the southwest part of its namesake city. From higher points, golfers enjoy great views of the surrounding countryside and the Coast Range to the west. The club is ringed by houses, farms and forests. Corvallis Country Club began in 1917 with nine founder-designed holes. It wasn't until nearly 40 years later that the second, Fred Federspiel-designed nine was built. Besides a well-manicured course, the members have access to a restaurant and lounge, tennis courts and a swimming pool. Big annual events include the Corvallis Invitational Chapman in June, a Ladies Best-Ball in July, and the Guys & Dolls Couples in August.

Corvallis boasts some of the most spectacular stands of oaks and firs found on a Northwest golf course. Lining most fairways, these stately trees are truly magnificent. The course also features a nice mix of old-style and modern holes. Some of Corvallis' old-style "push-up" greens are big, round affairs that, when mowed low, are very slick. Over the years the greens have sagged and developed some interesting tiers and whorls. The putting surfaces are usually ringed by modern bunkers, not the deep, high-banked affairs found at Waverley or Gearhart. Other contemporary flourishes include lovely flower gardens, paved cart paths, and an automatic irrigation system.

The 8th hole at Corvallis Country Club is a tight 469-yard par-5.

Memorable Corvallis holes include the 3rd, a 385-yard par-4 that runs steeply uphill. Fairly wide initially, the fairway gradually tapers en route to a large and oval, left-tilting green with a steep right side. The 570-yard, par-5 6th ascends for 225 yards, then curls downhill to the right to a big, front-banked green trapped left and right-front. The 7th, a 201-yard par-3, drops down to a front-sloping, trapped-right-rear putting surface crossed in front by a creek. Tee shots at the 7th can be blown off-line by westerly winds. The 469-yard, par-5 8th follows an uphill path flanked on the left by a big bunker; the fairway slopes steeply rightward toward jail. Over its final 200 yards, the hole descends over greatly rolling ground to a small, hill-cut and severely left-leaning green trapped on the right. Oaks shadow the green's right-front entry, while a solitary oak sentinel stands guard on the left. The 285-yard, par-4 9th features a tee in trees and a narrow, right-turning fairway. Over its concluding 100 yards, the hole curls rightward and up to a smallish, laterally-trapped green guarded right-front by a massive oak.

The 494-yard, par-5 12th is a lengthy left-bender that tilts sharply rightward all the way to the 100-yard mark. The tidy putting surface is imperiled by a tall ledge, grass bunkers and a steep back side. The top-rated 15th, a 589-yard par-5, heads tightly uphill between oaks right and firs left. The fairway bears leftward for 225 yards or so, then curls to the right and descends to a sizable green trapped right-front. The 16th, a 386-yard par-4, is an uphill dogleg-left shadowed by huge trees. At the 150-yard mark, the left-tilting fairway curls 90 degrees left and rises to a skinny and semi-deep green trapped twice right. A great oak towers over the green's left-front entry. The 432-yard, par-4 17th starts at an elevated tee then shoots down a trough-like, right-sloping path. The narrowish hole winds uphill to the left over its final 100 yards to a severely right-front-tilting green. A steep hill and a grass trap squeeze the right edge of this green, which has two tiers. Also in play is the pond off the 18th tee.

Illahe Hills Country Club

18 *3376 Country Club Drive SE, Salem, OR 97302. (503) 581-3233. Ron Rawls, pro. 18 holes. 6,709 yards. Par 72. Grass tees. Course ratings: men—B72.5/129, M71.0/ 126, I69.0/122; women—M77.2/135, I74.8/130, F72.3/122. Year Opened: 1961. Architect: William P. Bell; John Harbottle III (remodel). Members, guests & reciprocates.*

Following the demise of Salem's original 1914-built Illahe course, a layout designed by Arthur Vernon Macan, Illahe Hills Country Club was begun in 1960 by a group of golfers who wanted a private club. After trying unsuccessfully to purchase Salem Golf Club from the Kay family, the group acquired a 330-acre parcel of farmland and filbert orchards along the Willamette River, and commissioned architect William P. Bell to design an 18-hole layout. An all-new Illahe Hills Country Club opened in 1961.

The course lies in a quiet area. Upscale residences occupy some peripheries of the course; more housing will be built on lots subdivided from the club's original acreage. Filbert trees, pears, cherries, cottonwoods, sweet gums, pines, firs, sequoias and willows line fairways. Illahe Hills crosses generally flat ground, with a few holes traversing some fairly steep slopes. The course's proximity to the Willamette caused it to be flooded in the winter of 1996 but, by that summer, the layout was fully restored. Also that year, Illahe Hills was in the midst of a four-year master plan overseen by Tacoma architect, John Harbottle. Slated to be finished by 1998, the work involves a redesign of the 4th and 17th holes and a renovation of the bunkers.

Illahe Hills features mid-width fairways and quite a bit of length for a west-of-the-Cascades track. The course is imperiled by more than 55 bunkers, some of which contain high, difficult-to-escape lips. Sundry water hazards also vie for errant shots. Noteworthy tests include the 2nd, a 527-yard par-5 with a raised tee and a left-bending, tree-lined fairway. A bunker lurks along the left at the 225-yard mark, at which point the hole winds downhill to the left over rolling ground. The hole concludes at a hill-perched green trapped right-front and left. The top-rated 5th, a 565-yard par-5, is wide and straight off the tee. The fairway eventually curls rightward between trees, passing a large pond along the right 300 yards out. Here, the hole begins an ascent to a mid-sized, creek-fronted green trapped twice in front.

The 5th is a lovely 152-yard par-3 with a pond-fronted, steeply front-sloping green trapped front and left-rear. The 396-yard, par-4 12th is right-bending and narrow along an initial descent. Over its final 100 yards, the fairway climbs to a good-sized green trapped twice in front. The 538-yard, par-5 14th curls rightward between two bunkers about 250 yards out. The medium-sized 14th green tilts frontwards and is trapped twice on the right. The 16th, a 516-yard par-5, sports a pond along the left of its left-turning path; there's ample landing area to the right, however. The fairway goes straight to the 150-yard mark, then rises past a pond along the left to a steeply front-banked green trapped twice right and once left. The 176-yard, par-3 17th may have the slickest putting surface at Illahe Hills. This two-tiered beauty slopes rear- and leftward, and is bunkered twice left.

Michelbook Country Club

1301 Michelbook Lane, McMinnville, OR 97128. (503) 472-8079. Mel Chaufty, pro. 18 holes. 6,581 yards. Par 72. Grass tees. Course ratings: men—B71.4/126, M69.9/124; women—M75.9/127, F72.2/122. Years Opened: 1964 (original nine); 1984 (second nine). Architect: Shirley Stone. Members, guests & reciprocates.

18

This stockholder-owned club is an integral part of Michelbook Estates, a 235-acre subdivision on McMinnville's northwest end. Michelbook Country Club was initiated by a group of local folks who sought to build a course in golf-starved Yamhill County. When the Yamhill Golf & Country Club closed during the Depression, the only place to play was nine-hole Riverwood Golf Course. After making several failed attempts to buy land for a new links, the founders convinced Francis Michelbook (pronounced "My-kel-book") to sell his farm. The sale of memberships ensued when Michelbook Estates was incorporated into McMinnville in 1963. After selling $150,000 in stock certificates to 30 golfers, the club hired Shirley Stone of Western Turf Company to design a course. Portland's Keith West transformed Michelbook's old dairy barn into a clubhouse.

The initial nine holes opened in 1964 and, after selling homesites to generate capital, the members built a second nine in 1984. In 1985, the original side was remodeled with bunkers, a couple of ponds, and new tees and greens. The course has several distinctive features, including a pair of mighty oaks on the 8th hole, and a 610-yard par-5—the 9th—that ranks among Oregon's longest holes. Sporting very large bunkers, Michelbook is graced with spectacular deciduous, fruit and ornamental trees on the back side. The front nine is set quite tightly within housing; some residences are ringed by nets to protect them from wayward shots. Conversely, the back crosses ample acreage and is virtually unhoused. Having more variety than their counterparts, holes 10 through 18 are also more easily affected by prevailing winds.

Good tests include the top-rated 3rd, a 376-yard par-4 that goes leftward between traps and trees, passing homes on the right. The raised 3rd green is trapped left-front. The 397-yard, par-4 4th curls to the right on a route lined left by a creek. Trees, homes and OB sit inside the turn, after which the hole angles slightly uphill to a wide-but-shallow green trapped once in front and twice rear. The 5th, a 500-yard par-5, doglegs right and is bunkered left; a pond lurks inside trees along the right. The fairway ends at to a narrowly-entered, kidney-shaped green guarded by a bushy tree left-front and a trap right. The 509-yard, par-5 7th goes straight for 300 yards or so before veering left. A pond enters the right side of the fairway about 200 yards from a rolling green trapped twice left and once right-front. The mammoth 9th is a flattish hole lined on the left by OB. The fairway winds 60 degrees to the right toward a medium-sized green trapped laterally.

The 387-yard, par-4 10th curls leftward along a path lined by two sand traps and three grass bunkers left, and a pond right. Another trap sits left-front 100 yards from a big, right-front-sloping putting surface trapped twice left. A fir towers over the green's right-front entry. The pretty 15th, a 337-yard par-4, is lined by a towering row of oaks along the right, with a creek and pond left. The pond starts about 150 yards out, and the fairway goes rightward around the oaks. The water hazard fronts a bowl-shaped green trapped right and left-front. The 18th, a 479-yard par-5, has a pond off the tee that runs up to line the right side of its uphill path. The hole winds rightward, skirting two bunkers in the lay-up area en route to a steeply front-sloping green trapped twice in front and once right.

Salemtowne Golf Club

9 *2906 Oakcrest Drive NW, Salem, OR 97304. (503) 362-2215. 9 holes. 1,690 yards. Par 30. Grass tees. Course rating: men—C55.9/82, M55.0/79; women F58.5/86. Year Opened: 1967. Architect: Bill Schafer. Members & guests.*

Located in West Salem off Wallace Road, this nine-hole executive track is the centerpiece of a retirement community with nearly 500 homes. Salemtowne was built in the 1960s by Jim Watts, the same fellow who built Oregon State University's Gill Coliseum. Salemtowne's dual-tee set-up winds between well-kept dwellings.

Nine traps encircle the small and slick greens, and Wilson Creek enters play at the 7th, 8th and 9th holes. A pond adds beauty while attracting mishit golf shots. Recent improvements include a new 17th tee, which made the "back nine" hole a par-4 and boosted Salemtowne's 18-hole par to 61. Future plans include another water hazard. The course is visited by nutrias, ducks, blue herons and Canada geese.

Senior Estates Golf & Country Club

18 *1776 Country Club Drive, Woodburn, OR 97071. (503) 981-0189. Jim White, pro. 18 holes. 5,398 yards. Par 72. Grass tees. Course ratings: men 65.0/100, women 67.7/109. Years Opened: 1961 (original nine); 1969 (second nine). Architect: Bill Graham. Members, guests & reciprocates.*

The course at Senior Estates is used by homeowners who reside in the surrounding retirement community. The subdivision on Woodburn's northeast edge contains 1,500 homes. The course is visible east of Interstate 5. Besides golf, residents have access to a swimming pool, exercise room, dance floor, billiards and shuffleboard areas, and an arts and crafts center. Senior Estates is the site of many golf tournaments for men and women in summer.

Former Seattle golf pro Bill Graham designed the 18-hole course, which sits on one-time wetlands used by locals for duck-hunting. Opened with nine holes in 1961, Senior Estates received a second Graham-designed side in 1969. Guyle Fielder, former professional hockey player for Portland's and Seattle's Western Hockey League teams, is one of two residents who've shot the course record of 63.

At 5,400 yards, Senior Estates' layout is short and easy to walk. Players encounter minimal hazards, but some fairways are squeezed by cottonwoods, willows and pines. The generally small greens are elevated and slick. Golf activities at Senior Estates have been overseen by Class A pro Jim White since 1979.

Spring Hill Country Club

18 *155 Country Club Lane, Albany, OR 97321. (541) 928-5454. Bill Raschko, pro. 18 holes. 6,416 yards. Par 72. Grass tees. Course ratings: men—B70.5/120, M69.0/118; women—M75.2/131, F71.0/123. Years Opened: 1960 (original nine); 1964 (second nine). Architects: Albert Fortier, Bud Fortier & Fred Federspiel. Members, guests & reciprocates.*

A private 18-hole venue located about a mile north of Highway 20, this club is accessible off the Spring Hill Drive exit. The club was initiated by two brothers, Albert and Bud Fortier, who had operated the nearby Albany Golf Club (now The Golf

Club of Oregon) from 1945 to 1959. When their lease on the public course expired in 1959, the Fortiers acquired acreage and began the Spring Hill development. A country club association was formed, and two years after the original nine (now played as the back) opened in 1960, it was sold to the members. The Fortiers built another nine holes four years later and, again, sold them to the club. Homes border parts of the course, which is visited by foxes and coyotes.

Spring Hill features old-style bunkers filled with grayish river sand; some of the traps are quite deep. The course crosses generally flat ground—a floodplain beside the Willamette River. In February 1996, Spring Hill experienced its worst flooding since 1964. The Willamette spilled over its banks and the only greens not awash were the elevated swards at the 9th and 18th. According to locals, the 1st fairway was a "raging river." The course was repaired and back to normal by spring.

William Robinson has been asked to do a course-wide remodel but, as of late 1996, had not received member authorization to begin the project. As it is, Spring Hill is a nice track, with fairways lined by tall ash, fir, cedar, sequoia and birch trees. Homes border several holes, with farms to the north. Besides a back nine circuiting around the front side, Spring Hill is unique in that it has six par-3s, six par-4s, and six par-5s, with no like pars running in succession. The members named a tree grove next to the 17th hole "Pierce's Park," after a member who routinely endured dark moments in the area.

Another unusual aspect of Spring Hill is that it starts with the top-rated hole, a 420-yard par-4. The tree-lined opener has a long and wide, right-sloping fairway that eventually runs up to a big, right-tilting green trapped left. The 480-yard, par-5 6th is a narrow left-bender through trees. Lovely spruces line the left side of the hole, which winds leftward over its final 150 yards to a large, V-shaped green trapped at the right-front. The rolling 8th, a 540-yard par-5, heads fairly straight between dense arbors to a mid-sized and round, knoll-perched putting surface that leans left-rear. The 330-yard, par-4 10th is a downhill dogleg-left bordered by pretty trees; wetlands lurk along the left. The fairway winds up to a high-centered green guarded at the right-front and left-front by a pair of deep bunkers.

The 11th, a 551-yard par-5, features a mid-width and flat fairway lined by trees. At the 150-yard mark, the hole curls around two mounds to a tree-tucked, rolling green. The 221-yard, par-3 12th stretches out to a front-left-sloping green. The 13th, a 484-yard par-4, starts at a pond-fronted tee then winds leftward, passing trees left and a bunker right. The hole tapers as it runs up to a banked putting surface trapped twice in front. The 509-yard, par-5 15th traverses undulating ground before ascending past a pond on the right at the 100-yard mark. The round, steeply front-tilting 15th green is protected by a deep bunker at the right-front.

Willamette Valley Country Club

18

900 Country Club Place, Canby, OR 97013. (503) 266-2102. Pat Akins, pro. 18 holes. 7,008 yards. Par 72. Grass tees. Course ratings: men—B74.2/132, M71.2/ 131, I69.9/126; women—I75.4/130, F71.6/120. Years Opened: 1963 (original nine); 1969 (second nine). Architect: Shirley Stone; William Robinson (remodel). Members, guests & reciprocates.

Willamette Valley lies just east of the Willamette River, northeast of Canby. The original nine holes (played as the back) were ready for play on Columbus Day

One of Willamette Valley's many tough holes is the 6th, a 637-yard par-5.

1962, but the powerful storm that ravaged the Pacific Northwest that day delayed the opening until the following year. The generally flat 18-holer sprawls across 163 acres of riverside land, and recently benefited from a major remodel overseen by William Robinson. The project included many new tees, an automatic irrigation system, two ponds, six greens, a driving range, over 40 bunkers (including fairway-side), improved drainage, and extensive mounding. In March 1997, the old clubhouse was razed in preparation for a new structure in the same spot. Though more and more houses have been built around it, Willamette Valley's course remains pastoral in nature and is visited by deer, foxes, hawks, raccoons and possums.

The equity-type club enjoys a full 500-member roster, a group amenable to turning their course over to major tournaments. When I visited Willamette Valley in September 1996, the Oregon Seniors' tourney was underway. Other events have included Oregon PGA Championships, Oregon Amateur, Oregon Juniors, Oregon Open, and regional qualifying for the U.S. Amateur, Mid-Amateur and Senior Amateur. That Willamette Valley is in demand as a tournament site is not surprising, considering its championship-caliber challenge and outstanding conditioning. Other hallmarks of the course include smallish and slick greens, towering trees, and understated but elegant gardens and landscaping.

Exceptional tests include the 2nd, a 546-yard par-5 with a tree-pinched fairway lined left by bunkers about 225 yards out. The narrow and rolling hole meanders between oaks and firs to a mid-sized, right-tilting green trapped twice left-front and once right. The tree-lined 6th, a 637-yard par-5, descends for its first 300 yards. Halfway through, the fairway veers left, skirting a boulder left and a pond right. A bunker lines the fairway along the left, while another pond lurks along the right at the 120-yard mark. The water hazard goes up to guard the right-front edge of the mid-sized, two-tiered 6th green, which leans to the left-front and is bunkered left-rear. The 7th, a 419-yard par-4, runs slightly uphill past a bunker on the left about 250 yards out. The 7th green slopes to the left-front, and is trapped right-front and left-rear.

Golfers must execute a precise drive from the back tees at the 11th, a 579-yard par-5, as a fat tree squeezes the right portion of the landing area. The left-tilting hole crosses rolling ground, bearing leftward about 280 yards from an undulating, left-sloping green trapped twice in front and once rear. The 413-yard, par-4 12th is a rising dogleg-left skirting OB left. The fairway winds over left-leaning ground en route to a right-front-sloping green trapped in front. A ridge runs through the back-left quadrant of this putting surface, which is further guarded by a pot bunker at the right-front. The 164-yard, par-3 13th features a trapped-left, two-tiered target lined by a pond right-front and pot bunkers back-right. Willamette Valley's home hole, a 452-yard par-4, crosses an up-angled path lined by houses and OB left, with bunkers along both sides. The fairway crests at the bunker (200-yard mark), then descends slightly to what may be the course's largest green, a front-banked affair engirded by traps right-front, right and left-rear.

Par-3 Courses

Frontier Golf Course

2965 North Holly Street, Canby, OR 97013. (503) 266-4435. 9 holes. 1,063 yards. Par 27. Grass tees. No course ratings. Economical, sr. rates. No reservations.   **9**

Frontier's par-3 layout began in 1964 as a 4-holer built on property behind the house of its owners, Joe and Kit Sisul. The area was in need of a clean-up, so Sisul—with help from his four sons and a few friends—arrayed the golf holes. Five more holes were added over the next few years. Frontier's green fees are kept low since most of its play is from seniors on fixed incomes. When the clubhouse is closed, golfers pay green fees on the honor system. Surrounded by farms, Frontier is flat and easy to walk. Wildlife includes raccoons, skunks and deer, and views of Mount Hood are available from the 2nd and 5th holes. Frontier's abbreviated fairways are lined by sycamores, birches, deodoras, pines, maples and flowering plums, and flower beds adorn some of the tees.

Driving Ranges

Caddieshack Driving Range
5201 State Street, Salem, OR 97301.
(503) 581-7045. Jim Hynds, Jr., pro.

Cordon Road Driving Range
4205 Cordon Road SE, Salem, OR 97302.
(503) 362-3694. Mike Dwyer, pro.

Westside Driving Range & Golf Center
6050 Highway 22, Independence, OR 97351.
(503) 364-3615.

Upcoming Courses

    Grand Ronde — Grand Ronde Tribe Project (1999). In 1996, a development/construction company out of Ashland, Willamette Valley Golf, was working with the Grand Ronde Indian tribe on an 18-hole course at a site near a tribe-operated casino. The Polk County project may also involve housing, an RV park and hotel. Peter Jacobsen and Jim Hardy will tentatively co-design the layout.

14

Eugene &
Southwest
Oregon

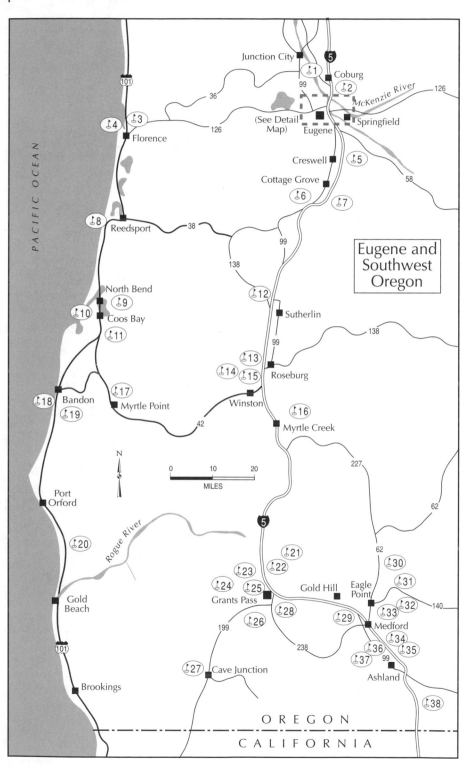

Eugene and
Southwest
Oregon

PACIFIC OCEAN

OREGON
CALIFORNIA

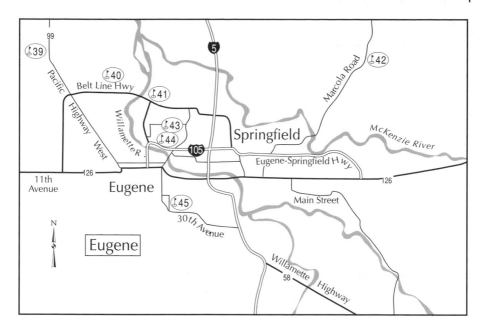

1. **Shadow Hills Country Club** — private 18
2. **Coburg Hills Golf Club** — public 18 & driving range
3. **Ocean Dunes Golf Links** — public 18 & driving range
4. **Sandpines Golf Resort** — public 18, driving range
   & 9-hole putting course
5. **Emerald Valley Golf Club** — public 18 & driving range
6. **Hidden Valley Golf Course** — public 9
7. **Middlefield Village** — public 18 & driving range
8. **Forest Hills Country Club** — semiprivate 9 & driving range
9. **Kentuck Golf Course** — public 18
10. **Sunset Bay Golf Club** — public 9
11. **Coos Country Club** — semiprivate 9
12. **The Club at Sutherlin** — public 18 & driving range
13. **Roseburg Country Club** — private 18
14. **Stewart Park Golf Course** — public 9 & driving range
15. **Roseburg Veterans Hospital Golf Course** — private 9
16. **Myrtle Creek Golf Course** — public 18 & driving range
17. **Coquille Valley Elks Golf Club** — private 9
18. **Bandon Face Rock Golf Course** — public 9
19. **Jack Creek Driving Range**
20. **Cedar Bend Golf Club** — semiprivate 9 & driving range
21. **Colonial Valley Golf Course** — public 9
22. **Red Mountain Golf Course** — public 9
23. **Hillebrand's Paradise Range Resort** — public 3 (par-3)
24. **Dutcher Creek Golf Course** — public 9 & driving range
25. **Grants Pass Driving Range**
26. **Applegate Golf** — public 9
27. **Illinois Valley Golf Club** — semiprivate 9 & driving range
28. **Grants Pass Golf Club** — semiprivate 18 & driving range

29. **Laurel Hill Golf Course** — public 9 & driving range
30. **Veterans Administration Domiciliary Golf Course** — private 9
31. **Eagle Point Golf Course** — public 18 & driving range
32. **Stoneridge Golf Club** — public 18 & driving range
33. **Cedar Links** — public 18 & driving range
34. **Rogue Valley Country Club** — private 27
35. **Quail Point Golf Course** — semiprivate 9 & driving range
36. **Stewart Meadows Golf Course** — public 9 & driving range
37. **Bear Creek Golf Course** — public 9 & driving range
38. **Oak Knoll Golf Course** — public 9
39. **Fiddler's Green Golf Course** — public 18 (par-3) & driving range
40. **Eagles on the Green** — private 9 (par-3)
41. **Riveridge Golf Course** — public 18 & driving range
42. **Springfield Country Club** — private 18
43. **Oakway Golf Course** — public 18
44. **Eugene Country Club** — private 18
45. **Laurelwood Golf Course** — public 9 & driving range

This geographically diverse part of the Northwest is also one of the biggest, incorporating coastal dunelands, the densely wooded Klamath Mountains, the beautiful Rogue River Valley, and the southern Cascades. The area contains Oregon's second largest city, Eugene, as well as the growing metropolises of Medford and Grants Pass. Several different climates characterize the region, including temperate zone 5 and winter-cold zone 1; the Rogue River Valley lies in zone 7. Greater Medford has seen several new golf courses open of late. With an influx of Californians and a sunny but mild climate attractive to retirees, the Rogue River Valley should continue to draw Golden Staters. Though Medford and Grants Pass have plenty of players for the new golf courses, there comes a time when supply outstrips demand. This part of the Northwest will be interesting to watch in the upcoming decade.

Public Courses

Applegate Golf

7350 New Hope Road, Grants Pass, OR 97527. (541) 955-0480. 9 holes. 2,677 yards. Par 36. Grass tees. Course ratings: men—B65.8/104, B/F64.8/101; women—B70.4/120, B/F69.1/118, F67.8/115. Year Opened: 1994. Architect: John Briggs. Economical, jr./sr. rates. Call for reservations. Walk-on Chances: Good. Walkability: Good. Playability: Owners to rebuild course in aftermath of disastrous flood.

Applegate Golf lies south of Grants Pass off the Williams Highway (238); head toward Murphy and travel west on New Hope Road for a mile and a half to the course. The nine-hole venue opened on Thanksgiving Day 1994, and is owned by John Briggs and Nancy Swinney. Briggs, a longtime construction worker who moved to Oregon from Texas in 1974, designed and built the course—laying it out "naturally" with help from golfing friends. Though neither Briggs nor Swinney golf, they wanted to convert their acreage into something useful and attractive. The former dairy farm lies in a rural-residential area called "Memphis." The Josephine County layout spans a flat, 45-acre parcel beside the Applegate River. When I visited the place in September 1996, there were plenty of folks taking swings at the course. Indeed, Briggs and Swinney had built a golf facility which was growing in popularity and repaying their investment.

All that changed on January 1, 1997. Heavy rains and snowmelt backed up a lake behind the Applegate River Dam. The Army Corps of Engineers warned residents of the Applegate River Valley that it had to release water to prevent the dam from breaching. Finally, the water rose so high that the corps opened the floodgates, creating a wall of water that tore through the valley. Briggs and Swinney helplessly watched the deluge from higher ground, shocked as huge oak trees on the property were ripped out by their roots. Cars, trucks and other large objects flowed past them. A boat taken off its trailer and carried downstream was later returned to a neighbor. A 1956 Thunderbird and a Cadillac never were found, buried under deep rocks and mud far from their garages. Farms were awash, and dikes and bridges were wiped out by the flood.

Applegate Golf suffered considerable damage. A series of ponds on the course were gouged out, replaced by 12-foot-deep gullies, some as wide as 200 feet. The 9th hole was buried under four feet of rock. The 3rd, 4th and 5th holes were underneath thousands of tons of gravel—valued at $1 million—swept away from a nearby county-operated gravel pit. The new irrigation system was lost. Ancient oak trees along the course's boundary with the river were wiped out. News services from around the U.S. ran video and print stories of Applegate's destruction. One local golfer learned about the flood while watching a news program in the Midwest.

Shortly after the flood, Briggs and Swinney put up a sign next to the clubhouse that read: "Winter Rates — $800 for 9 holes; $1,300 for 18 holes. Play at your own risk." Besides reflecting their dark humor, the sign somehow speaks of the owners' resiliency. Applegate Golf will be rebuilt. Its strong men's and women's clubs immediately volunteered to help with the clean-up. Hundreds of yards of gravel and rock must be moved into the chasms now cutting through the property. Bridges will be erected to allow golfers passage over the deep washes. Another irrigation system must be installed. A couple of months after the flood, Briggs was upbeat, saying he wanted to have a modified nine-holer ready for play in March of 1997. Applegate's regulars were also positive; some even saw a silver lining in the devastation. An old oak tree in the 9th fairway had the nasty habit of batting down golf shots into the green. The members were tickled to learn it was removed by the flood.

When Applegate Golf (there's no "course" or "club" in the name) is returned to normal operations, visitors will enjoy the place's low-key ambiance. Briggs used his contractor skills to build a comfortable clubhouse (untouched by the flood), siding it with timbers from an old barn. The pastoral attractions of the usually serene river valley include much wildlife; deer and many birds visit the course. Briggs watched bemusedly as skunks ferreted out ground bees during the hot summer of '96. Briggs and Swinney plan to replace the bentgrass greens and ryegrass fairways, and return Applegate to its rightful place as a recreational outlet for residents of Josephine County. Hopefully, the only future hardships the couple will have to endure will be golfers carping about faulty golf swings.

Bandon Face Rock Golf Course

9

3225 Beach Loop Road, Bandon, OR 97411. (541) 347-3818. 9 holes. 2,132 yards. Par 32. Grass tees. Course ratings: men B60.0/99; women—B61.2/104, F60.2/ 102. Year Opened: 1927. Architect: Lee Smith. Economical, jr. rates, credit cards. No reservations. Walkability: Good. Playability: Though on the short side, course is made difficult by fierce winds and wild weather.

Bandon Face Rock's shortish nine sits about 200 yards from the roaring Pacific Ocean. Wild weather, wind and heavy rains complicate play on the layout, which is named after a monolith that sits in surf just to the west. Located beside the Inn at Face Rock, the course has been owned by Margaret Miller and Jerry Brown since 1991. The layout dates back to 1927, when it was built on the old Ledgerwood farm. Lee Smith, who had just designed Alderbrook's original nine up north, was hired by local golfers to array a 4-hole layout. The venue's original name was Bandon Westmost Golf Course since it was, and still is, the westernmost place to golf in the contiguous

United States. During World War II, Bandon's course was converted to a cattle and sheep pasture. After reopening in 1947, a series of owners ran it until 1980, at which time Face Rock Development Company bought the property and built condominiums and an inn next door.

During their tenure, Miller and Brown have installed automatic sprinklers and made other improvements. When playing both sets of tees over two circuits, the layout extends 4,154 yards, an ideal configuration for infrequent golfers on vacation. Primary hazards include Johnson Creek—which meanders across several holes, and "gorse traps," dense ball-swallowing yellow-flowered thorn patches. From some holes, the Pacific Ocean is visible; howling, often rain-flecked winds are invariably aloft. Bandon Face Rock's best hole is the 2nd, a 348-yard par-4. The fairway parallels the creek en route to a small, domed green. Another good test is the 8th, a 189-yard par-3 that heads through trees—directly into the teeth of the Pacific's winds—to a postage-stamp target.

Bear Creek Golf Course

2355 South Pacific Highway, Medford, OR 97501. (541) 773-1822. Tara Staal, pro. 9 holes, 1,501 yards. Par 29. Grass tees. Course ratings: men 56.6/84, women 56.0/82. Year Opened: 1965. Architect: Ray Offord. Economical. No reservations. Walkability: Very good. Playability: Amenable to the whole family.

9

Medford's Bear Creek is co-owned by Marla Corbin and Ray Offord. Corbin is the daughter of Bear Creek's previous head pro, Guy Hupe. Offord designed the layout for Dixon and Crawford—the course's developer—in the mid-1960s. During its early years, Bear Creek was known as Roxy Ann Links. One of its early golf pros and owners was the late Jim Sheldon, who went on to a long tenure as the head pro at Grants Pass Golf Club. Since taking over active management of the course, Corbin has instituted changes to make it more comfortable for golfers. She coined a slogan, "The perfect place to begin," dedicating Bear Creek to families, women, seniors and beginners. LPGA member Tara Staal, a California native and the wife of Stoneridge Golf Club's head pro Jim Staal, serves as the head pro.

Bear Creek lies beside baseball fields and a bowling alley south of Medford's city center. Upcoming plans include building new tees and adding 300 yards to the course. The par-4 9th will be stretched out, and the 8th will be given another 175 yards and made into a par-4, making Bear Creek a par-30 layout. These modifications received a setback when portions of the course were flooded in January 1997. The layout, temporarily reduced to six holes after a couple of bridges were wiped out, was restored by that spring.

Besides an evolving layout, Bear Creek (one of three Northwest courses so named) features a driving range, large pro shop, and an 18-hole miniature track with artificial turf. The executive-length course occupies an L-shaped, 25-acre parcel, and averages about 40,000 rounds a year. The namesake creek crosses the the 6th, 7th and 8th holes. Most greens are raised and slick, with a few sporting peripheral bunkers and multiple tiers. Golfers enjoy lovely gardens and hit their drives from well-kept grass tees.

Cedar Bend Golf Club - semiprivate

9

34391 Squaw Valley Road, Gold Beach, OR 97444. (541) 247-6911. 9 holes. 2,984 yards. Par 35. Grass tees. Course ratings: men B67.6/115; women—M71.0/123, 170.0/122, F69.0/120. Year Opened: 1971. Architects: Founding members; Ed Giovanetti (remodel). Moderate, jr. rates, credit cards. Reservations: Call a week ahead. Walk-on chances: Fair. Walkability: Good. Playability: Tight fairways and ample hazards complicate play on remote track.

Dubbed "Curry County's Only Golf Course," this nine-hole facility lies 14 miles south of Port Orford and three miles from the Pacific Ocean in the secluded Squaw Valley. The road to the course from Highway 101 tunnels through a dense forest. Member-owned Cedar Bend arose in 1971 through the efforts of a group of local golfers, known as the "Gold Beach Orphans" for their lack of a golf course. The layout was funded by a $250,000 Farmers Home Association loan, the last such loan awarded by the FHA. The "orphans" sold 250 memberships, at $100 each, to become eligible for the funding. After securing financing, the 250 members cut down trees and built the course.

The 74-acre layout was remodeled in 1981 by Ed Giovanetti, who liked the area so much he became Cedar Bend's head pro. For several years the members have had plans for another nine holes. But as of early 1997, the expansion idea was still simmering on the back burner. A driving range and 11-slip RV park complement Cedar Bend's clubhouse, which contains a snack bar, lounge and pro shop. The course's isolated locale within dense cedar and alder forests sees it regularly visited by deer, elk, salamanders and other beasts indigenous to Oregon's South Coast country.

The dual-tee layout uses a double-flag arrangement; front-nine players aim at the yellow flags while back-niners fire at the red-flagged sticks. Good tests include the 3rd, a 535-yard par-5 crossed by Cedar Creek 300 yards from a right-tilting green trapped at the left-rear. The 470-yard, par-5 5th is a sharp dogleg-left around trees. An iron from the tee is recommended to avoid blowing over a tiny landing area. The entire left edge of the fairway leans toward jail, and grassy mounds line its right edge en route to a slippery putting surface. The 8th, a 320-yard par-4, has a large pond extending 150 yards out from the tee. The mid-sized 8th green is backed by a pond. The top-rated 9th, a 405-yard par-4, has a right-bending fairway that skirts OB left before arriving at a front-sloping, trapped-left green.

Cedar Links

18

3155 Cedar Links Drive, Medford, OR 97504. (541) 773-4373. Scott Lusk, pro. 18 holes. 6,142 yards. Par 70. Grass tees. Course ratings: men—B68.9/114, M67.9/110; women—M73.0/121, F68.5/112. Years Opened: 1972 (original nine); 1988 (second nine). Architects: Dale Coverstone (original nine); Robert Muir Graves (second nine). Moderate, sr. rates. Call for reservations. Walk-on chances: Fair. Walkability: Good. Playability: Nice variety of holes at full-service 18-holer.

Cedar Links crisscrosses a foothill on Medford's north end, offering choice views of the Rogue River Valley. The course is owned by two brothers, Mike and Monty Jantzer, and has been overseen by head pro Scott Lusk since 1977. The layout began when the Jantzers' father, Ted, built the original Dale Coverstone-designed nine in 1972. In 1988, a Robert Muir Graves-designed side was added. Besides a nice course with some challenging holes, Cedar Links features a large clubhouse with a restaurant and lounge. Widgeons, muskrats, quails, doves, pheasants and an occasional farmer's cow venture onto this suburban venue.

According to Lusk, the decreased play levels at Cedar Links in 1996 were a direct result of the new courses in greater Medford, particularly Stoneridge and Eagle Point. Nonetheless, the course remains a hotbed for private tournaments, with more than 50 held annually. Recent upgrades for Cedar Links include new tees at the 4th and 6th holes that lengthened it by 80 yards. The 4th is now a 546-yard par-5, while the par-4 6th went from 379 to 400 yards.

The layout features two different nines. The Coverstone side encompasses 2,815 gently rolling yards lined by maples, oaks and houses. Four ponds dot these holes, while seven traps guard the raised, steep-sided greens. The Graves nine—with the exception of the 10th and 18th holes—is etched within a pear orchard to the east. Golfers cross Cedar Links Drive to play the holes and to get to the driving range.

Good tests include the top-rated 7th, a 404-yard par-4 that follows a narrow path bordered along the right by residential yards and OB. A good-sized pond lies 150 yards from the skinny, knoll-perched 7th green—a narrowly-entered affair shaded left-front by a tall tree and trapped right-front. The 421-yard, par-4 12th has a wide, right-curling fairway that ascends over wavy terrain to a slender right-tilting putting surface. The 14th, a 377-yard par-4, winds 180 degrees around to the right. Over its initial leg, the hole heads downhill while sloping left, then makes a U-turn and goes up to a front-banked green. The fairway at the 18th, a 424-yard par-4, winds around a pond along a dogleg-left route. The hole ends at a left-front-leaning, bi-trapped green.

The Club at Sutherlin

1919 Recreation Lane, Sutherlin, OR 97479. (541) 459-4422. 18 holes. 6,543 yards. Par 72. Grass tees. Course ratings: men—B71.5/125, M69.8/121; women—M74.2/ 122, F71.5/116. Year Opened: 1969. Architects: Local golfers. Moderate, credit cards. Reservations: Call a week ahead. Walk-on chances: Good. Walkability: Good, with some uphill hikes. Playability: Course in need of repairs enjoys glimmer of hope from new owners.

This course lies on the east side of Interstate 5 west of Sutherlin. Originally funded through a Farm Home Administration loan, it was designed and built by local folks in 1969. The latest incarnation of the 18-holer is The Club at Sutherlin. Previous titles have included The Knolls and, before that, Sutherlin Knolls. At the end of 1996 the layout was the property of Sutherlin Resorts LLC, a group of local investors who acquired the 160-acre facility from Alaska Sutherlin Knolls. The latter group had big plans for the venue when they purchased it and a contiguous 273-acre plot in 1992: Alaska Sutherlin Knolls wanted to build 150 homesites and a 150-room hotel on the site. Unfortunately, those plans fell through. The current owner may proceed with the hostelry, but only after the playing conditions of this golf course are restored to respectability.

That task may be difficult. When I visited Sutherlin on a bone-chilling day in September 1996, parts of the course were torn up, with deep trenches cut in several fairways in an effort to carry off excess water. A sprinkler by the 3rd green was seeping out of control; the turf—never outstanding in the first place—was in terrible shape; and the two back roof supports on the cart in which I was riding were broken. The swaying, banging roof nearly decapitated me as I rode over rough spots. The owners hope the drainage work will return play levels at a course which, despite its upscale name, remains a downtrodden track.

The course is irrigated by treated effluent, and the ditches (many of which radiate through the first two lower holes) may eventually take water off the course. But the primary need here is an automatic irrigation system (which, it must be noted, may be installed in 1997 or '98). Antique pop-up sprinklers are used around the greens, but the rest of the course is hand-watered. Serious turfgrass maintenance is needed as weed patches and disease have overwhelmed much of the grass. Sutherlin's site is okay, but the clayey soil doesn't perk properly. Perhaps most importantly, an infusion of cash is needed to get the course sufficiently up to snuff so the owners can proceed with peripheral development plans.

As it is, decent golf tests are found at the 3rd hole, a 359-yard par-4 that runs narrowly uphill to the left along a ridge. The squarish 3rd green has a tall left side. The top-rated 6th, a 527-yard par-5, crosses rolling, slightly ascending ground en route to a small, right-leaning green. The 9th, a 426-yard par-4, goes straight out for 250 yards or so, then bends sharply right around a pond to a right-front-tilting green. The 462-yard, par-5 11th has an elevated tee and a fairway crossed by two ditches. The narrow path winds uphill between a rugged hill left and trees right to a hill-perched putting surface. The 290-yard, par-4 13th requires a tee shot over a ravine to reach an upwardly-angled fairway lined on the left by a tree and bunker. The 13th green tilts steeply toward the front. The 430-yard 14th is a par-4 that goes narrowly downhill, passing trees right and I-5 off to the left. The hole ends at an undulating, trapped-right putting surface with a tall rear edge.

Coburg Hills Golf Club

18 *Off Van Duyn Road, Coburg, OR 97408. (541) 334-1777. Mike Haggerty, pro. 18 holes. 7,030 yards. Par 72. Grass tees. Course ratings not available. Year Opened: 1997. Architect: Mike Stark. Moderate, credit cards. Call for reservations. Walk-on chances: Good. Walkability: Fair, with some hills. Playability: New course near I-5 has tremendous possibilities.*

Coburg Hills Golf Club is a new 18-hole venue located east of Interstate 5; take the Coburg exit and go east on Van Duyn Road to the course. The facility was scheduled to open with first nine holes in September 1997, with the second set of holes two months later (after this book went to press). The golf-only project was spearheaded by designer and co-owner Mike Stark, a Springfield native who worked in California with Robert Muir Graves for eight years before returning home. Other Stark-designed courses include Mallard Creek in Lebanon and the remodeled Riverwood Golf Course in Dundee. His primary partner in Coburg Hills is Les Eddy of Seattle, with other investors involved.

By early 1997, the irrigation system was installed in preparation for seeding that June. David Page of Bend shaped the fairways and greens. Drain tile and six inches of sand were deposited under fairways to ensure good drainage. Stark specified bentgrass for tees and greens, with the fairways a unique mix of Colonial bent and dwarf fescue. The bent-fescue blend has several attributes, being low-maintenance while tolerant to low mowing, low watering and low fertilization. Previously grazed by cattle, the property encompasses 248 acres, 75 of which are wetlands circuited by the 7,000-yard course.

The site involves over 350 feet of elevation, giving golfers a bit of a workout as well as a tough test. Nice westerly views of the Willamette Valley are on tap from the higher points. Douglas firs and 200-year-old oaks line fairways, Little Muddy Creek crosses five holes, and two ponds impede play. The plan calls for fairways and greens to be lined by 45 white-sand bunkers. In addition to what could become a difficult golf course, Coburg Hills includes a driving range and a 5,000-square-foot clubhouse with a restaurant. Stark and Eddy are hoping their layout will draw linksters from Albany, Salem and Eugene. I visited the site in fall of 1996 and found it naturally endowed. I'm looking forward to returning and seeing if Stark's vision for the property came out to his—and golfers'—liking.

Colonial Valley Golf Course

75 Nelson Way, Grants Pass, OR 97526. (541) 479-5568. Randy Blankenship, pro. 9 holes. 1,587 yards. Par 29. Grass tees. No course ratings. Year Opened: 1969. Architect: John Nelson. Economical. No reservations. Walkability: Good. Playability: Short but tight track renders fun rounds.

Executive-length Colonial Valley is four miles east of Interstate 5 off the Nelson Way exit. Colonial Valley has been owned since 1972 by its head pro, Randy Blankenship. The course, which averages about 30,000 rounds a year, was built in 1969 by John Nelson (namesake of Nelson Way and "settler" of the area). Blankenship lives in a house beside a pond on the course. From this vantage, he watches deer, quails, raccoons, squirrels, and an occasional bear cross fairways. Oak and pine trees line many holes.

As befitting the venue's colonial theme, the facility has a large, white clubhouse with a small bar, banquet area, a billiards room and bathrooms labeled "George" and "Martha." Meandering Soldier Creek borders one side of the flattish layout, which has seven par-3s ranging from 98 to 190 yards along with two par-4s—233 and 242 yards. Though the small, round greens can be quick when mowed low, play here is less a major test than an enjoyable country outing.

Coos Country Club - semiprivate

999 Coos City-Sumner Road, Coos Bay, OR 97420. (541) 267-7257. Jim Bartleson, pro. 9 holes. 2,921 yards. Par 34. Grass tees. Course ratings: men—B68.8/126, M68.1/124, women—M72.4/125, F71.3/123. Year Opened: 1923. Architect: H. Chandler Egan. Moderate. Call for reservations. Walk-on chances: Fair. Walkability: Good. Playability: Tight, old-style course to receive second nine.

Owned by 230 members, this semiprivate venue allows public play for golfers from outside a 50-mile area. In recent years, Coos Country Club has been slated to receive another set of holes. The project keeps getting delayed, however, as final construction permits have been tough to get. Nearly all approvals had been obtained in late 1996; the project was approved by the membership in 1997 and work on the William Robinson-designed addition was to start later that year.

The 1923-built original nine was designed by the legendary H. Chandler Egan, a great player from the early 1900s who won the U.S. Amateur and went on to design several historic layouts on the West Coast. Coos Country Club was built on land once owned by the pioneering Haynes family. A requirement of the land sale was that the grave of Charles T. Haynes, who died in 1876 at age 12, be preserved. Young Haynes' headstone resides next to the 226-yard, par-3 1st hole. The course has been overseen for many years by head pro Jim Bartleson.

Although traditional in scope and somewhat short, Coos Country Club plays tough. The layout is notorious for its slick, rolling and steep-sided greens. Robinson will try to create similar putting surfaces on the new nine. The dual-tee layout plays to 5,728 yards over two circuits, and features far-apart tees that simulate a genuine "18-on-9" feel. Sand bunkers and ponds guard several holes. The club's big annual event is the Southwest Oregon Amateur, a match-play tourney held on the Fourth of July for over 40 years. For the tournament—a relaxed, family-oriented function—128 players from around the Northwest are accepted on a first-come, first-served basis.

9 Dutcher Creek Golf Course

4611 Upper River Road, Grants Pass, OR 97526. (541) 474-2188. Jon Kukula, pro. 9 holes. 3,261 yards. Par 36. Grass tees. Course ratings: men—B71.2/118, M68.6/109, I66.6/106; women—M/F73.2/131, I70.3/124, F66.1/115. Year Opened: 1994. Architect: Dutcher Creek Enterprise. Moderate. Reservations: Call a week ahead. Walk-on chances: Fair. Walkability: Good. Playability: Water and some slick greens daunt shotmakers.

Named for the stream that runs through it, this nine-hole layout opened in July 1994. The course arose through the efforts of a handful of local landowners and golfers who converted a former dairy farm into a nice recreational facility. Majority stockholder Jack Boersma heads the group, which calls itself Dutcher Creek Enterprise. Each owner had input in the design of the course. Besides several danger-filled holes, Dutcher Creek features an airy clubhouse that offers excellent views of the surrounding valley. The nine-hole record of 30 was shot by head pro Jon Kukula, a Class A PGA member who previously worked at Agate Beach on the Oregon coast.

Dutcher Creek hosted 35,000 rounds in 1996, pretty good numbers for a nine-hole layout in a rural area southwest of Grants Pass. The layout, popular during the summer with private tournaments, is ringed by houses and farms. There's some room across Upper River Road for another nine, but such an expansion is not imminent. The nicely-appointed venue is adorned with pretty flower gardens, clear signage and raised tees. The greens are rather perfunctory, and some of the bunkers are in odd places (generally apart from greens and target zones). The layout crosses generally flat ground, with a ledge near the clubhouse serving as starting and ending points for the 1st and 9th holes, respectively.

Good tests include the 1st, a 304-yard par-4 with an elevated tee fronted by wetlands and a pond. The hole curls leftward past two big bunkers in mounds outside the turn, while a pond runs up the left side. The wide-but-shallow 1st green sits at a 45-degree angle to the fairway. The 593-yard, par-5 4th has a pond-fronted tee and a right-turning route ending at a mound-engirded, humped-in-the-middle green. The top-rated 6th, a 435-yard par-4, is a wide dogleg-left that bends around a fat trap. The fairway stretches out to a rolling green trapped twice in front. The putting surface is also protected by a pond on the right. The interesting 9th, a 314-yard par-4, sports a ledged fairway that sits about 50 feet above the tee. The route drops off steeply along the left as it ascends to a berm-backed, trapped-left-front, hill-cut green that tilts toward the front.

Eagle Point Golf Course

100 Eagle Point Drive, Eagle Point, OR 97524. (541) 826-8225. Brian Sackett, pro.
18 holes. 7,099 yards. Par 72. Grass tees. Course ratings: men—T74.3/131, B71.7/
129, M68.7/120; women—M73.4/132, F68.9/113. Year Opened: 1996. Architect:
Robert Trent Jones, Jr. Moderate, credit cards. Call for reservations. Walk-on
chances: Fair. Walkability: Fair; layout generally efficient except for lengthy gaps
between the 9th and 10th, and 15th and 16th holes. Playability: Great new
addition to the Rogue Valley golf scene.

Eagle Point Golf Course opened to great fanfare on May 15, 1996. Owned
and operated by its famed designer, Robert Trent Jones Jr., the upscale layout was
constructed by Greenscape Ltd., a division of RTJ, Jr., the name of Jones' firm. The
venue lies about two miles north of Stoneridge Golf Club—on the north side of
Highway 140, making this area east of Medford suddenly a hotbed for golf. Eagle
Point Golf Course is part of a residential project. Overseen by local developer Greg
Adams, the subdivision may ultimately contain 600 houses, approximately 175 of
which will be alongside some golf holes. Homes already have been built near the 11th
tee. Currently served by a temporary clubhouse, Eagle Point may eventually be
augmented by a permanent structure with all the amenities. In January 1997, Eagle
Point was named in *Golf Magazine's* list of the "Top Ten Layouts You can Play" for
courses opened in 1996.

After designing over 175 courses around the world, Jones' first self-owned
golf facility is Eagle Point. The course crosses a former pear orchard and cattle ranch.
Four lakes were built on the 180-acre layout, which was prepared with extensive
subsurface drainage and six inches of sand underneath fairways. (While other local
courses were heavily flooded in January 1997, Eagle Point went unscathed.) Fourteen
acres were reserved for the expansive grass-teed driving range. The course, an enrollee
in the Audubon Program, features man-made wetlands to encourage the proliferation
of native deer and game birds, especially pheasants. About 100 birdhouses were placed

Eagle Point's 10th hole is a 348-yard par-4.

around the course, which offers great vistas of Mount McLaughlin. Golfers are spaced a relaxing 10 minutes apart.

During my visit in September 1996, the course was in very impressive condition, a status that will probably become a hallmark of the place. Jones fashioned large mounding along the generally wide and forgiving ryegrass fairways, and lined the routes with native fescues. Concrete cart paths wind throughout, and pure-white Emmett, Idaho sand fills bunkers. Many traps are positioned anywhere from 50 to 75 yards from the putting surfaces. These bunker placements create optical illusions, and may delude shotmakers into thinking the targets are closer than they really are. Also, in several instances the bentgrass greens are fronted by low-cut grassy swales. While perhaps not puttable, these areas are eminently chippable. With the exception of two junctures—between the 9th and 10th, and 15th and 16th holes—Eagle Point is walker-friendly.

Memorable holes include the 2nd, a 456-yard par-4 with a right-sloping fairway lined on the right by a pond and left by two bunkers. The gradually rising hole is crossed by a creek, which feeds into a pond. The fattened water hazard runs up the fairway's left side to guard the left-front flank of a mid-sized, trapped-right-front green. The top-rated 6th, a 474-yard par-4 into the prevailing wind, has a pond left of the tee which merges into a creek that diagonally crosses the hole. There's adequate bail-out area for tee shots to the right. The 6th resumes on the far side of the stream, skirting a pot bunker in a mound 75 yards from a wide-but-shallow, front-trapped green. The 522-yard, par-5 9th winds leftward around wetlands, passing trees on the right. The creek and adjoining wetlands cross the hole at the 200-yard mark. The two-tiered, trapped-right 9th green is crossed in front by the creek, which also snuggles against its left flank. The nifty 10th, a 348-yard par-4, features a pond right-front of the tee and a "channel" fairway that slopes steeply left toward jail. The hole gradually tapers en route to a tidy, left-front-tilting green trapped right-front and left.

The 526-yard, par-5 12th is a gradually ascending left-bender bordered on the left by wetlands and right by bunkers. Over its concluding 120 yards, the 12th curls rightward around wetlands to a rolling green trapped left-front; the putting surface is steeply banked and guarded on the right by more wetlands. Eagle Point's toughest par-3 may be the 206-yard 13th, which ascends to a hill-cut green that leans rightward toward a phalanx of bunkers. The 591-yard, par-5 16th contains a wide, bi-level fairway (the left side is higher than the right) that goes straight for 260 yards or so. It then drops precipitously down a route lined on the left by five traps and right by a pond. The small, left-front-tilting 16th green has a tier through its front one-third; three traps pinch the left-front side. Eagle Point's home hole is a dandy 471-yard par-4. Wetlands and scrub growth lurk off the tee, with three bunkers along the right between the 225- and 275-yard markers. Once past these traps, the fairway tips to the right toward wetlands while curling left to a mid-sized, left-front-leaning green trapped at the left-front. The putting surface also has a big dip in its right half. A nice touch to the Eagle Point golf experience—a towering totem pole—is situated left of the 18th green.

Emerald Valley Golf Club

83293 Dale Kuni Road, Creswell, OR 97426. (541) 895-2174. Rob Lindsey, pro. 18 holes. 6,851 yards. Par 72. Grass tees. Course ratings: men—B73.0/126, M70.8/122; women—M76.6/131, F70.8/122. Year Opened: 1996. Architect: Bob Baldock. Moderate, jr./sr. rates, credit cards. Reservations: Call a week ahead. Walk-on chances: Fair. Walkability: Good. Playability: Length and ample hazards merge into a challenging course.

18

Located south of Eugene on the east side of Interstate 5 (take exit 182 and go north on Dale Kuni Road to get here), Emerald Valley features a championship-length track and a 54,000-square-foot clubhouse. The golfing grounds were acquired in 1993 by Paloma Golf Group, a Southern California company that owns several other courses in the West. A peripheral 150-acre parcel—owned by Ernest Jaffarian and Steven Klemen—was put on the market in September 1996. The property, which includes the clubhouse/athletic facility, some condominiums and vacant residential land, had not been sold by the time this book went to press. Jaffarian and Klemen wanted to develop Emerald Valley's periphery into a residential subdivision along with a hotel, RV camp and restaurant, but have not had much luck.

The year 1996 was also not kind to Paloma, as Emerald Valley's play levels were down 10 percent over previous years. The course was closed for two months due to flooding by the nearby Willamette River, which at certain times, was redirected through the 4th fairway. Though cart paths are now paved around the course and all-new women's tees are finished, Paloma's progress on other upgrades was slowed because of the closure. The layout spans a 160-acre parcel alongside the Willamette. The mostly flat track often plays longer than its 6,850 yards. Designer Bob Baldock fashioned ample bunkering and water hazards for the layout which, thanks to its riverside locale, is visited by deer, foxes, beavers and sundry waterfowl.

Emerald Valley's fairways are lined by pine, maple, cedar, red oak, cherry, apple and plum trees. Besides three ponds, a tributary of the Willamette enters play on a few front-nine holes. A signature feature of the course is its large, saddle-shaped greens, targets that are invariably surrounded by grassy mounds. These raised putting surfaces permit direct entry from fairways, but cascading flanks leaning toward peripheral tree groves severely penalize the errant.

Particularly tough holes include the 5th, a 438-yard par-4 that winds leftward on a path bordered left by a creek. A tall maple looms in mid-fairway, driving distance out. At the 115-yards mark, the route is squeezed along the left by a pond and on the right by trees. The raised 5th green is trapped laterally, and a pond lurks close by its right edge. The 430-yard, par-4 15th doglegs right. The fairway leans toward a hidden bunker and duck pond inside the turn; once past this juncture, the hole crosses wavy ground to a domed green fronted by two bunkers.

Forest Hills Country Club - semiprivate

9

1 Country Club Drive, Reedsport, OR 97467. (541) 271-2626. Kevin Winston, pro. 9 holes. 3,214 yards. Par 36. Grass tees. Course ratings: men—B70.8/123, M69.8/ 120; women—M75.4/124, F71.4/120. Year Opened: 1962. Architect: William R. Martin. Moderate, credit cards. Call for reservations. Walk-on chances: Fair. Walkability: Good. Playability: Enjoyable golf near the ocean.

Forest Hills Country Club is a semiprivate nine on Reedsport's west side, not far from the Pacific Ocean. The course was built by International Paper in the early 1960s. The late owner of Agate Beach, William R. Martin, designed the 45-acre layout. In 1988, International Paper sold the club to the 150 members who, previously, had rented the course and clubhouse. The members held a 35-year anniversary in 1997. Forest Hills is overseen by Kevin Winston, a Class A pro from Reedsport.

Though semiprivate, unlimited public play is allowed at Forest Hills. The dual-tee nine is unique in that its first five holes loop back to the clubhouse, with the latter four interior holes similarly arrayed. This cyclical arrangement allows tournament contestants to start at both the 1st and 6th tees. The east side of the course is lined by well-tended homes, while a spruce forest to the west is a habitat for deer. Herons are also frequent visitors. In summer, golfers often wander off fairways to pick blueberries in adjoining roughs.

Forest Hills may experience standing water after heavy rains, but drainage has been improved in recent years. Some of its better holes include the top-rated 1st, a right-bending 412-yard par-4 that skirts trees right and a pond left en route to a large green. The dogleg-right 3rd, a 477-yard par-5, curls around a creek that penetrates the fairway after the turn. The 519-yard, par-5 8th occupies a good portion of the "back-four loop." This right-curling hole borders a tree grove and drainage ditch along the right before ending at a wavy green.

Grants Pass Golf Club - semiprivate

18

230 Espey Road, Grants Pass, OR 97527. (541) 476-0849. Ed Fisher, pro. 18 holes. 6,367 yards. Par 72. Grass tees. Course ratings: men—B71.1/130, M69.8/128; women—M75.7/130, F73.5/126. Years Opened: 1946 (original nine); 1974 (second nine). Architects: Founding members (original nine); Bob Baldock (second nine & remodel). Moderate, credit cards. Reservations: Call two days ahead. Walk-on chances: Ok for singles. Walkability: Good, with players getting a workout traversing the higher points. Playability: A fine variety of flat and not-so-flat holes at venue southwest of Grants Pass.

Unless member events are underway at this semiprivate course, public golfers are allowed. The full-service facility lies southwest of its namesake town off Highway 238 and Espey Road. Begun with nine holes in 1946 by founding members, the course underwent a massive remodel that added nine more holes in the mid-1970s. California architect, Bob Baldock, oversaw the project. Recent upgrades include new front tees at the 4th, 6th, 7th and 9th holes, a move which helped make the course more playable for women. A new men's tee at the 13th stretched the par-3 to 140 yards, and a new back tee at the 18th added 50 yards and made the hole a more legitimate par-5. It's expected the members will endorse the construction of a new clubhouse within the next decade.

With a relatively mild climate and long playing season, Grants Pass Golf Club hosts upwards of 80,000 rounds annually. The course is a hotbed for junior golf; the boys' and girls' golf teams at Grants Pass High School have garnered several state championships over the years thanks to the junior program. While serving as the head pro at Grants Pass from 1976 to 1990, Jim Sheldon, helped develop such fine players as Amanda Nealy. Tutored by Sheldon since age 11, Nealy went on to win two state golf championships and four Oregon Amateur titles, and enjoyed a fine college career at the University of Arizona. Others out of Grants Pass' stable have included Walt Porterfield, Glen Luikart and Kevin Miskimins. Head pro Ed Fisher continues the junior program originated by Sheldon, who succumbed to cancer in early 1997.

The 117-acre layout contains two different nines, with the front relatively flat and the up-and-down back arrayed over a hillside. From its higher points, nice views of the Rogue River Valley are on tap. Colorful gardens brighten many tees, and the grounds are nicely manicured. Challenging holes include the top-rated 9th, a 425-yard par-4 that winds between OB right and trees left. A small pond sits driving distance out, and the hole concludes at a slick, bi-trapped green. The 506-yard, par-5 15th is a tight left-bender that heads through trees to a well-bunkered green.

The 16th, a 407-yard par-4, is an uphill and narrow dogleg-right that eventually reaches a trapped-right-front green. The 231-yard, par-3 17th begins at an elevated tee that offers outstanding vistas. The skinny, tree-ringed 17th green is bunkered right-front. The 18th, a 513-yard par-5, also features a heightened tee. The right-turning hole skirts OB left as it goes to a two-tiered putting surface guarded right-front by a pond and left by a large bunker.

Hidden Valley Golf Course

775 North River Road, Cottage Grove, OR 97424. (541) 942-3046. 9 holes. 2,881 yards. Par 35. Grass tees. Course ratings: men M66.6/108; women—M72.0/120, F68.4/114. Year Opened: 1929. Architect: Bill Zimmerly. Moderate, jr. rates, credit cards. Reservations: Call for weekends. Walk-on chances: Good. Walkability: Good. Playability: Steady improvements over the years have enhanced challenge at older course.

Etched within a forest of firs and 300-year-old oaks, Hidden Valley Golf Course has been a popular sporting hub since it opened in 1929. The course is owned by Linda Levings, who's also the greens superintendent. Bill Zimmerly designed and built the 69-acre course, financing it through the sale of 20 $100 shares. During the Depression, Zimmerly repurchased the shares from the original investors and ran the course until 1966. He built a clubhouse with a restaurant and lounge in 1959. That same year, local golfer DeRoss Kinkade set an amazing endurance record, playing 365 holes in 39 hours and finishing 55 strokes under par. During the marathon performance, Kinkade broke Hidden Valley's 18-hole record of 65 four times and set a world record for consecutive holes played.

The current 18-hole record, a 57, is still held by the indomitable Kinkade. Hidden Valley's nine holes are imperiled by towering trees and Bennett Creek, with the stream particularly nettlesome on the 6th, 7th and 8th holes. Golfers may encounter deer, porcupines, beavers, raccoons and squirrels while playing the course. As might be expected due to its relatively old age, Hidden Valley is a conventional layout with small and slick, steep-sided greens. The dual-tee layout stretches 5,625 yards over two circuits, and features such testers as the 6th, a 316-yard par-4 with a creek-crossed fairway and a trapped-right green.

Illinois Valley Golf Club - semiprivate

9 *Highway 199, Cave Junction, OR 97523. (541) 592-3151. Rex Denham, pro. 9 holes. 3,049 yards. Par 36. Grass tees. Course ratings: men B69.1/117; women— B73.9/126, F71.1/120. Year Opened: 1977. Architect: Bob Baldock. Moderate, jr./sr. rates. Reservations: Call a week ahead. Walk-on chances: Fair. Walkability: Good. Playability: Tight fairways and slick greens create challenge at forested track.*

Illinois Valley Golf Club lies within the confines of a forested valley 12 miles north of the California border. The "Illinois" identifying many local landmarks came from a family from that state who settled the valley in the late 1800s. Cave Junction is surrounded by snowcapped peaks; Kalmiopsis Wilderness Area and the Illinois River lie to the west. Located at 1,300 feet above sea level, the layout is home to deer, foxes, coyotes, skunks, eagles, hawks, wood ducks and pheasants.

A decade-long effort by Illinois Valley's member-owners for another nine holes was put on hold in 1996. Construction permits had been received for the project, but new courses in the area caused the members to shy away from financing a costly expansion. Instead of building another nine holes, the current course will be up-graded with some new tees and enhanced drainage. The existing dual-tee track is quite nice, though it lacks bunkers. Tall and fat, ball-snagging firs are of considerable concern, however, as are Illinois Valley's slick and fast greens. George Creek and Kerby Ditch also enter play. Good tests include the top-rated 5th hole, a 390-yard par-4 with one of Oregon's tightest fairways.

Kentuck Golf Course

18 *680 Golf Course Road, North Bend, OR 97459. (541) 756-4464. Martin Culp, pro. 18 holes. 5,394 yards. Par 70. Grass tees. Course ratings: men B65.5/99, women—M69.8/ 107, F64.1/95. Years Opened: 1961 (original nine); 1964 (second nine). Architects: Don Houston & Gene Carver. Economical, jr. rates, credit cards. Reservations: Call a week ahead. Walk-on chances: Good. Walkability: No problems except for returning to the hill-perched clubhouse. Playability: Abbreviated length and straightforward holes combine for a suitable beginning-to-intermediate test.*

Kentuck is an 18-hole facility north of Coos Bay and east of Highway 101, off East Bay Drive. The course is within eyeshot of 101 traffic crossing McCullough Bridge. Kentuck, an old Native American name affixed to a nearby inlet, crosses flat, reclaimed tideflats situated below sea level. The low-lying nature of the site precludes sand traps; the water table is just too high to allow any digging of bunkers. The S-shaped, 135-acre layout was an old dairy farm before Don Houston and Gene Carver built the first nine holes. After installing a back nine three years later, the two ex-loggers sold the course to Wallace Wickett. Wickett's son-in-law, Martin Culp, is now Kentuck's head pro and greens superintendent.

The rather short course is arrayed at the base of the hill upon which the clubhouse roosts. From Kentuck's lofty outdoor patio, golfers enjoy choice views of Coos Bay and points northwest. West and north of the course is Kentuck Inlet, a haven for stilts, egrets and other shorebirds which, along with deer and elk, often find their way here. A few of the holes descend from the clubhouse over hilly terrain. But most of the course lies on the floodplain, which can lead to soggy conditions in the rainy seasons. On the other hand, the turf hardens in dry weather to generate much more roll.

A mile-long dike restrains the waters of Coos Bay and of the ocean, which lies 10 miles to the west. In addition to a drainage ditch, which eases flooding, two ponds enter play on Kentuck. Good holes include the 4th, a 476-yard par-5 with a straight fairway crossed by the ditch driving distance out. Trees border the left edge of the small 4th green. The 343-yard, par-4 12th traverses corrugated turf to a knoll-perched green backed by trees. The 13th, a 401-yard par-5, has a tight fairway intersected by the drainage ditch before reaching a small, rolling green.

Laurel Hill Golf Course   9

9450 Old Stage Road, Gold Hill, OR 97525. (541) 855-7965. 9 holes. 1,9101 yards. Par 31. Grass tees. Course ratings: men—B62.0/102, B/F61.5/102; women F62.3/ 103. Year Opened: 1977. Architect: Harvey Granger. Economical, jr./sr. rates, credit cards. Call for reservations. Walk-on chances: Good. Walkability: No problems for bag-packers. Playability: Tight, tree-lined track in the Rogue River Valley.

Executive-length Laurel Hill Golf Course winds through dense forests between Gold Hill and Central Point, off Old Stage Road (also called the Jacksonville Highway). Laurel Hill is a favorite haunt for local players as well as for tourists visiting the area on Rogue River rafting trips. The layout was begun in 1977 by Harvey Granger, who designed the tight track in woodlands. Granger's daughter Jan Fish and her husband Pete now run the facility. Recent improvements include a covered driving range, which opened in December 1996.

Generally open year-round, the 33-acre course runs beneath a canopy of towering trees. Several greens are protected by bunkers filled with crushed quartz from a local plant, while two ponds also enter play. Dubbed by its owners as the "Toughest Nine Holes in Southern Oregon," the layout sports narrow fairways between dense stands of madronas, pines and maples. The course may be considered a scaled-down version of Chewelah in northeast Washington; the "whacks" of golf balls banging against tree trunks are common at both places.

Laurel Hill's fairways are close-cropped, and its lush postage-stamp greens are slick. Cain Creek severs the 1st and 9th holes from the rest of the course, and a slim waterway lines the left flanks of the 2nd and 3rd fairways. A duck pond borders the edge of the 280-yard, par-4 9th—the course's top-rated hole. With its wooded locale, Laurel Hill is home for deer and gray squirrels. Cain Creek harbors steelhead trout, and great horned owls reside in treetops safely above the field of play.

Laurelwood Golf Course   9

2700 Columbia Avenue, Eugene, OR 97403. (541) 687-5321. Shawn Goben & Kit Wilbur, pros. 9 holes. 3,130 yards. Par 35. Grass tees. Course ratings: men—B70.0/ 121, M67.3/112; women—M72.2/130, F70.4/124. Year Opened: 1931. Architect: Charles Sutton. Economical, jr./sr. rates, credit cards. Call for reservations. Walk-on chances: Fair. Walkability: Good, though some hills make for a few steep climbs. Playability: Tough nine-holer near the U of O campus.

When it opened in the early 1930s as an 18-holer, Laurelwood quickly became one of the Northwest's premier golf facilities, hosting such tournaments as the Oregon Amateur on a regular basis. The course, located about six blocks from the University of Oregon beside Skinner's Butte, was later reduced to nine holes to make way for houses. Prior to its development as a golf layout, the site was a dairy farm. Laurelwood's pro shop is in an old barn, a vestige of its farmland-past. The city-owned track is leased to Herb Carlisle, who hires golf pros to run the shop and give lessons at Laurelwood's busy driving range. A big annual event is the Frostbite Championship, held annually on the first Saturday of December.

Recent improvements include drainage upgrades; new drain tile was placed in previously wet places around the course. Laurelwood stretches across a hillside bordered on the east by a forest and on the west by homes and university recreation fields. The venue is frequented by the members of Laurelwood's large men's and women's clubs and university students. The dual-tee layout stretches 6,260 yards over two circuits. Its fairways are lined by giant oak, filbert, black and English walnut, pear, plum, cherry and apple trees. An occasional deer scampers down from the woodlands on the east.

Middlefield Village

18

91 Village Drive, Cottage Grove, OR 97424. (541) 942-8730. Jim Dodd, pro. 18 holes. 5,100 yards. Par 68. Grass tees. Course ratings: men 63.7/104, women 63.4/102. Year Opened: 1991. Architect: Gene "Bunny" Mason. Moderate, jr./sr. rates. Call for reservations. Walk-on chances: Fair. Walkability: Good. Playability: Though on the short side, contemporary layout tests golfers of all abilities.

Opened in 1991, this executive-length track is divided by Interstate 5. Ten holes lie on the west side of the freeway, with the remainder of the course and the clubhouse to the east. The two sections of the layout are accessed by a tunnel underneath the freeway that was once used to herd dairy cows back and forth. Middlefield Village is the brainchild of Kim Woodard, whose family has owned the property for years and previously leased it to dairymen and corn growers. Besides the course, the 150-acre venue features a driving range, pro shop and 100 housing lots, about 60 of which now contain houses. A 200-space RV park has since been pared from the original plans.

The course skirts the Row River, crossing generally flat ground reshaped during construction with mound-lined fairways. Recent improvements include new tees at the 4th and 15th holes. The one-time par-3 at the 4th is now a 340-yard par-4 (bumping the course's par to 68), while the 15th went from a 515-yard par-5 to a 600-yarder from the tips. Upcoming plans may include converting the 205-yard, par-3 17th into a 260-yard par-4, thus raising the course's par to 69. Though somewhat short, Bunny Mason-designed Middlefield Village plays tough, with narrowish fairways winding through trees and considerable hazards along the way. Five ponds enter play and dozens of traps guard the well-conditioned fairways and greens. The saddle-shaped, bentgrass putting surfaces here are on the small side, and they have plenty of tilt.

Particularly good tests include the top-rated 6th, a narrow 332-yard par-4 that runs straight between mounds along the right and I-5 left. The concave 6th green is trapped twice at the left-front and has a steep back side. The recently-lengthened 15th features an "S-shaped" fairway that initially goes left, then curls back around to the right. This serpentine hole is squeezed by trees on the right before ending at a trapped-left, well-canted green.

Myrtle Creek Golf Course

Day's Creek Cutoff Road, Myrtle Creek, OR 97457. (541) 86304653. 18 holes. 6,900 yards. Par 72. Grass tees. Course ratings not available. Year Opened: 1997 (original nine); 1998 (second nine). Architect: Graham Cooke & Associates. Moderate. Call for reservations. Walk-on chances: Good. Walkability: Fair; mountain-goat affair crosses sides of a steep valley. Playability: Though very tough from the tips, women and mid-handicappers should have some success if playing the appropriate tees.

18

Located in Douglas County on Day's Creek Cutoff Road, this new course is two miles northeast of its namesake city. Scheduled to open with nine holes in spring 1997 (after this book went to press), with the second nine following that summer, the Graham Cooke-designed track sprawls across precipitous terrain. Situated at 850 feet above sea level, the course lies in an area referred to as the "100 valleys of the Umpqua" by that local Indian tribe. The course's backer, the Myrtle Creek Building Authority, hopes visitors to the Umpqua's Seven Feathers Resort, a gambling and convention center west of town, will find their way here for rounds of golf. If the building authority can draw these tourists while generating steady local play, Myrtle Creek may host upwards of 30,000 rounds a year.

The course was built by Jack Moss of British Columbia-based BMR Golf International, and is managed by Golf Resources, Inc., a Tacoma firm that runs several other Northwest facilities. Jerry Whiteaker, previously at Roseburg Country Club, was hired as the superintendent during grow-in. While visiting the unopened course in September 1996, I was struck by its severe topography: nicely-mowed stretches of green grass splay up and down some radical terrain. The course is split by Day's Creek Cutoff Road; players must cross this rural lane to get from one group of holes to the other. Holes 2 through 8 cross a steep hillside south of the road, while the remainder of the course encompasses foothills to the north. During construction, over four inches of sand were deposited under the course to help the ryegrass fairways and Providence bent greens drain properly. The Myrtle Creek area receives 32 to 34 inches of rain annually. Unseasonally heavy downpours in spring 1996 washed out sections of some holes, causing a delay in the work.

Other salient construction facts: Nearly 750 sprinkler heads were installed by Chuck Ewanchuk, of Terra Tech Design. Six miles of cart paths were paved (riding may be the best option at the hilly, 180-acre layout). Each hole has four to five tees, making Myrtle Creek quite player-adaptable. The course is irrigated with level 3 sewage effluent. Half of the course's $7.5-million price tag was funded by a federal grant for a sewage treatment plant. For years the city had dumped untreated sewage into the Umpqua River; using treated effluent to irrigate the course will correct a nasty environmental problem. Though cascading ravines and severely tilting terrain characterize the site, wetlands are found on lower parts of the course. The layout on the old McFarland farm is bordered by a few homes. The building authority hopes a neighboring landowner will execute plans for an RV park on adjoining property to attract even more golfers.

Myrtle Creek will punish those who play from the way-back "Tiger Tees." Good tests include the 3rd, a 485-yard par-5 that goes rightward and steeply uphill. The Day's Creek lines the right side of the hole, which is squeezed by oaks along the left as it rises past two bunkers on the right, 75 yards from a raised, hogbacked green. The 280-yard 6th is an interesting par-4 with a steeply rising, right-leaning fairway and a radical, hill-cut green trapped left-front. The 9th, a 500-yard par-5 with a pond-fronted tee, tilts left toward wetlands and a bunker. About 250 yards out, a pond lurks in mounds on the left. The hole then curls up to a small, left-sloping green trapped thrice on the left.

Myrtle Creek's signature hole may be the 13th, a 145-yard par-3 with a pond from tee to green. A sinuous bunker winds around the left and rear edges of the front-right-leaning green to give it an island-like appearance. The 415-yard, par-4 15th shares a huge teeing area with the par-3 17th. The 15th has a pond left of the tee and a bi-level fairway that winds rightward around a fescue-blanketed knoll. After skirting two pot bunkers on the right, the fairway angles up to a hill-cut green with a steep, bunker-engirded right flank. Myrtle Creek's home hole, a 475-yard par-5, features a creek-fronted tee and an uphill and sharply right-turning—yet left-sloping—fairway. A bunker sits along the right, 150 yards from a mid-sized green trapped front-left and right-rear. Wetlands cross the hole 75 yards before the green to test the mettle of players who must decide whether to gamble and shoot for the green or play it safe.

Oak Knoll Golf Course

9 *3070 Highway 66, Ashland, OR 97520. (541) 482-4311. Bob Harvey, pro. 9 holes. 3,020 yards. Par 36. Grass tees. Course ratings: men B69.1/119; women—B75.0/ 127, F70.5/116. Year Opened: 1927. Architects: Founders. Economical, jr. rates, credit cards. Call for reservations. Walk-on chances: Fair. Walkability: Good. Playability: Decent challenges await at public nine east of Ashland.*

Owned by the city of Ashland, Oak Knoll Golf Course was built on a farm once owned by the Wells family. The cemetery plot of this pioneering clan borders the 4th hole. The Wells' patriarch, born in 1789, was one of southern Oregon's earliest settlers. Oak Knoll's interesting heritage was once discussed in a *Golf Digest* article. Ashland is the home of the internationally-recognized Oregon Shakespearean Festival, as well as the Oregon State Ballet, Oregon Dance Theatre, and Southern Oregon University.

The 1927-opened course was designed and built by local golfers. Following a temporary conversion to a sheep ranch, the nine-holer reopened in the late-1930s. The 100-acre layout sprawls over a meadow and foothills situated at an elevation of 2,000 feet. The city may make significant changes to the layout by the year 2000. The plan involves rebuilding some holes to make room for a driving range. Earlier plans to add a back nine are on hold indefinitely. Head pro Bob Harvey replaced Oak Knoll's long-time pro and former PGA Tourer, Buddy Sullivan, in 1996.

The course is visited by deer and geese, while vistas include the towering Siskiyou Mountains and Pilot Rock on 7,500-foot Mount Ashland. Nine-hole rounds at Oak Knoll can generally be accomplished in less than two-and-a-half hours. The dual-tee layout traverses terrain ranging from gently rolling to fairly steep, and stretches 6,035 yards over two circuits. Oak Knoll's players enjoy lush conditions, white-sand bunkers around greens, good directional signs, and some slick and tricky putting surfaces. Tough holes include the 455-yard, par-4 3rd, which spans a sidehill, and the 5th, a 520-yard par-5 with a water-fronted tee.

Oakway Golf Course

2000 Cal Young Road, Eugene, OR 97401. (541) 484-1927. Tom DeCuman, pro. 18 holes. 3,576 yards. Par 61. Grass tees. Course ratings: men 58.6/91, women 59.0/92. Years Opened: 1929 (original course); 1972 (current course). Architects: Founders (original course); John Zoller Sr. (current course). Moderate, jr./sr. rates, credit cards. No reservations. Walkability: Good. Playability: Goodly amount of hazards complicate executive-length course.

18

During its original incarnation, Oakway was a regulation 18-holer. Today, it's a nicely-manicured, well-hazardized 18-hole executive track. The course occupies farmland once tilled by Cal Young, the Eugene pioneer who settled the area in the late-1800s. Young's homestead, part of which is now underneath Eugene Country Club as well as this course, was at one time crossed by Indians who came to fish for steelhead in the nearby Willamette River. In addition to being one of Lane County's first land commissioners, Cal Young was the University of Oregon's original football coach.

Oakway opened with nine holes in 1929. Ralph Hope bought the course and part of Young's homestead in 1947. He later turned it over to his son, Bob Hope, who designed and built a championship-length layout that stretched 7,000 yards. Hope reduced the course to its current 60-acre parcel in 1972, building houses on the western half of the original venue. Before it was shortened and the residences were constructed, Oakway was a prime habitat for foxes, raccoons, pheasants, skunks, possums and deer.

The current 3,576-yard layout was designed by John Zoller, Sr., the father of Portland's golf director and a leading golf administrator in northern California. In September 1992, Hope and co-owners Alice and Dave Shirey sold Oakway to Eugene businessman, John Hammer, who's added several bunkers and upgraded maintenance practices. In 1996, Hammer removed a troublesome trap on the 10th fairway. Future plans include building a new 9th tee, a move that will force players to drive over a pond.

Considered by its owner as "Oregon's Finest Executive 18," Oakway winds through towering groves of oak, ash, fir, and maple trees. The parkland layout involves three ponds and nearly three dozen sand traps. Six holes—the 12th through 17th—are separated from the rest of the course by Spyglass Road, a residential thoroughfare leading to upscale homes. Oakway's holes range in length from 104 to 333 yards, with the par-4s featuring left- and right-turning fairways that need accuracy to stay within their tight confines.

Ocean Dunes Golf Links

3345 Munsel Lake Road, Florence, OR 97439. (541) 997-3232 or 1-800-468-4833. 18 holes. 6,200 yards. Par 72. Grass tees. Course ratings (to be re-rated in 1997): men—B68.5/124, M67.4/122; women—M72.8/134, F69.5/124. Year Opened: 1959 (original nine); 1990 (second nine). Architects: Fred Federspiel (original nine); William Robinson (second nine & remodel). Moderate, credit cards. Call for reservations. Walk-on chances: Fair. Walkability: Fair, with some up-and-down traverses over sand dunes. Playability: Very tight fairways gaining width with ongoing remodels.

18

Ocean Dunes Golf Links is owned by golf architect William Robinson and his partner, Ted Johnson of Hadley, Massachusetts. Johnson co-owns Hickory Ridge Country Club in Hadley with his brother, and operates Montgomery Rose Company, the largest rose grower east of the Mississippi River. After becoming part-owner of Ocean Dunes in the late 1980s, Robinson designed a second nine holes and initiated a major remodel resulting in 16 new or rebuilt holes. The most recent changes—aimed at adding length to the former 5,700-yard, par-70 layout—are new 4th and 5th fairways in 1996. Both par-4s, the 4th is now a 380-yarder while the 5th stretches 417 yards. In 1997, the par-4 16th became a par-5, and the 2nd got 150 more yards and is now a 510-yard par-5. Future plans include moving the 3rd hole—making it a par-3 with a ravine-fronted tee, and widening the 16th hole.

All the changes have added 500 yards to the course and bumped its par to 72. The original front nine is now considerably stronger, with wider and fairer holes. Greens superintendent Mark Shephard has overseen the work. Ocean Dunes began in 1959 with nine holes lined by pines and rhododendrons. Appropriately, it was named Rhodo Dunes. In 1979, a Gladstone construction firm, Lam and Irving, bought the facility and changed its name to Florence Golf Club. The scorecard during that period described the venue as "a beautiful course bordered by the world's largest sand trap." The name still fits as towering dunes, some over 60 feet tall, define the personality of Ocean Dunes Golf Links.

During their ownership, Robinson and Johnson have added land to their 120-acre parcel. The extra acreage has allowed the development of homesites and a cart barn. It's possible that a new clubhouse will be built in the future. Florence receives 70-plus inches of precipitation annually. The rainy climate, however, has no ill effect on this course, which sits on 100 inches of sand. Because Ocean Dunes is close to the Pacific Ocean, with views of crashing surf available from higher points, wind raises havoc with golf shots, particularly in the afternoons. According to Shephard, who's worked here since 1979, the best time to play is in the morning when the wind is negligible. Other natural attributes include visits from deer, bears, raccoons, nutrias and shorebirds.

Ocean Dunes warrants a "links" designation, with its well-conditioned f airways running between sand dunes marked by sparse vegetation and clumps of coastal grasses. Sand traps aren't needed as sand engirds every fairway. Straying off the beaten path is not advised at Ocean Dunes; golf balls lying in the sand are not often observable because of glare from the sun. Good tests include the 6th, a 472-yard par-5 that runs narrowly over a dune. The "S-shaped" fairway bears west—into the teeth of the prevailing winds—on a path that skirts sand along its entire left edge. The 6th eventually curls downhill and left to a small front-tilting green. The 385-yard, par-4 8th heads windward and slightly uphill. The hole runs between trees and OB right and dunes left to a front-banked, trapped-left green. Perhaps the most difficult hole on the back side is the 16th, which can play two or three clubs longer when the wind is high. The hole descends off a raised tee, then rises up to a large, right-front-sloping green ringed by dunes covered with bunch grass.

Quail Point Golf Course - semiprivate

9

1200 Mira Mar Avenue, Medford, OR 97504. (541) 857-7000. Tom Kohler, pro. 9 holes. 3,369 yards. Par 35. Grass tees. Course ratings: men—B69.4/123, M68.0/120, 164.8/109, F64.2/108; women—M73.4/131, 169.0/117, F68.4/115. Year Opened: 1993. Architect: Bob Foster. Moderate. Reservations: Call 10 days ahead. Walk-on chances: Fair. Walkability: Fair, with some steep hills. Playability: Nine-holer crosses promontory overlooking Interstate 5 and Rogue River Valley.

Nine-hole Quail Point is within Rogue Valley Manor, a Medford retirement community. The layout spans a hill; its fairways and greens tip side-to-side. Quail Point originally opened as a private course for manor residents, but it couldn't survive with that restricted number of players. The $1.7-million course was designed by Bob Foster of San Diego, and was built by Oregon Landscaping and Design. Rogue Valley Manor's owners have plans for another nine holes, to be situated on a former pear orchard to the southeast. The project backers have permits for the expansion, and work may begin as early as 1997. The 252-acre plan also includes a driving range, three practice greens and open-space buffers.

Though situated amid homes and alongside a freeway, Quail Point is quiet. The elevated site offers tremendous views of Medford and the Rogue River Valley. When visiting here in September 1996, I found some of fairway turf in so-so condition; the greens, however, were fine. The tees are square-shaped, a la Pumpkin Ridge, with taller grass around the short-cut areas. Quail Point golfers park in a lot across Mira Mar Avenue from the small pro shop, and must cross this road three times during a nine-hole round.

Among the better holes is the 2nd, a 381-yard par-4 with a creek-fronted tee and an uphill fairway skirting OB and houses on the left. The hole concludes at a front-banked green trapped twice at the left-front. The 371-yard, par-4 5th features an elevated tee and a dogleg-left fairway that winds around a pond and residences. A sign at the tee warns, "Don't Attempt to Hit Over Homes." The rolling hole tilts to the right en route to a mid-sized, left-front-leaning green trapped right-front; trees lurk close to its left edge. The 366-yard, par-4 6th crosses severely right-tilting ground. Over its last leg, the hole angles uphill leftward to a hill-cut, right-sloping green with a wood-planked trap on the right. The top-rated 7th, a 417-yard par-4, is lined by OB and I-5 on the left. The trench-like, left-sloping fairway curls uphill to a radical two-tiered putting surface trapped (oddly in my estimation) about 40 yards before its left-front flank.

Red Mountain Golf Course

324 North Schoolhouse Creek Road, Grants Pass, OR 97526. (541) 479-2297. 9 holes. 1,118 yards. Par 28. Grass tees. No course ratings. Year Opened: 1988. Architect: Bob Snook. Economical. No reservations. Walkability: Good. Playability: Conditions improving at short nine.

Red Mountain Golf Course lies about 10 miles north of Grants Pass. Take the Merlin exit off Interstate 5 and go to Monument Drive; travel to North Schoolhouse Creek Road and the course. The 13-acre layout was originated by Bob Snook. Snook called the place Shoestring Golf Course after his "shoestring" operating budget for the place. Since taking over the course after his father died, Dave Snook renamed it and began making improvements. Snook's work has included revamping the greens to USGA specifications, upgrading landscaping, and adding power carts.

The dual-tee track features a 1,118-yard, par-28 front nine and a par-29, 1,127-yard back. The course name comes from Red Mountain, located about a half-mile away. The peak's colorful moniker came through its high concentration of oxenite, a rubescent mineral. The layout is generally flat, with a couple of its tree-lined fairways imperiled by water hazards. Red Mountain is home to deer, bobcats, squirrels, birds and elk, and affords a pleasant outing in the countryside.

Riveridge Golf Course

18 *3800 North Delta Highway, Eugene, OR 97401. (541) 345-9160. Ric Jeffries, pro. 18 holes. 6,256 yards. Par 71. Grass tees. Course ratings: men—B68.6/116, M67.2/ 112; women—M69.0/116, F67.7/112. Years Opened: 1989 (original nine); 1990 (second nine). Architect: Ric Jeffries. Moderate, sr. rates, credit cards. Reservations: Call a week ahead. Walk-on chances: Fair. Walkability: Good. Playability: Newer course gradually getting upgrades which make it tougher.*

Eighteen-hole Riveridge stretches across 107 acres beside the Willamette River in Eugene's north end. Take the North Delta Highway exit off Beltline to get here. The layout was designed by Ric Jeffries, who also owns the place with his wife Debbie. Jeffries, a Class A pro, plied his trade in Florida before returning to his Oregon roots and becoming a proprietor of this course. Besides a lush and enjoyable layout, the facility features a clubhouse and a state-of-the-art driving range. The practice facility contains 25 covered and lighted stalls as well as grass tees and laser-measured target greens. Jeffries and his staff offer extensive lesson programs.

Riveridge opened with nine holes on June 1, 1989; the second (back) side was finished the following year. Recent improvements include new bunkers at the 1st, 6th and 12th holes, and a pond on the 14th. Parts of the course traverse open ground, with fairways lined by recently-planted English oak, fir, hemlock and maple trees. The remainder of Riveridge winds through old-growth trees and wetlands off the Willamette. Water hazards—creeks and ponds—are a considerable threat on the more restrictive back nine.

Each hole has three tees, enabling Riveridge to be player-adaptable. Interesting tests include the top-rated 2nd, a 532-yard par-5 with a straight and rolling fairway guarded by a water-filled ditch and pond on the left, with OB right. The hole concludes at a saddle-shaped, front-tilting green backed by the Willamette. A challenge typical of the tight back side is found at the 12th, a 319-yard par-4 with a pond-fronted tee. The right-turning hole curls through trees en route to a shallow-but-wide green. This tough target is guarded by a depression that fills with water in winter and spring, then metamorphoses back into a grass bunker in summer and fall.

Sandpines Golf Resort

18 *1201 35th Street, Florence, OR 97439. (541) 997-1940 or 1-800-917-4653. Jim Skaugstad, pro. 18 holes. 6,954 yards. Par 72. Grass tees. Course ratings: men—T74.0/ 129, B71.7/125, M69.5/120; women—M75.7/129, F71.1/123. Year Opened: 1993. Architect: Rees Jones. Expensive, jr. rates. Reservations: Call two weeks ahead. Walk-on chances: Fair. Walkability: About as good as can be expected considering sprawling nature of course. Playability: Among the finest links layouts on the West Coast.*

Named the Best New Public Course of 1993 by *Golf Digest*, this exceptional layout was designed by noted architect, Rees Jones. Venturing to Florence for his first project west of the Mississippi River, Jones took a rugged site and transformed it into something special. The layout lies 400 feet from the Siuslaw River's entrance into the Pacific Ocean. Twelve holes cross dunes while the rest of the course weaves through a pine forest. Despite an annual rainfall average of 65 inches, the layout enjoys excellent drainage because of a 10-foot sandy base.

Sandpines was originated by Floreco, a limited partnership headed by Jack Roack and Ellis Vandehey. Initially, the developers had a tough time attracting players to the course. As a result, the 290-acre project—which was to include 147 single-family homes, over 170 townhouses, an RV park and hotel—was taken over by its primary creditor, Kenzo Ariki, a businessman who owns Izu Golf Club in Tokyo. At the end of 1996, the residential part of the project was on hold, since only 10 houses had been built. An upscale clubhouse has also been tabled for a later date. But Ariki has provided stability for Sandpines, improving the playing conditions and drawing more and more players. Course upgrades have included a greenside bunker at the 11th, and a nine-hole putting course that may eventually be expanded to 18. Drainage was also modified in wet areas between the 3rd and 13th holes, and on the 2nd.

The turf—bentgrass fairways and tees, fescue roughs and Pennlinks greens—grows remarkably well in this salty environment. Though sprawling over 175 acres, the Scottish-style links is easy to walk. The course lies on a 55-million-gallon aquifer called the Clear Lake Watershed; samples are taken from five irrigation wells to make sure chemicals are not contaminating the groundwater. Another interesting aspect of the course is that it follows a dune-stabilization program, which involves planting native seagrasses and erecting fences. The plan has halted an annual shift of 10 to 12 feet of dunes, thus preventing sand from overrunning the course.

Sandpines has at least four tees per hole to make it very player-adaptable. Concrete cart paths extend to the ends of tees, but not alongside or in fairways. The layout contains over 70 bunkers and three lakes—encompassing 14 acres—in the field of play. Views of Pacific surf are available from several holes, while deer, elk and shorebirds inhabit the grounds. Indigenous flora includes shore pines and salal, with huge rhododendrons and wildflowers scattered about. In 1996, *Golf Digest* once again recognized Sandpines, giving the course the Number 1 spot in its listing of the nation's "Top-75 Affordable Courses." It also received four-and-a-half stars in the magazine's "Places to Play 1996-'97" guide.

Sandpines' toughest holes include the 6th, a 426-yard par-4 that winds right-ward over rolling ground to a knoll-perched green fronted by grass bunkers. The 9th, a 471-yard par-4, runs straight and long toward a bi-bunkered green. The 13th, a 449-yard par-4, contains a pine-ringed tee and a right-curling, mound-lined fairway that stretches to a slick putting surface trapped twice in front. Perhaps the most treacherous par-3 on the course is the 203-yard 17th. The par-3 features a massive, tee-to-green pond that guards a skinny-but-deep, trapped-right green.

Stewart Meadows Golf Course

1301 South Holly Street, Medford, OR 97501. (541) 770-6554. Dan Coughlin, pro. 9 holes. 2,658 yards. Par 35. Grass tees. Course ratings: men—B67.6/119, B/M66.5/116, M65.4/113; women—M69.6/114, M/F68.1/114, F66.6/114. Year Opened: 1994. Architect: Chuck Mangum. Moderate, jr./sr. rates. Reservations: Call a week ahead. Walk-on chances: Fair. Walkability: Good. Playability: Bunkers and ponds dot newer nine-hole track.

Stewart Meadows Golf Course lies south of Medford off Interstate 5's Barnett Street exit. The course was originated by the owners of Medford's KOGAP Manufacturing Company, a firm headed by Jerry Lausman. Jerry's son Craig helped build the course and is the greens superintendent. The Lausmans own property south of this 62-acre layout; in the future, they may convert the pear orchard currently there into a back nine.

Stewart Meadows' enjoyable, easy-to-walk course provides a good challenge for beginning to intermediate players. The dual-tee layout features a modest-sized, modern clubhouse and a driving range (located to the north and accessible by a separate road). The back nine stretches about 250 yards farther than its alter ego. When here on a warm afternoon in September 1996, I observed many youngsters plying these fairways, some searching their bags for replacements to balls lost in Stewart Meadows' water hazards.

Good tests include the top-rated 2nd, a 349-yard par-4 with "Doc's Pond" right of the tee. The right-tilting fairway winds leftward around a bunker before rising to a wide, rolling green trapped right-front, left and rear. The 324-yard, par-4 4th heads straight. Two trees sit in mid-fairway, and a hidden bunker-backed pond lurks along the right at the 150-yard mark. The raised 4th green is trapped twice in front and once on the rear. The right-curling 6th, a 330-yard par-4, has a creek along the right and two traps at the turn. The creek fattens into a pond that runs up to guard the right-front flank of a large, trapped-left-front green. Another water hazard shimmers behind this putting surface. The 450-yard, par-5 9th receives another 50 yards when played as the 18th, making it the course's longest hole. The tee bears a pond along the right, then the narrow route goes to a front-banked green trapped right-front and left-rear.

Stewart Park Golf Course

9 *1005 West Stewart Parkway, Roseburg, OR 97470. (541) 672-4592. Steve McNelly, pro. 9 holes. 3,123 yards. Par 35. Course ratings: men—B69.8/114, M67.6/110; women—M73.8/119, F73.5/118. Year Opened: 1956. Architect: Roseburg Parks Department. Economical, sr. rates, credit cards. Reservations: Call a week ahead. Walk-on chances: Fair. Walkability: Good. Playability: Decent course within Roseburg's most popular park.*

Owned by the city of Roseburg, this nine-holer lies within a like-named park with recreational fields. Also nearby is the Roseburg VA Golf Course, which is open only to patients and hospital volunteers. A wildlife refuge north of Stewart Park's course is a habitat for ducks and deer. The city built the public course and adjoining athletic fields in 1956. Stewart Park's golf operations are overseen by head pro Steve McNelly, an employee of the concessionaire, Fore Golf Enterprises. Recent upgrades include a covered and lighted driving range.

The 45-acre course crosses generally flat terrain, and lies on clayey soil that drains poorly after heavy rains. For well over a decade, the city has discussed joining the VA Hospital course with this one to create an 18-hole track. But the linkage of courses has not come about as this facility serves alcohol, a taboo element at the VA venue. When mowed low, Stewart Park's "push-up" greens are quick; six holes are imperiled by sand traps and water hazards. Noteworthy tests include the left-turning 4th, a 435-yard par-4 that skirts a pond en route to a knoll-perched green. The 6th, a 306-yard par-4 rated among Oregon's "worst holes" in a recent poll conducted by Portland's *Oregonian* newspaper, fishhooks 180 degrees to the left. The hole initially ascends onto a well-treed hill, then curls left and backward past oaks and a pond to a tiny green. The 403-yard, par-4 9th runs straight between trees to a front-tilting green.

Stoneridge Golf Club

500 East Antelope Road, Eagle Point, OR 97524. (541) 830-4653. Jim Staal, pro. 18 holes. 6,738 yards. Par 72. Grass tees. Course ratings: men—C72.5/132, B70.6/ 127, M68.3/118; women—M72.8/130, F68.4/114. Year Opened: 1995. Architect: Jim Cochran. Moderate, credit cards. Reservations: Call a week ahead. Walk-on chances: Fair. Walkability: Fair; once past the first few holes, course is flat and easy to walk. Playability: Tough, danger-filled track loaded with interesting holes.

18

Stoneridge Golf Club is the brainchild of its owner, Jim Cochran. This is the first golf course designed by Cochran, who prepared for the task by traveling up and down the West Coast researching layouts and absorbing all that he found interesting and tough for golfers. Such intense preparation paid off, as Stoneridge is one helluva course. Built by the Ashland firm, Hawaiian Island Golf, to Cochran's specifications, Stoneridge features two distinctly different sets of holes. The initial section of the course follows the steep slope of a hillside, while the majority of the holes are flat and involve water hazards. The tippier fairways are lined by pines, while oaks line the flatter portions of the course. Regardless of the hole type, Stoneridge offers an arresting series of challenges.

The course was named after a previous use of the site. During World War II, troops here practiced building the kinds of stone fences found in battles in the European theater. Some stoneridges cross a few holes. Also, an active rock quarry is in operation up the hill above the course. Quarry workers call the pro shop to tell Stoneridge's staff of their blast schedule. In turn, the employees warn golfers not to be too alarmed when a loud boom causes them to jump out of their socks in mid-swing. According to golfers, these quarry explosions feel like an earthquake.

While touring the course in fall of 1996, I didn't experience any blasts from above. Instead, I found a thoroughly modern, upscale layout that rivals Robert Trent Jones Jr.'s new Quail Point track in all ways except price; Stoneridge is quite a bit cheaper. Though not quite up to Eagle Point's lofty conditioning standards, Stoneridge enjoys a more topographically-diverse site, a comparable amount of hazards, and some wild and wavy greens. Some of these putting surfaces are very tricky, with assorted humps and bumps, tiers and "buried elephants" complicating their negotiability. Sections of the fairway turf were patchy and rough, owing to Stoneridge's newness, and the paths were graveled and dusty. This latter deficiency would be addressed in 1997 when, I was told, all the paths will be asphalted.

Stoneridge's initial leg heads up the hill, making the first two holes dandies. The tree-lined 1st, a 544-yard par-5, goes left, then reverses itself and rises steeply rightward to a right-tilting, bi-tiered green trapped right-front and left. The 2nd, a 380-yard par-4, has a tee fronted by a stone fence. The rolling fairway skirts trees right and jail left. A hidden pond lurks along the right 100 yards from a severely left-tilting, terraced green. The 4th, a 326-yard par-4, features a panoramic tee and a downhill, jail-lined fairway that leans to the right. Bunkers pinch the front and left edges of the long and deep 4th green, which is further squeezed by a pond on the right. The top-rated 5th, a 428-yard par-4, features a towering tee and a lake right of the landing area. Over its final 100 yards, the hole narrows before reaching a mid-sized, right-front-sloping green with a tall back end. The 400-yard, par-4 7th has the right half of its fairway eaten up by a huge pond that extends all the way to the green. Highway 140 parallels the hole's left side, and a bunker sits along the left driving distance out. Another water hazard guards the left-front of a large, rolling green protected on the right by a grass trap and the aforementioned pond.

The 529-yard, par-5 12th contains a pond left of its wide and flat route. The hole goes straight for 450 yards or so, then winds sharply left between a pond and a bunker to a water-fronted green. The slightly uphill 13th, a 434-yard par-4, has a pond lining its entire left edge, while mounds are on the right. The rolling 13th green is protected left by a pond. The par-3 16th may be Stoneridge's signature hole. The 163-yarder ascends to a steeply front-tilting green trapped left-front; a creek and pretty waterfall embellish the scene along the right. The 398-yard, par-4 18th descends off a raised tee toward a fairway-crossing creek at the 150-yard mark. Here, the hole winds precisely rightward around oaks. The radically undulating 18th green has very steep tiers in its right-rear edge and left half. A tree towers over its right-front entry, bunkers guard the right-rear and left-front edges and, oh, I almost forgot, the target is crossed in front by another stream.

Sunset Bay Golf Club

9

11001 Cape Arago Highway, Coos Bay, OR 97420. (541) 888-9301. 9 holes. 3,020 yards. Par 36. Grass tees. Course ratings: men 68.0, women 69.7 (no slope). Year Opened: 1967. Architect: John Zoller, Sr. Moderate, jr. rates, credit cards. No reservations. Walkability: Good, overall. Playability: Excellent conditioning a hallmark of this coastal venue.

Considered a "labor of love" by its owners, Larry and Rosalie Hyatt, Sunset Bay is a fine nine-hole layout on Cape Arago. The facility adjoins Sunset Bay State Park on Oregon's rugged central coast. The Hyatts have owned the course—and a total of 600 acres—since 1983. A back nine designed by Sunset Bay's architect, John Zoller Sr., has been roughed in, but won't be open for several years. The Hyatts are taking their time with this addition, concentrating instead on upgrading conditioning of the existing layout, improving drainage, and paving cart paths.

Despite Hyatts' large land holdings, Sunset Bay will remain in its natural form; the couple will never develop peripheral housing. The dual-tee track—extending 5,700 yards over two circuits—is popular with RVers staying in nearby Charleston State Park. It's also a hot spot for private tournaments; events with upwards of 120 players are permissable. According to Larry, many families and groups return year after year. Wildlife visitors include black-tailed deer, muskrats and a variety of coastal birdlife. Sea lions can be heard barking on rocks in the nearby bay.

The allure of the place is understandable. Sunset Bay's holes span an impressive 100-acre plot. Crossing a wooded valley close to the Pacific Ocean, the course is split by Big Creek, a troublesome water hazard involved on eight holes. Fairways are squeezed by old-growth hemlocks, blue and Sitka spruces, alders and berry bushes. The greens are mowed low and have quite a bit of pace. A representative hole of Sunset Bay is the 5th, a 330-yard par-4 with a creek-fronted tee and a fairway that winds leftward between woodlands to a fast green guarded left-front by a pond.

Private Courses

Coquille Valley Elks Golf Club

Off Highway 42, Myrtle Point, OR 97458. (541) 572-5367. 9 holes. 2,342 yards. Par 33. Grass tees. Course ratings: men—B62.0/100, B/M61.5/97; women F66.0/ 103. Year Opened: 1938. Architect: Clarence Sutton. Elks Lodge members, guests & reciprocates.

This facility in southwest Oregon is used exclusively by Elks club members. It's located four miles from Coquille in a verdant valley above Highway 42. Designed by Oregon golf pro Clarence Sutton, the course was built in 1938 by a local farmer. The dual-tee layout involves a 2,216-yard front nine and a 2,342-yard back. Both play to a par of 33. Parts of the course involve wide fairways, while holes on the northwest edge are hillier and more densely treed. A creek runs through the midsection of this tidy track, where golfers might spot deer, raccoons, minks and ducks. Coquille Valley's big annual event is the Oregon State Elks tournament on Labor Day.

Eagles on the Green

1375 Irving Road, Eugene, OR 97404. (541) 688-9471. 9 holes. 1,295 yards. Par 27. Grass tees. No course ratings. Year Opened: 1962. Architect: Jack Davis. Eagles members & guests.

Originally a public 18-hole par-3 called Green Acres, this venue in northwest Eugene is now a private nine played by members of the Fraternal Order of Eagles Lodge #275 and their guests. The course was built in 1962 by Jack Davis, who sold it to Max Bayless in 1966. In 1972, Bayless sold eight of the course's 18 acres to the Eugene Water and Electric Board, which built a substation on the property, a move that cut the layout in half. Six years after buying the course in 1981, the Eagles built a clubhouse with a 400-seat banquet space which is converted into a dance floor for member events. The structure also contains a restaurant, lounge and game room.

Though short, the Eagles' track plays tough, with full-grown trees squeezing fairways, water hazards invading five holes, and the greens small and slick. The layout is ringed by homes, filbert trees and railroad tracks. Overseen by managers Dick Cramer and Gene Hoover, Eagles on the Green receives maintenance help from a revolving group of 35 member-volunteers.

Eugene Country Club

255 Country Club Road, Eugene, OR 97401. (541) 344-5124. Ron Weber, pro. 18 holes. 6,837 yards. Par 72. Grass tees. Course ratings: men—B73.9/136, M71.7/ 133, I68.9/123; women—M78.1/149, I74.7/138, F73.4/135. Year Opened: 1926 (current course). Architect: H. Chandler Egan; Robert Trent Jones, Jr. (remodel). Members, guests & reciprocates.

Founded in 1899, Eugene Country Club is one of the region's oldest continuously-operated golf clubs. It's also home for one of the Northwest's revered courses, one regularly in *Golf Digest's* list of America's 100 Greatest Golf Courses. Only

One of Eugene's fine par-3s is the 200-yard 7th.

Sahalee in Redmond, Washington and, more recently, Pumpkin Ridge near Portland, approximate Eugene's high regard among the recognized appraisers of superior golf courses. The layout has certainly hosted its share of top tournaments. Among these are the Oregon Open in 1928, the Trans-Mississippi Women's tournament in 1961 and 1974, USGA Junior Amateur in 1964 (won by Johnny Miller), several men's and women's PAC-10 golf championships, two NCAA Men's Championships and the 1993 USGA Mid-Amateur. It also serves as the site for the Pacific Coast Amateur every four years (1999 is the next date). My only question is: Why hasn't Eugene Country Club been selected to host a men's or women's U.S. Open?

Eugene Country Club was begun by a handful of local businessmen and professors from the University of Oregon. The original course was a primitive nine-holer with sand greens located off South Willamette Street. The founders "conditioned" the layout by burning tall grass off fairways and pouring oil on the sand greens to smooth their surfaces. A herd of goats mowed fairways. By 1912, the members began a subscription drive to acquire more land for a new course. In 1922, they purchased 135 acres and, the following year, hired noted Medford amateur golfer, H. Chandler Egan, to design an 18-hole course. The new layout was formally dedicated in 1926, with Ted Gardner the head pro. In 1936, Wendell Wood succeeded Gardner and began a 40-year term at the club. Eugene's head pro today is Ron Weber, a Prineville native who previously worked at The Woodlands in Texas.

In 1967, the club had Robert Trent Jones, Jr. renovate the 40-year-old course. Jones enlarged and raised the greens, repositioned and reversed tees and greens, and replaced the irrigation system. The current course has changed little since Jones' exquisite remodel, which retained Egan's traditional design while lending modern elements. A magnificent combination of new and old golf architecture, Eugene features awesome landscaping; gardens, manicured ponds and carefully-cut trees lend it a regal beauty. The immaculately conditioned course is noted for its huge and deep, tough-to-escape bunkers; towering deciduous and coniferous trees along fairways and near greens; generally small and wildly sloping, steep-sided greens; hazard-strewn par-3s; and relentless hole-after-hole challenge.

Well-established, upscale residences ring the course which, despite its position amid homes, hosts lots of wildlife—especially ducks and geese. The layout is eminently walkable. Gravel cart paths border tees but stop there; there are no cart paths through fairways. Particularly tough holes include the straight and rolling 4th, a 408-yard par-4 that runs past a tree-veiled pond and a bunker along the right. The fairway winds up to an undulating, front-left-tilting green trapped right-rear, front-left and front-right. The lovely 5th, a 185-yard par-3, contains a pond-fronted, hill-cut green. The wide-but-shallow target leans toward the water, while three traps squeeze its back edge. The top-rated 6th, a 545-yard par-5, is a long, uphill dogleg-right that winds around two traps while passing another bunker outside the turn. At about the 300-yard mark, the fairway descends rightward over right-leaning ground to a pond-fronted, two-tiered green trapped along the back.

The 450-yard, par-4 9th is a lengthy right-turner that skirts a trap along the left. The fairway winds narrowly uphill between fruit trees to a large, crowned green trapped twice in front. The 10th, a 401-yard par-4, follows a slightly right-bending route between spruces, firs and maples on the right and fruit trees left. Two bunkers squat along the left as the fairway heads to the right toward a raised, domed green with a tier through its midsection and traps right and left. The 400-yard, par-4 11th traces a tight path that descends somewhat off the tee. At the 165-yard mark, an eight-foot-high berm crosses the fairway. The route then curls narrowly rightward to a steeply right-front-tilting green guarded by a hidden pond and two traps in front, with a bunker and another pond behind.

Yet another great Eugene par-3 is the 12th, a 183-yarder that requires a precise drive between trees to an elevated, pond-fronted and steeply front-banked green trapped twice on the rear. The 525-yard, par-5 13th heads straight past OB on the left. The rolling fairway is flanked along the right by trees and houses and a bunker left before rising to a small, knoll-perched green trapped front, right, right-rear and left. The 15th, a 410-yard par-4, is a lengthy, tree-etched left-bender that concludes at a steeply front-sloping green trapped twice in front and once each left and rear. The 433-yard, par-4 18th goes slightly downhill along a—for Eugene Country Club anyway—fairly wide path. Bunkers lurk along the right about 140 yards from a very slick, severely right-front-tilting green trapped laterally.

Rogue Valley Country Club

2660 Hillcrest Road, Medford, OR 97504. (541) 772-4050. Jim Wise, pro. 27 holes. Grass tees. Course ratings: Original Course (6,729 yards, par 72): men—B72.6/130, M70.5/128, I69.8/125; women—M76.8/134, F73.9/129. Number 1 Course (6,666 yards, par 72): men—B72.1/128, M70.3/126, I68.2/121; women—M74.5/130, F70.1/122. Number 2 Course (6,550 yards, par 70): men—B72.0/128, M70.0/124; women—M77.1/133, F75.3/132. Years Opened: 1920 (original nine); 1928 (second nine); 1961 (third nine). Architects: H. Chandler Egan (original and second nines); Ron Caperna (third nine); Robert Muir Graves (remodel). Members, guests & reciprocates.

A private 27-holer on Medford's eastern edge, Rogue Valley lies amid homes off Black Oak and Hillcrest roads. Rogue Valley's scrolls list 675 golfing members and 500 social members, and the course averages 90,000 rounds a year. Rogue Valley has annually hosted the Southern Oregon Amateur for over 60 years. This Labor Day tournament is the largest match-play event west of the Mississippi River, with a

The 16th at Rogue Valley's Rogue Course is a 486-yard par-5.

464-player field. The course has also been the site of the Oregon Amateur, USGA Junior Qualifying, as well as other regional tourneys.

Rogue Valley began with nine holes in 1920; the second nine followed eight years later. Designed by former U.S. Amateur champion and Medford's best-ever golfer, H. Chandler Egan, Rogue Valley's original 18 slaked the members' needs until 1961, when a third nine was built. The final set of holes was designed by Rogue Valley's head pro at the time, Ron Caperna. The golf operations are now overseen by Jim Wise, the head pro here since 1981.

The nines are arranged as follows: The Number One Course (also called "The Rogue") involves holes 1 through 18, while Inside Course Number Two (also called "The Oaks") is routed separately, with its holes numbered 1 through 9. (The above ratings are a mix-and-match of the three nines.) Over 1994-95, the Number One Course was extensively remodeled by Robert Muir Graves. The work, done by Transpacific Construction, involved building four tees per hole and adding five new greens. Also during that time a new clubhouse was erected. Hallmarks of Rogue Valley's 27 holes include excellent conditioning, efficient and easy-to-walk passages, great views of its namesake valley and the Siskiyou Mountains, and mature ornamentals, firs, pines and oaks along fairways.

Tough holes on The Rogue include the 3rd, a 380-yard par-4 that ascends along a gradually tapering path that crests 200 yards out. Here, the right-sloping hole winds rightward to a raised, mound-ringed green trapped left. The top-rated 5th, a narrow 428-yard par-4, heads straight between a bunker right and a trap, trees and creek left. The route rises over its last 100 yards to a mid-sized and rolling, trapped-left green. The pretty 7th, a 335-yard par-4, goes downhill and straight. A pond eats up the right two-thirds of the fairway over its final 75 yards. The water runs up to protect the right-front edge of a diminutive, front-tilting green trapped twice in front.

The 423-yard, par-4 10th heads narrowly uphill along a right-turning route, sloping toward mounds and trees on the left. At the 150-yard mark, the hole drops to a smallish, front-tilting green with grass bunkers in front.

The 193-yard, par-3 11th heads down to a wide-but-shallow, V-shaped green guarded right-front by a pond and right-rear by a bunker. The 12th, a 603-yard par-5, goes straight before winding sharply rightward 225 yards out. Trees occupy the turn while a power station and OB line the hole along the left. At the 200-yard mark, the 12th descends to a severely front-leaning, hill-cut green trapped twice right and once rear. The 201-yard, par-3 13th ascends to a knoll-perched, steeply front-banked green guarded by grass bunkers in front and a sand trap right. Missing the elusive 13th green comes with a stiff penalty. The 18th, a 373-yard par-4, rises slightly along a tree-lined path. At the 150-yard mark, the hole curls rightward around a bushy spruce and climbs to a two-tiered putting surface engirded by five traps.

Lacking the recent modernization work recently done on The Rogue, the Inside nine is traditional in scope. Surprisingly, it may be tougher than its sister course. The bunkers here are deeper, the greens smaller and more severe, and the shots into greens more demanding. Tough tests include the 2nd, a 308-yard par-4 with an uphill, left-bending fairway and a very slick, hill-cut green guarded by five bunkers. The top-rated 3rd, a 429-yard par-4, veers to the right over downhill, left-tilting ground. At the 150-yard mark, the fairway narrows en route to a diminutive, left-rear-sloping green protected by high-lipped traps left and right-rear. The 5th, a 385-yard par-4, bends sharply left off the tee. Drives must carry the oaks at the corner to avoid going too far right and into deep trouble. The fairway winds up to a ridge-roosting, front-banked green trapped laterally. The 525-yard, par-5 9th is an uphill left-bender around fat bunkers. Over its last 200 yards, the hole is jailed on both sides as it curls rightward up to a large, left-sloping green trapped twice in front.

Roseburg Country Club
18

5051 NW Garden Valley Road, Roseburg, OR 97470. (541) 672-4041. Pat Huffer, pro. 18 holes. 6,329 yards. Par 71. Grass tees. Course ratings: men—B70.3/123, M68.6/121; women—M73.5/123, F70.8/116. Years Opened: 1923 (original nine); 1980 (second nine). Architects: George Junor & W.H. Nash (original nine); Gary Roger Baird (second nine); Pat Huffer & Jerry Whiteaker (remodel). Members, guests & reciprocates.

Roseburg Country Club sits west of its namesake city off Garden Valley Road. The layout sprawls over a hillside; from its higher points, golfers enjoy arresting views of the Umpqua Valley. The club began in 1923 with 97 members and nine holes. The initiation fee was $200 and monthly dues were $2.50. George Junor and W.H. Nash designed the original nine, which contained sand greens. Roseburg's first clubhouse burned to the ground in 1961. The present structure—with a pool, pro shop, locker rooms and restaurant—was dedicated in 1962. In 1979, the club purchased 55 acres and hired Gary Roger Baird, an associate of Robert Trent Jones, Sr., to design a second nine. On July 12, 1980, the expanded layout was inaugurated, with PGA touring pro Gay Brewer driving the first ball.

The golf operations at Roseburg Country Club have been overseen by head pro Pat Huffer since 1982. Besides being a good "stick" and holding Roseburg's course record of 62, Huffer was honored by the Pacific Northwest Section of the PGA with the Bill Strausbaugh Award each year from 1993 to 1996. The award goes to the PGA member who has helped bring about dramatic improvements in employment conditions at the section level.

After nixing a master plan devised by architect William Robinson in the early '90s, the members proceeded with upgrades overseen by Huffer and former greens superintendent Jerry Whiteaker, who is now at the new Myrtle Creek course. The work included remodeling the practice green; adding a new pond at the 7th; widening the 4th green; inserting a pond front-left of the 16th green; and a complete makeover of the notorious putting surface at the 17th, a three-tiered affair that caused heartbreak among nearly every golfer who tried to negotiate it. Portland's Bernhardt Golf did the work. The result is a thoroughly enjoyable layout, one with a nice mixture of contemporary putting surfaces and raised, old-style greens (such as the 12th, a severe front-leaner). Gardens embellish tee boxes and, with the addition of the ponds, considerable hazards now enter play.

Bordered by the North Umpqua River, the layout is highlighted by such holes as the 2nd, a left-sloping, 380-yard par-4 that runs straight uphill to a small, oak-ringed green. The top-rated 5th, a 413-yard par-4, winds downhill past a pond along the right. This water hazard feeds into a creek that crosses the fairway 90 yards from a front-tilting green trapped once right and twice left. The 187-yard, par-3 6th descends to a large green guarded by a pond right and two bunkers rear-left. The 7th, a 402-yard par-4, is a downhill right-bender between trees and bunkers. A pond crosses the hole 100 yards from a ridge-perched, steeply right-front-tilting green. The 8th, a 506-yard par-5, starts at an elevated tee, then winds downhill to the right past a big pond outside the turn. At the 230-yard mark, the hole curls sharply right. A big tree lurks in mid-fairway, and a pond that starts 100 yards out runs up to guard the left-front flank of an expansive green trapped left-rear. Two traps sit 30 yards in front of this target.

The 387-yard, par-4 10th has a raised tee and a dogleg-left fairway circuiting around a pond. The hole bends 70 degrees left en route to a mid-sized, sharply front-leaning green trapped right-rear. The toughest pin placement at the 10th is back-left. The 13th, a 417-yard par-4, contains a bunker-backed pond along the left about 200 yards out. Trees and dense jail line the right side of the tight landing area. The 13th ends at a two-tiered green, guarded right-front by a pond and left-rear by a trap. The 193-yard, par-3 17th rises up to a hill-cut, three-tiered green. Traps at the green's front and left-rear flanks—and a steep hill to the left—make the the 17th one of Roseburg's most difficult holes. The home hole is a left-bending 568-yard par-5. The 18th is skirted by trees right and a pond left on the way to a trapped-left-front green. This target is shadowed at its right rear by a towering oak, and has a steep left side.

Roseburg Veterans Hospital Golf Course

9 *East Stewart Parkway, Roseburg, OR 97470. No phone. 9 Holes. 2,374 yards. Par 35. Grass tees. No course ratings. Year Opened: 1961. Architect: VA Hospital staff. Patients & hospital volunteers.*

Fondly called "Aspirin Acres" by the staff at the Roseburg VA Hospital, this straightforward nine-holer was built in 1961 to provide a source of relaxation and recreation for hospital patients and volunteers. The course winds in front of the red-brick buildings in the VA Hospital section of Stewart Park. The structures at Oregon's largest military infirmary were built in the 1930s. Flat in topography, the fairways are lined by black oaks, maples and firs, and end at small, untrapped greens.

Shadow Hills Country Club

18

92512 River Road, Junction City, OR 97448. (541) 998-8441. Mark Keating, pro. 18 holes. 7,007 yards. Par 72. Grass tees. Course ratings: men—T73.8/135, B72.5/ 133, M71.2/128; women—M76.6/136, I73.2/124, F70.4/118. Year Opened: 1962. Architect: Alex Kindsfather; William Robinson (remodel). Members, guests & reciprocates.

Named after the faint-blue hills surrounding it, Shadow Hills Country Club crosses former farmland. The Alex Kindsfather-designed course opened for play in 1962. Over the years, Shadow Hills has hosted such tournaments as the Oregon Open, PNGA Ladies, and various state and regional events. Annual events include the Me & My Shadow Couples in June and the Shadow Hills Men's Invitational in August. With its locale near farms and plant nurseries, the venue is visited by foxes, deer, rabbits, squirrels, chipmunks and ducks. The club's 450 members enjoy access to a full-service clubhouse and a swimming pool.

In the early 1990s, Shadow Hills' layout underwent a massive remodel overseen by Florence architect, William Robinson. The course was stretched 400 yards and received fairway mounding, an automatic irrigation system, and large, contemporary bunkers. The generally flat layout is easy to walk. Drainage was also improved on the formerly wet track, with players enjoying drier underfooting and more roll on shots hit in fairways. Shadow Hills is increasingly in demand for tournaments as it features one of the strongest concluding six-hole sets in the Northwest.

Challenges are found at the top-rated 3rd, a 402-yard par-4 with a creek-fronted tee and a tight, bunker-squeezed area for drives. The fairway skirts a pond along the right en route to a front-sloping green trapped right-front, left and right-rear. The 182-yard, par-3 4th houses a pond that runs from the tee to the right-front edge of a big green trapped left-front. The 6th, a 428-yard par-4, has one trap in mid-fairway and two others right of the landing zone. Over its final 150 yards, the hole is narrowed by trees before reaching a front-banked green protected by a bunkers right and left-front. The right-bending 9th, a 578-yard par-5, has bunkers along the left and a hidden pond right, driving distance out for big hitters. The last leg of the hole climbs slightly to a smallish, rolling and front-leaning green trapped left-front and right-rear.

Shadow Hills' concluding six begin with the 13th, a tree-lined and left-winding 408-yard par-4. At the 210-yard mark, the hole skirts big bunkers left-front of a severely front-leaning green trapped right-rear. The 403-yard, par-4 14th has a gradually rising fairway that involves two bunkers in mounds along the right. A hidden pond crosses before the humped-in-the-middle green, which is trapped right and left-rear. The right-turning, 533-yard, par-5 15th bears bunkers inside and trees outside of its path, which horseshoes 120 degrees around a pond 200 yards out. A bunker on the left lurks 110 yards from a right-front-tilting green trapped left-front and right-rear. The 197-yard, par-3 16th features a long pond that guards the right-front edge of a rolling green trapped left-front and rear. The 433-yard, par-4 17th winds rightward between trees and a pond before arriving at a steeply front-banked green trapped right-front and right-rear. A second pond guards the green's left edge. The 541-yard, par-5 18th bends rightward around two traps; the pond from the 17th lurks along the left and is reachable. The final 250 yards rise to a medium-sized, right-front-leaning putting surface. A huge bunker located 60 yards out runs up to guard the right-front edge of the 18th green, which is also guarded by a pot bunker left-front and a slender trap in back.

Springfield Country Club

18 *90333 Marcola Road, Springfield, OR 97478. (541) 747-2517. Sadel Nahle, pro. 18 holes. 6,316 yards. Par 71. Grass tees. Course ratings: men—B70.7/123, M69.1/ 118; women—M73.9/123, F71.1/116. Years Opened: 1957 (original nine); 1983 (second nine). Architects: Sid Milligan (original nine); John Zoller, Jr. (second nine). Members, guests & reciprocates.*

Springfield Country Club is a former public course that went private in January 1992 after it signed up 550 club members. With its 1957-opened original nine (played as the back) crossing flat ground beside the Mohawk River, Springfield is frequently awash when that waterway goes over its banks. In February 1996, the course received its worst flooding in 25 years. Though most of the lower portions of the layout came through relatively unscathed, the 15th green was damaged and had to be replaced.

In 1996, the members approved a Mike Stark-designed master plan that will result in a reworking of several holes. The project also involves rebuilding several tees and greens, the addition of one and a half holes, and a new practice facility. The work may be completed by 1998. Recent upgrades include a new women's tee at the 4th.

Sid Milligan's original layout was augmented by a John Zoller, Jr.-designed nine holes in 1983. These holes, played as the front, cross the side and foot of a hill on the club's western and southern sections. From the higher points at this section of the course, golfers enjoy panoramas of a Mohawk River Valley enriched by farmlands and wildlife, including deer, birds and possums. A quirk of the newer holes are power poles and cabling off the tees at the 4th and 9th holes.

Springfield's layout is imperiled by over 20 bunkers and several ponds. The Mohawk penetrates four back-nine holes, with the 15th, a 176-yard par-3, requiring players to drive over two jogs of the river to reach a recently rebuilt green. Springfield's golf operations were recently turned over to head pro, Sadel Nahle, who stepped in to replace longtime pro, Ron Wells. Roger Vandehey is the greens superintendent.

Veterans Administration Domiciliary Golf Course

9 *Department of Veterans Affairs, White City, OR 97503. (541) 826-2111. Jim Morgan, director of golf. 9 holes. 2,018 yards. Par 33. Grass tees. No course ratings. Year Opened: 1970. Architect: Department of Veteran's Affairs. Patients & hospital staff.*

Located north of Medford in White City, this course is played by patients and employees of the VA's Domiciliary. As part of the White City Domiciliary Recreation Program, the par-33 layout serves as a recreational outlet for the patients. The tree-lined nine crosses flat, easy-to-walk terrain en route to straightforward putting surfaces. Recent improvements include drainage upgrades and a new bunker guarding the right-front edge of the 7th green. As part of a therapy program, the course and clubhouse are maintained and operated by patients and volunteers. Director of golf Jim Morgan oversees these workers. Domiciliary Golf Course hosts various tournaments throughout the year for hospitalized veterans, employees and outbound patients.

PAR-3 COURSES

Fiddler's Green Golf Course

18

91292 Highway 99 North, Eugene, OR 97402. (541) 689-8464 or 1-800-999-6565. 18 holes. 2,378 yards. Par 54. Grass tees. No course ratings. Economical, jr./sr. rates, credit cards. No reservations. Driving range.

Hosting upwards of 80,000 rounds annually, this par-3 18-holer is not only one of the region's busiest courses but it contains the Northwest's top-selling golf-equipment outlet. Situated in a building over 10,000 square feet in size, the Fiddler's Green pro shop is regularly ranked among the nation's top-100 on-course retailers by *Golf Course Operations* magazine. Also available at the full-service facility is a driving range and golf-teaching center.

The roots of Fiddler's Green stretch back to the course's previous incarnation. Originally called Country Place and opened in 1964, the layout—originated by Ben and Virginia Simpson—was designed by John Zoller, Sr. After moving to Oregon from Minnesota in 1976 and despite a lack of golf experience, Dan and Gerri Whalen bought Country Place, which had gone into decline by that time. After changing the name to Fiddler's Green, the Whalens used their retailing background to revitalize the venue. By upgrading and advertising the course, and expanding the pro shop, the Whalens gradually saw Eugene-area linksters return. Fiddler's Green is now managed by the Whalens' sons, Tim, Al and Matt.

The layout crosses 43 acres of flat terrain bordered on the west by a farm. Wildlife include nutrias, with ducks and fish in the ponds. Despite considerable play and a somewhat marshy site, Fiddler's Green endures well. The track is a cut above the par-3 genre, having ample hazards and good conditioning. A four-pronged pond enters play—off tees, in fairways and around greens—on eight holes; bunkers ring many of the small, slick greens. Holes range from 76 to 206 yards, the latter of which is considered the toughest.

Hillebrand's Paradise Ranch Resort

3

7000 D Monument Drive, Grants Pass, OR 97526. (541) 479-4333. 3 holes. 1,310 yards (three circuits). Par 28. Grass tees. No course ratings. Economical. No reservations.

Hillebrand's Paradise Ranch Resort is a dude ranch-style getaway located northwest of Grants Pass. The 380-acre reserve offers overnight accommodations, two tennis courts and horseback-riding trails. Acquired in 1989 from Computerland's founder Bill Millard by West German developer Herbert Hillebrand, owner of recreational properties around the world, the resort has been in the throes of expansion. The plan includes 125 housing units as well as a Robert Muir Graves-designed 18-hole course. In late 1996, Hillebrand halted plans for the course in order to concentrate on the homes. The project also involves a 75-unit lodge, more tennis courts, a swimming pool, spa, 250-seat conference room and restaurant.

Until the new golf course is built (at an undetermined date), resort guests can play a three-hole course that winds around the inn's biggest lake. This body of water—along with two other ponds—offer anglers catch-and-release fishing for bass, trout and Chinese koi. The triad of holes, designed by Ollie Raymond, the resort's owner before Millard, features three tees that can be circuited thrice for a par-28 layout. One of the holes is a 285-yard par-4, while another requires golfers to hit from the lake's shore up to an elevated green. The entry to another green is blocked by tall trees.

DRIVING RANGES

Grants Pass Driving Range
2540 NW Vine Street, Grants Pass, OR 97526.
(541) 479-9500. Eric Robertson, pro.

Jack Creek Driving Range
Off South Bank-Chetco Road, Brookings, OR 97415.
(541) 469-2606. Bruce Alexander, pro.

UPCOMING COURSES

Ashland — Marriott Clear Springs Resort (1999/2000). In the works since the mid-1980s, this resort project—which includes a Jerry Pate-designed 18-hole course, a 96-room hotel and 110 homesites—was still awaiting permits in early 1997. Ongoing appeals by neighbors and various state agencies show just how many obstacles can be thrown in the path of an Oregon golf developer.

Ashland — Muni Project (1999/2000). The city of Ashland has proposed building an 18-hole golf course on a 142-acre site northwest of the city. The course may be developed in tandem with a wastewater treatment facility.

Bandon — Bandon Dunes Project (1998-2000). Perhaps one of the most exciting projects to come along in recent times, this resort will include 45 golf holes— designed by the Gleneagles Group of Scotland— along with a hotel, conference center, lodge and 300 homesites. The project was approved by Coos County in August 1996, and no groups had filed an appeal by the December '96 deadline. The project's backer, Michael Keiser of Chicago, owns Recycled Paper Products, a leading publisher of greeting cards. Work on the first 18 could begin as early as the summer of 1997.

Brookings — Jack Creek Golf Course (1999/2000). This long-delayed project finally made progress in 1996 with the opening of Jack Creek Driving Range. The 187-acre site lies four miles east of Brookings. Financing has not been secured for an 18-hole course designed by Bob Baldock & Son, though it has received governmental approval.

Grants Pass — Hillebrand's Paradise Ranch Inn (1999/2000). Though German tycoon Herbert Hillebrand has received permits for a resort-type course designed by Robert Muir Graves, work has not yet started. Before course construction will commence, Hillebrand plans to expand the resort with 125 single-family lots and 75 overnight units.

Grants Pass — Rogue Golf Club (1999/2000). In 1996, the backers of this upscale project submitted an application for a 7,100-yard, Rees Jones-designed course to the Josephine County Planning Department. The developer has encountered hurdles in the form of wetlands and Native American archaeological findings. The 390-acre site is zoned for exclusive farm use.

Medford — Airport Project (1998/1999). A 3,000-yard public nine may be in the works for a site near Rogue Valley International Airport. The course will be designed and built by Ashland-based Hawaiian Island Golf, and include a driving range, clubhouse and golf school.

Shady Cove — Rogue River Estates & Golf Course (1999/2000). The local backers of this semiprivate 18 and 400 residential units were seeking permits in fall 1996. Rogue Development Group has tentatively pegged Peter Jacobsen and Jim Hardy to design the golf course. Also under consideration is a 95-room hotel.

Winchester Bay — Salmon Harbor Project (1999). In late-1996, one of the uses proposed for the west spit on Salmon Bay was a nine-hole golf course. Other possible tourist amenities include a restaurant, inn and an RV park.

Winston — Brockway Oaks Golf Course (1998/1999). Though work had commenced on this 18-hole, 6,811-yard course in 1996, construction was halted that fall as the developer needed to obtain final permits from the state. Wetlands were found on the 275-acre site, which is west of Winston off Highway 42. The Peter Thompson-designed course will abut the historic Brockway Store. The $15-million project also includes 380 homes, shops, a hotel and convention center.

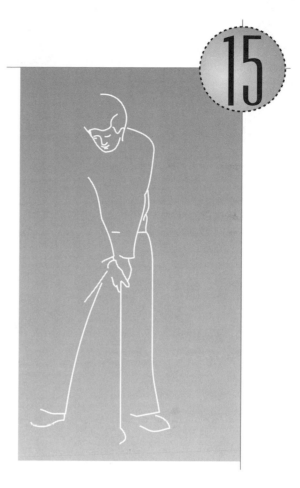

15

NORTH-CENTRAL OREGON

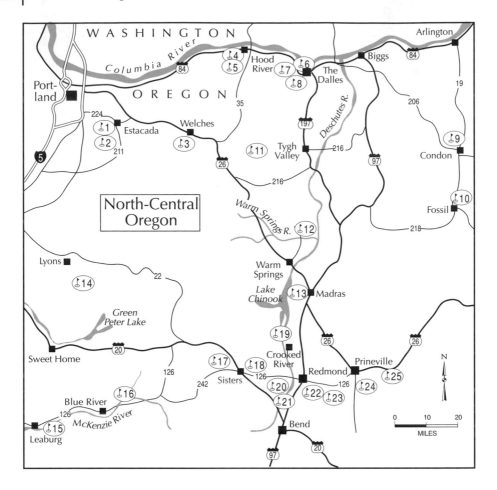

WASHINGTON

Columbia River

OREGON

Arlington

Biggs

84

Hood River

The Dalles

Portland

Welches

Estacada

224

211

35

197

Deschutes R.

Tygh Valley

216

97

206

19

Condon

9

10

Fossil

216

North-Central Oregon

218

Warm Springs R.

12

Lyons

22

14

Warm Springs

Green Peter Lake

Lake Chinook

13

Madras

Sweet Home

20

19

Crooked River

17

18

126

242

Sisters

126

20

21

Redmond

22

23

126

24

Prineville

25

N

Blue River

126

McKenzie River

16

15

Leaburg

Bend

97

20

0   10   20
MILES

1

2

3

5

4

5

6

7

8

11

1. **Springwater Golf Course** — public 9
2. **Eagle Creek Golf Course** — public 9
3. **The Resort at the Mountain** — public 27 & driving range
4. **Indian Creek Golf Course** — public 18 & driving range
5. **Hood River Golf & Country Club** — public 18 & driving range
6. **Northwest Aluminum Golf Club** — private 9 (par-3)
7. **The Dalles Country Club** — private 9
8. **Lone Pine Village Driving Range**
9. **Condon Golf Course** — public 9
10. **Kinzua Hills Golf Club** — semiprivate 6
11. **Pine Hollow Golf Course** — public 9
12. **Kah-Nee-Ta Resort** — public 18 & driving range
13. **Nine Peaks Golf Course** — public 18
14. **Elkhorn Valley Golf Course** — public 9
15. **McKenzie River Golf Course** — public 9
16. **Tokatee Golf Club** — public 18 & driving range
17. **Black Butte Ranch** — semiprivate 36 & driving range
18. **Aspen Lakes Golf Course** — public 18 & driving range
19. **Crooked River Ranch Golf Course** — semiprivate 18 & driving range
20. **Eagle Crest Golf Course** — public 18 & driving range
21. **Eagle Ridge Golf Course** — public 18, driving range
    & 18-hole putting course
22. **Juniper Golf Club** — semiprivate 18 & driving range
23. **The Greens at Redmond** — public 9
24. **Meadow Lakes Golf Course** — public 18 & driving range
25. **Prineville Golf & Country Club** — private 9

This section of the Northwest extends from the Columbia River south to Redmond and Prineville. Major wheat-growing operations spread across these high plains which sit, on average, about 2,000 feet above sea level. Between the Cascades and Blue Mountains lie the sparsely populated counties of Wasco, Sherman, Gilliam, Morrow, Jefferson and Wheeler. Though dominated by the wintry chill of zone 1, north-central Oregon can enjoy warm weather in autumn, which extends the golf season beyond its usual eight-month term. New courses are popping up in this area, thanks to central Oregon's expanding role as a recreational hotbed.

Public Courses

Aspen Lakes Golf Course

18 *17204 Highway 126, Sisters, OR 97559. (541) 549-4653 or 1-800-866-3981. James Spadoni, director of golf. 18 holes. 7,000 yards. Par 72. Grass tees. Course ratings not available. Years Opened: 1997 (original nine); 1998 (second nine). Architect: Bill Overdorf. Expensive (moderate for Central Oregon residents), jr. rates, credit cards. Call for reservations. Walk-on chances: Fair. Walkability: Good, with some uphill hikes. Playability: From what I've seen, this course could become a star among Central Oregon's stellar tracks.*

After several years of planning and preparation, ground was finally broken for this course in spring 1996. Aspen Lakes fulfills a longtime dream of the Cyrus family who, with their forefathers, have farmed this 564-acre property east of Sisters since the late 1800s. Keith and Connie Cyrus and their children, Matt and Pam, work on the project. Matt and Pam, graduates of Oregon State University, have used their OSU business training to market Aspen Lakes. In 1996, ads were placed in *The Nugget*, Sisters' newspaper, detailing progress on the course. Among the tidbits related during these updates was news that the Cyruses are seeking entry into Audubon International's Signature Cooperative Sanctuary Program. The program involves establishing a citizens advisory committee to ensure the venue adheres to Audubon's stringent guidelines. As of 1996, the program had 39 courses enrolled nationwide; Aspen Lakes will be the first in the Northwest. Among the wildlife to be preserved in these pastoral environs are deer, eagles, ospreys, owls and hawks.

The Cyruses built the course with equipment from their company, Sisters Aggregate and Construction. Par-Five of Bend shaped the Bill Overdorf-designed layout, which will debut with the front nine in spring 1997. Work on the back nine commenced in early '97 for an opening later that fall or spring '98. A third nine will be built after the first 18 opens. Other plans include a driving range and a 7,500-square-foot clubhouse with a restaurant, locker rooms and pro shop. Also in the works are 115 houses on one-acre lots. James Spadoni was hired as director of golf in 1997; he'd previously worked at courses in Hawaii, Arizona and California. Matt Peltier is the superintendent.

Aspen Lakes crosses a plateau and foothills situated at 3,100 feet above sea level. On clear days, views of nearby mountains—Broken Top, Washington,

Three-Fingered Jack, Black Butte, Jefferson and Sisters—are on tap. To help preserve the natural beauty of the site, only underground, fiber-optic cables will be installed. Power and water utilities were brought into the site in 1996. The Cyruses gave Overdorf's design priority over the housing needs, so the fairways utilize the premium parcels. The three nines will be called North, South and West; the North Nine will be the first to open.

Aspen Lakes features all-bentgrass fairways, tees and greens. Its hallmark will be the massive water hazards along many holes. The left side of the 2nd hole, a 415-yard par-4, is bordered by a 15-acre lake. A lobe of the lake—which also serves as the course's main irrigation source—cuts into the fairway before running up to protect the green's left and rear edges. The 165-yard, par-3 3rd requires a tee shot over part of the lake at the 2nd to reach a huge green. This putting surface is engirded by a 180-foot-long bunker along the right. After two par-4s at the 390-yard 4th and 470-yard 5th, the 220-yard par-3 6th comes along. Three lakes enter play on this hole, the latter two of which line the green's front and right flanks. The ponds—to be stocked with trout and other fish—are linked by a lovely waterfall. The 440-yard, par-4 7th contains a stream and pools beside the tees. Three ponds run up the left side of this dogleg-left, while a bunker squeezes it outside the turn. Another pond crosses before the hill-cut 7th green. The 8th is a straightaway par-4, while the 9th is a lengthy par-5 that rises up to a green which provides wonderful mountain panoramas.

Black Butte Ranch - semiprivate

36

Off Highway 20, Black Butte Ranch, OR 97759. (541) 595-6689 (Big Meadow), 595-6400 (Glaze Meadow) or 1-800-399-2322. J. D. Mowlds, director of golf. 36 holes. Grass tees. Course ratings: Big Meadow (6,790 yards, par 72) men—B72.0/127, M70.0/124; women—M74.9/122, F70.5/115. Glaze Meadow (6,568 yards, par 72) men—B71.5/128, M69.9/124; women—M75.5/127, F72.1/120. Years Opened: 1972 (Big Meadow); 1980 (Glaze Meadow). Architects: Robert Muir Graves (Big Meadow); Gene "Bunny" Mason (Glaze Meadow). Expensive, credit cards. Call for reservations. Walk-on chances: Fair. Walkability: Good. Playability: Two fine representations of Central Oregon golf.

Located northwest of Sisters, Black Butte Ranch is an independent town with permanent residents and seasonal guests. The 1,950-acre recreational enclave offers such sports as tennis, trout fishing, swimming, horseback riding, hiking, cross-country skiing and golf at two top-notch, 18-hole courses. The resort on the old Corbett cattle ranch sits at an elevation of 3,345 feet; golf balls travel far in this rarified air. Since all the housing lots have been sold, with no more planned, about the only future changes planned for Black Butte are an expanded pro shop and maybe another restaurant.

Though classified as expensive, with green fees in the $50 range, Black Butte's courses are priced less than those at Sunriver. Perhaps one of the best aspects of playing the layouts is that they're walkable; too many of Central Oregon's courses are set up for carts. Despite the many bag-toters here, the pace of play is brisk, much faster than, say, a resort course like Eagle Crest. Clocks at the first tee underscore Black Butte's "Keep Pace" concept, letting potential laggards know they'll be expected to play 18 holes in around four hours. Another plus is that peripheral houses are apart from fairways, with Big Meadow's back nine—which to my thinking is the best set of holes here and perhaps anyplace in this golf-rich part of the Northwest—particularly undeveloped.

Both courses are imperiled by considerable sand and water hazards, and both offer spectacular Cascade vistas. Big Meadow lies in a valley carved smooth by glaciers, with towering conifers along fairways. Among its better holes is the 8th, a 228-yard par-3 that runs up to a large, tri-trapped green. The 526-yard, par-5 10th is a long dogleg-right between trees. Bunkers along the right squeeze the landing zone for drives. The 10th eventually rises to a mid-sized green trapped laterally. The 390-yard, par-4 12th runs straight uphill past a pond along the left. The mid-width, moguled fairway winds to a narrowly-entered, steeply front-tilting green trapped on both sides. Perhaps Big Meadow's toughest test is the 17th, a 228-yard par-3 that plays very long, despite Black Butte's shot-enhancing elevation. The deep 17th green is trapped right and left.

Glaze Meadow was designed by Black Butte's former director of golf, Bunny Mason. It sprawls across rolling ground near *the* Black Butte, a towering precipice overlooking the resort. This course is a bit hillier and perhaps more densely-treed than Big Meadow, and may have tighter fairways. Tough holes include the 4th, a par-4 of 379 yards that winds rightward around a pond—skirting bunkers left—en route to a well-canted, pine-ringed green. The 160-yard, par-3 5th boasts an elevated tee and a mid-sized green enisled by sand. A pond behind the green further pinches the target. The top-rated 7th, a 523-yard par-5, doglegs left over rolling ground to a smallish green trapped twice in front. The 590-yard, par-5 12th stretches along a left-curling route to a trap-fronted, right-tilting green. The 15th, a 514-yard par-5, has a right-turning fairway that slopes left. The 15th green is narrow and well-trapped.

Condon Golf Course

9

North Lincoln Street, Condon, OR 97823. (541) 384-4266. 9 holes. 3,118 yards. Par 36. Grass tees. Course ratings: men 69.4/112, women 70.3/109. Year Opened: 1967. Architect: Don Lehman. Economical. No reservations. Walkability: Good. Playability: Straightforward course winds over a slope.

Condon's nine-hole course lies on the northwest edge of town between a grain silo and a residential neighborhood. Condon, population 700, serves the commercial needs of farmers and ranchers within a 40-mile radius. Amber-hued wheatlands ring the town. A list of the local businesses supporting the town's sole golf course is displayed on the scorecard and on a sign outside the clubhouse. When the pro shop is unattended, golfers pay green fees on the honor system.

The Don Lehman-designed layout spans 40 acres along a gentle slope. The virtually treeless track is imperiled by a few sand traps, and the greens are well-maintained. The single-tee nine features holes such as the top-rated 2nd, a 444-yard par-4 that heads straight over rolling terrain. At the 100-yard mark, the fairway bends left to a small, rolling green. The 392-yard, par-4 4th is a dogleg-right ending at a front-tilting sward. And the 9th, a 492-yard par-5, runs straight to an undulating green.

Crooked River Ranch Golf Course - semiprivate

18

Seven miles off Highway 97, Crooked River, OR 97760. (541) 923-6343. Gary Popp, pro. 18 holes. 5,661 yards. Par 71. Grass tees. Course ratings: men—B66.3/ 107, M65.0/101; women F67.2/109. Years Opened: 1971 (original nine); 1994 (second nine). Architects: William R. McPherson (original nine): Jim Ramey (second nine). Moderate, jr. rates, credit cards. Call for reservations. Walk-on chances: Fair. Walkability: Fair, with some distance between holes. Playability: Upgraded course gains excitement through its greens.

This recently expanded layout is part of Crooked River Ranch (CRR), a self-contained community inhabited mainly by retirees. CRR was developed in the early 1970s by William R. McPherson of Seattle, and occupies roughly 11,000 acres of sagebrush- and juniper-covered mesas. The ranch is ringed by ancient canyon walls—cut prehistorically by the Crooked River—which seem to change colors throughout the day, offering a psychedelic palette of browns, blues, purples and oranges from dawn to dusk. Marmots, porcupines, coyotes, jackrabbits, deer and sundry birdlife inhabit these high-desert environs. Also on display are vistas of the surrounding mountains and Deschutes River Valley.

CRR sits in a banana belt at 2,500 feet above sea level; the course is usually open in February and March—months that bring snow to nearby areas. The development is home (either full-time or seasonally) to approximately 1,600 property owners. Ranch facilities include a full-service RV area, solar-heated swimming pool, tennis courts, shops and a western-style clubhouse with an Astroturfed putt-putt course outside. Decisions regarding modifications to CRR's facilities are overseen by a board of directors. In 1993, the board approved an $800,000 project that doubled the size of the course. A year later, nine new holes were in play.

Though rather perfunctory, the new holes sport tricky greens with considerable undulations and a few traps along their sides. But CRR's hazards—outside of a few watery graves—are minimal; the wide fairways are quite compatible

The 15th hole at Crooked River Ranch is a 318-yard par-4.

for mid- to high-handicappers. Good tests on the original front nine include the 5th, a 260-yard par-4 that winds sharply rightward to a steeply front-banked green trapped along the left. The 7th, a 149-yard par-3 once rated the course's toughest hole, heads straight uphill to a two-tiered, trapped-left green etched into a steep hill. Negotiating putts from above the hole at this green are quite dicey.

Noteworthy back-siders include the 14th, a 494-yard par-5 that runs mostly straight. A pond lurks along the left at the 150-yard marker, while scrub growth on the right further squeezes this juncture. The mound-backed 14th green is small and square. The 17th is a dandy 405-yard par-4. The left-tilting hole starts off a raised tee fronted left by a pond and trees. Water hazards line the hole on the left as it descends to a mid-sized green guarded left by another pond. The 401-yard, par-4 18th is an uphill dogleg-right around sagebrush. Over its final 150 yards, CRR's home hole rises to a small, squarish green with a ridge through its middle.

Eagle Creek Golf Course

9

25805 SE Dowty Road, Eagle Creek, OR 97022. (503) 630-4676. 9 holes. 3,179 yards. Par 35. Grass tees. No course ratings. Year Opened: 1994. Architect: John Bastasch. Economical. No reservations. Walkability: Good. Playability: A little rough around the edges, but nine-holer is the only place to golf in Eagle Creek.

Named after a nearby waterway and a neighboring Clackamas County town, this nine-hole track lies south of Highway 212 (take the Folson exit and go right to Dowty). The layout was originated by brothers Frank and John Bastasch, who own a total of 450 acres along the Clackamas River. Because of its isolated locale beside a major river, wildlife is plentiful. According to greenskeeper Daryl Gardner, Eagle Creek is visited by wolves, deer, beavers, muskrats, skunks and all types of ducks. The generally flat layout is lined by massive oaks, with farms on its peripheries.

Eagle Creek's layout is rather rudimentary, with fairways consisting of mowed pastures. Its greens are satisfactory but, when I visited the course in May 1996, they were a bit brown from not being thatched or top-dressed since the course opened two years before. Players will encounter a few bunkers, but they sit in rather odd places; some traps 10 to 15 yards from the greens are not serious threats. Nonetheless, during my visit, there were several groups plying the spread-out fairways. Eagle Creek's operations are handled out of an old farm building; if there's no one in, pay green fees on the honor system.

The Bastasches have plans for another nine; in mid-1996, the fairways were routed but the greens hadn't been completed. And Gardner said that yet another 18 holes may be in the offing. Interesting holes include the 2nd, a 384-yard par-4 with a fairway that must be 200 yards wide. The runway-fairway goes straight over wavy ground to a raised and round green trapped in front. The 401-yard, par-4 3rd curls rightward and has two trees in mid-fairway. The left-sloping 3rd green is trapped in front, and bears another bunker 20 yards behind it. The drive at the 4th, a 351-yard par-4, must go over or through trees 150 yards off the tee. The hole ends at a mid-sized green "guarded" by a bunker 15 yards from its right-front edge. The 617-yard, par-5 5th was cited by *The Oregonian* in a 1994 poll as one of the state's worst holes. A large wetland off the tee is driveable, and another bog can be reached with second shots. There is no safe route around either area, thus raising the ire of the voters. The 5th concludes at a raised green with a pond close to its left edge.

Eagle Crest Golf Course

1522 Cline Falls Road, Redmond, OR 97756. (541) 923-4653. Terry Anderson, pro. 18 holes. 6,673 yards. Par 72. Grass tees. Course ratings: men—B71.5/123, M69.3/124; women—M74.2/119, F68.8/109. Years Opened: 1986 (original nine); 1988 (second nine). Architect: Gene "Bunny" Mason. Moderate, credit cards. Reservations: Call two weeks ahead. Walk-on chances: Fair. Walkability: Not as amenable to bag-toters as its sister course, Eagle Ridge. Playability: Play on nice layout sometimes slowed by infrequent golfers on vacation.

18

The first of Eagle Crest Resort's two courses, this layout began with nine holes in 1986, with the back nine opening two years later. The resort's condominiums and facilities are closer to these fairways than those on its sister layout, Eagle Ridge, but that may change once residential development occurs on the latter venue. And play is a bit slower here in summer because of the many vacationing and infrequent golfers, who aren't quite so prevalent on Eagle Ridge. I like the amenities at this resort, which is less populated than Sunriver and has much less car traffic. Guests have access to many activities, including horseback riding, biking and swimming. An athletic club offers swimming, a weight room and spa, and racquetball and pickelball courts. For Northwest time-share owners, Eagle Crest is an excellent choice as a "local" destination.

Wonderful vistas of the Three Sisters and other Deschutes River Valley mountains are available from the course. Recognized as a five-star resort, Eagle Crest was developed by Jeld-Wen, a wood-products firm that, in conjunction with a subsidiary, Trendwest Resorts, is developing the Running Y Ranch near Klamath Falls. The superintendent of the two "Eagle" courses is John Thronson, co-designer of Running Y's new course and architect of Eagle Ridge. Head pro Terry Anderson has been here since the resort opened. Over the next several years, Eagle Crest will be one of the three courses (with Awbrey Glen and Running Y Ranch) hosting the Northwest Open.

Bunny Mason-designed Eagle Crest crosses pine-covered hills and curls between lava-filled meadows; some holes occupy canyon floors. Dozens of sand traps dot the track, and two lakes (named Eagle and Bogey) enter play on the 17th hole. Paved cart paths wind over the sometimes-steep terrain (a cart is a good idea here). Good tests include the 2nd, a 481-yard par-5 with a raised, ravine-fronted tee. The narrow, ditch-like hole heads straight before curling sharply to the right, 100 yards from a raised, right-front-sloping green trapped laterally. The 550-yard, par-5 6th is a wide left-bender skirting bunkers outside the turn. Once around the corner, the hole narrows en route to a front-left-sloping, tri-trapped green.

Lovely panoramas are on tap from the tee of the 504-yard 15th, a par-5 traversing a basalt-lined path that tilts toward traps. A gnarled, 800-year-old juniper tree stands in mid-fairway, and the kidney-shaped 15th green is fronted by trees and guarded left by two bunkers. The 388-yard, par-4 17th bends rightward along a slight descent. The hole is pinched by the two lakes: Eagle left and Bogey right. Two bunkers also lurk right of the fairway, driving distance out. The 17th ends at a triangular green trapped left and rear, with water close to its left flank.

Eagle Ridge Golf Course

18 *1521 Cline Falls Road, Redmond, OR 97756. (541) 923-5002. Terry Anderson, director of golf. 18 holes. 6,992 yards. Par 72. Grass tees. Course ratings: men—T73.0/131, B70.7/125, M68.6/115; women—M73.2/131, I70.3/124, F66.1/115. Year Opened: 1993. Architect: John Thronson. Moderate, credit cards. Reservations: Call two weeks ahead. Walk-on chances: Fair. Walkability: Well-designed layout is walker-friendly. Playability: One of the more enjoyable courses in Central Oregon.*

Eagle Ridge Golf Course sits across Cline Falls Road from Eagle Crest Resort and its sister course. The newer of the resort's two golf tracks, Eagle Ridge is an efficient, walkable layout involving length, ample hazards and great vistas. The resort's superintendent, John Thronson, designed Eagle Ridge and did an excellent job making the layout playable for all golfers. The only blot is power lines across a few holes. The track is augmented by a modular clubhouse, a driving range and a fun-filled putting course. This two-acre, bentgrass gem contains dipsy-doodle holes lined by traps and ponds. It's secluded enough for players to have a rip-roaring good time without bothering anyone. One memorable hole (called "The Pit") has an oval, 20-foot-deep abyss between the tee and pin. The only safe route around it is to hit the ball hard along the edge of the chasm. Unfortunately, many players don't putt firmly enough. It's quite comical watching the golf ball go 'round and 'round all the way to the bottom of the pit. On this hole anyway, an improperly hit shot looks like it's going down the toilet.

My wife and I and another couple spent a week in Central Oregon in the summer of 1996. Of the five courses we played, Eagle Ridge was the most enjoyable for all concerned. We could comfortably walk it; the play was brisk but unrushed; and peripheral residential construction had not begun. This section of the resort spans 700 acres. The 132-acre course will be augmented by houses on half-acre lots and

Eagle Ridge's 7th hole is a 173-yard par-3.

time-share condos. A permanent clubhouse and possibly another 18-hole course are on the drawing board.

Eagle Ridge is more Arizona-ish than its counterpart, with large juniper pines dotting the grounds and scrub growth bordering fairways. The track features huge tees, excellent signage, paved cart paths and sizable greens with entertaining personalities. Good tests include the 2nd, a 418-yard par-4 affected by crosswinds. Over its last 150 yards, the straightahead hole drops to a front-banked green bunkered twice at the rear. The 497-yard, par-5 5th is an uphiller that bends to the right around a deep, mound-ringed swale; two large traps sit outside the turn. Once past the dogleg, the fairway ascends to a ridge-perched, hogbacked green trapped rear and right-front. The top-rated 8th, a 430-yard par-4, goes directly along a mid-width route to a steeply front-tilting green guarded by deep grass bunkers left and two sand traps rear.

The 501-yard, par-5 9th winds to the right around juniper trees; three fat bunkers lurk along the left. The rolling 9th green has three traps right-front and a pond along its right and rear edges. The 190-yard 12th drops off an elevated tee to a huge, front-leaning green trapped right-rear and left-front. A pond at the right-front makes this par-3 pretty but treacherous. The 13th, a 509-yard par-5, runs fairly straight over an assortment of heaves and hollows. A depression fronts its right-front-tilting green, which is trapped right-rear and left. The 17th, a 357-yard par-4, follows a wide, right-leaning route trapped along the right. Bunkers lurk at the right-rear, right and left flanks of its crowned and slick putting surface.

Elkhorn Valley Golf Course — 9

32295 Little North Fork Road, Lyons, OR 97358. (503) 897-3368. 9 holes. 3,169 yards. Par 36. Grass tees. Course ratings: men—C71.4/136, B/M70.1/131, M68.8/126, M/I66.2/117; women—I69.6/126, I/F66.7/121, F63.8/116. Year Opened: 1976. Architect: Don Cutler. Moderate, credit cards. Reservations: Call a week ahead. Walk-on chances: Good. Walkability: Good. Playability: Perhaps the premier nine-hole course in the Northwest.

Elkhorn Valley is an outstanding nine-hole course located 10 miles north of Highway 22 off the Little North Fork Road exit. Elkhorn Valley was originated by Don Cutler, who acquired a 480-acre parcel along the Santiam River in 1964. After waging a 10-year fight with various state agencies to get construction permits, Cutler was able to begin work and finally opened the course in 1976. Though he'd originally planned a full-blown resort with an 18-hole course and overnight accommodations, the regulators would only let him proceed with these nine holes. But, boy, are they special.

Cutler's design for Elkhorn Valley stemmed from his own desire (not the regulatory agencies') to protect native plants and animals, while presenting a layout challenging for all golfers. And he fulfilled that goal, with hawks and other birds flying past while elk and deer forage in nearby forests. Birdhouses serve as 150-yard markers. Wildflowers, rhododendrons, tall grasses, maples, pines and other trees border fairways. Creeks and pools enter play on six holes, and 28 bunkers vie for errant shots. As shown above, Elkhorn Valley has some of the highest ratings in the Northwest—for nine- and 18-hole courses. The 18-hole record from the tips is a 67 shared by Randy Wolf and former PGA Tourer, Pat Fitzsimons. PGA Tour pro Bob Gilder has played here, shooting a par 36 and proclaiming the course "great."

Open from March 1 through October 31, Elkhorn Valley is a Cutler family affair. Don's son Bruce is the greens superintendent, and daughter Elizabeth is the manager. Especially tough holes include the 1st, a 380-yard par-4 that curls rightward around a large trap. Finding the elevated, creek-fronted 1st green requires a delicate second shot. The top-rated 4th, a 543-yard par-5, is crossed by a creek that billows into a pond 250 yards out. Another water hazard fronts its rolling, bunker-backed putting surface. The 310-yard, par-4 5th bends sharply right along a route squeezed by a pond. A 175-yard shot off the tee will provide a clear view of a bi-trapped, clover-shaped green. The picturesque 8th is a 175-yard par-3 with a ravine-fronted green imperiled laterally by a pond and a trap. A waterfall cascades from the pond into the ravine. The 386-yard, par-4 9th doglegs sharply left, passing a bunker outside the turn en route to a shallow green ringed by three bunkers.

The Greens at Redmond

9
2475 SW Greens Boulevard, Redmond, OR 97756. (541) 923-0694. Dick Mason, pro. 9 holes. 1,662 yards. Par 29. Grass tees. Course ratings: men—B59.0/100, B/M58.3/97, M57.6/95; women M57.2/93. Year Opened: 1995. Architect: Robert Muir Graves. Economical, credit cards. Call for reservations. Walk-on chances: Good. Walkability: Good. Playability: Surprisingly tough short course near Redmond.

The 1995-opened Greens at Redmond is part of a subdivision being developed by Redmond realtor, Pete Wilson. The course occupies a section of Wilson's 91-acre site south of Redmond off Highway 97. The tricky Robert Muir Graves-designed track is augmented by a clubhouse with a pro shop and food service. The golf operations are overseen by longtime Northwest pro Dick Mason—who previously owned Golf City in Corvallis—and his wife Jeannette.

The layout crosses varied though generally flat terrain, giving it considerable interest. Additionally, Graves fashioned many sand and water hazards, with the top-rated, 205-yard 9th featuring a narrow fairway squeezed by two ponds. A total of five water hazards enter play on eight holes. The course contains par-4s of 304 and 294 yards, and its seven par-3s range in length from 109 yards to the 205-yard 9th. Also of concern on this good-looking track are greens with plenty of slopes and undulations.

Hood River Golf & Country Club

18
1850 Country Club Road, Hood River, OR 97031. (541) 386-3009. Dave Waller, pro. 18 holes. 6,400 yards. Par 72. Grass tees. Course ratings not available. Years Opened: 1922 (original nine); 1997 (second nine). Architects: Hugh Junor (original nine); Dave Waller & Tennyson Engineering (second nine). Moderate, jr./sr. rates, credit cards. Reservations: Call a week ahead. Walk-on chances: Fair. Walkabilty: Fair. Playability: Nine new holes and other upgrades prepare course for the 21st century.

Work began on revitalizing Hood River Golf & Country Club in 1996. The plan involves adding three new holes and rebuilding two holes on the original 1922-built nine, while constructing an all-new back side. Where the three old holes were will be a driving range. The course renovations, which came on the heels of a clubhouse remodel in 1996, were built by Brian Whitcomb, the Oregon native who owns Lost Tracks Golf Club in Bend and operates several Arizona courses. Hood River's head pro Dave Waller, with help from Tennyson Engineering, designed the new holes. According to Waller, the revamped course may be open in late fall 1997 or spring 1998 (after this book went to press).

Hood River Golf & Country Club has been an integral part of the community for 75 years. Its owner, Orchard Machinery Corporation (OMC), is financing the expansion on portions of a 230-acre parcel. The new holes will occupy hilly terrain west of the original track. Appropriately for this agricultural hub, Hood River is surrounded by apple, cherry and pear orchards. Vineyards and wineries are also nearby. Mount Hood is visible from the course; Mount Adams in Washington peeks over the Columbia River's northern banks. Besides enjoying pleasant vistas, golfers may spot deer and many birds.

Hood River's golf season typically runs from March 1 to November. When the snows come, the clubs are put away and the skis removed from storage. Hood River's original Hugh Junor-designed nine was notorious for its small and slick, "push-up" greens. Only four holes from that side will be retained. It'll be interesting to see how the new fairways and greens blend with Junor's. The grounds are dotted with full-grown firs, oaks and maples. These trees—along with the tipped topography over which the new holes cross—will set the tone for a revived Hood River Golf & Country Club.

Indian Creek Golf Course

18

3605 Brookside Drive, Hood River, OR 97031. (541) 386-7770. Treve Gray, pro. 18 holes. 5,906 yards. Par 72. Grass tees. Course ratings: men—B70.2/124, M67.7/ 112; women—M71.7/126, F67.7/116. Year Opened: 1990. Architect: Dave Martin. Moderate, jr./sr. rates. Reservations: Call two weeks ahead. Walk-on chances: Fair. Walkability: Fair, with some distances between holes. Playability: Idiosyncratic layout close to Hood River.

Throughout the early and mid-1990s, this 18-hole course was the target of heated legal action from a neighboring farmer, who repeatedly appealed Indian Creek's conditional-use permit. In late 1995, for the third time in seven years, the Hood County Board of Commissioners approved the permit. The neighbor, who had received support from the 1000 Friends of Oregon, claimed the course altered his farming practices, saying chemicals sprayed on his fruit trees would drift over golfers and make them sick. In early 1997, no further appeals had been filed, so maybe Indian Creek is over its legal imbroglios.

Named after one of the three streams that wind through the site (Squaw and Dribble creeks are the others), the layout occupies much of a 170-acre parcel owned by its co-developers, Brookside, Inc. and Hanel Lumber Company. Beside the 6,000-yard layout are 40 homes and 36 condos the owners are developing in a subdivision called Indian Creek Meadows. The facility lies on Hood River's southwest corner next to a residential neighborhood and fruit orchards. From the higher points are vistas of mounts Adams and Hood.

Indian Creek traverses some hilly terrain and is split by Brookside Drive; the separated holes are accessed via a tunnel. One of Brookside's partners, Dave Martin, designed the course. When the $4-million venue was built, over a thousand young trees were planted to augment the full-grown oaks, pines and firs on the property.

Additional embellishments include nearly 30 white-sand bunkers, water hazards on 11 holes, and concrete cart paths. Ponds were created by widening sections of the three creeks. A unique feature of the course is its "flowered bunkers." These clumps of daisies lurk in target zones and before greens; players get a free drop if in them.

Martin's design of Indian Creek—his first-ever golf course—has some problems, including way too many OB stakes. Other quibbles include a bunker in the middle of the 14th fairway that swallows decent drives; unsightly telephone poles and wires over the 11th, 12th, and 13th holes; too many blind and potentially dangerous shots into greens; and some pretentious greens, one of which (the 11th) bears a two-foot-high tier. But there are some good and tough holes as well, including the 2nd, a 334-yard par-4 with a pond off the tee, a downhill fairway, and a blind second shot into a pond-backed, heart-shaped green 50 feet below the fairway. The top-rated 4th, a ravine-like 497-yard par-5, winds 90 degrees to the right and leans toward a creek along the right. The waterway lines the hole all the way to a long and skinny green with a hump in its center.

The 562-yard, par-5 11th runs straight—bypassing OB left and telephone cabling right—toward two bunkers in the landing area. The tree-tapered fairway eventually reaches a trapped-left, hogbacked green. Indian Creek's 17th is a pretty but treacherous 322-yard par-4. Long-hitters are advised to use an iron from the tee as this narrow downhiller is lined left by dense jail. A fat part of a creek also lurks unseen 220 yards out. Backed by a hump and a grass bunker, the 17th's triangular putting surface tilts steeply toward the front and a shimmering pond.

Juniper Golf Club - semiprivate

18 *139 SE Sisters Avenue, Redmond, OR 97756. (541) 548-3121. Bruce Wattenburger, pro. 18 holes. 6,533 yards. Par 72. Grass tees. Course ratings: men—B70.8/127, M69.4/124; women—M74.7/121, F70.9/115. Years Opened: 1951 (original nine); mid-1980s (second nine). Architects: Fred Sparks (original nine); Tim Berg (second nine). Moderate, jr. rates, credit cards. Call for reservations. Walk-on chances: Fair. Walkability: Good. Playability: Nice layout winds between junipers and sagebrush.*

Semiprivate Juniper is owned by over 400 members, each of whom plays a role in the club's business and golf decisions. Unless member events are planned, unrestricted public play is allowed. Juniper Golf Club, Inc.'s operations are overseen by its longtime head pro, Bruce Wattenburger. The 150-acre facility is in Redmond's southern section, just east of Highway 97 near the city airport. The course was named after the low-growing, shrubby conifers that cover central Oregon's desertlands. A juniper plant, with its scalelike, prickly foliage and deep roots, can survive in these arid environs for over 600 years.

The course began as a dual-tee nine in 1951. Designed and built by Fred Sparks, Juniper's original holes were appended with another nine in the mid-'80s. The latter holes were fashioned by Tim Berg, formerly the director of golf at Sunriver. After Berg's side opened, several front-nine holes were shuffled to create the current configuration. The two sets of holes are quite different, with the generally hazardless originals crossing flat terrain en route to small but slick greens. Berg's nine features narrow and contoured fairways, a few water hazards, quite a few bunkers, and large rolling putting surfaces. Perhaps the prettiest juncture on the course is where the side-by-side par-3s at the 4th and 17th holes share a pond.

Juniper's verdant grounds contrast starkly with the juniper- and sage-filled between-hole recesses, areas which golfers should avoid at all costs. Wildlife visitors include deer, rabbits and coyotes. Good tests include the 3rd, a 527-yard par-5 with a tight dogleg-left fairway and a small, quick green. The 540-yard, par-5 9th skirts the driving range and OB along the left en route to a green guarded on the right by a pond. The 16th, a 488-yard par-5, curls leftward between tawny scrub. A pond squeezes the fairway about 100 yards from a large, rolling green.

Kah-Nee-Ta Resort

100 Main Street, Warm Springs, OR 97761. (541) 553-1112 or 1-800-831-0100. Joe Rauschenburg, pro. 18 holes. 6,374 yards. Par 72. Grass tees. Course ratings: men—B71.4/123, M69.0/118; women—M73.8/124, F69.7/116. Years Opened: 1972 (original nine); 1976 (second nine). Architects: William P. Bell (original nine); Gene "Bunny" Mason (second nine). Moderate, jr./sr. rates, credit cards. Reservations: Call two weeks ahead. Walk-on chances: Fair. Walkability: Not bad overall. Playability: One of central Oregon's original golf destinations. **18**

The 18-hole course at Kah-Nee-Ta Resort was the first in the United States fully owned and operated by a Native American tribe. Kah-Nee-Ta is run by a confederation of the Warm Springs, Wasco and Paiute tribes. Several similarly-owned courses have sprouted up of late. In the Northwest, the most recent is the Wildhorse layout in Pendleton, which was built by the Confederated Tribes of the Umatilla Indian Reservation. Located alongside the Warm Springs River on part of the tribes' 560,000-acre reserve, Kah-Nee-Ta's layout exemplifies desert golf in central Oregon, with lush fairways winding between tan-colored scrublands. The golf course is augmented by swimming and tennis facilities, with overnight guests staying in an arrowhead-shaped lodge atop a panoramic promontory.

Locals are quick to say that the sun shines, on average, 340 days a year at Kah-Nee-Ta. Desert fauna includes lizards, hawks, eagles, and an occasional bull snake. Except for holes near the Warm Springs River, which winds through the site, Kah-Nee-Ta's fairways are virtually treeless. Most holes are separated by dry grass, hard clay, sagebrush and junipers. But some between-fairway spaces are green, thanks to an expanded irrigation system installed in the early 1990s. The resort's locale at an elevation over 2,000 feet creates about a one-club difference than at sea level.

Kah-Nee-Ta contains some narrowish fairways, with adequate bunkering and the river prominently in play. Good tests include the 4th, a 396-yard par-4 that winds rightward around the Warm Springs River to a laterally trapped green. The 491-yard, par-5 6th curls slightly right off a 100-foot-high tee. Traps squeeze the landing area; farther down, a willow protects the right-front entry to a bi-trapped green. The dogleg-left 11th, a par-5 of 504 yards, skirts jail en route to a narrow and slick, trapped-in-front green. The 515-yard, par-5 17th curls leftward for most of its length. At the 50-yard mark, the route is crossed by the river, but well-placed shot should find the 17th's large oval green.

Kinzua Hills Golf Club - semiprivate

6

Off Highway 19, Fossil, OR 97830. (541) 763-2698. 6 holes. 1,463 yards. Par 32 for 9 holes. Grass tees. Course ratings: men 60.8/99, women 61.3/97. Year Opened: 1951 (current course). Architects: Local golfers. Economical. No reservations. Walkability: Very good. Playability: The only course in Wheeler County slakes the appetite of local linksters.

Besides being the only six-hole course in Oregon, Kinzua Hills is also the only place to golf in Wheeler County. Owned by the Kinzua Corporation, the Fossil layout is leased to the nonprofit Kinzua Hills Golf Club. The course off Highway 19 offers views of the Blue Mountains. Pine trees surround Kinzua Hills and a creek grabs errant shots.

The course originated in 1931, but was later converted into a baseball diamond used by a local semipro team. Restarted in 1951, the nine-hole course sported sand greens. In 1954, three holes were pared and a sprinkler system was installed, thus allowing the growth of grass putting surfaces. Three sets of tees on the six-hole track enable golfers to play 18-hole rounds. When played to a par of 65 over three circuits, the layout stretches 4,232 yards.

McKenzie River Golf Course

9

41723 Madrone Street, Walterville, OR 97489. (541) 896-3454. 9 holes. 2,755 yards. Par 35. Grass tees. Course ratings: men B65.6/102; women—B/M71.2/116, I/F65.7/107. Year Opened: 1961. Architects: Earl, Lloyd & Ken Omlid. Moderate, jr./sr. rates. Reservations: Call a day ahead. Walk-on chances: Good. Walkability: Good. Playability: Though not overly daunting, family-owned track beside the McKenzie River provides a nice outing.

Named for the waterway that flows just beyond its property line, this layout east of Springfield is readily accessible off Highway 126 in the small town of Walterville. McKenzie River Golf Course has long been a family affair. The corporation that runs it is now owned by two couples: Rod and Diane Omlid and Ivan and Sally Holte, children of the course's founders. McKenzie River was built in 1961 by the Omlid brothers—Earl, Lloyd and Ken. Near the venue are vacation retreats, hot springs resorts, hiking trails and state parks.

The verdant 50-acre layout sits at 630 feet above sea level, and is surrounded by the river and homes with lovely flower gardens. Golfers may spot deer, raccoons, ducks, muskrats, eagles and hawks. Some visitors bring fishing gear as the McKenzie is replete with fat rainbow trout. Meandering Haugen Creek trickles below the deck behind the clubhouse, entering play on three holes, and most fairways are squeezed by towering firs, maples and cedars. The course gains difficulty from its wavy, knoll-perched greens. A prime example of these slick putting surfaces is the triple-tiered affair at the 1st. A few sand traps sprinkle the grounds but, in general, the rather shortish layout is a mid-level test. The toughest holes are the 435-yard, par-4 4th and the 487-yard, par-5 7th.

Meadow Lakes Golf Course

300 Meadow Lakes Drive, Prineville, OR 97754 (541) 447-7113. 18 holes. 6,731 yards. Par 72. Grass tees. Course ratings: men—B73.1/131, M71.8/128, I69.1121; women—I73.3/130, F69.0/121. Year Opened: 1993. Architect: William Robinson. Moderate. Call for reservations. Walk-on chances: Fair. Walkability: Good. Playability: Tight layout involves plenty of water hazards.

Municipally-owned Meadow Lakes was created by the city of Prineville to provide recreation for local citizens and visitors. But its 10 ponds are actually a series of lagoons used to store 1.1 million gallons of treated wastewater. The golf project arose through the efforts of Prineville city administrator Henry Hartley, and various state and federal agencies. In 1988, the city was faced with daily $25,000 fines by the Environmental Protection Agency if it couldn't come up with an alternative to dumping wastewater into the Crooked River. Because the course was considered part of a new water-treatment facility, the city received a $2.5 million federal grant to help finance it. Once funding was in place, work (by Trecon of Anchorage, Alaska) began on the Bill Robinson-designed course.

Since Meadow Lakes opened in 1993, it has garnered several awards, including *Golf Digest's* inaugural Environmental Leaders in Golf Award in March 1996. Also, the average monthly sewer bill in Prineville is less than it costs to play a round of golf. And the city expects the course to begin turning an annual $500,000 profit by the end of 1998. Quite a coup for a town and governmental agencies that considered spraying the effluent over a 400-acre "leach field" of alfalfa, a plan that would have doubled monthly sewer bills.

Fortunately, after a 14-month review, all concerned settled on this 160-acre golf course as the preferred method of disposal. Each day, 600,000 gallons of Prineville's treated wastewater is pumped into on-course ponds. Some of the water evaporates, while most of it is used for irrigation. None of it has an odor. Robinson designed the fairways so they surface-drain into the ponds, a configuration that also causes balls hit into these peripheral areas to sometimes bounce into the water hazards. Other unique engineering aspects Meadow Lakes include a deep-tile drainage system that prevents contamination of groundwater or the Crooked River, and moisture-tolerant grasses rather than the drought-resistant turf usually found on central Oregon's high-desert layouts.

Meadow Lakes boasts a fine clubhouse with a popular restaurant, and a driving range. Paved cart paths wind throughout, and each hole has four sets of tees. Blue herons frequently alight on ponds. The links-like venue, which was once a cow pasture, will gradually be landscaped with deciduous and evergreen trees. Besides water hazards on every hole, Meadow Lakes is imperiled by nearly 60 sand traps. Another concern for golfers are prevailing winds out of the northwest, which tend to kick up in mid-afternoon.

Good tests include the 390-yard, par-4 9th. Crooked River crosses before its perched green, which is trapped twice in front. The 240-yard, par-3 13th requires a long and accurate shot to reach a sizable, tri-trapped green. The 14th, a 600-yard par-5, curls leftward between three ponds en route to a clover-shaped, bi-bunkered green guarded left-front by water. The 15th, a 430-yard par-4, winds to the right around a pond near the landing zone. The rolling 15th green is ringed by three bunkers.

Nine Peaks Golf Course

18 *1152 NW Golf Course Road, Madras, OR 97741. (541) 475-3511. 18 holes. 6,582 yards. Par 72. Grass tees. Course ratings: men 67.8/103, women 70.0/107. Years Opened: 1958 (original six); 1958 (next three holes); 1992 (second nine). Architects: Don Lehman (original nine); Kevin, Bill and Pat O'Meara (second nine). Moderate. No reservations. Walkability: Good. Playability: Though not one of central Oregon's toughest tracks, family-operated layout is enjoyable.*

Recently-expanded Nine Peaks was once known as Madras Golf & Country Club. The 120-acre layout crosses tablelands at 2,300 feet above sea level, offering views of area farms and the ennead of mountains for which it's named: Hood, Jefferson, Brokentop, North Sister, South Sister, Middle Sister, Three-Fingered Jack, Washington and Bachelor. The town of Madras is a trading center for area farmers, with peppermint, seed vegetables (garlic, carrots and dill), wheat and alfalfa the predominant crops.

Nine Peaks has been owned by Kevin and Deidre O'Meara since 1987. The course began with six holes in 1958, and received three more in 1960. Kevin O'Meara, with help from his brothers Bill and Pat, designed and built the second nine on a 60-acre parcel south of the original holes. The brothers are part of Oregon's golfing O'Mearas; Bill owns Wildwood west of Portland and Pat is the proprietor of Springwater in Estacada. Father Joe, owner of Killarney West in Hillsboro, also helped with the work. Besides a small clubhouse that serves hearty breakfasts and lunches, Nine Peaks has a popular swimming pool used mainly by local kids. The O'Mearas may develop 40 homesites on peripheral acreage and build a driving range in the future.

The new holes at Nine Peaks are quite like the originals—relatively flat with minimal hazards, except they're lined with mounds and sport large greens. Three ponds also enter play. The new holes occupy a city-owned site—once part of a U.S. Air Force bomber base with the state's longest runway—that the O'Mearas lease, and are irrigated by treated wastewater. Good tests include the 8th, a 548-yard par-5, and the 570-yard 15th, a par-5 that winds around a pond en route to a green lined on the left and front by another pond.

Pine Hollow Golf Course

9 *8A South County Road, Tygh Valley, OR 97063. (541) 544-2035. 9 holes. 2,224 yards. Par 34. Grass tees. Course ratings: men 61.6/95, women 60.9/101. Year Opened: 1991. Architect: Irl Davis, Jr. Economical, sr. rates, credit cards. Call for reservations. Walk-on chances: Good. Walkability: Good. Playability: Water and trees spice up remote course.*

Pine Hollow is a nine-hole course in a remote part of north-central Oregon. Though the venue has a Tygh Valley address, it's actually closer to Wamic, southwest of Tygh Valley and 38 miles south of The Dalles off Highway 197. The course is within a resort still being built by Irl Davis, Jr., a local rancher who has converted his 700-acre property near Pine Hollow Reservoir into a recreational center with water skiing, boating, camping and RV parking. He's also developing 600 housing lots, which range in size from one to 10 acres. The reservoir is a popular place in summer, and Davis hopes his resort will fill the recreational needs of visitors. Also on site is a clubhouse, restaurant and gas station; Davis may eventually build a bed and breakfast.

Davis designed the self-built course, which is made verdant by an automatic sprinkler system. The layout involves some elevation changes, three ponds and tree groves. From its higher points, golfers enjoy views of Mount Hood. Davis, in his mid-70s, had never golfed before he began Pine Hollow. That may be evident on some parts of the course. The 2nd hole, a 212-yard par-4, was included in a list of the state's worst golf holes in a 1994 poll by *The Oregonian* newspaper. Pine Hollow's 2nd, complete with a sign identifying it as "The Hole From Hell," has a double-dogleg, 10-yard-wide fairway that sits just below Davis' home. During course construction, Davis left trees as tall as 60 feet in the fairway. He now watches golfers try to hack their way through the maze. Other holes involve forced carries over water, pines and oaks.

The Resort at the Mountain   27

68010 East Fairway Avenue, Welches, OR 97067. 1-800-669-4653. Rick Seven, pro. 27 holes. Grass tees. Course ratings: Pine Cone/Foxglove (6,016 yards, par 70) men 68.0/114, women 69.3/113. Thistle/Pine Cone (5,757 yards, par 70) men 67.2/116, women 68.9/116. Foxglove/Thistle (6,443 yards, par 72) men 70.0/119, women 71.8/123. Years Opened: 1928 (Pine Cone); 1966 (Foxglove); 1978 (Thistle). Architects: Waale & Chattuck (Pine Cone); Gene Bowman (Foxglove & Thistle). Moderate, credit cards. Reservations: Call two weeks ahead. Walk-on chances: Fair. Walkability: Fair, with some between-hole distances. Playability: Though not particularly lengthy, the three nines feature narrow fairways, small and slick greens, and considerable hazards.

The 27 holes at this 350-acre resort in the Mount Hood Wilderness Area evolved gradually over the years. Billy Welches, founder of the adjoining town, built the original nine (called Welches Golf Course then but since renamed Pine Cone) in 1928. The venue was later acquired by Gene Bowman, who designed and built the second and third nines (Foxglove and Thistle) in 1966 and 1978. At that time the resort was called Bowman's at Rippling River, a name later amended to Rippling River Resort and Convention Center. In 1989, Ed and Janice Hopper of Hillsboro bought the resort, and invested $3.5 million in renovations to the lodge, restaurant and golf shop. They built a fitness center, and renamed the place yet again, calling it The Resort at the Mountain. The Hoppers also gave the resort a Scottish theme (ergo the names of the nines), even opening a shop with "Mac" knickknacks. The new owners may one day proceed a fourth nine holes.

Over the years, this getaway spot has been what its various owners have intended it to be: a place of relaxation and recreation, one that's also a good choice for business functions. In addition to condos, lodges and meeting rooms, the resort offers tennis, swimming pools, volleyball and basketball courts, and 10 miles of hiking trails. A massive RV park is nearby. The resort holds over 200 conventions a year, with two-thirds of its golfers being conventioneers. Because of the resort's proximity to Mount Hood's year-round skiing, it's not unusual to find guests arriving with skis, golf clubs and windsurfing boards (for use on the nearby Columbia River). If there's room, a fishing pole may be brought as well since there are plenty of trout-filled streams and lakes nearby.

The Resort at the Mountain's course is usually closed from December to April, though the clubhouse is open year-round. Since the area receives about 100 inches of rain and snow annually, the Hoppers have retrofitted the fairways with improved drainage. In 1997, the 4th and 5th holes on the Foxglove Nine were rebuilt, and further upgrades are planned. Besides views of Mount Hood's glorious cone, golfers might spot deer, elk and bald eagles while circuiting the course. The Foxglove and Pine Cone nines are fairly straightforward; the Thistle side features tight fairways, tricky greens, and the Salmon River beside seven holes. The 27-holer winds between forests, residences and resort facilities, and is imperiled by numerous water and sand hazards. Perhaps the best test here is Thistle's 8th, a tight, 413-yard par-4 that *The Oregonian* once included in a list of the state's most difficult holes.

Springwater Golf Course

9 *25230 South Wallens Road, Estacada, OR 97023. (503) 630-4586. 9 holes. 3,001 yards. Par 36. Grass tees. Course ratings: men—B68.8/124, B/M67.9/120; women F67.8/108. Year Opened: 1962. Architect: Bob Rehberg. Moderate, jr./sr. rates. Reservations: Call five days ahead. Walk-On chances: Fair. Walkability: Good, with some hills. Playability: Steady improvements have stiffened challenge at rural nine.*

Springwater Golf Course lies in a pastoral valley surrounded by Christmas-tree farms and fruit orchards. Pat and Vickie O'Meara have been its sole proprietors since 1986. Pat and his brother Kevin, now the owner of Nine Peaks in Madras, operated Springwater for a few years prior to '86. The 60-acre course was designed and built by Bob Rehberg, who called it Estacada Springwater. Rehberg later sold the facility to C. B. Stauffacher; Greg and Gary Hartman ran the course before the O'Mearas.

The layout crosses well-treed hills and dales, with four ponds entering play on several holes. Pat O'Meara has built several new tees in recent years, a move that stretched the dual-tee layout to 6,002 yards over two circuits. Springwater's rural locale allows unhurried rounds and frequent visits from deer. Interesting holes include the tree-lined 5th, a 503-yard par-5 along a ridgetop that winds leftward to an undulating green. The left-bending 6th, a 445-yard par-5, goes between evergreens. A large pond crosses the fairway midway to a raised green. The sporty 9th, an uphill par-3 of 135 yards, contains a creek in a ravine off the tee and a small and slick, knoll-perched putting surface.

Tokatee Golf Club

18 *54947 McKenzie Highway, Blue River, OR 97413. (541) 822-3220 or 1-800-452-6376 (in Oregon only). Dan King, pro. 18 holes. 6,842 yards. Par 72. Grass tees. Course ratings: men—B72.0/126, M69.7/119; women F71.0/115. Years Opened: 1965 (original nine); 1970 (second nine). Architect: Ted Robinson. Moderate. Reservations: Call 30 days ahead. Walk-on chances: Fair. Walkability: Good. Playability: One of Oregon's premier layouts.*

Tokatee Golf Club is one of central Oregon's toughest courses. Though located 48 miles east of Eugene and a bit removed from civilization, the course lures the golfing cognoscenti, who have no qualms about traveling to the place. No less an authority than *Golf Digest* has concurred that the drive is worth it, often ranking Tokatee in its list of the nation's top-25 public courses. In 1996, the magazine gave Tokatee a Number 8 ranking in its list of the nation's "Top-75 Affordable Courses." Conceived by timber baron N. B. "Nat" Giustina, Tokatee—a Chinook Indian word describing a place of restful beauty—provides a great test for a golfer's physical and mental abilities. The challenging course is often used for high school championships, and has hosted some top collegiate and amateur tournaments over the years.

The track crosses a 200-acre site that, in pre-golf days, was used as a cattle ranch, a stopover place for stagecoaches, and an apple orchard. Located at 1,300 feet above sea level, Tokatee enjoys a porous, well-draining base but, because of snowfall, is open only from February 1st to November 15th. The Ted Robinson-designed layout—immaculately conditioned for years by superintendent Ray Telfer—features slick greens, ample sand and water hazards, and considerable length. Also of concern are winds roiling off the nearby Cascades that clash with Pacific westerlies to skew shots.

The first four holes cross a treeless tract and are fairly open. At the 362-yard par-4 5th, the course moves into woodlands, where ponds, creeks, bunkers, trees and deep roughs pinch fairways and penalize the misdirected. Top holes include the 6th, a 508-yard par-5 narrowed by a lake driving distance out. Two large traps front its small and quick green. The beautiful 11th, a 204-yard par-3, contains a pond that skirts the right edges of the fairway and a skinny-but-deep, trapped-left-front green. The 509-yard, par-5 12th winds sharply right initially, then bends back leftward to a trapped-left green. The 16th, a 532-yard par-5, has a fairly wide landing area for drives. But the second and third shots here are very tough as a ditch across the fairway wreaks havoc with club selection. A trap right and a pond left squeeze the two-tiered 16th green. The lovely 17th, a 152-yard par-3, requires an uphill tee shot to a tidy green fronted by a pond and a trap.

Private Courses

Northwest Aluminum Golf Club

9

3313 West 2nd, The Dalles, OR 97058. (541) 296-6161. 9 holes. 1,183 yards. Par 27. Grass tees. No course ratings. Opened: 1950s. Architect: Harvey Aluminum Company. Northwest Aluminum employees only.

This par-3 layout lies within a private park at the 180-acre Northwest Aluminum plant in The Dalles. The plant's 500 employees have access to the course as well as to adjoining softball fields, tennis courts and archery range. The layout was built in the 1950s by the plant's original owner, Harvey Aluminum. Martin-Marietta then acquired the facility, which was sold to Northwest Aluminum in 1986. The relatively flat track sports tree-lined fairways and a few greenside traps, and is used for employee tournaments.

Prineville Golf & Country Club

18

232204 Highway 26, Prineville, OR 97754. (541) 447-7225. Jeff Bright, pro. 9 holes. 2,525 yards. Par 33. Grass tees. Course ratings: men B/M64.1/112; women—B68.5/116, F66.3/113. Year Opened: 1950. Architects: Bob Hogan, Eddie Hogan, Ted Longworth & Larry Lamberger Sr. Members, guests & reciprocates.

Prineville's only private club lies about three miles east of town on the south side of Highway 26. The layout is surrounded by farms, and is home to such wildlife as yellow-bellied marmots, quails, foxes and coyotes. Deer are frequent visitors in fall and winter, while frogs croak in ponds and rabbits scurry across the fairways in

Prineville's 3rd hole is a dandy 399-yard par-4.

summer. Llamas—owned by former pro Mark Payne and his partner Tonia Angel—are occasionally "rented" as caddies for charity golf tournaments. Prineville's 185 members, many of whom live outside the area, enjoy a nice clubhouse and lovely mountain views from the course. Among the club's more enduring events is the Prineville Invitational and Pro-Am, held since 1954.

Well-maintained and blessed with considerable character, the 1950-opened layout was designed by four golf pros from Portland: Bob and Eddie Hogan, Ted Longworth and Larry Lamberger Sr. Most of Prineville's holes cross gently rolling terrain, with a few winding over a hill at the southern edge of the property. Fairways are lined by juniper, pine, Dutch elm and Russian olive trees, and 20 bunkers dot the grounds. Ochoco Creek enters play on four holes. Prineville's dual-tee course extends 4,977 yards over two circuits, and is known for its small and slick putting surfaces.

Particularly interesting tests include the 3rd, a 399-yard par-4 that runs narrowly downhill off the tee. The fairway then rises to a round, left-sloping green trapped right-front and left. The 281-yard, par-4 5th starts with a blind tee shot to a descending fairway with a tiny landing area. The small, hill-cut 5th green, which tilts left toward a trap, can be driven but only by a powerful and well-placed tee shot. The narrow 6th, a 323-yard par-4, is a flat dogleg-left lined along the right by OB. The hole winds around a trap, rocks and trees, then shoots straight uphill to a rolling, right-leaning green with a steep right edge. A detritus-filled chasm called "Garrett's Gorge" lurks right of the green. The top-rated 8th, a 532-yard par-5, has a pond 100 yards left of the tee. The tree-lined hole then winds rightward—passing a bunker along the right—en route to a diminutive, laterally-trapped green.

The Dalles Country Club

4550 Highway 30 West, The Dalles, OR 97058. (541) 296-5252. Bob Sproule, pro. 9 holes. 3,060 yards. Par 36. Grass tees. Course ratings: men B69.4/120; women— M74.5/121, F73.6/118. Year Opened: 1921. Architects: Founding members. Members, guests & reciprocates.

9

The Dalles Country Club boasts a tricky nine-hole track that butts against a towering basalt escarpment. Rocky outcroppings enter the field of play, serving as fairway separators and ball-battering hazards. Full-grown trees line these rolling and narrow routes, and white-sand bunkers guard greens. It's obvious that a lot of care goes into The Dalles' lush, well-maintained track. Located off Highway 30 about six miles west of its namesake city, the dual-tee venue stretches 6,038 yards over two circuits.

Because it's close to the Columbia River Gorge, which generates winds averaging 20- to 30-mile-an-hour year-round, The Dalles Country Club has been the site of many "windy" anecdotes over the years. Golf balls hit safely onto greens are blown onto fairways, into traps or, for those lucky enough, into the hole. The winds are at their strongest from September through March. From higher points on the course, players can spot the river and Washington state to the north. Several men's and women's events are included on the club's calendar.

The Dalles Country Club was built in 1921 by a small band of founding members, and has served as a sporting and social center for the city, an important inland port for east-of-the-Cascades farmers. Besides tight fairways and small greased-lightning greens, two ponds enter play on three holes and there's a number of greenside traps. Good tests include the top-rated 2nd, a 523-yard par-5 that winds narrowly over corrugated terrain to a slippery putting surface. The 369-yard, par-4 9th heads straight to a slick green guarded left by a pond.

DRIVING RANGES

Lone Pine Village Driving Range

355 Lone Pine Drive, The Dalles, OR 97058. (541) 298-2800. Steve Welker, pro.

UPCOMING COURSES

Madras — Crystal View Golf Course (1999/2000). This 623-acre project was moving toward fruition in early 1997. The project's backer, Albert Zemke of Madras, proposes to build an 18-hole, Robert Cupp-designed layout, a modest clubhouse and an undetermined number of houses on a portion of his wheat and cattle ranch.

Redmond — Canyon Lakes Golf Course (1999). This off-and-on project reemerged from the back burner in late 1996 when its local supporters came up with a new plan for Dry Canyon's south end. The latest proposal involves a par-3 18-holer on 32 acres of privately-owned land and six acres of city land. The project, which would allow the city of Redmond to extend a bicycle and walking path through the course, will probably continue to meet opposition from locals who want to preserve the Dry Canyon.

The Dalles — Lone Pine Village Golf Course (1999). With a driving range already operating, owner William Van Nuys may proceed with an executive nine in the next few years.

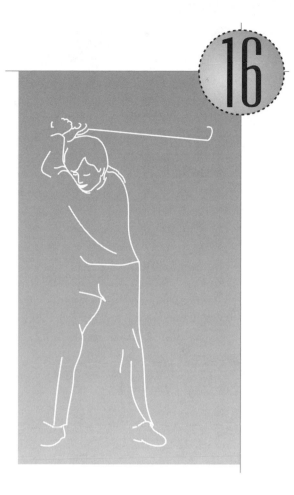

16

SOUTH-CENTRAL
OREGON

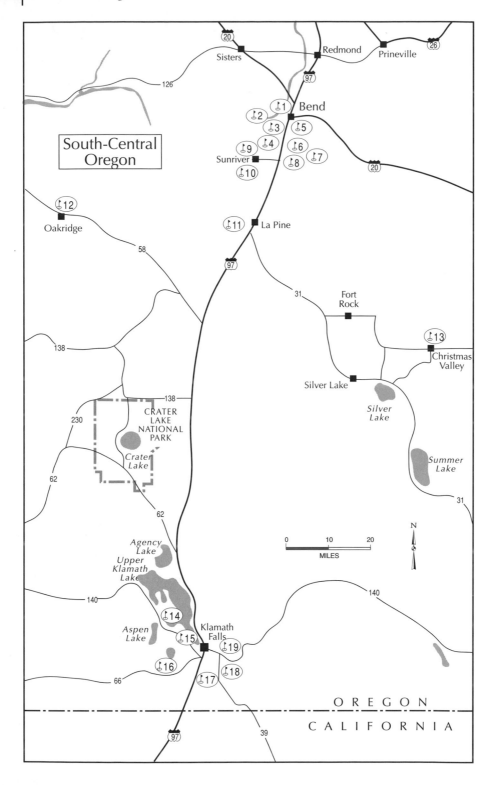

South-Central
Oregon

1. **River's Edge** — public 18 & driving range
2. **Awbrey Glen Golf Club** —private 18
3. **Broken Top Club** — private 18
4. **Widgi Creek Golf Club** — semiprivate 18 & driving range
5. **Orion Greens Golf Course** — public 9
6. **Mountain High Golf Course** — public 18 & driving range
7. **Lost Tracks Golf Club** — public 18 & driving range
8. **Bend Golf & Country Club** — private 18
9. **Sunriver Resort** — public 36 & driving range
10. **Crosswater** — private 18
11. **Quail Run Golf Course** — public 9 & driving range
12. **Circle Bar Golf Club** — public 9
13. **Christmas Valley Golf Course** — public 9 & driving range
14. **Running Y Ranch Resort** — public 18 & driving range
15. **Harbor Links Golf Course** — public 18 & driving range
16. **Round Lake Golf Course** — public 9
17. **Reames Golf & Country Club** — private 18
18. **Raymax Driving Range**
19. **Shield Crest Golf Course** — public 18 & driving range

Widely regarded among Northwesterners as "The Palm Springs of the North," these high desert environs have turned into a year-round recreational mecca with golf leading the way. In the winter when cold weather brings snow, area resorts switch to ski season, both downhill and cross-country. Once-sleepy Bend has led the renaissance, going from a cowboy town to a booming city with traffic problems created by its new inhabitants, many of whom hail from California.

The region stretches from Bend on the north to Klamath Falls on the south. Lying in climate zone 1, south-central Oregon experiences four distinct seasons. Summers are sunny and warm, winters are frigid. Though a few banana belts break up the hot-in-summer-icy-in-winter pattern— especially south and west of Bend, golf remains a May-to-November activity.

Several new golf courses have been built near Bend, while Klamath Falls boasts a new golf-oriented resort, Running Y Ranch. The explosion of new courses in the late 1980s and early 1990s may lead an observer to ask: Has Bend's market been tapped out? It probably has for the time being, at least until more new residents arrive. But the question goes beyond having more supply than demand. How long can course proprietors expect local golfers to keep paying the high green fees charged by resort facilities? Maybe Bend and its neighboring cities should employ a two-tiered, resident-guest system similar to Hawaii's. At least during the slow (non-summer) periods, the facilities can sustain play levels.

Public Courses

Christmas Valley Golf Course

9 *Christmas Valley, OR 97641. (541) 576-2216. 9 holes. 3,517 yards. Par 36. Grass tees. No course ratings. Year Opened: 1963. Architect: Joe Ward. Economical, credit cards. No reservations. Walkability: Good. Playability: A place to whale away with (relative) impunity.*

Christmas Valley Golf Course lies in Oregon's high desert country, about 20 miles southeast of Fort Rock. The town of Christmas Valley was named by Union General John C. Fremont, who was stranded near here during a Christmas Day snowstorm in the mid-1800s. Each year, Christmas Valley's small post office is deluged with thousands of greeting cards from around the world from people who want to have the town's name postmarked on yuletide mail. The golf course adjoins Christmas Valley Lodge, a hostelry built in 1961.

Many of the town's 450 citizens were lured here by one of the largest land swindles ever perpetrated in Oregon. In the early-1960s, the M. Penn Phillips

Company of California bought over 450 square miles of land around Christmas Valley. The company's glossy brochures, depicting a posh resort surrounded by palm trees, attracted a hundred or so families. When the newcomers arrived, they discovered barren scablands and other forlorn takers. Penn Phillips promised there was industry here; over the years, the only business of significance is a kitty litter plant with 25 employees west of town. The new inhabitants also learned that the brochure's elegant lake was actually a small pond behind the lodge, and that the teeming resort had but modest facilities. Palm trees have yet to be seen in Christmas Valley.

But the folks soon moved on to growing alfalfa and barley, farming, and raising cattle. By the early 1970s Christmas Valley was on the upswing as the U.S. government gave low-interest loans for pivot irrigation systems, thus making feasible the irrigation of vast acreage. Soon, however, the subsidies stopped, land prices tumbled to three dollars an acre, and some residents moved on. In 1987, the business climate temporarily improved with the installation southeast of town of a $500-million missile detector system called an Over-the-Horizon Backscanner. The military personnel from the radar site helped boost the local economy and patronized Christmas Valley's golf course. But, with the threat of Russian missiles targeting U. S. soil now nonexistent, the backscanner is closed and only security guards man the site.

Local golfers and visitors from Bend and LaPine play the course, which is owned and operated by Christmas Valley's parks and recreation department. The 1963-built layout is one of Oregon's longest nine-holers at 3,517 yards. Golfers don't encounter many trees or man-made hazards, and the aforementioned "lake"—usually filled with honking geese—enters play only at the 5th hole. Generally, players shoot for distance to tame these expansive fairways. The number-one-ranked hole is the 6th, a 600-yard par-5.

Circle Bar Golf Club 9

West Oak Road, Oakridge, OR 97463. (541) 782-3541. 9 holes. 3,367 yards. Par 36. Grass tees. Course ratings: men B70.8/119; women—B76.8/125, M74.7/ 121, F73.0/118. Year Opened: 1954. Architect: Clarence Sutton. Economical. Call for reservations. Walk-on chances: Good. Walkability: Not too bad overall. Playability: Bowl-shaped layout has some tough holes.

Circle Bar Golf Club occupies a scenic valley near Oakridge. In autumn, deciduous trees around it turn brilliant reds, oranges and yellows. Called Circle Bar Ranch when opened in July 1954, the course occupies land owned by Hines Lumber Company. In 1984 when Hines Lumber closed its local operations, 54 golfers formed a proprietary club and began leasing the course from the company for $10 a year.

Clarence Sutton-designed Circle Bar crosses a bowl-shaped site once logged by Hines Lumber. Stately oaks and maples border fairways, and the layout is bisected by a thin creek. The 45-acre, dual-tee nine stretches across 6,648 gently sloping yards over 18 holes. Situated at 1,200 feet above sea level, Oakridge does not receive much winter snow, and the course has been known to stay open year-round. Circle Bar features a two-story clubhouse with a small pro shop on the ground floor and a banquet room above.

The venue is watered by a manual irrigation system connected to four spring-fed ponds, and its small, raised greens are healthy and well-conditioned. Good tests at the pastoral track include the 2nd, a 425-yard par-4 that curls rightward around the creek to an undulating green. The 4th, a 565-yard par-5 rated the second-toughest hole (its alter ego, the 13th, is deemed the most difficult), bears a pond along the right, 200 yards from a small putting surface. At the 9th, a 515-yard par-5, golfers find a creek-crossed fairway that rises to a knoll-perched and slick, steeply front-tilting green.

Harbor Links Golf Course

18 *601 Harbor Isles Boulevard, Klamath Falls, OR 97601. (541) 882-0609. Rocky Warner, pro. 18 holes. 6,194 yards. Par 72. Grass tees. Course ratings: men— B69.3/117, M68.5/115; women—M73.4/122, F71.2/119. Years Opened: 1986 (original nine); 1990 (second nine). Architect: Ken Black. Moderate, credit cards. Reservations: Call a day ahead. Walk-on chances: Fair. Walkability: Good. Playability: Links layout on the corner of massive Upper Klamath Lake.*

Harbor Links is an 18-hole layout on the north end of Klamath Falls, next to Upper Klamath Lake. The locale is one of the Northwest's prettiest; players enjoy western views of the shimmering lake as well as towering Cascade spires. Though beautiful, the lake and mountains generate howling winds, particularly in late afternoon, skewing golf shots all over the place. That can lead to problems as the 95-acre course is adequately hazardized with five ponds and two dozen sand traps. Other amenities include a driving range, pro shop and the Greygull Restaurant and Lounge.

Designed by its manager and co-owner, Ken Black, Harbor Links began with a front nine in 1986; the back nine followed in spring 1990. The two sides, separated by Harbor Isles Boulevard, are joined by a tunnel. Most holes are lined by mounds and, with few trees, Harbor Links justifies its name. Good holes include the top-rated 5th, a 513-yard par-5 that curls left between ponds to a heart-shaped green backed closely by Upper Klamath Lake. Water hazards are more of a concern on the back side. A representative hole is the 413-yard 17th, a right-bending par-4 that swings around a pond en route to a trapped-right, front-sloping green guarded left by another pond.

Lost Tracks Golf Club

18 *60205 Sunset View Drive, Bend, OR 97702. (541) 385-1818. Steve Bruening, director of golf. 18 holes. 6,855 yards. Par 72. Grass tees. Course ratings: men— B72.4/129, M69.6/122; women—M74.4/132, F70.2/111. Year Opened: 1996. Architect: Brian Whitcomb. Moderate, jr./sr. rates, credit cards. Call for reservations. Walk-on chances: Fair. Walkability: Good, with some hills. Playability: Tough course with blind shots, feral rough and length.*

Opened in mid-1996, Lost Tracks Golf Club joins the growing ranks of top-flight Bend-area courses. The layout was named for an old logging train that once ran through the property but was never found. Helping to sustain the railroad theme, co-owner and designer Brian Whitcomb renovated a 1947 dining car and placed it alongside the 16th green. Golfers walk through the car to enter and leave the green. Whitcomb, a Prineville native who owns Lost Tracks with his brother Paul, moved back to central Oregon to build the course. After playing on the Asian Tour in the early 1980s, the Arizona State University grad went on to develop and own Arizona courses such as 500 Club West, Paradise Valley and Sierra Estrella. Steve Bruening, a Midwesterner, is the director of golf.

Lost Tracks opened with a modular clubhouse and driving range. A local builder, Bill Bundy, is developing 50 houses in and around the 350-acre site. The Whitcombs want to build a 9,000-square-foot clubhouse. But, during the permit process, local residents complained about the size of the building and plans for it to serve food and alcohol. It's uncertain if and when this structure will be built.

Playing the course a few weeks after it opened, I had mixed feelings about Lost Tracks. The layout is characterized by some very tight holes confounded by blind landing areas; an efficient layout suitable for bag-toters; and low-lipped, escapable bunkers filled with gray river sand. These random observations followed a somewhat lousy round. Though not an excellent golfer, I can usually find a fairway when I see it. But with no yardage markers in sprinkler heads (which will be remedied) and Bend's 3,700-foot elevation, I was hitting through these twisting fairways all day. First-timers are thus warned: beware the view-blocking rises off tees which, combined with the twisting fairways, make hitting perceived targets tough. Bring an extra sleeve of balls since, when you're off fairways, you're not likely to find your ball. Even if you can find it, recoverability is impeded by uncleared sagebrush, juniper and dense groundcover.

Typical of a new course, the greens at Lost Tracks were a bit shaggy in summer 1996, but the putting surfaces will be mowed lower as the turf ages. Because it was built earlier and the grass was better grown in, the back nine was more mature and more open than the restrictive front side. Besides the stroll through the dining car, nice touches include wooden benches mounted atop rocks at tees, little steel trains for tee markers, and paved cart paths. The women's tees at Lost Tracks are quite close to the tips on several holes, a fact readily pointed out by my playing-partner wife.

Tough front-nine tests include the 3rd, a 426-yard par-4 with an elevated tee and a mid-width fairway lined by a tall pine on the left. The fairway winds 90 degrees to the right, and involves a patch of scrub growth and pines at the 100-yard mark. Another large pine guards the right-front entry of the small and round, front-tilting 3rd green. The 453-yard, par-4 4th has a raised tee fronted (oddly) 125 yards along the right by a mound and two pot bunkers. A fat trap sits outside the turn of the right-curling hole, which rises to a two-tiered green trapped left-front, right-front and right-rear. From the back tees at the 7th, a 501-yard par-5, golfers must drive between two pines to find a left-turning fairway. Three pot bunkers lurk inside the turn at the 250-yard mark. The hole then ascends to a ridge-cut green trapped five times in front. The left-front-tilting putting surface sits in a bowl and is smaller than it looks. The top-rated 573-yard, par-5 9th is a very tight, 90-degree dogleg-left around a pond. Well-hit second shots can clear the pond and perhaps find a landing area left-front of a hill-cut, wide-but-shallow green trapped twice on the left. For those laying up to the right, precision is a must as trees and scrub lurk 50 yards before the green.

From the tips at the 10th, a 448-yard par-4, the drive must cross over the entry road. A pond sits along the right of this left-turning hole, which is squeezed at the 150-yard mark by trees and rocks along the right. A swale fronts the steeply front-sloping 10th green, which is trapped on the right and has two levels. The 417-yard, par-4 13th is long left-turner with two traps outside the dogleg. The hole curls around to a large, left-rear-tilting green trapped right-rear and right. Of perhaps more concern is a hidden-from-the-fairway pond that runs up to green's right-rear edge. The 15th, a 341-yard par-4 called "Blind Draw," is an uphill dogleg-left with two traps outside the knee. Trees along the right line the hole before it ends at a steeply front-banked green with three tiers and deep jail left and rear. The 141-yard 16th is a pretty par-3 with an island green engirded by water laterally and in front. The "Lost Tracks Railway" car provides a rear-right entry to the putting surface, which is bunkered left-rear and rear. The 508-yard, par-5 18th has a sizable landing area lined by three pines on the right. Don't overhit this target as a pond sits invisibly 250 yards out. The lake runs for 125 yards along the route's right side; trees on the left also squeeze this juncture. The 18th's latter leg curls left to a front-leaning green with a grass trap in front and sand bunkers right, right-rear and rear.

Mountain High Golf Course

18

60650 China Hat Road, Bend, OR 97701. (541) 382-1111. 18 holes. 6,656 yards. Par 72. Grass tees. Course ratings: men—B72.0/131, M69.2/122, I67.3/115, F65.4/110; women—M73.5/136, I71.6/126, F69.2/120. Years Opened: 1987 (original nine); 1990 (second nine). Architects: Michael Currie (original nine): Jan Ward (second nine). Moderate, credit cards. Reservations: Call a week ahead. Walk-on chances: Fair. Walkability: Good, overall. Playability: Well-conditioned course has some idiosyncratic holes.

Mountain High's course winds through a like-named, 300-unit subdivision originated by Bend native, Jan Ward. The facility began with nine holes in 1987 and received a second side three years later. The venue has a roundhouse-like clubhouse with a pro shop and food service. Mountain High residents have access to swimming pools, tennis courts, and biking and hiking paths (also used by golf carts) at the development.

These verdant fairways wind between Bend's ubiquitous lava outcrops. From higher parts of the course, golfers enjoy choice mountain vistas, while rabbits, chipmunks and quails scurry across fairways. Impediments to success on this mid-length (for Bend) course include dozens of white-sand bunkers and 10 ponds, which lurk off tees, alongside fairways and in front of greens. Each hole has five tees,

Mounain High's 5th hole is a 348-yard par-4.

making the course adaptable for a wide variety of golfers. Mountain High employs a "target time" system—similar to that used at Black Butte—which encourages players to finish a round in four hours and 15 minutes. The suggested time to play a hole is listed on the scorecard.

The original nine (played as the back) offers a challenging and generally fair set of golf holes. Its designer, landscape architect Michael Currie, made good use of the site's rolling topography. These holes offer golfers some tough tests (the 460-yard par-4 16th in particular) as well as birdie opportunities (the 282-yard par-4 18th). With its subtle design and variable tee locations, these holes are well-suited to Bend's many vacationing—and infrequent—golfers.

Contrarily, Ward's 3,556-yard front nine has several contrivances. Among the most pretentious is the 496-yard 7th, Oregon's longest par-4 by quite a margin. The thin air created by Bend's 3,700-foot elevation alleviates the distance somewhat, but the 7th exceeds the maximum length for a regulation par-4 by some 20 yards. Another oddity is the 9th, a driveable par-4 less than 240 yards from the white tees. I also have a problem with the white OB stakes along nearly every Mountain High fairway, including many interior holes. Narrow routes lined by pines, sagebrush, lava, and considerable sand and water hazards—legitimate concerns all—should not have OB stakes along them. It's penalty enough trying to get safely back to the fairway from these rugged peripheries.

Orion Greens Golf Course   9

61525 Fargo Lane, Bend, OR 97702. (541) 388-3999. 9 holes. 2,075 yards. Par 31. Grass tees. Course ratings: men—B59.6/96, M58.8/95; women—I62.0/95, F59.3/90. Year Opened: 1982. Architects: the Reed family. Moderate, credit cards. Call for reservations. Walk-on chances: Fair. Walkability: Very good. Playability: Fun executive course on Bend's southeast end.

This executive-length nine lies about a mile-and-a-half east of Highway 97 off Reed Market Road. The layout, which is augmented by a large clubhouse with a full-service restaurant, is part of a subdivision known as Orion Greens Golf Course & Estates. The facilities were developed by the Reed family in 1982. Orion Greens extends 2,075 yards from the back tees, and provides enjoyable rounds. When tired of getting their brains beaten out by Bend's numerous championship tracks, many golfers come here for a respite.

Though Orion Greens doesn't provide a supreme test, trouble can be found on the well-tended layout, which features fairways winding between lava beds and houses. Several ponds enter play and most greens are guarded by traps. The track sports four par-4s ranging from 306 to 346 yards, and five par-3s from 124 to 201 yards. The layout crosses a plateau, so there are nice views of the mountains around Bend.

Noteworthy holes include the 1st, a 346-yard par-4 that winds leftward around a bunker to a green backed by a pond. The 326-yard, par-4 4th has a narrow, dogleg-left fairway with a swale midway along a route lined by homes and pine trees. The 4th green is backed by lava and jail. The pretty 9th, a par-3 of 124 yards, features a tiny and slick, trapped-front green guarded behind by a pond.

Quail Run Golf Course

9 *16725 Northridge Drive, LaPine, OR 97739. (541) 536-1303. Jon Noack, pro. 9 holes. 3,450 yards. Par 36. Grass tees. Course ratings: men—B72.2/126, B/M70.9/ 123, M69.6/119; women—I73.4/124, I/F71.5/120, F69.6/116. Year Opened: 1991. Architect: Jim Ramey. Moderate. Call for reservations. Walk-on chances: Fair. Walkability: Good. Playability: Length and hazards combine in challenging nine-hole package.*

Quail Run lies nine miles south of Bend, two miles west of Highway 97 off the East Lake/Lake Paulina exit. The nine-holer is owned by two brothers, Jerry and Art Larsen, and was designed by Jim Ramey, Sunriver's longtime greens superintendent. The 110-acre layout crosses generally flat ground, and is bordered by a few homes. Quail Run features a nice clubhouse, a practice green, chipping green with practice bunker, and a grass-teed driving range. Earlier in the '90s, the Larsens sought to acquire a neighboring 90-acre parcel for a back nine, but that project remains a future consideration.

Because of its sizable plot, the lengthy dual-tee layout—extending 6,900 yards over two circuits—has no paralleling holes. Located at 4,000 feet above sea level, Quail offers great views of the local mountains, and is frequented by its namesake bird. Though containing but nine holes and a bit removed from the city, moderately-priced Quail Run is a good choice for Bend-area linksters tired of spending big bucks at the upscale courses. Ramey did an excellent job weaving holes over the site's gently rolling terrain and incorporating sand and water hazards into the field of play. Most fairways present ample landing areas, and the large greens are not overly tricked up. Quail Run's signature hole is the 9th, a 451-yard par-4 that winds leftward around a pond with a landscaped island. The fairway concludes at a two-tiered, trapped-left green guarded along the right by two pot bunkers.

River's Edge Golf Course

18 *400 Pro Shop Drive, Bend, OR 97701. (541) 389-2828. Lyndon Blackwell, pro. 18 holes. 6,618 yards. Par 72. Grass tees. Course ratings: men—B72.6/137, M71.6/ 135, I70.5/129; women—I76.3/144, F71.8/135. Years Opened: 1988 (original nine); 1992 (second nine). Architect: Robert Muir Graves. Moderate, credit cards. Reservations: Call a week ahead. Walk-on chances: Fair. Walkability: Fair, with some steep terrain. Playability: Dipsy-doodle fairways and plenty of hazards make this track above Bend very challenging.*

An 18-hole layout, River's Edge traverses a steep hill behind Riverhouse Inn, a four-diamond hotel according to AAA. The course and hostelry are owned by River's Edge Investments, a consortium made up of Clyde and Mary Lou Purcell, their son Wayne, and Anne Swarens. Since the original nine was built in 1988, the owners have developed 325 homes in and around the course. From the higher points on River's Edge, wonderful views of Mount Hood, Smith Rock and the Ochoco Mountains are available.

Because of a rocky site, thousands of yards of topsoil and dirt were hauled in during course construction. Rock walls were dynamited and ponderosa pines removed where necessary. The tipped topography leads to all sorts of side-, up- and downhill lies. Combined with length and more-than-ample hazards, it's easy to see why the OGA arrived at River's Edge's high ratings. But each hole has four tees, so the course is player-adaptable. Cart paths wind throughout and good signage helps golfers negotiate the layout. Fit golfers shouldn't have too many problems packing their clubs at this track. But others might, as steep hikes are common.

Particularly tough holes include the 4th, a 513-yard par-5 with a left-bending fairway that rises to a narrow point, then bends sharply left around a pond to a trapped-left, tree-backed green. The 344-yard, par-4 5th is the signature hole at River's Edge. Starting at a raised tee, the fairway heads toward two tree-covered rock walls above a waterfall-bedecked pond. The green roosts atop a mesa behind the water. The three-tiered, front-banked putting surface is reached by a bridge. From the elevated tee at the 10th, a 524-yard par-5, golfers enjoy wonderful views of Bend and environs. From here, the hole heads slightly uphill to the right. Two bunkers guard the right edge of the domed, steeply left-front-tilting 10th green.

The tough 14th, a 461-yard par-4, starts at a raised tee and follows a narrow route that leans left toward grass bunkers and trees. Second shots must be hit straight up to a hill-cut, shallow green whose throat is squeezed by pines at the right-front. A second River's Edge signature hole is the 15th, a 215-yard par-3 that drops down to a figure-eight-shaped green trapped right-front and rear. A pond also lurks right-front of the target. Water fronts the tee of the 16th, a 515-yard par-5 that requires a blind drive to a right-curling, uphill fairway. Grass bunkers line the left edge of the hole before it rises narrowly to a slippery green protected by a trap and jail left.

Round Lake Golf Course   9

4000 Round Lake Road, Klamath Falls, OR 97601. (541) 884-2520. 9 holes. 1,512 yards. Par 29. Grass tees. No course ratings. Year Opened: 1978. Architect: Bob Caine. Economical, jr./sr. rates. No reservations. Walkability: Good. Playability: Short track good choice for vacationing RVers.

The abbreviated nine here is part of Round Lake Resort, a recreational-residential enclave located eight miles north of Highway 66, west of Klamath Falls. The course and resort were built in 1978 by its founder and current owner Bob Caine, a Bend resident. Resort facilities include an RV park, a clubhouse with banquet and recreation hall, and a swimming pool. RVers who spend two or more nights enjoy free golf. Nearly 30 trailer houses used by residents are also on the grounds. The resort is named for its namesake body of water, which shimmers to the north and west.

Lying at about 4,000 feet above sea level, Round Lake's course closes when the snow comes. It's often visited by deer, bears, porcupines, skunks, muskrats, bald eagles and hawks. Mosquitos are a problem in summer. The perfunctory single-tee nine is easy-to-walk, with the only hazards a creek on the 1st and 2nd holes, and a pond at the 3rd. The course has two par-4s of 260 and 345 yards, and seven par-3s—from 109 to 160 yards. Fairways are squeezed by alders, and Round Lake's postage-stamp greens can be elusive.

Running Y Ranch Resort

18 *Off Highway 140, Klamath Falls, OR 97601. (541) 882-6135 (resort headquarters). 18 holes. 7,300 yards. Par 72. Grass tees. Course ratings not available. Year Opened: 1997. Architects: John Thronson & Palmer Design. Moderate, credit cards. Call for reservations. Walk-on chances: Fair. Walkability: Fair, with spread-out holes. Playability: Upscale course has potential to be one of central Oregon's finest.*

The 165-acre golf course at Running Y Ranch is the first of many recreational facilities planned for the new resort, which is located six miles west of Klamath Falls off Highway 140. The $68-million project will eventually include 1,250 houses and condos, a 250-room hotel, restaurant, indoor sports facility, tennis courts, swimming pools, small town center, and trails for horseback riders, bicyclists and hikers. Also planned is a 6,000-square-foot clubhouse/lodge, 12-acre driving range and an 18-hole putting course. In 1997, the backers were working on an Environmental Impact Statement for a federal permit to build a ski resort on nearby Pelican Butte. At full build-out, probably after the year 2000, the resort will cover 3,525 acres of the 9,600-acre site.

Running Y Ranch was previously used as a summer place by Roy Disney, brother of the famed cartoonist and fantasylander, Walt. The project is backed by Jeld-Wen and its development subsidiary, Trendwest Resorts. Jeld-Wen, the biggest door manufacturer in the world and emerging as a leader in the window market, developed Eagle Crest Resort and has plans for a similar project in Roslyn, Washington. The south-central Oregon site is beautiful—a wide valley at an elevation of 4,200 feet that offers wonderful Cascade vistas. The venue is on the migratory path for deer and, as part of the Pacific Coast Flyway, is a regular stop for ducks and geese. Cows graze lazily in pastures beside several holes.

The course was a co-design of Eagle Crest's superintendent John Thronson and Palmer Design. Thronson worked closely with Erick Larsen of Palmer Design, creating what appears to be a magnificent track. I visited Running Y during the height of construction in September 1996. The work, overseen by Richard Page of Terrebonne, Oregon, was being performed by a huge crew of 97. Superintendent Larry Rashko was hired during grow-in. All holes were shaped before the snows came, with seeding to commence in spring '97 (after this book went to press). While touring the site with Thronson, I was struck by the epic scope of many holes. The course involves four lakes, several natural and man-made wetlands, and 100 white-sand bunkers. The five miles of paved cart paths around the layout will be used by cross-country skiers in winter.

Running Y Ranch will be one of the three courses (with Eagle Crest and Awbrey Glen) hosting the Northwest Open over the next several years. The course involves 100 feet of elevation change, and should prove worthy of any tournament. Here's a brief sketch of some of the better tests: The 580-yard, par-5 2nd winds leftward around a canal which guards the hole along its entire length. The 4th, a 440-yard par-4, has wetlands off the tee and on the fairway's right edge. Following a short par-3 at the 5th, the 430-yard, par-4 6th boasts a steep uphill fairway and a big green enveloped by pot bunkers. The 8th is a 575-yard par-5 that angles uphill to the left. The par-3 12th involves a 75-foot drop; prevailing winds will boggle club selections at the tee. The 13th and 14th are 400-plus-yard par-4s, and the 15th is a 222-yard par-3. The 16th is a beautiful tree-lined par-4, while the 440-yard 18th sports towering elevated tees and great views. I can't wait to return to Running Y Ranch and see the course when it's green.

Shield Crest Golf Course

3151 Shield Crest Drive, Klamath Falls, OR 97603. (541) 884-1493. John Humphrey, pro. 18 holes. 7,005 yards. Par 72. Grass tees. Course ratings: men—B72.1/122, M70.6/120; women—M75.7/122, F73.4/118. Years Opened: 1989 (original nine); 1990 (second nine). Architects: Mike Whitmore (original nine); Charles Mangum (second nine). Moderate, sr. rates, credit cards. Reservations: Call three days ahead. Walk-on chances: Fair. Walkability: Good, overall. Playability: Long-ballers should do well here.

Shield Crest's 7,000-yard course occupies 156 acres of a like-named, 265-acre subdivision. The facility lies off Highway 97 east of Klamath Falls on the way to Altamont. Begun by Klamath Falls natives Robert and Helen Cheyne, the development has 76 lots and 33 condo units. Also on-site is a clubhouse with a pro shop and cafe, and a 10-acre, grass-teed driving range. From the course's upper points are views of nearby mountains, especially Mount Shasta in California.

The fairways wind past soon-to-be-developed homesites and existing residences. The front nine was designed by Mike Whitmore of Portland, and the back by Salem's Charles Mangum. Despite being arrayed by different architects, the two sets of holes are quite similar. Fairways are lined by shortish saplings and are generally wide-open. Shield Crest Creek meanders through, entering play—along fairways or behind greens—on five holes. White sand fills the bunkers, some of which are small and a bit removed from critical junctures. The course derives its difficulty from several 400-plus-yard par-4s where good drives and accurate second shots are needed to get home in regulation.

Noteworthy tests include the 2nd, a 539-yard par-5 that follows a wide and fairly straight path lined on the right by the creek. The stream crosses the hole 120 yards from a left-leaning, trapped-in-front green. The 522-yard, par-5 8th curls rightward between OB and a pasture en route to a squarish, unbunkered putting surface. The hardest hole on the course is the 18th, a 466-yard par-4 that runs straight for 250 yards or so, then curls 70 degrees to the left around a pond. The water hazard almost laps at the two bunkers fronting a hill-carved green.

Sunriver Resort

36 *Sunriver Lodge & Resort, Sunriver, OR 97707. (541) 593-1221 or 1-800-962-1769. Pros: Dave Hall (South Meadows); Brad Bedortha (North Woodlands). 36 holes. Grass tees. Course ratings: South Meadows Course (6,880 yards, par 72) men— B72.7/133, M68.8/124; women—M73.0/122, F70.3/118. North Woodlands Course (6,898 yards, par 72) men—B72.6/132, M70.7/131, I70.0/129; women—M74.8/ 123, F71.7/116. Years Opened: 1968 (South Meadows); 1981 (North Woodlands). Architects: Fred Federspiel (South Meadows); Robert Trent Jones Jr. (North Woodlands). Expensive, credit cards. Reservations: Call a week ahead. Walk-on chances: Ok for singles. Walkability: Fair, with some long treks over asphalt paths. Playability: Northwest's original golf resort still packing 'em in.*

Sunriver, the Northwest's first major golf-oriented resort, continues its popularity. The 36 holes at this sprawling, 3,368-acre retreat represent just one of the sports available to guests. Also listed on the summer-season agenda are river-rafting, horseback riding, miles of interwoven biking and hiking trails, swimming pools, tennis and fishing. Eight-and-a-half miles of the Deschutes River meander through the resort, and over 300 lakes lie within 40 miles. In winter, Sunriver tunes in to the cross-country and downhill skiing at nearby Mount Bachelor.

The resort's 3,200 homesites are owned by individuals who belong to the Sunriver Owners Association. In the peak days of July and August, the resort has a population in excess of 6,000. Gridlock happens frequently as motorists negotiate the two-lane roads, trying to get from one end of Sunriver to the other. The 600-acre Crosswater part of Sunriver is an upscale development with 98 expensive lots and a separate 18-hole course, which is playable only by members and resort guests. Sunriver is owned by Lowe Enterprises, the Los Angeles-based firm behind the proposed Arrowleaf Resort in north-central Washington.

Like other Bend-area courses, Sunriver is pricey, with summer green fees around $60 and cart rentals at $25. For that cost, golfers should expect premier conditions and outstanding courses. Though they're often extolled in national publications, North Woodlands Course (previously called North) and South Meadows have lost some of their luster in recent years. I've heard complaints from players of deteriorating playing conditions and rock-hard fairways and greens. I don't believe the first claim, but the latter allegation is certainly true as the winds pick up in the afternoon, desiccating Sunriver's fairways and greens such that shots are often deflected into unintended places. Also, south-central Oregon's arid mountain air allows golf balls to fly far, and many "flatlanders" from the coast aren't used to balls jumping off their clubs as they do here at 3,700 feet above sea level.

National authorities still lavish praise on Sunriver's courses; North Woodlands received four stars in *Golf Digest's* "1996-'97 Places to Play Guide" and South Meadows got three. These high marks follow such accolades as North being voted Oregon's top resort course in 1992 by *GOLFWEEK* readers, and a regular ranking among *Golf Digest's* "America's 75 Best Resort Courses." Certainly both layouts have the earmarks of top-flight tracks, with paved paths for motorized chariots and yardages on brass sprinkler heads. On the down side, South Meadows is lined throughout by houses and condos, so enjoying a quiet round here is well nigh impossible. North Woodlands is a bit less developed on the periphery.

Among the better tests at the 1968-opened South Meadows is the 1st, a 524-yard par-5 that bends left en route to a bunker-ringed green. The 423-yard, par-4 7th doglegs slightly right to a trap-fronted green. A 539-yard par-5, the 17th curls rightward around a lake to a bunker-squeezed green backed by a pond. The 392-yard, par 4 18th curls 90 degrees left around a fat part of the lake behind the 17th green. The putting surface here is small and bunkered laterally.

Robert Trent Jones Jr.-designed North Woodlands is hillier and more interesting than South Meadows. For years it was the site of the Oregon Open, which moved to Crosswater in 1996. Good holes here include the top-rated 1st, a 506-yard par-5 that rises past a pond along the right. Several fairway bunkers squat 50 yards from an elevated, bi-trapped green. The 438-yard, par-4 9th winds rightward past bunkers left and a pond right en route to a wavy, bi-trapped green. The 15th, a 543-yard par-5, has a trap-littered fairway and a boomerang-shaped green. The 416-yard, par-4 18th is a sharp dogleg-left with ponds inside and outside the turn. The inside water hazard can be carried but, hmmm, how much of the water does one bite off? The 18th green is guarded on the right by traps and left by the latter part of the pond.

Widgi Creek Golf Club - semiprivate

18707 Century Drive, Bend, OR 97709. (541) 382-4449. Jeff Jarvis, pro. 18 holes. 6,911 yards. Par 72. Grass tees. Course ratings: men—T73.4/134, B71.3/132, M68.7/122; women—I74.5/135, F69.2/124. Year Opened: 1991 (original nine); 1992 (second nine). Architect: Robert Muir Graves. Expensive, credit cards. Reservations: Call a week ahead. Walk-on chances: Ok for singles. Walkability: Fair, with some hills and long between-hole hikes. Playability: Restrictive fairways lined by trees, hazards and inescapable jail.

Though relatively new, this course has already undergone several name changes. Originally called Seventh Mountain Golf Village, it was named Pine Meadow Country Club during an aborted purchase attempt by a group that included PGA Tour member and golf commentator Johnny Miller. After that deal fell through, its current name—taken from the creek winding through—was given in 1994. The Yamazoe family (developers of the Inn at Seventh Mountain), Sho Dozono and former Olympic swimming champ Don Schollander are the proprietors.

Widgi Creek lies five miles southwest of Bend near the ski slopes of Mount Bachelor, and traverses property next to the Inn at Seventh Mountain. On-site facilities include a clubhouse, pro shop, lockers, showers, driving range, paved cart paths and excellent signage. A swimming pool and tennis courts are used by homeowners. The layout sports up to five tees per hole, 11 lakes and 60 bunkers. When designing the course, architect Robert Muir Graves made sure that the surrounding housing lots were situated well apart from the fairways. Widgi Creek's Penncross bent greens are tricky and fast, with assorted slopes and hogbacks lending them much difficulty.

Winding over rolling terrain and through densely-packed ponderosa pines, Widgi Creek involves potential problems on each of its narrow holes. This is a "thinking player's" course, one that requires pre-shot planning and careful execution. One mistake can lead to major calamity. Particularly difficult holes include the 6th, a pretty 334-yard par-4 lined along the left by two ponds and a bunker. A long iron is a reasonable choice from the tee. A larger pond skirts the front and right edges of the narrow but deep, three-tiered 6th green, which is trapped twice on the right.

The 216-yard, par-3 11th has a heart-shaped pond running from the tee to a large, mound-ringed green that tilts steeply left-front toward a bunker. The 551-yard, par-5 12th winds leftward through pines. The fairway rises to a peak, then flattens 130 yards from a skinny and raised green trapped left. The 13th, a 377-yard par-4, follows a narrow and rolling, left-curling route. A deep ravine, partially filled by a "lava trap," fronts a knoll-perched, shallow-but-wide green squeezed by three sand traps.

Private Courses

Awbrey Glen Golf Club

2500 NW Awbrey Glen Drive, Bend, OR 97708. (541) 385-6011. Mark Amberson, pro. 18 holes. 6,980 yards. Par 72. Grass tees. Course ratings: men—B73.7/135, M71.9/132, I69.6/124; women—I74.0/130, F69.6/119. Year Opened: 1993. Architect: Gene "Bunny" Mason. Members, guests and some outside play (call for details).

Situated within Awbrey Glen, a 407-acre "Private Residential Golf Community" three miles from downtown Bend, this course is classified as private. But it does allow some outside play (call for details). In June 1996, my wife and I arranged a tee time. But the going rate was pricey: $158 for two rounds and a cart. Developed by Brooks Resources (which also did Canyon Lakes in the Tri-Cities and Black Butte Ranch in Sisters, Oregon), the gated Awbrey Glen community involves 330 residential lots, a large clubhouse, tennis courts, a park, and walking and biking trails. Awbrey Glen features one of the region's premier driving ranges/practice facilities. The 400-yard-long range has grass tees at each end. Five practice holes—the longest at 180 yards—wind around the range. Also on-site is a classroom with swing-analysis equipment; a parcel next to the clubhouse has been set aside for an 18-hole putting course.

Several houses have been built along fairway peripheries; fortunately, they're suitably apart from play. Brooks Resources hopes to eventually sell 450 non-proprietary memberships. Once these have been sold, Brooks will turn the course over to the members. Awbrey Glen was open for only two years when it hosted the 1995 Northwest Open, won by John McComish of Oak Knoll Golf Course in Independence, Oregon. Big John (he's 6'6" and 260 pounds) shot 11-under for three rounds, firing a course-record 65 on one of the days. Over the next several years, Awbrey Glen will be one of the three courses (with Eagle Crest and Running Y Ranch) hosting the Northwest Open.

The Bunny Mason-designed layout crosses hilly, forested terrain, and harbors all manner of ill intent. Yet Mason made the course adaptable for golfers of all skills, building four or five tees per hole, including blocks for seniors and children. As an example of this, the par-3s play anywhere from 130 to 230 yards. Other than tipped topography (a cart is a good idea here), Awbrey Glen's is known for its ultra-slick greens. If Bend can be labeled "The Land of the Fast, Domed Greens," then Awbrey Glen may well be the county seat. Perhaps the severest case of these is the 17th green, which is bowed in the middle and trapped both sides. I got in the right-hand trap and hit what looked like a nice shot near the pin. The ball should have stopped, since we'd just endured a very heavy rainstorm. But no. It skittered across the green and rolled into the left trap. Back out again, this time uphill, and a painful two-putt. Let's just say that the game plan for Awbrey Glen is to hit it close to the hole.

Other hallmarks are excellent conditioning, white-sand bunkers (which I experienced too many times), paved paths, and great signage (with yardages on sprinkler heads and on buttons on cart paths every 25 yards). Difficult holes include the 4th, a 393-yard par-4 that goes uphill and straight. A fat pine tree sits at the 75-yard mark, squeezing the right-hand entry to a steeply front-tilting green trapped front-right. The 398-yard, par-4 5th involves a tee shot slammed into a steeply rising, well-moguled fairway. The ascending route eventually curls left to a smallish, untrapped green with a tall front edge. The second shot into the 5th green is one of the course's toughest. The top-rated 9th, a 536-yard par-5, is a downhill dogleg-left with mounds and a solitary tree inside the turn. Once around the corner, the fairway skirts a huge bunker left en route to a severely left-sloping, triple-tiered green trapped left.

I consider Awbrey Glen's back nine one of the most entertaining sets of holes in the Northwest. Following a 441-yard par-4 at the 10th comes a 205-yard par-3, which rises to a large, rolling green trapped twice in front. The 591-yard, par-5 12th is an engineering marvel, with towering tees cut out of a steep cliff. Drives are fired off this precipice toward a landing area that leans rightward to a huge bunker. The right-tilting fairway gradually arrives at a huge green guarded by a bunker left-front and two ponds right. Though ranked Awbrey Glen's 18th-toughest hole, the 190-yard 13th is a dandy par-3. The hole descends between ruddy rock walls to a steeply left-front-leaning green trapped right-front and left-rear. The putting surface sits in a hollowed-out section of solid rock; tee balls pushed to the right may very well carom onto the green.

The 439-yard 14th is another uphill par-4, bypassing a pine in the right half of the fairway and mounds left. The big 14th green is raised and mound-ringed, and has swales and trees along the left. Another candidate for signature hole status (besides the 12th and 13th) is the 15th, a 559-yard par-5 that runs slightly downhill off the tee. The right-tilting hole goes for 400 yards or so—skirting bunkers, rocks and a well-treed escarpment—before winding 90 degrees to the right around trees and jail to a sunken, trapped-right green. If positioned properly off the tee (left-center), the 15th is a definite eagle or birdie opportunity. The 222-yard, par-3 16th rises to a ridge-perched green trapped left-front and right-rear. Perhaps of more concern is a grass bunker in front that sits five feet below the putting surface. The 18th, a 561-yard par-5, features a towering tee and a left-sloping fairway that descends about 200 yards out. A pond lurks along the left at the 250-yard mark, a point where the fairway rises and straightens out. The slick, trapped-left 18th green is guarded closely by trees along the right.

Bend Golf & Country Club

18

20399 Murphy Road, Bend, OR 97702. (541) 382-7437. Thomas Tirrill, pro. 18 holes. 7,035 yards. Par 72. Grass tees. Course ratings: men—B73.8/132, M71.4/ 127; women—I74.6/133, F72.5/129. Year Opened: 1925 (original nine); 1973 (second nine). Architects: H. Chandler Egan (original nine); Bob Baldock & Son (second nine); William Robinson (remodel). Members, guests & reciprocates.

With its original nine holes opened in the mid-1920s, this became the second course built in central Oregon. The first was Central Oregon Golf Club, which locals played in the early 1900's. Located on the Fred Stanley Ranch at Deschutes Junction beside what is now Highway 97, that club was the precursor of the many golf courses now thriving in Bend. The demise of Central Oregon Golf Club was expedited in 1924 when Bend residents wanted golfing grounds closer to the city. Local businesses and residents invested $100 apiece in the club and, in 1924, the founders acquired 172 acres southeast of town from the Brooks-Scanlon Lumber Company. Medford's H. Chandler Egan designed Bend's original "outside" nine, which opened May 7, 1925.

Various club structures—caddie house, machinery shed, pro shop and locker room—were donated by the Shevlin-Hixon Company and Brooks-Scanlon. By 1930, Bend Golf Club enjoyed an active ladies club. In the early 1930s, central Oregon was afflicted by a severe water shortage, but the nine-hole course survived. The club maintained a 100-strong membership through the Depression, but World War II severely depleted the scrolls. Thankfully, Camp Abbott outside of town had several thousand troops who made use of the club's facilities. In 1948, Brooks-Scanlon donated 309 undeveloped acres south of the course. The tract was later used for nine more holes as well as homesites, which were sold to raise capital for the expansion. In the 1950s when the club was in the midst of recovery, improvements were made to the clubhouse. Slot machines helped raise capital before the state cracked down on gambling, a move that cost the club as much income as it generated through dues. Other private clubs in Oregon also suffered when the gambling devices were deemed illegal. Nonetheless, in the early 1950s Bend's members financed a sprinkler system and, in 1965, a new clubhouse opened along Murphy Road.

In 1971, the club began planning nine more holes, hiring Bob Baldock & Son for the design of the long-missing "inside" part of the course. The project was completed in 1973. By 1978, the club had a new swimming pool, indoor tennis and handball/racquetball courts, and outdoor tennis courts. When Deschutes County assessed Bend Golf Club's land and improvements at over $2 million in 1981, the club was dissolved and Bend Golf & Country Club was formed. Throughout Bend's golf boom, the club has enjoyed a full membership.

The course has held many tournaments over the years. Annual events include the Mirror Pond Invitational (held since 1953), the Ponderosa Invitational, Southern Oregon Seniors, Central Oregon Pro-Am and Women's President Trophy. The course hosted the 1980 Equitable Savings Northwest Open, and has been the site of the Oregon Open. Over its lengthy history, the club's listing of head pros includes Bill Reed, John Gravon, Walter Sopke, Bill Lindgren, Dave Duvall, Woody Lamb, Harvey Bunn, Einer Allen, Bud Davis, Lou Kokal, Ken Spence, Mike Dudik, Stan Hogan, Mickey Sullivan, Jim French, Larry Novak and Jim Wilkinson. Wilkinson holds Bend's noncompetitive record, a 62, while the competitive record is a 65 set by PGA Senior Tourer Don Bies during U.S. Open Qualifying.

In the early 1990s, the course received a $1-million remodel from Bill Robinson. The project included 14 new tees, 39 new or reshaped bunkers, mounding, six remodeled greens, and renovations to the ponds and irrigation system. Bend's two modernized nines are now similar. The efficient and easy-to-walk layout is lined by a few homes and, except for western holes along Highway 97, offers quiet rounds. The Three Sisters mountains are on display from open areas, and deer and chipmunks occasionally visit. Good holes include the top-rated 2nd, a 567-yard par-5 that goes 200 yards before winding narrowly to the right. The hole rises past a bunker along the left and, at the 100-yard mark, curls leftward to a small, ridge-perched green trapped twice right-front and once each left and right. The 4th, a 423-yard par-4, runs straight along a rising path. At the 125-yard mark, the fairway drops to a large green trapped left, front and rear. The 410-yard, par-4 8th is wide over its initial length, then narrows as it bears left. After the turn, a fat pine in mid-fairway veils a pond to its left. The small, left-sloping 8th green is pinched left by a trap and right by three pines.

Perhaps Bend's prettiest hole is the 11th, a 145-yard par-3 whose tee and green are separated by a pond. Its wide-but-shallow green is trapped left-rear and along the back. The right-bending 12th, a 424-yard par-4, gradually tapers before ascending to a rolling and ridged green trapped rear. The 539-yard, par-5 13th doglegs right around a big pine, skirting two traps outside the turn. Once around the corner, the fairway stretches to a small, flattish green trapped twice rear and once right. A hidden pond lurks left-front of the 13th green. The 15th, a par-5 of 535 yards, has a knoll in front of the tee; a periscope helps golfers view the fairway. Trees right of the landing area must be avoided before the hole angles off to the right. Pines squeeze both sides of the fairway as it rises over rolling, right-leaning ground to a small, front-left-sloping green trapped once in front and twice rear. The 482-yard 17th is one of the region's longest par-4s. The hole ascends over moguled ground to a peak, then descends along a tight, tree-lined path to a rear-sloping green bunkered laterally and rear.

Broken Top Club

61999 Broken Top Drive, Bend, OR 97702. (541) 383-0868. Randy Shannon, pro. 18 holes. 7,161 yards. Par 72. Grass tees. Course ratings: men—B74.4/138, M71.5/ 130, 168.8/121, F65.9/111; women—M76.7/138, 173.4/131, F70.3/122. Year Opened: 1993. Architects: Tom Weiskopf & Jay Morrish. Members & guests. **18**

Opened on July 4th, 1993, Broken Top Club is an exclusive venue with all the amenities. The project was originated by investors from Portland, San Francisco, and Japan's largest trading company, C. Itoh. Club president Bill Criswell oversaw the development of the 528-acre project, which has grown to include this outstanding course, 500 homesites, equestrian facilities, 30 guest cottages, a driving range, an 18-hole putting course, and a 27,000-square-foot clubhouse with a restaurant and indoor swimming pool and tennis courts. Only the club's homeowners and guests may play this course. Golf memberships are limited to 395. In the May 1997 issue of *Golf Magazine*, Broken Top placed third in a listing of the nation's "Top-20 Communities to Semi-Retire."

Broken Top's site encompasses three parcels previously used by timber, livestock and pumice-mining concerns. Crossing a broad expanse, the holes fashioned by designers Weiskopf and Morrish vary from well-treed, Northwest-traditional to high-desert to links style. The track features bentgrass tees and greens, bluegrass fairways, white-sand bunkers, and extra-wide cart paths. It even has three USGA-specified target greens in the driving range. A six-acre pond in front of the clubhouse is stocked with fish and "landscaped" with indigenous reeds and cattails.

Rock formations were left intact and remnants of the old mining operation were woven into the field of play. Though Broken Top's contour is generally flat, tall ridges afford elevated tees and cascading fairways. Top holes include the 5th, a 232-yard par-3 with a pond and a vast bunker guarding the left edge of a slick green. The 468-yard, par-4 7th winds leftward off an elevated tee along a tree-lined path. The rolling 7th green is bunkered left. One of Weiskopf's design hallmarks is a reachable par-4. At Broken Top that comes at the 9th, a 356-yarder with a "left" and "right" fairway. Longer hitters can aim at the miniscule left fairway on the dogleg-left hole, and hopefully find the midsized 9th green. But for this to happen, towering pines at the corner and a huge bunker on the green's facing flank must be avoided. The safer two-shot route is to the right fairway.

Broken Top's signature hole is the 11th, a 364-yard par-4 with the Northwest's largest bunker at its right-front.

Broken Top's signature hole is the 11th, a 364-yard par-4. The hole descends slightly off the tee and slopes steeply rightward to the region's longest and deepest bunker. This 45-foot-deep, 120-yard-long trough is an old pumice excavation pit. If a golfer is unlucky enough to land in this abyss, a lofted shot over a "wall" between it and the green is the only way out. Two smaller traps—which Morrish calls "thank-you" bunkers—line the raised green's right-front edge and capture shots that aren't hit quite badly enough to find Broken Top's pumice grave. The 552-yard, par-5 15th begins at a towering tee where golfers view a beautifully-framed, descending and dogleg-right fairway lined by pines. A swale occupies the second-shot landing area, and the 15th's skinny, boomerang-shaped green is amply bunkered. The 18th, a 417-yard par-4 with bunkers along its left-bending route, boasts a well-trapped green cut into a red-colored hillside. Surrounding the green at Broken Top's home hole is a grassy amphitheater, giving promise that tournaments may one day be held at this top-of-the-line track.

Crosswater

18 *Sunriver Lodge & Resort (PO Box 3609), Sunriver, OR 97707. (541) 593-6196. Brad Myrick, pro. 18 holes. 7,657 yards. Par 72. Grass tees. Course ratings: men—C76.9/150, B74.8/144, M72.4/133, I69.4/126; women—M78.0/154, I74.0/146, F69.8/125. Year Opened: 1995. Architects: Robert Cupp & John Fought. Members, resort guests & reciprocates.*

Measuring well over 7,600 yards from the tips, Crosswater is the Northwest's longest course. It's also the highest-rated for men from the championship tees and for women from the middle blocks. Crosswater is part of a 600-acre development on Sunriver's southern edge that includes 98 lots, a vast driving range and a 17,000-square-foot clubhouse. From the clubhouse and course are panoramic

Cascade vistas. After it opened in 1995, Crosswater was named by *Golf Digest* as that year's Best New Resort Course in the U.S. The "resort course" designation comes with a caveat; Crosswater is playable only by its members, resort guests, and members of other private clubs on a reciprocal basis. The venue hosts the Oregon Open, which moved about a mile to the site from Sunriver's North Woodlands course. In March 1997, Sunriver officials were working on putting together a nationally televised tournament featuring four of the top LPGA players in match-play competition.

Crosswater was developed by Lowe Enterprises, Sunriver's owner. The marketing plan for the course involves enlisting 300 members; so far, the 200 or so members hail from such exotic places as Japan, Saudi Arabia, Portland and Seattle. Members are attracted to the 217-acre heathland layout, which occupies a portion of the old Joel R. Allen homestead. The conditional-use permit for the course mandated that the Allen family's burial plot be kept intact. The cemetery along the 11th hole is a collection of a dozen or so headstones inside a picket fence. The site also crosses the "Big Meadow" area of old Camp Abbott. World War II soldiers practiced their bridge-building skills on property where two rivers—the Deschutes and the Little Deschutes—form a confluence. During course construction, damage caused by cattle to the riparian areas along the rivers was repaired. A great variety of wildlife (deer, river otters, coyotes, elk and ospreys) are on view.

The rivers wind in and out of the holes, creating forced carries off tees and invading target zones. An extensive bridge system gets golfers around the course. Crosswater features bentgrass fairways, greens and tees, the latter of which sit like toadstools amid wetlands. Holes are lined by fescue and blue grasses, giving the place a links appearance. Winds out of the west whip across the flattish terrain, shoving shots into unintended places. The greens feature shaved fringes—a la those at Langdon Farms, another Cupp and Fought track, thus allowing chips or putts from aprons. The venue is first-class all the way, with wide and curbed concrete cart paths, outstanding signage (yardage and directional), white-sand bunkers, and meticulous care. Though it costs resort guests $100 to play, Crosswater provides an opportunity to test one's game against a truly tough track. When the 18th-rated hole on a course is a 582-yard par-5 (the 2nd), you know you're in for a rugged challenge.

Among Crosswater's most memorable holes is the 5th, a 460-yard par-4 that involves a brutal forced carry over wetlands and the Little Deschutes from the back tees. The river runs along the fairway's left side, and a series of bunkers squeeze the landing area to the right. The severely left-sloping 5th green has a hogback in its midsection, and is guarded left by wetlands. The 427-yard, par-4 8th begins with another forced-carry opening shot, with the Little Deschutes right and wetlands left. The river borders the hole on the right and crosses before a ridge-perched green. This elusive target has two pot bunkers in front, three traps behind and a fat bunker right. The back tees at the 9th, a 456-yard par-4, are fronted by the river, which then curls along the right side of the hole. The good-sized fairway tilts to the right. Trees along the left squeeze the throat of the 9th's large and rolling, untrapped putting surface.

Starting at a scrub-fronted tee, the 480-yard, par-4 11th bends leftward around four bunkers. The hole passes traps left and right—with the Allen cemetery left—en route to a rolling, hill-perched green with steep sides. The par-5 12th, a 687-yard behemoth, is a yawning left-bender lined along its entire left edge by a massive pond. Two bunkers outside the turn may enter play on second shots. The 12th eventually reaches a rolling green trapped left, right (twice) and rear, with the pond near its left flank. The 468-yard, par-4 14th requires a long drive over wetlands to find a right-curling fairway, which winds around a huge bunker. The Deschutes borders the hole's right flank all the way to a right-tilting, laterally-trapped green. The 16th, a 598-yard par-5, follows a wide, right-curling path engirded along the right by scrub and wetlands, which cross the hole at the 280-yard mark. Bunkers pinch the hole as it ascends to a huge and slick, undulating green with a steep left side and bunkers right. The 17th, a 244-yard par-3 rated Crosswater's second-toughest hole, involves a titanic carry over wetlands to land on a left-sloping, humped-in-the-middle green trapped right-front and left-rear. Winds out of the left really batter tee shots here.

Reames Golf & Country Club

18 *4201 Highway 97 South, Klamath Falls, OR 97603. (541) 884-7446. Michael Oberlander, pro. 18 holes. 6,564 yards. Par 72. Grass tees. Course ratings: men— B71.2/124, M70.3/123; women—M76.0/134, F73.3/127. Year Opened: 1924 (original nine); 1965 (second nine). Architects: H. Chandler Egan (original nine) & Bob Baldock & Son (second nine & remodel). Members, guests & reciprocates.*

The 18-hole course at Reames Golf & Country Club is found south of Klamath Falls off Highway 97. Other than a wood-products plant to the east, peripheries are quiet and relatively undeveloped. Reames Golf & Country Club opened with nine H. Chandler Egan-designed holes in 1924. The venue was named after the donor of the property, who required that his 160-acre parcel be dedicated to golf. In 1965, the club hired Bob Baldock & Son to lay out another nine and remodel the original holes (played as the back). There are nice views of the Cascades, Mount Shasta and a lovely valley from the course.

Several events mark the club's calendar, including a member-guest in July. Other tournaments include a men's invitational, two pro-ams (one each for men and women), a ladies invitational, and various fundraisers. Reames hosted the Ladies Pro West tournament in 1995 and '96. During the '95 go-round, the women's course record of 66 was set by Debbie Parks. Greg Brosterhous owns the men's record of 65. The club has been overseen since May 1993 by Class A pro Michael Oberlander.

Besides a fine golf course, members enjoy a swimming pool, full-service restaurant and bar, and a driving range. Reames features such nice touches as excellent signage, strategically-placed drinking fountains, and pretty gardens around tees. As might be expected, the older back nine is more densely treed than the front. In combination, the two sides offer an interesting mix of wide-open and tight holes. Good tests include the 1st, a rolling, 445-yard par-4 that winds downhill past trees along the right. Over its final 100 yards, the hole rises slightly to a small, front-leaning green backed by trees. The 2nd, a 354-yard par-4, is an uphill right-bender across left-tilting terrain. The fairway winds past jail on the right to a steeply front-sloping green bunkered both sides.

Reames' prettiest hole is the 3rd, a 162-yard par-3 with a right-sloping, laterally-trapped green backed by a pond. The 385-yard, par-4 8th descends over undulating ground, passing trees, a pond and bunkers along the right. The diminutive and slick 8th green is trapped front-left. The top-rated 9th, a 556-yard par-5, heads uphill and straight off the tee. Scrub growth and OB are a concern to the right, while two traps on the 8th fairway are in play along the left. About 300 yards out, the fairway horseshoes about 120 degrees to the right around OB and scrub; OB also lurks on the left. The small 9th green tilts to the right-front, with OB close to its left edge. Nice views of Mount Shasta are available from this spot.

The 446-yard, par-4 11th curls uphill to the right. At the 150-yard mark, the hole dips before rising to a right-front-leaning, hill-cut green. The 15th, a 514-yard par-5, heads downhill past tall trees along the left. At the 200-yard mark, the fairway veers left and rises slightly along a tree-tapered path. The 15th green is small and tilts rightward. The area off the tee at the 17th, a 373-yard par-4, is squeezed by bushy trees. Farther down, a pond with a fountain lurks along the left, driving distance out. The hole then bears left, ascending slightly to a steeply front-banked green trapped twice in front. Reames' home hole, a 366-yard par-4, goes straight uphill past bunkers right and left. Over its final 100 yards, the fairway rises to a mid-sized, two-tiered green trapped twice in front. The tiers in the ultra-slick 18th green are about two feet apart.

Driving Ranges

Raymax Driving Range
3707 Aberlein, Klamath Falls, OR 97603.
(541) 883-2143.

Upcoming Courses

Bend — Cascade Highlands Project (1999/2000). In early 1996, the developers of Broken Top proposed building a resort-like community on 500 acres near Broken Top. The project would include an 18-hole course, hotel and affordable homes.

Bend — Deschutes Municipal (1999). Under consideration since 1992, the county is still pursuing a Peter Jacobsen-designed course northwest of the Bend Airport. The city of Bend and a private golf firm might also be involved in the project, which includes a small clubhouse and driving range. The course may be irrigated by treated effluent from Bend's wastewater treatment plant.

Klamath Falls — Shasta Heights (1999/2000). This 1,200-acre project received considerable publicity in the mid-1990s, but has been quiet of late. Local developer Hank Albertson proposed building a semiprivate 18-hole course, commercial areas, parks and upwards of 3,000 houses and condos on a site near Basin View Drive.

EASTERN
OREGON

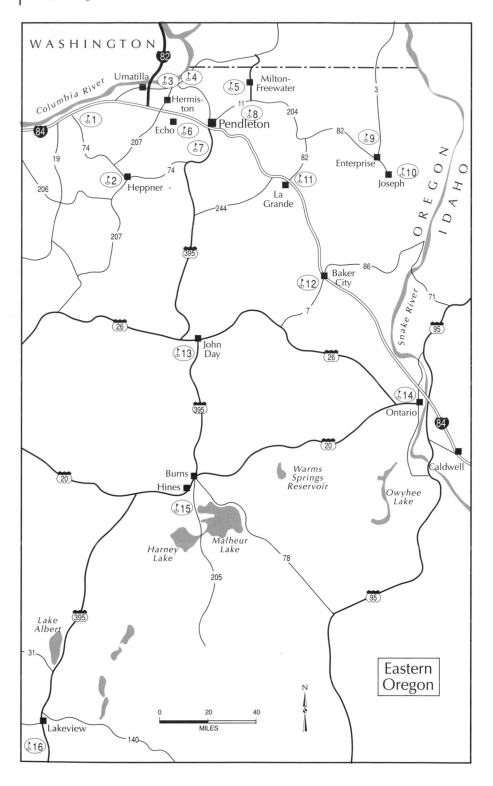

WASHINGTON

Columbia River

84

Umatilla

19

74

207

206

207

Heppner

Echo

Hermis-ton

82

11

204

Pendleton

Milton-Freewater

3

82

82

Enterprise

Joseph

OREGON

IDAHO

74

244

La Grande

395

86

Baker City

7

Snake River

71

26

John Day

26

95

395

Ontario

84

Caldwell

20

20

Warms Springs Reservoir

Owyhee Lake

Burns

Hines

Malheur Lake

Harney Lake

78

205

95

Lake Albert

395

31

Lakeview

140

N

0   20   40
MILES

Eastern Oregon

1. **Wilson's Willow Run Executive Golf Course** — public 9
2. **Willow Creek Country Club** — semiprivate 9
3. **Umatilla Golf Course** — public 18
4. **Kik's Driving Range**
5. **Milton-Freewater Golf Course** — public 18
6. **Echo Hills Golf Course** — public 9 & driving range
7. **Pendleton Country Club** — private 18
8. **Wildhorse Golf Course** — public 18 & driving range
9. **Alpine Meadows Golf Course** — public 9
10. **Eagle Driving Range**
11. **La Grande Country Club** — private 9
12. **Baker City Golf Club** — public 9
13. **John Day Golf Club** — semiprivate 9 & driving range
14. **Shadow Butte Municipal Golf Course** — public 18 & driving range
15. **Valley Golf Club** — public 9
16. **Lakeridge Golf & Country Club** — public 9 & driving range

The eastern half of Oregon is home to rugged mountain ranges, high plains and massive lakes, but not many people. The area is defined on the north by the Columbia River, south by Oregon's borders with California and Nevada, and east by the state of Idaho. Within these confines are the Umatilla Indian Reservation, the Blue and Wallowa mountain ranges, rolling timberlands and sparkling lakes. Oregon's fabled rangelands, also called "shrub steppe" and "scrublands," contain cattle ranches as large as 900,000 acres. The region's biggest towns are Pendleton, La Grande, Baker, Burns and Ontario. Dominated by the frigid winters and dry summers of climate zone 1, eastern Oregon also has the more moderate, Snake River-area climates of zones 2 and 3.

For years, eastern Oregonians played the same courses. But in the mid-1990s several proposals were announced that may not only result in new golf holes, but more tourists coming to the area as well. Most of the planned courses are located in small towns off Interstate 84, the major route through the northern part of this vast region. It'll be interesting to see if and when these projects come to fruition, and what effects they'll have on the local economies.

PUBLIC COURSES

Alpine Meadows Golf Course

9 *Golf Course Road, Enterprise, OR 97828. (541) 426-3246. Jim Chestnut, pro. 9 holes. 3,033 yards. Par 36. Grass tees. Course ratings: men 66.8/113, women 69.9/116. Year Opened: 1933. Architects: Founding members. Economical. No reservations. Walkability: Good. Playability: Though not all that tough, old-style course offers tremendous views of the mountains around Wallowa Valley.*

Alpine Meadows is a nine-hole layout at Enterprise's northern end. Crossing a flat meadow at an elevation of 3,900 feet, the course offers wonderful views of the picturesque Wallowa Mountains. The permanent population of Wallowa County is about 5,000, but in summer tourists flock to Wallowa Lake, a popular recreation area with RV facilities, campsites, a lodge, cabins, horseback-riding, miniature golf and several restaurants. A gondola travels 7,000 feet up Sacajawea Peak in summer, and skiers schuss these slopes in winter. The 6,982-foot-deep Hell's Canyon, the continent's deepest gorge, lies 40 miles to the east. Alpine Meadows' season runs from April to October.

The golf course opened in 1933 on the site of a former sheep pasture. Originally equipped with sand greens, it was updated with grass putting surfaces in the mid-'60s. The 50-acre course is owned by the city of Enterprise; the Wallowa County Golf Association leases the site. With help from his wife Flo, head pro Jim Chestnut runs Alpine Meadows' shop. Club members form work parties to improve a course that hosts a number of private and public tournaments. Alpine Meadows is visited by deer, elk, badgers, squirrels and upland birds. Trout Creek enters play on the 7th, 8th and 9th holes. An interesting anecdote of the course occurred during World War II, when a B-29 fighter plane made an emergency landing on it. By sheer coincidence, one of the crewmen was a resident of Enterprise.

Alpine Meadows is a dual-tee affair that stretches 6,060 yards over two circuits. Good holes include the 5th, a 476-yard par-5 that curls leftward around full-grown trees to a rolling green. The 343-yard, par-4 7th heads straight over corrugated ground to a small green fronted by Trout Creek. The top-rated 9th, a 388-yard par-4, is skirted by the stream over its initial leg, then doglegs left to a tree-ringed putting surface.

Baker City Golf Club   9

2801 Indiana, Baker City, OR 97814. (541) 523-2358. 9 holes. 3,046 yards. Par 35. Grass tees. Course ratings: men 67.2/117, women 71.0/118. Year Opened: 1936. Architect: John Junor. Economical, jr. rates, credit cards. No reservations. Walkability: Good, with a few hills. Playability: Tipped topography can lead to ungainly stances and difficult shots.

Baker City officials and area golfers have been planning another nine holes at this course for several years. At the end of 1996, the city and the local golf board were still working on the project. Architect William Robinson has come up with a design; now it's just a matter of generating a financial plan for the new holes, which could be ready for play as early as 1999. The new holes will be situated on a 60-acre site west of the existing track. In early 1997, the city was in the process of selecting a course manager and, for the first time, a superintendent. The hirees will be private contractors, not city employees. I must have 30 news clippings from the *Baker City Herald* that discuss the expansion project and other events at the course. It's obvious by these reports that the community really cares for it.

The course crosses a hilltop along Baker City's southwest edge, offering views of the town as well as of the Elkhorn Mountain Range, Wallowa Mountains and Whitman National Forest. The Blue Mountains form a semicircle along the western and northern horizons. The area around Baker City served as the backdrop for the movie, "Paint Your Wagon," starring Clint Eastwood and Lee Marvin, who ventured here for between-scene rounds. Another celebrity link is Sam Snead, who golfed here a couple of decades ago. This is actually the second course in Baker City. The original Baker Golf Course was built in 1912, but closed a few decades later.

Wildlife such as deer, coyotes, skunks, badgers and game birds—including owls—visit the grounds. A bronze plaque outside the clubhouse says the course was built in 1936 by the Works Progress Administration, under the sponsorship of the municipality of Baker, which has always owned it. As might be expected, the John Junor-designed layout is traditional in scope, with trees delineating rolling fairways, grassy mounds around small and slick greens, and a few greenside bunkers. Decent tests include the 5th, a 400-yard par-4 that winds over wavy terrain. The latter part of the fairway rises to a mid-sized green perched beside the clubhouse. The top-ranked 7th, a 500-yard par-5, has a ditch off its raised tee. OB lines the entire right edge of the hole, which concludes at a large, wavy green. The 385-yard, par-4 9th skirts a pond along the right, then ascends to a steeply front-tilting green bunkered twice in front.

Echo Hills Golf Course

9 *100 Golf Course Road, Echo, OR 97826. (541) 376-8244. 9 holes. 2,983 yards. Par 36. Grass tees. Course ratings: men 68.1/113, women 68.8/117. Year Opened: 1955. Architects: Founding members. Moderate, jr./sr. rates, credit cards. No reservations. Walkability: Good. Playability: Nice track off Interstate 84.*

Echo Hills Golf Course lies a mile south of Interstate 84 off the Echo/Lexington exit. The course is actually the town's second. The original Echo Hills Golf Club was built in the early 1930s and sat next to the Echo Rod and Gun Club west of the Umatilla River, which runs through town. After the gun club closed, local golfers decided to move the course to another place because "there were too many rattlesnakes on that [west] side of the river," according to early records. The old clubhouse was moved to the new site—it's still here—and a new course with sand greens was built in 1955. In 1960, mayor C.H. "Brick" Esseltyn helped raise $30,000 for a sprinkler system through a municipal bond. Grass greens were added soon after, and a few holes were repositioned to comprise the current layout.

Today, Echo Hills is a fine track thanks in good measure to Randy Sperr, its manager and superintendent. The layout crosses a hill that offers southerly views of Echo Valley's wheat fields, and is the habitat for rabbit, deer, pheasants and quail. Rattlesnakes are not a problem. Over a nine-month season, Echo Hills is played by its 200 or so club members as well as motorists traveling on I-84. The dual-tee course stretches 5,867 yards and plays to a par-72 over two circuits. Good tests include the 1st, a 455-yard par-5 that crosses wavy terrain en route to a knoll-perched green. The 484-yard, par-5 5th is similar to the 1st in that it spans rolling ground and concludes at a small and slick putting surface. The top-rated 6th, a ribbonish 418-yard par-4 lined by tawny native grasses, splits OB and deep rough on its way to a front-sloping green.

John Day Golf Club - semiprivate

9 *Off West Highway 26, John Day, OR 97845. (541) 575-0170. 9 holes. 3,055 yards. Par 35. Grass tees. Course ratings: men 67.1/111, women 71.2/111. Year Opened: 1954. Architects: Founding members. Moderate, credit cards. No reservations. Walkability: Good, with some hills. Playability: A fine rural course offers nice mountain views.*

Previously called Mountain View Golf Course, this semiprivate nine changed its name to John Day Golf Club in 1991 to prevent confusion with the Mountain View in Boring, Oregon. The venue lies west of its namesake town off Highway 26, and boasts a spacious clubhouse with a bar, restaurant and pro shop. Despite the course's revised moniker, vistas of the Blue, Dixie and Strawberry mountains remain an essential ingredient. The facility sits at an elevation of 3,000 feet.

The club's founders designed and built the layout in 1954 after raising capital through the sale of stock certificates. The dual-tee nine—extending 6,010 yards over two rounds—crosses up-and-down terrain. Most fairways are lined by maples, elms and junipers. The lush course is irrigated by water from the nearby John Day River, and sports an assortment of man-made hazards, with ponds involved at the 4th and 7th holes. Top tests include the 3rd, a 371-yard par-4 with a right-bending fairway that winds over a hill at the site's southern edge to an elusive green. The top-rated 6th, a 411-yard par-4, doglegs left between trees to a fast, knoll-perched putting surface. The 360-yard, par-4 7th contains a pond driving distance out and a small, trapped-left green.

Lakeridge Golf & Country Club

Highway 140 West, Lakeview, OR, 97630. (541) 947-3855. 9 holes. 3,324 yards. Par 36. Grass tees. Course ratings: men 70.0/119, women 71.6/121. Year Opened: 1960. Architect: Mark Clark. Moderate, jr. rates, credit cards. No reservations. Walkability: Good. Playability: Length and hazards complicate play at rural layout.

9

Lakeridge is a public nine off Highway 140 and west of Lakeview, population 2,500. The venue offers wonderful views of the Goose Lake Valley as well as the Warner Mountains to the northeast, and Fremont National Forest, Quartz Mountain and the Cascades to the west. Wildlife on and around the course include deer, antelopes, geese, hawks and eagles. The improving Lakeridge Golf & Country Club features a converted barn-clubhouse with a deli and pro shop. Lakeridge's owners, Ed and Diane Almojuela, live on the second floor of this structure.

Lakeridge was originated in 1960 as a seven-holer by Mark Clark. It served as a replacement to the original Lakeview course, which later became the local airport. Clark sold the course to the men's club, which ran it until encountering financial difficulties. Lakeridge changed hands several more times before the Almojuelas bought it in 1987. During their tenure the couple has remodeled the pro shop, added bunkers, and built a driving range.

The dual-tee nine is open from April through October, and spans 6,647 yards over two circuits. Of primary concern to golfers is a ditch that runs across many fairways. Good tests include the rolling 1st, a 500-yard par-5 that skirts OB and a bunker. The ditch intersects the fairway 200 yards from a trapped-in-front green. The 421-yard, par-4 5th heads into the Goose Lake Valley's often-powerful prevailing winds. The ditch crosses at the 100-yard mark, and the 5th ends at a right-tilting green. The 6th, a 524-yard par-5, heads straight past OB along the left en route to a left front-leaning, trapped-right green.

Milton-Freewater Golf Course

West 301 Catherine Street, Milton-Freewater, OR 97862. (541) 938-7284. George Gillette, pro. 18 holes. 3,346 yards. Par 60. Grass tees. Course ratings: men 55.4/ 80, women 58.1/83. Years Opened: 1973 (original nine); 1985 (second nine). Architects: Founding members (original nine); Gene "Bunny" Mason (second nine). Economical, jr./sr. rates. Reservations: Call a week ahead. Walk-on chances: Good. Walkability: Good, except for the mountain-goat back nine. Playability: Though short, trouble can be found on course with two distinctly different nines.

18

The 18-hole layout here crosses the base and top of a prominent hill on the west side of Milton-Freewater (hereafter called M-F). The city of 6,800 people was named when the neighboring towns of Milton and Freewater were united. Milton was named after the English writer and philosopher, John Milton; Freewater arose through the "free-water" rights accorded early settlers. Upon entering town, motorists are greeted by a sign bearing the rather modest legend: "Home of Low-Cost Utilities."

M-F is within one of eastern Oregon's few banana belts, a climatic anomaly that allows the course in some years to be open year-round. A portion of the 40-acre track crosses land by the local high school. M-F's course can be classified as executive-length, as no hole is beyond 300 yards; but the routing was done so nicely as to make it appear longer than 3,346 yards. M-F's track began with the member-designed front nine in 1973. These holes at the base of the hill feature flattish, tree-pinched routes and small, well-bunkered greens. The Bunny Mason-designed back opened in 1985 on a steep hill that towers 100 feet over the front. Considerably different than its counterpart, these holes were built by volunteers for a mere $20,000—the cost of an automatic sprinkler system. Offering great views of the Blue Mountains and the city below, the back nine is marked by swales and uprises, ungainly lies, and knoll-perched greens with steep back ends. Wind is a much greater factor on this part of the course.

M-F's layout is well-conditioned and has quite a few white-sand bunkers at greensides. Future plans include an upgrade to the irrigation system. Good tests include the 3rd, a 207-yard par-3 lined by trees right and a creek left en route to a small green. One of M-F's six par-4s, the 299-yard 5th is bordered left by a creek that crosses in front of its diminutive and slick green. A hole typical of the hilly back nine is the 15th, a 249-yard par-4 with a corrugated path skirted by OB left, and a left-tilting green. The 121-yard, par-3 17th has a tee-to-green drop of some 150 feet. Jammed against the bottom of the hill, the large 17th green is backed by the creek.

Shadow Butte Municipal Golf Course

18 *Butler Boulevard, Ontario, OR 97914. (541) 889-9022. John Wallace, pro. 18 holes. 6,847 yards. Par 72. Grass tees. Course ratings: men—B70.4/112, M69.3/110; women F73.3/120. Year Opened: 1965. Architect: Bob Baldock & Son; Brooks Farnsworth (remodel). Economical, credit cards. No reservations. Walkability: Good. Playability: Ontario track has considerable length and will be getting improvements soon.*

Named for the flat-topped monolith that dominates the horizon to the west, Shadow Butte Golf Course is set amid onion, potato and sugar beet fields. Ontario, population 10,000, calls itself "The Onion Capital of the World" and serves as the business center for the Jordan Valley. These environs at 2,000 feet above sea level receive moderate winter snowfall. The city of Ontario owns Shadow Butte, which is a member club of the Idaho Golf Association. Wildlife at the course includes foxes, deer, coyotes and an occasional badger. The municipal venue is appointed with a sizable clubhouse with a restaurant and lounge; a grass-teed driving range is also on-site.

In recent years, Ontario has been considering how to improve Shadow Butte's operations. The city spent $18,000 for a feasibility study by National Golf Foundation to analyze how best to finance improvements and where the upgrades should occur. NGF's recommendations were for the city to raise green fees; improve customer service; hire a permanent superintendent; amend accounting practices; and allow the golf advisory committee to become more instrumental in addressing customer concerns. In March 1997, the city signed a lease with Bill Johnson, a native of nearby Vail and resident of Carnation, Washington. Johnson will gradually implement improvements in the clubhouse and on the course. Sometime in the next couple of years, Johnson and the city may complete four new holes on property to the east.

When opened in 1965, the Bob Baldock & Son-designed track extended over 7,200 yards, but was shortened in the mid-'70s to accommodate the elderly regulars who found it too long. Good tests include the 1st, a 390-yard par-4 that passes OB left en route to a small, right-tilting green bunkered laterally. The 505-yard, par-5 5th curls to the right 300 yards out, then ascends to a raised green trapped at the left-front. The top-rated 6th, a 424-yard par-4, winds leftward to a bi-trapped green backed by *the* Shadow Butte. The dogleg-right 11th, a 430-yard par-4, has a large pond along the right edges of its fairway and green. Another good hole is the 17th, a 212-yard par-3 often afflicted by Jordan Valley winds.

Umatilla Golf Course

705 Willamette Street, Umatilla, OR 97882. (541) 922-3006. Todd Demarest, pro. **18**
18 holes. 6,033 yards. Par 70. Grass tees. Course ratings: men 69.1/115, women 72.5/119. Years Opened: 1948 (original nine); 1968 (second nine). Architects: U.S. Army Corps of Engineers (original nine); members (second nine). Moderate, jr. rates, credit cards. No reservations. Walkability: Good. Playability: Mid-length course borders full-service resort.

Begun with nine holes in the late 1940s, this course has grown with the nearby town and neighboring Nendel's Resort. Located above the Columbia River, which is visible from a few holes, the site was converted into a golf course by the Army Corps of Engineers when the federal agency was building McNary Dam. Local golfers and workers on the dam played the layout, storing power carts in corps offices. Called McNary Golf & Country Club at the time, it evolved into a member-owned, semiprivate facility with public play. But the members couldn't keep the ball rolling at the course and, in 1984, Umatilla Golf Course was auctioned to Larry Grayson who owned it for a year before Dale Miller of Vancouver, Washington, bought it.

Umatilla caters to local linksters as well as Nendel's guests. Reserved tee times are available only for groups of 20 or more. Umatilla's 2,665-yard original (front) nine is 700 yards shorter than the 1968-built back. A sizable lake in the course's midsection enters play on the 5th, 16th and 17th holes; 20 sand traps guard the generally small and rolling greens. Notable holes include the 4th, a 500-yard par-5 that stretches over flat ground to a front-tilting, well-bunkered green. The 515-yard, par-5 10th skirts a bunker at a point where views of the Columbia are available. The top-rated 17th, a 400-yard par-4, winds sharply left past a pond along the right en route to an undulating green.

Valley Golf Club

345 Hines Boulevard, Hines, OR 97882. (541) 573-6251. 9 holes. 3,190 yards. **9**
Par 36. Grass tees. Course ratings: men 69.4/107, women 73.2/115. Year Opened: 1951. Architect: Shelby McCool. Economical. No reservations. Walkability: Good. Playability: Some decent holes for local players and Hines-Burns visitors.

Valley Golf Club is situated between the neighboring towns of Hines and Burns, the commercial centers for farmers and ranchers in this vast part of eastern Oregon. Hines' and Burns' 5,000 residents represent most of the population of Harney County. The course sits at an elevation of 4,100 feet, making its short golf season run from April to October. Hines Lumber Company built Valley for its employees in 1951. The city of Hines now owns the course, leasing it to Valley Golf Club's 175 members on a year-to-year basis.

The dual-tee layout stretches 6,469 yards over two circuits, and is augmented by a small pro shop and banquet room in a cavernous building by the 1st tee. The

40-acre layout is crossed by Sylvie's River—actually a creek—which causes the alkali-leaching whiteness seen on some holes. Valley's fairways are generally flat, with a few lined by full-grown trees such as Russian olives. The course, with five holes over 400 yards, features such tests as the 5th, a sharply right-turning par-5 of 455 yards. The 9th, another 455-yard par-5, runs out to a small, pond-backed green.

Wildhorse Golf Course

18 *72787 Highway 331, Pendleton, OR 97801. (541) 276-5588. 18 holes. 7,000 yards. Par 72. Grass tees. Course ratings not available. Year Opened: 1997. Architect: John Steidel. Moderate, credit cards. Call for reservations. Walk-on chances: Good. Walkability: Good, overall. Playability: New links-like course a welcome addition to northeastern Oregon golf scene.*

This new 18-hole course is an integral part of the Wildhorse Gaming Resort, a recreational venue backed by a joint venture of the Cayuse, Umatilla and WallaWalla Tribes. The facility lies five miles east of Pendleton and a mile north of Interstate 84 (take exit 216). The three tribes, combined, are known as the Confederated Tribes of the Umatilla Indian Reservation. The layout will be adjoined by a driving range, a 3,600-square-foot modular-type clubhouse with a pro shop and food/beverage service, RV park, 100-room hotel, pool, spa and exercise area on 640 acres of tribal land. A casino is already in place, while the Tamustalik Cultural Center—which tells the story of the Oregon Trail from the Indians' perspective—is in the works. In late 1996, 13 holes were seeded before the snows came. The tribes hoped to have the course open by late-summer or fall 1997 (after this book went to press).

Wildhorse was spearheaded by two tribal leaders, Gary George and Alan Wagner, the latter of whom served as the project manager. Teufel Golf of Portland built the layout, which spans a former wheatfield. To vary a flat site with only 30 feet of elevation change, architect John Steidel had Teufel move over 300,000 cubic yards of earth, reshaping the landscape into a lengthy, links-like layout with fairway-bordering mounds. Wildhorse features bentgrass tees and greens, with a rye-bluegrass blend for fairways. The holes are lined by natural fescue grasses; resident ponderosa pines and aspens were spared.

During construction a tooth from an ancient woolly mammoth was found, a discovery that temporarily shifted work to other parts of the course. To preserve the archaeological site, two tees were moved. The 150-acre course should be walker-friendly because of its flatness and the tight spacing of holes. Views from Wildhorse encompass the Umatilla River Valley and Blue Mountains. The playing experience should be decidedly pastoral, with wildlife visitors including deer and many birds. In late 1996, the course was chosen to host the season-ending Central Washington Pro-Am series in 1997, an autumnal event that draws players from Leavenworth to Pendleton.

The course has water on nine holes and, according to Steidel, features some huge bunkers (one of which is 70 yards long). Par-3s range from 165 to 225 yards, par-4s stretch from 355 to 460, and the four par-5s measure 505 to 570 yards from the tips. Potential signature holes include the 190-yard 8th, which involves a pond-guarded green; and the 165-yard 16th, with another water-ringed putting surface. Another dandy is the 2nd, a 365-yard par-4 that offers a great view of the Umatilla River. Since Wildhorse was being built and I wasn't able to tour or play it before this book went to print, I look forward to paying a visit after it opens. Knowing Steidel's work (Canyon Lakes in the Tri-Cities, Whitefish Lake in northwest Montana, Lynnwood Muni near Seattle, et al.), and having a general concept of the site, I think Wildhorse could be an exciting track. Certainly it'll be a welcome addition to the golf menu for players in northeast Oregon and southeast Washington.

Willow Creek Country Club - semiprivate   9

State Route 74, Heppner, OR 97836. (541) 676-5437. 9 holes. 1,736 yards. Par 30. Grass tees. Course ratings: men 56.7/83, women 59.2/85. Year Opened: 1960. Architects: Local golfers. Economical. No reservations. Walkability: Very good. Playability: Executive venue in remote part of the state.

Willow Creek is a dual-tee, executive-length nine off Highway 74, about a half-mile from the town of Heppner. With a population of 1,500, Heppner is Morrow County's largest city. Despite its solitude in eastern Oregon's wheat country, Willow Creek Country Club—named for the slender stream running through it—has over 250 members. A set of infrequently-used railroad tracks cuts through the course just outside a small clubhouse. A lumber mill across the highway clatters away, periodically interrupting the calm at an otherwise quiet course.

The semiprivate track is ringed by tawny hills. Local golfers designed and built member-owned Willow Creek, which opened in 1960. The layout began as a three-holer with sand greens; six more holes and grass greens were added in 1968. A major flood in 1971 forced the reconstruction of three greens. The layout features three par-4s ranging from 215 to 311 yards, and six par-3s from 121 to 190 yards. The 8th plays as a par-4 on the front side and a par-3 on the back. The 9th plays just the opposite: par-3 on the front, a par-4 as the 18th. Willow Creek is known for its domed greens and tight, tree-lined fairways. The top rated hole is the 7th, a 190-yard par-3 that stretches to a small green lined by the creek and willows on the right.

Wilson's Willow Run Executive Golf Course   9

Wilson Road, Boardman, OR 97818. (541) 481-4381. 9 holes. 1,805 yards. Par 31. Grass tees. Course ratings: men 59.0/88, women 56.1/79. Year Opened: 1972. Architect: Dallas Wilson. Economical. No reservations. Walkability: Good. Playability: Excellent conditioning at Boardman layout.

Located southwest of Boardman, Willow Run lies amid golden wheatfields. The facility was built by Dallas Wilson, a businessman who co-owns a truck-equipment company in Portland. Wilson came up with the course's name during a cross-country flight. After being told by the pilot that the plane was over Ford's (now-closed) Willow Run plant, he liked the name so much he used it for his golf course. Wilson's Willow Run is played by many employees of the Lamb-Weston potato-processing plant in Umatilla, as well as visitors to the area. As with many rural courses, Willow Run's small clubhouse is closed on slow days and fees are paid on the honor system.

Wilson built the course on his family's ranch, having literally grown up on the property. The 20-acre layout gains distinction from fairways pinched by Rocky Mountain junipers, Russian olives, dwarf fruit trees and other ornamentals. The small, rolling greens are elusive. Water hazards—a lake, creek and a few irrigation ditches—curl through the dual-tee track, which involves a 1,731-yard front nine and a 1,805-yard back. Willow Run boasts 11 greens, with dual putting surfaces at the 2nd/11th and 6th/15th holes. The longest hole is the 332-yard 16th, a par-4 that runs through the course's midsection. Wildlife visitors include seagulls, quails and pheasants; trout swim in the irrigation ditches.

Private Courses

La Grande Country Club

9 *10605 South McAlister Road, La Grande, OR 97850. (541) 963-4241. Bill Rosholt, pro. 9 holes. 3,267 yards. Par 36. Grass tees. Course ratings: men 70.6/123, women 70.9/120. Year Opened: 1916. Architect: Dr. Ross. Members, guests, reciprocates and golfers from outside Union County.*

La Grande Country Club is one of the few private courses in the Northwest that allows some public play. If you're from outside Union County, call and see if a tee time is available; green fees are in the moderate range. The historic course opened in 1916. A previous layout was located near Perry, about two miles west of La Grande along the Oregon Trail. A Dr. Ross from Walla Walla designed the course and the club's founders built it, using horse-drawn scrapers to mold the fairways and greens. Besides a tight, well-manicured course, La Grande's 300 members have access to a full-service clubhouse, tennis courts and a driving range. Class A pro Bill Rosholt has been here since 1980. Annual events include an Elks Tournament in August; this tourney began in 1952. A Two-Man Best-Ball in late August has fields in excess of 100 players.

La Grande's course lies in the beautiful Grande Ronde Valley at 2,750 feet above sea level. Golf can be a year-round sport, but temporary greens are used from mid-December through early spring. Wildlife visitors include deer, minks, raccoons, red squirrels and an occasional badger. The dual-tee setup, with a 3,267-yard front and 3,247-yard back, winds through a former apple orchard. Its rolling fairways are now lined by mature trees. A creek enters play on seven holes, and three long par-4s—stretching 448, 406 and 432 yards from the tips—can play tough. The valley's prevailing winds are usually a factor, with added difficulty stemming from La Grande's raised and slick, postage-stamp greens.

Pendleton Country Club

Off Highway 395, Pendleton, OR 97801. (541) 278-1739. Doug Newman, pro. 18 holes. 6,317 yards. Par 72. Grass tees. Course ratings: men—B69.8/116, M68.6/ 113; women—M74.2/127, F70.3/117. Years Opened: 1957 (original nine); 1984 (second nine). Architects: Francis L. James (original nine); Gene "Bunny" Mason (second nine). Members, guests & reciprocates.

Pendleton's 450-member club lies nine miles south of the city along the west side of Highway 395. This is actually Pendleton's second golf club; the original 1903-built course was on a hilltop west of the city, but it was sold to the Pendleton School District in 1950. The city was without a course until 1957, when a new club was formed and work was completed on nine Frank James-designed holes. In 1984, the layout was appended by nine holes designed by Bunny Mason. Pendleton's golf operations have been overseen by Doug Newman since 1990. The Eugene native previously worked at Glendale and Walla Walla country clubs in Washington. Among Pendleton's more popular tourneys are the Birch Creek Couples Chapman & Scramble in May, the Men's Roundup City Amateur in June, and September's Ladies' Two-Person Best-Ball, which is held on the weekend prior to the famed Pendleton Roundup.

Surrounded by wheat fields, the course lies in an area where the western way of life is common; a sign by the 3rd tee admonishes, "No Hunting." Featuring paved cart paths, white-sand bunkers and some interesting arboreal specimens, Pendleton's layout is impressive. As might be expected, the original (front) nine involves taller trees, and its small greens are domed and slick. Mason's back side is equipped with bigger putting surfaces and more fairway mounding. Birch Creek splits the layout and a large pond on the back penetrates two holes.

Among Pendleton's tougher holes is the 1st, a 455-yard par-4 (played as a par-5 by women) that winds 90 degrees to the right at the 150-yard mark. The fairway curls around a bunker and trees to a small, front-leaning green. The 476-yard, par-5 2nd is a slight dogleg-left that skirts a steep drop-off and creek on the left. The fairway tightens at the 200-yard mark as it tilts left toward the creek. The hole drops into a swale before rising to a laterally-trapped green. The top-rated 6th, a 546-yard par-5, bends leftward between mounds left and OB right. The saddle-shaped, trapped-right 6th green tilts toward the fairway. The 364-yard, par-4 7th curls left around a pond with an island that spells "PCC" in crushed white rock. A bunker on the far side of the water hazard stymies corner-cutters; the hole then ascends to a raised and slick green.

The 10th, a 399-yard par-4, starts at an elevated tee just outside the clubhouse. The narrow, tree-lined route winds rightward over left-leaning ground to a small, rolling green. The 435-yard, par-4 12th crosses fairly flat terrain, bending rightward on a path bordered along the right by Birch Creek. The 12th green is trapped-left. Pendleton's signature hole is probably the 17th, a pretty 159-yard par-3 with a creek-fronted tee and a large and undulating, trapped-in-front green.

DRIVING RANGES

Eagle Driving Range

63977 Imnaha Highway, Joseph, OR 97946.
(541) 432-4001.

Kik's Driving Range.

Off Highway 730, McNary, OR 97882.
(541) 922-2844. Todd Sprong, pro.

UPCOMING COURSES

Haines — Granite Springs Ranch (1999/2000). A local couple announced plans in late 1995 for a destination-type resort on their 989-acre parcel just north of Haines. Besides an 18-hole golf course designed by Robert Cupp, the resort—which will feature a working cattle-ranch theme—includes overnight accommodations, equestrian facilities, a lodge, conference center and 300 homes.

Joseph — O'Rourke Project (1999). The O'Rourkes, owners of Eagle Driving Range in Joseph, would like to build a 2,500-yard nine-hole course next to their practice facility. The couple has permits, but still need financing.

Perry — Hoyt Project (1999/2000). In late 1996, a father-and-son team was seeking permits to build an 18-hole course on 140 acres two miles east of La Grande. In June of that year, Union County officials approved the project, but the decision was later appealed by the Confederated Tribes of the Umatilla Indian Reservation, which sought an inventory of Indian artifacts on the property.

Seneca — Bear Valley (1999). Work on this public nine has been underway for several years. The course is being built by local golfers, and may eventually contain 18 holes.

Union — Municipal Project (1999). In 1997, the town of Union—located about 12 miles southeast of La Grande—put an 18-hole golf course and a sewage treatment plant at the top of its "wish list." The course will be used as a disposal site for the plant's treated effluent. Earlier, the city had received a grant from Union County to study the feasibility of the course.

IDAHO PANHANDLE
& SUN VALLEY

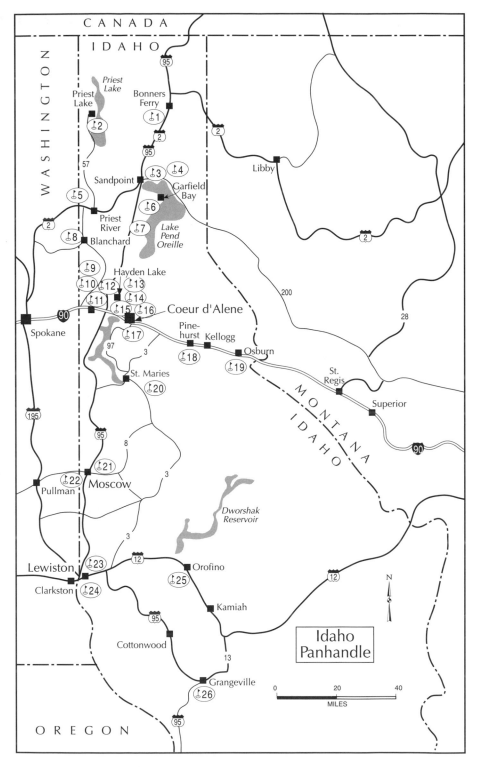

CANADA

IDAHO

WASHINGTON

Priest Lake

Priest Lake ⚲2

Bonners Ferry ⚲1

57

⚲4

Sandpoint ⚲3

Garfield Bay

Libby

⚲5

⚲6

Priest River

⚲7

Lake Pend Oreille

⚲8 Blanchard

200

28

⚲9

Hayden Lake

⚲10 ⚲12 ⚲13

⚲11 ⚲14

Spokane ⚲15 ⚲16 Coeur d'Alene

⚲17 Pine-hurst Kellogg

97 3 ⚲18 Osburn

⚲19

St. Regis

St. Maries

⚲20 Superior

MONTANA

IDAHO

195

95

8

⚲21

⚲22 Moscow

3

Pullman

90

Dworshak Reservoir

3

Lewiston ⚲23

12 Orofino

Clarkston ⚲24 ⚲25

12

N

Kamiah

95

Idaho Panhandle

Cottonwood

13

0 20 40

Grangeville

⚲26 MILES

95

OREGON

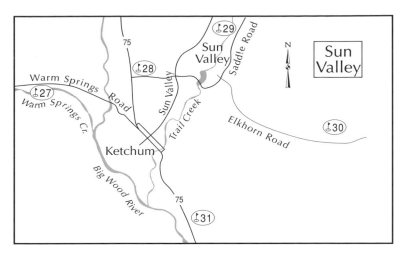

1. **Mirror Lake Golf Course** — public 9 & driving range
2. **Priest Lake Golf Course** — public 9 & driving range
3. **Sandpoint Elks Country Club** — public 9
4. **Hidden Lakes Golf Resort** — public 18 & driving range
5. **Ranch Club Golf Course** — public 9
6. **Midas Golf Club** — public 9
7. **Rimrock Golf Course** — public 9 (par-3)
8. **Stoneridge Golf Club** — semiprivate 18 & driving range
9. **Twin Lakes Village Golf & Racquet Club** — semiprivate 18 & driving range
10. **Prairie Falls Golf Course** — public 9 & driving range
11. **The Highlands Golf & Country Club** — public 18 & driving range
12. **Pumpkin Patch Golf & Restaurant** — driving range
13. **Avondale Golf Club** — semiprivate 18 & driving range
14. **Hayden Lake Country Club** — private 18
15. **Ponderosa Springs Golf Course** — public 9 (par-3)
16. **Coeur d'Alene Golf Club** — public 18 & driving range
17. **The Coeur d'Alene Resort Golf Course** — public 18 & driving range
18. **Kellogg Country Club** — public 9 & driving range
19. **Shoshone Golf Club** — semiprivate 9 & driving range
20. **St. Maries Golf Course** — public 9
21. **Moscow Elks Golf Club** — private 9
22. **University of Idaho Golf Course** — public 18 & driving range
23. **Lewiston Golf & Country Club** — private 18
24. **Bryden Canyon Golf Course** — public 18 & driving range
25. **Orofino Golf & Country Club** — semiprivate 9
26. **Grangeville Country Club** — semiprivate 9 & driving range
27. **Warm Springs Golf Course** — public 9 & driving range
28. **Bigwood Golf Course** — semiprivate 9 & driving range
29. **Sun Valley Golf Course** — public 18 & driving range
30. **Elkhorn Resort Golf Course** — semiprivate 18 & driving range
31. **The Valley Club** — private 18

The beautiful Idaho Panhandle runs from Grangeville north to the Canadian border. Within its boundaries lie the Selway-Bitterroot Wilderness and the Nez Perce, Clearwater, Saint Joe, Coeur d'Alene and Kaniksu national forests. Coeur d'Alene, north Idaho's major city, has emerged as one of the region's premier resort areas. A special section in this chapter is devoted to Sun Valley, a year-round playground southeast of the Sawtooth National Recreation Area. The high elevations of the Idaho Panhandle and Sun Valley are dominated by the cold winters and toasty summers of climate zone 1; greater Coeur d'Alene and Moscow are in milder zone 2. Clarkston, in zone 3, has the same weather as Washington's Tri-Cities and Walla Walla. In recent years, this part of the Northwest has burgeoned with new and proposed golf courses.

Public Courses

Avondale Golf Club - semiprivate

18 *10745 Avondale Loop Road, Hayden Lake, ID 83835. (208) 772-5963. Tim Morton, pro. 18 holes. 6,573 yards. Par 72. Grass tees. Course ratings: men—B71.8/124, M70.6/122, FF69.1/119; women—M76.5/140, FF74.7/135, F70.9/123. Years Opened: 1968 (original nine); 1972 (second nine). Architect: Jim Kraus; John Steidel & Mark Rathert (remodels). Moderate, credit cards. Reservations: Call a week ahead. Walk-on chances: Fair. Walkability: Despite a few hills, course suitable for bag-toters. Playability: Much improved following massive remodel.*

Formerly called Avondale-on-Hayden, this venue near Hayden Lake Country Club is ringed by homes, though none are within the course proper. A red barn near the clubhouse contains tennis courts for Avondale's 500 stockholders. The original Jim Kraus-designed nine opened in 1968, with the second Kraus nine following four years later. The land was owned by a group of doctors who sold it to Avondale's members. The semiprivate facility underwent a massive, $2-million remodel between August 1995 to spring 1996, when it was closed. Avondale's previously traditional layout received three new lakes, a state-of-the-art irrigation system, extensive mounding along fairways, nine rebuilt greens, new cart paths, all-new tees, renovations to the bunkers, 14 new traps, recontoured fairways, a new 400-foot-long creek, 30 new trees, added yardage, a parking lot expansion, three ponds, and a new practice green. Designed by Rathert International Golf Design of Englewood, Colorado, the renovations were done by Ed Adair of AdairCo, based in Post Falls.

Avondale's revisions are the result of a decisive membership. When the course opened at the start of the 1995 season, 60 leaks were found in the irrigation system. Instead of simply fixing the sprinklers, the members decided to proceed immediately with a five-year master plan that had been awaiting implementation. Closing the course for the 1995 season was a difficult option, and each member was assessed $3,000 to fund the work. About 50 people chose to forfeit their memberships instead of paying the assessment. But, in general, the members stood firm and construction got underway.

When I toured Avondale with Adair in September 1995, all manner of heavy equipment was huffing and puffing to resculpt the course. The hillside holes to the north—once straightforward up-and-down affairs—were completely changed, but still retain their hilliness. Ponds and a creek now grace the foot of the hill. Avondale's new signature hole, the par-3 11th, is fronted by a pond with a lovely waterfall. New ponds are also involved at the 9th, 10th and 18th holes. The all-new course opened to rave reviews in spring 1996. As it heads into its third decade, Avondale, thanks to a strong board of directors and a resolute membership, should be in great shape for years to come.

Bigwood Golf Course - semiprivate

125 Clubhouse Drive, Ketchum, ID 83340. (208) 726-4024. Herbert Fash, pro. **9**
9 holes. 3,200 yards. Par 36. Grass tees. Course ratings: men 68.8/113, women 71.2/114. Year Opened: 1971. Architects: Course founders; Robert Muir Graves (remodel). Moderate, credit cards. Call for reservations. Walk-on chances: Fair. Walkability: Good. Playability: Considerable hazards make this a tough track.

Owned by Dave Sellgren since 1979, this layout on Ketchum's north end crosses rolling terrain and boasts many water hazards and sand traps. The current course is the result of an extensive remodel in 1987 by Robert Muir Graves, who built three new holes, re-routed fairways and added the hazards. Bigwood has been lauded by such sources as the USGA's *Golf Journal*, which once deemed it one of the nicest nine-holers west of the Mississippi. The National Golf Foundation also rated it "outstanding."

Sellgren owns 100 acres to the south and north of a neighboring subdivision called The Club at Bigwood. In the early 1990s, he hired Coeur d'Alene architect, Jim Kraus, to design an 18-hole course. But the expansion efforts have been thwarted by the city of Ketchum and citizen groups, which oppose the project. The Kraus plan calls for using six of the existing holes and building 12 new ones.

Bigwood's course has several tees per hole; over two dozen sand traps imperil fairways and greens. Eight holes contain water hazards, with the top-rated 1st, a 495-yard par-5, guarded along its entire right flank by a pond. This hole ends at a wavy green ringed by three traps. The 4th, a right-turning par-4 of 407 yards, has its route split by a creek. A bunker lurks inside the turn, and the fairway ends at another tri-trapped green. Though ringed by houses, Bigwood is visited by deer, elk, sheep and foxes. The towering Sawtooth and Smoky mountains are also on view. Bigwood hosts two annual events: a Best-Ball tournament and the "Blaine County Closed," an invitation-only affair.

Bryden Canyon Golf Course

18 *445 O'Connor Road, Lewiston, ID 83501. (208) 746-0863. Lee Roberts, pro. 18 holes. 5,827 yards. Par 71. Grass tees. Course ratings: men 66.7/106, women 69.3/111. Year Opened: 1974. Architects: Course founders. Moderate, jr. rates, credit cards. Reservations: Call a week ahead. Walk-on chances: Good. Walkability: Fair, with plenty of up-and-down terrain. Playability: Intermediate challenges found on mid-length course.*

Built in 1974, this course overlooks the cities of Clarkston, Washington, and Lewiston, Idaho. On display from the promontory-perched course are vistas of Idaho's Waha Mountains, the Blue Mountains in Washington and Oregon, and the Snake and Clearwater rivers. The hilltop locale generates many odd-angled lies, with nearly all fairways crossing slanted ground. Several holes begin with cliff-side, elevated tees, and a few holes curl blindly around rocks and sagebrush. Bryden Canyon is home to ring-necked pheasants, chukars, owls, hawks, quails and marmots, known locally as rockchucks.

The city of Lewiston owns Bryden Canyon, which has only a few sand traps and two water hazards. The course gains its difficulty from deep dips and tall ridges in fairways. Good holes include the 369-yard, par-4 4th, which winds leftward around a pond to a small unbunkered green. The 332-yard, par-4 12th bears a dogleg-right, left-tilting fairway that cuts around and just below the crest of a hill, resulting in a tiny landing zone. A sagebrush-covered slope guards the left side of the 12th, whose elusive green is backed by a wall of rock and jail. The 14th, a par-4 of 345 yards, curls rightward around a pond to a small front-banked green.

Coeur d'Alene Golf Club

18 *2201 Fairway Drive, Coeur d'Alene, ID 83814. (208) 765-0218. Dave Lowe, pro. 18 holes. 6,295 yards. Par 72. Grass tees. Course ratings: men—B69.5/116, M68.3/113; women—M73.1/121, F70.4/115. Years Opened: 1957 (original nine); 1961 (second nine). Architects: M.F. "Curley" Hueston (original nine); Bill Boughton (second nine); John Steidel (remodel). Moderate, jr./sr. rates, credit cards. Reservations: Call two days ahead for weekdays; call Thursdays for weekends. Walk-on chances: Fair. Walkability: Good overall. Playability: Excellent alternative to pricey resort east of town.*

Coeur d'Alene Golf Club boasts a modern yet established course, a full-service clubhouse, a nice driving range, and a price structure that is far more affordable than the expensive similarly-named resort to the east. Originating with nine Curley Hueston-designed holes in 1957, followed by a Bill Boughton-designed back nine in 1961, the course underwent extensive renovations in the early 1990s. Architect John Steidel directed the remodel, which brought contemporary scope to a traditional track. Where dense forests and the southward slope of the hilly site once dominated Coeur d'Alene's personality, expanded tees, reshaped bunkers, enlarged greens and extensive fairway mounding transformed the course.

The course arose through the efforts of local businessmen. As one of the original stockholders, Boughton helped build the course and estimates that, though 500,000 trees were removed during construction, Coeur d'Alene still contains some 300,000 trees—primarily ponderosa pines and firs. The facility is well-supported locally, with nearly 800 season passes sold each year. During peak season, as many as

300 rounds a day are played, making this northern Idaho's busiest course. Call ahead for reservations during the summer.

Coeur d'Alene's course record is a 61 shot by its former head pro, Chris Mitchell. Players are challenged by holes that wind narrowly through trees. Flat lies are rare on the tilted site, which is within an established neighborhood northwest of downtown. Dense canopies of fir and pine branches arch over fairways as the holes ascend and traverse sloping terrain. The tall timber along holes poses as many problems to golfers as the recently introduced man-made hazards. A few elevated tees offer glimpses of a lovely valley to the south. The course is blessed with excellent signs, an automatic irrigation system, an attentive staff, and diligent maintenance.

Typical of Coeur d'Alene's tree-lined holes is the 3rd, a par-5 of 483 yards that begins as a dogleg-right, then ascends leftward to an elevated, two-tiered green. Rated Coeur d'Alene's most difficult hole, the 414-yard, par-4 7th has a left-bending route and an undulating, trapped-right green. The fairway at the 12th, a 435-yard par-4, crosses rolling terrain en route to a raised, 110-foot-deep green.

The Coeur d'Alene Resort Golf Course   18

2255 Mullan Avenue, Coeur d'Alene, ID 83814. (208) 667-4653 or 1-800-688-5253. Mike DeLong, pro. 18 holes. 6,309 yards. Par 71. Grass tees. Course ratings: men—B69.9/121, M68.2/117; women—M72.6/123, FF70.3/118, F64.6/104. Year Opened: 1991. Architect: Scott Miller. Expensive, credit cards. Reservations: Call three days ahead. No walk-on players. Walkability: Good, but cart is part of green fees. Playability: Outstanding conditioning will make you feel guilty for taking divots—go ahead and do it anyway.

The plushly manicured golf course here is part of its namesake resort, a towering hotel beside Lake Coeur d'Alene. Golfers who stay at the 338-room inn are brought to the layout by boat. The nautical theme extends to the course, where players are motored out from the tee to the famous, floating 14th green. Golfers are pampered here unlike any other Northwest course. Upon arrival at the club drop-off area, one's bag is whisked away and the contents washed. A tag stating, "(your name)— At the Coeur d'Alene—Every Guest is a Member," is then affixed to the bag. The course is the only one in the world using custom-fit Henry-Griffitts clubs for rentals. The $100-plus green fees include an unlimited number of range balls. The resort is the first in the Northwest to offer players laser guns for determining yardages to pins.

Each group—spaced 10 minutes apart—is paired with a forecaddie. These helpers perform duties usually handled by the duffer him- or herself: fixing divots and ball marks, choosing and recommending clubs, raking traps, tending flagsticks, finding wayward balls and reading putts. First-timers may find the assistance a bit cloying, particularly while experiencing a bad round better left unwitnessed. But the forecaddie is part of the resort's overwhelming attention to detail, and one of the reasons it received four-and-a-half stars in *Golf Digest's* "Places to Play 1996-97" guide.

Regardless of how golfers view service, once out on the course everyone is amazed by the meticulous condition of the all-bentgrass venue. In spring and summer, the carpeted surroundings are enlivened with thousands of wild roses, azaleas, red geraniums and assorted annuals. Lining fairways are junipers and hundreds of imported Austrian pines. Coeur d'Alene's carts—rigged with spoked wheels, whitewall tires, upholstered seats, ball and club washers, a front trunk and a cooler—follow curbed, concrete paths fitted with distance markers every 25 yards.

The brainchild of North Idaho businessman and publisher, Duane Hagedone, the course on a northern bank of Lake Coeur d'Alene occupies the site of the old Potlatch Mill. The 130-acre layout is tended by a crew, overseen by superintendent John Moore, that works at night; divots are sanded and reseeded each evening. Scott Miller's design mandate was to make the course playable for all skills. Though not long nor particularly difficult, the course's exquisite care lingers long after the round.

In addition to the lake, trout- and bass-bearing Fernan Creek enters play. Most fairways are separated by two-inch-high bluegrass, wildflowers and mounds. The course contains three short par-4s (277, 313 and 257 yards), and its four par-5s—from 491 to 566 yards—are birdieable if winds off the lake are light. Interesting holes include the 2nd, a tree-lined, 436-yard par-4 that bends to the right. A bunker along the right pinches the fairway 50 yards from a small and rolling, figure-eight-shaped green. The top-rated 9th, a 566-yard par-5, is a slight dogleg-left with two traps on the right driving distance out. Another bunker farther down may snare second shots, and four pot bunkers right and two traps left-front squeeze a wavy green. The 530-yard, par-5 11th slopes left toward Fernan Creek. This treacherous hole ends at a two-tiered green fronted by a fat part of the creek, and it's backed by two pot bunkers.

The floating 14th, a par-3 with a green that is moved daily from 100 to 175 yards from shore (a kiosk by the tee shows the day's length), is considered, depending on your view of golf design, a treat or an abomination. In his 1994 book, *America's Worst Golf Courses*, John Garrity found the 14th loathsome, adding, "Someone should run back to the clubhouse and tell the attendant that this hole belongs in Davey Jones's locker." In *Golf* magazine, Tom Doak commented, "Let's hope this baby dies in drydock." On the other hand, the placement of the $2.3-million floating green in a lake is a boon to golf ball reprocessors. In 1996 alone, scuba divers surfaced with some 24,000 balls.

Why all the hubbub? Maybe these pundits were rankled because they didn't come up with such a unique way to present a golf hole. The highly-publicized green comes with some mighty weird statistics: it cost $1.5-million to build; weighs 5,000,000 pounds; sits on 104 styrofoam-filled concrete blocks; and has an intricate cable-and-pulley system to move it back and forth. From the tee, the panoramic view of Lake Coeur d'Alene is almost as stunning as the odd sight of a putting green bobbing in a vast expanse of water. The 17,000-square-foot island provides an ample target, though one's tee shot must be airborne to find it since railroad ties run across the front. Bunkers guard the front and rear of the rolling, wide-but-shallow (pardon the pun) green, which is dressed with red geraniums at the back.

18 | Elkhorn Resort Golf Course - semiprivate

Elkhorn Road, Sun Valley, ID 83354. (208) 622-4511, 1-800-635-9356 (out of state) or 1-800-632-4101 (within Idaho). Jeff Steury, pro. 18 holes. 7,101 yards. Par 72. Grass tees. Course ratings: men—B72.4/133, M70.3/128; women F72.5/126. Year Opened: 1974. Architect: Robert Trent Jones, Jr. Expensive, credit cards. Reservations: Call two two days ahead or 30 days with a credit card. Walk-on chances: Fair. Walkability: Mandatory carts. Playability: Tough sledding for all skills.

Designed by Robert Trent Jones, Jr. and opened for play in 1974, this course and the surrounding resort were purchased in 1996 by Buena Vista Golf Holdings, a joint venture of Hanover Capital Holdings Corporation and Buena Vista Hospitality Group. After buying Elkhorn Resort from Milt Kuolt, the new owners announced plans to invest $4 million worth of upgrades to the resort and course, including a new clubhouse. The position of the new clubhouse may result in the realignment of holes. The hotel has had its ups and downs over the years. Co-developed by the Johns-Manville Corporation and Dollar Mountain Corporation in 1972, the hotel was shut down in 1981 after Johns-Manville foreclosed on the property. The company reopened the resort the following year, and Kuolt, founder of Horizon Air, bought it in 1984.

Sitting at 6,000 feet above sea level, the resort is a year-round facility that greets skiers in winter and golfers in summer. Appropriately, a ski lift skirts several fairways. On-site amenities include a restaurant and lounge, overnight accommodations, shops, a driving range and asphalt cart paths used by walkers, bicyclists and skaters. Mountain vistas are available from nearly every hole.

Once considered Idaho's toughest course, Elkhorn has recently slipped in the state rankings. In *Golf Digest* 's "Places to Play 1996-'97" booklet, Elkhorn received a modest three stars. The course hosts about 20,000 rounds a year. Elkhorn and Sun Valley co-host the Danny Thompson Memorial Golf Tournament, a fundraiser for the University of Minnesota Leukemia Research Foundation and Boise's Mountain States Tumors Institute. The event is played by dozens of sports, television and movie stars.

Elkhorn gains difficulty from its length (eased somewhat by Sun Valley's mile-high elevation) and daunting array of sand and water hazards. Fairways traverse up-and-down terrain and wind past condos and houses. Elkhorn is known for its hill-perched greens, targets invariably fronted by huge, upwardly-angled bunkers—a signature of Jones' courses. Players must be able to loft approaches to these undulating swards—a tough act for infrequent golfers on vacation—or be very adept at sand shots from uphill lies.

Top holes include the 5th, a 644-yard par-5 that offers great territorial views from its elevated tee. The hole curls past a bunker on the left before steeply descending over a left-sloping path. The fairway is squeezed by two bunkers right and one left, 210 yards from a small, boomerang-shaped green trapped in front. The tree-lined 10th, a 386-yard par-4, starts at a creek-fronted tee and then goes slightly downhill. Two traps left and a creek right shrink the "garden spot" for drives. The creek lines the entire length of the hole up to the green, a front-banked affair guarded by three traps left. The 434-yard, par-4 17th doglegs left around two vast bunkers. A creek flanks the right side of the hole before it ends at a knoll-perched green with a ridge through it. Large traps at the front and left, and an invisible creek at the rear, render this a slippery target.

Grangeville Country Club - semiprivate

9

Off Highway 95, Grangeville, ID 83530. (208) 983-1299. Greg Stone, pro. 9 holes. 2,854 yards. Par 35. Grass tees. Course ratings: men—B65.4/104, MF64.3/102; women—B72.0/117, F70.7/114. Year Opened: 1933. Architects: Founders. Economical. No reservations. Walkability: Good. Playability: Suitable for all concerned.

Located in central Idaho, Grangeville Country Club lies in a valley called "The End of the World." The Camas Valley is set amid wheat country; Grangeville, with a population of 3,700, serves as its trading center. Views from the 1933-built venue include the Bitterroot Range, Cottonwood Butte, 22 miles to the south, and White Bird Hill, five miles distant. The spectacular 6,982-foot-deep Hell's Canyon, the continent's deepest gorge, lies about 25 miles to the west. Golfers from the city of

Grangeville and surrounding communities take care of the member-owned course, and hold banquets and post-tournament festivities in a modest clubhouse. Situated at an elevation of 3,300 feet, Grangeville is visited by raccoons, moose, blue herons, deer and seagulls.

Grangeville Country Club's original sand greens were replaced by grass putting surfaces in 1961. A gun club and automotive racetrack once bordered the rural layout. John Creek runs through and enters play on four holes. Black locust trees line most fairways, and an automatic irrigation system keeps the course verdant over its seven-month season. The flattish layout, which sits on an underlayment of "dole," a non-porous clay, doesn't drain well after rainstorms.

The 40-acre, dual-tee layout extends 5,629 yards over two circuits, and features domed, "push-up" greens. Good holes include the top-rated 4th, a 450-yard par-4 (510 yards and a par-5 as the 13th). The fairway is a 90-degree dogleg-right, with the creek crossing at the turn; its green is trapped right-front. The 8th, a 350-yard par-4 that becomes a 401-yarder when played as the 17th, ascends over rolling ground. A black locust tree lies in mid-fairway, and the 8th/17th ends at a small, crested green. The 160-yard, par-3 9th requires a lofted shot over John Creek—and telephone poles with cabling—to reach a trapped-right green.

18 Hidden Lakes Golf Resort

8838 Lower Pack River Road, Sandpoint, ID 83864. (208) 263-1642. Ken Parker, director of golf; Tony Cuchessi, pro. 18 holes. 6,655 yards. Par 72. Grass tees. Course ratings: men—B71.7/128, M69.5/123, FF66.4/116; women—FF71.7/126, F69.1/119. Year Opened: 1987. Architect: Jim Kraus. Moderate, credit cards. Reservations: Call a week ahead. Walk-on chances: Fair. Walkability: Fair, with some hills and length between holes. Playability: One of the Northwest's toughest unsung courses.

Hidden Lakes is an 18-hole gem situated in deep forests six miles east of Sandpoint, off Highway 200. Opened in May 1987, the venue has undergone three ownership changes over its relatively short life. After financing and building it, Sandpoint developer Jim Berry sold the course to Sequoia Properties of Torrance, California. In 1994, Sequoia sold it to a group of investors that included Pack River Management, owner of Schweitzer Mountain Resort; Villeli Enterprises, a Bonners Ferry real estate firm; and Holson Syndicate, a Chicago-based furniture distributor. In March 1997, this group was in receivership and a sale of the ski resort and Hidden Lakes was imminent. Director of golf Ken Parker has been at Hidden Lakes since the beginning.

Despite the various owners, continuous improvements have been made to the course. I've visited Hidden Lakes three times over the years; during the most recent stopover in September 1995, it looked better than ever. The course's location by the Pack River had previously caused poor drainage on some holes. But after being stuck in a deluge that unleashed over an inch of rain in an hour, I observed no puddles on fairways and greens. Besides upgrading drainage, other recent changes include more peripheral houses and a driving range—on the other side of the highway and accessible by a tunnel. Landscaping enhancements have resulted in pretty flower gardens around tees and in other areas. Once the ownership situation straightens out, a lodge, marina and new clubhouse may be built.

Coeur d'Alene architect, Jim Kraus, designed this course in the northern tip of Idaho's Panhandle. I'm not sure whether its name was predetermined, but Kraus made sure the moniker fit. Water hazards—ponds, wetlands, creeks, canals and the Pack River—enter play at least once on 14 holes. The aptly-named layout finds many of the liquid ball-grabbers invisible from tees and fairways. Some lurk driving distance out and appear as slender rills. But on closer observation, the water extends 30 to 40 feet across; shots originally thought safe are gone forever. Hidden Lakes' signage shows both lay-up and carrying distances to the water hazards. Golfers should heed these guidelines.

Hidden Lakes lies in an alpine valley at 2,100 feet above sea level. Moose, deer, elk, geese, coyotes, bobcats, eagles, osprey and woodpeckers inhabit the pastoral grounds. The course occupies well over 200 acres and, with its forested environs, offers a peaceful round—other than the splashing of golf balls. Terrestrial hazards include over two dozen bunkers and feral fairway-side rough. Particularly tough holes include the 3rd, a 215-yard par-3 that requires a mighty poke to circumnavigate the large pond before a rolling green trapped right and left-front. The shot from the back tee at the 4th, a 380-yard par-4, must carry wetlands and a deceptively fat creek. The round 4th green is bunkered right-front and left. The 5th, a 388-yard par-4, has a pond—adorned with a pretty garden and a fountain—along the left. Also of concern is a hidden pond along the right 200 yards out. Over the 5th's final leg, the lake on the left runs up to protect the left-front edge of a wide-but-shallow green trapped right. The 6th, a 435-yard par-4, winds 90 degrees to the right around a pond; two big bunkers squat outside the turn. The small and round 6th green is laterally trapped.

The top-rated 7th, a narrow 406-yard par-4, has water off the tee and again 240 yards out. Once past the second hazard, the fairway ascends to a ridge-perched, left-tilting green trapped once right and twice left-front. The 150-yard, par-3 8th sports a tiny hill-cut green with a very steep left side. Traps left-rear and left-front further

The 11th hole at Hidden Lakes is a 495-yard par-5.

imperil this treacherous little hole. The 11th, a 495-yard par-5, has an elevated tee and a large landing area for drives. Water crosses the fairway 300 yards out, and traps lurk in front of a mid-sized green. The 404-yard, par-4 13th is a very restrictive driving hole with the Pack River right; ponds and trees are scattered along the left. Water guards the right-bending fairway all the way to the green, which has a bunker and more aqueous stuff along the left. The long and S-shaped 18th, a 542-yard par-5, gradually ascends to a hill-cut, left-leaning green trapped laterally.

The Highlands Golf & Country Club

18

North 701 Inverness Drive, Post Falls, ID 83854. (208) 773-3673. Sean Fredricksen & Bob Rannow, pros. 18 holes. 6,369 yards. Par 72. Grass tees. Course ratings: men—B70.7/125, M68.9/122; women—M75.5/135, F70.3/120. Opened: 1990-91. Architect: Jim Kraus. Moderate, credit cards. Reservations: Call a week ahead. Walk-on chances: Fair. Walkability: Fair, with some long between-hole hikes. Playability: Course can play tough.

The Highlands Golf & Country Club lies about a quarter-mile east of Highway 41, just north of Post Falls. The venue was initiated by local businessman Robert W. Coles, whose family settled in Post Falls in the early 1900s. In addition to a Jim Kraus-designed layout, The Highlands' 250 acres involves 285 lots, many of which have houses built on them. An attempt in 1995 to turn The Highlands into a private course failed. A 3,200-member fitness facility in the Lilac City, the Spokane Club, said it wanted to purchase all the 1996 tee times for its members, a move that would have essentially locked the gates to public players. After striking a deal with Coles, the Spokane Club found its members either weren't interested in golf or didn't want to travel to Post Falls. The news of The Highlands remaining a public facility was greeted with cheers by local golfers, who often find themselves struggling to get tee times at area courses.

All clubs in the bag must be used at this track, which is amply imperiled by water and sand hazards. The course sits atop a promontory; from the clubhouse are splendid views of the Spokane Valley and Rathdrum Prairie. Despite being fenced in, the layout—a former state-run pheasant farm—is visited by deer, coyotes, Canada geese, wild foxes and red-tailed hawks. Nice touches include a sculpture and a sand trap, both shaped like a bear, alongside the 12th hole.

Good golf tests are found at the 2nd hole, a 320-yard par-4 with a rolling fairway lined by a bunker driving distance out. The 2nd green squats in a depression and is guarded left-front by a hidden, bunker-backed pond. The 468-yard, par-5 6th crosses rolling ground interrupted by a shot-blocking pine. The OB-lined route winds downhill to the left, skirting bunkers left and right. Another trap lurks 125 yards from a tree-enveloped, wavy green squeezed by three traps. The 16th, a beautiful par-4 of 322 yards, is The Highlands' signature hole. The tree-lined fairway rises up to a ridge. From here, golfers can spot a boomerang-shaped, pond-ringed green surrounded by mounds, trees and sand traps.

Kellogg Country Club

Country Club Lane, Pinehurst, ID 83850. (208) 682-2013. Stan Edwards, pro.
9 holes. 3,042 yards. Par 36. Grass tees. Course ratings: men B67.9/112; women—
B73.6/124, F70.6/115. Opened: 1920s. Architects: Founding members. Economi-
cal, jr./sr. rates. Reservations: Call a day ahead. Walk-on chances: Good. Walkability:
Good. Playability: Old-style course with new-wave black bunkers.

Kellogg Country Club's 1920s-built course lies in the town of Pinehurst, and is accessible off Interstate 90. The member-owned facility comes with nine holes and a modest clubhouse. Many of Kellogg's small and dome-shaped greens are guarded by traps filled with black "sand." The bunker material is actually slag from nearby lead and silver smelters. Kellogg is the only Northwest course equipped with the black bunkers, though the new Jack Nicklaus-designed layout in Anaconda, Montana—another old mining town—uses slag traps.

The dual-tee setup extends 5,988 yards over two circuits, and a creek enters play on five holes. A good golf hole is the rolling and wide 3rd, a 503-yard par-5. The tree-lined route heads directly to a creek-fronted green guarded left by one of Kellogg's signature bunkers. The 8th, a 400-yard par-4, is invaded by the creek 230 yards from a small, trapped-left green. The creek also weaves through the 9th, a 405-yard par-4, 250 yards off the tee. A looming evergreen protects the right-front entry to the small 9th green.

Midas Golf Club

7145 Garfield Bay Road, Sagle, ID 83860. (208) 263-1087. 9 Holes. 1,121 yards.
Par 29. Grass tees. No course ratings. Year Opened: 1974. Architects: Local players.
Economical. No reservations. Walkability: No problems. Playability: Quite facile.

Located within a secluded neighborhood, Midas is a short track near Lake Pend Oreille. The facility is owned by the Post Falls-based Steckman & Linnebach Financial Group. Plans by the company to add another nine holes have been shelved indefinitely, though it may proceed with developing homesites on a neighboring 130-acre parcel. The 1974-built layout is played mainly by locals seeking a golf fix. The 10-acre course has seven par-3s (ranging from 95 to 127 yards) and two par-4s, both about 180 yards. The tiny greens, which are about the same size as the tees, are basically shaved pastures. Players pay green fees at a nearby store, Anchor Gas and Boat Storage, whose owner, Bill Daly, manages the course.

Mirror Lake Golf Course

Off Highway 95, Bonners Ferry, ID 83805. (208) 267-5314. Dan Robertson, pro.
9 holes. 2,894 yards. Par 36. Grass tees. Course ratings: men—B69.2/124, M68.3/
121; women M/F70.6/122. Year Opened: 1974. Architect: Jim Kraus. Economical,
credit cards. Reservations: Call two weeks ahead. Walk-on chances: Good.
Walkability: Good. Playability: Surprisingly good challenges from nine-holer.

Mirror Lake Golf Course sits alongside Highway 95 and overlooks the Kootenai National Wildlife Refuge, a haven for birds as well as deer, black bears and elk. Also on view are the Selkirk Mountains and Paradise Valley. Managed for several years by head pro Dan Robertson, Mirror Lake is owned by the city of Bonners Ferry. The genesis for a golf course at the site dates back to 1959 when local golfers bought the property. Unfortunately, they could barely keep up with payments on the note. Luckily, a local benefactress stepped forward in 1964 and paid off the contract.

After considering various offers, she gave the land to the city of Bonners Ferry in 1972. The city applied for matching state funds and received $34,000 to build a golf course; the city hired Coeur d'Alene architect Jim Kraus to design it. Once an irrigation source was obtained (Burlington Northern deeded nine acres of railroad land to allow the project to move forward), work began in summer 1973. After enduring heavy rains that washed away the first planting of grass seed, the course finally opened in fall 1974. The clubhouse was built in 1975. A few years ago, a local landowner offered to donate acreage for a back nine. But, after much deliberation, civic officials declined due to a shortage of funds.

As it stands, Mirror Lake is quite nice. The dual-tee track, which extends 6,100 yards over two circuits, traverses a gently sloping hill. Fairways are lined by pines, ponds and sand traps. Tough tests include the par-5 4th, a 496-yard right-bender that skirts a bunker along the right en route to a green trapped laterally. The 7th, a 339-yard par-4, is a 90-degree dogleg-right. The corner can be cut with a high, well-placed drive, but gamblers beware: inside the turn lurks dense jail. The 7th green is flanked by traps and trees.

Orofino Golf & Country Club - semiprivate

9

3430 Debertin Drive, Orofino, ID 83544. (208) 476-3117. 9 holes. 2,696 yards. Par 35. Grass tees. Course ratings: men B66.1/110; women—B70.8/114, F68.1/ 110. Year Opened: 1966. Architects: Founding members. Economical, jr. rates, credit cards. Call for reservations. Walk-on chances: Good. Walkability: Though hilly in parts, layout amenable to bag-toters. Playability: Sidehill lies and up-and-down terrain make for interesting shot selections.

Orofino Golf & Country Club is a semiprivate nine in the Clearwater Valley. It lies three miles east of Orofino and is readily accessible off scenic Highway 12. The area is a haven for outdoor recreationalists, with Clearwater River rafting trips and outstanding trout and bass fishing available. Elk, white-tailed and mule deer, bears, upland game birds and waterfowl also inhabit this slice of the Gem State, which sits at 1,000 feet above sea level. Another nearby attraction is Dworshak Dam, the country's highest straight-axis dam, and Dworshak National Fish Hatchery, the world's largest steelhead hatchery.

The greater Orofino area—dubbed "The Land of Clear Waters"—receives 26 inches of precipitation a year. The golf season generally runs from April to late October. Opened in 1966, the course crosses some flat meadows and a hill. Electrical cables are strung above some holes, but Orofino players are more challenged by the sidehill lies and blind shots created on the tilted parts of the course. Good tests include the 4th, a rolling 421-yard par-4 that doglegs sharply left to a green in a gully. The fairway at the 7th, a 343-yard par-4, is peaked in the middle and bends rightward to a knoll-perched green fronted by a swale. The 404-yard, par-4 9th has an elevated tee, with OB and forests lining the left side of its S-shaped, right-sloping fairway. The 9th green is guarded in front by a pond and fir tree and backed by a knoll.

Prairie Falls Golf Course

3000 Spokane Street, Post Falls, ID 83854. (208) 667-1551. 9 holes. 3,500 yards. Par 36. Grass tees. Course ratings not available. Year Opened: 1997. Architects: Ed Adair & Mark Rathert. Moderate, credit cards. Call for reservations. Walk-on chances: Good. Walkability: Good. Playability: New course opens with nine holes; second nine to follow soon.

9

Prairie Falls is a new venue located north of Post Falls at the intersection of Poleline Road and Spokane Street. Built by Prairie Falls Development L.L.C., a local firm whose partners include Bill Radobenko and Bob Thomlinson, the course will ultimately be surrounded by 400 homes. Before being converted into a place for golfers, the 285-acre site was a bluegrass seed farm, a previous usage that is ideal for a links. The initial (front) nine was scheduled to open in the summer of 1997 (after this book went to press). Work on a second nine to the north will commence in 1997, and should be ready the following year. The course was built by Ed Adair of the local firm, AdairCo, which oversaw the recent modernization of Avondale Golf Club. A driving range and clubhouse should be completed in time for the 1997 opening.

When I visited the site in fall 1995, a few holes had been built. The front nine involves a 30-foot elevation change, while the back will involve 50 feet. Six hundred spruce, Scotch pine, Canadian red, crabapple and golden willow trees were planted along the new fairways. Prairie Falls features bentgrass greens, bluegrass-rye tees, and a four-way ryegrass blend for fairways. Bunkers are filled with a white composite sand from Roach, Idaho. The well-draining holes are lined by peripheral mounding, with several dozen bunkers squeezing fairways and greens. According to Adair, the putting surfaces will be "quite interesting," though fair overall. Perhaps the most radical of these is the 4th, a three-tiered, 120-foot deep affair.

Man-made features include a large lake fronting the 9th green. Prairie Falls' signature hole may be the 155-yard 6th, a par-3 with a green guarded by, according to Adair, Idaho's largest bunker. The 9,000-square-foot pit sweeps in front of the target. Another interesting hole is the par-4 8th, which bears seven traps along its narrow route. Prairie Falls' original nine contains two par-5s of 545 and 555 yards, five par-4s ranging from 329 to 444 yards, and a pair of 155- and 185-yard par-3s. Vistas from the course take in the Rathdrum Mountains and the rolling foothills near Spokane. From the view holes, Adair fashioned mounds that duplicate the outlines of the mountains in the background. Once a regular haunt of deer and elk, the course is now the habitat for many birds.

Priest Lake Golf Course

Off Highway 57, Priest Lake, ID 83856. (208) 443-2525. Roy Reynolds, pro. 9 holes. 3,097 yards. Par 36. Grass tees. Course ratings: men M69.5/118; women— M76.0/130, F71.6/121. Year Opened: 1968. Architects: Founding members. Moderate, credit cards. Call for reservations. Walk-on chances: Good. Walkability: Pretty good. Playability: Challenge at course in popular resort area should broaden when new holes are built.

9

Owned by Priest Lake Golf Club, Inc., this course lies within forests beside its namesake lake. Vast Priest Lake, one of Idaho's largest bodies of water, borders majestic Chimney Rock and Lookout Mountain, and is within Kaniksu National Forest. The town of Priest Lake, accessible only by Highway 57, is a popular year-round resort offering water sports and golf in summer, and cross-country and downhill skiing in winter.

The nine-hole, 1968-built layout is open from April through October, and is regularly visited by much wildlife, including moose. The proprietors have planned to add nine Del Hatch-designed holes since 1992 but, for various reasons, have not broken ground. As of 1996, financing and permits were in place, and the 100-acre site was cleared and ready for construction. Besides nine new holes totaling 3,000 yards, 141 homesites are planned.

The course expansion follows on the heels of an upgrade to the original 3,097-yard course. These holes stretch across a meadow, with a few holes wandering up and through a forested hillside. Ponds are a concern, and bunkers dot many greensides. Top tests here include the 2nd, a 375-yard par-4. The fairway skirts woodlands along the right before reaching a pond-fronted green. The 401-yard, par-4 6th bends slightly right toward a narrow tree-pinched juncture. Once beyond this point, the fairway widens before ending at a small, tree-ringed green. The 8th, a 505-yard par-5, curls rightward between the driving range and a pond. Conifers loom inside the turn; the 8th features a raised and front-tilting green.

Ranch Club Golf Course

9

Off Highway 2, Priest River, ID 83856. (208) 448-1731. 9 holes. 2,530 yards. Par 33. Grass tees. Course ratings: men B63.2/94; women—B67.5/103, F66.1/ 101. Opened: 1950s. Architect: Rivercrest Association. Economical, credit cards. Call for reservations. Walk-on chances: Fair. Walkability: Good. Playability: Suitable for beginning-intermediate linksters.

Nine-hole Ranch Club is alongside Highway 2 in the small town of Priest River, a neighbor of Newport, Washington. The venue is owned by Bill and Melodye Tait and Dennis Napier who, since purchasing it in 1986, have made many improvements, including an upgraded irrigation system. Ranch Club is very popular with locals, particularly the Rivercrest Association and a group called the "Old Goats," a fun-loving band of retirees. The Old Goats have been instrumental in building the golf program at Priest River High School, a past winner of Idaho scholastic golf championships.

The course was built in the early 1950s by the Rivercrest Association, which still runs the men's and women's clubs. Ranch Club originally had sand greens, which were later converted to grass. The previous owner had planned to replace the course with a drive-in movie theater, going so far as to bulldoze an escarped amphitheater on land beside Highway 2. This aborted effort results in a course with a down-sloped (away from the highway) contour. The 29-acre layout is not difficult; it's ideal for junior golfers and those not seeking a gut-wrenching test. Over two nine-hole circuits, dual-tee Ranch Club extends 5,060 yards.

Among the better holes is the 2nd, a 348-yard par-4 that runs straight toward a one-time pond—now a grassy swale—200 yards out. The domed 2nd green is backed by trees. The 4th, a 215-yard par-3, descends to another small, convex putting surface. The top-rated 6th is a 407-yard par-4 that winds over a narrow path squeezed on the left by woods and OB. Its squarish green is trapped left.

Sandpoint Elks Country Club

Highway 200 East, Sandpoint, ID 83864. (208) 263-4321. Tom Tharpe, pro. 9 holes. 2,897 yards. Par 35. Grass tees. Course ratings: men 65.9/106, women 71.1/108. Year Opened: 1927. Architects: Founding members. Moderate, jr./sr. rates, credit cards. No reservations. Walkability: Good. Playability: Interesting "track" lined by railroad thoroughfares.

9

A wedge-shaped layout near the town of Ponderay, Sandpoint Elks Country Club is lined on two of its three sides by railroad tracks. One hole, the 7th, requires a drawn tee shot to carry the tracks. The course began with five holes in 1927; the remaining holes were added later. Local families owned the venue before the Elks Club bought it in the 1960s. The dual-tee affair extends 5,701 yards over two circuits.

Tall evergreens line most holes on the flattish layout, which has six par-4s on the front nine. Decent tests include the 4th, a 355-yard par-4 (a 316-yarder as the 13th) that runs straight through a treed corridor to a front-tilting, two-tiered green flanked by two traps. The par-5 7th, a 449-yarder, is much tougher than its alter ego, the 342-yard, par-4 16th. As the 7th, the hole requires a tee shot that must arc over the course's southwest corner and a stretch of track. A copse of trees blocks the left half of the landing zone, and the right-bending fairway is bordered on the right over its entire length by OB and tracks. Traps and mounds ring the 7th/16th green.

Shoshone Golf Club - semiprivate

Off Interstate 90 at exit 54, Osburn, ID 83849. (208) 784-0161. Wayne "Sano" Haldi, pro. 9 holes. 3,176 yards. Par 36. Grass tees. Course ratings: men M70.1/ 121; women—M75.5/131, F73.8/127. Year Opened: 1979. Architect: Keith Hellstrom. Moderate, jr. rates, credit cards. Reservations: Call a week ahead. Walk-on chances: Fair. Walkability: Fair, with some rather steep hills. Playability: Hillside track can play quite tough (note ratings).

9

Shoshone Golf Club is a member-owned venue located a couple of miles northeast of Osburn and south of Interstate 90. Designed by Spokane landscape architect, Keith Hellstrom, the course sprawls over a forested hillside 300 feet above a valley floor. This is actually Osburn's second course. The original layout, now the site of a landfill, was built in 1923. Shoshone (pronounced "show-shone") is a semiprivate facility; call ahead to make sure no member events are underway. Deer, elk, coyotes and black bears occasionally visit the grounds. Views from the course include the Bitterroots and Steven's Peak.

The layout extends 6,270 yards over its "18-on-9" configuration, and boasts paved cart paths, pretty flower gardens, birdhouse-style 150-yard markers, and a spacious clubhouse and restaurant. Tough holes include the 5th, a 365-yard par-4 named "Tamarack" in honor of a lightning-struck tree in mid-fairway. The hole rises up to a severely left-tilting green backed by a hidden trap. Dubbed "Terrible Edith," the 538-yard, par-5 6th starts at an elevated tee (with ball-pecked "Chuck's Tree" to the right). The top-rated 6th bears a wildly rolling fairway that leans left toward OB en route to a squeezed-by-trees, oval green. The 9th, a 366-yard par-4, doglegs left around a pond, then ascends to an undulating, trapped-left green.

St. Maries Golf Course

9

909 Main Street, St. Maries, ID 83804. (208) 245-3842. 9 holes. 2,644 yards. Par 35. Grass tees. Course ratings: men—B67.4/113, B/M66.7/111, M66.0/109; women—B/M70.3/117, M/FF67.6/112, F65.8/108. Year Opened: 1924. Architects: Founding members. Economical, jr. rates. Reservations: Call a day ahead. Walk-on chances: Fair. Walkability: Outside of one hole, not too bad. Playability: Tight, bowl-shaped layout can cause problems.

Situated a mile east of its namesake town, this course is owned by the city of St. Maries and Benewah County. In 1995, the owners partially logged a 30-acre tract nearby and used the sale of the timber to help finance course improvements. The venue sits at nearly 3,000 feet above sea level, and is open from March through October. Elk, bears and deer occasionally cross the site; fences are placed around the greens in winter and early spring to prevent elk from dancing on the turf. Besides a well-manicured golf course, the facility has a comfy clubhouse with a restaurant and bar.

St. Maries opened as a six-holer in 1924. In 1968, its greens were converted from sand to grass and three holes were added. According to local lore, caddies were used to point out golf balls buried in knee-high fairway grass. Also, golfers are known to play St. Maries barefoot, treading over its incredibly soft, unthatched greens. The multiple-tee set-up has front- and back-nine holes with different starting points; over two circuits it stretches 5,586 yards.

Four ponds and several bunkers dot the layout which, overall, presents an intermediate challenge. Good tests are found at the 2nd/11th. The 11th tee perches on a hill above the entry road, while its alter ego, the 2nd, lies on the course proper. Although short par-4s, the 2nd/11th has a pond that guards the front of its small, trapped-left-front green. The 9th/18th, par-4s of 348 and 363 yards, doglegs 90 degrees leftward around evergreens. A screen by the tees prevents players from shooting over the trees at the corner. One must hit a long-iron drive—or risk going into jail, then lob an accurate shot to reach the trapped-left green in regulation.

Stoneridge Golf Club - semiprivate

18

Blanchard Road (off Highway 41), Blanchard, ID 83804. (208) 437-4682. Doug Phares, pro. 18 holes. 6,522 yards. Par 72. Grass tees. Course ratings: men—B71.4/127, M69.4/123; women—M75.6/129, F72.8/126. Year Opened: 1971. Architect: Jim Kraus. Moderate, jr./sr. rates, credit cards. Reservations: Call a week ahead. Walk-on chances: Fair. Walkability: Pretty good overall. Playability: Can play quite tough, particularly when course is washed by westerly winds.

The 18-hole layout here is part of 600-acre Stoneridge Golf Club, a resort-like community with tennis courts, a swimming pool, equestrian facilities and an increasing number of homes. Originated in the early 1970s, the course endured bankruptcy proceedings and resultant disrepair in 1974 and 1975, but emerged from that down period in decent shape. The development and some neighboring land were purchased in 1992 by Keith Garner, a Salt Lake City developer. After trying to turn the course into a private venue, Garner acquiesced to the wishes of the Stoneridge homeowner's association and kept it open on a semiprivate basis. The area around Stoneridge is a prime recreational zone, with skiing at nearby Mount Spokane in winter and boating and fishing on the Hoodoo, Spirit, Pend Oreille and Twin lakes in summer.

Well-appointed Stoneridge features excellent conditioning. On-course touches include gardens filled with colorful flowers, good signage and a goodly number of water and sand hazards. The gently rolling site stretches across meadows south of the Kaniksu National Forest, and nice panoramas are on tap from the more open holes. Top tests include the 8th, a par-3 of 230 yards with an elevated tee and a green guarded left by a pond and right by a bunker. The wavy fairway at the 490-yard, par-5 9th bears a pond off the tee before ascending between bunkers en route to a slender green trapped twice in front. The narrow fairway off the raised 14th tee requires a precise drive. The 512-yard par-5 is squeezed by traps driving distance out, and two bunkers pinch its mid-sized green. The 17th, a par-5 of 531 yards, winds uphill leftward to a raised putting surface with steep sides.

Sun Valley Golf Course   18

Sun Valley Village (off Highway 75), Sun Valley, ID 83353. (208) 622-2251 or 1-800-634-3347 (resort). Rick Hickman, pro. 18 holes. 6,565 yards. Par 72. Grass tees. Course ratings: men—B71.1/128, M68.6/122; women F70.4/125. Years Opened: 1938 (original nine); 1964 (second nine). Architects: George P. Bell (original nine); Robert Trent Jones, Jr. (second nine & remodel). Expensive, credit cards. Reservations: Call up to 30 days ahead. Walk-on chances: Fair. Walkability: Cart mandatory. Playability: One of Idaho's best courses.

Sun Valley's 18-hole layout provides the summertime yin to the resort's winter-skiing yang. An integral part of the Sun Valley's recreational personality, the course has lots of variety, some very interesting holes, and a good-time ambiance not found in some upscale venues. Located on a former sheep ranch, the layout began as a dual-tee nine in 1937. The course was built by Union Pacific Railroad, which then offered the only means of transportation into this remote area of Idaho. A second set of holes was added in 1964; in 1978, the entire venue was extensively renovated by Robert Trent Jones, Jr.

Sun Valley is annually ranked among Idaho's best courses; its most recent accolade was a four-star rating in *Golf Digest*'s "Places to Play 1996-'97" guide. The layout occupies a 100-acre parcel in Sun Valley Village, a resort with lodging, restaurants, lounges, pools, shops, tennis courts and hiking trails. A long-time home for *Golf Digest* schools, Sun Valley also co-hosts—with Elkhorn Valley—the annual Danny Thompson Memorial Golf Tournament, a benefit honoring the former Minnesota Twins player that has raised over $2 million for leukemia research since it began in 1977.

The course crosses terrain that ranges from flat to downright hilly. Trail Creek is involved on five front-nine holes and three holes on the back. Six ponds are strategically placed, and over 50 traps vie for shots to fairways and greens. Tough tests include the 2nd, a 428-yard par-4 with a tee fronted by Trail Creek. The tree-lined fairway doglegs sharply left along a route bisected by the creek. The mid-sized 2nd green is trap-fronted. Perhaps Sun Valley's signature hole is the 12th, a seemingly benign par-4 of 382 yards that looks wide-open from the tee. There's a generous landing area before the fairway curls leftward. From here, players must launch second shots up to a towering, precipice-perched green fronted by two gigantic traps and guarded left by trees and shrubs. Escaping these bunkers at the 12th may leave one climbing the walls.

Twin Lakes Village Golf & Racquet Club - semiprivate

18 *2600 East Village Boulevard, Rathdrum, ID 83858. (208) 687-1311. Randy Buchenberger, pro. 18 holes. 6,277 yards. Par 71. Grass tees. Course ratings: men— B70.0/121, M68.4/117; women—M73.5/124, F70.5/118. Years Opened: 1974 (original nine); 1987 (second nine). Architects: Jim Kraus (original nine); Carl Thuesen (second nine). Moderate, jr./sr. rates, credit cards. Reservations: Call a week ahead. Walk-on chances: Fair. Walkability: Fair, with some steep uphill walks and distances between holes. Playability: Two different nines set within growing residential community.*

The golf course at Twin Lakes Village winds through a like-named community four miles north of Rathdrum, on Highway 41's west side. Besides the golfing venue, which is owned by the homeowners association, the village contains swimming and tennis facilities, a clubhouse and restaurant, and a mini-mart. The community is home to many Spokaners and Californians, who play golf here about seven months a year.

The community has considered making the course a private club. During a recent visit, I was struck by the two very different types of players here. On one hand, this is a resort-type facility with infrequent (read: not very good) golfers. Conversely, the other group is made up of residents who have more skill at the game, along with a proprietary sense the course is exclusively their's. Unfortunately, the two factions don't mix well. One redneck resident repeatedly hit into our group, glaring at us the whole time like we were pariahs who should stand aside, even though we were in step with the group ahead. Yet another regular hit one of our group's balls and got very rude when the gaffe was pointed out. Perhaps the best thing would be for the community to close the course to the general public, then deal with the small group of classless jerks who have no manners.

Twin Lakes Village's Jim Kraus-designed front nine is 300 yards shorter than the Carl Thuesen-designed back. Holes 1-9 involve seven flat fairways winding between residences, with the 5th and 6th going up and down a hill. The best of these is the 6th, a 433-yard par-4 with an elevated tee and a pine-lined, dogleg-right fairway. The garden spot for drives is squeezed by bunkers and a pond; the 6th ends at a squarish, laterally-trapped green.

Several back-nine fairways are bordered by rugged, ball-digesting rough, a condition that will change as peripheral homesites are developed. A good hole is the 10th, a 365-yard par-4 that follows a slender, rolling path through trees. Out-of-bounds and a road line the route closely along the left before it rises to a round, hill-backed green trapped at the left-front. The 488-yard, par-5 16th has a fairway pinched by trees left and a pond right. The hole then curls leftward before descending to a small green fronted by two bunkers.

University of Idaho Golf Course

1215 Nez Perce Drive, Moscow, ID 83843. (208) 885-6171. Don Rasmussen, pro. **18**
18 holes. 6,637 yards. Par 72. Grass tees. Course ratings: men—B72.3/130, M69.8/
123; women—M75.3/128, F73.0/122. Years Opened: 1933 (original nine); 1971
(second nine). Architects: Francis L. James (original nine); Bob Baldock & Son
(second nine). Moderate, student & sr. rates, credit cards. Reservations: Call a
week ahead. Walk-on chances: Fair. Walkability: Fair; have a good set of lungs and
some strong legs for this mountain-goat course. Playability: A tough customer with
length and tilted terrain.

Located on the edge of the University of Idaho campus, this course is the toughest in the Palouse country of Washington and Idaho. The layout sits at an elevation of 2,700 feet, and offers great views of the surrounding countryside. The University of Idaho track gains much difficulty from its arrayal across a hillside. Fairways span declivitous ridges and arroyos; sagebrush and scrub line most holes; and a flat lie is impossible to find. Though tough, the course is quite popular with students at WSU and UI, who get price breaks at this and Wazzu's course. There are also discounted rates for high school students, faculty members, juniors, seniors, adults and families.

As the home track for UI's men's and women's golf teams, the layout has hosted several conference championships. The facility originated with nine Francis L. James-designed holes in 1933. James, an early-day Northwest golf pioneer who designed several other courses in the region, was also UI's first head pro. When the second Bob Baldock & Son-designed nine was completed in 1971, it was combined with the original holes to form the present layout. Besides severe terrain, play is affected by prevailing westerlies.

Tough tests—and there are many of them—include the par-3s at the 5th and 8th, 227- and 232-yarders, respectively. These three-pars play more like par-4s when

The steepness of the University of Idaho course is evidenced by its 12th hole, a 400-yard par-4.

the Palouse winds are at their nastiest. The 13th, a rolling par-5 of 556 yards, is a double-dogleg that goes left, then right to a very slick green. The 526-yard, par-5 16th heads straight over rolling ground before curling left to an undulating green.

9 Warm Springs Golf Course

1801 Warm Springs Road, Ketchum, ID 83346. (208) 726-3715. 9 holes. 2,604 yards. Par 35. Grass tees. Course ratings: men 69.3/111, women 71.5/119. Year Opened: 1960. Architect: Owen Simpson. Moderate, credit cards. Reservations: Call a day ahead. Walk-on chances: Fair. Walkability: Good. Playability: Quirky layout in Ketchum.

This nine-hole course lies off Warm Springs Road on the northwest edge of Ketchum. The Owen Simpson-designed layout opened in 1960. Warm Springs has been managed by Simpson's grandson Pat, and his wife Karen, since 1972. The course spans 40 well-treed acres beside Warm Springs Creek. As part of the Warm Springs Resort, the course is adjoined by a restaurant and tennis courts; sleigh rides are available in winter. Wildlife guests include deer, foxes, black bears and an occasional elk.

The well-tended layout is tucked between the creek—which crosses two holes and borders two others—and Bald Mountain. Warm Springs has no sand traps but, with its water hazards and tightness, trouble can be found. Some adjoining fairways seem to blend together. Signs indicate the hole you're playing and the direction of the corresponding green. Just be aware of other players and incoming golf balls. The first three holes are regulation in length, but holes 4 through 9 are quirky, with several short par-4s resulting from the compressed space. The top-rated 6th, a 203-yard par-3, plays tough. One's tee shot must be placed squarely between two groves of trees to find a slippery, ridge-perched putting surface.

PRIVATE COURSES

18 Hayden Lake Country Club

1800 East Bozanta Drive, Hayden Lake, ID 83835. (208) 772-3211. Dan Hill, pro. 18 holes. 6,020 yards. Par 70. Grass tees. Course ratings: men—B67.4/114, M66.0/113; women—M71.7/122, F71.0/118. Year Opened: 1907 (original nine); 1912 (second nine). Architect: J.C. Olmstead. Members, guests & reciprocates.

The lovely 18-hole course here is an integral part of a private club overlooking Hayden Lake, which has served as a recreational retreat for Inland Empire residents for nearly a century. Users of the lake have ranged from members of the Coeur d'Alene Indian tribe to Lilac City folks on vacation. The area became "civilized" in the early 1900s when an electric railway linked Spokane and Coeur d'Alene, with a spur to Hayden Lake. The lake itself was named after Matt Hayden, a former cavalryman who settled near the present-day Honeysuckle Ranch. According to legend, Hayden and another ex-soldier played a card game for the right to name the lake, and Hayden won.

The 14th hole at Hayden Lake Country Club is a 186-yard par-3.

The club began in 1906, when the Hayden Improvement Company purchased 145 acres and announced plans for a large hotel and resort. Master landscaper J.C. Olmstead (of the distinguished Brookline, Massachusetts, firm that designed New York's Central Park and Seattle's park system) laid out the grounds; Spokane's leading architect, Kirtland K. Cutter, designed the buildings. Though a golf course was not part of the plan, Olmstead proclaimed that he wanted "parts of the grounds to be laid out (with) a golf links which (will) equal any in the East." Olmstead got his way.

The resort was originally named "Bozanta Tavern," Bozanta being an Indian term for the phrases, "the house by the lake" or "meeting place by the lake." Bozanta Tavern was dedicated on July 20, 1907. By then, the grounds featured a nine-hole, 3,000-yard golf course as well as courts for box ball, lawn bowling, quoits, ring quoits, croquet and tennis. During its early years, Bozanta Tavern was heralded as "The Switzerland of America." By 1912, the resort boasted an 18-hole golf course.

In 1919, the founders sold the resort to Great Northern Railway. The course was played mainly by Coeur d'Alene-area families, who began leasing it and a caddy shop from the railroad under the auspices of Coeur d'Alene Golf Club. The members bought the course and Tavern property from the railroad in 1928, and soon established the private Hayden Lake Golf Club. In 1937, the Mug-Hunter Tournament was begun for junior members; it's still played today. Among the early-day entrants were entertainer Bing Crosby's four children. In 1971, the course was remodeled.

Today, Hayden Lake's manicured layout winds through towering evergreens. The greens are small and slick, and its bunkering is traditional (i.e., usually one on each side of the green). Lovely flower gardens are sprinkled throughout the parkland venue. Hayden Lake's massive clubhouse—renovated several times over the years—affords wonderful views of the lake. Outside of homes on the periphery and along the entry road, the course is unfettered by civilization. Among the tougher holes is the

3rd, a 345-yard par-4 with a dogleg-right fairway that gradually narrows en route to a laterally-trapped green with a ridge through its middle. The top-rated 8th, a 424-yard par-4, bends to the right around four tall firs. At the 200-yard mark, the fairway widens before reaching a small green guarded in front by two upwardly-angled traps.

The right-curling 10th, a 529-yard par-5, winds even sharper to the right over its last 75 yards as it runs up to a steeply front-tilting green trapped both sides. The 11th, a 396-yard par-4, passes lovely flower gardens en route to a raised, saddle-shaped green trapped laterally. The 395-yard, par-4 13th has a yawning dogleg-left fairway that tightens before arriving at a domed green trapped twice in front. The 15th, a 171-yard par-3, features peekaboo views of the lake and a well-trapped, two-tiered target. The 16th, a 292-yard par-4, bears a very narrow, Hogan's Alley-like fairway that meanders between trees to a tiny, kidney-shaped green trapped left and front-right.

Lewiston Golf & Country Club

18 *3985 Country Club Drive, Lewiston, ID 83501. (208) 746-2801. Paul McCarthy, pro. 18 holes. 6,689 yards. Par 72. Grass tees. Course ratings: men—B71.9/125, M70.3/124; women—M75.7/127, F72.3/119. Year Opened: 1978. Architects: Founding members. Members, guests & reciprocates.*

Built in 1978, this private 18-hole course offers golf, social, student, junior and associate memberships. During its early years, Lewiston Golf & Country Club was a semiprivate venue open to the public. It went private on January 1, 1989, when the membership grew to a self-sufficient level. In addition to a tough golf course, members enjoy a swimming pool, restaurant and lounge. Views from Lewiston's fairways encompass the Snake River and a rugged valley. The club's driving range is equipped with a lake, a set-up similar to that at some Spokane-area courses.

Beyond landscaping enhancements, there haven't been many recent changes to this course. Regular Lewiston Golf & Country Club events include the Rockchuck Ladies in May, Safeco Open on Memorial Day, Margaret Spencer Invitational in July, and the Labor Day Wing Ding, a five-day tourney. Tournament contestants and members are challenged by a course that crosses rolling topography. Dozens of bunkers—mainly at greensides—enter play, and a couple of water hazards grab errant shots. An unusual Lewiston hole is the double-greened 11th. The women play the 11th as a 201-yarder; their green lies in front of a rugged canyon. The men play the 11th as a 344-yard par-4. Their bi-trapped green on the far side of the ravine is reached only by a well-placed second shot.

Moscow Elks Golf Club

9 *3300 Highway 8, Moscow, ID 83843. (208) 882-3015. Hank Hendrickson, pro. 9 holes. 3,220 yards. Par 35. Grass tees. Course ratings: men 70.4/122, women 71.5/ 125. Opened: 1920s. Architects: Founding members. Elks Club members & guests.*

Built in the mid-1920s, Moscow Elks Golf Club is one of the Gem State's oldest courses. Always owned by the Elks Club, the dual-tee nine crosses two hills and a flat meadow. When played in its "18-on-9" configuration, the course extends 6,445 yards. Players encounter assorted ponds and several sand bunkers. A snaking creek invades the 2nd, 7th, 8th and 9th holes, and winds behind the 1st green. As its relatively high ratings indicate, the course is no snap.

Hank and Carol Hendrickson have managed the Elks facility for several years. The Hendricksons have also overseen golf courses in Burns and Baker City, Oregon, as well as Orofino, Idaho. An Air Force retiree, Hank once supervised the golf and recreation programs at Mountain Home AFB near Sandpoint. In addition to a fine golf course, the Moscow Elks facility boasts a spacious, airy clubhouse with an attractive patio where barbeques and other social functions take place.

The Valley Club

Ohio Gulch Road, Ketchum, ID 83340. (208) 788-1441. John Weeks, director of golf; Scott Syms, pro. 18 holes. 7,102 yards. Par 72. Grass tees. Course ratings: men—C72.2/123, B70.1/117, M68.0/111; women F71.5/120. Year Opened: 1996. Architects: Hale Irwin & Richard Phelps. Members & guests. **18**

The Valley Club is an equity-type 18-holer that began greeting golfers in the summer of 1996. The course opened with a driving range and 18,000-square-foot clubhouse. The venue lies just south of the small burg of Gimlet, east of Highway 75 off Ohio Gulch Road, and six and a half miles south of Ketchum. Developed by HGW, Inc., a group that includes Isaac Kalisvaart of Portland, John Williams of Colorado, Ketchum City Councilman David Hutchinson, and Bill Criswell, the president of the Broken Top Club in Bend, The Valley Club represents the Ketchum-Sun Valley area's first private club. The course is an integral part of the 524-acre Valley Club, an upscale community in the scenic Wood River Valley.

The need for such a private club was apparently great in this year-round recreational mecca; over 300 of the 400 total golf memberships were sold before The Valley Club even opened. Once the membership totals 375, the golf course will be turned over to the members. The club also offers golf-social and tennis-social memberships. On-site facilities include four tennis courts and a swimming pool. Further proof of the club's guaranteed success is that over 70 of the 99 single-family homesites on the property were quickly snatched up, mainly by golfing members. The project was originally proposed by Dick Toomey and Roy Tinker, two Southern Californians who later sold the site to HGW.

Fellow Coloradans, architect Richard Phelps and PGA Senior Tour star and two-time U.S. Open winner, Hale Irwin, designed the championship-length track, which was built by Wadsworth Construction. The course crosses generally flat ground, with tall mounds lining most holes and odd-angled fairway lies common. The Valley Club is almost links-like in character, with only a few trees dotting the site. Par is thwarted by over 70 bunkers; water hazards—a man-made creek and ponds—invade 12 holes. Irwin shot a 71 at the grand opening, and the course record is a 70 shot by first-year club champion Jim Greenwood. As might be expected, wildlife is plentiful at The Valley Club. Herds of elk—which damaged some greens in fall 1996, coyotes, badgers, bobcats and deer visit the well-tended grounds. Views from the course take in the mountains ringing the Wood River Valley.

Par-3 Courses

Ponderosa Springs Golf Course

9 *2814 Galena Drive, Coeur d'Alene, ID 83814. (208) 664-1101. Dean Fotis, pro. 9 holes. 1,211 yards. Par 27. Grass tees. No course ratings. Economical. No reservations.*

Ponderosa Springs Golf Course lies east of downtown Coeur d'Alene on Galena Drive. It was designed by local architect Jim Kraus and built in 1966 by Russ Morbeck, who also developed the area around the facility. Richard Lynch acquired the par-3 layout in 1989 from French Gulch Partnership, which owned Ponderosa for 13 years. Lynch's son-in-law, Don Bartell, operates the course, a putting green and batting cage.

Ponderosa Springs is a step above most par-3 tracks, featuring water hazards, fairway-pinching pines, seven bunkers, and tiny greens. A ditch runs enters play on three holes, and a one-acre pond impedes progress on six holes. Two natural springs also serve as hazards. A course policy says that anyone who shoots par 27 or better on the course is entitled to a free round. No one has succeeded in this quest since 1989.

Rimrock Golf Course

9 *North 21600 Highway 95, Athol, ID 83858. (208) 762-5054. 9 holes. 1,269 yards. Par 27. Grass tees. No course ratings. Economical. No reservations.*

Par-3 Rimrock Golf Course is on the east side of Highway 95, about three miles south of Silverwood Theme Park. The facility is owned by John and Mary Veylupek. The holes cross a portion of the Veylupeks' 26-acre parcel, which is just west of the course's namesake rock formation. Veylupek says that he and a neighbor laid out the holes in 1994 after consuming a case of beer. A shaper moved the dirt around the empty cans, which were used to stake out the course. As might be expected, Veylupek is a fun-loving guy who's found Rimrock to be a surprising success. The Nebraska native and Air Force retiree says much of the play comes from Californians and Canadians passing through this scenic part of Idaho's Panhandle.

The flat course is equipped with Penncross bentgrass greens; about 10 greenside bunkers vie for errant shots. The longest hole is a 220-yarder. The operations are currently run out of the Veylupek's mobile home; a permanent structure will be built in the future. Other plans include planting more trees and building a pond or two. Wildlife visitors include graytail hawks, elk and moose. In July '95, a bull moose made a surprise appearance. Wisely, all golfers stopped in their tracks and waited until the beast left. The big annual event here is the Greater Chilco Open, held the third weekend in May.

DRIVING RANGES

Pumpkin Patch Golf & Restaurant
7130 Prairie Avenue, Coeur d'Alene, ID 83814.
(208) 772-4533.

UPCOMING COURSES

Coeur d'Alene — Arrow Point Resort (1999). In early 1997 the backer of this residential and golf resort was proceeding with plans for a $7-million golf course on the east side of Lake Coeur d'Alene. The semiprivate layout, which will be appended by 142 houses and 100 condominiums, will be designed by nationally-recognized architect, Michael Hurdzan.

Hailey — Stanton's Crossing Golf Course (1999/2000). In late 1996 momentum was growing for a municipal-type course near Hailey. The Blaine County Recreation District would operate the facility, which would be built adjacent to a planned sewage treatment plant. Effluent from the plant would irrigate the fairways.

Harrison — Powderhorn Ridge Project (1999). In early 1997 a group of local landowners was working with Kootenai County officials to obtain permits for a public nine-hole course and 220 houses. The project, located five miles north of Harrison, would also include a clubhouse, equestrian facilities, tennis courts and trails. Ed Adair of Post Falls may be the designer and builder of the course.

Lewiston — Red Pheasant Golf Course (1999). In mid-1996 the owner of Schaub Farm donated land to a local group which wants to develop an 18-hole course and upwards of 300 homes. The site is east of Lewiston off Lapwai Road. Blue T Golf has come up with a preliminary design for the course.

NORTHWEST
MONTANA

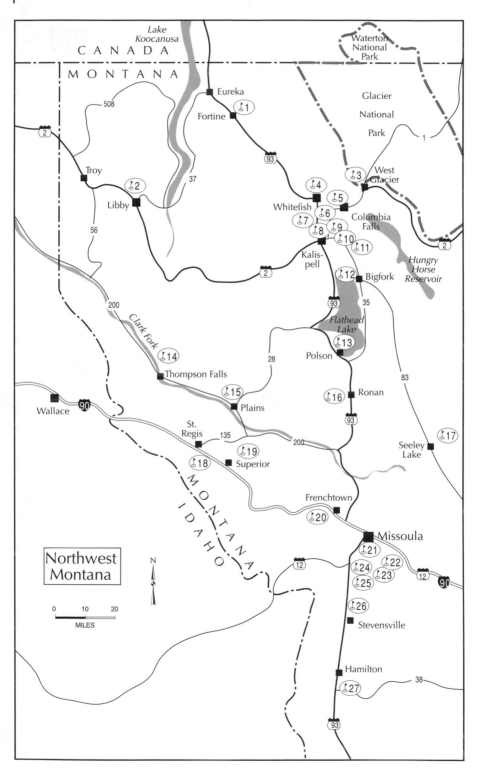

Northwest
Montana

N

0   10   20
MILES

1. **Meadow Creek Golf Course** — public 9 (par-3)
2. **Cabinet View Country Club** — public 9 & driving range
3. **Glacier View Golf Club** — public 18 & driving range
4. **Whitefish Lake Golf Club** — public 36 & driving range
5. **Meadow Lake Resort** — public 18 & driving range
6. **The Par-3 on 93 Golf Course** — public 9 (par-3) & driving range
7. **Northern Pines Golf Club** — public 18 & driving range
8. **National Golf Driving Range**
9. **Buffalo Hill Golf Club** — public 27 & driving range
10. **Village Greens Golfing Community** — public 18 & driving range
11. **Mountain Crossroads Golf Course** — public 9
12. **Eagle Bend Golf Club** — public 27 & driving range
13. **Polson Country Club** — public 18 & driving range
14. **Thompson Falls Golf Club** — public 9 & driving range
15. **Plains Golf Course** — public 9 & driving range
16. **Mission Mountain Country Club** — semiprivate 18 & driving range
17. **Double Arrow Golf Resort** — semiprivate 9 & driving range
18. **Trestle Creek Golf Course** — public 9 & driving range
19. **Cedar Creek Golf Course** — public 9 (par-3) & driving range
20. **King Ranch Golf Course** — public 18 & driving range
21. **Larchmont Golf Course** — public 18 & driving range
22. **University of Montana Golf Course** — public 9 & driving range
23. **The Highlands Golf Club** — public 9
24. **Missoula Country Club** — private 18
25. **Linda Vista Public Golf Course** — public 9 & driving range
26. **Whitetail Golf Club** — public 9 & driving range
27. **Hamilton Golf Club** — semiprivate 18 & driving range

Western Montana—from Glacier National Park on the north and Hamilton on the south—contains some of the Northwest's most spectacular scenery. Jutting into this section of "Big Sky Country" are the Rocky, Salish, Mission and Bitterroot mountain ranges. The national forests of Kootenai, Flathead, Bitterroot and Beaverhead are habitats for abundant wildlife. Miles upon miles of glacier- and snow-fed rivers cut through jagged canyons. Koocanuso and Flathead lakes and Noxon and Hungry Horse reservoirs rank among the West's largest lakes. Northwest Montana's alpine environs put it squarely in winter-cold climate zone 1, with the golf season generally running from mid-March to mid-October. To get a tee time at most of Northwest Montana's courses, call the Flathead Convention and Visitor Association at 1-800-392-9795.

As evidenced by the half-dozen new courses opened since 1994, golf has become a major recreational attraction for the area. These facilities have pretty much sated the market, so it'll be interesting to see how they and the existing courses do over the next decade. New nines are in the works at Cabinet View in Libby, King Ranch in Frenchtown, Polson Country Club, and Trestle Creek in St. Regis. Other large-scale 18-holers have been mentioned in the past but, as they say in Montana, many of the backers have "big hats but no horses." But the proposed projects listed at the end of this chapter are backed by developers with both the "hats" and the "horses."

PUBLIC COURSES

Buffalo Hill Golf Club

27 *North Main Street, Kalispell, MT 59901. (406) 756-4547 or 756-4545. Dave Broeder, pro. 27 holes. Grass tees. Course ratings: Cameron Nine (3,001 yards, par 35) men 68.3/122, women 73.7/132. Championship 18 (6,525 yards, par 72) men—B71.4/ 131, M70.2/128; women F70.3/125. Years Opened: 1936 (Cameron Nine); 1978 (Championship 18). Architects: Works Progress Administration (Cameron Nine); Robert Muir Graves (Championship 18). Moderate (Championship 18) & economical (Cameron Nine), credit cards. Call for reservations. Walk-on chances: Ok for singles. Walkability: Fair, with some steep hills and a few lengthy between-hole hikes. Playability: Outstanding conditions and stiff challenges for all concerned.*

Buffalo Hill features one of the region's best municipal courses and golf programs. Occupying a promontory above Kalispell and the west entrance to Glacier National Park, the facility is often ranked as one of Montana's top two layouts by *Golf Digest*. The venue was named after the hill it occupies; buffalo grazed here before Kalispell was settled, and city founder Charles Conrad later kept a buffalo herd on the site. Buffalo Hill is run by the Kalispell Golf Association (KGA), a nonprofit organization that emphasizes junior golf and events for its 2,000 members. Though its golf season is relatively brief, Buffalo Hill hosts over 80,000 rounds a year. The 27 holes are lined with birches, spruces, Douglas firs, poplars and cottonwoods. Wildlife visitors include deer, woodchucks, minks, woodpeckers, bluebirds, pheasants, ducks and red-winged blackbirds.

Just to the east of Buffalo Hill is the Stillwater River which, following heavy rains and prolonged snowmelt, goes over its banks to flood the Championship 18's lower fairways. Raising a roadway (which acts as a dike) has helped prevent flooding, although a few holes were awash in spring 1996; by July the Championship 18 was back to normal. Recent improvements include a new tee at the 4th hole.

When it opened in 1936, the Cameron Nine had sand greens. Minutes from the club's early meetings note that founding members discussed "renting" sheep from a local farmer to "mow" fairways. In 1964, a second nine was built on land north of the Cameron Nine. Then, in 1978, architect Robert Muir Graves designed 14 new holes and incorporated four old ones to create the Championship 18, which Arnold Palmer helped christen. Named after the mayor who spearheaded the site's acquisition and the creation of a golf course, Cameron Nine contains holes exclusively from the original layout. Fairways are bordered by full-grown trees and bunkers, with its challenge based on some fast, tilted greens and the southward slope of Buffalo Hill.

The Championship 18 is tighter and hillier; in other words, this is a shotmaker's track. The course is made difficult by large and slick greens ringed by grassy mounds; vast arrays of sand and grass bunkers; prevailing winds off the Mission Mountains; and tricky water hazards in target zones. A unique characteristic of the course is that the 10th tee, a site normally near the clubhouse, is situated at the farthest point from the pro shop. Noteworthy holes include the top-rated 2nd, a 598-yard par-5 with a fairway that ascends off the tee. After reaching a ledge, the hole curls uphill to the right toward a knoll-perched green with steep front entry. Another gem is the 17th, a 412-yard par-4 with a sharply-banked, dogleg-left fairway that winds around woods and OB. Drives must be aimed to the right side of the fairway to allow balls to roll down the hill onto a flat area. But a solitary pine right of the tee often waylays this plan. No traps guard the oval 17th green, which squats in a depression.

Cabinet View Country Club

378 Cabinet View, Libby, MT 59923. (406) 293-7332. 9 holes. 3,105 yards. Par 36. Grass tees. Course ratings: men 68.5/112, women 69.4/113. Year Opened: 1954. Architects: Founding members. Moderate, jr./sr. rates, credit cards. Call for reservations. Walk-on chances: Fair. Walkability: Good. Playability: Ongoing improvements to original course and potential for new nine make this a place to watch.

Stockholder-owned Cabinet View Country Club is kept busy by its 290 members and many vacationing golfers. Helping to boost the play levels are economically-priced punch cards and season passes. The venue lies on the west edge of Libby, a timber town in the northwest corner of the state. The club, named for its vistas of the nearby Cabinet Mountains, has been planning a second nine for years. As of early 1997, the Carl Theusen-designed, 3,400-yard side is still in the works. A major stumbling block to the project is Cabinet View's site, which sits atop a 400-foot-deep strata of clay; the city hasn't been able to extend sewer services because of the "non-perking" substrate. That may all change in late-1997 (after this book went to press) when the city may finally install the utilities. If the utilities are installed and financing is arranged, work on the new nine may commence in 1998 or '99.

The club has made other improvements in recent years, with more planned. In an effort to reduce debt, it sold the driving range to a residential developer. Cabinet View's member-owners will build a new range in 1997 on part of the land reserved for the new holes. Greens superintendent Steve Richard has put in new tees at the 1st and 7th holes; new tee blocks will be built on other holes over the next few years.

With all the upgrades, the dual-tee layout has garnered its share of praise from the visitors who venture to this remote area from all over the world. Good golf holes include the top-rated 5th hole, a 409-yard par-4 with a dogleg-right, pine-pinched fairway that leads to a domed, trapped-left green. The 382-yard, par-4 6th bends leftward over rolling ground to a large, tree-ringed green backed by a hidden trap. The 478-yard, par-5 9th runs—over its initial leg—straight and narrow. It then curls to the right 150 yards from a two-tiered, trapped-right green fronted by a pond.

9 Double Arrow Golf Resort - semiprivate

Off Highway 83, Seeley Lake, MT 59868. (406) 677-3247. Ed Bezanson, pro. 9 holes. 3,167 yards. Par 36. Grass tees. Course ratings: men—B68.9/119, M67.2/116; women F68.1/118. Year Opened: 1994. Architect: Ed Bezanson. Moderate, credit cards. Reservations: Call two weeks ahead. Walk-on chances: Good. Walkability: Rolling site suitable for walking. Playability: Surprising difficulty with hazards galore.

Double Arrow's nine-hole course is part of a 290-acre four-season resort. Located on part of the old Double Arrow Guest Ranch, a 10,000-acre retreat founded earlier this century, the resort offers an assortment of activities. Golf, swimming, flyfishing, horseback riding, hiking and tennis are on the summer agenda. In winter, the resort is turned over to cross-country skiing, horse-drawn sleigh rides and snowmobiling. Participants in the latter sport have access to over 400 miles of groomed trails that crisscross the Seeley-Swan Valley. Located at 4,000 feet above sea level, the resort is inhabited by white-tailed deer, moose and elk. An occasional black bear will lumber down a fairway, causing quite a stir among golfers.

Double Arrow's layout was designed by its head pro, Ed Bezanson, a Helena native and Class A PGA member who worked in Idaho, Texas, San Diego and Palm Springs before returning to his home state. Bezanson also manages the resort. The course, which traverses rolling and well-treed terrain, was built by Roe & Son, the fine golf course builders from Big Timber, Montana. Bezanson has designed a 3,300-yard back nine; work on this addition may commence in fall 1997. Parts of the new side will be lined by 50 or 60 townhouses. Over 200 homes now dot the resort, with upwards of 600 more lots available for sale.

Owned by 150 stockholders, the course is played primarily by Double Arrow residents and guests. Lot owners include people from as far away as Seattle and Spokane, with many folks from Great Falls making the trip down Highway 200 for getaways. Overnight accommodations are available at the resort, which is equipped with a restaurant and bar. Double Arrow borders the Bob Marshall Wilderness, a vast and pristine area with magnificent scenery and abundant wildlife. In summer, guests often take single- or multi-day horse trips into the wilderness. Double Arrow is part of RCI, a time-share cooperative with vacation destinations world-wide.

Double Arrow is a shotmaker's track with narrow, evergreen-lined fairways and water hazards (streams and ponds) on seven holes. Most of the greens are protected by traps filled with a fine-screened sand dredged from a nearby river. The course boasts bentgrass greens, bluegrass tees and fairways, and fescue roughs. Among the better holes is the 7th, a 402-yard par-4 with a rolling fairway that ends at a tri-trapped green. The 445-yard, par-4 8th is a dandy dogleg-left that winds tightly around trees to a front-tilting green guarded right-front by a pond and left by a bunker.

Eagle Bend Golf Club

27

279 Eagle Bend Drive, Bigfork, MT 59911. (406) 837-7312 or 1-800-255-5641. Tom Clary, director of golf; Jack Saunders, pro. 27 holes. Grass tees. Course ratings: Championship 18 (6,802 yards, par 72) men—B71.4/124, M69.3/119; women F70.0/119. Nicklaus Nine (3,419, par 36) ratings not available. Years Opened: 1984 (original nine); 1988 (second nine); 1995 (Nicklaus Nine). Architects: Bill Hull & Associates (Championship 18); Jack Nicklaus Jr. (Nicklaus Nine). Moderate, jr./sr. rates, credit cards. Reservations: Call three days ahead. Walk-on chances: Fair. Walkability: Some distance between holes may lead one to cart it. Playability: Fine 27-holer with oodles of variety and tremendous vistas.

Located on the northeast corner of Flathead Lake, Eagle Bend is bordered on the west by the Flathead River and on the south by a federally-protected waterfowl area. The naturally-endowed site is home for eagles, hawks and deer. The resort includes permanent residences, vacation rentals, a clubhouse, restaurant, bar, driving range, tennis courts, health club and marina. Eagle Bend was originated in the 1980s by an investment consortium led by Mike Felt. Between 1995 and 1996, Felt and his group tried to sell the 27-hole venue and clubhouse. In early '97, the owners of Northern Pines—Golf Northwest—bought the course as well as some housing lots and property on the resort's northwest edge. Golf Northwest restored Eagle Bend's original course, calling it the Championship 18; the third set of holes, designed by Jack Nicklaus Jr. and built in 1995, became the standalone Nicklaus Nine. The owners also rearranged the clubhouse's floor plan and put in a new restaurant. Future plans include a 75-slip RV park, marina-side condominiums, new women's tees, and renovations to the irrigation system. The company offers "combination passes" for Eagle Bend and Northern Pines.

Eagle Bend has garnered several accolades over the years; in 1989, *Golf Digest* made it the runner-up as the Best New Public Course of the Year. Often ranked among Montana's top tracks, Eagle Bend was the site of the 1994 National Public Links Championship and hosted the 1996 and 1997 Montana State Match Play Championships. I've made regular sojourns to Eagle Bend ever since the original nine opened. One of those visits was on the day following the Publinx (won in an upset by Guy Yamamoto). The rough along fairways was eight inches high, the pin placements were dastardly, and the playing conditions were as tough as they could be. Though shot-making was of paramount concern, I couldn't help be enthralled by the lovely flower gardens; the rapid maturation of the hole-bordering deciduous trees; and the course's outstanding condition. Golf Northwest will further Eagle Bend's status as a well-conditioned and challenging course, while making the operations more user-friendly.

During a subsequent visit in fall 1995, I checked out the Nicklaus nine. It, too, bears the flourishes of the Championship 18, though with a hillier and more topographically diverse site. Soon after the newer holes opened, Felt's group mixed them in with holes from the original course. Golf Northwest now lets golfers play the Nicklaus Nine separately. Eagle Bend has always been one of my favorite courses—anywhere in the Northwest. Though not one of the most difficult tracks around, there are plenty of challenges to sustain interest. Perhaps more invigorating than the golf are the magnificent views of Flathead Lake—the largest freshwater lake in the Rocky Mountains—and the surrounding mountain ranges. Some PGA pros (notably Bruce Crampton, Nicklaus Sr., Lon Hinkle—Eagle Bend's original director of golf—and Phil Blackmar) are so smitten with the place they regularly visit.

Top holes on the Bill Hull-designed Championship 18 include the 4th, a 402-yard par-4 with a pond off the tee. The hole winds through alders, bypassing a pond on the right 100 yards from a big and rolling, trapped-rear green. The 434-yard, par-4 5th is narrow and lined by birch trees. A pond and two bunkers lurk along the right before the fairway winds to a ridge-perched green trapped laterally and rear. The 200-yard 6th is one of the prettiest and most treacherous par-3s around. During an exhibition, the Golden Bear himself said Eagle Bend's 6th was among the best par-3s he'd ever played. A cattail-laden pond off the tee runs all the way up to the left side of the green. A large, amoeba-shaped bunker fronts this wide-but-shallow putting surface, which is marked with many undulations. The vistas from the 6th tee are simply spectacular. The 15th, a 461-yard par-4, rises to a ridge about 260 yards out. The hole then drops down to a wide and rolling green trapped right, rear and left.

Among the toughest tests on the Nicklaus Nine is the 1st, a 546-yard par-5. The uphill tee shot must avoid trees left, and both grass and sand bunkers along the right. The rising fairway stretches out to a ridge-perched green trapped laterally and guarded right by a pond. The photogenic 9th, a 446-yard par-4, starts at a raised tee, then descends along a reasonably wide path engirded by bunkers on both sides. The prow-shaped 9th green is imperiled by a pond left and bunker in front.

Glacier View Golf Club

18 | *Off Highway 2, West Glacier, MT 59936. (406) 888-5471 or 1-800-843-5777. Mike Micklewright, pro. 18 holes. 5,176 yards. Par 69. Grass tees. Course ratings: men 64.1/88, women 64.6/96. Year Opened: 1969. Architect: Bob Baldock & Son. Moderate, credit cards. Reservations: Call a week ahead. Walk-on chances: Fair. Walkability: Good. Playability: Though on the short side, course's challenge increased by new sand and water hazards.*

Glacier View lies near the entrance to Glacier National Park; turn into the town of West Glacier and follow the signs to the course. Located at 3,190 feet above sea level, the facility is played primarily by tourists who flock to the park in summer. The layout spans a meadow between the Middle Fork of the Flathead River; the area's spectacular mountain ranges are on view from every hole. Glacier View's proximity to federally-protected wildlife refuges makes it home to some 600 bald eagles that nest in trees along nearby McDonald Creek. In spring, rutting elk tear the bark off trees. Grizzly bears have been spotted, with moose and deer also stopping by.

The course was originally the site of a dude ranch that catered to wealthy bankers and oil men from eastern Montana. Glacier View is now owned by Ross Wilde and family, who've made several changes since purchasing it in 1991. Bunkers have been added, a pond was built between the 9th and 10th holes, a condominium project continues, and a new tee gave the 3rd hole 50 more yards. During a visit in 1995, I found an upgraded course with better conditioning than the one observed five years earlier. Though it looks much better, Glacier View remains flat, short and easy-walking: an ideal set-up for infrequent golfers on vacation.

Good tests include the 1st, a 396-yard par-4 that doglegs left around trees and houses. Once past a tree in the landing area, the hole curls up to a mid-sized green. The 3rd's new back tee has taken the hole from a 435-yard par-4 to a 485-yard par-5. The left-bender skirts OB along the left en route to a rolling putting surface. The 383-yard, par-4 9th winds rightward past a pond along the left before reaching a wildly undulating green. The 284-yard 10th is a right-turning par-4 that ventures between water and sand. The pond runs up to guard much of the large 10th green. The 14th, a 203-yard par-3 rated Glacier View's second-toughest hole, descends slightly to a mound-ringed, wavy green. The 389-yard, par-4 17th skirts a pond along the right. The water hazard lines the hole's right side until 30 yards from a dome-like, slick green.

Hamilton Golf Club - semiprivate   18

570 Country Club Lane, Hamilton, MT 59840. (406) 363-4251. Jason Lehtola, pro. 18 holes. 6,847 yards. Par 72. Grass tees. Course ratings: men 69.9/115, women 71.9/118. Opened: 1930s (original nine); 1978 (second nine). Architects: Founding members (original nine); Keith Hellstrom (second nine). Economical, credit cards. Reservations: Call a week ahead. Walk-on chances: Fair. Walkability: Overall, quite good. Playability: Old-style front and modern back nines add spice to mountain-ringed course.

Member-owned Hamilton Golf Club lies about three miles southeast of Hamilton in a scenic valley. From the course, which sits at 3,800 feet elevation, there are wonderful views of the Bitterroot and Sapphire mountains. Usually open from March 15 to October 15, Hamilton hosts Montana's first tournament of the year, the Snowbird Open on the first Sunday in April. The course had been overseen by its head pro, Wayne Jones, for nearly 20 before he retired at the end of 1996. His former assistant, Jason Lehtola, now runs the show. Jones' final year was a banner one for the club, which set all-time records for rounds played. Besides considerable play from members, the venue is popular with tourists traveling along Highway 93, which lies about three miles to the west.

Hamilton's founder-designed front nine had sand greens for a couple of decades before the putting surfaces were converted to grass in 1954. Holes 1 through 9 feature small and domed greens, flat terrain, and tiny tees. The 1978-built, Keith Hellstrom-designed back side is much more modern, with larger greens and tees and more man-made hazards woven through the field of play. In recent years, bunkers have been built along the 13th, 14th and 15th fairways. Future plans include more fairway traps, a pond at the 11th to toughen the hole while enhancing drainage, and a new clubhouse.

Besides slick greens, the front nine is imperiled by several water hazards, including trout-stocked Gird Creek. It's not uncommon for players to wield both golf clubs and fishing poles when making the rounds at Hamilton. The back side crosses a view-encompassing plateau, making it one of the most picturesque sets of holes in Montana. Hamilton's 10th through 18th holes also feature large, undulating greens and more hazards than the front. Hamilton's well-tended course has such flourishes as flower boxes at tees. A couple of comical, straw-stuffed "cowboys" sit drunkenly under trees at a few junctures.

Good tests include the top-rated 3rd, a 421-yard par-4 with a rolling and tree-lined, dogleg-left route and a radical two-tiered green that looks like a Dali-esque tabletop. The 520-yard, par-5 5th skirts two poplar trees along the right as it runs straight to a small, raised green guarded at the front, right and rear by a creek. The 11th, a 501-yard par-5, contains a narrow, right-tilting fairway bordered along the right by a creek. The mid-sized 11th green is bunkered left. The 524-yard, par-5 15th is a 90-degree dogleg-left that stretches to a steeply right-leaning green trapped in front. Hamilton's 430-yard, par-4 home hole is lined by OB right; a cattail-laden pond squeezes the left side of the tee-shot landing area. The 18th then gradually tapers as it goes to a right-sloping, saddle-shaped green backed by trees.

The Highlands Golf Club

9 *102 Ben Hogan Drive, Missoula, MT 59803. (406) 728-7360. Richard Hoffmaster, pro. 9 holes. 3,200 yards. Par 35. Grass tees. Course ratings: men 68.3/116; women 70.6/114. Year Opened: 1954. Architects: Founding members. Moderate, credit cards. Reservations: Call a week ahead. Walk-on chances: Fair. Walkability: Good overall, with some uphill hikes. Playability: Fair, with homes along fairways squeezing the field of play.*

The Highlands is a nine-hole course on the southeastern edge of Missoula atop Far View Hill. With an elevation of 3,600 feet, Missoula's golf season generally runs from March through November. The Highlands' holes curl through a residential neighborhood; some fairways are quite close to backyards. The site once contained the Greenough Mansion, an 1897-built structure that was moved here from a position alongside Rattlesnake Creek earlier this century. Sadly, the mansion—which contained the pro shop and clubhouse-restaurant—burned to the ground in 1992. It's since been replaced by a new clubhouse and eatery operated by The Highlands' pro, Richard Hoffmaster.

The layout crosses up-and-down terrain, with various sand and water hazards squeezing fairways and greens. Westerly winds howling through the Missoula Valley often skew airborne shots hit at the generally treeless track. Among the better tests is the 2nd, a 465-yard par-4 that winds slightly leftward off an elevated, pond-fronted tee. The narrow, right-sloping fairway eventually arrives at a laterally-trapped green. The 515-yard, par-5 9th has water left-front of the tee. The rising hole then bends left around bunkers to a trapped-right green.

King Ranch Golf Course

18 *Wild Goose Lane, Frenchtown, MT 59834. (406) 626-4000. Greg Van Natta, pro. 18 holes. 6,600 yards. Par 72. Grass tees. Course ratings (original nine): men— 69.0/113, women 66.8/107. Years Opened: 1992 (original nine); 1997 (second nine). Architects: Bud King (original nine); Greg Van Natta (second nine). Economical, credit cards. Reservations: Call a week ahead. Walk-on chances: Good. Walkability: Good. Playability: Though straightforward, layout is enjoyable and laid-back.*

King Ranch Golf Course lies in the scenic Frenchtown Valley, 15 miles west of Missoula off Interstate 90 (exit 89). The venue started with nine holes in 1992, and work commenced on a second nine in 1995. Unfortunately, the nearby Clark Fork River flooded in the winter of 1996 and wiped out much of the work on the new holes. Shaping of the holes began anew in summer and fall 1996. If nature obliges, King Ranch's expanded layout should be open in summer or fall 1997 (after this book went to press).

The course is the brainchild of the late Bud King. His family—daughter Trudy, her husband and greens superintendent Tod Green, and Bud's grandson Todd King—run the facility. In late 1996, Dennis Washington, Trudy's cousin, bought the course for upwards of $3 million, erasing some debt associated with construction of the new holes. The King family members are friendly folks, greeting golfers with open arms just as their father would have done. Once a private duck-hunting reserve, 700-acre King Ranch sits on a Clark Fork floodplain on Frenchtown's west end. Many ducks, geese and deer visit the site, which also has a bass-stocked pond. Trudy Green once adopted a pet fawn, calling it Fairway.

Depending on how the par-37 second nine pans out, King Ranch may eventually contain 27 holes and 30 homesites. The venue has a driving range as well as a nice restaurant and bar overlooking the valley. The golf course is not particularly difficult; but it's fun, easy to walk, and provides an enjoyable outing in some lovely country. The holes cross flat ground intersected by meandering ponds and creeks. Because of its floodplain locale, the course can be wet in spring. Top tests on the par-35 front include the 329-yard par-4 3rd, a straight and wide hole lined by a creek right and tall rough left. The 3rd ends at a diabolical bi-level green with a two-foot difference between tiers. The 213-yard par-3 4th starts at a raised tee and ends at a pond-fronted, undulating green. Crosswinds from the west (right) boggle the tee shots here. Another good hole is the 7th, a 490-yard par-5 with a route squeezed by a pond, bunker and trees. The small and raised 7th green is fronted by a pond and backed by a bunker and yet more water.

Larchmont Golf Course

3200 Old Fort Road, Missoula, MT 59801. (406) 721-4416. Bill Galiher, pro. 18 holes. 7,093 yards. Par 72. Grass tees. Course ratings: men—B71.9/117, M69.9/114; women F69.4/110. Year Opened: 1982. Architects: Keith Hellstrom & Randy Lilje. Moderate, credit cards. Reservations: Call a day ahead. Walk-on chances: Fair. Walkability: Good. Playability: Length, considerable bunkering and ample water hazards give players plenty to think about. **18**

Located on Missoula's west side, Larchmont is owned by Missoula County and run by Summit Golf Management, a local firm overseen by pro Bill Galiher and his partner Eileen Nordwick. The venue boasts fine conditioning, considerable length, ample water hazards, and a plethora of Scottish-style pot bunkers. Regularly ranked among the state's top-five tracks, Larchmont plays host to the Montana Open each year. The three-day event has golf pros from around the Northwest flocking to Missoula for a share of the $23,500 purse. The 1996 winner, Mike Hamblin of Idaho, took home a check for $4,500.

These pros and Larchmont's regulars seek to overcome a layout that can be sideswiped by winds out of the west. The flattish track is efficiently arrayed and walker-friendly. Fairways are lined by pine, spruce, green ash, poplar and apple trees. The course in the panoramic Missoula Valley offers vistas of the Bitterroots and Rockies. The front side, at 3,623 yards, is among the region's longest sets of holes. Larchmont's considerable yardage is mitigated somewhat by Missoula's 3,200-foot elevation. The course was co-designed by Spokane landscape architect Keith Hellstrom and Missoula park planner Randy Lilje.

Water hazards (small lakes and ponds) invade eight holes. Memorable tests include the top-rated 4th, a 570-yard, par-5 that doglegs right between bunkers to an undulating green guarded left-front by a trap and right-front by a pond. The 468-yard, par-4 13th is a slight dogleg-right with a pond outside the turn and a vast bunker before its small, rolling green. The 15th, a 453-yard par-4, winds rightward around pine trees to a pond-backed green. The 16th, a par-5 of 515 yards, curls slightly leftward to a slick green.

Linda Vista Public Golf Course

9 *4915 Lower Miller Creek Road, Missoula, MT 59801. (406) 251-3655. John Galiher, pro. 9 holes. 1,745 yards. Par 29. Grass tees. Course ratings: men—C55.7/85, M53.8/81; women 54.0/77. Year Opened: 1994. Architect: Carl Thuesen. Moderate, credit cards. Reservations: Call two weeks ahead. Walk-on chances: Good. Walkability: Good. Playability: Executive track sports many sand and water hazards.*

Executive-length Linda Vista is in the Lower Miller Creek area south of Missoula. Linda Vista ("beautiful view" in Spanish) was developed by Twite Family Partnership, a local firm headed by Lloyd Twite. The course occupies a 100-year floodplain and is bordered by the Bitterroot River. The river reached a 30-year high in spring of 1996 and flooded its banks. Several fairways were under water as late as June. Later that summer, after some fairways were rebuilt, the course was back in good shape. Besides a nicely arrayed nine holes, Linda Vista boasts a grass-teed driving range and an upscale clubhouse with food service and banquet space. The Twites are developing homesites to the south. Future plans include adding new back tees to lengthen the course.

The watery 3rd hole at Linda Vista is a 140-yard par-3.

Well-appointed Linda Vista features mound-lined fairways, adequate bunkering, troublesome water hazards, paved cart paths, tee benches, flower gardens and large, USGA-spec. greens. The course is occasionally visited by foxes, ducks and geese; bleating sheep graze alongside the 8th hole. The par-29 venue contains seven par-3s and a couple of par-4s. Among its tougher holes is the 1st, a 350-yard par-4 that winds slightly right around a bunker; wetlands and OB sit outside the turn. The opening hole ends at a large, left-front-tilting green trapped twice on the left. A pond looms along the right. The 193-yard, par-3 5th has a pond-fronted tee and a front-sloping, trapped-left putting surface. Linda Vista's top-rated hole is the 8th, a fine 365-yard par-4. The dogleg-right curls narrowly between a pond (right) and bunker (left). Another pond lines the fairway's last leg and runs up to guard the left edge of the 8th green, which is also trapped right and rear.

Meadow Lake Resort   18

100 Saint Andrews Drive, Columbia Falls, MT 59912. (406) 892-2111 or 1-800-321-4653. Kyle Long, pro. 18 holes. 6,601 yards. Par 72. Grass tees. Course ratings: men—B70.2/126, M69.1/123; women F69.9/122. Years Opened: 1974 (original nine); 1986 (second nine). Architect: Richard Phelps. Moderate, credit cards. Reservations: Call two weeks ahead. Walk-on chances: Fair. Walkability: Fair, with some lengthy hikes between holes. Playability: Varied, interesting challenges found at resort course.

Meadow Lake's 18-hole layout is within a full-service resort northeast of Columbia Falls. In recent years, more houses have been built along these fairways, particularly on the front nine. The appeal of moving here is simple: a vast array of outdoor activities are close by, the resort features many amenities, and the Richard Phelps-designed course is a joy to play. While staying here for a few days in the summer of 1994, I attended an Emmy Lou Harris concert at the resort. After golfers had cleared the 17th hole late one Sunday afternoon, 3,000 or so concertgoers began arriving with kids, blankets and picnic baskets. It was wonderful sitting on a fairway—where I'd dug divots just a few hours before—while sipping a local microbrew as Harris played her Montana-tuned country rock. The resort offers other types of fun-filled activities on its busy summer programs.

Meadow Lake is owned by High Country Development, a group that includes Peter Tracey, Ron Holliday, Paul Benn and other stockholders. Besides developing the golf course and a clubhouse with a restaurant ("Tracey's") and bar ("Mulligan's"), the group has built time-share townhouses, dozens of single-family homes, a lodge and villas on the 700-acre site. Accommodations at the lodge are spacious and affordable; outdoor decks off the units provide western views of the lush layout and magnificent sunsets. In 1995, Meadow Lake became the first Flathead Valley course certified by the National Audubon Society. A staff environmentalist and local birders cooperated in building houses for bluebirds, swallows and chickadees along fairways. A special box attracts bats to parts of the course where mosquitoes have bothered golfers. Some roughs have been allowed to grow, providing cover for birds and a buffer zone for ponds. The course inventories mammals, birds and plants, and monitors the seepage of fertilizers into water hazards.

Located at an elevation of 3,100 feet, Meadow Lake is known for its herds of deer and elk; ducks and geese alight on the ponds. The front nine is more developed on peripheries, while the newer back nine is still mostly forested. Noteworthy golf tests include the 3rd, a 579-yard par-5 that runs narrowly between trees and OB. The hole curls leftward over its final 125 yards to a small, trapped-right-front green. The 357-yard, par-4 4th is a sharp dogleg-left through trees. The first leg of the hole goes 200 yards, then veers abruptly uphill to the left around a pair of firs to a mid-sized, kidney-shaped green. The serpentine 7th, a 526-yard par-5, goes straight downhill, then turns left and, finally, ascends rightward to a left-leaning, trapped-left-front green fronted by a creek.

The 369-yard, par-4 9th has a pond right of the tee and OB and homes along the left. The tight hole heads between alders and a bunker left before curling rightward to a creek-fronted, bi-trapped and steeply front-banked green with a ridge through it. The 10th, a 352-yard par-4, has homes left and two bunkers right of the tee-shot landing zone. The left-tilting hole ends at a ledged green trapped right and left-front. The 11th, a 377-yard par-4, is a sharp dogleg-right around pines. OB and bunkers line the left side of the hole before it rises to a slick knoll-perched green. Great views are available from the elevated tee at the 14th, a 503-yard par-5 that sweeps leftward past bunkers outside the turn. A pond guards the right edge of a heart-shaped, front-right-sloping green trapped right, rear and left. The 15th is a dandy par-4 of 449 yards. OB and a road border the hole on the left, and its round, trapped-left green sits in a hollow and is protected in front by a tall fir.

Mission Mountain Country Club - semiprivate

18 *640 Stagecoach Trail, Ronan, MT 59864. (406) 676-4653. Marlin Hanson, pro. 18 holes. 6,478 yards. Par 72. Grass tees. Course ratings: men—B69.7/114, M68.7/ 112; women F66.5/105. Year Opened: 1988 (original nine); 1992 (second nine). Architect: Roger Gary Baird. Moderate, credit cards. Reservations: Call two days ahead. Walk-on-chances: Fair. Walkability: Good. Playability: Quite tough, with lots of variety among the holes.*

Mission Mountain Country Club is a semiprivate track east of Ronan off Highway 93. The course's former isolation has been mitigated in recent years as more and more homesites are built along its periphery. Mission Mountain began with several dozen members; its scrolls now list 260 members and counting. Recent improvements to the course, which hosts about 27,000 rounds a year, include a new 13th tee that added 50 yards to the hole. Another change is a full-service clubhouse— with bar, restaurant and pro shop—out of which head pro Marlin Hanson operates.

The club was originated by a local banker, Don Olson, and was built by Roe & Son of Big Timber, Montana. Mission Mountain's course crosses 160 acres of rolling terrain. Magnificent views of nearby mountain ranges are available from nearly every hole. The original (front) nine traverses generally flat ground, while the back side involves wavier topography. The holes are gradually losing their links-like appearance as evergreen, birch, aspen and maple trees along fairways grow taller. Mud Creek invades several back-nine holes.

Many Mission Mountain fairways are lined by "chocolate drops" (mounds), while its large bentgrass greens are guarded by many grass and sand bunkers. Seasonal winds are a factor at the rural course, especially at the 1st hole, a 543-yard par-5. The right-bender heads into the prevailing wind as it stretches out to a front-tilting green ringed by three white-sand traps. Another Mission Mountain beauty is the 611-yard, par-5 15th, a relatively straight hole crossed by Mud Creek. The latter part of the 15th is also lined by the creek along the right-hand side. The water hazard runs up to protect the right edge of a figure-eight-shaped, trapped-left-front green.

Mountain Crossroads Golf Course   9

100 Highway 206, Creston, MT 59902. (406) 755-0111. Peter LeDonne, pro. 9 holes. 1,600 yards. Par 31. Grass tees. Course ratings not available. Year Opened: 1997. Architect: Peter LeDonne. Moderate, jr. rates, credit cards. Call for reservations. Walk-on chances: Good. Walkability: Good. Playability: Nice place for a quick fix.

Nine-hole Mountain Crossroads is located at the northeast corner of Flathead Lake. The course is next to the Crossroads Restaurant at the intersection of highways 206 and 35. The layout was built by Roe & Son from a design by Mountain Crossroads' owner and head pro, Peter LeDonne. A longtime area pro who previously worked at Glacier View and Village Greens, LeDonne also runs the restaurant that now serves as a temporary clubhouse. Besides adding a permanent clubhouse—to contain an art and gift gallery, offices and pro shop, LeDonne may build a putting course as well as another nine holes.

Mountain Crossroads enjoys a good location beside one of the main routes into Glacier Park. Previously used as a sheep farm, the site crosses gently rolling ground in the Lake Blaine area of the Flathead Valley; Kalispell lies five miles to the west. Blaine Creek runs through the course, which offers clear vistas of the Glacier and Mission mountains, Whitefish Range, Jewel Basin, Swan Peak and Bob Marshall Wilderness.

Augmented by a trout-stocked fishing pond, the executive-length track contains four par-4s and five par-3s. The L-shaped layout features ponds and the creek on six holes. Cottonwood, willow, spruce, ponderosa pine and fir trees line fairways, with bunkers on three holes. The large, bentgrass greens bear quite a few undulations. LeDonne wanted his course to be amenable to juniors. Appropriately, there's a special "green" tee for neophytes.

Northern Pines Golf Course   18

3230 Highway 93, Kalispell, MT 59901. (406) 752-7950 or 1-800-255-5641. Tom Clary, director of golf; Chad Poirot, pro. 18 holes. 7,015 yards. Par 72. Grass tees. Course ratings: men—C72.5/121, B70.7/119, M68.6/115; women F69.5/117. Year Opened: 1996. Architects. Andy North & Roger Packard. Moderate, credit cards. Call for reservations. Walk-on chances: Fair. Walkability: Good. Playability: Sublime conditioning and a variety of challenges come together in a fine package.

Located on the west side of Highway 93 four miles north of Kalispell, this new 18-hole venue is a great addition to the Flathead Valley golf scene. The course's backers, Golf Northwest, LLC, are headed by Brian Cloutier. In early 1997, Golf Northwest completed the purchase of Eagle Bend in Bigfork. The company now offers "combination passes" at these two top-flight tracks. Northern Pines features a fine golf course, a 3,200-square-foot clubhouse and grass-teed driving range; 28 homesites will also be developed on the property. The 160-acre layout skirts the Stillwater River, which enters play on the 14th through 17th holes. Prior to being converted into an entertaining course, the site was a potato farm. During construction very few rocks were found as the tubers had broken apart the soil.

Northern Pines' course is separated from Highway 93 by a tall grassy berm. The earthen hill was part of the over 400,000 yards of dirt shaped during construction. While the course was being built, a bevy of turtles was found along a stretch of the Stillwater. The Montana Wildlife Department determined that these river holes contained the state's most populous turtle habitat. The operators call this part of the course "Turtle Bay." Of more mundane concern to golfers are a four-acre lake, over 40 sand traps and 20 grass bunkers. The track features four to five tees per hole; Penncross bentgrass greens and tees; bluegrass fairways; and wheatgrass-blue flax roughs.

Northern Pines had a "soft" opening in August 1996. News that a new course was open didn't take long to circulate among local linksters, who made repeated visits that fall. Northern Pines' non-river holes resemble a links layout with tall heaves and deep swales marking the fairways; that characteristic may change in the years ahead when upwards of 3,000 trees will be planted. Players here enjoy great views of the mountains ringing the Flathead Valley, most especially Big Mountain to the north. Among the players who've visited the new course are some of designer Andy North's PGA Tour contemporaries: Gary McCord, Craig Stadler and Bruce Lietzke.

The most naturally-endowed holes at Northern Pines are those along the Stillwater. The front side includes such daunting tests as the top-rated 2nd, a 448-yard par-4, and the 9th, a rolling par-4 of 430 yards. Noteworthy back-nine holes include the 404-yard, par-4 14th, which winds rightward off an elevated tee. Traps lie inside the turn and the river meanders alongside the fairway's left flank as the hole goes toward a rolling, tree-ringed green. The signature hole at Northern Pines may be the 16th, a 193-yard par-3 that crosses the river and Turtle Bay.

Plains Golf Course

9 *Highway 200, Plains, MT 59859. (406) 826-3106. Walter Martin, pro. 9 holes. 2,900 yards. Par 36. Grass tees. Course ratings: men 65.7/102, women 65.5/101. Opened: 1930s; reopened 1954. Architects: Founding members. Economical. Reservations: Call a week ahead. Walk-on chances: Very good. Walkability: Good, despite a prominent hill. Playability: Fair.*

About 100 club members operate and maintain this city-owned course. A local man, Walter Martin, does the brunt of the work. If Martin or other volunteers aren't inside "The Shelter," a small building that serves as the clubhouse, use a pay box for green fees. Plains' course was built in the 1930s on land donated by the Johnson brothers, a local family. The layout, which sported sand greens until 1987, was open for play until World War II. It was closed during the war but reopened in 1954. Though the course now has all-grass greens, the major problem remains getting irrigation water on the putting surfaces through an ancient sprinkler system. Recent improvements include a new 2nd green, which converted the former par-4 into a par-5; the 3rd, previously a par-4, is now a three-par.

The primary degree of difficulty here stems from a towering hill, which is shadowed by Bonneville power lines. (Players get to reload with no penalty if a ball strikes them.) Seven holes traversing the hill are lined by tall grass and scrub growth. Good views of the Plains Valley are available from the higher points. Decent tests include the 2nd, a 459-yard par-5 that doglegs left toward the new green. The 466-yard, par-5 5th ascends over rolling ground to a tiny green cut into a steep hillside. The 9th, a 299-yard par-4, has an elevated tee fronted by a rock-filled, overgrown ravine. Players must circumnavigate this to reach a tight landing zone before the small 9th green.

Polson Country Club

18

111 Bayview Drive, Polson, MT 59860. (406) 883-2440. Roger Wallace, pro. 18 holes. 6,756 yards. Par 72. Grass tees. Course ratings: men—B70.9/119, M67.9/ 115; women F68.4/114. Years Opened: 1936-37 (original nine); 1989 (second nine). Architects: Works Progress Administration (original nine); Frank Hummel (second nine). Moderate, credit cards. Reservations: Call two days ahead. Walk-on chances: Fair. Walkability: Good. Playability: Nice mix of old and new holes.

Polson Country Club adorns the southern end of Flathead Lake; its "Take a swing by the lake!" slogan is quite apt. The original nine (played as the back) was one of a handful of courses built in the Northwest by Works Progress Adminstration labor in the 1930s. A 3,500-yard front nine, designed by Colorado architect Frank Hummel, opened for play in summer 1989. In early 1997, discussions were underway on arranging funds for a third nine at the city-owned facility. If the project proceeds, perhaps as early as summer 1997, architect John Steidel will design it. Recent course upgrades include adding white sand to all the bunkers.

The course is located off Highway 93 between the shops, restaurants, hotels and RV parks that line this thoroughfare through Polson. The front side is generally flat, with now-short trees along most fairways. Outside of a few water hazards, players can whale away at the ball with relative impunity on this wide-open set of holes. The original back nine, however, is completely different, with towering firs, maples and other arboreal giants squeezing target zones. Magnificent views of Flathead Lake are available from holes 10-18.

Good front-nine tests include the 2nd, a 355-yard par-4 that runs downhill along a left-bending path to a knoll-perched, trapped-left green guarded right by a pond. The top-rated 3rd, a 608-yard par-5, has a wide, ascending fairway that skirts OB and a road left. A pond lurks before the back tee, and the 3rd ends at a small, front-banked green trapped left. Polson's signature hole is the 15th, a 182-yard par-3 that descends to an oval, trapped-rear green with Flathead Lake close behind.

Thompson Falls Golf Club

9

46 Golf Course Road, Thompson Falls, MT 59873. (406) 827-3438. 9 holes. 3,022 yards. Par 36. Grass tees. Course ratings: men 67.2/109, women 68.9/112. Years Opened: 1962 (original five holes); 1965 (four new holes). Architects: Local players. Economical. Reservations: Call two weeks ahead. Walk-on chances: Very good. Walkability: Good. Playability: Slick greens and narrow, pine-lined fairways comprise the brunt of the challenge.

Located about a mile north of Thompson Falls, this nine-hole layout sits along the banks of the sparkling Clark Fork River. The course's rural locale leads it to be visited by a host of whitetailed deer. Other local wildlife include bears, moose and Canada geese in spring. Nice views of Flatiron Ridge are available from some holes. The layout originated in 1962 with five holes; four more followed in 1965 and its original sand greens were sodded in 1973. Volunteers are primarily responsible for conditioning the city-owned course, which is leased to members for one dollar a year. A new clubhouse was built in 1996 after a windstorm destroyed the old structure.

The layout follows a bend in the Clark Fork. Fairways are carved within stands of ponderosa pine and fir, and the greens are generally small and slick. Judging the distances of shots within these wood-paneled corridors can be chancy. Among the better holes at the dual-tee setup is the 2nd, a 480-yard par-5 bordered left by the river. The hole ascends rightward over its last 150 yards to a domed, tree-ringed green. The top-rated 4th, a 440-yard par-4, begins at a sunken tee in trees, and ends at a steeply front-banked putting surface. The tree-ringed, humped-in-the-middle green at the 180-yard 8th can make for some tough pin placements at the par-3.

Trestle Creek Golf Course

9

Frontage Road, Saint Regis, MT 59866. (406) 649-2680. Marv Clover, pro. 9 holes. 3,227 yards. Par 36. Grass tees. Course ratings: men—B69.9/119, M68.5/116; women—M71.5/119, F68.5/116. Year Opened: 1994. Architects: Keith Hellstrom & Ed Hunnicutt. Moderate. Reservations: Call two weeks ahead. Walk-on chances: Good. Walkability: Good. Playability: Considerable challenge found at course alongside I-90.

Observable along the south side of Interstate 90 just east of Saint Regis, this modern nine-holer provides a nice challenge for area linksters and motorists. Though the course is close to a major freeway, traffic noise is not audible from it. Trestle Creek is the brainchild of Grant Lincoln, a Saint Regis native who owns Lincoln Development Company and the Heidel House Restaurant in Missoula. An uncle operates the famed Lincoln 10,000 Silver Bar tourist attraction in Saint Regis. The course is part of a larger development that includes 108 housing lots, a driving range and clubhouse. Original plans called for another nine holes, but that addition is several years away.

Trestle Creek's 4th is a 356-yard par-4.

Trestle Creek's layout adjoins the meandering South Fork River, and its rolling fairways wind between tall trees. Deer and elk (the latter were once hunted here) inhabit the grounds. Moose damaged the greens during construction of the course, whose name came from railroad tracks and a bridge to the south. When I visited the facility in the fall of 1995, superintendent Rick Meier had the greens stimping at 8.5. They'll get even quicker in the years ahead.

Trestle Creek was designed for popular tastes and built with sound engineering. The mid-sized greens, usually ringed by white-sand bunkers, have friendly level entries and mounds behind; though there's plenty of trouble to be found, there are escape hatches. I found the turf outstanding. And barring a major South Fork flood, it should stay that way. The site preparation of the course was excellent, with the well-draining, weedless fairways offering easy-to-pick lies.

Holes of note include the 3rd, a 348-yard par-4 with a lovely flower-boxed-in tee and a trestle off to the right. The narrow right-bender is interrupted by a tall pine in mid-dogleg. Two conifers 60 yards left-front of the small, trapped-right 3rd green will block errant shots. The 523-yard, par-5 5th is a slight downhiller with an S-shaped—left, then right—route lined by mounds right and trees left. The squarish, trapped-right green leans front-left. The top-rated 6th, a 384-yard par-4, goes between OB and trees to a steeply front-tilting green guarded along the right by a hidden pond. Trestle Creek's prettiest par-3 is the 155-yard 7th. The green is surrounded by water: a big pond in front and rocked-in creek to the right. The rock wall-fronted putting surface slopes toward the red-staked hazard in front.

University of Montana Golf Course   9

515 South Avenue East, Missoula, MT 59812. (406) 728-8629. Bob Crandall, pro. 9 holes. 3,086 yards. Par 35. Grass tees. Course ratings: men 68.6/110, women 72.4/116. Year Opened: 1916; 1924 (revised layout). Architects: Founding members. Moderate, student/sr. rates, credit cards. Reservations: Call two weeks ahead. Walk-on chances: Fair. Walkability: Good. Playability: Traditional nine ranks as one of Missoula's most popular courses.

Situated on the University of Montana campus in east Missoula, this course is the original site of the Missoula Country Club, founded here in 1916. University—subsequently revised in 1924—is Montana's third-oldest course, after Butte Country Club (1899) and Pine Ridge Country Club in Roundup (1908). When the private club moved to its present site in the late 1920s, the nine-hole venue was donated to the university. In 1958, UM's greens were converted to grass. With a convenient locale beside one of Montana's two major universities, affordable green fees and a driving range, the facility is quite popular.

University's dual-tee nine crosses flat terrain. The course has a par-35 front side, with a par of 36 on the back (the par-4 3rd hole is a par-5 as the 12th). Full-grown pines, spruces, cottonwoods and Russian olives define the holes. In general, the fairways are narrow and the greens small and sloped. Good tests include the 3rd, a 405-yard par-4 that skirts scrub growth and rocks as it winds to an oval green trapped right-front. The 393-yard, par-4 4th bends slightly left around trees en route to a bunker-fronted, rolling green. The 8th, a 391-yard par-4, is a 90-degree dogleg-left that curls around trees and a small pond 200 yards out. Three traps occupy the front and left flanks of its small green.

Village Greens Golfing Community

18 *500 Palmer Drive, Kalispell, MT 59901. (406) 752-4666. Jim Skurvid, pro. 18 holes. 6,227 yards. Par 70. Grass tees. Course ratings: men—B68.5/111, M67.0/109; women F67.9/111. Opened: 1992-93. Architect: William Robinson. Moderate, credit cards. Reservations: Call two weeks ahead. Walk-on chances: Fair. Walkability: Good. Playability: Ample water and sand hazards impede pursuit of par at contemporary course on Kalispell's east side.*

Though its front nine opened in 1992 and its back side the following year, this course near Kalispell is still evolving. By 1996, new back tees had added 300 yards to the layout. Upcoming plans include more back tees (ultimately stretching the course to 6,300 yards), expanding the driving range, and sanding the remaining bunkers. In the meantime, lot sales are continuing in the 300-acre community off Whitefish Stage Road. At full build-out, Village Greens will have 350 houses described in promotional literature as "affordable golf course living." Golf is interwoven into the residential ambience; streets crossed to get to holes are equipped with cute "Duffer Crossing" signs to warn motorists and linksters.

The course lies on the old Schulze Farm, a dairy operation that also grew alfalfa. Three of the Schulze brothers—George, Roger and Gerald—backed the project along with local businessman, Duane Bitney. The layout is fairly close to the Whitefish River and, in spring 1996, it was flooded when ground water rose up over the turf. Though play continued during this period, some fairways were resodded. By fall of that year, the course was fully restored.

Village Greens' course is enjoyable, featuring three par-5s from 480 to 589 yards, 10 par-4s from 311 to 417 yards, and a sixsome of par-3s. Six ponds enter play on over half the holes. Once all the bunker pits are filled with sand, the challenge will stiffen even more. Interesting tests are found at the top-rated 1st, a right-bending par-5 of 589 yards. Two bunkers squeeze the fairway 75 yards from a shallow-but-wide green trapped rear and left. The 140-yard, par-3 5th bears a large pond—dubbed Lake Martello—before a trap-squeezed, terraced green. The 7th, a 490-yard par-5, follows a tight right-bending route skirted by OB left and grass bunkers right. A sand trap sits 50 yards before its humped-in-the-middle, trapped-right-front green.

The back nine sits on a horseshoe-shaped parcel to the north, and contains extensive mounding and hazards. This side has six par-4s, a tough par-5 (the 15th), and two par-3s. "Amen Corner" at Village Greens is found at the 13th through 15th holes. The 407-yard, par-4 13th winds leftward, passing a pond along the right as it ventures to a raised, rolling green bunkered left-front. The 14th, a 387-yard par-4, backtracks alongside the 13th, with the fairway winding rightward around the aforementioned pond to a trapped-right putting surface. The 500-yard 15th runs fairly straight along a fairway that tilts rightward to a pond about 250 yards out. Two bunkers guard its undulating green.

Whitefish Lake Golf Club

Highway 93 North, Whitefish, MT 59937. (406) 862-4000. Mike Dowaliby, pro. **36**
36 holes. Grass tees. Course ratings: North (6,556 yards, par 72) men—B69.8/
118, M68.7/116; women F70.1/115. South (6,561 yards, par 72) men—B70.5/
122, M69.0/120; women F70.3/120. Years Opened: 1935 (North Course); 1978
(South original nine); 1994 (South second nine). Architects: Works Progress
Administration (North Course); Keith Hellstrom (South original nine); John Steidel
(South second nine & North remodel). Moderate, jr./sr. rates, credit cards. Reser-
vations: Call two days ahead. Walk-on chances: Fair. Walkability: Good on North
18 and fair on South. Playability: North's old-style character and South's newer
architecture are both outstanding.

Whitefish Lake Golf Club straddles Highway 93 next to Grouse Mountain
Lodge. The completion of the South 18 in 1994 helped make this city-owned facility
become one of the Northwest's finest places to golf. With a clubhouse, driving range
and a friendly staff, the 36-hole venue is certainly well-endowed. In the lodge-like
clubhouse is the Whitefish Restaurant, a fine eatery and a popular local gathering
spot. Renovated between 1983 and 1985, the well-treed North course is comparable
in difficulty to the newer South, yet retains the feel of a classical course. Once finished
with a round on the North course, golfers are encouraged to ring a large bell that
hangs on a tree near the 18th green. The South course involves more water, larger
greens and hillier terrain. The North is easy to walk; the South, with its tilted
topography and longer between-hole distances, is more of a cart course. Both tracks
have automatic irrigation systems, white-sand bunkers, excellent signage and
outstanding territorial views.

Whitefish Lake's charter stipulates that the courses cater to local citizens. The
Whitefish Golf Association has in excess of 1,700 members who pay a mere $400 annually
for unlimited golf privileges. Head pro Mike Dowaliby has overseen the course for over a
dozen years, and is one of the Flathead Valley's leading proponents of junior golf.

The 195-yard, par-3 4th hole at Whitefish Lake's North Course.

Good holes on the North 18 include the top-rated 3rd, a 435-yard par-4 that runs straight and downhill between trees to a raised, saddle-shaped and wavy green trapped right. The 4th, a 195-yard par-3 with nice views of Big Mountain, contains a lovely pond that runs up to guard the left side of a large green trapped right and left-rear. The 550-yard, par-5 5th runs straight and slightly uphill as it skirts two bunkers left. Another trap sits 125 yards from a raised green trapped left-rear. The 10th is one of those short (280-yard) and tricky par-4s from yesteryear. The tree-lined hole winds narrowly past OB on the right. Trees and a deep bunker guard the right-front flank of the small 10th green, which is also trapped rear. Another dandy is the 17th, a 371-yard par-4 that heads off an elevated tee toward a pond-squeezed landing area. Once past this point, the fairway ascends to a ridge-perched green trapped twice on the right.

A difficult South hole is the top-rated 4th, a 407-yard par-4 that runs uphill over rolling terrain toward a deep swale driving distance out. The 4th then narrows and bends left over its concluding 150 yards before reaching a wide-but-shallow, heart-shaped green ringed by three traps. A tier through the green's gut enables tough pin placements. The 470-yard, par-5 6th requires a 220-yard drive to carry the pond off the tee and find a broad landing area. The fairway then narrows and rises steeply to a big green with a tall left side, two bunkers right-front, and a three-foot-high tier in its rear section. The 7th, a 207-yard par-3, is a beautiful hole with wetlands stretching from tee to green. The front-tilting putting surface is further guarded in front by a long and sinuous bunker.

The straight-running 8th, a 402-yard par-4, is defined by wetlands left and alders right. Over its last 100 yards, the hole tapers before arriving at a front-sloping green trapped left; trees are close right and rear. The 429-yard, par-4 11th bears a tree-lined and left-leaning fairway. Its V-shaped, front-left-sloping green is lined on the right by a bunker, and has a steep left edge that directs errant shots toward jail. The chute-like 13th, a 354-yard par-4, begins at a raised tee and contains a fairway-crossing pond 215 yards out. A clump of trees stands guard along the right of the right-front-leaning green, which has three bunkers around it. The South's home hole, a 465-yard par-4, has a mid-width fairway and a rolling green engirded by three bunkers.

9 Whitetail Golf Club

4295 Wildfowl Lane, Stevensville, MT 59870. (406) 777-3636. David Aller, pro. 2,844 yards. Par 35. Grass tees. Course ratings: men 65.8/104, women 67.9/107. Opened: 1920s. Architects: Founding members. Economical. Reservations: Call two weeks ahead. Walk-on chances: Good. Walkability: Good. Playability: Quiet golf rounds in rugged area.

Previously known as Stevensville Golf Club, this nine-hole track lies about 20 miles south of Missoula on the west side of Highway 93. The member-owned course near the Lee Metcalf Wildlife Refuge offers wonderful views of the Bitterroot Valley, Saint Mary's Peak and the Bitterroot Range. Non-golfing visitors include white-tailed deer, ducks and geese. In the past, newborn fawns have occasionally followed golfers on their appointed rounds. When Whitetail's small clubhouse is unattended, green fees are paid on the honor system.

Originally the site of a ranch, the course occupies a 100-year floodplain alongside the Bitterroot River. In spring 1996, the river flooded its banks and forced the course to close for a month. It's since been returned to normal. Recent upgrades include greenside bunkers at the 1st, 5th and 7th holes. More traps will be added in the years ahead by superintendent, Gary Geer. The layout was founded, designed and built by local golfers in the 1920s; construction was supported by the sale of 42 stock certificates. The original sand greens were gradually replaced by grass greens by the mid-1980s.

Over the years, pines and other conifers have been planted in the course's midsection. Besides trees, hazards include a ditch and a pond which cross several holes. Among Whitetail's better tests is the 345-yard 6th, a left-curling par-4 that goes between a bunker left and pond right en route to a small rolling green. The 8th, a 423-yard par-4, follows a tree-paneled path to a slippery, mid-sized green.

PRIVATE COURSES

Missoula Country Club

18

3850 Old Highway 93, Missoula, MT 59806. (406) 251-2751. Skip Koprivica, pro. 18 holes. 6,575 yards. Par 71. Grass tees. Course ratings: men—B69.9/118, M68.9/ 117; women F71.1/118. Year Opened: 1928 (original nine); 1949 (second nine). Architects: Dr. Don Barnett, Tim Clowes, R. E. "Jack" Rice & Ted Barker (original nine); Francis L. James (second nine); William Hull & Chip Roe (remodels). Members, guests & reciprocates.

Missoula's only private club lies in the city's west end near the Bitterroot River. Ironically, Missoula Country Club was one of the few courses in western Montana that wasn't hard hit by the floods of spring 1996. Water surrounded Missoula's 17th green—converting the putting surface at the par-3 into an island configuration—and the driving range was flooded. But, overall, the course went relatively unscathed. Other events in 1996 included the club's hosting of the Montana State Amateur, a Memorial Day event that began in the 1930s. Missoula's next big tournament is the Montana State Seniors in 1998.

Missoula Country Club officially began in 1916 at the current site of the University of Montana Golf Course. The members eventually sought a new site, and found land available at Fort Missoula. The officers at Fort Missoula had built a nine-hole golf course of their own before the club approached them. The military brass accepted the members' proposal with the condition that the soldiers who helped construct the course be allowed free play. Work began in 1927, with mules pulling scrapers and the members providing labor. Upon completion, the new course was the only one between Minneapolis and Spokane with grass fairways. After several unsuccessful attempts, Missoula Country Club became one of Montana's first courses with grass greens when it debuted in 1928. (Unfortunately, those putting surfaces were destroyed by winterkill in 1989. New greens—designed by Bill Hull and Chip Roe—finally grew into good shape in 1992.)

In the mid-1930s, Norway spruces, black locusts, Scotch pines, junipers, golden willows, Russian olives, box elders, lindens and Chinese elms were planted along Missoula's fairways. These trees now tower over the course, providing shade in summer and color in fall. In 1949, a new nine designed by architect Francis L. James opened for play. The new holes were initially played as the back side but have since been reversed. Recent improvements include new tees at the 2nd and 13th holes. Superintendent Jon Heselwood, one of the state's best turf tenders as well as a fine tournament golfer, oversees the improvements. Skip Koprivica, here for nearly a dozen years, previously worked at Buffalo Hill in Kalispell, Thunderbird Country Club in Palm Springs, and Oak Hill Country Club in Rochester, New York.

Par-3 Courses

Cedar Creek Golf Course

10 Wadsworth Lane, Superior, MT 59872. (406) 822-4443. 9 holes 1,427 yards. Par 27. Grass tees. No course ratings. Economical. No reservations. Driving range.

Cedar Creek is a new par-3 track that debuted in August 1995. In effect, the venue replaces the old Superior course that arose in the 1920s but was later paved over when Interstate 90 was built. This course alongside the Clark Fork River is part of a small housing development with 16 lots. The project backers—Ed Hollenbach, Bernie Anderson, Guy Moats, Ken Kuhl and Dave Sanchez—are all from Superior. Golf operations will be conducted from a house on the property until a permanent clubhouse is built. A driving range sits across Wadsworth Lane from the course.

Anderson designed and built the layout with his own equipment. He did a surprisingly good job; Cedar Creek boasts sizable bentgrass greens, an interesting cross-section of well-shaped holes, and better-than-average conditioning. Nice touches include a covered bridge across a creek near the 7th hole. A towering tamarack in mid-course is home to ospreys, and a garden-adorned waterfall embellishes the 100-yard 1st hole. Mounds line some fairways, with other routes squeezed by water hazards. The holes by the Clark Fork are particularly tough, with some up-and-down tee shots involving a hill along the river.

Meadow Creek Golf Course

1st Street South, Fortine, MT 59918. (406) 882-4474. 9 holes. 1,382 yards. Par 27. Grass tees. No course ratings. Economical. No reservations.

Meadow Creek, a par-3 track near Fortine, was originated by Jerry and Noreen Syth. The year 1996 was a sad one for the Syth family. Jerry passed away early in the year, forcing Noreen to become the sole proprietor of this course as well as operator of the adjoining "Jerry's Saloon"—a casino and steakhouse—and an 18-slip RV park. Then spring floods came and washed out most of the golf season. After *the* Meadow Creek returned to its banks, repairs were made to the course and play didn't resume until late July.

The layout occupies the former site of a state fish hatchery. Fortine's Carl Goble designed the course, which was built by local residents Roger and Charlie Parker. Hazards include 80 blue spruces along fairways, seven water hazards and eight bunkers. Golfers enjoy views of the Salish Mountains and Whitefish Range from most sections of the course.

The Par-3 on 93 Golf Course

6145 Highway 93, Whitefish, MT 59937. (406) 862-7273. 9 holes. 1,065 yards. Par 27. Grass tees. No course ratings. Economical, credit cards. Call for reservations. Walk-on chances: Good. Driving range. **9**

This par-3 venue is owned by Jim Kane, a New York City native who's lived in Montana since 1971. Kane once owned a nearby steakhouse, but sold it in the early 1990s. The John Steidel-designed track opened in 1989. Upcoming plans include stretching the 5th, 7th and 9th holes 20 or 30 yards each by the addition of new back tees.

The Par-3 on 93 features bentgrass greens and ample water and sand hazards. Golfers here enjoy sweeping vistas of the peaks around the Flathead Valley. The layout was built by Bob Soushak of Fore, Inc., a Maple Valley, Washington company that has constructed many championship courses in recent years. Souchak supervised the project for awhile, then turned the remaining work over to his crew to finish up. The workers had never built a par-3 layout; they ended up building large, regulation-sized tees and greens. The 17-acre nine contains seven traps and a pond that enters play on three holes. There's also a driving range next to the course.

DRIVING RANGES

National Golf Driving Range

3159 Highway 93 North, Kalispell, MT 59901.
(406) 752-4653. Ken Olson, pro.

UPCOMING COURSES

Hamilton — Bitter Root Stock Farm Golf Club (1999/2000). In late 1996, it was learned that billionaire accountant Charles Schwab is backing a private 18-hole course east of Hamilton. The Tom Fazio-designed layout will occupy land donated by property owner Harold Mildenberger. The original plan called for 90 members, but local regulatory agencies may scoff at such exclusivity and require Schwab to broaden his horizons.

Whitefish — Iron Horse Golf Club (1999/2000). This 825-acre project off East Lakeshore Drive includes a private 18-hole course designed by Tom Fazio, 450 housing units, a 20,000-square-foot clubhouse and some rentable cottages. The backers, Montana Capital Partners, include native Montanan and former Dallas Cowboy Pat Donovan and the majority owner of Dallas-based Hunt Oil, Ray Hunt.

ALPHABETICAL INDEX

A

Agate Beach Golf Course	414
Alderbrook Golf Course (Tillamook)	400
Alderbrook Golf & Yacht Club (Union)	210
Allenmore Public Golf Club	178
Alpine Meadows Golf Course	542
Alta Lake Golf Course	254
American Lake VA Golf Course	193
Apple Tree Golf Course	274
Applegate Golf	453
Arrowhead Golf Club	439
Ashford Driving Range	249
Aspen Lakes Golf Course	494
Astoria Golf & Country Club	408
Auburn Golf Course	179
Auburn Center Golf Club	415
Avalon Golf Club	70
Avondale Golf Club	556
Awbrey Glen Golf Club	530

B

Baker City Golf Club	543
Ballinger Park Municipal Golf Course	117
Bandon Face Rock Golf Course	454
Banks Lake Golf Club	255
Batstone Hill Practice Golf	223
Battle Creek Golf Course (Marysville)	118
Battle Creek Golf Course (Salem)	415
Bay Breeze Golf & Driving Range	409
Bayou Golf Club	416
Beacon Hill Golf Center	314
Beacon Rock Public Golf Course	276
Bear Creek Golf Course (Medford)	455
Bear Creek Golf Course (Winthrop)	256
Bear Creek Country Club (Woodinville)	152
Bellevue Municipal Golf Course	119
Bellingham Golf & Country Club	85
Bend Golf & Country Club	531
Big Bend Golf & Country Club	294
Bigwood Golf Course	557
Birch Bay Village Golf Course	86
Birdies Golf Place	314
Black Butte Ranch	495
Blue Boy West Golf Course	120

Bowyer's Par 3 Golf	392
Brae Burn Golf & Country Club	152
Broadmoor Golf Club (Seattle)	153
Broadmoor Golf Course (Portland)	346
Broken Top Club	533
Brookdale Golf Course	179
Bryden Canyon Golf Course	558
Buckhorn Par-3	313
Buffalo Hill Golf Club	584

C

Cabinet View Country Club	585
Caddieshack Driving Range	448
Camaloch Golf Club	96
Canterwood Golf & Country Club	194
Canyon Lakes Golf Course	318
Capitol City Golf Club	228
Carey Lakes Golf Course	276
Carnation Golf Course	121
Cascade Golf Course	121
Cedarcrest Municipal Golf Course	122
Cedar Bend Golf Club	456
Cedar Creek Golf Course	604
Cedar Links	456
The Cedars Golf Club	347
Centralia Public Golf Course	229
Charbonneau Golf & Country Club	348
Chevy Chase Golf Club	211
Chewelah Golf & Country Club	295
The Children's Course	349
Christmas Valley Golf Course	518
Christy's Golf Course & Driving Range	203
Chuck Milne's 82nd Avenue Golf Range	394
Circle Bar Golf Club	519
Claremont Golf Club	349
Clarkston Golf & Country Club	334
Classic Country Club	180
Clover Valley Golf & Country Club	97
Cloverdale Golf Club	123
The Club at Sutherlin	457
Club Green Meadows	374
Coburg Hills Golf Club	458
Coeur d'Alene Golf Club	558
The Coeur d'Alene Resort Golf Course	559
Colfax Golf Club	319
Colonial Valley Golf Course	459
Columbia-Edgewater Country Club	375
Columbia Park Golf Course	320
Columbia Point Golf Course	320

Colville Elks Golf Course   296
Colwood National Golf Club   350
Condon Golf Course   496
Cooper's Golf Range   91
Coos Country Club   459
Coquille Valley Elks Golf Club   479
Cordon Road Driving Range   448
Corvallis Country Club   440
Cottonwood Lakes Golf Course   416
The Country Club of Seattle   105
The Creek at Qualchan   296
Creekside Golf Club   417
Crescent Bar Resort   277
Crestview Hills Public Golf Course   418
Crooked River Ranch Golf Course   497
Cross Creek Golf Course   419
Crossroads Park Golf Course   171
Crosswater   534
Crystal Springs Golf Center   269

D

Dakota Creek Golf & Country   71
Dallas Golf Course   420
Deer Meadows Golf Course   297
Deer Park Golf & Country Club   298
Delphi Golf Course   229
Desert Aire Golf & Country Club   278
Desert Canyon Golf Resort   257
Desert Lakes Driving Range   340
Diamond Woods Golf Course   420
Dino's Driving Range   394
Double Arrow Golf Resort   586
Downriver Golf Course   299
Druids Glen Golf Club   124
Dungeness Golf Course   212
Dutcher Creek Golf Course   460

E

Eagle Bend Golf Club   587
Eagle Creek Golf Course   498
Eagle Crest Golf Course   499
Eagle Driving Range   552
Eagle Point Golf Course   461
Eagle Ridge Golf Course   500
Eagle View Golf Center   249
Eaglemont Golf Course   72
EagleQuest at Golf Park   172
EagleQuest at Linksman Golf Center   204

Eagles on the Green   479
Eastmoreland Golf Course   351
Echo Falls Country Club   126
Echo Hills Golf Course   544
Elk Run Golf Course   126
Elkhorn Resort Golf Course   560
Elkhorn Valley Golf Course   501
Ellensburg Golf Club   278
Emerald Links Driving Range   204
Emerald Valley Golf Club   463
Enumclaw Golf Course   181
Esmeralda Golf Course   300
Eugene Country Club   479
Everett Golf & Country Club   154
Evergreen Golf Club (Mount Angel)   421
Evergreen Golf Center (Vancouver)   394
Evergreen Golf Course (Everson)   73

F

Fairway Village Golf Course   352
The Fairways at West Terrace
   Golf Course   300
Fairwood Golf & Country Club   155
Fiddler's Green Golf Course   487
Fircrest Golf Club   195
Fisher Park Golf Course   288
Flowing Lake Golf Course   127
Forest Hills Golf Course (Cornelius)   401
Forest Hills Country Club (Reedsport)   464
Fort Lewis Golf Course   196
Fort Steilacoom Golf Course   182
Foster Golf Links   128
Frontier Golf Course   447

G

Gallery Golf Course   97
Gateway Golf Center (Clarkston)   340
Gateway Golf Course (Sedro-Woolley)   74
Gearhart Golf Links   401
Gig Harbor Golf & Country Club   183
Glacier View Golf Club   588
Glen Acres Golf & Country Club   156
Glendale Country Club   157
Glendoveer Golf Course   352
Gleneagle Golf Course   129
Gold Creek Tennis & Sports Club   172
Gold Mountain Golf Course   98

Golden Bear Family Golf Center
  at Interbay   130
Golden Bear Golf Center at Sunset   394
Goldendale Country Club   279
Golf City   422
The Golf Club at Newcastle   130
The Golf Club of Oregon   422
Golfgreen Golf Center   248
Grand Mound Driving Range   249
Grandview Golf Course   74
Grangeville Country Club   561
Grants Pass Driving Range   488
Grants Pass Golf Club   464
Grays Harbor Country Club   221
Green Lake Golf Course   171
Greenlea Golf Course   353
The Greens at Redmond   502
Gresham Golf Course   354

H

H & H Driving Range   394
Hamilton Golf Club   589
Hangman Valley Golf Club   301
Harbor Links Golf Course   520
Harbour Pointe Golf Club   131
Harrington Golf & Country Club   302
Hartwood Golf Course   354
Harvest Valley Golf Center   289
Hat Island Golf Club   158
Hawk Creek Golf Course   423
Hayden Lake Country Club   574
Heron Lakes Golf Course   355
Hidden Lakes Golf Resort   562
Hidden Valley Golf Course   465
High Cedars Golf & Country Club   183
High Valley Country Club   244
The Highlands at Gearhart   402
The Highlands Golf & Country Club
  (Post Falls)   564
Highland Golf Course (Cosmopolis)   230
The Highlands Golf Club (Missoula)   590
Highlands Golf & Racquet Club
  (Tacoma)   184
Hillebrand's Paradise Range Resort   487
Holmes Harbor Golf Course   100
Home Place Golf Course   258
Homestead Golf & Country Club   75
Hood River Golf & Country Club   502
Horn Rapids Golf & Country Club   321

Horseshoe Lake Golf Course   101
Hot Springs Golf Course   280
Jim Colbert's Hound Hollow
  Golf Center   356
Husum Hills Golf Course   280

I

Illahe Hills Country Club   442
Illinois Valley Golf Club   466
Indian Canyon Golf Course   303
Indian Creek Golf Course   503
Indian Summer Golf & Country Club   244
Inglewood Golf Club   158
Iron Eagle Sport Center   172
Ironwood Green Golf Course   231
Island Greens   110

J

Jack Creek Driving Range   488
Jackson Park Municipal Golf Course   132
Jade Greens Golf Course   185
Jefferson Park Municipal Golf Course   133
John Day Golf Club   544
Juniper Golf Club   504

K

Kaddyshack Golf Center   172
Kahler Glen Golf Course   259
Kah-Nee-Ta Resort   505
Kayak Point Golf Course   134
Kellogg Country Club   565
Kentuck Golf Course   466
Kenwanda Golf Course   135
Kik's Driving Range   552
Killarney West Golf Club   357
King City Golf Course   357
King Ranch Golf Course   590
Kinzua Hills Golf Club   506
Kitsap Golf & Country Club   105

L

La Grande Country Club 550
Lake Chelan Golf Course 260
Lake Cushman Golf Course 213
Lake Josephine Riviera Golf
  & Country Club 198
Lake Limerick Country Club 214
Lake Oswego Golf Course 358
Lake Padden Municipal Golf Course 76
Lake Spanaway Golf Course 186
Lake Wilderness Golf Club 135
Lake Woods Golf Course 261
LakeLand Village Golf & Country Club 214
Lakeridge Golf & Country Club 545
Lakeside Golf & Racquet Club 423
Lakeview Golf Challenge 392
Lakeview Golf & Country Club 335
Lam's Links 102
Langdon Farms Golf Club 359
Larchmont Golf Course 591
Laurel Hill Golf Course 467
Laurelwood Golf Course 467
Leavenworth Golf Club 262
Legion Memorial Golf Course 136
Lewis River Golf Course 231
Lewiston Golf & Country Club 576
Liberty Lake Golf Course 304
Linda Vista Public Golf Course 592
Linden Golf & Country Club 198
Lipoma Firs Public Golf Course 187
Lobo Country Club 171
Lone Pine Village Driving Range 513
Longest Drive 340
Longshots Driving Range 172
Longview Country Club 245
Loomis Trail Golf Club 87
Lopez Island Golf Club 77
Lost Tracks Golf Club 520
Lower Valley Golf Club 281
Lynnwood Municipal Golf Course 137

M

MA-8 + 1 Golf 263
Madrona Links Golf Course 188
Mallard Creek Golf Course & RV Camp 424
Manito Golf & Country Club 310
Manzanita Golf Course 403
Maple Grove Golf 232
Maplewood Golf Course 138
Marysville Golf Center 172
Marysville Golf Course 425
McCormick Woods Golf Club 102
McKay Creek Golf Course 361
McKenzie River Golf Course 506
McNary Golf Club 425
Meadow Creek Golf Course 604
Meadow Lake Resort 593
Meadow Lakes Golf Course 507
Meadow Park Golf Course 189
Meadow Springs Country Club 336
Meadowlawn Golf Club 426
Meadowmeer Golf & Country Club 103
MeadowWood Golf Course 304
Meridian Greens 190
Meridian Valley Country Club 160
Meriwether National Golf Club 362
Meriwood Golf Course 233
Michelbook Country Club 443
Midas Golf Club 565
Middlefield Village 468
Mill Creek Country Club 161
Milton-Freewater Golf Course 545
Mint Valley Golf Course 234
Mirror Lake Golf Course 565
Mission Mountain Country Club 594
Missoula Country Club 603
Monroe Golf Course 139
Moscow Elks Golf Club 576
Moses Lake Golf & Country Club 337
Mount Adams Country Club 282
Mount Si Golf Course 139
Mountain Crossroads Golf Course 595
Mountain High Golf Course 522
Mountain View Golf Club 363
Myrtle Creek Golf Course 469

N

National Golf Driving Range 605
Neskowin Beach Golf Course 427
New World Pro Golf Center 90
Newaukum Valley Golf Course 235
Nile Golf & Country Club 140
Nine Peaks Golf Course 508
Nisqually Valley Golf Course 236
North Bellingham Golf Course 78
North Shore Golf & Country Club 190
Northern Pines Golf Club 595
Northwest Aluminum Golf Club 511
Northwest Golf Range 111

O

Oak Knoll Golf Course (Ashland) 470
Oak Knoll Golf Course (Independence) 428
Oakbrook Golf & Country Club 199
Oaksridge Golf Course 216
Oakway Golf Course 471
Oasis Park 339
Ocean Dunes Golf Links 471
Ocean Shores Golf Course 216
Odessa Golf Club 306
OGA Members Course at Tukwila 429
Okanogan Valley Golf Club 263
Olalla Valley Golf Course 431
Olympia Country & Golf Club 247
Orcas Island Golf Club 78
Orchard Hills Country Club 376
Oregon City Golf Club 363
The Oregon Golf Club 377
Orenco Woods Golf Club 364
Orion Greens Golf Course 523
Orofino Golf & Country Club 566
Oroville Golf Club 264
Oswego Lake Country Club 378
Othello Golf Club 323
Overlake Golf & Country Club 162
Overlook Golf Course 79

P

Pacific Golf Center 237
Painted Hills Golf Club 306
Par IV Golf Learning Center 249
The Par-3 on 93 Golf Course 605
Pasco Golfland 339
Peaceful Valley Country Club 79
Pend Oreille Golf & Country Club 307
Pendleton Country Club 551
Peninsula Golf Club (Port Angeles) 222
Peninsula Golf (Long Beach) 237
Persimmon Country Club 365
Pine Crest Golf 393
Pine Hollow Golf Course 508
Pineacres Par-3 Golf Course 313
Pineway Golf Course 431
Plains Golf Course 596
Plateau Golf & Country Club 163
Pleasant Valley Golf Club 380
Polson Country Club 597
Pomeroy Golf Course 323
Ponderosa Springs Golf Course 578
Port Ludlow Golf & Meeting Retreat 217
Port Townsend Municipal Golf Course 219
Portland Golf Club 381
Portland Meadows Golf Course 366
Potholes Golf Course 324
Prairie Falls Golf Course 567
Priest Lake Golf Course 567
Prineville Golf & Country Club 511
Progress Downs Municipal Golf Course 366
Puetz Evergreen Golf Range 172
Pumpkin Patch Golf & Restaurant 579
Pumpkin Ridge Golf Club — Ghost Creek (public) 367
Pumpkin Ridge Golf Club — Witch Hollow (private) 383

Q

Quail Point Golf Course 472
Quail Ridge Golf Course 324
Quail Run Golf Course 524
Quail Valley Golf Course 369
Quincy Valley Golf Course 283

R

Rainbow Golf Driving Range 249
Rainier Golf & Country Club 164
Ranch Club Golf Course 568
Ranch Hills Golf Club 432
Raspberry Ridge Golf Community 80
Raymax Driving Range 537
Reames Golf & Country Club 536
Red Mountain Golf Course 473
Red Wood Golf Center 172
The Reserve Vineyards Golf Club 370
The Resort at the Mountain 509
Rimrock Golf Course 578
Ritzville Municipal Golf Course 325
Riverbend Golf Complex 141
Riveridge Golf Course 474
River's Edge Golf Course 524
Riverside Country Club (Chehalis) 238
Riverside Golf & Country Club
 (Portland) 384
Riverside Golf Course (Ferndale) 80
Riverwood Golf Course 433
Rock Creek Country Club 385
Rock Island Golf Course 265
Rodarco Golf Range 91
Rogue Valley Country Club 481
Rolling Hills Golf Club 104
Rose City Golf Course 371
Roseburg Country Club 483
Roseburg Veterans Hospital
 Golf Course 484
Round Lake Golf Course 525
Royal City Golf Course 326
Royal Oaks Country Club 386
Running Y Ranch Resort 526

S

Sage Hills Golf Club 327
Sah-Hah-Lee Golf Course 393
Sahalee Country Club 165
Saint Helens Golf Course 404
Salem Golf Club 434
Salemtowne Golf Club 444
Salishan Golf Links 434
San Juan Golf & Country Club 81
Sand Point Country Club 166
Sandelie Golf 372
Sandpines Golf Resort 474

Sandpoint Elks Country Club 569
Sandy Point Golf Course 88
Santiam Golf Club 436
Scott Lake Golf Course 239
Sea Links 90
Seaside Golf Course 404
Seattle Golf Club 167
Semiahmoo Golf & Country Club 81
Senior Estates Golf & Country Club 444
Shadow Butte Municipal Golf Course 546
Shadow Hills Country Club 485
Shelter Bay Golf Course 88
Shelton Bayshore Golf Club 220
Sheridan Greens Golf Course 307
Shield Crest Golf Course 527
Shoshone Golf Club 569
Shuksan Golf Club 82
Similk Beach Golf Course 84
Skagit Golf & Country Club 88
Skamania Lodge Golf Course 284
Skyline Golf Course 239
Snohomish Public Golf Course 142
Snoqualmie Falls Golf Course 143
Snoqualmie Ridge TPC Golf Course 169
South Campus Public Golf Course 328
Southcenter Golf 172
Spokane Country Club 311
Spring Hill Country Club 444
Springfield Country Club 486
Springwater Golf Course 510
St. John Golf & Country Club 328
St. Maries Golf Course 570
Steamboat Golf 249
Stewart Meadows Golf Course 475
Stewart Park Golf Course 476
Stoneridge Golf Club (Blanchard) 570
Stoneridge Golf Club (Medford) 477
Straight Arrow Driving Range 289
Sudden Valley Golf & Country Club 84
Summerfield Golf & Country Club 372
Sumner Meadows Golf Links 191
Sun Country Golf Resort 285
Sun Valley Golf Course 571
Sun Willows 329
Sundance Golf Course 308
Sunland Golf & Country Club 220
Sunny Meadows Golf
 & Four Seasons Resort 267
Sunriver Resort 528
Sunset Bay Golf Club 478

Sunset Grove Golf Club   405
Suntides Golf Course   285
Surfside Golf Course   240
Super Range   172

T

Tacoma Country & Golf Club   200
Tall Chief Golf Club   144
Tam O'Shanter Golf & Country Club   170
Tapps Island Golf Course   192
The Course at Taylor Creek   144
Tekoa Golf Club   329
The Dalles Country Club   513
Thompson Falls Golf Club   597
Three Lakes Golf Course   265
Three Rivers Golf Course   240
Tokatee Golf Club   510
Top O'Scott Public Golf Course   373
Touchet Valley Golf Course   330
Tour Fairways Golf Range   340
Trestle Creek Golf Course   598
Tri-City Country Club   331
Tri-Mountain Golf Course   241
Trysting Tree Golf Club   437
Tualatin Country Club   387
Tualatin Island Greens   394
Tumwater Valley Golf Club   242
Twin Lakes Golf & Country Club   201
Twin Lakes Village Golf
    & Racquet Club   572
Twin Rivers Golf Course   146
Tyee Valley Golf Club   146

U

Umatilla Golf Course   547
University Golf Club   193
University of Idaho Golf Course   573
University of Montana Golf Course   599
University of Washington
    Driving Range   172
Useless Bay Golf & Country Club   107

V

The Valley Club   577
Valley Golf Club   547
Valley View Golf Course   308
Vanco Driving Range   394
Vashon Island Driving Range   111
Vashon Island Golf & Country Club   108
Vernonia Golf Club   406
Veterans Administration Domiciliary
    Golf Course   486
Veteran's Memorial Golf Course   331
Vic Meyers Golf Course   266
Village Greens (Port Orchard)   104
Village Greens Golfing Community
    (Kalispell)   600

W

Walla Walla Country Club   338
Walter E. Hall Memorial Golf Course   147
WSU Golf Course   332
Wandermere Golf Course   309
Warm Springs Golf Course   574
Waverley Country Club   389
Wayne Public Golf Course   148
Wellington Hills Golf Course   149
Wenatchee Golf & Country Club   267
West Richland Municipal Golf Course   333
West Seattle Municipal Golf Course   149
Westside Driving Range & Golf Center
    (Salem)   448
Westside Golf Range (Vancouver)   394
Westwood West   286
Whidbey Golf & Country Club   108
Whispering Firs Golf Course   202
Whitefish Lake Golf Club   601
Whitetail Golf Club   602
Widgi Creek Golf Club   529
Wildhorse Golf Course   548
Wildwood Golf Course   407
Willamette Valley Country Club   445
Willapa Harbor Golf Club   243
Willow Creek Country Club   549
Willows Run Golf Club   150
Wilson's Willow Run Executive
    Golf Course   549
Wing Point Golf & Country Club   109
Woodall's World Driving Range   111
Woodburn Golf Club   438

Y

Yakima Country Club   286
Yakima Elks Golf & Country Club   287

Geographical Index

Washington

**Northwest Washington
& the San Juan Islands**
Avalon Golf Club   70
Bellingham Golf & Country Club   85
Birch Bay Village Golf Course   86
Cooper's Golf Range   91
Dakota Creek Golf & Country   71
Eaglemont Golf Course   72
Evergreen Golf Course   73
Gateway Golf Course   74
Grandview Golf Course   74
Homestead Golf & Country Club   75
Lake Padden Municipal Golf Course   76
Loomis Trail Golf Club   87
Lopez Island Golf Club   77
New World Pro Golf Center   90
North Bellingham Golf Course   78
Orcas Island Golf Club   78
Overlook Golf Course   79
Peaceful Valley Country Club   79
Raspberry Ridge Golf Community   80
Riverside Golf Course   80
Rodarco Golf Range   91
San Juan Golf & Country Club   81
Sandy Point Golf Course   88
Sea Links   90
Semiahmoo Golf & Country Club   81
Shelter Bay Golf Course   88
Shuksan Golf Club   82
Similk Beach Golf Course   84
Skagit Golf & Country Club   88
Sudden Valley Golf & Country Club   84

**Kitsap Peninsula
& Puget Sound Islands**
Camaloch Golf Club   96
Clover Valley Golf & Country Club   97
The Country Club of Seattle   105
Gallery Golf Course   97
Gold Mountain Golf Course   98
Holmes Harbor Golf Course   100
Horseshoe Lake Golf Course   101
Island Greens   110
Kitsap Golf & Country Club   105
Lam's Links   102

McCormick Woods Golf Club   102
Meadowmeer Golf & Country Club   103
Northwest Golf Range   111
Rolling Hills Golf Club   104
Useless Bay Golf & Country Club   107
Vashon Island Driving Range   111
Vashon Island Golf & Country Club   108
Village Greens   104
Whidbey Golf & Country Club   108
Wing Point Golf & Country Club   109
Woodall's World Driving Range   111

Seattle, Everett & Vicinity
Ballinger Park Municipal Golf Course   117
Battle Creek Golf Course   118
Bear Creek Country Club (Woodinville)   152
Bellevue Municipal Golf Course   119
Blue Boy West Golf Course   120
Brae Burn Golf & Country Club   152
Broadmoor Golf Club   153
Carnation Golf Course   121
Cascade Golf Course   121
Cedarcrest Municipal Golf Course   122
Cloverdale Golf Club   123
Crossroads Park Golf Course   171
Druids Glen Golf Club   124
EagleQuest at Golf Park   172
Echo Falls Country Club   126
Elk Run Golf Course   126
Everett Golf & Country Club   154
Fairwood Golf & Country Club   155
Flowing Lake Golf Course   127
Foster Golf Links   128
Glen Acres Golf & Country Club   156
Glendale Country Club   157
Gleneagle Golf Course   129
Gold Creek Tennis & Sports Club   172
Golden Bear Family Golf Center
   at Interbay   130
The Golf Club at Newcastle   130
Green Lake Golf Course   171
Harbour Pointe Golf Club   131
Hat Island Golf Club   158
Inglewood Golf Club   158
Iron Eagle Sport Center   172
Jackson Park Municipal Golf Course   132
Jefferson Park Municipal Golf Course   133
Kaddyshack Golf Center   172
Kayak Point Golf Course   134
Kenwanda Golf Course   135

Lake Wilderness Golf Club	135
Legion Memorial Golf Course	136
Lobo Country Club	171
Longshots Driving Range	172
Lynnwood Municipal Golf Course	137
Maplewood Golf Course	138
Marysville Golf Center	172
Meridian Valley Country Club	160
Mill Creek Country Club	161
Monroe Golf Course	139
Mount Si Golf Course	139
Nile Golf & Country Club	140
Overlake Golf & Country Club	162
Plateau Golf & Country Club	163
Puetz Evergreen Golf Range	172
Rainier Golf & Country Club	164
Red Wood Golf Center	172
Riverbend Golf Complex	141
Sahalee Country Club	165
Sand Point Country Club	166
Seattle Golf Club	167
Snohomish Public Golf Course	142
Snoqualmie Falls Golf Course	143
Snoqualmie Ridge TPC Golf Course	169
Southcenter Golf	172
Super Range	172
Tall Chief Golf Club	144
Tam O'Shanter Golf & Country Club	170
The Course at Taylor Creek	144
Twin Rivers Golf Course	146
Tyee Valley Golf Club	146
University of Washington Driving Range	172
Walter E. Hall Memorial Golf Course	147
Wayne Public Golf Course	148
Wellington Hills Golf Course	149
West Seattle Municipal Golf Course	149
Willows Run Golf Club	150

Tacoma & Vicinity

Allenmore Public Golf Club	178
American Lake VA Golf Course	193
Auburn Golf Course	179
Brookdale Golf Course	179
Canterwood Golf & Country Club	194
Christy's Golf Course & Driving Range	203
Classic Country Club	180
EagleQuest at Linksman Golf Center	204
Emerald Links Driving Range	204
Enumclaw Golf Course	181
Fircrest Golf Club	195
Fort Lewis Golf Course	196
Fort Steilacoom Golf Course	182
Gig Harbor Golf & Country Club	183
High Cedars Golf & Country Club	183
Highlands Golf & Racquet Club	184
Jade Greens Golf Course	185
Lake Josephine Riviera Golf & Country Club	198
Lake Spanaway Golf Course	186
Linden Golf & Country Club	198
Lipoma Firs Public Golf Course	187
Madrona Links Golf Course	188
Meadow Park Golf Course	189
Meridian Greens	190
North Shore Golf & Country Club	190
Oakbrook Golf & Country Club	199
Sumner Meadows Golf Links	191
Tacoma Country & Golf Club	200
Tapps Island Golf Course	192
Twin Lakes Golf & Country Club	201
University Golf Club	193
Whispering Firs Golf Course	202

Olympic Peninsula

Alderbrook Golf & Yacht Club	210
Batstone Hill Practice Golf	223
Chevy Chase Golf Club	211
Dungeness Golf Course	212
Grays Harbor Country Club	221
Lake Cushman Golf Course	213
Lake Limerick Country Club	214
LakeLand Village Golf & Country Club	214
Oaksridge Golf Course	216
Ocean Shores Golf Course	216
Peninsula Golf Club	222
Port Ludlow Golf & Meeting Retreat	217
Port Townsend Municipal Golf Course	219
Shelton Bayshore Golf Club	220
Sunland Golf & Country Club	220

Olympia & Southwest Washington

Ashford Driving Range	249
Capitol City Golf Club	228
Centralia Public Golf Course	229
Delphi Golf Course	229
Eagle View Golf Center	249
Golfgreen Golf Center	248
Grand Mound Driving Range	249
High Valley Country Club	244
Highland Golf Course	230
Indian Summer Golf & Country Club	244
Ironwood Green Golf Course	231
Lewis River Golf Course	231
Longview Country Club	245
Maple Grove Golf	232
Meriwood Golf Course	233
Mint Valley Golf Course	234
Newaukum Valley Golf Course	235
Nisqually Valley Golf Course	236
Olympia Country & Golf Club	247
Pacific Golf Center	237
Par IV Golf Learning Center	249
Peninsula Golf	237
Rainbow Golf Driving Range	249
Riverside Country Club	238
Scott Lake Golf Course	239
Skyline Golf Course	239
Steamboat Golf	249
Surfside Golf Course	240
Three Rivers Golf Course	240
Tri-Mountain Golf Course	241
Tumwater Valley Golf Club	242
Willapa Harbor Golf Club	243

North-Central Washington

Alta Lake Golf Course	254
Banks Lake Golf Club	255
Bear Creek Golf Course (Winthrop)	256
Crystal Springs Golf Center	269
Desert Canyon Golf Resort	257
Home Place Golf Course	258
Kahler Glen Golf Course	259
Lake Chelan Golf Course	260
Lake Woods Golf Course	261
Leavenworth Golf Club	262
MA-8 + 1 Golf	263
Okanogan Valley Golf Club	263
Oroville Golf Club	264
Rock Island Golf Course	265
Sunny Meadows Golf & Four Seasons Resort	267
Three Lakes Golf Course	265
Vic Meyers Golf Course	266
Wenatchee Golf & Country Club	267

South-Central Washington

Apple Tree Golf Course	274
Beacon Rock Public Golf Course	276
Carey Lakes Golf Course	276
Crescent Bar Resort	277
Desert Aire Golf & Country Club	278
Ellensburg Golf Club	278
Fisher Park Golf Course	288
Goldendale Country Club	279
Harvest Valley Golf Center	289
Hot Springs Golf Course	280
Husum Hills Golf Course	280
Lower Valley Golf Club	281
Mount Adams Country Club	282
Quincy Valley Golf Course	283
Skamania Lodge Golf Course	284
Straight Arrow Driving Range	289
Sun Country Golf Resort	285
Suntides Golf Course	285
Westwood West	286
Yakima Country Club	286
Yakima Elks Golf & Country Club	287

Spokane & Northeast Washington

Beacon Hill Golf Center	314
Big Bend Golf & Country Club	294
Birdies Golf Place	314
Buckhorn Par-3	313
Chewelah Golf & Country Club	295
Colville Elks Golf Course	296
The Creek at Qualchan	296
Deer Meadows Golf Course	297
Deer Park Golf & Country Club	298
Downriver Golf Course	299
Esmeralda Golf Course	300
The Fairways at West Terrace Golf Course	301
Hangman Valley Golf Club	301
Harrington Golf & Country Club	302
Indian Canyon Golf Course	303
Liberty Lake Golf Course	304
Manito Golf & Country Club	310
MeadowWood Golf Course	304
Odessa Golf Club	306
Painted Hills Golf Club	306
Pend Oreille Golf & Country Club	307
Pineacres Par-3 Golf Course	313
Sheridan Greens Golf Course	307
Spokane Country Club	311
Sundance Golf Course	308
Valley View Golf Course	308
Wandermere Golf Course	309

Southeast Washington

Canyon Lakes Golf Course	318
Clarkston Golf & Country Club	334
Colfax Golf Club	319
Columbia Park Golf Course	320
Columbia Point Golf Course	320
Desert Lakes Driving Range	340
Gateway Golf Center	340
Horn Rapids Golf & Country Club	321
Lakeview Golf & Country Club	335
Longest Drive	340
Meadow Springs Country Club	336
Moses Lake Golf & Country Club	337
Oasis Park	339
Othello Golf Club	323
Pasco Golfland	339
Pomeroy Golf Course	323
Potholes Golf Course	324
Quail Ridge Golf Course	324
Ritzville Municipal Golf Course	325
Royal City Golf Course	326
Sage Hills Golf Club	327
South Campus Public Golf Course	328
St. John Golf & Country Club	328
Sun Willows	329
Tekoa Golf Club	329
Touchet Valley Golf Course	330
Tour Fairways Golf Range	340
Tri-City Country Club	331
Veteran's Memorial Golf Course	331
Walla Walla Country Club	338
WSU Golf Course	332
West Richland Municipal Golf Course	333

Greater Vancouver

Bowyer's Par 3 Golf	392
The Cedars Golf Club	347
Club Green Meadows	374
Evergreen Golf Center	394
Fairway Village Golf Course	352
H & H Driving Range	394
Hartwood Golf Course	354
Lakeview Golf Challenge	392
Orchard Hills Country Club	376
Pine Crest Golf	393
Royal Oaks Country Club	386
Vanco Driving Range	394
Westside Golf Range	394

Oregon

Portland & Vicinity

Broadmoor Golf Course	346
Charbonneau Golf & Country Club	348
The Children's Course	349
Chuck Milne's 82nd Avenue Golf Range	394
Claremont Golf Club	349
Columbia-Edgewater Country Club	375
Colwood National Golf Club	350
Dino's Driving Range	394
Eastmoreland Golf Course	351
Glendoveer Golf Course	352
Golden Bear Golf Center at Sunset	394
Greenlea Golf Course	353
Gresham Golf Course	354
Heron Lakes Golf Course	355
Jim Colbert's Hound Hollow Golf Center	356
Killarney West Golf Club	357
King City Golf Course	357
Lake Oswego Golf Course	358
Langdon Farms Golf Club	359
McKay Creek Golf Course	361
Meriwether National Golf Club	362
Mountain View Golf Club	363
Oregon City Golf Club	363
The Oregon Golf Club	377
Orenco Woods Golf Club	364
Oswego Lake Country Club	378
Persimmon Country Club	365
Pleasant Valley Golf Club	380
Portland Golf Club	381
Portland Meadows Golf Course	366
Progress Downs Municipal Golf Course	366
Pumpkin Ridge Golf Club — Ghost Creek (public)	367
Pumpkin Ridge Golf Club — Witch Hollow (private)	383
Quail Valley Golf Course	369
The Reserve Vineyards Golf Club	370
Riverside Golf & Country Club	384
Rock Creek Country Club	385
Rose City Golf Course	371
Sah-Hah-Lee Golf Course	393
Sandelie Golf	372
Summerfield Golf & Country Club	372
Top O'Scott Public Golf Course	373
Tualatin Country Club	387
Tualatin Island Greens	394
Waverley Country Club	389

Northwest Oregon

Alderbrook Golf Course	400
Astoria Golf & Country Club	408
Bay Breeze Golf & Driving Range	409
Forest Hills Golf Course	401
Gearhart Golf Links	401
The Highlands at Gearhart	402
Manzanita Golf Course	403
Saint Helens Golf Course	404
Seaside Golf Course	404
Sunset Grove Golf Club	405
Vernonia Golf Club	406
Wildwood Golf Course	407

Salem, Corvallis & Central Oregon Coast

Agate Beach Golf Course	414
Arrowhead Golf Club	439
Auburn Center Golf Club	415
Battle Creek Golf Course	415
Bayou Golf Club	416
Caddieshack Driving Range	448
Cordon Road Driving Range	448
Corvallis Country Club	440
Cottonwood Lakes Golf Course	416
Creekside Golf Club	417
Crestview Hills Public Golf Course	418
Cross Creek Golf Course	419
Dallas Golf Course	420
Diamond Woods Golf Course	420
Evergreen Golf Club	421
Frontier Golf Course	447
Golf City	422
The Golf Club of Oregon	422
Hawk Creek Golf Course	423
Illahe Hills Country Club	442
Lakeside Golf & Racquet Club	423
Mallard Creek Golf Course & RV Camp	424
Marysville Golf Course	425
McNary Golf Club	425
Meadowlawn Golf Club	426
Michelbook Country Club	443
Neskowin Beach Golf Course	427
Oak Knoll Golf Course (Independence)	428
OGA Members Course at Tukwila	429
Olalla Valley Golf Course	431
Pineway Golf Course	431
Ranch Hills Golf Club	432
Riverwood Golf Course	433

Salem Golf Club   434
Salemtowne Golf Club   444
Salishan Golf Links   434
Santiam Golf Club   436
Senior Estates Golf & Country Club 444
Spring Hill Country Club   444
Trysting Tree Golf Club   437
Westside Driving Range & Golf Center 448
Willamette Valley Country Club   445
Woodburn Golf Club   438

Eugene & Southwest Oregon
Applegate Golf   453
Bandon Face Rock Golf Course   454
Bear Creek Golf Course (Medford)   455
Cedar Bend Golf Club   456
Cedar Links   456
The Club at Sutherlin   457
Coburg Hills Golf Club   458
Colonial Valley Golf Course   459
Coos Country Club   459
Coquille Valley Elks Golf Club   479
Dutcher Creek Golf Course   460
Eagle Point Golf Course   461
Eagles on the Green   479
Emerald Valley Golf Club   463
Eugene Country Club   479
Fiddler's Green Golf Course   487
Forest Hills Country Club   464
Grants Pass Driving Range   488
Grants Pass Golf Club   464
Hidden Valley Golf Course   465
Hillebrand's Paradise Range Resort   487
Illinois Valley Golf Club   466
Jack Creek Driving Range   488
Kentuck Golf Course   466
Laurel Hill Golf Course   467
Laurelwood Golf Course   467
Middlefield Village   468
Myrtle Creek Golf Course   469
Oak Knoll Golf Course (Ashland)   470
Oakway Golf Course   471
Ocean Dunes Golf Links   471
Quail Point Golf Course   472
Red Mountain Golf Course   473
Riveridge Golf Course   474
Rogue Valley Country Club   481
Roseburg Country Club   483
Roseburg Veterans Hospital
  Golf Course   484

Sandpines Golf Resort   474
Shadow Hills Country Club   485
Springfield Country Club   486
Stewart Meadows Golf Course   475
Stewart Park Golf Course   476
Stoneridge Golf Club   477
Sunset Bay Golf Club   478
Veterans Administration Domiciliary
  Golf Course   486

North-Central Oregon
Aspen Lakes Golf Course   494
Black Butte Ranch   495
Condon Golf Course   496
Crooked River Ranch Golf Course   497
Eagle Creek Golf Course   498
Eagle Crest Golf Course   499
Eagle Ridge Golf Course   500
Elkhorn Valley Golf Course   501
The Greens at Redmond   502
Hood River Golf & Country Club   502
Indian Creek Golf Course   503
Juniper Golf Club   504
Kah-Nee-Ta Resort   505
Kinzua Hills Golf Club   506
Lone Pine Village Driving Range   513
McKenzie River Golf Course   506
Meadow Lakes Golf Course   507
Nine Peaks Golf Course   508
Northwest Aluminum Golf Club   511
Pine Hollow Golf Course   508
Prineville Golf & Country Club   511
The Resort at the Mountain   509
Springwater Golf Course   510
The Dalles Country Club   513
Tokatee Golf Club   510

South-Central Oregon
Awbrey Glen Golf Club   530
Bend Golf & Country Club   531
Broken Top Club   533
Christmas Valley Golf Course   518
Circle Bar Golf Club   519
Crosswater   534
Harbor Links Golf Course   520
Lost Tracks Golf Club   520
Mountain High Golf Course   522
Orion Greens Golf Course   523
Quail Run Golf Course   524
Raymax Driving Range   537

Reames Golf & Country Club   536
River's Edge Golf Course   524
Round Lake Golf Course   525
Running Y Ranch Resort   526
Shield Crest Golf Course   527
Sunriver Resort   528
Widgi Creek Golf Club   529

Eastern Oregon
Alpine Meadows Golf Course   542
Baker City Golf Club   543
Eagle Driving Range   552
Echo Hills Golf Course   544
John Day Golf Club   544
Kik's Driving Range   552
La Grande Country Club   550
Lakeridge Golf & Country Club   545
Milton-Freewater Golf Course   545
Pendleton Country Club   551
Shadow Butte Municipal Golf Course   546
Umatilla Golf Course   547
Valley Golf Club   547
Wildhorse Golf Course   548
Willow Creek Country Club   549
Wilson's Willow Run Executive
   Golf Course   549

Idaho Panhandle
Avondale Golf Club   556
Bryden Canyon Golf Course   558
Coeur d'Alene Golf Club   558
The Coeur d'Alene Resort Golf Course   559
Grangeville Country Club   561
Hayden Lake Country Club   574
Hidden Lakes Golf Resort   562
The Highlands Golf & Country Club   564
Kellogg Country Club   565
Lewiston Golf & Country Club   576
Midas Golf Club   565
Mirror Lake Golf Course   565
Moscow Elks Golf Club   576
Orofino Golf & Country Club   566
Ponderosa Springs Golf Course   578
Prairie Falls Golf Course   567
Priest Lake Golf Course   567
Pumpkin Patch Golf & Restaurant   579
Ranch Club Golf Course   568
Rimrock Golf Course   578
Sandpoint Elks Country Club   569
Shoshone Golf Club   569

St. Maries Golf Course   570
Stoneridge Golf Club   570
Twin Lakes Village Golf
   & Racquet Club   572
University of Idaho Golf Course   573

Sun Valley
Bigwood Golf Course   557
Elkhorn Resort Golf Course   560
Sun Valley Golf Course   571
The Valley Club   577
Warm Springs Golf Course   574

Northwest Montana
Buffalo Hill Golf Club   584
Cabinet View Country Club   585
Cedar Creek Golf Course   604
Double Arrow Golf Resort   586
Eagle Bend Golf Club   587
Glacier View Golf Club   588
Hamilton Golf Club   589
The Highlands Golf Club   590
King Ranch Golf Course   590
Larchmont Golf Course   591
Linda Vista Public Golf Course   592
Meadow Creek Golf Course   604
Meadow Lake Resort   593
Mission Mountain Country Club   594
Missoula Country Club   603
Mountain Crossroads Golf Course   595
National Golf Driving Range   605
Northern Pines Golf Club   595
The Par-3 on 93 Golf Course   605
Plains Golf Course   596
Polson Country Club   597
Thompson Falls Golf Club   597
Trestle Creek Golf Course   598
University of Montana Golf Course   599
Village Greens Golfing Community   600
Whitefish Lake Golf Club   601
Whitetail Golf Club   602

Since 1990, Jeff Shelley has written three editions of *Golf Courses of the Pacific Northwest*. Beginning research on the book in 1986, he's traveled some 150,000 miles and taken over 2,000 photographs of the region's 550-plus courses. A writer for 20 years, he lives in Seattle with his wife Anni and daughter Erica. Jeff and Anni, the book's designer, own Fairgreens Media, the publisher of this edition.

Jeff has served on the PNGA's Publication Committee since its inception, helping define the association's successful magazine, *Pacific Northwest Golfer*. A member of the Golf Writers Association of America, he's been editor for two regional golf magazines and penned many articles for other publications. He's currently the media director for the Fred Couples Invitational, an annual two-day tournament in Seattle. Jeff and Erica team up as volunteer media coordinators for the Washington Junior Golf Association. Jeff's next golf project will be a pictorial history of the PNGA, which will celebrate its centennial in 1999.